VIRTUAL HISTORY

Niall Ferguson is Fellow and Tutor in Modern History at Jesus College, Oxford. He recently published *Paper and Iron: Hamburg Business and German Politics in the Era of Inflation 1897–1927* which was shortlisted for the *History Today* Book of the Year award. He has also written numerous articles on nineteenth- and twentieth-century financial history, including a critique of Keynes's *Economic Consequences of the Peace* and is the author of a history of the Rothschilds. A prolific commentator on contemporary politics, he lives with his wife and two children in Oxfordshire.

VIRTUAL HISTORY:

Alternatives and Counterfactuals

EDITED BY

Niall Ferguson

BASIC
BOOKS

A Member of the
Perseus Books Group

Virtual History was first published in hardcover in Great Britain by Picador in 1997. The Basic Books edition is reprinted by arrangement with Papermac, an imprint of Macmillan Publishers Ltd.

This collection copyright © Niall Ferguson 1997
Published 1999 by Basic Books,
A Member of the Perseus Books Group.

Typeset by CentraCet, Cambridge

A CIP catalog record for this book is available from the Library of Congress.
ISBN 0-465-02322-3

99 00 01   10 9 8 7 6 5 4 3 2

CONTENTS

....

....

Contributors

NIALL FERGUSON is Fellow and Tutor in Modern History at Jesus College, Oxford. He recently published *Paper and Iron: Hamburg Business and German Politics in the Era of Inflation 1897–1927* (1995), which was shortlisted for the *History Today* Book of the Year award. He has written numerous articles on nineteenth- and twentieth-century financial history, and is currently writing a history of Rothschilds.

JOHN ADAMSON is a Fellow of Peterhouse, Cambridge, and has published extensively on the political and cultural history of seventeenth-century Britain. He won the Royal Historical Society's Alexander Prize in 1990, and is currently editing the official history of *The Commons: 1640–1660* for the History of Parliament Trust.

JONATHAN CLARK is Joyce and Elizabeth Hall Distinguished Professor of British History at the University of Kansas. His publications include *The Dynamics of Change* (1982), *English Society 1688–1832* (1985), *Revolution and Rebellion* (1986), *The Language of Liberty, 1660–1832: Political Discourse and Social Dynamics in the Anglo-American World* (1993) and *Samuel Johnson: Literature, Religion and English Cultural Politics from the Restoration to Romanticism* (1994). He has edited *The Memoirs and Speeches of James, 2nd Earl Waldegrave 1742–1763* (1988) and *Ideas and Politics in Modern Britain* (1989).

ALVIN JACKSON is Reader in Modern History at the Queen's University of Belfast, and has been Lecturer in Modern Irish History at University College Dublin and John Burns Visiting Professor of Irish Studies at Boston College. He is author of *The Ulster Party* (1989), *Sir Edward Carson* (1993) and *Colonel Edward Saunderson: Land and Loyalty in Victorian Ireland* (1995). He is at present working on the Blackwell History of Modern Ireland.

ANDREW ROBERTS was an Honorary Senior Scholar at Gonville and Caius College, Cambridge. His books include *The Holy Fox, A Biography of Lord Halifax* (1991), *Eminent Churchillians* (1994) and *The Aachen Memorandum* (1995). He is currently writing the authorized biography of the 3rd Marquess of Salisbury.

MICHAEL BURLEIGH is Distinguished Research Professor of History at the University of Wales, Cardiff. His books include *Prussian Society and the German Order* (1984), *Germany Turns Eastwards: A Study of 'Ostforschung' in the Third Reich* (1988), *The Racial State: Germany 1933–1945* (with Wolfgang Wippermann, 1991), *Death and Deliverance: 'Euthanasia' in Germany, 1900–1945* (1994) and *Confronting the Nazi Past* (1996). His essays, *Ethics and Extermination: Essays on Nazi Genocide* will be published shortly. His award-winning Channel 4 Documentaries include *Selling Murder* and *Heil Herbie*.

JONATHAN HASLAM is a Fellow and Director of Studies in History at Corpus Christi College, Cambridge, and Assistant Director of Studies in International Relations at the Cambridge University Centre of International Studies. He is the author of *The Soviet Union and the Struggle for Collective Security in Europe 1933–1939* (1984) and *The Soviet Union and the Threat from the East 1933–1941* (1992). He has recently completed a biography of E. H. Carr and is currently writing *The Realist Tradition in International Relations: from Machiavelli to Waltz*.

DIANE KUNZ is Associate Professor of History at Yale University. She is the author of *The Battle for Britain's Gold Standard in 1931* (1987) and *The Economic Diplomacy of the Suez Crisis* (1991). Her most recent book is *Butter and Guns: America's Cold War Economic Diplomacy*.

MARK ALMOND is Lecturer in Modern History at Oriel College, Oxford. His most recent book is *Revolution: 500 Years of Struggle for Change* (1996). His other books include *Europe's Backyard War: the War in the Balkans* (1994) and *The Rise and Fall of Nicolae and Elena Ceausescu* (1992).

Acknowledgements

In a collaborative volume, it is for individual contributors to express their gratitude in their notes. The editor, however, has the right to a list of acknowledgements in a larger typeface. I would like to express my thanks to: the Modern History Faculty, Oxford; the Acting Principal and Fellows of Jesus College, Oxford; my agent, Georgina Capel, of Simpson, Fox Associates; Peter Straus and Tanya Stobbs, my editors at Macmillan; Glen O'Hara of Jesus College, Oxford, for his indispensable assistance with the research for both the introduction and my chapter; and Vivien Bowyer at Jesus College, Oxford. I am especially indebted for their comments on my sections of the book to Dr Christopher Andrew of Corpus Christi College, Cambridge; Professor Jonathan Clark of the University of Kansas; Professor Roy Foster of Oxford University; Dr Jonathan Steinberg of Trinity Hall, Cambridge; Dr John Stevenson of Worcester College, Oxford; and Professor Norman Stone of Oxford University. Many other friends and colleagues too numerous to name have assisted me by patiently fielding questions about the theory and practice of counterfactual history over coffee, lunch and dinner. Above all, I would like to thank my wife Susan for providing inspiration.

INTRODUCTION

Virtual History: Towards a 'chaotic' theory of the past

Niall Ferguson

Acted history ... is an ever-living, ever-working Chaos of Being, wherein shape after shape bodies itself forth from innumerable elements. And this Chaos ... is what the historian will depict, and scientifically gauge!

THOMAS CARLYLE

There is no privileged past ... There is an infinitude of Pasts, all equally valid ... At each and every instant of Time, however brief you suppose it, the line of events forks like the stem of a tree putting forth twin branches.

ANDRÉ MAUROIS

The enduring achievement of historical study is a historical sense – an intuitive understanding – of how things do not happen.

LEWIS NAMIER

The historian must ... constantly put himself at a point in the past at which the known factors will seem to permit different outcomes. If he speaks of Salamis, then it must be as if the Persians might still win; if he speaks of the coup d'état of Brumaire, then it must remain to be seen if Bonaparte will be ignominiously repulsed.

JOHAN HUIZINGA

What if there had been no English Civil War? What if there had been no American War of Independence? What if Ireland had never been divided? What if Britain had stayed out of the First World War? What if Hitler had invaded Britain? What if he had defeated the Soviet Union? What if the Russians had won the Cold War? What if Kennedy had lived? What if there had been no Gorbachev?

The obvious objection to such hypothetical or 'counterfactual' questions is simple: why bother asking them? Why concern ourselves with what *didn't* happen? Just as there is no use crying over spilt milk, runs the argument, so there is no use in wondering how the spillage might have been averted. (Even more futile to speculate what would have happened if we *had* spilt milk that's still safe in the bottle.)

One easy response to that objection is that we constantly ask such 'counterfactual' questions in our daily lives. What if I had observed the speed limit, or refused that last drink? What if I had never met my wife or husband? What if I had bet on Red Rum instead of Also Ran? It seems we cannot resist imagining the alternative scenarios: what might have happened, if only we had or had not ... We picture ourselves avoiding past blunders, or committing blunders we narrowly avoided. Nor are such thoughts mere day-dreams. Of course, we know perfectly well that we cannot travel back in time and do these things differently. But the business of imagining such counterfactuals is a vital part of the way in which we learn. Because decisions about the future are – usually – based on weighing up the potential consequences of alternative courses of action, it makes sense to compare the actual outcomes of what we did in the past with the conceivable outcomes of what we might have done.

Hollywood never tires of exploiting our fascination with what grammarians call the subjunctive conditional ('But for X, there might not have been Y'). In Frank Capra's *It's a Wonderful Life*, Jimmy Stewart's guardian angel catches him on the brink of suicide and gives him a glimpse of how much worse the world – or at least his home town – would have been if he had never lived.

Peggy Sue Got Married revolves around Kathleen Turner's middle-aged regrets about her choice of husband years before; while in *Back to the Future*, Michael J. Fox very nearly prevents his own conception by travelling back in time and unwittingly luring his mother-to-be away from his father-to-be. Appalled at the death of his girlfriend in an earthquake, Christopher Reeves's *Superman* reverses time and extricates her from the 'future' disaster he and the audience have just witnessed. Authors of science-fiction have returned time and again to the same fantasy. In John Wyndham's *Random Quest*, for example, the physicist Colin Trafford is catapulted into a parallel universe where there has been no Second World War and no atom bomb, to find that his *alter ego* is a womanising, wife-abusing novelist. In a similar story, Ray Bradbury imagines the entire world subtly but profoundly altered by a time traveller who inadvertently treads on a prehistoric butterfly.[1]

Of course, Hollywood and science fiction are not academically respectable. However, the same idea has engaged the attention of impeccably reputable writers too. In his Weimar masterpiece, *The Man without Qualities*, Robert Musil reflected at length on our predisposition to think counterfactually:

> If there is such a thing as a sense of reality – and no one will doubt that it has its *raison d'être* – then there must also be something that one can call a sense of possibility. Anyone possessing it does not say, for instance: Here this or that has happened, will happen, must happen. He uses his imagination and says: Here such and such might, should or ought to happen. And if he is told that something *is* the way it is, then he thinks: Well, it could probably just as easily be some other way. So the sense of possibility might be defined outright as the capacity to think how everything could 'just as easily be', and to attach no more importance to what is than to what is not.... [For] the possible covers ... the not yet manifested intentions of God. A possible experience or possible truth does not equate to real experience or real truth minus the value 'real'; ... in the opinion

of its devotees, it has in it something out and out divine, a fiery, soaring quality, a constructive will, a conscious utopianism that does not shrink from reality but treats it, on the contrary, as ... an invention.

Nevertheless – as Musil also suggested – there will always be those for whom this sense of the possible is deeply suspect:

Unfortunately [the consequences of such a disposition] not infrequently make the things that other people admire appear wrong and the things that other people prohibit permissible, or even make both a matter of indifference. Such possibilitarians live, it is said, within a finer web, a web of hazy imaginings, fantasy and the subjunctive mood. If children show this tendency it is vigorously driven out of them, and in their presence such people are referred to as crackbrains, dreamers, weaklings, know-alls, and carpers and cavillers. When one wants to praise these poor fools, one sometimes calls them idealists.[2]

And that, it might be said, rather neatly sums up the attitude of generations of historians, for whom, in the dismissive phrase of E. H. Carr, 'counterfactual' history is a mere 'parlour game', a 'red herring'.[3] In this view, there are and were literally no two ways about it, and questions beginning 'What if?' are simply not worth asking. To contemplate 'the things that might have happened' is not only to subscribe to 'the Bad King John' or 'Cleopatra's Nose' theory of history. It is to be a bad loser too:

Plenty of people who have suffered directly or vicariously from the results of the Bolshevik victory ... desire to register their protest against it; and this takes the form, when they read history, of letting their imagination run riot on all the more agreeable things that might have happened.... This is a purely emotional and unhistorical reaction.... In a group or a nation which is riding in the trough, not on the crest, of historical events, theories that stress the role of chance or accident in history will be found to prevail. The view that examination results are a lottery will always be popular among those who have been placed in the third class. . . . History is . . . a record of what people did, not what they failed to do. . . . The historian is concerned with those who . . . achieved something.[4]

This hostility to counterfactual arguments has been and remains surprisingly widespread among professional historians. Indeed, E. P. Thompson has gone so far as to dismiss 'counterfactual fictions' as mere '*Geschichtswissenschlopff*, unhistorical shit'.[5]

To be sure, not all historians would call themselves 'determinists', even in the loose sense of the term favoured by Anglo-Marxists like Carr and Thompson. There are important differences between believers in historical predestination – the idea that events are in some way preprogrammed, so that what was, had to be – and believers in more limited notions of causation. Not all believers in a linear chain or stream of causation, in which all events are the sole possible consequences of their 'determining' antecedents, share the belief of many nineteenth-century determinists that it has a purpose or meaningful direction. There are certainly profound differences between religious historians, who see divine agency as the ultimate (but not necessarily the sole) cause of events; materialists, who regard history as intelligible in terms analogous to, or derived from, those of the natural sciences (such as universal laws); and idealists, for whom history is the transformation of past 'thought' into an intelligible (and often teleological) structure by the imagination of the historian. Nevertheless, there is a consensus which transcends all these differences. All three schools of thought regard 'what if' questions as fundamentally inadmissible.

Although a firm opponent of the materialist determinism favoured by the likes of Carr and Thompson, Benedetto Croce's attack on the 'absurdity' of counterfactual questions was unequivocal:

When judgement is brought to bear upon a fact, the fact is taken as it is and not as it might otherwise have been ... Historical necessity has to be affirmed and continually reaffirmed in order to exclude from history the 'conditional' which has no rightful place there.... What is forbidden is ... the anti-historical and illogical 'if'. Such an 'if' arbitrarily divides the course of history into necessary facts and accidental facts ... Under the sign of this 'if', one fact in a narrative is graded as necessary and another one as accidental, and the second is mentally eliminated in order to espy how the first would have developed along its own lines if it had not been disturbed by the second. This is a game which all of us in moments of distraction or idleness indulge in, when we muse on the way our life might have turned out if we had not met a certain person ..., cheerfully treating ourselves, in these meditations, as though we were the necessary and stable element, it simply not occurring to us ... to provide for the transformation of this self of ours which is, at the moment of thinking, what it is, with all its experiences and regrets and fancies, just because we did meet that person ... For if we went on to such a full exploration of reality, the game would soon be up ... When the attempt is made to play this sort of game on the field of history, where it is thoroughly out of place, the effect is too wearisome to be long maintained.[6]

Still more fiercely antagonistic to counterfactualism was the English idealist philosopher Michael Oakeshott. In Oakeshott's view, when the historian 'considers by a kind of ideal experiment what might have happened as well as what the evidence obliges him to believe did happen' he steps 'outside the current of historical thought':

It is possible that had St Paul been captured and killed when his friends lowered him from the walls of Damascus, the Christian religion might never have become the centre of our civilisation. And on that account, the spread of Christianity might be attributed to St Paul's escape.... But when events are treated in this manner, they cease at once to be historical events. The result is not merely bad or doubtful history, but the complete rejection of history ... The distinction ... between essential and incidental events does not belong to historical thought at all; it is a monstrous incursion of science into the world of history.

And Oakeshott went on:

The question in history is never what must, or what might have taken place, but solely what the evidence obliges us to conclude did take place. Had George III not been King of England when the trouble arose in the American colonies, it is possible that the differences there might never have led to war; but to conclude from this that George III was an odd chance which at this critical point altered the 'natural' sequence of events is to have abandoned history for something less profitable if more entertaining. . . . The Historian is never called upon to consider what might have happened had circumstances been different.[7]

To imagine alternative courses of events is thus, in Oakeshott's words, 'a pure myth, an extravagance of the imagination'. This must be one of the few things about which he agreed with Carr and Thompson.

Such hostile views from such disparate figures partly explain why answers to the kind of counterfactual questions I began by listing have more often been provided by writers of fiction than by historians – one thinks, for example, of Robert Harris's recent novel *Fatherland*, a detective story set in an imaginary Europe twenty years after a Nazi victory.[8] As such books go, it is well researched. But it is irredeemably fictional, in as much as the narrative follows the classic pattern of a popular thriller; and as such it tends to diminish the plausibility of the historical setting. Instead of being a catastrophe which very nearly happened – and to avert which millions perished – a Nazi victory in the Second World War becomes merely a titillating backdrop for a good departure-lounge yarn. Numerous other works of fiction have been predicated on such counterfactual historical assumptions: Kingsley Amis's *The Alteration*, which wishfully undoes the English Reformation, is another good example.[9] But they have no more to do with history than the books of 'futurology' which the London Library politely categorises as 'Imaginary History'. Futurologists offer guesses as to which of the plausible alternatives which confront us today will prevail in the years ahead, and usually base their predictions on the extrapolation of past trends. To judge by the accuracy of such works, however, they might as well be based on astrology or tarot cards.[10]

Nevertheless, there have been serious historians who have ventured to address (or at least to pose) counterfactual questions. Gibbon was always fascinated by the tenuousness of certain historical developments, and occasionally allowed himself to write in an explicitly counterfactual way. A good example is his brief sketch of what might have happened had it not been for the victory of Charles Martel over the Saracens in 733:

> A victorious line of march had been prolonged above a thousand miles from the rock of Gibraltar to the banks of the Loire; the repetition of an equal space would have carried the Saracens to the confines of Poland and the Highlands of Scotland; the Rhine is not more impassable than the Nile or the Euphrates, and the Arabian fleet might have sailed without a naval combat into the mouth of the Thames. Perhaps the interpretation of the Koran would now be taught in the schools of Oxford, and her pulpits might demonstrate to a circumcised people the sanctity and truth of the revelation of Mohammed.[11]

This, of course, was a mere ironical aside, a Gibbonian joke at the expense of the university which had taught him so little. Altogether more ambitious was the French writer Charles Renouvier, whose *Uchronie* (published exactly a hundred years after the first volume of Gibbon's *Decline and Fall*) was nothing less than a 'Historical and apocryphal essay on the development of European civilisation as it has not been, but as it might perhaps have been'. Renouvier described himself as 'a sort of Swedenborg of history – a visionary who dreams the past', and characterised his book as a 'mixture of real facts and imaginary events'.[12] Presented as the testament of a seventeenth-century anti-determinist, relayed and supplemented by his descendants, *Uchronie*'s central counterfactual is not wholly dissimilar to Gibbon's. Christianity fails to establish itself in the West, as a result of a slight change in the course of events at the end of the reign of Marcus Aurelius. Only in the East does Christianity take root, leaving the West to enjoy an extra millennium of classical culture. As a consequence, when Christianity does reach the West, it is merely one of many religions tolerated in an essentially secular Europe. As might be expected in view of Renouvier's liberal sympathies, the book has a marked anti-clerical thrust.[13]

In 1907 – six years after Renouvier published a second edition of *Uchronie* – that most self-consciously literary of Edwardian historians G. M. Trevelyan wrote (at the suggestion of the editor of the *Westminster Gazette*) an essay entitled: 'If Napoleon had won the Battle of Waterloo'. Like Gibbon's, Trevelyan's is an alternative past calculated to unnerve rather than inspire. With Napoleon supreme on the continent following his victory at Waterloo, Britain remains stuck on the 'beaten track of tyranny and obscurantism'. A revolution led by Byron is brutally suppressed and a generation of young radicals is driven to fight for freedom on the distant South American pampas. Napoleon dies at last in 1836, 'the enemy alike of the ancien regime and of democratic liberty'. In short, no Waterloo, no Whig history.[14]

Yet, despite Trevelyan's example, this was not a genre which many serious historians sought to develop. When J. C. Squire put together a collection of similar counterfactual essays twenty-five years later, his eleven contributors were a motley crew, mainly composed of novelists and journalists.[15] The whole tone of Squire's *If It Happened Otherwise* was self-deprecating; it was even subtitled '*lapses* into imaginary history'. Not all his contributors, Squire admitted at the outset, had written 'on precisely the same plane of reality. Some mingle more satire with their speculations than others'; indeed, some of their fantasies put him in mind of Johnson's remark that 'a man is not on his oath in a lapidary inscription'. Unfortunately, Squire's own introduction was itself something of a lapidary inscription. Counterfactual history 'doesn't help much', he concluded lamely, 'as nobody is to know'. Small wonder the volume was soon dead and buried.

Did Squire's book discredit the notion of counterfactual history for a generation? Certainly, some of the contributions help explain why it came to be seen by so many historians as a mere parlour game. Philip Guedalla's 'If the Moors in Spain had won', for example, is based on the counterfactual of a Spanish defeat at Lanjaron in 1491, which allows the Islamic kingdom of Granada to become the centre of an Arab-led Renaissance and an eighteenth-century empire. (In this alternative world, Disraeli ends up as a Granadian Grand Vizier.) Still more whimsical is G. K. Chesterton's 'If Don John of Austria [Philip II of Spain's illegitimate brother] had married Mary Queen of Scots', a Counter-Reformation romance in which the royal couple together snuff out Calvinism in Scotland, inherit the English throne, and suspend the Reformation *sine die*. H. A. L. Fisher's 'If Napoleon had escaped to America' imagines Bonaparte crossing the Atlantic (rather than giving himself up to the *Bellerophon*) and joining forces with Bolivar to liberate Latin America from Popery and monarchy. Harold Nicolson offers more of the same in 'If Byron had become King of Greece', which has Byron surviving the fever which killed him at Missolonghi in 1824 and finally achieving an incongruous apotheosis as a henpecked and increasingly addled King George I of Greece (1830–54). (Typically, Nicolson has as Byron's most enduring achievement, 'removing the litter from the summit of the Acropolis and erecting in its place an exact replica of Newstead Abbey'.) Milton Waldman's 'If Booth had missed Lincoln' is rather less frivolous, portraying Lincoln as a grotesquely ageing 'thwarted autocrat', discredited by a lenient peace settlement which has satisfied neither North nor South, at loggerheads with his own more vengeful party in Congress and finally expiring in 1867, worn out by a last, doomed election campaign.[16]

But as for Squire's own 'If it had been discovered in 1930 that Bacon really did write Shakespeare', the most that can be said is that it would not have been out of place in the *Punch* of its day (the laboured pay-off line is that, conversely, Shakespeare wrote the works of Bacon). The same goes for Ronald Knox's spoof edition of *The Times* of 'June 31, 1930' purporting to postdate a successful General Strike.[17]

To be fair, not everything in *If...* is devoid of historical value. André Maurois's chapter avoids the French Revolution by imagining, not implausibly, a successful financial reform carried to its conclusion by Turgot, with the assistance not only of greater royal resolve, but also of a conclusive defeat of the Parlements in 1774 and a reform of the Paris police. Churchill raises equally interesting questions about a Southern victory in the American Civil War, assuming a Confederate victory at Gettysburg. And Emil Ludwig's piece argues – as was widely believed at the time – that if the German Emperor Frederick III had not died in 1888 (after just ninety-nine days on the throne), German political development might have taken a more liberal course. Yet even the better essays in *If...* are very obviously the products of their authors' contemporary political or religious preoccupations. As such, they tell us a good deal less about nineteenth-century alternatives than – for example – about 1930s views of the First World War. Thus Maurois imagines French security permanently underwritten by a united Anglo-America (Britain having won the American War of Independence); Churchill beats his drum for the same transatlantic combination (Britain having managed to reconcile the South and the defeated Union); and Ludwig sings the old German liberal lament for the missed chance of an Anglo-German alliance (which he imagines a longer-lived Frederick concluding). In other words, rather than approaching past events with a conscious indifference to what is known about later events, each takes as his starting point the burning contemporary question: How could the calamity of the First World War have been avoided? The result is, in essence, retrospective wishful thinking. Interestingly, only Hilaire Belloc imagines a counterfactual outcome worse than the historical reality. Like Maurois, Belloc undoes the French Revolution, but this time France's decline as a power is simply accelerated, allowing the Holy Roman empire to wax into a federation of Europe 'stretching from the Baltic to Sicily and from Königsberg to Ostend'. Thus, when war breaks out with this Greater Germany in 1914, it is Britain which loses, ending up as a 'Province of the European Commonwealth'.

The same defects recur in another, more recent collection of counterfactual essays entitled *If I Had Been*.[18] Two of the contributors avert the American War of Independence (one as the Earl of Shelburne, the other as Benjamin Franklin), another (as Juarez) averts the Mexican civil war by pardoning the Emperor Maximilian of Mexico in 1867, and another (as Thiers) prevents the Franco-Prussian War of 1870–1. Owen Dudley Edwards (as Gladstone) solves the Irish Question by opting for more land reform instead of Home Rule, Harold Shukman (as Kerensky) avoids the Bolshevik coup by treating Kornilov more carefully and Louis Allen (as Tojo) wins the war for Japan by attacking the British and Dutch Empires instead of Pearl Harbor – wishful thinking from an American as well as a Japanese point of view. As if that were not enough, Germany is reunified in 1952, thanks to Roger Morgan's Adenauer; the Prague Spring is not crushed, thanks to Philip Windsor's Dubček; and Chilean democracy is preserved by Harold Blakemore's Allende. The obvious objection is that all this is so much wisdom after the event. In each case, the argument is based more on what we know about the consequences of what was done than on the options and data actually available to the figures in question at the time.

Another weakness of both Squire's and Snowman's collections is that in a number of the chapters a single, often trivial, change has momentous consequences. Now, while there is no logical reason why trivial things should *not* have momentous consequences, it is important to beware of the reductive inference that therefore a trivial thing is *the* cause of a great event. The theory of Cleopatra's nose (originally Pascal's) is just the most notorious of many such reductive explanations: thus Anthony's passion for her proboscis determines the fate of Rome. Another attributes Richard III's fall to a lost nail:

> *For want of a nail, the shoe was lost;*
> *For want of a shoe, the horse was lost;*
> *For want of a horse, the rider was lost;*
> *For want of a rider, the battle was lost;*
> *For want of a battle, the kingdom was lost!*

And the same logic underlies Gibbon's suggestion that it was only the fourteenth-century Ottoman Sultan Bajazet's gout which prevented him sacking Rome;[19] the die-hard Southerner's that the American Civil War was lost only because of the fortuitous discovery of Lee's Special Order no. 191 by the Union General George B. McClellan; and Churchill's that a major war between Greece and Turkey was caused by the infected monkey bite which killed King Alexander of Greece in 1920.[20] Just as such reductive explanations imply counterfactuals (no monkey bite, no war), so, conversely, a number of the counterfactuals in the Squire collection are inferred from reductive explanations: that Louis XVI's lack of firmness led to the French Revolution, that the early death of Frederick III caused the First World War, and so on. Likewise, Snowman's book from beginning to end rests on the assumption that it was the mistaken decisions of a few 'great men' which led to major crises like the loss of the American colonies, the Franco-Prussian War and the Bolshevik Revolution. As with the other reductive explanations discussed above, this may sometimes have been the case; but it has to be demonstrated rather than simply assumed, or the explanations are simply not plausible – and the counterfactual outcomes on which they rest collapse.[21]

A related problem is the effect of humour. The essays in the Squire collection are, to varying degrees, supposed to be funny. But the funnier they are, the less plausible they are. This is true of most reductive explanations: formulated differently, they can become more plausible. 'Had Anthony not delayed leaving Egypt, he might have defeated Caesar'; 'Had Richard III won at Bosworth, he might have stabilised Yorkist rule'; 'Had Bajazet chosen to attack Italy after his Hungarian victory, he might well have been able to sack Rome'; 'Had it not been for their knowledge of Lee's intentions, the armies of the Union might well have been defeated at Antietam'; 'Had it not been for the death of the King of Greece, war with Turkey might not have broken out.' Less funny, in each case; but more believable. Similarly, it is not nonsense to suggest that, if the General Strike had been more successful, Labour governments might have lasted longer and achieved more than they did between the wars. Only when couched as a send-up of *The Times* does the counterfactual become incredible.

If nothing else, Squire's volume firmly established the character of the counterfactual essay as a *jeu d'esprit*, a vehicle for wishful thinking or reductive explanation – and, above all, high table humour. In his characteristically mischievous critique of Marxism in *Freedom and Organisation* (1934), Bertrand Russell maintained the standard which Squire had set:

> It may be maintained quite plausibly [*sic*] that if Henry VIII had not fallen in love with Anne Boleyn, the United States would not now exist. For it was owing to this event that England broke with the Papacy, and therefore it did not acknowledge the Pope's gift of the Americas to Spain and Portugal. If England had remained Catholic, it is probable that what is now the United States would have been part of Spanish America.

In the same facetious vein, Russell suggested 'without undue solemnity, the following alternative theory of the causation of the Industrial Revolution':

> Industrialism is due to modern science, modern science is due to Galileo, Galileo is due to Copernicus, Copernicus is due to the Renaissance, the Renaissance is due to the fall of Constantinople, the fall of Constantinople is due to the migration of the Turks, the migration of the Turks is due to the desiccation of Central

Asia. Therefore the fundamental study in searching for historical causes is hydrography.[22]

This tradition lives on in the collection of essays published in 1984 by John Merriman, *For Want of a Horse*.[23] These include three American speculations: What if Pocahontas had not saved Captain John Smith?, What if Voltaire had emigrated to America in 1753? and What if Governor Hutchinson's daughter had persuaded him not to send back the *Dartmouth* (the incident which precipitated the Boston tea party)? In addition, there are two on French subjects: What if the flight from Varennes had been successful? and What if the Bourbon line had not failed in 1820?; as well as one on Britain: What if William III had been defeated at sea by James II? On the whole, this is after-dinner history. The overall tone is set by the opening chapter, which speculates what would have happened if Fidel Castro had signed a contract to play baseball with the New York Giants, and is maintained by an absurd piece by Peter Gay, which implies that psychoanalysis would have been taken more seriously if its founder had not been a Jew. Only Conrad Russell's essay on 1688 – entitled 'The Catholic Wind' – has any real historical value.[24]

Here, Russell revives the question originally (but whimsically) addressed by Chesterton in the Squire collection: could the English Reformation have been undone, in this case by a wind which favoured James II's fleet rather than William III's? A variation on the same theme had in fact been suggested just a few years before by Hugh Trevor-Roper, who disputed the inevitability of Stuart failure in the 1640s and 1680s, asking: 'Could not a wiser king than [Charles I or James II] have preserved or restored an authoritarian monarchy in England, as was done in many European countries?' If Charles had been granted 'a few more years', Trevor-Roper suggested, the ageing of his parliamentary opponents might have told against them. If James, 'like his brother, had set politics above religion' the 'Stuart reaction' might have 'taken root': 'And then would not the Whig grandees of England, like the Huguenot grandees of France, have turned to worship the risen sun?'[25] John Vincent has recently developed this theme further, matching Renouvier's 'alternative' history of a pagan Europe with an alternative history of a Catholic England. Vincent takes an earlier starting point than Russell and Trevor-Roper:

> [T]he Spanish conquest of the sixteenth century [involved] a relatively bloodless imposition of rationality, but ... a novel consistency in taxation which led to sporadic revolts such as the Iconoclasm of Norwich. More seriously, it left England without the option of playing the part of a demilitarised satellite. In the Thirty Years War, no less than four foreign armies contended for mastery of English soil, and the putting of Bristol to the sword entered folk memory.

In the wake of this disaster Vincent imagines a period of 'stability' lasting well into the eighteenth century; but this ends with another calamity: 'the collapse of state credit after defeat in the French war, and the concession to France of its "natural frontier" on the Thames'.

After this, things deteriorate rapidly, so that the nineteenth century becomes England's nadir, rather than its zenith:

> The subsequent abdication led to intermittent civil war between the gentry republic of Citizen Burke, and the Navy Radicals, ending only in the protectorate of Marshal Wellesley and entry into the French mercantilist system. Despite disinterested government, England under the Wellesleys, deprived of its trade, moved inexorably towards demographic disaster, exacerbated by reliance on a single crop as it became the granary of a rapidly industrialising France. The wheat rust and mass starvation of the Wet Years initiated catastrophic depopulation. Politically, failure of French relief efforts inspired obsessive nationalism centred on liberating the so-called 'lost' French province south of the Thames, a movement abruptly ended by the flight of the Whig earls to Madeira and the internment of Gladstone on St Helena.

But the worst was still to come:

> Next century, the determining event was the German war. Long-standing English scientific backwardness made it structurally inevitable that Germany would be first with the atomic bomb. The clinical elimination of Leeds and Sheffield brought speedy surrender, and at least saved England from invasion. Indeed, no event did more to bring England into the European Union...[26]

Unlike so many of the contributors to Squire and Merriman, neither Russell, Trevor-Roper nor Vincent can really be accused of wishful thinking. Nor are their assumptions reductive to the point of being merely humorous. In each case, a serious historical point is being made about the contingency of English 'exceptionalism'. Yet their various contributions remain no more than suggestions, with only the sketchiest of supporting evidence. They are brilliantly formulated counterfactual *questions*, not answers.

A wholly different use of counterfactual argumentation has been made by exponents of the so-called New Economic History.[27] The first serious venture into quantitative counterfactual argumentation, R. W. Fogel's work on the contribution of railways to American economic growth, sought to construct a model of US economic development without railways in order to challenge the traditional assumption that they had been indispensable to American industrialisation. According to his calculations, if no railways had been built, US GNP would have been only slightly lower than it actually was in 1890, though the area of cultivated land would have been substantially smaller.[28] Similar methods have been used by McCloskey and others in the debate on Britain's relative economic decline after 1870.[29]

There is no wishful thinking here, and certainly no humour. However, there are serious objections to such 'cliometric' arguments. The most frequent is that the relatively narrow base of nineteenth-century statistics cannot sustain the edifice of extrapolation and calculation built upon it.[30] In so far as this objection has been directed at Fogel's work on the economics of slavery, it clearly has a political subtext: his argument that, but for the Civil War, slavery could have been sustained economically was naturally an unpopular one with many American liberals.[31] But it applies with considerable force to his work on railways too. Only by making fairly heroic assumptions about 'backward and forward linkages' was Fogel able to conjure up – even if only on a computer print-out – an America without railways. A more serious objection to his approach is that the counterfactual scenarios in question lack historical plausibility – not because they are reductive or frivolous, but because they are anachronistic. Contemporary debates about railways were generally not about *whether* to build them but about *where* to build them. The best defence of Fogel is that the purpose of calculating the 'social savings' afforded by railways is not to conjure up a plausible alternative history but to test a hypothesis about the role of railways in economic growth. No one is in fact trying to 'imagine' nineteenth-century America without railways. Indeed, the ultimate effect of this kind of counterfactual is to show precisely why the railways *were* built, by quantifying their (quite considerable) contribution to the economy as a whole. In a similar way, the debate on economic policy options in the last years of the Weimar republic has tended to show that there were no politically viable alternatives to the deflationary measures implemented by Chancellor Brüning between 1930 and 1932.[32]

There are, in other words, two distinct kinds of counterfactual which have been used by historians: those which are essentially the products of imagination but (generally) lack an empirical basis; and those designed to test hypotheses by (supposedly) empirical means, which eschew imagination in favour of computation. In the case of the former, it is the tendency to rely for inspiration on hindsight, or to posit reductive explanations, which leads to implausibility. In the case of the latter, it is the tendency to make anachronistic assumptions. Just how hard it is to overcome these difficulties can be seen in the path-breaking attempt by Geoffrey Hawthorn to combine elements of both approaches.[33] In one of his supposedly 'plausible worlds', he 'subtracts' the plague from French medieval history, imagining a consequent fall in rural fertility in France and a consequent acceleration in the pace of French economic and political modernisation in the eighteenth century. In another, he imagines the consequences of American non-intervention in Korea after the Second World War; and in a third he diverts the course of Italian art of the late Duecento and early Trecento away from the innovations which were the harbingers of the Renaissance. The second example has perhaps the greatest plausibility, rooted as it is in the American diplomatic documents.[34] But Hawthorn's other 'worlds' are less credible. The first involves an argument about the links between medieval demography and eighteenth-century economic and political development which even the boldest cliometrician would view with suspicion; while his vision of a 'non-Renaissance' in art depends almost entirely on questionable assumptions about the dynamics of stylistic change in art.[35] As for his less detailed introductory sketches for a Labour Party renaissance in the 1980s and a Moorish superstate in the twentieth century (in fact, an extension of Guedalla's essay of 1932), these would not look out of place in a new edition of Squire's *If...*.[36]

By themselves, the defects of all these attempts at explicit counterfactual analysis could almost explain the failure of counterfactualism to catch on. Whether by posing implausible questions or by providing implausible answers, counterfactual history has tended to discredit itself. Yet there are clearly other reasons why so few historians have attempted to argue in this way – or, when they have acknowledged the possibility of alternative outcomes, have left the counterfactual implicit, as a kind of subtext. Such veiled counterfactualism has been a striking feature of a great many recent 'revisionist' works of history – not altogether surprisingly, in that most revisionists tend to be challenging some form of deterministic interpretation. To take one example, R. F. Foster's justly acclaimed *Modern Ireland* repeatedly calls into question the nationalist teleology of inevitable independence from 'English' rule. Yet at no point does Foster make the implicit alternatives (for instance, continued Irish membership of the Union, perhaps as a result of a successful passage of one of the early Home Rule Bills) explicit.[37] Much the same can be said of John Charmley's polemical critique of Churchill, which implies that the British empire could have been preserved after 1940 by means of alternative policies such as peace with Hitler, without spelling out how this might have worked.[38] Clearly, something more than the defects of past attempts at counterfactual history has deterred such historians from spelling out the historical alternatives their books imply. A more profound suspicion of counterfactualism is at work – a suspicion which has the deepest of roots in the philosophy of history.

Divine Intervention and Predestination

There was nothing inevitable about the triumph of historical determinism. As Herbert Butterfield suggested, the world in pre-literate societies probably seemed anything but deterministic. Life was dominated by the effects of natural forces, some rhythmic and predictable (the seasons), others intelligible only with reference to supernatural forces:

> Whenever the causes seemed incommensurate with the results or the mundane explanation seemed inadequate, whenever chance or a curious conjuncture produced something that conflicted with expectations, whenever extraneous factors not normally brought into the reckoning ... give the narrative a surprising twist, in all these cases one would ... believe that [God] had intervened. This recourse to divine intervention to explain the unexpected illustrates the importance of contingency in history; the inability at early stages in the development to see all the connections between the events; the cataclysmic character of the happenings; the fact that great consequences can proceed out of little causes; the fears that men have in a world, the proceedings of which they do not understand; the feeling men

have that history is a thing that happens to them rather than something that they are making; the feeling of dependence which they would doubtless have when they were unable to understand or master the operations of nature, the mystery of natural happenings ...; all these things would lead men to feel in life that much depended on the gods ...[39]

Divine agency thus originated as a kind of explanation of last resort. In polytheistic religions, however, this was often merely a matter of giving names to conflicting natural forces. Indeed, the unsatisfactory nature of polytheism prompted the Epicureans' rejection of any kind of divine agency: perhaps the earliest statement of an anti-determinist philosophy. Lucretius proclaimed the existence of an infinite universe composed of atoms with an essentially random dynamic:

> Our world has been made by nature through the spontaneous and casual collision and the multifarious, accidental, random and purposeless congregation and coalescence of atoms ... *Nature is free and uncontrolled by proud masters* and runs the universe by herself without the aid of gods. For who ... can rule the sum total of the measureless? Who can hold in coercive hand the strong reins of the unfathomable? ... Who can be in all places at all times, ready to darken the clear sky with clouds and rock it with a thunderclap – to launch bolts that may often wreck his own temples, or retire and spend his fury letting fly at deserts with that missile which often passes the guilty and slays the innocent and blameless?[40]

The only remotely deterministic element in Lucretius' thought was his primitive theory of entropy: 'Everything is gradually decaying and going aground onto the rocks, worn out by old age.'[41]

It was thus only slowly that the idea developed of an ultimate and purposeful supernatural arbiter. A good illustration of the evolving classical conception of 'Fortune' in this role can be found in Polybius' *Rise of the Roman Empire* (written in the second century BC):

> It is precisely the element of the unexpected in the events I have chosen to describe which will challenge and stimulate everyone alike ... to study my systematic history ... Just as *Fortune has steered almost all the affairs of the world in one direction and forced them to converge upon one and the same goal,* so it is the task of the historian to present to his reader under one synoptical view the process by which she has accomplished this general design. ... The general and comprehensive scheme of events, when it began, whence it originated, and how it produced the final result [was] the achievement of Fortune ... For although Fortune is forever producing something new and forever enacting a drama in the lives of men, yet she has never before in a single instance created such a composition or put on such a show-piece as that which we have witnessed in our own times.[42]

Polybius' suggestion that the 'vicissitudes' of Fortune in fact had a purpose – the triumph of Rome – was an important historiographical step towards a more deterministic notion of divine agency. A similar conception can be found in the work of Tacitus, though here it is Rome's destruction which is the divine objective: 'Rome's unparalleled sufferings supplied ample proof that the gods are ... eager for our punishment.' For Tacitus, as for Polybius, 'the outcome' of 'the actual course of events' was 'often dictated by chance'; but events 'also had their underlying logic and causes'.[43]

An additional superhuman factor which Polybius acknowledged was the Stoic notion of historical cycles, culminating in periodic natural catastrophes:

> When a deluge or a plague or a failure of crops ... result[s] in the destruction of much of the human race ... all the traditions

and arts will simultaneously perish, but when in the course of time a new population has grown up again from the survivors left by the disaster, as a crop grows up from seed in the ground, a renewal of social life will begin.[44]

The same idea of history as a cyclical process can, of course, be found in the Old Testament book of Ecclesiastes: 'The thing that hath been, it is that which shall be; and that which is done is that which shall be done.'[45] However, the divine Plan of the Hebrew God was rather more complex than that of the Graeco-Roman Fortune. In the Old Testament, Yahweh's purpose unfolds itself in a complex historical narrative: the Creation, the Fall, the election of Israel, the prophets, the Exile and the rise of Rome. To this the early Christians' New Testament added a revolutionary coda: the Incarnation, the Crucifixion and Resurrection. Jewish and Christian history thus had from an early stage a far more deterministic structure than classical historiography: 'Not only did God direct the events of the world, but his intervention (and its underlying purpose) was for the early Christians *the only thing that gave any meaning to history*.'[46] In the writing of Eusebius (c. AD 300), events and individuals are generally portrayed as either pro-Christian, therefore favoured by God, or anti-Christian, therefore doomed.[47]

It would be wrong, however, to exaggerate the determinism of ecclesiastical history. In Augustine's *The City of God,* God is not crudely biased in favour of Christians, rewarding them and punishing the wicked; for the good as much as the wicked have been contaminated by original sin. Augustine's God is omnipotent and omniscient, but He has given men free will – albeit a will which has been weakened by original sin and is therefore biased towards evil. In theological terms, this put Augustine somewhere between the absolute fatalism of Manichaeism, which denied the existence of free will, and the Pelagian view that free will could not be compromised by the imperfection of original sin. In historical terms, it allowed him to combine the Judaeo-Christian idea of a preordained divine plan with a relatively autonomous portrayal of human agency – a distinct refinement of earlier Greek and Roman formulations.

From a practical point of view, this provided a relatively flexible framework within which to write Christian history. Indeed, much the same flexibility can still be found more than a millennium later in Bossuet's *Discourse on Universal History* (1681). As with Augustine, secondary causes appear to have some autonomy, despite the overarching theme of divine intention:

> The long concatenation of particular causes which make and undo empires depends on the decrees of Divine Providence. High up in His heavens God holds the reins of all kingdoms. He has every heart in His hands. Sometimes he restrains passions, *sometimes He leaves them free*, and thus agitates mankind. By this means God carries out his redoubtable judgements according to ever infallible rules. He it is who prepares vast results through the most distant causes, and who strikes vast blows whose repercussion is so widespread. Thus it is that God reigns over all nations.[48]

Of course, the line from Augustine to Bossuet was anything but straight. During the Renaissance, for example, there had been something of a revival of the original classical conception of the relationship between divine purpose and human freedom of action. In Machiavelli's historical writing, *Fortuna* is the ultimate arbiter of the individual's destiny – though a capricious, feminine arbiter who can be wooed by the 'virtuous' man. By contrast, in Vico's essentially cyclical model of 'the ideal eternal history' (composed of successive divine, heroic and civil periods), the role of Providence is distinctly Augustinian. Free will is:

> the home and seat of all the virtues and among the others of justice.... But men because of their corrupted nature are under the tyranny of self-love, which compels them to make private utility their chief guide.... Therefore it is only by divine

providence that [man] can be held within these orders to practise justice as a member of the society of the family, the state and finally of mankind.

Vico's *New Science* was therefore 'a rational civil theology of divine providence ... a demonstration, so to speak, of the historical fact of providence, for it must be a history of the forms of order which, without human discernment or intent, and often against the designs of men, providence has given to this great city of the human race'.[49] There is a close parallel between Vico's approach and that of Arnold Toynbee, certainly the most ambitious of twentieth-century Christian historians, who retained a firm belief in 'free will' despite subscribing to a similar – and, to some critics, fundamentally deterministic – cyclical theory about the rise and fall of what he called 'civilisations'.[50]

Of course, there was always a more strongly deterministic tendency (of which Augustine had been well aware) within Christian theology. It was a logical enough conclusion to draw from the fact of God's omniscience that He had already determined upon whom to bestow his grace. This raised a problem, however, which first surfaced in the predestinarian controversy of the ninth century. If God had predestined some for salvation, according to Godescalc of Orbais, he must also have predestined others to damnation; it was logically incorrect to speak of Christ dying for this second group, as on their account he would have died in vain. This doctrine of 'double predestination' persisted in the teaching of medieval theologians like Gregory of Rimini and Hugolino of Orvieto and resurfaced again in Calvin's *Institutes* (though it was actually Calvin's followers like Theodore Beza who elevated predestination to the position of a central Calvinist principle). Yet once again it would be misleading to equate Calvinist predestinarianism with historical determinism. For the theologians' arguments about predestination were largely concerned with the afterlife, and did not have any very clear implications for human affairs of the world.

In short, ideas of divine intervention in history circumscribed, but did not eliminate, the idea that individuals have some freedom to choose between possible courses of action. In that sense, neither classical nor Judaeo-Christian theology necessarily precluded a counterfactual approach to historical questions – though clearly the notion of an ultimate divine purpose did not encourage such an approach either. If there is a connection from theology to fully fledged historical determinism, it must therefore be an indirect one, mediated by the self-consciously rationalistic philosophies of the eighteenth century. That century is often associated with 'secularisation' and the decline of religion relative to science. But in historiography, as in so much of the 'Enlightenment', this distinction is less clear-cut than at first appears. Much Enlightenment thought, as Butterfield has said, was merely 'lapsed Christianity', with 'Nature', 'Reason' and other nebulous entities simply taking the place of God. Doctrines of progress were clearly secularised adaptations of Christian doctrine, although supposedly based on empirical foundation. The difference was that these new doctrines were often significantly more rigid in their determinism than the religions from which they were descended.

Scientific Determinism: Materialism and Idealism

Newton's 'revelation' of gravity and three laws of motion marked the birth of a truly deterministic conception of the universe. After Newton, it seemed self-evident (as Hume put it) that 'every object is determin'd by absolute fate to a certain degree and direction of its motion. . . . The actions, therefore, of matter are to be regarded as instances of necessary actions.' Whether one chose to see these laws as divinely ordained or not was, as it still is, to some extent a question of semantics. Hume invoked 'absolute fate'. Leibniz put it differently: 'As God calculates, so the world is made.' The important point is that science appeared to have eliminated contingency from the physical world. In particular, Leibniz's emphasis on the 'complex attributes' of all phenomena – the interrelatedness of everything – seemed to imply the unalterable nature of the past, present and future (save in other, imaginary worlds). From this it was but a short step to the rigid determinism of Laplace, in whose conception the universe could 'only do one thing':

> Given for one instant an intelligence which could comprehend all the forces by which nature is animated and the respective situation of the beings who compose it – an intelligence sufficiently vast to submit these data to analysis – it would embrace in the same formula the movements of the greatest bodies of the universe and those of the lightest atom; for it, nothing would be uncertain and the future, as the past, would be present before its eyes.[51]

The only limit to this kind of determinism was the possibility raised by Descartes and others that thought and matter were distinct substances, only the latter of which was subject to deterministic laws. A modified version of this distinction can be found in the work of Laplace's contemporary Bichat, who insisted that determinism only really applied to inorganic entities, whereas organic entities 'defy every kind of calculation . . . ; it is impossible to foresee, predict, or calculate, anything with regard to their phenomena'.[52] However, this kind of qualification could be countered in one of two ways.

The first was simply to explain human behaviour in materialistic terms. Such arguments had been attempted before. Hippocrates, for example, had explained 'the deficiency of spirit and courage observable in the human inhabitants of Asia' with reference to 'the low margin of seasonal variability in the temperature of that continent'. In addition, he cited 'the factor of institutions' – specifically, the debilitating effect of despotic rule – in his explanation of Oriental pusillanimity.[53] Precisely these kinds of explanation were taken up and developed by French Enlightenment writers like Condorcet and Montesquieu, whose *Spirit of the Laws* related social, cultural and political differences to climatic and other natural factors. Montesquieu gave characteristic expression to the new confidence of such materialistic theories: 'If a particular cause like the accidental result of a battle has ruined a state, there was a general cause which made the downfall of this state ensue from a single battle.' For: 'Blind fate has [not] produced all the effects which we see in the world.' In Britain, Adam Smith's *Wealth of Nations* laid the foundation for a strictly economic analysis of society which implied a cyclical historical process. Here too, it was not 'blind fate' but an 'Invisible Hand' which led individuals to act, unwittingly, in the common interest even while pursuing their own selfish ends.

A similar shift towards determinism occurred in German philosophy, though it took a very different form. Like Descartes, Kant left some room for human autonomy in his philosophy. But this was only in an unknowable parallel universe of 'noumena'. In the material world, he insisted, 'the manifestations of the will in human actions are determined, like all other external events, by universal natural laws':

> When the play of the freedom of the human will is examined on the great scale of universal history a regular march will be discovered in its movements; and ... in this way, what appears to be tangled and unregulated in the case of individuals will be recognised in the history of the whole species as a continually advancing, though slow, development of its original capacities and endowments.... Individual men, and even whole nations, little think, while they are pursuing their own purposes ... that they are advancing unconsciously under the guidance of a purpose of nature which is unknown to them.[54]

In his *Idea for a Universal History*, Kant spelt out the task for the new historical philosophy: 'To attempt to discover *a purpose in nature* behind this senseless course of events, and to decide whether it is after all possible to formulate in terms of a definite plan of nature a history of creatures who act without a plan of their own.'[55]

It was Hegel, more than any other German philosopher, who rose to this challenge. For Hegel as for Kant, 'human arbitrariness and even external necessity' had to be subordinated to 'a higher necessity'. 'The sole aim of philosophical inquiry,' as he put it in the second draft of his 'Philosophical History of the World', was 'to eliminate the contingent.... In history, we must look for a general design, the ultimate end of the world. We must bring into history the belief and conviction that the realm of the will is not at the mercy of contingency.' However, Hegel's 'higher necessity' was not material but supernatural – indeed, in many ways it closely resembled the traditional Christian God, most obviously when he spoke of 'an eternal justice and love, the absolute and ultimate end [of] which is truth in and for itself'. Hegel just happened to call his God 'Reason'. Thus his basic 'presupposition' was 'the idea that reason governs the world and that history therefore is a rational process':

> That world history is governed by an ultimate design ... whose rationality is ... a divine and absolute reason – this is the proposition whose truth we must assume; its proof lies in the study of world history itself, which is the image and enactment of reason.... Whoever looks at the world rationally will find that it assumes a rational aspect.... The overall content of world history is rational and indeed has to be rational; a divine will rules supreme and is strong enough to determine the overall content. Our aim must be to discern this substance, and to do so, we must bring with us a rational consciousness.[56]

This somewhat circular argumentation was the second possible way of dealing with the Cartesian claim that determinism did not apply to the non-material world. Hegel had no desire to give precedence to materialism: 'The spirit and the course of its development are the true substance of history,' he maintained; and the role of 'physical nature' was emphatically subordinate to the role of 'the spirit'. But 'the spirit', he argued, was just as subject to deterministic forces as physical nature.

What were these forces? Hegel equated what he called 'the spirit' with 'the idea of human freedom', suggesting that the historical process could be understood as the attainment of self-knowledge by this idea of freedom through a succession of 'world spirits'. Adapting the Socratic form of philosophical dialogue, he posited the existence of a dichotomy within (to take the example which most concerned him) the national spirit, between the essential and the real, or the universal and the particular. It was the dialectical relationship between these which propelled history onwards and upwards in what has been likened to a dialectical waltz – thesis, antithesis, synthesis. But this was a waltz, Fred Astaire style, up a stairway. 'The development, progress and ascent of the spirit towards a higher concept of itself ... is accomplished by the debasement, fragmentation and destruction of the preceding mode of reality.... The universal arises out of the particular and determinate and its negation.... All this takes place automatically.'

The implications of Hegel's model were in many ways more radical than those of any contemporary materialist theory of history. In his contradiction-driven scheme of things, the individual's aspirations and fate counted for nothing: they were 'a matter of indifference to world history, which uses individuals only as instruments to further its own progress'. No matter what injustice might befall individuals, 'philosophy should help us to understand that the actual world is as it ought to be'. For 'the actions of human beings in the history of the world produce an effect altogether different from what they themselves intend' and 'the worth of individuals is measured by the extent to which they reflect and represent the national spirit'. Hence 'the great individuals of world history ... are those who seize upon [the] higher universal and make it their own end'. Morality was therefore simply beside the point: 'World history moves on a higher plane than that to which morality properly belongs.' And, of course, 'the concrete manifestation' of 'the unity of the subjective will and the universal' – 'the totality of ethical life and the realisation of freedom' – was that fetish-object of Hegel's generation: the (Prussian) state.[57]

With such arguments, Hegel had, it might be said, secularised predestination, translating Calvin's theological dogma into the realm of history. The individual now lost control not only of his salvation in the afterlife, but also of his fate on earth. In this sense, Hegel represents the culmination of a theological tendency towards out-and-out determinism: a logical enough conclusion, perhaps, if the existence of a supreme deity is accepted, but one which Augustine and others had done much to temper. At the same time, there was at least a superficial resemblance between Hegel's idealist philosophy of history and the materialist theories which had developed elsewhere. Hegel's 'cunning of Reason' was perhaps a harsher master than Kant's 'Nature' and Smith's 'Invisible Hand'; but these other quasi-deities performed analogous roles.

A Hegelian would presumably say that a synthesis of the idealist and materialist approaches was inevitable. However, that would have seemed a remote possibility at the time of Hegel's death. The great idealist's British contemporaries may also have constructed their models of political economy on implicitly religious models (as Boyd Hilton and others have argued); but outwardly and self-consciously they continued to operate on empirical and materialist principles. Moreover, the striking feature of political economy as it developed in the early nineteenth century was its pessimism compared with the relative optimism of Hegel, who shared with Kant a basic assumption that history was progressive. Ricardo's economic laws of diminishing agricultural returns, the falling rate of profit and the iron law of wages, like Malthus's principle of population, portrayed the economy as self-regulating, self-equilibrating and morally retributive – a system in which growth must inevitably be followed by stagnation and contraction. The logical conclusion of British political economy was thus a cyclical rather than a progressive model of history.

Nor was there much obvious affinity between Hegel's idealist model of the historical process and the various materialist theories being developed at around the same time in France. Comte's *Cours de philosophie positive* claimed to discern yet another 'great fundamental law': 'That each of our leading conceptions – each branch of our knowledge – passes successively through three different theoretical conditions: the Theological, or fictitious; the Metaphysical, or abstract; and the Scientific, or positive'.[58] Taine offered another 'positivist' trinity, of milieu, moment and race. Both took pride in their empirical methods. According to Taine, the monograph was the historian's best tool: 'He plunges it into the past like a lancet and draws it out charged with complete and authentic specimens. One understands a period after twenty or thirty such soundings.'[59] In short, there was nothing preordained about the synthesis of British political economy and Hegelian philosophy which was to prove the most successful determinist doctrine of all.

What distinguished Marx from other nineteenth-century philosophers of history was that he did not worry much about free will; perhaps this was the secret of his success. When John Stuart Mill called on 'really scientific thinkers to connect by theories the facts of universal history' and to find 'the derivative laws of social order and of social progress', he was echoing Comte, and Kant before him. Yet like many other nineteenth-century liberals, Mill had a sneaking dread of slipping from determinism into fatalism. After all, it was not easy for a liberal to throw free will – the role of the individual – overboard. Mill's solution to the problem was to redefine 'the doctrine of Causation, improperly called the doctrine of Necessity', to mean 'only that men's actions are the joint result of the general laws and circumstances of human nature and of their own particular characters; those characters again being the consequence of the natural and artificial circumstances that constituted their education, *among which circumstances must be reckoned their conscious efforts*'. On closer inspection, however, this was a hefty qualification. Moreover, in a passage which explicitly posed counterfactual questions, Mill acknowledged openly that 'general causes count for much, but individuals also produce great changes in history':

> It is as certain as any contingent judgement respecting historical events can be that if there had been no Themistocles there would

have been no victory of Salamis; and had there not, where would have been all our civilization? How different, again, would have been the issue if Epaminondas, or Timoleon, or even Iphicrates, instead of Chares and Lysicles, had commanded at Chaeroneia?

Indeed, Mill quoted with approval two further counterfactual points: that without Caesar, 'the venue ... of European civilization might ... have been changed' and without William the Conqueror 'our history or our national character would [not] have been what they are'. After this, his conclusion that the individual's 'conscious efforts' would be subordinated to 'the law of human life' at the collective level, and over the long run, was unconvincing:

> The longer our species lasts ... the more does the influence of past generations over the present, and of mankind *en masse* over every individual in it, predominate over other forces; ... the increasing preponderance of the collective agency of the species over all minor causes, is constantly bringing the general evolution of the race into something which deviates less from a certain preappointed track.[60]

The same sort of uncertainty can be detected even in the work of Henry Thomas Buckle, whose *History of Civilization in England* (the first volume of which was published in 1856) appeared to answer Mill's description of a 'scientific' history. Here the parallel with the natural sciences was explicit and confident:

> In regard to nature, events apparently the most irregular and capricious have been explained and have been shown to be in accordance with certain fixed and universal laws.... If human events were subjected to a similar treatment, we have every right to expect similar results.... Every generation demonstrates some events to be regular and predictable, which the preceding generation had declared to be irregular and unpredictable: so that the marked tendency of the advance of civilization is to

strengthen our belief in the universality of order of method and of law.

For Buckle, study of social statistics (the volume of which was just beginning that exponential growth which continues today) would reveal 'the great truth that the actions of men ... are in reality never inconsistent, but however capricious they may appear only form part of one vast system of universal order ... the undeviating regularity of the moral world'.[61] Yet Buckle too was worried about free will. His model of causation, like Mill's, stated that 'when we perform an action, we perform it in consequence of some motive or motives; that those motives are the results of some antecedents; and that, therefore, if we were acquainted with the whole of the antecedents, and with all the laws to their movements, we could with unerring certainty predict the whole of their immediate results'. Thus 'the actions of men being determined solely by their antecedents, must have a character of uniformity, that is to say, must, under precisely the same circumstances, always issue in precisely the same results'. This would have been undiluted fatalism if Buckle had not added a rather lame rider: 'All the changes of which history is full ... must be the fruit of a double action; an action of external phenomena upon the mind, and another action of the mind upon the phenomena.'[62]

Perhaps no nineteenth-century writer wrestled harder with this problem – the contradiction between free will and deterministic theories of history – than Tolstoy in the concluding chapter of *War and Peace*.[63] Tolstoy ridiculed the feeble attempts not only of popular historians, memoir-writers and biographers, but also of Hegelian idealists, to explain the world-shaking events of 1789–1815, and particularly the French invasion of Russia and its ultimate failure – the historical setting of his great epic. The role of divine providence, the role of chance, the role of great men, the role of ideas – all these he dismissed as insufficient to explain the huge movements of millions of people which occurred during the Napoleonic period. For Tolstoy, 'the new school [of history] ought to be studying not the manifestations of power but the causes which create power.... If the purpose of history is the description of the flux of humanity and of peoples, the first question to be answered ... will be: What is the power that moves nations?' Borrowing the terminology of Newton, he insisted that 'the only conception capable of explaining the movement of peoples is that of some force commensurate with the whole movement of peoples'. He was dismissive of jurisprudential definitions of the relationship between ruler and ruled, especially those implying a contractual delegation of power from the latter to the former:

> Every command executed is always one of an immense number unexecuted. All the impossible commands are inconsistent with the course of events and do not get carried out. Only the possible ones link up into a consecutive series of commands corresponding to the series of events, and are carried out.... Every event that occurs inevitably coincides with some expressed desire and, having found justification for itself, appears as the product of the will of one or more persons.... Whatever happens it will always appear that precisely this had been foreseen and decreed.... Historical characters and their commands are dependent on the event.... The more [a] person expresses opinions, theories and justifications of the collective action, the less is his participation in that action.... Those who take the largest direct share in the event assume the least responsibility, and vice versa.

This line of argument appeared to lead him into something of a dead-end: 'Morally, power appears to cause the event; physically, it is those who are subordinate to that power. But inasmuch as moral activity is inconceivable without physical activity, the cause of the event is found in neither the one nor the other but in the conjunction of the two. Or, in other words, the concept of cause is not applicable to the phenomenon we are examining.' However, Tolstoy merely took this to mean that he had arrived at his goal: a law of social motion comparable with the laws of physics:

'Electricity produces heat; heat produces electricity. Atoms attract and atoms repel one another.... We cannot say why this occurs, and [so] we say that such is the nature of these phenomena, such is their law. The same applies to historical phenomena. Why do wars and revolutions happen? We do not know. We only know that to produce the one or the other men form themselves into a certain combination in which all take part; and we say that this is the nature of men, that this is a law.'

A moment's reflection will, of course, suffice to expose the hollowness of this definition of a natural law (that is, a law is a reciprocal relationship which we cannot explain). But what follows is even more baffling, as Tolstoy goes on to discuss the implications of his 'law' for the idea of individual free will. For 'if there is a single law controlling the actions of men, free will cannot exist'. Thus, for the sake of determinist theory, one of the greatest of all novelists – whose insights into individual motivations give *War and Peace* its enduring power – sets out to disprove the existence of free will. Can he really mean that all Pierre's long agonisings had no bearing whatever on his inevitable fate? So it would seem. According to Tolstoy, the individual is as much subject to the Tolstoyan law of power as he is to the Newtonian law of gravity. It is just that man, with his irrational sense of freedom, refuses to *acknowledge* the former law the way he acknowledges the latter:

> Having learned from experience and by reasoning that a stone falls downwards, man is convinced beyond doubt and in all cases expects to find this law operating ... But having learned just as surely that his will is subject to laws, he does not and cannot believe it.... If the consciousness of freedom appears to the reason as a senseless contradiction ... this only proves that consciousness is not subject to reason.

The implications of this dichotomy for history are spelt out in another (rather more intellectually satisfying) Tolstoyan law: 'In every action we investigate we see a certain measure of freedom and a certain measure of necessity.... The ratio of freedom to necessity decreases and increases according to the point of view from which the action is regarded; but their relation is always one of inverse proportion.' Tolstoy concludes that the historian will be less inclined to credit his subjects with free will the more he knows about their 'relation to the external world'; the further in time he is from the events he describes; and the more he apprehends 'that endless chain of causation demanded by reason, in which every phenomenon capable of being understood ... must have its definite place as a result of what has gone before and a cause of what will follow.'

Interestingly, at this point Tolstoy is forced to admit that 'there can never be absolute inevitability' in historical writing because 'to imagine a human action subject only to the law of necessity, without any freedom, we must assume a knowledge of an *infinite* number of spatial conditions, an *infinitely* long period of time and an *infinite* chain of causation':

> Freedom is the content. Necessity is the form.... All that we know of the life of man is merely a certain relation of free will to necessity, that is, of consciousness to the laws of reason.... The manifestation of the force of free will in space, in time and in dependence on cause forms the subject of history.

In fact, there is nothing in those lines which logically implies strict determinism. However, he then adds:

> What is known to us we call the laws of necessity; what is unknown we call free will. Free will is for history only an expression connoting what we do not know about the law of human life.... The recognition of man's free will as a force capable of influencing historical events ... is the same for history as the recognition of a free force moving heavenly bodies would be for astronomy.... If there is a single human action due to free will then not a single historical law can exist.... Only by reducing this element of free will to the infinitesimal ... can we

> convince ourselves of the absolute inaccessibility of causes, and
> then instead of seeking causes, history will adopt for its task the
> investigation of historical laws. ... The obstacle in the way of
> recognising the subjection of the individual to the laws of space
> and time and causality lies in the difficulty of renouncing one's
> personal impression of being independent of those laws.

Yet it is simply not clear why it should be desirable to reduce the
role of free will 'to the infinitesimal' when historical actors are
actually conscious of it, for the sake of deterministic laws which
the historian cannot truly apprehend without near-infinite knowledge. Ultimately, Tolstoy's attempt to formulate a convincing
deterministic theory of history is a heroic failure.

Only one man can really be said to have succeeded where he
(and many others) failed. Here – now that its day is apparently
done – we can at least set Marx's philosophy of history in its
proper context: as the most compelling among many brands of
determinism. It was an improbably neat synthesis of Hegelian
idealism and Ricardian political economy: a dialectical historical
process, but flowing from material conflicts rather than spiritual
contradictions, so that (as in *The German Ideology*) 'the real
processes of production' supplanted 'thought thinking itself' as
'the basis of all history'. Proudhon had tried it; Marx perfected it,
'correcting' Hegel by jettisoning the notion of state-sponsored
harmony between the classes and battering Proudhon out of
contention in *The Poverty of Philosophy*.[64] 'The history of all
hitherto existing societies', proclaimed the Communist Manifesto
of 1848 in one of the most enduring catch-phrases of the nineteenth century, 'is the history of class struggles.' Simple, and
catchy.

Marx took more from Hegel than just the dialectic; he also
imbibed his contempt for free will: 'Men make their own history
but they do not know that they are making it.' 'In historical
struggles, one must distinguish ... the phrases and fancies of
parties from their real ... interests, their conception of themselves
from the reality.' 'In the social production of their means of

production, human beings enter into definite and necessary relations which are independent of their will.' 'Are men free to choose this or that form of society for themselves? By no means.' But behind Hegel there is just visible the shade of Calvin, and still older prophets. For in Marx's doctrine, certain individuals – the members of the immiserated and alienated proletariat – formed a new Elect, destined to overthrow capitalism and inherit the earth. In a prophecy of detectably biblical provenance, it was foretold in *Capital*:

> The monopoly of capital becomes a fetter upon the mode of production, which has sprung up and flourished along with and under it. Centralisation of the means of production and socialisation of labour at last reach a point where they become incompatible with their capitalist integument. This integument is burst asunder. The knell of capitalist private property sounds. The expropriators are expropriated.[65]

Admittedly, Marx and Engels were not always as dogmatic as the majority of their later interpreters. Indeed, the failure of their more apocalyptic political predictions to be realised obliged them on occasion to temper the determinism of their best-known works. Marx himself acknowledged that 'acceleration and retardation' of the 'general trend of development' could be influenced by '"accidentals" which include the "chance" character of ... individuals'.[66] Engels too had to admit that 'history often proceeds by jumps and zigzags' which could lead, inconveniently, to 'much interruption of the chain of thought'.[67] In his later correspondence, he sought (vainly, as it proved) to qualify the idea of a simple causal relationship between economic 'base' and social 'superstructure'.

Precisely this kind of problem perplexed the Russian Marxist Georgi Plekhanov. Indeed, his essay 'The Role of the Individual in History' ends up making a far stronger case against Marxist socio-economic determinism than for it, despite Plekhanov's efforts to extricate himself from a welter of more or less persuasive examples of the decisive role played by individuals. If Louis XV had been a man of a different character, acknowledges Plekhanov, the territory of France could have been enlarged (after the War of the Austrian Succession) and as a result her economic and political development might have taken a different course. If Madame Pompadour had enjoyed less influence over Louis, the poor generalship of Soubise might not have been tolerated, and the war might have been waged more effectively at sea. If General Buturlin had attacked Frederick the Great at Streigau in August 1761 – just months before the death of the Empress Elisabeth – he might have routed him. And what if Mirabeau had lived, or Robespierre had died in an accident? What if Bonaparte had been killed in one of his early campaigns? Plekhanov's attempt to jam all these awkward contingencies and counterfactuals back into the straitjacket of Marxist determinism is, to say the least, tortuous:

> The [individual] serves as an instrument of ... necessity and cannot help doing so, owing to his social status and to his mentality and temperament, which were created by his status. This, too, is an aspect of necessity. Since his social status has imbued him with this character and no other, he not only serves as an instrument of necessity and cannot help doing so, but he passionately desires, and cannot help desiring, to do so. This is an aspect of freedom, and, moreover, of freedom that has grown out of necessity, i.e. to put it more correctly, it is freedom that is identical with necessity – it is necessity transformed into freedom.

Thus 'the character of an individual is a "factor" in social development only where, when, and to the extent that social relations permit it to be such'. 'Every man of talent who becomes a social force, is the product of social relations.' Plekhanov even anticipates Bury's later argument that historical accidents are the products of collisions between chains of deterministic causation; but he draws far more deterministic conclusions from it: 'No matter how intricately the petty, psychological and physiological causes may have been interwoven, they would not under any circumstances have eliminated the great social needs that gave rise to the French Revolution.' Even if Mirabeau had lived longer, Robespierre had died earlier and Bonaparte had been struck down by a bullet,

> nevertheless, events would have taken *the same course*. . . . Under no circumstances would the final outcome of the revolutionary movement have been the 'opposite' of what it was. Influential individuals can change the *individual features of events and some of their particular consequences*, but they cannot change their general *trend* . . . [for] *they are themselves the product of this trend; were it not for that trend they would never have crossed the threshold that divides the potential from the real.*[68]

Quite how 'the development of productive forces and the mutual relations between men in the socio-economic process of production' could have counteracted the effect of an Austro-Russian victory over Frederick the Great, Plekhanov does not say. Nor does he consider the possible ramifications of the one counterfactual outcome he does suggest in the case of a Napoleonless France: 'Louis-Philippe would, perhaps, have ascended the throne of his dearly beloved kinsmen not in 1830 but in 1820.' Would that really have been, as he implies, so inconsequential?

Yet just as doubts had begun to assail the Marxists, a breakthrough in an unrelated field of science provided a vital new source of validation for their model of social change. Darwin's revolutionary statement of the theory of natural selection was immediately seized upon by Engels as fresh evidence for the theory of class conflict[69] – though it was not long before the same claims were being made by theorists of racial conflict, who crudely misinterpreted and distorted Darwin's complex (and at times contradictory) message. Writers like Thomas Henry Huxley and Ernst Haeckel took the earlier racial theories of Gobineau and modernised them with a simplified model of natural selection in which competition between individual creatures became a crude struggle between races. Such notions became the common currency of much political debate at the turn of the century. In the absence of the sort of party-political discipline which kept socialist intellectual development under some kind of control, 'Social Darwinism' rapidly took on a host of different forms: the pseudo-scientific work of eugenic theorists; the overconfident imperialism of the English historian E. A. Freeman; the Weimar pessimism of Spengler; and ultimately, of course, the violent, anti-Semitic fantasies of Hitler, which combined racialism and socialism in what was to prove the most explosive ideology of the twentieth century. But what linked them was their deterministic (in some cases, apocalyptic) thrust, and indifference to the notion of individual free will. Given this apparent convergence of Marx and Darwin – despite their starkly different intellectual origins – it is hardly surprising that belief in the possibility of deterministic laws of history was so widespread during and after their lifetimes.

To be sure, not everyone in the nineteenth century embraced determinism. Indeed, the work of Ranke and his followers revealed that historians could draw very different lessons from the world of science. Ranke was suspicious of the way in which previous historians and philosophers had sought to pluck universal historical laws out of the air (or at best out of books by other historians and philosophers). It was his belief that only through properly scientific *methods* – meticulous and exhaustive research in the archives – could one hope to arrive at any understanding of the universal in history. This was the reason for his early pledge to write history 'wie es eigentlich gewesen' ('as it actually was') and his repeated stress on the uniqueness of past events and epochs. 'Historicism' – the movement which Ranke is often credited with having founded – was about understanding particular phenomena in their proper context. Yet this did not mean a complete rejection of determinism; for in a number of important respects Ranke remained beholden to Hegelian philosophy. The methodological direction might have been reversed – from the particular to the universal, rather than the other way round – but the nature and function of the universal in Ranke's work remained unmistakably Hegelian, as was his exaltation of the Prussian state. Above all, the idea that the historian should be concerned to describe the past as it actually was (or perhaps as it 'essentially' was) implicitly ruled out any serious reflection as to how it *might* have been. Ranke, like Hegel, held to the assumption that history was the working out of some kind of spiritual plan. He may not have had Hegel's certainty as to the nature of that plan; but that there was a plan he did not doubt, with the self-realisation of the Prussian state as its end point.

Even those historians who imported Ranke's methodology to England without its Hegelian subtext could base their work on an analogous teleology. In place of Prussia, Stubbs took as his theme that English constitutional evolution towards perfection which is traditionally associated with the less scholarly Macaulay.[70] That other great English Rankean, Acton, applied a similar conception to the history of Europe as a whole. Like the French positivists, the liberal historians of the turn of the century were proud of the way their scientific methods not only revealed practical political 'lessons', but also exemplified that generalised process of 'improvement' which had so enchanted Lecky before them. Indeed, Acton saw historical study itself as one of the engines of Europe's emergence from medieval darkness – a point he expressed in strikingly Germanic language: 'The *universal spirit* of investigation and discovery ... did not cease to operate and withstood the recurring efforts of reaction until ... it at length prevailed. This ... gradual passage ... from subordination to independence, is a phenomenon of primary import to us, because historical science has been one of its instruments.'[71] Thus the historian was not only concerned to describe the inevitable triumph of progress; in doing so, he was actually contributing to it. Hints of this kind of optimism can still be detected in more recent liberal historians like Sir John Plumb[72] and Sir Michael Howard.[73]

Contingency, Chance and the Revolt against Causation

Of course, such progressive optimism, whether idealist or materialist in inspiration, did not go unchallenged. In a powerful and justly famous passage of his essay 'On History', Thomas Carlyle had declared:

> The most gifted man can observe, still more can record, only the *series* of his own impressions; his observation, therefore, ... must be *successive*, while the things done were often *simultaneous* ... It is not acted, as it is in written History: actual events are nowise so simply related to each other as parent and offspring are; every single event is the offspring not of one, but of all other events, prior or contemporaneous, and will in its turn combine with all others to give birth to new: it is an ever-living, ever-working Chaos of Being, wherein shape after shape bodies itself forth from innumerable elements. And this Chaos ... is what the historian will depict, and scientifically gauge, we may say, by threading it with single lines of a few ells in length! For as all Action is, by its nature, to be figured as extended in breadth and depth as well as in length ... so all Narrative is, by its nature, of only one dimension.... Narrative is *linear*, Action is *solid*. Alas for our 'chains', or chainlets, of 'causes and effects' ... when the whole is a broad, deep immensity, and each atom is 'chained' and completed with all![74]

A still more extreme expression of this anti-scientific view came from Carlyle's Russian counterpart, Dostoevsky. In *Notes from Underground*, Dostoevsky fired a broadside of unequalled force against rationalist determinism, heaping scorn on the economists' assumption that man acted out of self-interest, on Buckle's theory of civilisation, on Tolstoy's laws of history:

> You seem certain that man himself will give up erring *of his own free will* ... that ... there are natural laws in the universe, and whatever happens to him happens outside his will.... All

human acts will be listed in something like logarithm tables, say up to the number 108,000, and transferred to a timetable.... They will carry detailed calculations and exact forecasts of everything to come.... But then, one might do anything out of boredom ... because man ... prefers to act in the way he feels like acting and not in the way his reason and interest tell him.... One's own free, unrestrained choice, one's own whim, be it the wildest, one's own fancy, sometimes worked up to a frenzy – that is the most advantageous advantage that cannot be fitted into any table.... A man can wish upon himself, in full awareness, something harmful, stupid and even completely idiotic ... in order to *establish his right* to wish for the most idiotic things.

Applied to history, this could only preclude the idea of progress. It might be 'grand' and 'colourful', but, for Dostoevsky's 'sick' *alter ego*, history was essentially monotonous: 'They fight and fight and fight; they are fighting now, they fought before, and they'll fight in the future.... So you see, you can say anything about world history.... Except one thing, that is. It cannot be said that world history is reasonable.'[75]

Yet even Dostoevsky did not sustain this line of argument throughout his greatest works. Elsewhere (perhaps most evidently in *The Brothers Karamazov*) he turned back towards religious faith, as if only Orthodoxy could inoculate against the plague of anarchy he prophesied in Raskolnikov's nightmare at the end of *Crime and Punishment*. Carlyle's thought took a similar turn, of course, though on closer inspection his sense of the divine will was much closer to Hegel's (and perhaps also to Calvin's) than to the Orthodoxy of Dostoevsky. Echoing (though amending) Hegel, Carlyle saw 'Universal History' as 'at bottom the History of Great Men': '[A]ll things that we see standing accomplished in the world are properly the outer material result ... of the thoughts that dwelt in the Great Men sent into the world; the soul of the whole world's history ... were [*sic*] the history of these ... living light fountain[s], ... [these] natural luminar[ies] shining by the gift of heaven.'[76] This was hardly a recipe for an anti-determinist philosophy of history. On the contrary, Carlyle simply rejected the new brand of scientific determinism in favour of the old divine version:

> History ... is a looking both before and after; as indeed, the coming Time already waits, unseen, yet definitely shaped, *pre-determined and inevitable*, in the Time come; and only in the combination of both is the meaning of either completed.... [Man] lives between two eternities, and ... he would fain unite himself in clear conscious relation ... with the whole Future and the whole Past.[77]

In fact, it is not until the work of turn-of-the-century English historians like Bury, Fisher and Trevelyan that we encounter a complete – if rather unsophisticated – challenge to deterministic assumptions, including even the atavistic Calvinism of Carlyle. Indeed, the mischievous stress on the role of contingency in turn-of-the-century Oxbridge historiography was perhaps informed more by anti-Calvinism than by anything else.[78] What Charles Kingsley called man's 'mysterious power of breaking the laws of his own being' was proposed as a new kind of historical philosophy by both Bury and Fisher. Fisher's *History of Europe* was prefaced with a bluff admission:

> Men wiser and more learned than I have discerned in history a plot, a rhythm, a predetermined pattern. These harmonies are concealed from me. I can see only one emergency following upon another as wave follows upon wave.... [P]rogress is not a law of nature.[79]

Accordingly, Fisher called on historians to 'recognise in the development of human destinies the play of the contingent and the unforeseen' (though whether he did so himself in the main body of the work is debatable). Bury went further. In his essay 'Cleopatra's Nose', he developed a fully fledged theory of the role of 'chance' – defined as 'the valuable collision of two or more independent chains of causes' – with reference to a series of decisive but contingent historical events, including those supposedly caused by the eponymous nose. In fact, this represented an attempt to reconcile determinism with contingency: in Bury's somewhat puzzling formulation, 'the element of chance coincidence ... helps to determine events'.[80] Yet neither Bury nor Fisher took the next step of exploring alternative historical developments in detail, despite the fact that the former's chains and the latter's waves could have collided at different points with different consequences. Indeed, Bury qualified his argument by suggesting that 'as time goes on contingencies ... become less important in human evolution' because of man's growing power over nature and the limits placed by democratic institutions on individual statesmen. This sounded suspiciously like Mill or Tolstoy on the decline of free will.

In his essay 'Clio, a Muse', Trevelyan went further than this, wholly dismissing the idea of a 'science of cause and effect in human affairs' as 'a misapplication of the analogy of physical science'. The historian might 'generalise and guess as to cause and effect', but his first duty was to 'tell the story': 'Doubtless ... the deeds of [Cromwell's soldiers] had their effect, as one amid the thousand confused waves that give the impulse to the world's ebb and flow. But ... their ultimate success or failure ... was largely ruled by incalculable chance'. For Trevelyan, battlefields provided the classic illustration of this point:

> Chance selected this field out of so many ... to turn the tide of war and decide the fate of nations and creeds.... But for some honest soldier's pluck or luck in the decisive onslaught round yonder village spire, the lost cause would now be hailed as 'the tide of inevitable tendency' that nothing could have turned aside.[81]

In the next generation, this approach informed much of the work of that other great writer of history, A. J. P. Taylor, who never tired of emphasising the role of chance ('blunders' and 'trivialities') in diplomatic history. Though Taylor was clear that it was 'no part of the historian's duty to say what ought to have been done',[82] he nevertheless took pleasure in hinting at what *might* have been.

Nor was this emphasis on the contingent nature of some, if not all, historical events uniquely British. For the later German historicists like Droysen, the task of historical philosophy was 'to establish not the laws of objective history, but the laws of historical investigation and knowledge'. Much more than Ranke, Droysen was concerned with the role of 'anomaly, the individual, free will, responsibility, genius ... the movements and effects of human freedom and personal peculiarities'.[83] This line of argument was elaborated on by Wilhelm Dilthey, who has a good claim to be considered the founder not only of history's theory of relativity, but also of its uncertainty principle.[84] In developing the historicist approach still further, Friedrich Meinecke sought to distinguish between several levels of causality, ranging from the determinists' 'mechanistic' factors to the 'spontaneous acts of men'.[85] It was a distinction he put into practice most explicitly in his last book, *The German Catastrophe*, which stressed not only the 'general' causes of National Socialism (a disastrous Hegelian synthesis of two great ideas), but also the accidental factors which brought Hitler to power in 1933.[86]

Yet there were important intellectual constraints which prevented a complete overthrow of nineteenth-century determinism. Of very great importance in the British context was the work of two English philosophers of history – Collingwood and Oakeshott, latter-day idealists whose work owed much to Bradley's *Presuppositions of Critical History*. Collingwood is best known for the aspersions he cast on the simple, positivist notion of a historical fact. As he saw it, all historical evidence was merely a reflection of 'thought': 'Historical thought is ... the presentation by thought to itself of a world of half-ascertained fact.'[87] The most the historian could therefore do was to 'reconstruct' or 're-enact' past thoughts, under the inevitable influence of his own unique experience. Not surprisingly, Collingwood was dismissive of determinist models of causation: 'The plan which is revealed in history is a plan which does not pre-exist in its own revelation; history is a drama, but an extemporised drama, cooperatively extemporised by its own performers.'[88] Unlike the plot of a novel, the 'plot of history' was merely 'a selection of incidents regarded as peculiarly significant'.[89] Historians were different from novelists because they sought to construct 'true' narratives, though every historical narrative was no more than an 'interim report on the progress of our historical inquiries'.[90]

Collingwood's reflections on the nature of time are especially insightful and, indeed, anticipate some of what modern physicists have to say on the subject:

> Time is generally ... imagined to ourselves in a metaphor, as a stream or something in continuous and uniform motion.... [But] the metaphor of a stream means nothing unless it means that the stream has banks.... The events of the future do not really await their turn to appear, like the people in a queue at a theatre awaiting their turn at the box office: they do not yet exist at all, and therefore cannot be grouped in any order whatever. The present alone is actual; the past and the future are ideal and nothing but ideal. It is necessary to insist on this because our habit of 'spatialising' time, or figuring it to ourselves in terms of space, leads us to imagine that the past and future exist in the same way ... in which, when we are walking up the High past Queen's, Magdalen and All Souls exist.

Yet Collingwood's conclusion was that the historian's goal could only be 'a knowledge of the present' and specifically 'how it came to be what it is': 'The present is the actual; the past is the necessary; the future is the possible'. 'All history is an attempt to understand the present by reconstructing its determining conditions.'[91] In this sense, he simply admitted defeat: history could only be teleological, because historians could write only from the vantage point, and with the prejudices, of their own present. The here-and-now was the only possible point of reference. This was a new and much weaker sort of determinism, but it clearly excluded any discussion of counterfactual alternatives.

It was possible, of course, to reject the very notion that the present had 'determining conditions' – by rejecting the notion of causation itself. There was a great fashion for this among idealist and linguistic philosophers between the wars. Ludwig Wittgenstein simply dismissed 'belief in the causal nexus' as 'superstition'. Bertrand Russell agreed: 'The law of causality ... is a relic of a bygone age surviving, like the monarchy, only because it is erroneously supposed to do no harm.'[92] So did Croce, who saw 'the concept of cause' as fundamentally 'alien from history'.[93]

At first sight, this seems like a profoundly anti-deterministic proposition. Nevertheless, as is clear from Oakeshott's definitive statement of the idealist position, it ruled out counterfactualism just as categorically as any determinist theory:

[W]e desert historical experience whenever we ... abstract a moment in the historical world and think of it as the cause of the whole or any part of what remains. Thus, every historical event is necessary, and it is impossible to distinguish between the importance of necessities. No event is merely negative, none is non-contributory. To speak of a single, ill-distinguished event (for no historical event is securely distinguished from its environment) as determining, in the sense of causing and explaining, the whole subsequent course of events is ... not bad or doubtful history, but not history at all.... The presupposi-tions of historical thought forbid it ... There is no more reason to attribute a whole course of events to one antecedent event rather than another.... The strict conception of cause and effect appears ... to be without relevance in historical explanation.... The conception of cause is ... replaced by the exhibition of a world of events intrinsically related to one another in which no *lacuna* is tolerated.

While this might have a certain philosophical logic to it, its practical implications are far from satisfactory. In Oakeshott's formulation, 'change in history carries with it its own explanation':

> The course of events is one, so far filled in and complete, that no external cause or reason is looked for or required.... The unity or continuity of history ... is ... the only principle of explanation consonant with the other postulates of historical experience ... The relation *between* events is always other events and is established in history by a full relation *of* the events.

Thus the only method whereby the historian can improve on the explanation of an event is by providing 'more complete detail'.[94]

As Oakeshott makes clear, this is not a recipe for 'total history'. Some kind of selection is necessary between 'significant relationships' and 'chance relationships', because 'historical enquiry, as an engagement to compose ... a passage of significantly related events in answer to an historical question, has no place for the recognition of such meaningless relationships'. [95] But what makes an event 'significant'? Here Oakeshott provides only an oblique answer, to the effect that the historian's answer to a given question must have some kind of internal logic. The aim is 'to compose an answer to an historical question by *assembling a passage of the past* constituted of related events which have not survived inferred from a past of artefacts and utterances which have survived'.[96] That would seem to imply a narrative structure of the sort envisaged by Collingwood, but in fact any kind of intelligible structure would logically suffice.

The idealist challenge to nineteenth-century determinism had an important influence on the work of a number of practising historians, notably Butterfield and Namier, whose researches into diplomatic history and political 'structures' respectively were informed by a deep hostility to determinism (especially its materialist variants). The same idealist tradition may be said to have been carried on by Maurice Cowling, whose preoccupations with high politics and the quasi-religious nature of nineteenth- and twentieth-century 'public doctrine' have set him apart from virtually all his Cambridge contemporaries.[97] In a more diluted form, traces of idealist anti-determinism can also be found in the work of Geoffrey Elton.[98]

The theoretical position as set out by Oakeshott was nevertheless incomplete. Having demolished the determinist model of causation derived from the natural sciences, Oakeshott effectively replaced it with another, equally rigid straitjacket. In his definition, the historian had to confine himself to the relation of significant past events *as they actually seem to have been* on the basis of the surviving sources. Yet the process whereby the historian distinguishes between the significant and the insignificant or 'chance' events was never clearly articulated. Clearly, it must be a subjective process. The historian attaches his own meaning to the surviving remnants of the past which he finds in his pursuit of an answer to a given question. Equally clearly, his answer, when it is published, must make some kind of sense to others. But who chooses the original question? And who is to say whether the reader's interpretation of the finished text will correspond to that intended by the author? Above all, why should counterfactual questions be ruled out? To these questions, Oakeshott had no satisfactory answers.

Scientific History – Continued

Conspicuously, many of the English historians associated with idealism were noted for their political conservatism. Indeed, as the conflicts within English history faculties in the 1950s and 1960s made clear, there was a fairly close connection between anti-determinism in historical philosophy and anti-socialism in politics. Unfortunately – from the point of view of idealism – these were conflicts which the other side effectively won.

For the determinism of the nineteenth century was not, as might have been expected, discredited by the horrors perpetrated in its name after 1917. That Marxism was able to retain its credibility was due mainly to the widespread belief that National Socialism was its polar opposite, rather than merely a near relative which had substituted *Volk* for class. The postwar renaissance of Marxism also owed much to the willingness of Italian, French and English Marxists to dissociate themselves not only from Stalin but also from Lenin – and increasingly from Marx himself. It is not necessary here to pay close attention to the various theoretical modifications introduced by the likes of Sartre and Althusser, the main aim of which was to extricate Marx from the inconvenient complexities of history and return him to the safety of the Hegelian heights. Nor need we dwell on the related but historically more applicable theories of Gramsci, who sought to explain the proletariat's consistent failure to behave as Marx had predicted in terms of hegemonic blocs, false consciousness and synthesised consent.[99] Suffice to say that such ideas helped give the Marxian version of determinism a new lease of life. True, continental influences were slow to make themselves felt in England. But here too, inspired more by a distinctively English sense of *noblesse oblige* – an elite sentimentality about lower-class radicalism – a Marxist revival took place.

Of all the English socialist historians, probably the least original thinker was E. H. Carr, the chronicler of the Bolshevik regime. Yet Carr's defence of determinism has been extraordinarily influential – and will doubtless continue to be so until someone else writes a better book with as seductive a title as *What Is History?* It is true that Carr seeks to distance himself from the strict monocausal determinism of Hegel or Marx. He himself is only a determinist, he says, in the sense that he believes that 'everything that happened has a cause or causes, and could not have happened differently unless something in the cause or causes had also been different'. This, of course, is a definition so elastic that it implies acceptance of the indeterminacy of events:

> In practice, historians do not assume that events are inevitable before they have taken place. They frequently discuss alternative courses available to the actors in the story, on the assumption

that the option was open ... Nothing in history is inevitable, except in the formal sense that, for it to have happened other-wise, the antecedent causes would have had to be different.

This is fine, as far as it goes. However, Carr quickly adds that the historian's task is simply 'to explain why one course was eventu-ally chosen rather than another'; to 'explain what did happen and why'. 'The trouble about contemporary history', he notes with impatience, 'is that people remember the time when all the options were still open, and find it difficult to adopt the atttitude of the historian for whom they have been closed by the *fait accompli*.' Nor is this the only respect in which Carr turns out to be an old-fashioned determinist. 'How', he asks, 'can we discover in a history a coherent sequence of cause and effect, how can we find any meaning in history' if (as he has to concede) 'the role of accident in history ... exists?' With a grudging nod in the direction of the idealists ('certain philosophical ambiguities into which I need not enter'), Carr decides, like Oakeshott, that we must select causes in order of their 'historical significance':

> From the multiplicity of sequences of cause and effect, [the historian] extracts those, and only those, which are historically significant; and the standard of historical significance is his ability to fit them into his pattern of rational explanation and interpretation. Other sequences of cause and effect have to be rejected as accidental, not because the relation between cause and effect is different, but because the sequence itself is irrele-vant. The historian can do nothing with it; it is not amenable to rational interpretation, and has no meaning either for the past or the present.

In Carr's version, however, this simply becomes another version of Hegel's view of history as a rational – and teleological – process. 'Dragging into prominence the forces which have triumphed and thrusting into the background those which they have swallowed up' is, he concludes, 'the essence of the historian's job'. For 'History in its essence is ... progress.' That this was an emotional position can easily be illustrated. In his notes for a second edition of *What Is History?*, Carr rejected *a priori* 'the theory that the universe began in some random way with a big bang and is destined to dissolve into black holes' as 'a reflexion of the cultural pessimism of the age'. A determinist to the last, he dismissed the implicit 'randomness' of this theory as an 'enthronement of ignorance'.[100]

By a not dissimilar route, E. P. Thompson also arrived back at the determinist position. Like Carr's, Thompson's attempt to find a middle way between the strictly anti-theoretical empiricism of Popper and the strictly unempirical theory of Althusser was motivated by a craving for meaning – a desire to 'comprehend ... the interconnectedness of social phenomena [and] causation'.[101] Like Carr (and indeed Christopher Hill), Thompson instinctively revolted against the whole notion of contingency. He yearned for an 'understanding of the rationality (of causation, etc.) of the historical process: ... an objective knowledge, disclosed in a dialogue with determinate evidence'. But the 'historical logic' Thompson proposed – 'a dialogue between concept and evidence, a dialogue conducted by successive hypotheses, on the one hand, and empirical research on the other' – was no more satisfactory than Carr's selection of 'rational' causes. At root, it was just reheated Hegel.

In the light of this, it is hardly surprising that both Carr and Thompson were as dismissive as they were of counterfactual arguments. Yet even the British Marxists found it hard to dispense with counterfactual analysis altogether. When Carr himself pondered the calamities of Stalinism, he could hardly avoid asking the question whether these were the inevitable consequence of the original Bolshevik project, or whether Lenin, 'if he had lived through the twenties and thirties in the full possession of his faculties', would have acted less tyrannically. In his notes for a second edition, Carr actually argued that a longer-lived Lenin would have been able 'to minimise and mitigate the element of coercion.... Under Lenin the passage might not have been altogether smooth, but it would have been nothing like what happened. Lenin would not have tolerated the falsification of the record in which Stalin constantly indulged.'[102] Exactly the same kind of argument underpins the last volume of what may be regarded as the British Marxists' greatest achievement – Eric Hobsbawm's four-volume history of the world since 1789. *The Age of Extremes* in many ways revolves around an immense, though implicit counterfactual question: What if there had been no Stalinist Soviet Union, sufficiently industrialised (and tyrannised) to defeat Germany and 'rescue' capitalism during the Second World War?[103] Whatever one thinks of the answers Carr and Hobsbawm provide to these questions, it is striking that, despite all their ideological commitment to determinism, both ultimately felt obliged to pose them.

Regrettably, such moves away from strictly teleological argumentation have been rare among the younger generation of Marxist historians. Inspired by Gramsci, they have tended to address themselves to questions about the oppression or manipulation of the working class and, with the growth of feminism (which substituted gender for class in the Marxist model of conflict), women. The new left's 'history from below' may have conclusively overturned Carr's dictum that history is about the winners (though in a sense yesterday's losers are being consciously studied as today's or tomorrow's winners). But it has only stuck the more firmly to the determinist model of historical development.

Not all modern determinists have been Marxists, of course. The emergence of sociology as a distinct subject has allowed a variety of less rigid theories to develop which historians have been quick to import. Like Marx, the intellectual 'fathers' of sociology, Tocqueville and Weber, retained a belief in the possibility of a scientific approach to social questions and distinguished analytically between the economic, the social, the cultural and the political. But they did not insist on any simple causal relationship leading from one to the others and propelling historical development inexorably forwards. Thus, in *L'Ancien Régime et la Révo-*

lution, Tocqueville discussed the roles of administrative change, class structure and Enlightenment ideas in pre-Revolutionary France without according primacy to one or other as a solvent of the 'old regime'. Moreover, the conclusion he drew from his pioneering study of regional administrative records was that the basic framework of government had not been significantly changed by the Revolution. The processes which interested him – of governmental centralisation and economic levelling, which he saw as posing an insidious threat to liberty – were long run; they preceded the events of the 1790s and continued long after 1815.[104] Weber went still further. In some respects, his idea of sociology was world history with the causation left out: in essence, a typology of social phenomena.[105] When he thought historically, he tended to illustrate selectively and with a broad brush, as (for example) in his *Protestant Ethic and the Spirit of Capitalism*, which linked the development of Western capitalism to the peculiar culture (not the theology) of the Protestant sects.[106] The key word here is 'linked': Weber was at pains to avoid suggesting a simple causal relationship between religion and economic behaviour: 'It is not . . . my aim to substitute for a one-sided materialistic an equally one-sided spiritualistic causal interpretation of culture and of history. Each is equally possible . . .'.[107] The historical tendencies which interested Weber – rationalisation and demystification in all walks of life – seemed to unfold themselves.

This relegation of causation – the elevation of structures above events, the preoccupation with long-run rather than short-run change – had important implications for the development of twentieth-century historiography. These were perhaps most obvious in France, where the sociological approach was first systematically applied by historians. The ultimate aim of what became known as the *Annales* school was to write 'total history', that is to say, to consider all (or as many as possible) of the aspects of a given society: its economy, its social forms, its culture, its political institutions and so on. As Marc Bloch conceived it, history was to become an amalgam of different scientific disciplines: everything from meteorology to jurisprudence would have a part to play, and the ideal historian would be a master of umpteen technical specialisms.[108] But this holism also applied to the periods which historians had to consider: in Braudel's characteristically heroic terms, the *Annales* historian would 'always wish to grasp the whole, the totality of social life ... bringing together different levels, time spans, different kinds of time, structure, conjunctures, events'.[109]

Of course, without some kind of organising principle, some hierarchy of importance, such history would be unwritable (for reasons Macaulay had spelt out a century before).[110] In practice, the historians of the *Annales* prioritised geography and long-run change, an ordering most explicit in the work of Braudel. As a self-proclaimed 'historian of peasant stock', Braudel instinctively assumed 'the necessary reduction of any social reality to the plane in which it occurs', meaning 'geography or ecology'.[111] 'When we say man, we mean the group to which he belongs: individuals leave it and others are incorporated, but the group remains attached to a given space and to familiar land. It takes root there.'[112] From this geographical determinism – which bore more than a passing resemblance to the materialist theories of French Enlightenment – followed Braudel's elevation of long-run development over short-run events. In his *Mediterranean World in the Age of Philip II*, he explicitly distinguished between three levels of history: firstly, the 'history whose passage is almost imperceptible, that of man and his relationship with the environment, a history in which all change is slow, a history of constant repetition, ever-recurring cycles'; secondly, 'history ... with slow but perceptible rhythms', the history of 'groups and groupings ... these swelling currents [of] economic systems, states, societies, civilisations and finally ... warfare'; and thirdly 'traditional history', that of 'individual men' and 'events', the 'surface disturbances, crests of foam that the tides of history carry on their strong backs. A history of brief, rapid, nervous fluctuations.'[113] Here, last was very definitely least. 'We must learn to distrust this history [of events],' warned Braudel, 'as it was felt, described and lived by contemporaries'; for it is merely concerned with 'ephemera ...

which pass across the stage like fireflies, hardly glimpsed before they settle back into darkness and as often as not into oblivion.'[114] The delusive smoke of an event might 'fill the minds of its contemporaries, but it does not last and its flame can scarcely ever be discerned'. For Braudel, the mission of the new sociological history was to demote 'the headlong, dramatic, breathless rush of [traditional history's] narrative'. The 'short time span' was merely 'the time of ... the journalist', 'capricious and delusive'.[115] Whereas:

> The long run always wins in the end. Annihilating innumerable events – all those which cannot be accommodated in the main ongoing current and which are therefore ruthlessly swept to one side – it indubitably limits both the freedom of the individual and even the role of chance.[116]

Clearly, this relegation of the 'trivia of the past' – 'the actions of a few princes and rich men' – beneath 'the slow and powerful march of history' was simply a new kind of determinism. Unconsciously, Braudel had even lapsed back into the distinctive language of the nineteenth-century determinists: once again, as in Marx, as in Tolstoy, mere individuals were being 'ruthlessly swept aside', trampled underfoot by superhuman historical forces. There are two obvious objections to this. The first is that, in dismissing history as it was felt and recorded by contemporaries, Braudel was dismissing the overwhelming bulk of historical evidence – even the economic statistics which were his bread and butter. 'In the long run,' as Keynes said, 'we are all dead'; and for that reason we are perhaps entitled to reverse the order of Braudel's hierarchy of histories. After all, if the short term was what primarily concerned our ancestors, who are we to dismiss their concerns as mere trivia? The second objection concerns Braudel's assumptions about the nature of environmental change. For, in assuming the imperceptible nature of long-run ecological change and the rhythmic, predictable quality of climatic change, he was perpetuating a serious misconception about the natural world.

In fairness to Braudel, he later qualified this dogmatic insistence on the 'longue durée'. With the development of capitalism, clearly the dominance of the terrain and elements was diminished: 'The chief privilege of capitalism ... [is] the ability to choose.'[117] In capitalist society, it was harder to prioritise. Which hierarchy was more important, Braudel asked himself in the third volume of *Civilisation and Capitalism*: that of wealth, that of state power or that of culture? 'The answer is that it may depend upon the time, the place and who is speaking.'[118] Thus the subjective element was at least temporarily rescued from the objective constraints of the long run: 'Social time does not flow at one even rate, but goes at a thousand different paces, swift or slow.'[119] There was at least some scope for the existence of 'free, unorganised zones of reality ... outside the rigid envelope of structures'.[120]

Such insights might have been developed further had Marc Bloch lived longer. It is clear from his notes for the later and never-written sixth and seventh chapters of *The Historian's Craft* that he had a far better grasp of the problems of causation, chance and what he called 'prevision' than Braudel.[121] As he made clear in the completed sections of the book, Bloch had no time for 'pseudogeographical determinism': 'Whether confronted by a phenomenon of the physical world or by a social fact, the movement of human reactions is not like clockwork, always going in the same direction.'[122] This raises a counterfactual question of its own: What if Bloch had survived the war? It seems likely that French historiography would not have succumbed to the implicit determinism of Braudel and the later *Annales*.

Sociological history outside France was never as concerned with environmental determinants (perhaps because other countries had witnessed far greater migrations of people and physical transformations of the land in the nineteenth and twentieth centuries). Nevertheless, similar kinds of determinism can be found. In the German case, this was partly due to a revival of Marxian ideas in the 1960s and 1970s. The school of 'societal history', whose John the Baptist had been the Weimar 'dissident' Eckart Kehr, posited a model of German historical aberrance based on the idea of a mismatch between economic development and social backwardness.[123] On the one hand, nineteenth-century Germany successfully developed a modern, industrial economy. On the other, its social and political institutions continued to be dominated by the traditional Junker aristocracy. At times, explanations for this failure to develop according to the Marxist rules (that is, to progress, like Britain, towards bourgeois parliamentarism and democracy) have been couched in unmistakably Gramscian terms; hegemonic blocs of manipulative elites became a wearisome feature of much German historiography after 1968. More recently, reviving interest in the ideas of Weber has led to less overt determinism, as in the most recent work of the doyen of societal historians, Hans-Ulrich Wehler. Yet, despite the efforts of non-German historians to question the validity of the ideal-typical relationship between capitalism, bourgeois society and parliamentary democracy,[124] there remains a deep reluctance within the German historical establishment to consider alternative historical outcomes. Societal historians remain deeply committed to the idea that 'the German catastrophe' had deep roots. Even conservative historians have relatively little interest in the role of contingency: some abide by the Rankean commandment to study only what actually happened; others, like Michael Stürmer, take refuge in an older kind of geographical determinism, in which Germany's location in the middle of Europe explains much, if not all, of the problem.[125]

Anglo-American historiography too has had its fair share of sociologically inspired determinism, some of it Marxian, some more Weberian. Lawrence Stone's *Causes of the English Revolution* is noteworthy for its reliance on another kind of three-tiered model, this time distinguishing between preconditions, precipitants and triggers. Unlike Braudel, Stone does not explicitly arrange these in order of importance: indeed, he explicitly avoids 'decid[ing] whether or not the obstinacy of Charles I was more important than the spread of Puritanism in causing the Revolution'.[126] But the strong implication of the book is that the combination of these and other factors made the Civil War inevitable. Equally cautious in tone is Paul Kennedy's *Rise and Fall of the Great Powers*, which posits nothing stronger than a 'significant correlation *over the longer term* between productive and revenue-raising capacities on the one hand and military strength on the other'.[127] Certainly, a close reading of the book acquits him of *crude* economic determinism. But the thrust of the argument is nevertheless that there is a causal relationship between economic factors and international power – subtle economic determinism maybe, but determinism nonetheless. Other attempts to propound grand theories on the basis of some sort of sociological model range from Wallerstein's Marxian *Modern World System* to Mann's more nuanced *Sources of Social Power*, Grew and Bien's *Crises of Political Development* and Unger's *Plasticity into Power*.[128] A classic illustration of grand theory at its pseudoscientific worst is 'catastrophe theory', with its reductionist topology of seven 'elementary catastrophes'.[129] The search for a unifying sociological theory of power will doubtless continue. It remains to be seen whether it will eventually be abandoned as futile, like the alchemists' search for the philosopher's stone; or whether it will go on for ever, like the search for a cure for baldness.

An alternative to colossal simplification – and the alternative favoured by many historians in recent years – has been evernarrower specialisation. It had, of course, been Bloch's hope that history would draw inspiration from as many other scientific disciplines as possible. In practice, however, this has tended to happen at the price of the holistic approach to which he and Braudel had aspired. Indeed, recent years have seen a bemusing fragmentation of scientific history into a multiplicity of more or less unconnected 'inter-disciplinary' hybrids.

This has certainly been true of attempts to import psychoanalysis to history. Freud himself was, of course, a positivist at heart, whose main goal was to reveal laws of the individual unconsciousness – hence his call for 'a strict and universal application of determinism to mental life'. A strict historical application of his theories, however, would seem to imply the writing of biography.

Even attempts to write the 'psycho-history' of social groups must depend heavily on the analysis of individual testimony;[130] and such testimony rarely lends itself to the sorts of analysis Freud could apply to his patients, whom he could interrogate with leading questions and even, on occasion, hypnotise. For this reason, Freud's real influence on historical writing has tended to be indirect: a matter of terminology which has passed into general, casual usage ('the unconscious', 'repression', 'inferiority complex' and so on) rather than strict imitation. Similar problems arise with the historical application of more recent forms of behaviourist psychology. Here too there is a determinist tendency, most obviously manifest in the attempts to import game theory and rational-choice theory into history. True, the assumptions about human behaviour made in the prisoner's dilemma game and its various derivatives are often more readily observable than those suggested by Freud. But they are no less deterministic – hence the tendency of psycho-historians to dismiss contemporary expressions of intention when they do not fit their model, using the old Gramscian excuse of 'false consciousness'. Game theory, like psychoanalysis, is also necessarily individualistic. The only way around this problem for historians who wish to apply it to social groups is to take up diplomatic history, where states can, in the time-honoured tradition, be anthropomorphised.[131]

Partly because of this individualising tendency, it has been anthropological models of *collective* psychology or 'mentality' which have been most popular with historians.[132] In particular, the approach of Clifford Geertz – 'thick description' which aims to fit a set of 'signifying signs' into an intelligible structure – has attracted influential imitators.[133] The result has been a new kind of cultural history, in which culture (broadly defined) has been more or less freed from the traditional determining role of the material base.[134] For a variety of reasons – partly the way anthropologists tend to do their fieldwork, partly the disrepute into which the notion of 'national character' has fallen and partly the political vogue for 'communities' – this has more often meant popular and local culture than high and national culture. Emmanuel Leroy

Ladurie's *Montaillou* and Natalie Zemon Davis's *Return of Martin Guerre* are perhaps the classic examples of what has become known as 'microhistory'.[135] But similar techniques have been applied to high culture at a national and even international level, most successfully by Simon Schama.[136]

There are obvious objections, however, to this new cultural history. Firstly, it can be objected that 'microhistory' chooses such trivial subjects for study that it represents a relapse into antiquarianism (though the historian's choice of subject is usually best left to him, his publisher and the book market). A better objection relates to the issue of causation. Anthropologists, like sociologists, are traditionally concerned more with structures than with processes of change. Historians seeking to adopt anthropological models therefore tend to be thrown back on their own discipline's traditional resources when seeking to explain – for example – the decline of belief in witchcraft.[137] Finally and most seriously, there is a tendency for the 'thick description' of mentalities to degenerate into rampant subjectivism, a game of free association with only tangential links to empirical evidence. The claims of this kind of history to be scientific in any meaningful sense seem dubious.

Narrative Determinism: Why Not Invent History?

It has been partly because of this creeping subjectivism and partly because of the historian's distinctive and perennial preoccupation with change as opposed to structure that recent years have seen a revival of interest in the narrative form.[138] Of course, the notion that the historian's primary role is to impose a narrative order on the confusion of past events is an old one. In their different ways, both Carlyle and Macaulay had seen their role in these terms. Indeed, Louis Mink was really rephrasing a Victorian idea when he summarised 'the aim of historical knowledge' as 'to discover the grammar of events' and 'convert congeries of events into concatenations'.[139] This explains the renewed interest of Hayden White and others in the great 'literary artefacts' of the previous century.[140] It also explains why the revival of narrative has been welcomed by some traditionalists, particularly those who (simplistically) equate scientific history with cliometric number-crunching.[141] In his critique of 'new' history, Barzun rejoiced in the subjectivism of historical writing, and echoed Carlyle's view of the fundamentally confused nature of past events:

> Whereas there is one natural science, there are many histories, overlapping and contradictory, argumentative and detached, biased and ambiguous. Each viewer remakes a past in keeping with his powers of search and vision, whose defects readily show up in his work: nobody is deceived. [But] the multiplicity of historical versions does not make them all false. Rather it mirrors the character of mankind ... There is no point in writing history if one is always striving to overcome its principal effect ... to show ... the vagarious, 'unstructured' disorder [of the past], due to the energetic desires of men and movements struggling for expression. ... The practices, beliefs, cultures, and actions of mankind show up as incommensurable ... [142]

To Barzun, this was plain 'common sense': the historian's task was not to be a social scientist but to 'put the reader in touch' with 'events' and 'feelings' – to feed his 'primitive pleasure in story'. On the other hand, the revival of narrative has been just as congenial to followers of fashion, who would like nothing better than to apply the techniques of literary criticism to the ultimate 'text': the written record of the past itself. The revival of narrative has therefore been Janus-faced: on one side, a revival of interest in traditional literary models for the writing of history;[143] on the other, an influx of modish terminology (textual deconstruction, semiotics and so on) for the reading of it.[144] Post-modernism has hit history,[145] even if the post-modernists are merely rehashing old idealist nostrums when they declare history 'an interpretative practice, not an objective, neutral science'. When Joyce writes that 'History is never present to us in anything but a discursive form' and that 'the events, structures and processes of the past are indistinguishable from the forms of documentary representation ... and the historical discourses that construct them', he is merely repeating what Collingwood said (better) over half a century ago.

There is only one problem with the narrative revival, and it is the perennial problem of applying literary forms to history. Literary genres are to some extent predictable: indeed, that is part of their appeal. Often, we read a favourite novel or watch a 'classic' film knowing exactly how it will end. And even if a piece is unknown to us – and there is no dustjacket or programme to give us the gist of the story – we can still often infer from its genre roughly how it will turn out. If a play is from the outset a comedy, we subconsciously rule out the possibility of carnage in the final act; if it is clearly a tragedy, we do the opposite. Even where an author notionally keeps the reader 'in suspense' – as in a detective whodunnit – the outcome is to some extent predictable: according to the conventions of the genre, a criminal will be caught, a crime solved. The professional writer writes with the ending in mind and frequently hints at it to the reader for the sake of irony, or some other effect. As Gallie has argued: 'To follow a story ... involves ... some vague appreciation of its drift or direction ... and appreciation of how what comes later depends upon what came earlier, in the sense that but for the latter, the former could not have, or could hardly have occurred in the way that it did occur.'[146] The same point is made by Scriven: 'A good play must develop in such a way that we ... see the development as necessary, i.e. can explain it.'[147] Martin Amis's novel *Time's Arrow* thus merely makes explicit what is implicit in all narratives: the end literally precedes the beginning.[148] Amis tells the life story of a Nazi doctor backwards, in the guise of a narrator within him who 'knows something he seems unable to face: ... the future always comes true'. Thus the old man who 'emerges' from his death bed in an American hospital is 'doomed' to perform experiments on prisoners in the Nazi death camps and to 'depart' the world as an innocent infant. In literature, to adapt a phrase of Ernst Bloch, 'the true genesis is not in the beginning but in the end': time's arrow always implicitly points the wrong way. Amis makes the point well when he describes a chess match in reverse: beginning in 'disarray', and going 'through episodes of contortion and crosspurpose. But things work out. . . . All that agony – it all works out. One final tug on the white pawn, and perfect order is restored.'

To write history according to the conventions of a novel or play is therefore to impose a new kind of determinism on the past: the teleology of the traditional narrative form. Gibbon, for all his awareness of contingency when considering particular events, subsumed a millennium and a half of European history under the supreme teleological title. If he had published his great work as *A History of Europe and the Middle East, AD 100–1400* rather than *The Decline and Fall of the Roman Empire*, his narrative would have lost its unifying theme. Likewise Macaulay: there is an undeniable tendency in the *History of England* to present the events of the seventeenth century as leading to the constitutional arrangements of the nineteenth. This was the form of teleology which Collingwood later saw as integral to history: the assumption that the present was always the end-point (and implicitly the only possible end-point) of the historian's chosen narrative. But (as with fiction) history written in this fashion might as well be written backwards, like the backwards history of Ireland which the writer 'AE' imagined in 1914:

> The small holdings of the 19th and 20th centuries gradually come into the hands of the large owners, in the 18th century progress has been made and the first glimmerings of self government appear, religious troubles and wars follow until the *last* Englishman, Strongbow, leaves the country, culture begins, religious intolerance ceases with the *disappearance* of Patrick, about AD 400, and we approach the great age of the heroes and gods.[149]

This, as AE himself joked, was merely the nationalist 'mythistory', mistakenly bound back to front.

The Garden of Forking Paths

The past – like real-life chess, or indeed any other game – is different; it does not have a predetermined end. There is no author, divine or otherwise; only characters, and (unlike in a game) a great deal too many of them. There is no plot, no inevitable 'perfect order'; only endings, since multiple events unfold simultaneously, some lasting only moments, some extending far beyond an individual's life. Once again, it was Robert Musil who put his finger on this essential difference between history proper and mere stories. In a chapter in *The Man without Qualities* entitled 'Why does one not invent history?', Ulrich – who, symbolically, is on board a tram – reflects on:

> mathematical problems that did not admit of any general solution, though they did admit of particular solutions, the combining of which brought one nearer to the general solution.... [H]e regarded the problem set by every human life as one of these. What one calls an age ... this broad, unregulated flux of conditions would then amount to approximately as much as a chaotic succession of unsatisfactory and (when taken singly) false attempts at a solution, attempts that might produce the correct and total solution, but only when humanity had learnt to combine them all.... What a strange affair history was, come to think of it.... This history of ours looks pretty safe and messy, when looked at from close at hand, something like a half-solidified swamp, and then in the end, strangely enough, it turns out there is after all a track running across it, the very 'road of history' of which nobody knows whence it comes. This *being the material of history* was something which made Ulrich indignant. The luminous, swaying box in which he was travelling seemed to him like a machine in which several hundred-weight of humanity were shaken to and fro in the process of being made into something called 'the future'.... Feeling this, he revolted against this impotent putting-up-with changes and conditions, against this helpless contemporaneity, the unsystematic,

submissive, indeed humanly undignified stringing-along with the centuries ... Involuntarily he got up and finished his journey on foot.[150]

Ulrich rejects the possibility that 'world history was a story that ... came into existence just the same way as all other stories', because 'nothing new ever occurred to authors, and one copied from another'. On the contrary, 'history ... came into existence for the most part without any authors. It evolved not from the centre, but from the periphery, from minor causes'. Moreover, it unfolds in a fundamentally chaotic way, like an order transmitted in whispers from one end of a column of soldiers which begins as 'Sergeant major to move to the head of the column' but ends as 'Eight troopers to be shot immediately':

> If one were therefore to transplant a whole generation of present-day Europeans while still in their infancy into the Egypt of the year five thousand BC, and leave them there, world history would begin all over again at the year five thousand, at first repeating itself for a while and then, for reasons that no man can guess, gradually beginning to deviate.

The law of world history was thus simply 'muddling through':

> The course of history was ... not that of a billiard-ball, which, once it has been hit, ran along a definite course; on the contrary, it was like the passage of clouds, like the way of a man sauntering through the streets – diverted here by a shadow, there by a little crowd of people ... – finally arriving at a place that he had neither known of nor meant to reach. There was inherent in the course of history a certain element of going off course.[151]

This line of argument disconcerts Ulrich – so much so (and as if to prove the point) that he loses his own way home.

In short, history is not a story any more than it is a tram

journey; and historians who persist in trying to write it as a story might as well follow Amis or AE and write it backwards. The reality of history, as Musil suggests, is that the end is unknown at the beginning of the journey: there are no rails leading predictably into the future, no timetables with destinations set out in black and white. Much the same point was made by Jorge Luis Borges in his short story 'The Garden of Forking Paths'. The author imagines a labyrinth-cum-novel devised by an imaginary Chinese sage, Ts'ui Pên, in which 'time forks perpetually toward innumerable futures':

'I lingered naturally on the sentence: *I leave to the various futures (not to all) my garden of forking paths*. Almost instantly, I understood: "The garden of forking paths" was the chaotic novel; the phrase "the various futures (not to all)" suggested to me the forking in time, not in space.... In all fictional works, each time a man is confronted with several alternatives, he chooses one and eliminates the others; in the fiction of Ts'ui Pên, he chooses – simultaneously – all of them. *He creates*, in this way, diverse futures; diverse times which themselves also proliferate and fork.... In the work of Ts'ui Pên, all possible outcomes occur; each one is the point of departure for other forkings.'

The work's imaginary translator goes on:

'*The Garden of Forking Paths* is an enormous riddle, or parable, whose theme is time ... an incomplete, but not false, image of the universe ... In contrast to Newton or Schopenhauer, [Ts'ui Pên] did not believe in a uniform, absolute time. He believed in an infinite series of times, in a growing, dizzying net of divergent, convergent and parallel times. This network of times which approached one another, forked, broke off, or were unaware of one another for centuries, embraces *all* possibilities of time ....'.[152]

Variations on this theme recur throughout Borges's work. In the idealists' imaginary world described in 'Tlön, Uqbar, Orbis Tertius', 'works of fiction contain a single plot with all its imaginable permutations'.[153] In 'The Lottery in Babylon', an imaginary ancient lottery evolves into an all-embracing way of life; what begins as 'an intensification of chance, a periodical infusion of chaos into the universe' becomes an infinite process in which 'no decision is final, all branch into others'. 'Babylon is nothing less than an infinite game of chance.'[154] The metaphor is changed, but the same theme developed, in 'The Library of Babel' and 'The Zahir'. Similar images can also be found in Mallarmé's poem 'Un Coup de dés'[155] or Robert Frost's 'The Road Not Taken':

> *I shall be telling this with a sigh*
> *Somewhere ages and ages hence:*
> *Two roads diverged in a wood, and I –*
> *I took the one less traveled by,*
> *And that has made all the difference.*[156]

For the historian, the implications of this are clear. As even Scriven has conceded:

[I]n history, given the data we have up to a certain point, there are a number of possible subsequent turns of fortune, none of which would seem to us inexplicable.... Inevitability is only in retrospect ...; and the inevitability of determinism is explanatory rather than predictive. Hence freedom of choice, which is between future alternatives, is not incompatible with the existence of causes for every event.... [W]e would have to ... abandon history if we sought to eliminate all surprise.[157]

Chaos and the End of Scientific Determinism

There is a close (and far from accidental) parallel between the questioning of narrative determinism by writers like Musil and

Borges and the questioning of classical Laplacian determinism by twentieth-century scientists. This is something which, regrettably, historians have tended to ignore (as E. H. Carr did when confronted by the theory of black holes), or simply to misunderstand. Thus a great many of those philosophers of history who have argued in this century about whether history was a 'science' seem not to have grasped that their notion of science was an out-of-date relic of the nineteenth century. What is more, if they had paid closer attention to what their scientific colleagues were actually doing, they would have been surprised – perhaps even pleased – to find that they were asking the wrong question. For it is a striking feature of a great many modern developments in the natural sciences that they have been fundamentally historical in character, in that they have been concerned with changes over time. Indeed, for this reason it is not wholly frivolous to turn the old question on its head and ask not 'Is history a science?' but 'Is science history?'

This is true even of the relatively old second law of thermodynamics, which states that the entropy of an isolated system always increases – that is, that disorder will tend to increase if things are left to themselves, and that even attempts to create order have the ultimate effect of decreasing the amount of ordered energy available. This is of profound historical importance, not least because it implies an ultimate and *disorderly* end to the history of human life and indeed the universe. Einstein's theory of relativity too has implications for historical thinking, since it dispenses with the notion of absolute time. After Einstein, we now realise that each observer has his own measure of time: were I to rise high above the earth, it would seem that events below were taking longer to happen because of the effect of the earth's gravitational field on the speed of light. However, even relative time has only one direction or 'arrow', principally because of entropy and the effect of entropy on our psychological perception of time: even the energy expended in recording an event in our memory increases the amount of disorder in the universe.

Disorder increases. Nothing travels faster than light. Contrary to the expectations of nineteenth-century positivists, however, not every process in the natural world can be summed up in such clear-cut laws. One of the most important scientific developments of the late nineteenth century was the realisation that the majority of statements about the relationships between natural phenomena were no more than probabilistic in nature. Indeed, the American C. S. Peirce proclaimed the end of determinism as early as 1892 in his book *The Doctrine of Necessity Examined*: 'Chance itself pours in at every avenue of sense: it is of all things the most obtrusive,' declared Peirce. 'Chance is First, Law is Second, the tendency to take habits is Third.'[158] Decisive evidence for this came in 1926 when Heisenberg demonstrated that it is impossible to predict the future position and velocity of a particle accurately, because its present position can only be measured using at least a quantum of light. The shorter the wavelength of light used, the more accurate the measurement of the particle's position – but also the greater disturbance to its velocity. Because of this 'uncertainty principle', quantum mechanics can only predict a number of possible outcomes for a particular observation and suggest which is more likely. As Stephen Hawking has said, this 'introduces an unavoidable element of unpredictability or randomness in science' at the most fundamental level.[159] Indeed, it was precisely this which Einstein, faithful as he remained to the ideal of a Laplacian universe, found so objectionable. As he put it in his famous letter to Max Born:

You believe in the God who plays dice, and I in complete law and order in a world which objectively exists, and which I, in a wildly speculative way, am trying to capture. I firmly *believe*, but I hope that someone will find a more realistic way, or rather a more tangible basis than it has been my lot to do. Even the great initial success of the quantum theory does not make me believe in the fundamental dice game, although I am well aware that your younger colleagues interpret this as a consequence of senility.[160]

But uncertainty has outlived Einstein; and it has no less disconcerting implications for historical determinism. By analogy, historians should never lose sight of their own 'uncertainty principle' – that any observation of historical evidence inevitably distorts its significance by the very fact of its selection through the prism of hindsight.

Another modern scientific concept with important historical implications is the so-called 'anthropic' principle, which in its 'strong' version states that 'there are many different universes or regions of a single universe each with its own initial configuration and perhaps with its own set of laws of science ... [but] only in the few universes that are like ours would intelligent beings develop'.[161] This naturally raises obvious problems: it is not clear what significance we should attach to the other 'histories' in which we do not exist. According to Hawking, 'our universe is not just one of the possible histories, but one of the most probable ones ... there is a particular family of histories that are much more probable than the others'.[162] This idea of multiple universes (and dimensions) has been taken further by physicists like Michio Kaku. The historian does not, it seems to me, need to take too literally some of Kaku's more fantastic notions. Because of the immense amounts of energy which would be required, it seems doubtful if time travel through 'transversible worm holes' in space–time can be described as even 'theoretically' possible. (Apart from anything else, as has often been said, if time travel were possible we would already have been inundated with 'tourists' from the future – those, that is, who had elected not to travel further back in time to avert Lincoln's death or to strangle the new-born Adolf Hitler.)[163] Nevertheless, the idea of an infinite number of universes can serve an important heuristic purpose. The idea that – as one physicist has put it – there are other worlds where Cleopatra had an off-putting wart at the tip of her celebrated nose sounds, and is, fanciful. But it provides a vivid reminder of the indeterminate nature of the past.

The biological sciences have made similar moves away from determinism in recent years. Although Richard Dawkins's work, for example, has a deterministic thrust to it, with its definition of individual organisms, including humans, as mere 'survival machines built by short-lived confederations of long-lived genes', he states explicitly in *The Selfish Gene* that genes 'determine behaviour only in a statistical sense . . . [they] do not control their creations'.[164] His Darwinian theory of evolution is 'blind to the future' – Nature has no predestinarian blueprint. Indeed, the whole point about evolution is that replicator molecules (such as DNA) make and reproduce mistakes, so that 'apparently trivial tiny influences can have a major impact on evolution'. 'Genes have no foresight, they do not plan ahead.' Only in one sense is Dawkins a determinist, in that he rules out the role of 'bad luck' in natural selection: 'By definition, luck strikes at random, and a gene that is consistently on the losing side is not unlucky; it is a bad gene.' Thus those organisms which survive the slings and arrows of fortune are those best designed to do so: 'Genes have to perform a task analogous to prediction . . . [But] prediction in a complex world is a chancy business. Every decision that a survival machine takes is a gamble . . . Those individuals whose genes build brains in such a way that they tend to gamble correctly are as a direct result more likely to survive, and therefore to propagate those same genes. Hence the premium on the basic stimuli of pain and pleasure, and the abilities to remember mistakes, to simulate options and to communicate with other "survival machines".'[165]

Other evolutionists, however, take issue with this line of argument, with its still deterministic implication that the race goes to the strong individual organism (or 'meme' or 'phenotype', Dawkins's other forms of replicator). As Stephen Jay Gould shows in his *Wonderful Life*, certain chance events – major environmental catastrophes like the one which apparently happened after the so-called 'Cambrian explosion' – do disrupt the process of natural selection.[166] By completely changing long-standing ecological conditions, they render valueless overnight attributes honed over millennia in response to those conditions. The survivors survive not because their genes have designed and built superior 'survival machines' but often because vestigial attributes suddenly turn up trumps. In short, there is no getting away from the role of contingency in prehistory. The traditional chains and cones of evolutionary theory, as Gould shows, are simply rendered obsolete by the diversity of anatomical designs revealed in the 530-million-year-old Burgess Shale in British Columbia. No Darwinian law of natural selection determined which of the organisms preserved in the Burgess Shale survived the great crisis which beset the earth 225 million years ago. They were just the lucky winners of a cataclysmic 'lottery'. Had the cataclysm taken a different form, therefore, life on earth would have evolved in quite different, and unpredictable, ways.[167]

Once again, it is easy to scoff at Gould's alternative worlds inhabited by 'grazing marine herbivores' and 'marine predators with grasping limbs up front and jaws like nutcrackers' – but not by *Homo sapiens* ('If little penis worms ruled the sea, I have no confidence that Australopithecus would ever have walked erect on the savannas of Africa').[168] But Gould's comments on the role of contingency in history are far from absurd. In the absence of the scientific procedure of verification by repetition, the historian of evolution can only construct a narrative – replay an imaginary tape, in his phrase – and then speculate as to what would have happened had the initial conditions or some event in the sequence been different. This applies not just to the fortuitous triumph of the polychaetes over the priapolids after the Burgess period, or the triumph of mammals over giant birds in the Eocene period. It applies to that brief eighteen-thousandth of the planet's history when it has been inhabited by man.

True, Gould's argument depends heavily on the role of major upheavals – like those caused by the impact of extraterrestrial bodies. Yet this is not the only way in which contingency enters the historical process. For, as the proponents of 'chaos theory' have demonstrated, the natural world is unpredictable enough – even when there are no falling meteors – to make the task of accurate prediction well-nigh impossible.

In its modern usage by mathematicians, meteorologists and others, 'chaos' does *not* mean anarchy. It does *not* mean that there are no laws in the natural world. It means simply that those laws are so complex that it is virtually impossible for us to make accurate predictions, so that much of what happens around us *seems* to be random or chaotic. Thus, as Ian Stewart has said, 'God can play dice and create a universe of complete law and order in the same breath,' since 'even simple equations [can] generate motion so complex, so sensitive to measurement, that it appears to be random'.[169] To be precise, the theory of chaos is concerned with stochastic (that is, seemingly random) behaviour occurring in deterministic systems.

This was originally a phenomenon of interest only to disciples of the pioneering French mathematician Henri Poincaré. Poincaré had maintained that periodicity must ultimately arise if a transformation were repeatedly applied in a mathematical system; but, as Stephen Smale and others came to realise, some dynamical systems in multiple dimensions did not settle down to the four sorts of steady state identified by Poincaré for two dimensions. Using Poincaré's topological system of mapping, it was possible to identify a number of 'strange attractors' (such as the Cantor set) to which such systems tended. The 'strangeness' of these systems lay in the extreme difficulty of predicting their behaviour. Because of their extreme sensitivity to initial conditions, it was necessary to have an impossibly accurate knowledge of their starting points to make accurate forecasts.[170] In other words, apparently random behaviour turns out not to be completely random – just non-linear: 'Even when our theory is deterministic, not all of its predictions lead to repeatable experiments. Only those that are robust under small changes of initial conditions.' Theoretically, we could predict the outcome when we toss a coin if we knew exactly its vertical velocity and rotations per second. In practice, it's too difficult – and the same applies *a fortiori* in more complex processes. So although the universe is notionally deterministic after all, 'all deterministic bets are off. The best we can do is [*sic*] probabilities . . . [because] we're too stupid to see the pattern.'[171]

The applications (and derivatives) of chaos theory are numerous. One of the first was in the classic physics problem of 'three bodies' – the unpredictable gravitational effects of two equally sized planets on a grain of dust – which astronomers have seen in practice in the apparently random orbit of Hyperion around Saturn. Chaos applies to turbulence in liquids and gases too: this was Mitchell Feigenbaum's main area of interest. Benoit Mandelbrot discovered other chaotic patterns in his work *The Fractal Geometry of Nature*: a fractal, as he defined it, 'continued to exhibit detailed structure over a large range of scales' – just as the Feigenbaum 'fig tree' does. Edward Lorenz's research on convection and the weather provides one of the most striking examples of chaos in action: he used the phrase 'Butterfly Effect' to characterise the climate's sensitive dependence on initial conditions (meaning that the flapping of a single butterfly's wing today could notionally determine whether or not a hurricane would hit southern England next week). In other words, tiny fluctuations in the state of the atmosphere could have big consequences – hence the impossibility of even roughly accurate weather forecasting (even with the biggest available computer) for more than four days to come. Chaotic patterns have also been found by Robert May and others in the fluctuations of insect and animal populations. In a sense, chaos theory finally confirms what Marcus Aurelius and Alexander Pope long ago instinctively knew: even if the world appears to be 'the effect of Chance', it still has a 'regular and beautiful' – if unintelligible – structure. 'All Nature is but art unknown to thee; / All Chance, direction, which thou canst not see.'

Clearly, chaos theory has important implications for the social sciences. For economists, chaos theory helps to explain why predictions and forecasts based on the linear equations which are the basis of most economic models are so often wrong.[172] The same principle 'that simple systems do not necessarily possess simple dynamic properties' can presumably be applied to the world of politics as well.[173] It is, if nothing else, a warning to all pundits to avoid simple theories about the determinants of elections. The most we can do with our understanding of chaotic systems, as Roger Penrose has suggested, is to 'simulate *typical* outcomes. The predicted weather may well not be the weather that actually occurs, but it is perfectly plausible as *a* weather.'[174] The same applies to economic and political predictions. The best the long-range forecaster can do is give us a number of plausible scenarios, and to admit that the choice between them can only be a guess, not a prophecy.

Towards Chaostory

But what are the implications of chaos for historians, who are concerned not with predicting the future, but with understanding the past? It is not enough simply to say that man, like all creatures, is subject to the chaotic behaviour of the natural world, though it is certainly true that, right up until the late nineteenth century, the weather probably was the principal determinant of most people's well-being. In modern history, however, the acts of other people have come to play an increasingly important role in this regard. In the twentieth century, more people have had their lives shortened by other people – as opposed to nature – than ever before.

The philosophical significance of chaos theory is that it reconciles the notions of causation and contingency. It rescues us not only from the nonsensical world of the idealists like Oakeshott, where there is no such thing as a cause or an effect and the equally nonsensical world of the determinists, in which there is only a chain of preordained causation based on laws. Chaos – stochastic behaviour in deterministic systems – means unpredictable outcomes even when successive events are causally linked.

In fact, this middle position was already implicit in much that had been said by philosophers of history about causation in the 1940s and 1950s – before the advent of chaos theory. The fundamental determinist idea that causal statements could only be predicated on laws can, as we have seen, be traced back to Hume. In his *Treatise of Human Nature*, Hume had argued that a causal link between two phenomena X_1 and Y_1 could only be posited if *series* of cases in which events X_1, X_2, X_3, X_4 ... had been followed by Y_1, Y_2, Y_3, Y_4 ... had been observed – a series sufficiently long to justify the inference that Xs are always (or very likely to be) followed by Ys. As refined by Hempel, this became known as the 'covering law' model of causation, which states that any statement of a causal nature is predicated on a law (or 'explicit statement of the [presupposed] general regularities') derived from repeated observation.[175]

However, Karl Popper cast doubt on the possibility of establishing such laws of historical change, if by 'law' was meant a predictive statement analogous to the classical laws of physics. Popper's point was simply that scientific methodology – the systematic testing of hypotheses by experimentation – could not be applied to the study of the past. Yet Popper's rejection of determinism – what he rather confusingly called 'historicism' – did not imply a rejection of the notion of causation altogether, in the way that Oakeshott's had.[176] Popper accepted that events or trends really were caused by 'initial conditions'. The critical point was that it was possible to have a causal explanation in history which did not depend on such a general statement or deductive certainty. Collingwood had already distinguished between the Hempelian (or nomological) type of causal explanation and the 'practical science' type of explanation, in which a cause is 'an event or state of things by producing *or preventing* which we can produce or prevent that whose cause it is said to be'.[177] Here the best criterion for establishing a causal relationship was not the Hempelian covering law, but the so-called 'but for' or *sine qua non* test, applying the principle that 'the effect cannot happen or exist unless the cause happens or exists'. Popper made the same point: 'There are countless possible conditions; and in order to be able to examine these possibilities in our search for the true conditions of a trend, we have all the time to try *to imagine conditions under which the trend in question would disappear.*'[178] Indeed, Popper's most telling charge against 'historicists' was their inability to ask such questions – 'to imagine a change in the conditions of change' (something of which idealists like Oake-shott, as we have seen, had been just as guilty).

The implications of this insight have been explored in more detail by Frankel, who cites some examples of historical explanations which are simply statements about 'conditions without which the events in question would not have taken place':

> Would the French Revolution have been different if Rousseau had not written the *Social Contract*? Would the Reconstruction period after the Civil War have been different if Booth, like most would-be assassins, had been a poor shot? Plainly, when we impute causal influences of a certain type to Rousseau or Lincoln we assume that these questions would be answered in the affirmative.... What exactly is the generalisation that lies behind a statement of historical causation such as 'Cleopatra's beauty caused Anthony to linger in Egypt'?[179]

In the words of Gallie, 'Historians ... tell us how a particular event happened by pointing out hitherto unnoticed, or at least undervalued, antecedent events, *but for which*, they claim on broadly inductive grounds, *the event in question would not or could hardly have happened.*'[180] One difference between science and history is that historians often have to rely on such explanations exclusively, whereas scientists can use them as hypotheses to be tested experimentally. In other words, if we want to say anything about causation in the past without invoking covering laws, we really have to use counterfactuals, if only to test our causal hypotheses.

Legal theorists of causation – who are, after all, as much concerned as historians with understanding the causes of past events – have arrived at the same conclusion by a different route. As Hart and Honoré demonstrate, there are practical problems from a lawyer's point of view with Mill's definition of a cause as 'the sum total of the conditions positive and negative taken together; the whole of the contingencies ... which being realised the consequence invariably follows'.[181] For, in their quests for responsibility, liability, compensation and punishment, lawyers have to establish *which* of a multiplicity of causes – of a fire, for example, or a death – 'made the difference'.[182] Here too, the only way of doing so is by posing the 'but for' or *sine qua non* question: only by saying whether or not a specific harm would have happened without a defendant's allegedly wrongful act can we say whether or not for legal purposes the act was the cause of the harm. In the words of R. B. Braithwaite, causally related events are thus those which are used:

> to justify inferences not merely as to what has happened or will happen, but 'counterfactual' inferences as to what *would* have been the case if some actual event, which in fact happened, had not happened. . . . The lawyer approaches the general element inherent in causal statements . . . [by asking] when it is suggested that A is the cause of B, . . . would B have happened without A?[183]

Hart and Honoré acknowledge the practical limitations of the *sine qua non* (for example, in the hypothetical case in which two men have simultaneously shot a third man dead).[184] But they have no doubt that it is nevertheless to be preferred to the no less subjective assumptions which 'realists' make about the intentions of law-makers.

The philosophical ramifications of the counterfactual are complex. As Gardiner has pointed out, much depends on the form the counterfactual question takes, which is often incomplete:

> 'Were shots on the boulevards the cause of the 1848 Revolution in France?' Does this mean: 'Would the Revolution have broken out at the precise time at which it did break out if they had not occurred?' Or does it mean: 'Would the Revolution have broken out sooner or later even if there had been no shots?' And if, after receiving an affirmative answer to the latter question, we ask: 'What then was the real cause of the Revolution?' further

specification is again required. For there are a number of possible answers.... And there are no absolute Real Causes waiting to be discovered by historians ...[185]

These problems of formulation have been explored at length by logicians.[186] But from the historian's point of view it is probably more important to decide *which* counterfactual questions to pose in the first place. For one of the strongest arguments against the whole notion of considering alternative scenarios is that there is no limit to the number which we can consider. Like Borges's Ts'ui Pên, the historian is confronted with an infinite number of 'forking paths'. This was what Croce saw as the main flaw of the counterfactual approach.

In practice, however, there is no real point in asking most of the possible counterfactual questions. For example, no sensible person wishes to know what would have happened in 1848 if the entire population of Paris had suddenly sprouted wings, as this is not a *plausible* scenario. This need for plausibility in the formulation of counterfactual questions was first pointed out by Sir Isaiah Berlin. Berlin's starting point in his critique of determinism, like Meinecke's, was its incompatibility with the historian's need to make value judgements about the 'character, purposes and motives of individuals'.[187] However, he went on to make an important distinction (originally suggested by Namier) between what did happen, what could have happened and what could not have happened:

[N]o one will wish to deny that we do often argue among the best possible courses of action open to human beings in the present and past and future, in fiction and in dreams; that historians (and judges and juries) do attempt to establish, as well as they are able, what these possibilities are; that the ways in which these lines are drawn mark the frontiers between reliable and unreliable history; that what is called realism (as opposed to fancy or ignorance of life or utopian dreams) consists precisely *in the placing of what occurred (or might occur) in the context of what could have happened (or could happen), and in the demarcation of this from what could not;* that this is all ... that the sense of history, in the end, comes to; [and] that upon this capacity all historical (as well as legal) justice depends ...[188]

This distinction between what did happen and what could plausibly have happened is of critical importance:

When an historian, in attempting to decide what occurred and why, rejects all the infinity of logically open possibilities, the vast majority of which are obviously absurd, and, like a detective, investigates only those possibilities which have at least some initial plausibility, it is this sense of what is plausible – what men, being men, could have done or been – that constitutes the sense of coherence with the patterns of life ...[189]

Another way of putting this is to say that we are concerned with possibilities which seemed probable in the past. This was a point which Marc Bloch well understood:

To evaluate the probability of an event is to weigh its chances of taking place. That granted, is it legitimate to speak of the possibility of a past event? Obviously not, in the absolute sense. Only the future has contingency. The past is something already given which leaves no room for possibility. Before the die is cast, the probability that any number might appear is one to six. The problem vanishes as soon as the dice box is emptied. ... In a correct analysis, however, the use which historical research makes of the idea of probabilities is not at all contradictory. When the historian asks himself about the probability of a past event, he actually attempts to transport himself, by a bold exercise of the mind, to the time before the event itself, in order to gauge its chances, as they appeared upon the eve of its realisation. Hence, probability remains properly in the future. But since the line of the present has somehow been moved back in the imagination, it is a future of bygone times built upon a fragment which, for us, is actually the past.[190]

Almost exactly the same point has been made by Trevor-Roper:

> At any given moment in history there are real alternatives ... How can we '*explain* what happened and *why*' if we only look at what happened and never consider the alternatives ... It is only if we place ourselves before the alternatives of the past ..., only if we live for a moment, as the men of the time lived, in its still fluid context and among its still unresolved problems, if we see those problems coming upon us, ... that we can draw useful lessons from history.[191]

In short, by narrowing down the historical alternatives we consider to those which are *plausible* – and hence by replacing the enigma of 'chance' with the calculation of *probabilities* – we solve the dilemma of choosing between a single deterministic past and an unmanageably infinite number of possible pasts. The counterfactual scenarios we therefore need to construct are not mere fantasy: they are simulations based on calculations about the relative probability of plausible outcomes in a chaotic world (hence 'virtual history').

Naturally, this means that we need to have some understanding of probability. We need, for example, to avoid the gambler's fallacy of believing that if red has come up five times running at the roulette wheel, the chance of black is greater at the next spin – it is not, and the same applies when we toss coins or roll dice.[192] On the other hand, historians are concerned with human beings who, unlike dice, have memories and consciousness. For dice, the past really does not influence the present; all that matters are the equations which govern their motion when thrown. But for human beings the past often does have an influence. To take a simple example (borrowed from game theory): a politician who has shirked military confrontation twice may be emboldened to take up arms the third time he is challenged, precisely because of the memory of those humiliations. Any statement about his likelihood to fight must be based on an assessment of his past conduct and his present attitudes towards it. So historical probability is more complicated than mathematical probability. Just as God does not play dice, humans *are* not dice. We come back to what Collingwood called the truly 'historical form' of causation, where 'that which is "caused" is the free and deliberate act of a conscious and responsible agent'.[193] And, as Dray has said, the 'principles of action' of agents in the past were not always what we would regard as strictly rational.[194]

There nevertheless remains an unanswered question. How *exactly* are we to distinguish probable unrealised alternatives from improbable ones? The most frequently raised objection to the counterfactual approach is that it depends on 'facts which concededly never existed'. Hence, we simply lack the knowledge to answer counterfactual questions. But this is not so. The answer to the question is in fact very simple: We should consider as plausible or probable *only those alternatives which we can show on the basis of contemporary evidence that contemporaries actually considered.*

This is a vitally important point, and one which Oakeshott seems to have overlooked. As has often been said, what we call the past was once the future; and the people of the past no more knew what their future would be than we can know our own. All they could do was consider the likely future, the plausible outcome. It is possible that some people in the past had no interest in the future whatever. It is also true that many people in the past have felt quite sure that they did know what the future would be; and that sometimes they have even got it right. But most people in the past have tended to consider more than one possible future. And although no more than one of these actually has come about, at the moment *before* it came about it was no more real (though it may now seem more probable) than the others. Now, if all history is the history of (recorded) thought, surely we must attach equal significance to *all* the outcomes thought about. The historian who allows his knowledge as to which of these outcomes subsequently happened to obliterate the other outcomes people regarded as plausible cannot hope to recapture the past 'as it actually was'. For, in considering only the possibility which was actually realised, he commits the most elementary teleological error. To understand how it actually was, we therefore need to understand *how it actually wasn't* – but how, to contemporaries, it might have been. This is even more true when the actual outcome is one which no one expected – which was not actually thought about until it happened.

That narrows the scope for counterfactual analysis down considerably. Moreover, we can only legitimately consider those hypothetical scenarios which contemporaries not only considered, but also committed to paper (or some other form of record) which has survived – and which has been identified as a valid source by historians. Clearly, that introduces an additional element of contingency, as there is nothing inevitable about which documents survive and which do not. But, at the same time, it renders counterfactual history practicable.

There is, then, a double rationale for counterfactual analysis. Firstly, it is a *logical* necessity when asking questions about causation to pose 'but for' questions, and to try to imagine what would have happened if our supposed cause had been absent. For this reason, we are obliged to construct plausible alternative pasts on the basis of judgements about probability; and these can be made only on the basis of historical evidence. Secondly, to do this is a *historical* necessity when attempting to understand how the past 'actually was' – precisely in the Rankean sense, as we must attach equal importance to all the possibilities which contemporaries contemplated before the fact, and greater importance to these than to an outcome which they did not anticipate.

Besides the first premise that *sine qua non* arguments are indispensable and should be made explicit, the key methodological constraint imposed in this collection is therefore that counterfactuals should be those which contemporaries contemplated. In each chapter, it is the alternatives which were seen at the time as realistic which provide the essential starting point for the argument.

A number of points emerge when we consider these. Firstly, what actually happened was often *not* the outcome which the majority of informed contemporaries saw as the most likely: the counterfactual scenario was in that sense more 'real' to decision-makers at the critical moment than the actual subsequent events.

Secondly, we begin to see where determinist theories really do play a role in history: when people believe in them and believe themselves to be in their grip. As noted above, the difference between chaos in the natural world and chaos in history is that man, unlike gases, fluids or lesser organisms, is conscious. Not only are his genes determined to survive; *he* generally is too, and he therefore seeks, prior to acting in the present, to make sense of the past and on that basis to anticipate the future. The trouble is that the theories on which he has generally based his predictions have so often been defective. Whether they have posited the existence of a Supreme Being, or Reason, or the Ideal, or the class struggle, or the racial struggle, or any other determining force, they have misled him by exaggerating his ability to make accurate predictions. Tocqueville once observed: 'One is apt to perish in politics from too much memory'; but he should have said 'from too much determinist historiography'. In different ways, belief in determinist theories made all the great conflicts studied here – the English Civil War, the American War of Independence, the Anglo-Irish conflict, the First World War, the Second World War and the Cold War – more rather than less likely. Ultimately, as this book seeks to argue, those who died in these conflicts were the victims of genuinely chaotic and unpredictable events which could have turned out differently. Probably as many people have been killed by the unintended consequences of deterministic prophecies as by their self-fulfilling tendencies. It is nevertheless a striking fact that their killers have so often acted in the name of deterministic theories, whether religious, socialist or racist. In this light, perhaps the best answer to the question 'Why bother asking counterfactual questions?' is simply: What if we don't? Virtual history is a necessary antidote to determinism.

There is therefore no need to apologise for the fact that this book is, in essence, a series of separate voyages into 'imaginary time'. It may smack of science fiction to offer the reader glimpses through a series of worm holes into eight parallel universes. But the assumptions on which each chapter is based are more than merely imaginary or fanciful. The world is not divinely ordered, nor governed by Reason, the class struggle or any other deterministic 'law'. All we can say for sure is that it is condemned to increasing disorder by entropy. Historians who study its past must be doubly uncertain: because the artefacts they treat as evidence have often survived only by chance, and because in identifying an artefact as a piece of historical evidence the historian immediately distorts its significance. The events they try to infer from these sources were originally 'stochastic' – in other words, apparently chaotic – because the behaviour of the material world is governed by non-linear as well as linear equations. The fact of human consciousness (which cannot be expressed in terms of equations) only adds to the impression of chaos. Under these circumstances, the search for universal laws of history is futile. The most historians can do is to make tentative statements about causation with reference to plausible counterfactuals, constructed on the basis of judgements about probability. Finally, the probability of alternative scenarios can be inferred only from such statements by contemporaries about the future as have survived. These points could be held up as the manifesto for a new 'chaostory' – a chaotic approach to history. But in many ways they simply make explicit what many historians have been doing for years in the privacy of their own imaginations.

One final question: if this book had not been published, would a similar (perhaps better) book have sooner rather than later appeared? It is tempting – and not just out of modesty – to say that it would. Ideas about causation in the sciences have changed so much in recent decades that it seems reasonable to assume that historians would have caught up sooner or later. Indeed, it might be said that, if the present generation of historians had paid as much attention to mathematics, physics and even palaeontology as they have paid to sociology, anthropology and literary theory, the book might have appeared ten years ago. However, history does not proceed as science does. Kuhn may be right about the convulsive quality of scientific revolutions – the tendency for outmoded 'paradigms' to persist for some time after their obsolescence has set in.[195] But at least the paradigm does eventually shift, not least because of the modern concentration of resources on research into what are thought to be important questions. (Even if the question turns out to be unimportant, that becomes apparent sooner or later as diminishing returns set in.) Historical paradigms change in a more haphazard way. In place of periodic 'shifts' forward, the modern historical profession has a sluggish 'revisionism', in which pupils are mainly concerned to qualify the interpretations of the previous generation, only rarely (and at a risk to their own careers) challenging its assumptions. If at times the history of history appears to have the kind of cyclical quality whose existence at a universal level this book denies, then that simply reflects the profession's inherent limitations. Indeed, fashions like 'the narrative revival' perfectly illustrate the historian's tendency to go backwards rather than forwards in search of methodological novelty. For that reason, it seems right to conclude on a resoundingly possibilitarian note. There was nothing inevitable about this book. Or rather, a book exactly like this would not have appeared had it not been for a succession of meetings between like-minded historians which might easily never have happened – bringing us neatly back to the authentically chaotic nature of everyday life, where this introduction began. It is for the reader to judge – as in the case of each of the counterfactuals discussed below – whether the actual outcome is to be preferred to the many unrealised, but plausible, alternatives.

ONE

ENGLAND WITHOUT CROMWELL:

What if Charles I had avoided the Civil War?

John Adamson

The grievances under which the English laboured, when considered in themselves, without regard to the constitution,
scarcely deserve the name; nor were they either burthensome on
the people's properties, or anywise shocking to the natural
humanity of mankind ... and though it was justly apprehended,
that such precedents, if patiently submitted to, would end in the
total disuse of Parliaments, and in the establishment of arbitrary
authority, Charles [I] dreaded no opposition from the people,
who are not commonly much affected with consequences, and
require some striking motive to engage them in a resistance of
established government.

> DAVID HUME, *The History of England* (1778), CH. LIII

Between 1638 and 1640, when not distracted by fiscal crises and
Scottish wars, Charles I turned his attention to a more congenial
task: the plans for a new royal palace at Whitehall.[1] Designed in
the Classical style by John Webb, Inigo Jones's gifted pupil and
collaborator, the project was the fulfilment of the King's long-
held ambition to replace the rambling and outmoded palace which
he had inherited from the Tudors. The new Whitehall was
conceived on a vast scale, a setting for the court which could rival
the grandeur of the Louvre or the Escorial. Given adequate
funding (an assumption which in 1638 was not yet wholly far-
fetched), it would probably have been completed by the mid- to

late 1640s. Here, at last, would be a seat of government appropriate to the system of 'Personal Rule' Charles I had established since dispensing with Parliament in 1629. At least until 1639, it was from here that Charles could expect to govern his realms, resplendent amid Webb's Baroque courtyards and colonnades, during the next decade and beyond.[2]

Implicit in such ambitious planning was the confident presumption that Charles I's regime would not only survive, but prosper. Was such confidence justified? Or was it, as many historians have held, the self-deluding folly of a remote and isolated regime – yet another instance of the sense of unreality which characterised the Caroline court? The answers to these questions have rarely been considered on their historical merits. To the two political philosophies most influential in historical writing during the last century, Whiggery and Marxism, the collapse of Charles I's regime during the 1630s appeared 'inevitable'. In seeking to enhance monarchical authority (in practice, the powers of the executive), Charles I was standing, Canute-like, against historical tides which were outside mere kingly control: the rise of parliamentary authority; the belief in individual liberty guaranteed by the common law; even, it was once believed, 'the rise of the gentry' (the nearest seventeenth-century England could get to Marx's 'bourgeoisie'). These forces swept inexorably on, so the theory ran, to produce a parliamentarian victory in the Civil Wars of the 1640s and the Glorious Revolution of 1688–9, before finally reaching the sunny uplands of parliamentary government in the heyday of Gladstone and Disraeli. To Samuel Rawson Gardiner – the Victorian historian whose work remains, a hundred years on, the most influential narrative of Charles I's reign – the King's opponents had the future on their side; the parliamentarians' proposals for the settlement of the kingdom during the 1640s 'anticipate[d], in all essential points, the system which prevails in the reign of Victoria'.[3] And in seeking to create a Personal Rule during the 1630s – a strong monarchical government unfettered by parliamentary control – Charles I was not merely up against his critics; he was up against History itself.

Of course, such assumptions about the inevitability of the regime's demise have recently been subjected to a battery of 'revisionist' criticism.[4] Yet, in subtler ways, the belief that Charles's experiment in government without Parliament was inherently unviable continues to enjoy currency, even among historians who reject the teleological approach of Marxists and Whigs. So unpopular were the King's policies that they were bound, at some point or other, to provoke rebellion; and, as the King could not mount a credible war-effort without parliamentary finance, the luxury of unfettered monarchical rule was one which Charles – quite literally – could not afford.[5] From this perspective, the King's great act of folly was his decision in 1637 to impose a 'Laudian' revision of the English Prayer Book on the Scottish Kirk – to which it reeked of 'Popery and superstition'. The sequence of events set in train by that decision revealed the political and financial impossibility of sustaining a non-parliamentary regime. Confronted with a full-scale rebellion in Scotland, for which the new Prayer Book had provided the catalyst, the King refused to compromise with his critics, and resolved to re-establish royal authority in Scotland at the point of the sword.[6] It was the King's adamant refusal to yield to the Covenanters' demands, and his determination to fight on – even after the débâcle of the 1639 campaign, the misgivings of his own Privy Councillors, and the failure of the Short Parliament in May 1640 to fund another war – which left his regime politically and financially bankrupt. The Covenanters won the 'Second Bishops' War' of August 1640. And, with a Scottish army of occupation in the north of England, Parliament met in November in conditions which – for the first time in Charles's reign – prevented the King from dissolving it when he willed. Once the two Houses had convened, it was only a matter of time before royal ministers were brought to book and the 'innovations' which had been at the heart of Charles's regime – from the exaction of ship money to the placement of the communion table 'altar-wise' in parish churches – were declared illegal, piece by piece.

The spate of research on the 'fall of the British monarchies' has stressed the highly contingent nature of the linkages which connected these events. At least until February 1641, Professor Russell has argued, Charles could have reached a *modus vivendi* with his Scottish and English critics which would have averted the Civil War.[7] This essay takes the enquiry one stage further: to ask not just whether Charles might have avoided a civil war, but whether he might have emerged from the Scottish crisis with the structures of the Personal Rule unscathed. Could Charles I have continued to govern his three kingdoms without referring to Parliaments – as he had done effectively at least until 1637 – into the 1640s and beyond? In considering these questions, it is clear that the critical moment was 1639. There is now broad agreement that, had he not failed to suppress the Covenanter rebellion at his first attempt (and so initiated the disastrous sequence of events which flowed from that failure), Charles would never have been forced to call the Long Parliament of November 1640, the body which set about dismantling the whole edifice of Personal Rule. But for the military failure of 1639, the future of Charles's regime would have taken a very different course. Success against the Scots would have brought the crown prestige, perhaps even popularity, and removed the need for a parliament for the foreseeable future – arguably, for decades to come.

Part of the difficulty in broaching such possibilities is that they touch on areas where the received account of England's past is so deeply embedded as to make alternative courses of development seem almost unimaginable: England without the evolution of a powerful Parliament; without the emergence of a religious settlement which was both Protestant and (at least in comparison with most of seventeenth-century Europe) relatively tolerant; without a system of common law in which the sanctity of private property was the cardinal principle governing the relationship between monarch and subject.[8] If the argument for the 'inevitability' of the Caroline regime's collapse does not stand, then there was nothing foreordained about any of these developments. The trajectory of British (and Irish) history would have looked very different: almost certainly no Civil War, no regicide, no

Glorious Revolution; and Oliver Cromwell pursuing a career of blameless obscurity among the rustic gentlefolk of Ely.

It would be reassuring if we could regard these questions as merely a self-indulgent toying with the what-ifs of history – those donnish 'parlour-games' so derided by E. H. Carr. Yet, in Hugh Trevor-Roper's famous phrase, 'history is not merely what happened: it is what happened in the context of what might have happened'.[9] And to contemporaries – as Edward Rossingham reported in August 1639 – the possibility of a royal victory in 1639 was real and plausible, not a matter of vaporous 'counter-factual' speculation.[10] As late as August 1640, the Comptroller of the King's Household, Sir Thomas Jermyn, was confident that 'we shall have a very good and successful end of these troubles'.[11] Weighing the probabilities, Secretary Windebanke agreed: 'I cannot much apprehend the rebels.'[12] Let us begin by examining the circumstances of the war in 1639. Were the King and his closest advisers the prisoners of events? Or was the campaign against the Covenanters a war that Charles I could have won?

Scotland in 1639: A Victory Forgone

Charles's decision to go to war in 1639 without summoning Parliament has been regarded as emblematic of a wider (and ultimately fatal) indifference on the part of his regime towards the sensibilities of England's local governing elites.[13] Not since Edward II in 1323 had an English king attempted to mount a major war-effort without the summons of the two Houses – admittedly, not a happy augury.[14] Yet there were more recent, and more auspicious, precedents. Elizabeth I, who disliked parliaments only marginally less than Charles I, had organised an effective military force to expel the French from the Lowlands of Scotland in 1559–60 without recourse to the legislature. And in 1562 she had gone to war again, despatching an expeditionary force to Le Havre, without convoking the two Houses.[15] Of course, Parliament *was* usually called upon in time of war; but it was not the *sine qua non* of an effective military campaign.

Nor was it just sycophantic courtiers who believed that the King could go to war in 1639 without needing parliamentary subsidies to buy his victory. Surveying the various resources at the King's disposal in February 1639, Edward Montagu – the son of the Northamptonshire Puritan Lord Montagu of Boughton – thought that it was obvious: 'the King will have no need of a Parliament'.[16] Charles and his Council planned to wage war in 1639 in a manner which tested, and (they hoped) simultaneously consolidated, the traditional institutions which the King had sought to make the buttresses of the Personal Rule. The crown's ancient fiscal prerogatives were revived and extended (including such feudal obligations as scutage and border service by the crown's tenants in the northern marcher counties); and in the mobilisation of the localities, the county hierarchies of lords lieutenant (responsible for each county's militia), their deputy lieutenants and the local magistracy (the justices of the peace) were all stretched to their limit. The results varied – from the exemplary to the farcical. But by the spring of 1639, without a parliament and relying exclusively on the administrative structures of the Personal Rule, England was in the throes of the largest mobilisation since the Spanish wars of the 1580s.

Charles's strategy for the defeat of the Covenanters, as devised over the winter of 1638–9, was an integrated programme of military and naval action. There were four principal elements.[17] The first was an amphibious force under the Marquess of Hamilton (the highly Anglicised Scottish magnate who was general of the King's forces in Scotland), to be made up of 5,000 men in eight warships and thirty transports (the tangible results of the 1630s' ship-money levies). Their task was to blockade Edinburgh and establish a bridgehead on the Scottish east coast.[18] Second, an attack on the west coast of Scotland led by that deft political survivor, Randall MacDonnell, 2nd Earl of Antrim; his task was to divide the Covenanter forces and pin them down in the west. From Ireland, Lord Deputy Wentworth, Charles's forceful and diligent viceroy, was to provide the third element of the assault: a landing on Scotland's west coast, reinforcing Antrim's proposed attack and placing 10,000 (mostly Catholic) Irish troops within striking distance of Edinburgh. The fourth, and principal, element in the offensive was the mobilisation of an English army. This was to advance towards the River Tweed (the natural frontier between England and Scotland), and be ready not only to repel Covenanter incursions across the English border, but also to cross the Tweed, if necessary, and take the war into the Covenanter heartlands. Whether or not Charles still intended to retake Edinburgh Castle – as he had first planned[19] – the Ordnance Office's preparations for the campaign were clearly such as to allow for the possibility of capturing Scottish strongholds by storm.[20] Charles wished to be in a position to mount an offensive war.

Little went according to plan. All wars, Parliament-sponsored or not, tend to test the Exchequer to breaking point, and in this the war of 1639 was no exception.[21] The amount actually allocated by the Exchequer in 1639 – some £200,000 – was relatively small, and almost certainly an under-assessment of the costs entailed.[22] But the inadequacy of the Exchequer's provision was partly offset by the often substantial sums raised by local gentry and expended on the trained bands. (By March 1639, the Yorkshire gentry alone claimed that they had expended £20,000 – none of which appears in the Exchequer's central accounts.)[23] Perhaps the strategy's principal shortcoming was its failure to offer timely support to the anti-Covenanter resistance led by the Catholic Marquess of Huntly and his son, Lord Aboyne, in the north-east Highlands of Scotland – with the result that the King forfeited the opportunity to create the nucleus of a 'royalist party' in Scotland in 1639.[24] Elsewhere, elements of Charles's strategy foundered and had to be abandoned. Wentworth's levies could not be mobilised in time. Antrim, too, failed to deliver his promised troops. Hamilton had grave reservations about the East Anglian recruits assigned to his command. And when the members of the peerage were summoned to York to endorse the campaign, Lords Saye and Brooke staged a damaging public protest against the non-parliamentary expedients which Charles was using to fight the war. On 22 May there was also, ominously, an eclipse of the sun.

But elsewhere, as the mobilisation progressed, there were grounds for hope. Yorkshire, which was expected to bear the brunt of any Scottish advance and where the gentry's support was seen as being crucial to the campaign's success, responded enthusiastically. Even that stern taskmaster, Wentworth – the President of the Council of the North – was impressed by the county's diligence, and wrote to the Yorkshire deputy lieutenants (responsible for mustering the trained bands), commending their 'loyalties and wisdom in [their] late cheerful and bounden offer ... in your promised readiness to attend [his Majesty's] commands'.[25] When the King arrived at York on 30 March 1639, to establish his court and oversee the preparations for the forthcoming campaign in person, he was greeted by spontaneous demonstrations of loyalty. There was 'great resort to court of the nobility and gentry of the northern parts; and such as were colonels of the trained bands expressed much forwardness to serve his Majesty in that expedition, in defence of the nation'.[26] By mid-April, Hamilton was pleased to find that his earlier pessimism had been unfounded, and that 'generally the bodies of men [under his command] are extremely good, well clothed, and not so badly armed as I feared'.[27] Stretched though it was, the Caroline regime did not break down. And by the end of May 1639 it had put into the field an army of between 16,000 and 20,000 men – comparable in size to the Civil War New Model Army (which rarely equalled its paper strength of 21,400), and more than three times the size of the English force which decisively defeated the Scots at Dunbar in 1650.[28] When Charles's forces marched out of York in 'great pomp and state' towards the border to begin the campaign, there was no hint that they considered any likely outcome other than victory for the King.[29] In May, as his army assembled and began to train, morale improved, and the once ragged levies gradually acquired the aspect of a serious fighting force. 'If we fight, it will be the bloodiest battle that ever was,' boasted Colonel Fleetwood, 'for we are resolved to fly in the very faces of [the rebels]; our spirits are good if our skill be according.'[30] The King was offering no more than an objective assessment when he described the forces that had assembled by the beginning of June as 'in notable good condition, pressing hard to see the face of their enemies'. Charles was bullish, 'now resolved to treat no more where he ought to be obeyed'.[31]

Yet when the two armies came close to engaging, on 4 and 5 June 1639, the King's response was one of doubt and indecision. The Earl of Holland, in command of a reconnaissance force of 3,000 infantry and 1,000 horse, had encountered the Scottish army at Kelso on the 4th, and decided to retreat before what he mistakenly believed to be a far larger Scottish force.[32] And on 5 June, the Covenanter commander, Alexander Leslie, reinforced this misapprehension, arraying the Scottish army on the heights of Duns Law, on the northern bank of the Tweed, within sight of the King's army, so as to create a misleading impression of their numbers.[33] It was as close as the two armies came to engaging. Over-suspicious of dissent within his own ranks, and gulled by the Covenanters' tactics into believing that they had fielded an army vastly outnumbering his own, the King decided that an invasion of Scotland was now impossible.[34] Instead, he opted for negotiations, to buy time rather than risk an encounter against what he believed were overwhelming odds. On 6 June, the Covenanter leadership – which was no less anxious to avoid a fight – invited the King to treat, a proposal which was promptly accepted.[35]

This decision to open negotiations with the Covenanters in June 1639 was arguably the greatest single mistake of Charles's life. The subsequent treaty, the Pacification of Berwick, allowed him to regain custody of his Scottish fortresses (including Edinburgh Castle), and met his demand for the dissolution of the Covenanters' rebel government, the Tables;[36] but, in return, he was obliged to concede the calling of a Scottish parliament and a General Assembly of the Scottish Kirk. The one was likely to impose stringent conditions on the exercise of Charles's absentee rule over Scotland; the other to endorse the removal of bishops from the Scottish church. As neither prospect was acceptable to the King, all he had purchased by the treaty was time. To bring Scotland to heel, he would need to go to war again. More serious was the reaction to this military failure in England. To those who had taken part in the English mobilisation, their investment of time and money seemed to have been frittered away, as it now appeared, 'unsuccessfully, fruitlessly, and needlessly'.[37] A formidable force had been mustered, and victory thrown away without a shot being fired.

Yet the King's decision to open negotiations was founded on an elementary miscalculation. The estimates of the size and strength of the Scottish army, on which Charles had based his decision, were grossly inflated. In fact, the King's army at the beginning of June 1639 either equalled or outnumbered the Covenanters' – perhaps by as many as 4,000 men.[38] As Sir John Temple reported at the time, the English army was growing daily, and the horse (tactically the most important element of the force) now stood at 4,000.[39] Even as Holland encountered Leslie's forces at Kelso, Scottish morale was crumbling. 'It is verily believed by those which were in the Scotch army [at Kelso]', ran one English intelligence report, 'that if we had come to blows, we [English] should have beaten them.'[40] Moreover, the Scots were beset with acute problems with regard to victualling, weapons and shortages of ready cash.[41] By the first days of June, Leslie's army had begun to desert. It was only a matter of time before the true state of his forces was disclosed. Even the severest modern critic of the Caroline regime's shortcomings in the campaign has argued that in June 1639 the King was on the brink of success. 'Ironically, Charles had been much closer to victory than he ever imagined. Had he postponed negotiations for another week or two, the Scottish army would probably have disintegrated, as its money and food were exhausted.'[42] At that point, with his own army intact, there would have been little standing between the King and Edinburgh. On 6 June the Covenanter leaders asked for peace; a fortnight later, and they would probably have been asking for surrender.

To Charles's contemporaries, the implication was clear. Edward Rossingham, perhaps the best informed of the newsletter writers, reported the consensus in August 1639: 'I have heard many men of good judgement say that if his Majesty would have taken his advantages to punish [the Scots'] insolencies, he might have marched to Edinburgh and bred such a confusion among them as that the common people must of necessity have deserted their [Covenanter] nobility.'[43] For all the problems that the King encountered – from laggardly muster-masters, obstreperous noblemen like Lords Saye and Brooke, overstretched Ordnance Office clerks – it appeared to contemporaries that the war of 1639 was one which Charles I could have won.

The Fortunes of Puritanism: Senescence and Decline?

Suppose the 'men of good judgement' were right in the summer of 1639, and that the King had engaged the Covenanter 'rebels' and defeated them – or had secured the upper hand simply by waiting for the Scottish force to dissolve. What were the regime's chances, in the event of a royal victory in 1639, for long-term survival into the 1640s and beyond? Several objections can be made to such a scenario. Even if Whig or Marxist teleology is discounted, it may still be retorted that examining the contingent circumstances of a given historical moment is a misleading gauge of a government's long-term chances of success. A victory in 1639 – so the counter-argument might run – would not have provided a long-term guarantee of the regime's survival, merely a temporary reprieve. Would not the regime have been toppled by its English critics at some point, even without the timely assistance of the Scots?

Any assessment of whether or not Charles I's regime could have survived must begin with its ability to resist, or at least to neutralise, potential sources of political coercion.[44] And in

England – the richest and most populous of Charles I's three kingdoms – possible sources of coercion were few and far between. Charles was the beneficiary of the 'demilitarisation' of the nobility, a process which had been virtually complete by the time of his accession in 1625. Rapid technological change in armaments and the techniques of warfare during the sixteenth century had rendered the old aristocratic arsenals redundant.[45] The fiasco of the Essex rebellion in 1601 marked, in Conrad Russell's phrase, 'the moment when the threat of force ceased to be a significant weapon in English politics'.[46] If there were those during the 1630s who wanted to coerce Charles I, they had to resign themselves to the fact that the means to do so were unlikely to be provided by his English subjects – however unpopular the regime might become.[47]

If Charles I was not merely to be challenged, but coerced, then the means to do so had to be found outside England. Ireland – from 1633 under the iron rule of Lord Deputy Wentworth (the future Earl of Strafford) – was occasionally troublesome, but posed no immediate threat of armed resistance to the crown.[48] Only in Scotland, which still remained virtually untouched by the 'military revolution', and where large arsenals remained in private hands, was there the possibility that the King's subjects could raise a private military force against the regime. Without the Covenanters' military successes in 1639 and 1640, and collusion between the victorious Scots and Charles's English opponents during 1640 and 1641, the Long Parliament would have been as powerless to bend the King to its will as any of its predecessors had been.[49] Had Scotland been defeated in 1639, the chances that Charles could have been coerced by his subjects would have been remote indeed.

But, if further armed revolt seemed unlikely in the event of a royal victory in 1639, there were other, potentially more insidious challenges which the regime would have had to confront. Two developments in English political culture, it is frequently argued, would have constituted insuperable obstacles to the policies of the Personal Rule: first, the rise of revolutionary Puritanism – which was to reach its zenith in the 1640s; and, second, the groundswell of legal and constitutionalist objections to 'arbitrary government' – the whole repertory of non-parliamentary exactions, from ship money to forest fines, the powers of Star Chamber and the prerogative courts, and the crown's high-handed indifference to the subject's liberties and the traditions of the common law.[50]

The force which perhaps did more than any other to destabilise English society during the late 1630s and early 1640s was the fear that government and the Church of England were about to succumb to some form of Popish plot.[51] In the immediate context of the last years of the Personal Rule, subventions from English Catholics to assist the war-effort in 1639 and the reception of Papal emissaries at court helped give substance to rumours of Catholic infiltration – tales which grew ever more extravagant in the telling.[52] Without the succession of anti-Popish scares and scandals of 1639–41, it is all but inconceivable that the political temperature at Westminster (and in the provinces) could ever have risen to the levels at which civil war became a possibility.[53]

Yet the extensiveness and plausibility of this Popish threat was conditioned at least as much by events in contemporary Europe as by any perceptions of the Caroline court and Privy Council at home. Reports of the disasters befalling Protestants in the Thirty Years' War inevitably coloured English assessments of the threat posed by indigenous Catholic conspiracies, endowing them with a menace out of all proportion to their actual threat. If the Habsburgs and their Spanish allies were to triumph in Europe, so the argument ran, the fate of Protestantism in England would hang precariously in the balance. To many committed English Protestants, the Thirty Years' War was an apocalyptic struggle, a contest between the Antichrist and the righteous: the actual historical playing out of the battle between St Michael and the Antichrist foretold in the Book of Revelation – and regarded as such not just by Puritan zealots, but also by such 'mainstream' English Protestants as Archbishop Abbot (Laud's predecessor at Canterbury).[54] The Scottish crises of 1639 and 1640 (and the Parliaments which they called into being) thus coincided with a time when the Thirty Years' War was nearing its climax, and when English apprehensions of Catholic militancy in Europe were as intense as they had been perhaps at any point since the Armada.

Yet if the English elite was at its most jittery about Habsburg belligerence during the late 1630s and early 1640s – and at its most susceptible to tales of Popish Fifth Columnists at home – there was a marked decline in the perceived level of threat from the early 1640s. The reduction continued steadily into the 1650s. Spain, once the most terrifying of the Catholic powers, was beset by internal rebellion in 1640; the Habsburg armies were smashed by Condé at Rocroi in 1643 (thereby abruptly losing their reputation for military invincibility); and by the mid-1640s the crusade to reimpose Catholicism in Europe had manifestly run out of steam. By 1648, the war was over.

Had Charles's regime withstood the immediate storms of the late 1630s, it should have benefited handsomely from the improved state of confessional politics in Europe, where, by the mid-1640s (and for the first time in the last quarter of a century), the survival of Protestantism seemed assured. As Professor Hirst has argued, this apocalyptic fear of militant Catholicism was one of the major influences sustaining Puritan militancy in England during the mid-seventeenth century. As the Catholic threat receded, 'the spectre of Antichrist dwindled', and 'the waning of anti-Catholicism ... helped sap reformist zeal'. By the late 1640s and 1650s, the claim that Protestantism was about to be devoured by the Catholic Leviathan rang distinctly hollow – a change in circumstances which contributed heavily to the 'failure of godly rule' during the 1650s.[55] Under a Caroline government during the 1640s and 1650s, and without the zealous support afforded by both the Long Parliament and the Cromwellian regime, Puritanism's 'failure' might well have come yet faster still.

Other influences seem likely, with time, to have weakened the ranks of Charles I's opponents. Many of the regime's leading critics were ageing men by the 1640s. Not all had the antiquity of that hoary old Elizabethan, the Earl of Mulgrave – one of the Twelve Petitioning Peers of August 1640 who called on Charles to convene the Long Parliament and whose proxy vote enabled the creation of the New Model Army in 1645: he had actually captained a ship in 1588 against the Spanish Armada. But the overwhelming majority of Charles's most influential adversaries belonged to the generation which had been born during the 1580s and 1590s – when the threat that English Protestantism might be extinguished by Habsburg Spain was imminent and real. Their religious outlook had been formed in the decades between 1590 and 1620 – the apogee of Calvinist influence on the theology of the English church. But by 1640 some of the most articulate (and, from Charles's perspective, the most mettlesome) of that generation were already dead: Sir John Eliot, who had been imprisoned after the dissolution in 1629, died in 1632 (no doubt hastened to the grave by the conditions of his incarceration); Sir Edward Coke (b. 1552), the legal sage who had caused the King such difficulties in the parliaments of the 1620s, died in 1634; Sir Nathaniel Rich, another trenchant critic of Charles's government who 'might well have emerged as the leader of the Parliamentarians', died in 1636.[56] Others were dead by the mid-1640s: Bedford (b. 1593), the lynchpin of the aristocratic coalition against the King in 1640, died in 1641; John Pym in 1643; William Strode in 1645; Essex (b. 1591), Parliament's commander-in-chief during the first years of the Civil War, in 1646. Indeed, of the Twelve Petitioning Peers of 1640, the vanguard of the movement to recall Parliament, no less than half were dead by 1646 – all but one of natural causes.[57] In 1639, Charles was still a monarch in his thirties; time was rapidly thinning the ranks of his leading critics. As Sir Keith Feiling once observed, 'While there's death, there's hope.' And in this respect the Caroline regime – had it successfully weathered the Scottish crisis – had much to be hopeful about.

A rather sharper light is thrown on the relation between age and attitudes towards the Caroline regime if we turn to the detailed statistics for the 1640s House of Commons. Taking the 538 members of the Commons whose allegiances can be known, a marked pattern emerges. 'It is at once clear that in every region the Royalists were younger men than the Parliamentarians,'

Brunton and Pennington concluded in their classic study of 1954. 'The median ages of the two parties for the whole country have been worked out at thirty-six and forty-seven respectively – a very large difference.'[58] Thus – in the Commons at least – Charles's opponents belonged predominantly to the (relatively elderly) generation of the 1580s and 1590s. Conversely, support for the King came disproportionately from the generation still in their thirties – those brought up in the years of the 'Jacobean Peace', when the crown pursued a policy of conciliation, if not quite amity, with Spain. A generation gap of almost eleven years – a huge gulf in a society where life expectancy was relatively low – separated those who went to war against Charles I from the younger generation which rallied to defend the royalist cause. The median age of the Twelve Peers who petitioned for a Parliament in 1640 was even older, with the most senior (Rutland and Mulgrave) being sixty and seventy-four respectively. An almost identical disparity between the ages of Parliamentarians and royalists can be found among the ranks of the peerage as a whole.[59]

A similar pattern also emerges from an examination of responses to the Caroline regime among those attending the universities during the 1630s – though here the statistical evidence is patchier still. In so far as the universities offer clues to the religious sensibilities of those under thirty, the age-group which included not only the undergraduates but also many of the college fellows, the general picture in the universities is one not just of forced compliance with the 'Laudian innovations' of the 1630s, but of willing acquiescence – even, at times, positive enthusiasm – and a strengthening of loyalty to the crown. In Oxford, where Laud was an active and interventionist chancellor between 1630 and 1641, the university emerged at the end of the decade, in Professor Sharpe's phrase, as the 'stronghold of church and crown'. When the Long Parliament divided between Cavaliers and Roundheads in 1642, 'most of those Oxford men who had matriculated during Laud's chancellorship supported the monarchy'.[60] In Cambridge, the picture was similar: by the early 1640s, 'the university was overtly royalist'.[61] Laudian ecclesiastical 'innovations' seem to have found an extensive constituency of support. In 1641, a Commons committee, chaired by the godly Sir Robert Harley, investigated the goings-on at the university during the 1630s and revealed 'an interest in catholic tradition, clearly shared by many [at the university]' which went far beyond the liturgical innovations which even Laud required.[62] Old-style Calvinism was not only erroneous in the eyes of the new Laudians; it was passé. As that baffled champion of Calvinism, Stephen Marshall, put it to the Long Parliament in 1641, it was 'as if we were weary of the truth which God has committed to us'.[63] To perhaps the majority of undergraduates during the 1630s, the handful of 'Puritan' colleges which remained – pre-eminently Emmanuel and Sidney Sussex at Cambridge – seemed not so much intimidating seminaries of sedition as quaintly old-fashioned backwaters, places where conservative fathers could ensure that sons were tutored in the divinity fashionable, twenty years before, in their youth. Yet even Emmanuel undergraduates, the Commons investigators of 1641 were appalled to find, were slipping out to taste the forbidden pleasures of chapel in the ultra-Laudian Peterhouse.[64] By 1639, Laudianism in Cambridge 'was in a commanding position. Complete dominance was only a matter of time.'[65]

Inferences from such necessarily imperfect data must be treated with the greatest caution.[66] In the case of the figures for age and allegiance within Parliament, there are interpretative problems in using information about allegiances in 1642 to suggest attitudes towards the regime three years earlier, in 1639 – not least because support for the King in the Civil War cannot be read as implying support for the regime's policies during the 1630s.[67] The averaging out of ages conceals the fact that there were, of course, younger men on the parliamentarian side – the likes of Brooke or Mandeville, still in their thirties in 1640 – who might have been a thorn in the regime's side for several decades to come. Similarly, the evidence for allegiance in the 1640s offers, at best, only a crude indication of the political nation's attitudes during the last years of the Personal Rule. But if the disparity in age and attitudes towards the regime evident among the 500-odd members of

Commons was even very roughly representative of trends within the nation at large, then the political implications were substantial – a conclusion which acquires additional force when viewed against the distribution of age-groups within society as a whole.

Between 1631 and 1641, the distribution of age-groups within the English and Welsh population remained roughly constant; those under thirty accounted for almost 60 per cent of the population; and roughly a third of the population were children aged under fifteen.[68] In 1640, half the population (49.7 per cent) had been born after 1616, and thus had been aged nine or younger when Charles I acceded to the throne in 1625. Or to put this in terms of political experience: in 1640 fully one-third of the population had known no other king but Charles. And, for this third of the population, even such recent events as the controversies over the 1628 Petition of Right probably seemed relatively distant – they had been aged four or younger when Charles had dissolved his most recent Parliament in 1629. Had Charles I's rule without reference to Parliament continued at least as long as his actual life – until 1649 – England would have been a country in which more than half the nation had no direct experience or recollection of Parliament. This was a gulf not only of politics, but of memory, and one which is likely to have had a profound effect upon the way in which the regime's 'innovations', in government as well as in the church, were perceived.

Of course, the transmission of cultural memory depends on a far subtler and more extensive range of influences than age alone. The traditions of Calvinist spirituality and the belief that Parliaments were an essential part of a rightly ordered commonwealth were unlikely to be forgotten merely because those who had actually experienced Elizabeth's and James's reigns ceased to constitute the majority of the population. Even when Parliament was not in session, pamphlets and treatises circulated (often in manuscript), relating its history, customs and powers; and there is no reason to suppose this would have ceased, even if Charles had won in 1639.[69] Yet, even so, the impact of age and generation on political perceptions cannot be lightly dismissed. At least part of

Parliament's success in rallying support in 1642 derived from its emotional appeal to those who had lived through the struggles for 'the subject's liberties' in the Jacobean and early Caroline Parliaments – in particular, the acrimonious sessions of 1626 and 1628–9. In 1639, this group was already a minority, albeit still a substantial one (roughly 40 per cent of the population). Had the call to arms to defend Parliament come five or ten years later, it might well have been greeted with a far less enthusiastic response. For the likes of Pym and St John, Bedford and Saye, 1639–40 was the real 'crisis of Parliaments': it was, perhaps, a matter of acting now or never.

The Remaking of the English Judiciary

Thus, looking beyond a hypothetical royal victory in 1639, the chances of Charles I being coerced by domestic rebellion or being forced to summon Parliament against his will would have been small – and possibly getting smaller by the year. However, there still remains one forum in which the King could have been forced to alter his policies, and where the legitimacy of his actions could have been subjected to public scrutiny: the courts of law. The judiciary still retained the power to inflict heavy damage on the fiscal policies (and prestige) of the crown, as was demonstrated by the great test case of 1637–8 over the legality of ship money, *Rex v. Hampden*. Heard before the entire bench of judges, the case was determined in the King's favour – upholding the legality of the levy, notwithstanding that it was imposed without parliamentary consent. But the strength of the dissenting judgements in the case left the crown with, at best, a Pyrrhic victory. The verdicts of Sir Richard Hutton and Sir George Croke – stating frankly that in point of law ship money was illegal – commanded wide authority, and left the legitimacy of ship money holed below the waterline.[70]

Hampden's case nevertheless provides a series of pointers to the way in which the law, and the role of the judges as its interpreters, might have developed had the Personal Rule extended into the 1640s. At stake was a question which had been canvassed in various forms during the early seventeenth century: did the common law guarantee the subject's rights in his property by demanding that taxation could not be levied without Parliament's consent?[71] To Hampden's counsel, and to a large swathe of legal opinion within the country at large, it clearly did. The subject's property could not be alienated except with the authority of a Parliament; ship money lacked parliamentary assent; *ergo*, it was unlawful.[72]

Yet for Charles (as for his father) the purpose of the law was instrumental: it was the practical means to achieve the end of 'good government' as defined by the crown; not a discrete body of wisdom (*à la* Sir Edward Coke) defining the law in conformity to abstract precepts of immemorial antiquity. Common lawyers were themselves divided as to which of these two interpretations should prevail. Here the contest was not necessarily between 'the common law' (as some fixed body of constitutional principles) and monarchical 'absolutism'; rather it was between two competing versions of what the common law should be. Already in James's reign, the idea that the common law was effectively an instrument of royal government had been extensively canvassed by Coke's arch-enemy, Lord Chancellor Ellesmere (d. 1617), and by Francis Bacon (later Viscount St Alban, d. 1626) – both men steeped in the common law. From their perspective, Coke's insistence on the primacy of the subject's rights was misplaced.[73] The crown could argue, and with some plausibility, that when faced with the task of paying for the defence of the realm in the 1620s, the amounts raised by parliamentary taxation had proved pitiably inadequate to the task.[74] The principal form of taxation, the subsidy, was beset by what amounted to institutionalised fraud, whereby the gentry rated themselves for the tax at a mere fraction of their real worth.[75] And by the 1620s the subsidy had been reduced in value to the point where (as Laud once tartly pointed out) it was hardly worth a king bargaining with Parliament about it. Ship money, on the other hand, was at least equitably imposed; was based on the subject's ability to pay; and brought in a realistic sum, commensurate with the actual cost of providing a fleet for the defence of the realm – the principal duty of government.[76] Since conquest extinguished all the laws of the conquered (as was almost universally agreed), it followed that without the defence of the realm there would be no liberties in general, still less the subject's individual liberties and property rights.[77] Hobbes, who was scarcely less impatient of Coke's views than Charles himself, neatly summed up the direction in which this line of argument was leading: there were circumstances, he contended, where a king actually had a moral obligation to rescind a promise not to tax without the subject's consent. 'If a king find that by such a grant he be disabled to protect his subjects if he maintain his grant, he sins; and therefore may, and ought, to take no notice of the said grant.'[78]

During the 1630s, the judiciary's refusal to provide unanimous approval for such an 'instrumental' view of the common law constituted one of the main obstacles to the creation of reliable, non-parliamentary sources of revenue for the crown. Altering the character of the bench was, however, a difficult and delicate matter. Judges held office until death; and, though they could be removed under exceptional circumstances, outright dismissal of a judge – as Charles had already learnt to his cost – was likely to be counterproductive, antagonising the bar and undermining the standing of the courts. If the courts were to work effectively as a buttress of the King's Personal Rule, their adjudications needed to be – or at least seem to be – freely given, not coerced by Whitehall.

Yet, when it came to his difficult judges, time seems once again to have been on Charles's side. By the late 1630s, he was well on the way towards achieving his goal: a judicial bench composed of men who could command respect among their peers while at the same time being broadly sympathetic towards a 'maximalist' interpretation of the relation between the crown's prerogatives *vis-à-vis* the common law. Of the five judges who found against the crown in the ship-money case of 1637–8, four were men in their seventies – Elizabethan survivors whose intellectual formation dated from the 1580s and 1590s. They were also at the end of their careers. The septuagenarian Sir John Denham

(b. 1559), who found for Hampden, was dead within a year of handing down his judgement against the crown. Sir Richard Hutton (b. *c*.1561) died a month after Denham (on 26 February 1639).[79] And Sir George Croke of the Court of Common Pleas (b. 1560), was compelled by declining health to seek permission to retire from the bench in 1641, and died on 16 February 1642. A fourth septuagenarian, Sir Humphrey Davenport (b. 1566), who found for Hampden on a technicality, lived on until 1645; but, as his judgement made clear, he was prepared to affirm the legality of this non-parliamentary levy.[80] Hutton, Croke and perhaps Denham were the three most trenchant critics of the regime on the bench. By 1641, Charles was rid of all three.[81] For critics of ship money, as for opponents of other aspects of the Caroline regime, the late 1630s were probably the last moment when an effective legal challenge to the regime could have been mounted.

By the early 1640s, in the absence of the parliamentary challenge, Charles would have been able to reconstitute the judiciary – without any rancorous purges or dismissals – so that the 'lions under the throne', when called upon to endorse novel fiscal exactions, would have purred their approbation from the bench. There would have been a price to pay for such subservience, in diminishing the judiciary's prestige.[82] Yet given a few more years, *Hampden's case* (had it ever come to court) would probably have concluded, not with the half-hearted approval for ship money given by the bench in 1638, but with a ringing endorsement for the fiscal policies of the crown.[83]

The implications for the future development of the law after a royal victory in 1639 seem clear. Under a Caroline government in the 1640s, England would still have been governed under the common law; but it would have been a system of law which developed in the directions adumbrated by Bacon and Ellesmere – towards the greater concentration of political authority in the crown; not along the paths laid down by Coke. The way forward had already been announced by Sir Robert Berkeley, in his ship-money judgement of 1638. Repudiating the argument of Hampden's counsel that the King could not 'exact from his subjects' without 'common consent in Parliament', Berkeley had no doubts. 'The law knows no such king-yoking policy. The law is of itself an old and trusty servant of the king's; it is his instrument or means which he useth to govern his people by.'[84] This was frankness that must have sent a chill through the hearts of all those who worshipped at the shrine of Sir Edward Coke.

Stuart Britain: The Refashioning of the State

With the Covenanter rebellion checked, an ever more compliant judiciary and the dwindling international 'Catholic threat', how would the three Stuart kingdoms have looked? Much depended on how a victory in 1639 would have affected the balance of power and influence at court. Undoubtedly, the figure who stood to gain most, in personal esteem and reputation, was the King himself. Kings victorious in war could normally expect the plaudits of the nation; and, notwithstanding the effective Scottish propaganda campaign directed to winning hearts and minds in England, there seems little doubt that a victory over the Coven-anters would have been widely popular, and have done much to silence domestic criticism of the regime. Military success would have offered Charles I the opportunity to realise his ambition to create an 'imperial' unity between the three kingdoms – in effect to make Scotland and Ireland yet further subservient to the English state. In government and law (as already in religion), England would have provided the models for the 'order and decency' to which the Celtic kingdoms were to be made to conform. Victory would have given the King the opportunity to press on with the agenda of his Personal Rule upon which, as he saw it, his subjects' welfare depended – in the somewhat sinister phrase the King was to use several years later: 'If any shall be so foolishly unnatural as to oppose their king, their country and their own good, we will make them happy, by God's blessing – even against their wills.'[85]

For Archbishop Laud, one of the chief enthusiasts in the Council for the decision to impose the English liturgy on Scotland in 1637, a royal victory in 1639 would have been more than just a personal triumph; it would have been a vindication by providence of the justness of his cause. His influence over the English church would have been powerfully consolidated, and the implementation of the ecclesiastical policies of the 1630s, interrupted by the war, would, it seems likely, have been vigorously resumed: the placement and railing of the communion-table 'altar-wise' in the east end of parish churches, the emphasis on catechising over preaching, the insistence on doctrinal and ceremonial conformity, and the enhancement of the wealth and social standing of the clergy. Had a modified version of English liturgy been successfully exported to Scotland in the late 1630s, other elements of the Laudian programme would likely have followed. In Ireland, Strafford and John Bramhall, Bishop of Derry, were already advanced in their plans to achieve liturgical conformity with England. And in all three kingdoms, the trend towards the clericalisation of government – epitomized by the appointment (engineered by Laud) of the Bishop of London to the lord treasurership in 1636 – was likely to have been further advanced. With Puritan celebrities such as Burton, Bastwick and Prynne languishing in their distant and chilly dungeons, Non-Conformists would have continued to smart under the Archbishop's ever vigilant (and at times vindictive) rule. Inigo Jones's remodelling of St Paul's, with the entablature of its sixty-foot-high Corinthian colonnade proclaiming Charles as the 're-edifier' of the church, would have continued into the 1640s: the visible monument to the triumph of the Laudian church.[86]

Catholics, too, stood to gain. Their timely subscriptions to the 1639 war-effort (which raised some £10,000) promised to yield a handsome dividend in the event of victory. On 17 April 1639, Queen Henrietta Maria had written to her principal secretary, the Catholic Sir John Wintour, undertaking to secure Catholics who assisted the King financially 'from all ... objected inconveniences' – a coded phrase for limited toleration.[87] Catholics would have stood to gain a further slackening of recusancy laws (much to the disgust of Laud, who remained, despite his public reputation, strongly anti-Papist) and a further opening of court office to Papists. The Catholic Earl of Nithsdale – one of the inner ring of counsellors with whom Charles took the decision to go to war in 1639 – stood to gain a major position of influence in Scotland;[88] so did the pro-Catholic Secretary of State and member of the King's Council of War, Sir Francis Windebanke, at Whitehall. Whether such moves would have created a further reaction against Roman Catholics or, in time, permitted the emergence of a *de facto* toleration (such as developed contemporaneously in the United Provinces) is difficult to gauge.[89] But there certainly would have been none of the vicious persecutions of Catholics which attended the Long Parliament's rule during the 1640s, when over twenty Catholic priests went to gruesome deaths by hanging, drawing and quartering. In comparison with the grisly penalties inflicted on religious dissidents by Parliament during the 1640s, the most rigorous of the punishments imposed under the Personal Rule (even those on Burton, Bastwick and Prynne) seem relatively benign.[90]

Among Charles's councillors, the repercussions of a victory in 1639 would have been extensive. The immediate beneficiaries would have been the architects of the royal victory: the circle within the Privy Council who supported the King's decision to go to war and who were most intimately involved in the planning and execution of the campaign against the Scots – none more so than the Marquess of Hamilton, the Earl of Arundel and Sir Henry Vane, the men whom the King described in April 1639 as the only counsellors who enjoyed his complete trust.[91] Hamilton, Charles's most loyal lieutenant in Scotland ever since the first signs of 'rebellion' in Edinburgh in 1637, stood to gain most. With his exalted rank, vast Scottish estates and polished English manners, Hamilton enjoyed an easy intimacy with the King, and was set to occupy an unrivalled position at the Whitehall court. Indeed, Hamilton was perhaps as close as Charles came to finding a surrogate for the murdered Duke of Buckingham (whose office as Master of the Horse passed to Hamilton on the Duke's death in 1628). His 'credit and power with the king' was reported to

have increased markedly in January 1639, 'since his late employ-
ments into Scotland'; by December 1640, he was described as
having 'sole power with the king'.[92] In the event of a Covenanter
defeat in 1639, Hamilton's position at court (and in the King's
affections) would have been unassailable.

The major institution to lose out as a result of the victory –
other than Parliament itself – would have been the English Privy
Council. It had already been effectively sidelined in the planning
of the King's response to the Scottish crisis on the ground that its
jurisdiction did not extend north of the Tweed. Its deliberative
role – the business of offering advice to the King – is likely to
have been increasingly weakened. Responsibility for the 'imperial'
aspects of government – those matters which concerned all three
kingdoms – would probably have been consolidated in the hands
of a small group of trusted confidants chosen by the King,
including Laud, Arundel, Hamilton, Sir Henry Vane the elder and
probably the Bedchamber men Patrick Maule, George Kirke and
Will Morray. This process had already begun during the crisis of
1637–9.[93]

Yet there are strong grounds for thinking that this trend
towards a more authoritarian royal government in the event of a
victory in 1639 would have been tempered by countervailing
influences at court which were themselves the consequences of
the Scots' defeat.[94] Many of those at court whose status would
have been enhanced by a royal victory in 1639 were on close
terms with the 'discourted' aristocratic leadership of 'country'
opinion during the 1630s. Hamilton's circle included Viscount
Saye and Sele (the initiator of the legal challenge, subsequently
taken over by Hampden, to ship money), and was shortly to
include Viscount Mandeville (later Cromwell's commanding
officer in the Eastern Association), Sir John Danvers (a future
regicide) and members of the Covenanter leadership in Scotland.[95]
Indeed, Hamilton's openness to discussion with the regime's
critics caused his loyalty to come under suspicion in some ultra-
royalist circles during 1639, precisely 'because of some private

correspondence which his lordship keeps with the ring leaders of the Covenanters' faction'.[96]

So, too, with the other major *dramatis personae* of 1639. The Earl of Arundel, the Lord General in the 1639 campaign, was second only to Hamilton in the trio of counsellors who, Charles declared, exclusively enjoyed his trust. Yet Arundel had been Buckingham's arch-enemy during the 1620s, and was widely regarded as a champion of the privileges of the 'ancient nobility' – the pre-Stuart peerage, from whose ranks the noble opposition to Charles was largely drawn.[97] Even closer to the regime's critics were Arundel's two field commanders, the Earls of Holland (the General of the Horse) and Essex (Arundel's lieutenant-general), both of whom were identified with patronage of the 'godly' cause.[98] Holland, the younger brother of the 'Puritan' 2nd Earl of Warwick, was detested by Laud for his interventions on behalf of Non-Conformist ministers threatened by the ecclesiastical authorities; his brother Warwick was an intimate of the circle which included such critics of the regime as the Earl of Bedford, Viscount Saye, Lord Brooke, John Pym, and Oliver St John. A military victory in 1639 would also have consolidated the Earl of Essex's position at court, where Holland (his first cousin) had worked hard to restore him to the King's favour.[99] As the son of the popular Elizabethan hero executed for the abortive coup of 1601, Essex was the closest England came to having a living Protestant hero.

Just as defeat forced the King into the promotion of policies and personnel during 1640 which gave substance to the damaging libel that there was a 'Popish conspiracy' afoot at court (Arundel, Essex and Holland were dismissed from their commands, and negotiations begun to secure loans from the Papacy), so a victory would have removed many of the factors which enabled such rumours to take hold. Holland, Essex and Hamilton (that 'zealous enemy to Popery')[100] were men of impeccable Protestant credentials. Holland and Essex had both seen service in Europe on the Protestant side against the Habsburgs; and Hamilton had actually campaigned with the sainted Protestant hero of the Thirty Years' War, Gustavus Adolphus of Sweden in 1631 – when his closest ally at court had been Sir Henry Vane, the Comptroller of the King's Household, and in 1639 the third member of the group Charles referred to as his 'most trusted counsellors'.[101] Their enhanced standing would probably have served as a counter-balance to the increased influence of Catholics at court in the aftermath of a royal victory in 1639, and have lessened the credibility that could be given to claims that the court was in the grip of a Popish plot. Charles might well have continued to deal courteously with Papal envoys;[102] but the humiliating need to negotiate with them in the hope of financial subventions from Rome would have gone – and, with it, the danger to the public image of the monarchy which such negotiations obviously entailed.

It would be naive, of course, to assume that opposition to Charles's policies would have been extinguished permanently by a victory against the Covenanters in 1639. What, then, might the likely flashpoints have been? Even if the Scottish crisis had been successfully resolved, the King would almost certainly have faced a factional struggle at court over the question of the proper extent of clerical power within the state. Episcopal influence at court had provoked a strong anti-clerical reaction in the Privy Council (where the Archbishop was despised by Pembroke, Northumberland and Salisbury); and clericalism would no doubt have become an increasingly sore point in the localities, where local squires were already disconcerted to find their parsons – newly appointed as JPs – taking their places during the 1630s on the Quarter Sessions bench. Here was a rich source for personal feuds and endless squabbles over precedence and jurisdiction. But, without the presence of a victorious Scottish army in England, such tensions were eminently containable. The relations between Laud and his fellow councillors would no doubt have continued to be prickly; but, with a victory in 1639, the Archbishop would have had every reason to assume that he would die, comfortably, in his Lambeth bed.

Scotland would have been more problematic. As earlier monarchs had learnt to their cost, defeating Scotland was one thing; holding the country down quite another. The scale and vehemence of the Covenanter revolt suggests that Scotland would have continued to present problems for the regime, even if Charles had won in 1639. But, so long as the Caroline regime's control of England remained secure, there is no reason to suppose that the remaining pockets of Covenanter resistance would not have been containable – much as the security of Elizabeth's regime had been frequently vexed, but rarely seriously threatened, by the rebelliousness of late sixteenth-century Ireland. Moreover, the Covenanter leadership was itself not without factional divisions and personal feuds.[103] Had Charles won in 1639, he would almost certainly have precipitated much sooner the split between hardliners (such as the Earl of Argyll) and more moderate nobles (such as Montrose) which eventually occurred in the summer of 1641.[104]

The decade or so after 1639 would inevitably have been a period which required political and fiscal consolidation; and that depended, in turn, on maintaining the diplomatic stance Charles had adopted since the early 1630s: the avoidance of foreign war. War with Spain seemed highly unlikely. Opinion within the Privy Council had moved strongly towards alliance with Spain from 1638; by July 1639, Bellièvre, noting the shift with dismay, reported that most councillors were in receipt of Spanish pensions.[105] And, after the 1640 Catalan revolt, Spain posed relatively little threat throughout the remainder of the decade. War with France, on the other hand, was more of a possibility. Charles had given sanctuary to Marie de Médicis, Richelieu's arch-enemy, in 1638 – and to the string of grand and tetchy dissidents (including the Duc de Vendôme and the Duc de Soubise) she had brought in her train. Yet, with France heavily committed against the Habsburgs and beset internally, from 1643, with the problems of a royal minority, the prospect of opening up war on another front against England had little to commend it. Commercial rivalries with the Dutch also constituted a potential source of conflict (as the wars of the 1650s and 1660s were to prove). But, in the immediate term, relations remained harmonious (in spite of the Dutch Admiral Tromp's incursion into English waters in October 1639 to harry the Spanish fleet), and they were further consolidated in 1641 by the marriage of Charles I's daughter, Mary, to the Stadholder's son and heir, Prince Frederik Hendrik of Orange-Nassau.[106]

In short, so long as Charles did not go out and seek a fight, there was a strong possibility that his government could have avoided war at least until the 1650s. After his experiences during the 1620s, Charles was all too well aware of the debilitating costs of foreign wars. Even had he been successful in 1639, the government's borrowings would have needed to be repaid; and re-establishing royal government in Scotland would have required substantial recurrent annual expenditure. It seems unlikely that the government would have been in the mood for military adventures abroad. As the Earl of Northumberland observed after the war of 1639, 'we are so set upon the reducing [of] Scotland, as, till that be effected, we shall not intend the re-establishing the broken estate of Europe'.[107]

The greatest area of uncertainty, however, remained the royal finances. Could the crown make ends meet in the absence of parliamentary subventions? The answer to this, in peacetime, seems an unequivocal yes. Charles had succeeded in doing what had consistently eluded his father: he had managed, by the mid-1630s, to balance his books. His major problem was liquidity and access to credit in times when there were exceptional calls on the Exchequer. The lesson of 1639 was that he could do this, without recourse to Parliament – but only just – by financing expenditure through loans from members of the nobility and affluent City merchants (£100,000 reportedly coming from the customs farmer Sir Paul Pindar alone).[108] About London there seems little doubt. Victory in 1639 would almost certainly have precluded the coup in the government of London which destroyed the dominance of the old aldermanic elite in 1640–1 and effectively cut the crown's line of City credit. With the Covenanters defeated, the crown's generally cosy relationship with the City's aldermanic government

– which had continued up until June 1639 – might well have carried on, to mutual advantage, indefinitely.[109]

The real question lay on the revenue side.[110] Could the crown move beyond its mid-1630s levels of income, and so augment its revenues that it could manage without Parliament – even, in the long term, to the extent of being able to finance a war? Two questions needed to be resolved. Was the political nation able to bear the cost of further non-parliamentary levies? And second, if such levies were imposed, would they be acceptable – politically and legally – to the bulk of the nation's taxpayers? About the first question there is little doubt. On the whole, England was one of the most lightly taxed nations in Europe, even taking into account the full weight of Charles's exactions during the 1630s. As we have seen, during the half-century between 1580 and 1630 the English gentry had effectively institutionalised a system of under-valuing their property for tax purposes; most properties were assessed in the subsidy rolls at probably little more than a tenth of their real worth.[111] The rating system which Charles introduced for ship money, however, was based on a far more realistic assessment of individuals' real worth (ironically, it was adopted by Parliament as the basis for its 'weekly assessment' in 1643). Had Charles succeeded in making ship money an annual levy, imposed throughout the country, as he was almost certainly planning to do, he would have been provided with a regular and highly lucrative revenue source – what Clarendon feared would become 'an everlasting supply of all occasions'.[112] Impositions were already bringing in around £218,000 per annum during the 1630s – the equivalent, in cash terms, of three parliamentary subsidies annually.[113]

There was the further likelihood that an excise or sales tax (which had long been considered as an option and was first introduced by the Long Parliament in 1643) would also probably have become one of the fiscal mainstays of the regime. With a reconstituted bench, there is little doubt that the King could have obtained the judiciary's imprimatur for such further extensions of prerogative finance. The experience of the 1640s and early 1650s leaves little doubt that the gentry could have sustained much higher levels of taxation: by 1651, taxation in most parts of the country was running at six or seven times what it had been at the height of the Personal Rule.[114] As Gerald Aylmer has observed, 'perhaps what is most astonishing' about the new fiscal exactions of the 1640s and 1650s 'is the amount raised in taxes and the paucity of the sustained opposition to their collection'.[115] Had Charles's Personal Rule continued into the same period, there is a high probability that the regime could have increased its revenues substantially, without provoking more than the minimal opposition encountered under Cromwellian rule. Moreover, so long as Charles avoided further large-scale wars, he would have had no need to raise taxation to anything like the levels imposed under the Commonwealth; an increase of two-fold or three-fold upon what he was already receiving in ship money would have made Charles an affluent king.

Not all the lawyers, of course, would have approved. Lincoln's Inn, in particular – where admirers of Sir Edward Coke abounded – would no doubt have fought a rearguard action against any judicial decisions which confirmed the crown's right to impose levies without parliamentary assent. Viewing the legal profession as a whole, however, a king victorious in 1639 would have been unlikely to face serious resistance from the bar. Lawyers, like politicians, are notorious toadies to power; and, had Charles's regime prospered beyond 1640, there seems little doubt that more than enough of them would have reconciled their consciences to the new fiscal expedients to ensure their success. Selden – the friend of Laud, and whose *Mare Clausum* was so much admired at court during the 1630s – would probably have served a victorious Caroline regime as devotedly as he served Parliament during the 1640s.[116] And for every rebarbative lawyer like Oliver St John or William Prynne, there was always an oleaginous Bulstrode Whitelocke ready to ingratiate himself with the regime of the day.

Indeed, during the Personal Rule, the legal profession had adapted with its usual flexibility to government without Parliaments, exploiting procedures (such as the collusive action) which in most cases circumvented the need for legislation. By 1640, Professor Russell has observed, the naturalisation of aliens and the changing of parish boundaries were almost the only things 'the lawyers had found themselves unable to achieve without statutory assistance'.[117] Dispensing with Parliament's function as a 'point of contact' between government and subject would prove more difficult. Yet, it is not inconceivable, in the absence of further Parliaments, that the county assizes – those regular meetings of the circuit judges and each county's nobility and gentry – would have assumed a far more assertive role in articulating local grievances, much as France's provincial *parlements* did after the demise of the Estates General in 1614.[118]

Had Charles I lived as long as his father, he would have died in 1659. Much was uncertain; but there was at least the possibility that Charles I could have bequeathed his son a powerful, well-funded, centralised kingdom, where the last few veterans of the 1629 House of Commons would have told tales by the fireside of its tumultuous final days, now thirty years before; and where historians would have written – with the glib confidence of hindsight – of the inevitability of Parliament's demise. Whether such a state could usefully be called 'absolutist' must remain highly dubious. In practice, Charles's power would have been limited – as was Louis XIV's in France – by the extent to which local elites were willing to cooperate with the crown. And in England, as in France, the possibilities for localised obstruction were legion. Yet, even without a standing army, by the end of the century there would have been the possibility of creating an English state far closer to Louis XIV's France than to the 'mixed monarchy' – in which sovereignty was shared between king, Lords and Commons – that Charles I had inherited from his father in 1625.[119] (Even at their worst, Charles's prospects of salvaging a strong royal government during 1639 were never as bleak as Louis's were to seem during the Fronde.)

But it was not just kings whose careers might have taken very different trajectories. How many of those who became parliamentarians during the 1640s would otherwise have become the loyal servants of a monarchical regime? In most cases this must remain an open question. However, of one, at least, there seems little doubt. In the 1640s, Sir Thomas Fairfax (b. 1612) was hailed as the 'champion' of Parliament: the commander of the New Model Army; the architect of the decisive victory over the royalists at Naseby in 1645; the general who had ensured Parliament's survival.[120] But in 1639 Fairfax championed the King. He was among the most zealous enthusiasts for the anti-Scottish cause; raised a troop of 160 Yorkshire dragoons; and earned his knighthood as one of the handful of officers whose services in that campaign were singled out by Charles I for particular reward. It is not the least of history's ironies that had the cause which Fairfax served so devotedly in 1639 prospered, it would probably have put an end to Parliaments in England for decades – possibly for centuries. Perhaps, even, until 1789?

TWO

BRITISH AMERICA:

What if there had been no American Revolution?

J. C. D. Clark

I think I can announce it as a fact, that it is not the wish or interest of that government [Massachusetts], or any other upon the continent, separately or collectively, to set up for independency.... I am as well satisfied as I can be of my existence that no such thing is desired by any thinking man in all North America; on the contrary, that it is the ardent wish of the warmest advocates for liberty, that peace and tranquility, upon constitutional grounds, may be restored, and the horrors of civil discord prevented.

GEORGE WASHINGTON TO CAPTAIN ROBERT
MACKENZIE, 9 October 1774[1]

The Inevitability of Anglo-American History

History labours under a major handicap in societies suffused with a sense of their own rightness or inevitability. Whether driven by secular ideologies, shared religious beliefs or consensual optimism, such societies devise intellectual strategies to blot out their earlier sense of the paths that were not taken, their number, their feasibility and their attractiveness to those who, knowingly or unknowingly, with foresight or without it, made the fatal choices. Although England has been archetypal in all these ways, no Western culture has been more systematic and more successful in this retrospective reordering than the United States. American exceptionalism is still a powerful collective myth, and one whose origins can be traced to the experience of the founding. It is not surprising that so few American historians have ventured seriously to question the 'manifest destiny' of the United States with counterfactual enquiries. Those few writers who have imagined American history without independence have tended to treat the idea as a joke.[2] The early American historians of the new republic at least tried to escape from the sense of inevitability created by the role of divine providence in their Puritan heritage, and to give proper attention to the importance of contingency; but the attempt did not last. The pressure to celebrate the manifest destiny of an independent United States made impossible any serious respect for the two greatest counterfactuals of modern Western history. For without the American Revolution, and the financial burden placed on the French government by its participation in the American war, it is unlikely that the old order in France would have collapsed as it did in 1788–9, and with widely acknowledged finality. What is at stake in the re-creation of the counterfactuals of 1776 is less the flattery of injured British sensibilities than the possible avoidance of that sequence of 'great' national revolutions of which 1789 was rightly seen as the second instalment, and which devastated the culture of the *ancien régime* across Europe. Their adopted role of celebrating this sequence of collapsing dominoes gave European historians no reason to question the inevitability of the American episode that triggered the sequence.

The lack of intellectual challenges to American self-sufficiency from outside the American republic is thus one of the French Revolution's unnoticed legacies. Yet, in the case of Britain's relations with its former North American colonies, the lack of constructively critical engagement is more remarkable. Partly the cause was definitional: independence in 1783 seemed to remove the American question from its former place as a problem integral to British history and to establish it as a separate subject, with questions and answers relevant only to itself. More importantly, though, the absence of British analyses of American counterfactuals reflected the substantial absence of such analyses within

British history itself. Until quite recently, British historians evidently felt little need to consider what might have been when the actual outcomes appeared, from their perspective, to be so agreeable. The teleology built into the 'Whig interpretation of history' was entirely congruent with its American counterparts. Whig historians might briefly allow themselves to dwell on the might-have-been, but only in order to highlight its abhorrent and unacceptable nature. With the counterfactual as with the ghost story, Victorians might frighten themselves with the intolerable, safe now in the knowledge of its impossibility.

However, a handful of writers have ventured to reopen the questions which English history has traditionally defined as closed. Geoffrey Parker used a counterfactual framework to set out evidence for the strength of the Spanish land forces in 1588 and the weakness of their English counterparts, and to speculate on the wider consequences of even limited military success had Spanish troops landed in England.[3] A still more provocative reversal of the orthodoxies was provided by Conrad Russell in a parody of an explanation of James II's victory over William of Orange's invasion force in 1688 which dismissed short-term contingencies and ascribed the triumph of Catholicism and absolute monarchy in England to deep-seated and long-term causes.[4] John Pocock too, examining the ideological consequences of the Revolution of 1688, pointed out that the governing classes would never have consented to James II's deposition had he not fled the country.[5] Such enquiries therefore have their justifications, for if, as Russell has suggested, there was nothing inevitable about the Glorious Revolution of 1688, then we can hardly avoid posing counterfactual questions about the American Revolution too. The term 'revolution' confers no special status on the collections of avoidable events to which it is applied.

Stuart Alternatives: An Empire of Many Parliaments – or None?

In the case of America, a counterfactual scenario extending back to the later Stuarts, and including their successors in exile, is necessary if the constitutional setting of Britain's transatlantic empire is to be established, since one option for a British America in the eighteenth century was as a British possession in an empire still ruled by that strangely fated dynasty. Such an outcome might have embraced either of two quite different constitutional settlements, both of which might have strengthened the long-term coherence of England's empire. The first would have applied had James II's plans for the reorganisation of colonial government succeeded, and had he retained his throne in 1688. The second might have obtained had one of his successors regained the throne which James lost, and had the relations between Britain and its colonies thereafter mirrored the constitutional relations between the component kingdoms of the British Isles.

It might be argued that James II's plans for the American colonies illustrated an inflexible commitment to bureaucratic centralisation and against representative assemblies. This was a considered response to American realities, however, for his involvement in colonial affairs was extensive, and came early. As Duke of York, James was granted the proprietorship of the colonies of New Jersey and New York in 1664 after their conquest in the Second Dutch War. While proprietor of New York, his experience of colonial conflicts made him consistently resist local demands for an assembly: he conceded such a body reluctantly in 1683, and promptly abolished it on his accession to the throne in 1685 when New York was reorganised as a crown colony.[6] Massachusetts, equally, lost its assembly when its charter was revoked and reissued in 1684. James then went further still, combining the colonies of Connecticut, Massachusetts, New Hampshire and Rhode Island into a new body, the Dominion of New England, under the control of a governor-general; later it was enlarged to include New Jersey and New York, raising fears that James intended it to be the model for amalgamating into two or three Dominions all the American colonies.[7] The suppression of colonial assemblies, and the magnification of the powers of the governor-general, was probably intended primarily to turn the colonies into defensible military units, and only secondarily to impose religious toleration on recalcitrant Congregationalists. But the combined effect of these two implications was to raise in full form the spectre of 'Popery and arbitrary power' already familiar in England, and to unleash sudden resistance when news arrived in the colonies of James's flight in December 1688: America, too, had its Glorious Revolution.[8]

Without the events of 1688 in England, however, it is not clear that American colonists at their then stage of development could have resisted the centralisation of their governments into three 'Dominions' and the elimination or diminution of colonial assemblies. And without the structure provided by those assemblies in the eighteenth century, it is unlikely that colonial constitutional debate would have taken the form it then did. An America effectively subordinated to an English executive at an early stage, and paralleled by a constitutional settlement at home in which the Westminster, Edinburgh and Dublin parliaments – but especially the first – played much lesser roles, would have been an America with a much smaller potential for resistance in the 1760s and 1770s.[9]

This first alternative, then, assumes – as Whigs at the time firmly believed – that Stuart rule would mean the end of parliaments. This is at least open to qualification: if it was chiefly conflicts over religion that made it so hard for Charles I, Charles II and James II to work with their parliaments, one might frame an alternative scenario in which a compromise on religious questions would have left the Stuarts no more averse to democratic assemblies in practice than other dynasties. Stuart history after 1688 gives some support to this, for James II's flight in 1688 did not settle the dynastic question. Conspiracies for a restoration 'were hatched, exploded or investigated in 1689–90, 1692, 1695–6, 1704, 1706–8, 1709–10, 1713–14, 1714–15, 1716–17, 1720–2, 1725–7, 1730–2, 1743–4, 1750–2 and 1758–9. Foreign invasions inspired by the Jacobites were foiled by the elements and the Royal Navy (in almost equal parts) in 1692, 1696, 1708, 1719, 1744, 1746 and 1759.'[10] These attempts were increasingly accompanied by proclamations from James II, his son and grandson professing elaborate respect for the constitutional forms they had previously seemed to threaten. After 1689, it was supporters of William of Orange, Whigs and Hanoverians in turn who tended to treat representative assemblies with minimal patience, and the Stuarts in exile who came to call for free parliaments, uncorrupted by ministerial largesse.[11] Along with the goal of the liberation of the Westminster, Edinburgh and Dublin parliaments went a legitimist constitutional theory which, by emphasising the monarchy, entailed that the unity of the kingdoms of England, Scotland and Ireland was expressed solely in terms of allegiance to a common sovereign. The restored monarchy in 1660 had deliberately undone the Cromwellian unions with Scotland and Ireland; the Stuarts, bidding for Scots support, were committed to undoing the union of 1707 also. Scots Jacobites looked for a restoration of a Stuart dynasty and the Edinburgh Parliament together, and Irish Jacobites anticipated by many decades the arguments most loudly made by Irish Whig politicians in the 1780s about the legislative equality of England and Ireland.[12] If James II had not been destroyed by his religious zeal, such a constitutional *modus vivendi* might have been feasible for him also.

Such a structure would have been as helpful in North America as in the British Isles. Until the 1770s, colonial Americans too sometimes expressed a desire for greater legislative autonomy within the reassuring framework of the empire. They reverted to an argument which, to Hanoverians, appeared shockingly Tory, associated with excessive deference to the crown: the assembly of each colony was claimed to be equal in authority to the Westminster Parliament, and the component parts of the empire were, Americans claimed, united only by their allegiance to a common sovereign. Nor was this argument confined to a handful of American colonists. It could be found in England too, in the writings of reformers like the Dissenting minister and philosopher Richard Price.[13] Just as Jacobitism in its later stages came to take on something of the air of a protest movement, adding to its dynastic doctrinal core a series of social grievances which anticipated the platform of John Wilkes, so too its constitutional doctrines came to find echoes at many unexpected points in the political spectrum. A Stuart Britain might have appealed to constituencies on both sides of the Atlantic.

After independence, it was made to seem that American colonists had always been ruggedly anti-monarchical. Parts of the writings of the founding fathers could indeed be made to bear this interpretation. In 1775, for example, John Adams, one of the earliest of his generation to campaign for full independence and later the second President of the USA, argued that the idea of a 'British empire' in America was unwarranted in constitutional law, 'introduced in allusion to the Roman empire, and intended to insinuate that the prerogative of the imperial crown of England' was absolute, not including Lords and Commons.[14] But most colonists were attracted by the convenient and seemingly patriotic argument that each colony was linked to the empire solely through its link with the crown. This remained an appealing model for many Americans even after independence. In 1800, reflecting on the then balance of power between the federal government and the states, James Madison, Virginia revolutionary, co-author of *The Federalist* and in 1809 fourth President of the USA, argued that:

> The fundamental principle of the Revolution was, that the Colonies were co-ordinate members with each other and with Great Britain, of an empire united by a common executive sovereign, but not united by any common legislative sovereign. The legislative power was maintained to be as complete in each American Parliament, as in the British Parliament. And the royal prerogative was in force in each Colony by virtue of its acknowledging the King for its executive magistrate, as it was in Great Britain by virtue of a like acknowledgement there.[15]

This was an old idiom of debate, revolving around charters, statutes and common law privileges. Of course, colonial arguments came finally to be expressed in a quite different natural law idiom which proved explosive. The origins of this can be traced back to the mid-1760s. In 1764, for example, the Boston lawyer James Otis, one of the first patriot controversialists, appealed to Locke's anti-Stuart natural law argument to contend that the government was dissolved whenever the legislative arm violated its trust and so broke 'this fundamental, sacred and unalterable law of self preservation', for which men had 'entered into society'.[16] The revolutionary doctrine that, by 'the law of nature', men leaving the mother country to found a new society elsewhere 'recover their natural freedom and independence' was heard at least as early as 1766 from the senior Virginia politician and pamphleteer Richard Bland. According to Bland, 'the jurisdiction and sovereignty of the state they have quitted, ceases'; such men 'become a sovereign state, independent of the state from which they separated'.[17] Such arguments were, after the Revolution, retrospectively organised into a high road to independence. Yet this transition to a natural law idiom was not inevitable and did not become widespread until the 1770s. Had the empire already, since 1688, been structured in terms of the separateness of the colonies and their personal tie to the king, natural law claims of this kind might not have been generated. Anglo-American disputes might have gone on being addressed in the concrete, negotiable context of specific liberties and privileges.[18]

English law provided another area in which the debate could have taken a different direction. Formally, all lands in America had been granted to settlers by the crown in 'free and common Soccage' as if they were located in the manor of East Greenwich in Kent.[19] They were, in law, merely part of the royal demesne. Benjamin Franklin ridiculed this ancient doctrine of English land law in 1766, but others were to put it to use in the republican cause.[20] It was a doctrine to which both sides might appeal. John Adams cited it in the interest of independence to establish that English law, to the reign of James I, made no provision for 'colonization', no 'provision ... for governing colonies beyond the Atlantic, or beyond the four seas, by authority of parliament, no nor for the king to grant charters to subjects to settle in foreign countries'.[21] The argument was still sufficiently powerful that colonists could use it in order to place a particular interpretation on the transatlantic constitution. Others could use the same doctrine differently, however: the argument that men reassumed their rights by the law of nature in quitting the kingdom was always vulnerable since the king had a common-law right to prevent such emigration (given effect by the writ *ne exeat regno*). If colonies were royal grants, some colonists could argue (contrary to Bland's claim that the colonies were free and independent states) that they were still part of the realm of England and therefore entitled to all the rights of Englishmen, including 'no taxation without representation'. Complete independence was not the only or inevitable outcome of the remarkable flowering of constitutional and political theory seen in America between 1763 and 1776.

Despite natural law arguments and the self-evident truths of the Declaration of Independence which natural law arguments generated, this older constitutional idiom remained basic up to the outbreak of the war. In 1775, the Lord Chief Justice, Lord Mansfield, in a debate in the House of Lords, argued that colonial grievances focused on the principle of British supremacy, not the detail of controversial legislation.

> If I do not mistake, in one place, the Congress sum up the whole of their grievances in the passage of the Declaratory Act [1765], which asserts the supremacy of Great Britain, or the power of making laws for America in all cases whatsoever. That is the true bone of contention. They positively deny the right, not the mode of exercising it. They would allow the king of Great Britain a nominal sovereignty over them, but nothing else. They would throw off the dependency on the crown of Great Britain, but not on the person of the king, whom they would render a cypher. In fine, they would stand in relation to Great Britain as Hanover now stands; or, more properly speaking, as Scotland stood towards England, previous to the treaty of Union.[22]

Constitutional doctrines and practical purposes were thus mutually dependent. In an eighteenth-century Britain ruled by Stuart monarchs, such doctrines might have been more easily used as a way of redefining imperial relationships to cope with increasing colonial population, prosperity and political maturity. Imperial devolution was to be the path eventually explored by the metropolis after the Durham Report of 1839; it is possible that a continued or a restored Stuart regime would have found itself committed to a constitutional formula within the British Isles which unintentionally promoted the process of imperial devolution at an earlier date, and so accommodated American ambitions rather than resisting them. No such Stuart restoration recast the political landscape, of course, and a forward-looking Britain found itself increasingly committed to the Blackstonian doctrine of the absolute authority of the crown in parliament which a backward-looking America, still obsessed with the seventeenth-century jurist Sir Edward Coke, finally resisted with armed force.

Two Types of Tragedy? 1688 and 1776

The revolutions of 1688 in the British Isles and 1776 in Britain's North American colonies shared a number of essential features: their initial seeming improbability; the reluctance of most men, however critical of the government, to resort to armed force; a high level of eventual unanimity that something had to be done; a considerable degree of disagreement, in historical retrospect, about the causes of what actually was done; but a powerful political need to claim that the meaning of the revolution was profound and unambiguous. Yet, in respect of causation, the two episodes now appear very different. The fall of James II came about in a narrow time frame, as the result of a set of events which contemporaries saw as bewildering and historians explain as dominated by contingency. It was a revolution which, then and later, seemed incomprehensibly under-determined. By contrast, historians of the conflicts of the 1770s and 1780s have always argued that the Revolution was over-determined, the long-delayed result of long-rehearsed social, religious or ideological conflicts in law and religion. This is equally true of those who pointed to British policy and of those who, more recently, explain the Revolution chiefly as the result of causes internal to the colonies themselves.[23]

Yet even this recognition of the powerful antecedents of the American Revolution is still consistent with the existence of counterfactuals, for that revolution was a *civil* war, each side embracing a plausible alternative, rather than a consensually supported war of colonial liberation aimed at driving out a wholly alien occupying power. Where the great majority of both English and Scots had sat on the fence in 1688, waiting to see which side would prevail, the pattern in the thirteen colonies in 1776 was strikingly different. There, men had often been politically mobilised and pre-committed to one side or other by principled conflicts and local coercion dating from the early 1760s. In England in 1688 a change of government was peacefully effected, but followed by agonisings over the theoretical implications of what had been done; in 1776 American colonists had had their theoretical debates already and were now swiftly drawn into bitter civil war with neighbouring communities of the opposite allegiance. Only the arrival of peace in 1783, the permanent exclusion of the loyalists and the subsequent wave of triumphalism created the illusion of a unity of national purpose and the inevitability of a wholly independent United States.

This over-determination therefore implies not inevitability but two counterfactuals, two distinct and irreconcilable alternatives: a British America, ever more securely integrated into a British modernity of church and king, commerce and science; or a republican America, stepping back into a mode of plebeian politics, sectarian conflict and agrarian self-sufficiency[24] which to many English observers recalled the 1640s and 1650s. Political contingencies defined these options, of course, for the British model of a future American society was not forcefully proselytising. It did not include any sustained attempt to export nobility and gentry to the plantations: colonial society was already sufficiently receptive to English patrician ideals. It did, however, include an attempt to promote the Church of England in America as the basis for a tolerant regime in a plural society, an ambition which many colonists, and not only Dissenters among them, saw quite differently as a sinister bid for spiritual power.[25]

English hegemony was often interpreted as insidious too, since it increasingly found its expression through the processes of cultural emulation: consumerism, with its cargo of English aesthetic and commercial norms, was giving American polite society an increasingly English orientation.[26] Later, these forms of English influence were quickly overlaid by the exultation of the new republic at its independence and at the initial success of its experiment in devising a constitution. The vision of a young society rejecting old-world political corruption in favour of republican innocence[27] and spurning the tainted luxury of modern consumerism for rustic simplicity[28] was so compelling that it fused in a national myth. When corruption and luxury returned, as return they must, they paid obeisance to that myth and were not allowed to overturn it: colonial cultural exceptionalism, it was assumed, had pointed the way to American political independence. Yet only in retrospect did it seem obvious that the evolution of American values had made independence inevitable.

Before the 1770s the path of rebellion and autonomy seemed anything but likely. The British *ancien régime*, a state form devised in the 1660s to make impossible any lurch back into the horrors of religious war and social upheaval that scarred early-seventeenth-century Europe, had done its work all too well. Many contemporaries regarded the momentous and atavistic events unfolding in the mid-1770s with awe and disbelief: it was a common reaction to say that the ostensible causes were wholly inadequate to explain the scale of the unfolding tragedy, and so they were.

Although some commentators had predicted the hypothetical independence of America at an unspecifically remote date, almost none had expected a crisis as soon as the mid-1770s. Benjamin Franklin, testifying before the House of Commons on 13 February 1766, during its deliberations on the repeal of the Stamp Act, classically identified what colonial republicans came to argue had been the status quo before 1763: the colonies then, he claimed,

> submitted willingly to the government of the Crown, and paid, in all their courts, obedience to the acts of parliament. Numerous as the people are in the several old provinces, they cost you nothing in forts, citadels, garrisons or armies, to keep them in subjection. They were governed by this country at the expense only of a little pen, ink and paper. They were led by a thread. They had not only a respect, but an affection, for Great Britain, for its laws, its customs and manners, and even a fondness for its fashions, that greatly increased the commerce. Natives of Britain were always treated with particular regard; to be an Old England-man was, of itself, a character of some respect, and gave a kind of rank among us.[29]

Even experienced colonial administrators might share this perspective. In 1764, Thomas Pownall, who had been Governor of Massachusetts from 1757 to 1759, looked to the strengthening of the hold of the metropolis on a mercantilist empire by reinforcing the tie between Whitehall and each colony individually, while carefully avoiding any possibility of a union of colonies. According to Pownall, developing commercial relations made a transatlantic breakdown impossible:

> if, by becoming independent is meant a revolt, nothing is further from their nature, their interest, their thoughts. If a defection from the alliance of the mother country be suggested, it ought to be, and can truly be said, that their spirit abhors the sense of such; their attachment to the protestant succession in the house of Hanover will ever stand unshaken; and nothing can eradicate from their hearts their natural, almost mechanical, affection to Great Britain, which they conceive under no other sense, nor call by any other name, than that of *home*.[30]

In the second edition of this work, published in 1765 after the colonial outcry against the Stamp Act, Pownall left this passage unchanged and merely prefaced his tract with a Dedication to George Grenville which explained how the recent tumults had been produced by 'demagogues':

> The truly great and wise man will not judge of the people from their passions – He will view the whole tenor of their principles and of their conduct. While he sees them uniformly loyal to their King, obedient to his government, active in every point of public spirit, in every object of the public welfare – He will not regard what they are led either to say or do under these fits of alarm and inflammation; he will, finally, have the pleasure to see them return to their genuine good temper, good sense and principles.[31]

These expectations explain men's astonishment at the Revolution. The Virginia Congressman Edmund Randolph wrote later of the famous protest of Patrick Henry in the Virginia House of Burgesses in May 1765 against the Stamp Act:

> Without an immediate oppression, without a cause depending so much on hasty feeling as theoretic reasoning; without a distaste for monarchy; with loyalty to the reigning prince; with fraternal attachment to the transatlantic members of the empire; with an admiration of their genius, learning and virtues; with a subserviency in cultivating their manners and their fashions; in a word, with England as a model of all which was great and venerable; the house of burgesses in the year 1765 gave utterance to principles which within two years were to expand into a revolution.[32]

Joseph Galloway, Speaker of the Pennsylvania Assembly between 1766 and 1775, argued from the perspective of 1779 that during the Seven Years' War 'there was no part of his Majesty's dominions contained a greater proportion of faithful subjects than the

Thirteen Colonies.... The idea of disloyalty, at this time, scarcely existed in America; or, if it did, it was never expressed with impunity.'

This only created the paradox: how could such deep-rooted attachment be so suddenly reversed?

> How then can it happen, that a people so lately loyal, should so suddenly become universally disloyal, and firmly attached to republican Government, without any grievances or oppressions but those in anticipation? ... No fines, no imprisonments, no oppressions, had been experienced by the Colonists, that could have produced such an effect ... If we search the whole history of human events, we shall not meet with an example of such a sudden change, from the most perfect loyalty to universal disaffection. On the contrary, in every instance where national attachment has been generally effaced, it has been effected by slow degrees, and a long continuance of oppression, not in prospect, but in actual existence.[33]

Galloway's solution to the paradox was a radical one: the colonists in general were not disaffected, as some zealots for republicanism had claimed, and might be won back to their allegiance. It was an argument which still challenges the received explanation of the Revolution as the culmination of long-prepared American nationalism.

Nor was Galloway alone. The Boston judge Peter Oliver argued that the Revolution was a *'singular'* phenomenon: 'For, by adverting to the historick Page, we shall find no Revolt of Colonies, whether under the *Roman* or any other State, but what originated from severe Oppressions.' But America had been 'nursed, in its Infancy, with the most tender Care & Attention ... indulged with every Gratification ... repeatedly saved from impending Destruction'; this was 'an unnatural Rebellion', instigated by a small minority of the colonists only, 'a few abandoned Demagogues'.[34] The Earl of Dartmouth's under-secretary for the colonies, Ambrose Serle, observing events in New York, reacted in the same way to news of the constitutions of New Jersey and Virginia: 'An Influenza more wonderful, and at the same time more general than that of the Witchcraft in the Province of Massachuset's Bay in the last Century! The Annals of no Country can produce an Instance of so virulent a Rebellion, of such implacable madness and Fury, originating from such trivial Causes, as those alledged by these unhappy People.'[35] 'Will not posterity be amazed,' wrote the Massachusetts lawyer and politician Daniel Leonard, 'when they are told that the present distraction took its rise from the parliament's taking off a shilling duty on a pound of tea, and imposing three pence, and call it a more unaccountable phrenzy, and more disgraceful to the annals of America, than that of the witchcraft?'[36] Only after their initial incomprehension at the justifications of the patriots did such men come to explain the Revolution as a volcano, erupting in response to enormous internal pressures.

The tragic quality of the Revolution of 1688 lies in the trope of Boccaccio's *De Casibus Virorum Illustrium*: 'the fall of great men'; the malign turn of fortune's wheel that reduces the most noble and splendid to the most base, and does so from trivial causes. It is, in retrospect, the tragedy of contingency. The same is true, it might be argued, of 1776; yet the need retrospectively to integrate the events of the mid-1770s into the founding myth of a great nation has created a different impression. The tragic quality of 1776 now seems to lie in the inexorable logic of an approaching doom, a chain of events, unfolding to catastrophe, triggered not by a tragic error but by the pursuit of high ideals and good intentions. The historian is entitled to doubt whether such chains of causation were as inevitable at the time as they were later made to seem. And to abolish inevitability is to open up counterfactuals.

'External Causes' and the Inadequacy of Teleology

Until recently, historians' accounts of the causes of the Revolution of 1776 tended to become a familiar – and teleological – litany of the stages of British policy and colonial responses to it, both expressed in a secular constitutional idiom: the Stamp Act, the Townshend duties, the Boston Tea Party, the 'Intolerable Acts'.[37] The decision to declare independence made it necessary to argue that the causes of the Revolution were external, so that the 'ostensible causes' of the conflict were the true ones: these innovations in British policy alone were sufficient to explain the colonial reaction to them.[38] Such a pattern of explanation was implicitly counterfactual, but inadequately so: it had to suggest (without conviction) that slight changes in colonial policy at Westminster and Whitehall would have left the empire intact. Although metropolitan policy should indeed be questioned in this way, presenting the problem in these terms alone obscured the options plausibly available for colonial Americans; in particular, it systematically removed their major counterfactual, the obvious and central path of peaceful colonial development within the empire in the direction of greater political and less cultural autonomy.

In deference to national cultural imperatives, it has been an assumption shared with remarkable unanimity by recent American historians of the American Revolution that the causes of that event were external to the colonies.[39] Two scholarly and powerful versions of that thesis are currently prevalent, though neither should be accepted as it stands. One is owed to Bernard Bailyn, and was devised in the 1960s. In this model, colonists in the early part of the eighteenth century adopted from England a political rhetoric derived from the 'Commonwealthmen', a rhetoric which identified political virtue in landed independence, representative institutions, religious scepticism, gentry dominance and a militia, and saw political corruption in standing armies, placemen, arbitrary taxation, priestcraft and assertive kingship. In the early 1760s, colonists thought they saw these evils in British policy. Given the nature of British politics and innovations in colonial policy, argued Bailyn, it was rational for them so to think.[40]

The second variant of that 'externalist' interpretation has much older origins, but its most modern version was formulated by Jack P. Greene. It depicts the emergence of a consensual, tacitly accepted constitutional structure for relations between colonies and metropolis by the early eighteenth century. That structure allegedly ensured *de facto* autonomy to each colonial assembly, and produced a quasi-federal system of colonial self-rule. According to this thesis, it was the colonists' consensual understanding of already extensive American autonomy that was challenged by British policy in the 1760s and, with the British persisting in their infringements, armed resistance was the final and natural response.[41]

Without substantiating the point, both Bailyn and Greene contended that the colonial tie with Britain could have survived unchallenged for a long period, but for metropolitan innovations.[42] Colonial demands, they argued, could all have been accommodated within the empire had the British government acted differently. If so, it made sense for many historians to frame counterfactuals in British politics rather than in American politics:

> The chance that brought one man and then another to the place of power in Whitehall played its part in bringing on the imperial civil war. At almost every turn events might have proceeded differently – if George III had not quarrelled with Grenville in the spring of 1765; if Cumberland had not died that autumn; if Grafton and Conway had not been so insistent in early 1766 that Pitt ought to lead the ministry; if Pitt, now Earl of Chatham, had not allowed the reluctant Townshend to be foisted on him by Grafton as his chancellor of the exchequer; if Chatham had kept his health, or if Townshend's had given way twelve months earlier than it did; if the Rockinghams had not, by combining in a trial of strength to bring down Grafton in 1767, forced him into the arms of the Bedford party; if Grafton as head of the Treasury had had the firmness of purpose to insist on his own fiscal policy (with regard to the tea duty) in 1769. Either armed conflict might have come earlier when the colonists' resources were less developed and when they were less prepared, materially and psychologically, than was the case by 1775; or prudence might have prevailed, causing adjustments within the

Empire, which clearly had to take place ultimately, to be pursued with less animosity and without violence.[43]

The two distinguished authors of that passage, one British, one American, in a work published in 1976, strikingly omitted a similar list of counterfactuals on the colonial side. Yet although these counterfactual insights into metropolitan politics have not been refuted, attention has increasingly shifted to the social and denominational conflicts, the ideological debates in law and religion, that explain the colonies' swift conversion from loyalism to disaffection.

Recent scholarship has steadily converted to the view that whatever the vicissitudes of British ministerial politics between 1765 and 1775, and whichever individuals were in office, the range of options available within British colonial policy was unlikely by itself to have made a major difference to the outcome. The best-informed colonial administrators of the 1750s adopted diametrically opposite views on whether the colonies should be subdued by force or won by kindness; yet even such contrasting figures as Henry Ellis, a hawk who favoured force, and Thomas Pownall, reputedly a dove, had much in common in asserting metropolitan authority. Pownall in 1764 looked to strengthen the hold of the metropolis over a mercantilist empire through strengthening the tie between Whitehall and each individual colony while carefully avoiding any possibility of a union of colonies. Nevertheless, argued John Shy, Pownall's supposedly pacific policy in fact anticipated 'The Sugar Act, the Currency Act, the Stamp Act, the Townshend Acts, the extension of vice-admiralty jurisdiction, the creation of West Indian free ports and a Secretary of State for the Colonies, even threats to the Rhode Island charter, the alteration of the Massachusetts Council, and adamant opposition to inter-colonial congresses'.

It follows that 'if Thomas Pownall and Henry Ellis are taken to represent the limits of what was conceivable in American policy between 1763 and 1775, then the range of historical possibilities was very narrow indeed'. By contrast,

A great deal of historical writing on the American Revolution contains at least the suggestion that there were available alternatives for British policy, and that what actually happened may be seen as a sad story of accident, ignorance, misunderstanding, and perhaps a little malevolence. George Grenville is narrow minded, Charles Townshend is brilliant but silly, Hillsborough is stupid and tyrannical, Chatham is tragically ill, Dartmouth is unusually weak, and the King himself is very stubborn and not very bright. But if politics had not been in quite such a chaotic phase, perhaps the Old Whigs or an effective Chathamite ministry would have held power, been able to shape and sustain a truly liberal policy toward the Colonies, and avoided the disruption of the Empire. So the story seems to run.

Given the absence (as historians now acknowledge) of a new, liberty-threatening master-plan for the empire in the minds of British politicians in 1763, especially George Grenville, it can seem even more plausible that 'A little more knowledge, a little more tact, a little more political sensitivity, and it all might have turned out differently.' But, if even so instinctively pro-American an observer as Thomas Pownall was not at odds with the policies adopted, there is a 'prima facie case that British colonial policy in this period was neither fortuitous nor susceptible of change.... The impulse that swept the British Empire toward civil war was powerful, and did not admit of any real choice.'[44]

The Strategic Counterfactuals

Before accepting so fatalist a diagnosis, however, we need to examine those points at which, as some have argued then or later, a different line of policy could have been adopted which would have retained the colonies within the empire (however that empire might have been redefined). One such set of policy options concerns the strategic setting of the thirteen colonies. Given the appeal by many Americans in the 1760s and 1770s to the status quo which, they claimed, prevailed before the Peace of Paris in

1763, the first such change of direction has been located in the Seven Years' War of 1756–63, an episode decisive, in some accounts, in re-establishing metropolitan control, abrogating customary relationships and asserting novel powers including a right of taxation. Many scholars, but especially Americans, once discerned a new attitude towards empire in these years as Britain adapted to the responsibilities and opportunities created by the defeat of France in North America.[45]

Even if this were the case, British military successes in the second half of that war were by no means assured, as a series of reverses in its first half, including the loss of Minorca, emphasised to contemporaries. Wolfe's victory at Quebec was a classic military contingency, and it could not be foreseen that Canada, once conquered, would be retained. The key French Canadian fortress of Louisbourg, captured by a colonial expedition in the previous war, had been returned at its end in 1748. A debate raged between 1759 and 1761 over whether Canada or more immediately valuable conquests in the French West Indies should be retained at the peace, if both could not be kept;[46] the eventual choice of the former might easily have gone the other way. Few statesmen at the time entertained the visionary belief in an empire of vast geographical extent in North America or saw its potential for commerce. Even William Pitt, speaking against the Treaty of Paris and in favour of the retention of Guadeloupe, argued that 'The state of the existing trade in the conquests in North America, is extremely low; the speculations of their future are precarious, and the prospect, at the very best, very remote.'[47]

Canada might not have been won; when won, it might not have been kept. True, in the debate over its retention, William Burke famously predicted that the removal of the French threat would remove also a powerful inducement which kept the other British colonies in subjection to the metropolis: Guadeloupe should be retained, Canada returned to France. The prospect of a colonial bid for independence was already entertained as a hypothesis: 'If, Sir, the People of our Colonies find no Check from *Canada*, they will extend themselves, almost, without bounds into the Inland Parts ... by eagerly grasping at extensive Territory, we may run the risque, and that perhaps in no very distant Period, of losing what we now possess.... A Neighbour that keeps us in some Awe, is not always the worst of Neighbours.'[48] But this was hardly a disinterested argument, for William Burke had obtained the posts of secretary and register of Guadeloupe when that island was conquered in 1759, and was to lose them again when it, rather than Canada, was returned at the peace in 1763. The possible future loss of the mainland colonies of British settlement was evidently a remote possibility to most observers. Despite warnings of the future independence of North America, what weighed more with British statesmen was the need to defend the colonies as a whole against the French threat. Canada was retained in order to make British possession of its more southerly colonies secure. That such a move would provide a necessary condition of their independence was, as yet, a counterfactual to which few people gave weight.

In 1760, Benjamin Franklin argued passionately in reply to William Burke's pamphlet that Canada should be retained at the peace, and that this posed no threat to Britain's hold over its other North American colonies. Writing anonymously, and adopting the character of an Englishman, Franklin argued: 'A people spread thro' the whole tract of country on this side of the Mississippi, and secured by Canada in our hands, would probably for some centuries find employment in agriculture, and thereby free us at home effectually from our fears of American manufactures.' Indeed, they would be tied by dependence on British manufactures. Franklin predicted that rapid population increase in America

> would probably in a century more, make the number of British subjects on that side of the water more numerous than they now are on this; but I am far from entertaining on that account, any fears of their becoming either *useless* or *dangerous* to us; and I look on those fears, to be merely imaginary and without any probable foundation.

Even the fourteen North American colonial governments already in existence found it impossible to combine:

> Those we now have, are not only under different governors, but have different forms of government, different laws, different interests, and some of them different religious persuasions and different manners. Their jealousy of each other is so great that however necessary an union of the colonies has long been, for their common defence and security against their enemies, and how sensible soever each colony has been of that necessity, yet they have never been able to effect such an union among themselves, nor even to agree in requesting the mother country to establish it for them.

If the colonies could not unite against the French and Indians, 'who were perpetually harassing their settlements, burning their villages, and murdering their people; can it reasonably be supposed there is any danger of their uniting against their own nation, which protects and encourages them, with which they have so many connections and ties of blood, interest and affection, and which 'tis well known they all love much more than they love one another?' Such a union, predicted Franklin, was 'impossible' (though he at once added a rider: 'without the most grievous tyranny and oppression').[49]

A second consequence of the Seven Years' War stemmed from the manner in which it was terminated, for the decision of a restructured British ministry to end the conflict in circumstances interpreted by Frederick of Prussia as abandonment of him was crucial. As a result of this decision, Britain went into the American war in 1776 without a major ally on the European continent. Britain, undistracted, might have been able to contain or suppress a rebellion in her American colonies, but in the 1780s it was drawn into a major war against both the Bourbon powers, France and Spain, and the League of Armed Neutrals. Continental alliances had been essential to sustaining British naval supremacy, argued one historian: 'Neither administrative weakness, nor military and naval ineptitude was responsible for the humiliating disaster' of Yorktown. 'The dominating factor was political isolation.'[50] A continental alliance might have made a difference in the years 1763–76. But the absence in this period of a French expansionary threat on the European continent meant that no other major continental power had an interest in fighting Britain's continental battles for it.[51] In this perspective, its failing hold on its American colonies was largely the consequence of its own over-stretched military resources. But this was not widely foreseen, any more than the consequences of the retention of Canada were foreseen.

Strategic speculation on the long-term future of transatlantic relations normally focused on another theme. Some commentators speculated that the changing balance of population between Britain and America would eventually bring about a redefinition of imperial relationships. By 1776, this could be used as a decisive argument for the inevitability of independence by a friend of America like Richard Price:

> They are now but little short of half our number. To this number they have grown, from a small body of original settlers, by a very rapid increase. The probability is, that they will go on to increase; and that, in 50 or 60 years, they will be *double* our number ... and form a mighty Empire, consisting of a variety of states, all equal or superior to ourselves in all the arts and accomplishments, which give dignity and happiness to human life. In that period, will they be still bound to acknowledge that supremacy over them which we now claim?[52]

Yet, even among those who so argued (and such arguments can be traced back many decades), none foresaw the immense cataclysm of the 1770s. Even Price himself had not done so, writing to Benjamin Franklin on colonial demographic data in 1769. In the version of his letter intended as a paper to the Royal Society, Price added a sentence on the colonists, 'Formerly an increasing number of FRIENDS, but now likely to be converted, by an unjust and fatal policy, into an increasing number of ENEMIES.'[53] But, even here, it was British policy that Price sought to blame, not some inexorable logic of demography.

Price's correspondence before the outbreak of the Revolution shows no anticipation of that momentous event, an apparent blindness that he shared with almost all of his contemporaries. The constitutional conflicts of the 1760s had, after all, been settled by negotiation; the explosion of the mid-1770s caught by surprise even colonists soon to be in the forefront of the movement for independence. The Dissenter Price's interest in American affairs was first attracted when the colonists were seen to be engaged in a battle like his own against those 'enemies to truth and liberty', bishops: 'If they once get footing there, it is highly probable that in time they will acquire a power (under the protection and with the aid of their friends *here*) that will extend itself beyond Spirituals, and be inconsistent with the equal and common liberty of other religious persuasions.'[54] These. atavistic English Dissenting phobias, not the imminent independence of America or its constitutional claims, were Price's starting point.

With the advantage of hindsight, of course, men were able to argue differently: by 1773, Thomas Hutchinson, Lieutenant Governor of the colony of Massachusetts, locked in controversy with his colony's assembly, looked back on the retention of Canada as the great mistake. Without it, 'none of the spirit of opposition to the Mother Country would have yet appeared & I think the effects of it [the acquisition of Canada] worse than all we had to fear from the French or Indians'.[55] In this sense, the acquisition of Canada is now acknowledged as 'a major cause' of the American Revolution.[56] But it was a necessary, not a sufficient, cause: it established the context in which a rebellion might occur, but it did not determine that such a rebellion would occur. The same causes (the removal of a neighbouring threat) obtained equally within Canada, but it was not Canada in the 1770s which sought to break its political ties with the metropolis.

Domestic Counterfactuals: Colonial Union, Taxation and Democracy

A second set of policy options concerned developments within the colonies. One reason for thinking an American revolution unlikely was, as Franklin suggested, the marked lack of enthusiasm for plans for colonial union in earlier decades. The scheme discussed at a conference at Albany, New York, in 1754, would have vested very substantial powers, including that of taxation, in a Grand Council nominated by the lower houses of colonial assemblies; but so dominant did such a unified government seem that the provincial assemblies themselves unanimously rejected the scheme.[57] When a more modest plan of inter-colonial cooperation in military and Indian affairs was drawn up by Lord Halifax at the Board of Trade in 1754, Charles Townshend dismissed it: 'It is ... impossible to imagine that so many different representatives of so many different provinces, divided in interest and alienated by jealousy and inveterate prejudice, should ever be able to resolve upon a plan of mutual security and reciprocal expense.' Nor would the colonial assemblies, thought Townshend, pass the Act of Supply necessary to fund a union: it would run counter to their 'settled design of drawing to themselves the ancient and established prerogatives wisely preserved in the Crown' by steadily gaining control of each colony's finances.[58]

Yet even this 'quest for power' on the part of colonial assemblies, if real, did not create an assumption that independence was inevitable. Even the man regarded as the greatest catalyst of the Revolution did not claim it to be the outcome of a trend which the colonists had long understood. In *Common Sense*, published in Philadelphia in 1776, Tom Paine wrote of the colonists' policies of 1775: 'Whatever was advanced by the advocates on either side of the question then, terminated in one and the same point, viz. a union with Great Britain; the only difference between the parties, was the method of effecting it; the one proposing force, the other friendship ...'.[59] In the words of Jack

Greene, the 'latent distrust' that lay behind transatlantic relations could not 'become an active cause of disruption between Britain and the colonies so long as the delicate and uneasy accommodation that had been worked out under Walpole continued to obtain. That it would not obtain was by no means predictable.'[60] Given the commitment of colonists to the constitutional practices they claimed as a shared inheritance, it is understandable that so many at the time regarded transatlantic controversies as open to negotiated settlement. However, Paine's claim was contradicted by much evidence of which, as a recent migrant, he was probably unaware. In the early 1760s, long before he set foot in America, the political rhetoric of many colonists had moved in a relatively short period from eulogies of the liberties they enjoyed, as Englishmen within the empire, to denunciations of the corruption and tyranny into which English society, in their perception, had fallen. 'It is when viewed amidst this widespread and enthusiastic acclamation for the English constitution', as Gordon Wood has observed, 'that the American Revolution takes on its tone of irony and incomprehensibility – a tone not lost to the Revolutionaries themselves.' By a rhetoric which sought to take its stand solely on the English constitution, 'the Americans could easily conceive of themselves as simply preserving what Englishmen had valued from time immemorial.... Yet this continual talk of desiring nothing new and wishing only to return to the old system and the essentials of the English constitution was only a superficial gloss.'[61]

On the classic constitutional points at issue, the 'ostensible causes' of the Revolution, the colonists themselves proposed a counterfactual. In the 1760s, responses to the Stamp Act assumed that all would be well if the novel legislation were repealed. John Dickinson's best-selling *Farmer's Letters* implied the same argument against the Townshend duties of 1767. Governments might adopt wrong measures; 'But every such measure does not dissolve the obligation between the governors and the governed. The mistakes may be corrected; the passion may subside.'[62] In 1769, Benjamin Franklin wrote:

Of late a Cry begins to arise, Can no body propose a Plan of Conciliation? Must we ruin ourselves by intestine Quarrels? I was ask'd in company lately by a noble Lord if I had no Plan of that kind to propose? My Answer was, 'Tis easy to propose a Plan; mine may be express'd in a few Words; *Repeal* the Laws, *Renounce* the Right, *Recall* the Troops, *Refund* the Money, *Return to the old Method of Requisition.*[63]

Congress itself, in its address *To the people of Great-Britain*, dated 5 September 1774, argued that the constitutional relationship prior to the Seven Years' War was legitimate; it was only at its conclusion that 'a plan for enslaving your fellow subjects in America was concerted ... Place us in the same situation that we were at the close of the last war, and our former harmony will be restored.'[64]

Yet this was a counterfactual substantially disproved by events, for the metropolitan government showed a repeated willingness to compromise on the points at issue in the 1760s.[65] It can now be shown that British policy towards colonial trade underwent no sea-change from mercantilism to imperialism in the early 1760s, as an older historiography once argued. The Sugar Act of 1764 attempted to raise a revenue in the colonies, at the same time attempting to encourage trade to flow within traditional mercantilist channels. The same was true in 1767 of Chatham's reduction of the duty on tea re-exported to the American colonies.[66] Likewise, inflation in the colonies, the result of colonial issues of paper money, was checked by Westminster's Currency Act of 1764; after colonial protests, this measure was relaxed in the case of New York by an Act of 1770 and in the case of the other colonies by an Act of 1773: on this basis, it is possible that the issue might have been resolved.[67] George Grenville later admitted in a debate in the Commons that he 'did not foresee' the degree of opposition to the Stamp Act, and, had he foreseen it, would not have proposed it.[68] This was plausible: given that revenue had to be raised by the imperial government in the colonies, a small stamp duty was an ineffective method of raising it. The anticipated revenue from the tax was only £110,000, of which £50,000 would come from the West Indies.[69] Without broaching issues of internal taxation, the ministry in London might have raised far larger revenues through the existing customs and excise legislation, vigorously enforced by the use of naval power and adjudicated by an augmented version of the existing vice-admiralty courts. After colonial protests, the Westminster Parliament repealed the Act.

If the Stamp Act was passed with no anticipation of colonial resistance, so too was Townshend's Revenue Act in 1767: it raised no questions of internal taxation, and seemed to be based on the colonists' own distinction between legitimate external and illegitimate internal taxation. Not even the colonial agents forecast what was to come, or warned against it.[70] Even Benjamin Franklin, in an article in the *London Chronicle* in April 1767, had accepted the constitutional correctness of imperial taxation on external trade, protesting only against 'internal taxes'.[71] In turn, it is difficult to resist the conclusion that the outcry against the reduction of the duty on tea from one shilling to three pence per pound was manufactured by colonial merchants who stood to lose from the suppression of the lucrative smuggling trade. If the earlier use of the Royal Navy in North American waters to eliminate smuggling might have pre-empted this before it became a political hot potato, it remains true that, in the absence of serious coercion, there was little room for compromise on the American side. Contingency was not dominant in 1776 as it had been in 1688.

Historians who adhered to the traditional scenario of 'ostensible causes' have, perhaps, framed too simplistic an alternative to conflict. On 1 May 1769, the Cabinet met to consider the mounting colonial protests against the duties passed by the Commons in June 1767 on the initiative of Charles Townshend, then Chancellor of the Exchequer. Now, the Cabinet voted for the repeal of all but one. By five votes to four, the conciliatory First Lord of the Treasury, the Duke of Grafton, was outvoted in his move to abolish the tea duty. 'This fateful decision', it has been claimed, 'was to prove the point of no return in the sequence of events leading to the American Revolution. Without a tea duty there would have been no Boston Tea Party and no consequent final quarrel between Britain and her colonies.'[72] This confident judgement seems less plausible as colonial causes of rebellion are admitted to the historical record. Counterfactuals can indeed be framed in respect of British policy, yet the more important counterfactuals all concern the patterns of social development and of ideological conflict within the colonies themselves.

These colonial counterfactuals do not chiefly involve the classic constitutional issues, the 'ostensible causes' of inevitable revolution. The problem of representation was the most obvious obstacle to a settlement, yet it may be that even this was not the insuperable barrier that it later appeared to have been. Taxation and representation were, of course, linked issues. Yet if questions of revenue seem more open to a negotiated settlement (taxation being a feature of all governments, including republican ones), questions of representation tend to be regarded as more principled, and more irreconcilable. This was not necessarily the case, however, even with the constitutional fiction generally identified as the weakest link in the metropolitan argument. As Thomas Whately argued, 'All *British* subjects are really in the same [situation]; none are actually, all are virtually represented in Parliament; for every Member of Parliament sits in the House, not as Representative of his own Constituents, but as one of that august Assembly by which all the Commons of *Great Britain* are represented.'[73] In other words, apart from those men sitting in Parliament as members of the House of Lords or House of Commons, all Britons related to their MP not as a delegate but as a representative, a representative unpaid by his constituents and not bound to accept instructions offered by them. The problem with this doctrine of virtual representation was not that it was self-evidently untrue, but that it was a truism, and was therefore introduced into the debate unrehearsed and with no theoretical explication. But it could have been given the sort of theoretical basis which would have contributed to a better understanding both of imperial relations and of the actual working of politics in Britain itself.

It was a truism that a British MP represented the whole polity, not just his constituency; represented all the inhabitants, of both sexes, including minors; represented the eight- or nine-tenths of the populace who were not voters; represented those electors who had voted against him, or had abstained, as well as those who had given him their votes. This was, of course, a necessary fiction of government. But it bore more relation to the daily working of government than did the succeeding myth that a man could be represented only if he himself cast a vote, a theory which, in a system of universal suffrage, by definition subjected to a majoritarian tyranny all non-voters, all voters for defeated candidates, and all voters for MPs on the losing side in parliamentary divisions. In both cases, states were effectively run by small minorities; in the first case this reality was less disguised, and more dignified. Except for the political elite, virtual and actual representation were equally formal concepts. Here too, just as in the replacement of divine-right monarchy by representative democracy, historians are now obliged to dispense with a scenario in which a logic of historical inevitability led men to replace early-modern 'fictions' with self-evident modern 'truths'.[74]

To be sure, William Pitt in 1766 declared that 'The idea of a virtual representation of America in this House, is the most contemptible idea that ever entered into the head of a man; it does not deserve a serious refutation.'[75] This was a political gambit, however, for Pitt himself represented only a variety of tiny constituencies including, as his first, the depopulated borough of Old Sarum, which boasted (on a good day) an electorate of about seven. From 1757 to 1766 he sat in the Commons as one of the two Members for Bath: it fielded an electorate of about thirty. Even in that seat, Pitt never had to face a poll.[76] Despite his rhetoric, it is not clear just whom William Pitt represented, either in the Commons or when elevated to the Lords as 1st Earl of Chatham. American adulation of him as a democrat overlooked the fact that he fought only one contested election in his entire parliamentary career. Even that was in the tiny Cinque Port of Seaford.

However contemptuous some orators might be of the concept of virtual representation, their desire to create an American nation reintroduced it. Thomas Paine hailed the cause of independence: ''Tis not the concern of a day, a year, or an age; posterity are virtually involved in the contest, and will be more or less affected even to the end of time by the proceedings now.'[77] Although the colonists rejected 'virtual' representation, their 'actual' representation in the Westminster Parliament was generally sought neither by themselves nor by their British supporters: since the relations of colonies and metropolis were debated in terms of mutual self-interest, this would only have imported the conflict into the House of Commons, not resolved it in a new context of Anglo-Saxon solidarity. The only viable alternative was to work with and through the growing power of the colonial assemblies. Even Joseph Galloway, later remembered as a resolute loyalist, was explicit at the First Continental Congress in Philadelphia in September 1774 that Acts of the Westminster Parliament did not bind the colonies;[78] and, if a man so well disposed could envisage a redefinition of imperial relations only along federal lines, it is unlikely that there would have been substantial backing in the colonies for a solution which failed to include the principle of equivalence between the Westminster and colonial assemblies.

The rise of these assemblies as against the power of the governors was, indeed, a marked feature of the half-century to 1776. Yet, although these assemblies showed a clear desire to assert growing colonial wealth and population, they had shown few overt signs of extrapolating these trends into a bid for separation from the mother country. Even in 1774–6, it was not the assemblies which articulated the claim of independence, but groups of zealots bypassing each assembly to set up a self-authorising representative body. Well-informed and practical individuals like Galloway continued until a late date to act on the belief that a negotiated compromise was still possible. Galloway proposed to the Continental Congress on 28 September 1774 a plan for reconciliation based on the establishment of an American legislative council, under a president-general appointed by the crown, its members chosen by the colonial assemblies.[79] Congress voted on that day by six colonies to five to lay the plan on the table for subsequent consideration, so effectively killing it;[80] but, had the vote gone the other way, a positive response from London might have cleared the way to negotiated settlement. For there, the ministry remained open to the idea.

In January 1775, the Cabinet agreed on North's so-called 'olive branch': backed up by coercive measures to halt the trade of those colonies perceived as being uncooperative, the proposal was for Parliament to forbear to exercise its right of taxing a colony if that colony, through its normal and legal channels, would contribute its proportion to the common defence and pay the expenses of its civil government and administration of justice.[81] It was a proposal which inevitably ignored the Continental Congress: for Parliament to have addressed it would have been to recognise its legitimacy, which was the point at issue. At the same time, it expressed the reasonable hope that, by dealing with each colony separately, their common front might have been broken. It was the Second Continental Congress which rejected North's proposal as inadequate: it did not meet the colonies' demand for recognition of a right of granting whatever they thought fit, at their sole discretion, and did not address Parliament's claim of a right to legislate for the colonies in other matters, most recently in the Coercive Acts and most generally in the right to alter colonial charters.[82] But, had Galloway's proposal been adopted, a compromise might still have been reached.

In its absence, the most dramatic and decisive solution to the problem was that proposed by the Dean of Gloucester, Josiah Tucker. He saw clearly that, by this stage, the claims of the two parties had been defined in terms which precluded compromise. Britain's interests, however, lay in trade with her colonies, not political control over them. Tucker's solution was 'to separate entirely from the *North-American* Colonies, by declaring them to be a free and independent People'.[83] Such a pre-emptive act would have at once deprived the republican movement of its *raison d'être*. If adopted at any time before the Declaration of Independence stigmatised George III personally, it would have caught the colonists at the moment of claiming equality with the Westminster Parliament by taking up their personal loyalty to the crown: independence would have removed most incentives to distance themselves from this royalism. Americans would have been locked into the position of subjects of George III, though a George understood as a very constitutional monarch.

Equally, the absence of a war to win independence would have prevented the emergence of the single main cause of colonial unity. Even the tenuously confederal system embodied in the Articles of Confederation was agreed to only in response to dire military necessities. Without war, the jealousies, rivalries and diversities of the North American colonies would probably have produced only a much weaker association, if any. The new states, lacking a natural focus of unity, would have been likely therefore to preserve their allegiance to the monarch as a valuable guarantor of the legitimacy of their civil governments and an emblem of their cultural equality with the old world. For a marked feature of political debate in the decades before 1776, even in the last decade before the Revolution, was the absence of a key component which, in retrospect, appears natural and obvious: republicanism.

Colonial Americans had seldom, before the publication of Paine's *Common Sense* in 1776, denounced monarchy as such and still less often had they speculated on alternative, republican, models for colonial governance or society.[84] *Common Sense* itself contained no extended discussion of republicanism: it was a negative critique of existing constitutional arrangements, not a blueprint for new ones in the future. Few such blueprints were available to colonists in 1776. Equally, although democracy became a shibboleth of the new republic, it was not a cause of the Revolution. Since these two 'ostensible causes' tell us little about why the Revolution occurred, they cannot be invoked as explanations of why it was inevitable. Without the breakdown of 1776, transatlantic relations would not have run on in unchanging tranquillity: the powerful ideological pressures mounting in the colonies would have seen to that. But it remains true that the traditional 'ostensible causes' did not make inevitable the exact form that the Revolution took.

The Problems of Repression in a Libertarian Polity

Early-modern rebellions were as often provoked by lax government, permitting the growth of practices and expectations of local self-rule, as by active tyranny. A more efficient exertion of Britain's legal sovereignty over the colonies from an earlier date was another route which might have offered prospects of retaining executive control, and it is necessary to explore the reasons why this was so difficult. For there is an immense contrast between the metropolitan responses to the threatened rebellion in Ireland in 1797–8 (which largely aborted a carefully prepared rising) or the Indian Mutiny in 1857 (similarly repressed by military force) and the relative restraint employed by Englishmen towards fellow Englishmen in America.

Even before the fighting, Whitehall officials might systematically have resisted the many small steps by which colonial legislatures built up their power. The metropolis might have stipulated that colonial grants of revenue to colonial budgets be for long periods, or indefinite; that the salaries of the governor and other officials be shielded from local political pressures; that the colonial treasurers be royal appointments; that the governors' powers of local patronage be built up, and exercised by the governor, not the ministry in London. Such steps might plausibly have been taken under the energetic and reformist Earl of Halifax, President of the Board of Trade from 1748 to 1761, had he received the necessary backing from his ministerial colleagues. One reason why he did not, of course, was that ministers were wholly preoccupied with the need to secure the full cooperation of the colonies in the war with France.[85] Yet there were other reasons too, especially ministers' unwillingness to revert to the administrative ethic associated with the later Stuart monarchy.

The rare exceptions to this administrative quiescence help to illustrate the rule. In Massachusetts, Lieutenant Governor Thomas Hutchinson sought to force the issue in January 1773 by instituting an exchange with the assembly on the questions of constitutional principle involved. This initiative had the opposite effect to that which Hutchinson wished, however, for the assembly, especially the House of Representatives, took the opportunity to turn their *de facto* resistance to certain metropolitan measures into a defiant *de jure* rejection of metropolitan authority. The Secretary for the Colonies was appalled: 'The governor had upset Dartmouth's hopes that the controversy might subside and even perhaps disappear in time if only the parties would avoid raising the critical issues that separated them. To Dartmouth, Hutchinson had reopened a wound that might have healed if only it had been neglected or ignored.'[86] Although this possibility seems implausible in the light of later events, it is open to argument that it represented one possible avenue of development.

Politics destabilised policy in London, too: throughout the 1760s, indeed up to the end of 1774, British policy towards the colonies was rendered indecisive and vacillating by the instability and internal conflicts of ministries. Had George III been the tyrant that Americans later painted him, this would not have been the case. As it was, with many possible policies being advocated by different groups in the Lords and Commons, the natural response of many politicians was to frame a compromise or leave policy ambiguous, firm in principle, indecisive in practice. True, in a world of greater consistency of conduct and clarity of intentions, American resistance might have come earlier. On the other hand, it might not have come at all.

In part, the ineffectual nature of British policy reflected early Hanoverian phobias about arbitrary power, represented by the hypostatised threat of a Stuart restoration. This meant that successive Whig ministries under the first three Georges were often inhibited about using the power of the executive against Whig opposition. Roman Catholics, Jacobites, Nonjurors and their fellow travellers had often been subjected to persecution, sometimes sanguinary, and the Tory and Jacobite press had suffered legal harassment and judicial suppression. But successive ministries, by contrast, treated Whig and Dissenting opponents gingerly, fearful of the charges of 'Popery and arbitrary power' that they could level against the authorities. So, in the colonies from the early 1760s, imperial officials did almost nothing to prevent a quasi-treasonable opposition from organising itself. Colonial governors largely failed to muzzle seditious newspapers and pamphlets, take printers and authors into custody, prosecute inciters of disaffection or prevent the growth of organisations like the Stamp Act Congress which might be the bases for rebellion. Countermeasures like these had often been used in England under the first two Georges to smash the Jacobite underground, and had been used with success. A self-consciously libertarian regime in England had then ruthlessly defended itself against the threat of populist subversion by whatever means were necessary to achieve its ends. With the defeat of the Stuart menace in the 1740s, however, the Hanoverian regime dropped its guard. It is worth considering what the outcome would have been in colonial America had the vigilance of the imperial authorities been main-tained at its former level, and redirected against the activities of Dissenters and Whigs.

This was, of course, not done. The British army in America, which, after some delay, was adopted as a symbol by agitators to play on colonial memories of late-Stuart rule, was – even in the occupation of Boston in 1768–70 – almost never used in the role of controlling civil disobedience: officers were still inhibited by the legal dangers which surrounded such interventions in Eng-land.[87] Even when the ministry decided in the summer of 1768 to send British army units to Boston, the troops found on their arrival that the civilian authorities who alone could requisition the assistance of troops (the Massachusetts Council and justices of the peace) were opposed to their very presence. Up to the outbreak of the Revolution, there was no such legal requisition. British troops in Boston were subject to continual harassment in local courts staffed by hostile colonists:[88] this had not been foreseen, and Parliament had taken no steps to change the statutory context within which military power was exercised in America. Had it done so, and from an early date, a preventive military occupation of colonial capitals might have been feasible. In February 1769 Lord Hillsborough, Secretary of State for the Colonies, indeed urged on the Cabinet and the King firmer measures against Massachusetts Bay, including vesting nominations to the colony's Council in the crown, and envisaged a forfeiture of Massachusetts' charter. George III accepted that such measures might be a last resort, 'but till then ought to be avoided as the altering of Charters is at all times an odious measure'. That, of course, had been James II's fatal policy. Nor was there agreement in the House of Lords on altering the charter, as Governor Bernard of Massachusetts had requested.[89] Although it was rumoured that a Bill for charter reform was imminent in 1770–1, at the outset of North's ministry, no such Bill was introduced into Parliament.[90]

The novel presence of a 'standing army' in America after the peace of 1763 was later elevated into a major grievance; it is not obvious that it need have been. Far from being part of a metropolitan plot to extinguish American liberties, the stationing of regular troops in America was a natural response to the strategic problems created by the conquest of vast new territories during the Seven Years' War, the need to hold down conquered populations and make real the claim to sovereignty. The distribution of British troops reflected this: of fifteen battalions deployed, it was intended to station three in Nova Scotia, four in Canada and four in Florida. Only four remained for Britain's older possessions, and many even of these troops would be assigned to defend the frontier.[91] At the time, it was natural that few colonists protested. 'The decision to maintain a British army in postwar America was not, as such, a matter of controversy. The size and deployment of the force were largely determined by the essential functions it would be called upon to perform.'[92]

Occasional military commentators in earlier decades had suggested that the stationing of British troops would help to ensure the loyalty of Americans, but the evidence does not suggest that the Grenville ministry considered the prospect of resistance to their policy of raising a colonial revenue or the prospect of coercing the colonies. George Grenville's lack of foresight was shared by many colonists, however, including Benjamin Franklin. Even when metropolitan taxation began to be challenged in the colonies, the target of colonists was the principle of taxation as such, not the army as such.[93] Only later, in a more heightened emotional atmosphere, were the thinly scattered detachments of redcoats built up into a symbol of tyranny. There was nothing inevitable about this invention of a demonology, however, and an alternative scenario is plausible in which no such heightened imagery was employed.

In most areas of Britain's North American possessions, the minimal presence of the army remained non-controversial. The troops sent to America brought with them the assumptions about their role in society which had, by then, become ingrained in the army's mentality in England: they attempted to stay out of politics. The army did not interfere in colonial elections, and did not coerce colonial assemblies. Only with great reluctance did it take on a police role, preserving civil order. The flashpoints, the moments of friction with the civilian population, were few. It is reasonable to ask whether this state of affairs might have continued. Certainly, it made coercion extremely difficult. In the autumn of 1774, the commander-in-chief in North America, General Gage, warned correctly that the situation in New England already amounted to rebellion, that imperial authority could be reasserted only by military force, that his own resources of 3,000 troops were inadequate, and that a force of 20,000 was needed to re-establish control. This advice, unwelcome in London, was not acted on.[94] But what course might the conflict have taken if large numbers of troops had been committed to New England at an early stage?

Even after the outbreak of fighting, many different outcomes remained possible. The war was long and indecisive partly because of its character as a civil war, driven by powerful social constituencies unwilling to accept defeat, and partly because the conflict revealed the existence of little outstanding military talent on either side. Neither the British nor the republican colonists produced a single dominant general: no Marlborough, no Wellington fought decisive campaigns, and the war dragged on, ebbing first one way, then the other. Thomas Gage offered his home government good advice, but was unable to snuff out the revolution in Massachusetts. The three major-generals sent to reinforce him (John Burgoyne, Henry Clinton, William Howe) did little better. On the other hand, neither the colonial rebels nor the colonial loyalists produced any military geniuses. The characteristics revealed in battle were generally ones of stubborn determination and dogged endurance rather than swift and triumphant conquest. But from the British point of view the war was worth fighting even if the possibility of a sweeping reconquest of the colonies was remote: military force had good prospects of compelling a negotiated peace in which the constitutional points at issue would have been compromised, and some form of political tie retained. The forces of both sides recorded victories during the land campaigns in North America; it is easy to imagine scenarios in which even slightly more successful British commanders could have made an important difference.[95]

As it turned out, British military action was fatally divided between the alternative goals of a negotiated settlement based on the conciliation of fellow countrymen, and the decisive military defeat of an enemy at any cost to their lives and property.[96] It was similarly divided between a strategy of maintaining major bases on the American seaboard, seeking thereby to control American trade, and a strategy of attempting to conquer large tracts of territory inland, often in liaison with loyalist forces.[97] The failure of the British authorities to exploit this social constituency was an important feature of the conflict. As a result of lack of preparedness in previous decades, during the Revolution 'the potentially enormous military strength of Loyalism remained inert, almost untapped as a means to put down rebellion'.[98] In return, loyalists were the best-informed and most unsparing critics of British military commanders. Joseph Galloway posed the question:

> How then, since the British Commander had a force so much superior to his enemy, has it happened that the rebellion has not been long ago suppressed? The cause, my Lord, however inveloped in misrepresentation on this side of the Atlantic, is no secret in America.... Friends and foes unite in declaring that it has been owing to want of wisdom in the plans, and of vigour and exertion in the execution.[99]

Howe's failure to destroy Washington's army in Long Island and on the Delaware River in the autumn of 1776, when he seemed able to do so; Burgoyne's failure to lure the American forces into an ambush that would have reversed the outcome of the subsequent Battle of Saratoga; the escape of the American army from its British pursuers after the Battle of Cowpens; Washington's decision to strike south in late 1781 rather than adhere to his intended attack on New York, a decision which led to Yorktown: the military history of the Revolutionary War is thick with pivotal incidents which, decided otherwise, might have had major effects on the final result.

Manifest Destinies? The Denial of American Counterfactuals

The details of military conflict have a wider significance. Had the course of the war been different, it has been suggested, the shape of the America that emerged from the fighting might have been different also. Had British arms been more successful, and been overcome only by a more systematic American response, 'The consequence might have been a very different American public culture, one that stressed the national state more than the individual, obligations more than rights.'[100] Yet military conflict is as uncertain in prospect as the result seems triumphantly assured in retrospect. Contemporary American historians of the Revolution knew this, for they were close to and often confronted by the awkward fact that the outcomes of battles had hinged on minor events. They uneasily reflected, as did William Gordon: 'On incidents of this kind may depend the rise and fall of mighty kingdoms, and the far distant future transfer of power, glory, and riches, of arts and sciences, from Europe to America.'[101] Gordon's inconclusive discussion of such incidents, suggests a modern analyst, marks a point at which historians broke with their Puritan, predestinarian past by attempting to give some historical rigour to the force of contingency and to equip their new republic with a serious, professional account of its origins; but they emancipated themselves only in part. They

> destroyed the traditional concept of providence by blurring the line between providence and chance. They used the terms interchangeably and they used both descriptively to suggest only that the improbable, unexpected, inexplicable event had indeed occurred. In addition, they used both the language of providence and the language of chance not as modes of historical explanation but precisely to reserve judgement about causes when they were unknown. By destroying the distinction between providence and chance, the historians made clear that providence was no longer for them an adequate mode of historical explanation.

Providence survived only for 'ideological and aesthetic purposes'.[102] Not God but American manifest destiny became the final cause.

It might be suggested that the American Revolution thus achieved an important stage in the secularisation of historical explanations. Henceforth, trivial events (inexplicable contingencies) and grand counterfactuals (providential destinies) were no longer united within a providential order, and so were potentially at odds with each other. Yet this too may have been an unintended outcome, if Lester Cohen's account of early patriot historians of the Revolution is correct: 'by conflating providence and chance, by destroying the traditional use of providence as a mode of explanation, and by using chance independently of providence', those historians meant to achieve the same ends as Hume and Gibbon: 'to reinfuse history with a sense of contingency, and to present causation as a complex problem'.[103] They succeeded only, however, in giving America's history a new, though secular, purposiveness.

These historians 'wanted it both ways. On the one hand, they aimed to write impartial history, dedicated to truth and the service of humanity and pure in language and style; while on the other, they meant to develop a distinctively *American* history, intended to justify the Revolution and to inculcate the principles of republicanism in future generations of Americans.' Moreover, they 'saw no contradiction between their efforts to be objective and their insisting upon the principles and values of the Revolution',[104] a problem which, it might be suggested, has persisted in some quarters. The counterfactual was not to be entertained in the new American republic, any more than it had been in the Puritan phase of colonial history. Puritan theology, the revolutionaries' heritage, had regarded the future as unknown only to man: the future had, however, already been predetermined from the Creation by God, and man lacked the power to change it by acts of free will. By contrast, the new 'zealous rhetoric' of the revolutionaries manifested 'the sense of urgency, anxiety and challenge presented by an indeterminate future and by the feeling that people are responsible for the future's shape'.[105] They were to be free to shape it, but in only one way.

The Revolutionary historians, then, attempted to devise a more sophisticated, more professionally historical version of their nation's founding. They did so not least by qualifying Puritan predestinarianism with a new sense of the force of chance. But they were unable to proceed more than a part of the way towards this professionalism, because the logic of contingency had to be made subservient to a single, predetermined end, the rightness and inevitability of an independent United States. The alternative counterfactual, which pointed to another and equally feasible scenario for the development of a British North America, was implicitly excluded from the outset. So the real dynamic of history, the interplay between counterfactuals and contingencies, was never grasped. Instead, the Revolutionary historians used a residual notion of providence as a way of hinting at their purposive understanding of American destiny, and were led to use contingency only as a device to secularise providence rather than as a means of eliminating teleology. In this way were the broad outlines of the problem established at an early date.

The Marginalised, the Expropriated and the Oppressed

It was not only the white colonists whose futures were at stake, however. If a British America might have taken a more libertarian, less populist direction, it is worth considering the implications of such a polity for the two groups which were to be so massively disadvantaged in the new republic: Native Americans and African-American slaves.

Before the Seven Years' War, each colony had determined its own policy toward the Native Americans. These policies had enjoyed little success in alleviating the continual friction, sometimes flaring into savage conflict, which resulted as the settlers dispossessed the natives. Assimilation largely failed: Native Americans showed a marked unwillingness to accept enslavement or to surrender a nomadic for a settled way of life, and pastoral for arable farming. Settlers, especially when they were Calvinist predestinarians, showed little of the practical desire to convert the natives to Christianity that the Anglican discoverers of the new world in the early seventeenth century had promised. Britain had, however, a major rival on the North American continent. French relations with the Indians were far better: the Catholic drive to convert the natives implied far more respect than could be inferred from New England Puritanism; the French reliance on the fur trade similarly argued for a certain reciprocity, where English-speaking settlers aimed at settlement and expropriation.

It was the need to compete with France for the favour of

Indian tribes in wartime, especially the Seven Years' War, that induced the government in London to involve itself in Indian policy. So pressing was this need, as Anglo-French conflicts on the American frontier escalated into a major international conflict, that London was willing not only to regulate Anglo-Indian trade but to address the major problem: land. Three times during the war the metropolitan government signed treaties with Indians (Easton, 1758; Lancaster, 1760; Detroit, 1761) which committed the unwilling white colonists to respect the line of the Appalachian mountains as the limit of settlement: these treaties remained in force after the war was over, and Indian policy was quickly expressed in the royal proclamation of 7 October 1763. From Georgia to Quebec, the same principle now applied: land west of the Appalachians was reserved for Indians, and permission of the imperial government was required before purchase or settlement. Licences were made necessary for traders. *De facto* authority in this area rested with the British commander-in-chief in North America, working through two Indian superintendents. Clearly, the metropolitan authorities were establishing a structure intended to implement a comprehensive Indian policy. It was not proposed to halt westward expansion permanently but to regulate it, in the wake of controlled imperial purchases of Indian territory.

A major Indian rebellion in 1763, Pontiac's uprising, and the haphazard colonial response to it, made metropolitan control of Indian policy more essential, as the imperial government saw it, and a standing army more necessary to police the frontier. It was the cost of these forces that gave additional urgency to metropolitan attempts to raise revenue from the colonists. Whatever the difficulties this caused, the final objective – to free both colonists and Indians from the threat of periodic massacre – was intelligible enough. A British army would have been needed in North America anyway, to secure the older British colonies against the strategic threat posed by newly acquired Canada and Florida, and this in itself would have required a colonial revenue: for the imperial government to have ignored the Indian problem would not have solved the constitutional problems raised by imperial taxation.[106] But a British America might have been one in which the westward migration of peoples was regulated and humanised, freed in part from the stains of massacre and exploitation which were later to characterise it.

Black slaves might equally have enjoyed a radically different lot in a continuing British America. White colonists interpreted as treachery the decision of the Governor of Virginia, Lord Dunmore, in November 1775, to offer emancipation to slaves who rallied to the British cause,[107] but aside from pressing military needs this episode may also have reflected the faster and further evolution in Britain of opinion on the question of chattel slavery. Similarly, where many groups in the colonies remained rabidly anti-Catholic in a way which recalled seventeenth-century traumas, British opinion was already moving towards a lifting of Catholic disabilities. In 1772 Lord Mansfield's judgement in *Somersett's case* established that the common law at once dissolved the bonds of slavery for blacks on English soil: with a British America loudly claiming the rights of Englishmen, it would only have been a matter of time before the same principle was communicated to the colonies. How long would it have taken? Within the empire, a supreme political authority in the metropolis, combined with the power of the Royal Navy, was able to end the slave trade following legislation of 1806–11 and proceed to the emancipation of slaves in British possessions overseas after legislation of 1833; in America, political realities compelled the deletion of Jefferson's condemnation of slavery in his initial draft of the Declaration of Independence. Black colonists who fought for the crown during the Revolutionary War (as many did) fought with some reason.[108] Historians have debated whether the American war of the 1860s was essentially about slavery, or essentially about the rights of the subordinate legislatures to resist Sir William Blackstone's doctrine of the indivisibility and absoluteness of sovereignty by secession. In either case, the events of the 1860s can be analysed as the second American Civil War, a reversion to the problems left unresolved in the first. Had the events of the 1770s developed differently, therefore, it is possible that avenues of negotiation and compromise would have developed which might have skirted the second great catastrophe to afflict the North American continent.

The Long Shadow of the Transatlantic Counterfactual

Not only the British and their former colonists but continental European observers also entertained counterfactual reflections on the Revolution's result. The French political economist Turgot, in a memorandum written in April 1776, expected an independent America to emerge from the conflict; but, should the outcome of the war be the opposite, the scale of British military resources committed to the colonies would inevitably lead to a British conquest of the whole continent from Newfoundland to Panama, expelling the French from Louisiana and the Spaniards from Mexico.[109] A transatlantic world of peace and trade would have promoted the economic development and population growth of Britain's American colonies: without the war of 1776–83, which devastated the colonial economy and delayed its development by decades, the wealth and power of a libertarian North Atlantic polity might have promoted meliorist reform in France rather than *philosophe*-inspired revolution. The point is so obvious that it rarely needs to be stressed: had the American Revolution not taken the form it did in 1776–83, it is highly unlikely that the French state would have staggered vainly beneath a fatal fiscal burden, and collapsed in ruin in 1788–9.

Such a counterfactual is so large, and so far removed from the actual outcome, that it loses touch with historical enquiry. Analysts of the counterfactual must beware of that easy escape which is offered by the argument that, but for some initial mistake, some tragic error, all would have been well, and mankind released from avoidable conflicts into a golden age of peaceful progress. From the perspective of 1914 or 1939, British observers might easily look back regretfully on the great opportunity missed, the opportunity to create a peaceful and prosperous North Atlantic Anglophone polity, united in its commitment to libertarian and commercial values. The Whig–Liberal tradition of English histo-riography could make such a course seem plausible by ascribing the American Revolution to easily avoidable errors of British policy, especially the personal failings of George III. This expla-nation has become increasingly unlikely, however. Even if conflict had been avoided in the 1770s, as it well might, this would not have guaranteed future tranquillity *sine die.*

Slavery might, after all, have shattered the peace of this resplendent empire in the 1830s or 1840s, as it tore apart the new American republic shortly afterwards. For if the Stamp Act in the 1760s produced a near-unanimous outcry from American colonies incensed by even so modest an infringement (as they saw it) of their property rights, how much more violent would have been American resistance to a British attempt to emancipate America's slaves? Such a metropolitan intervention in the affairs of the colonies, had it come, as it did for Britain's other colonies, in 1834, might have united American colonists with far greater vehemence around an economic institution of vastly greater significance than tea. As it was, the conflict over slavery in the 1860s was one from which Britain was able to stand aside; the result was a victory for the northern states, and emancipation. Had the conflict been fought within a transatlantic polity, American victory might have had the effect of entrenching that peculiar practice even more deeply in the life of the nation.

The world of the actual draws a veil over happier possibilities as well as over the darker ones, and our need to reconcile ourselves with the world in which we live forbids us to raise that veil. Yet an alternative methodology might explain many momentous episodes in British history as improbable and unforeseen events which some men found ways of portraying, in retrospect, as inevitable: 1660, 1688 and 1776 fall into that category. Equally, attempted actions which had a considerable chance of success are explained away by the hegemonic ideology, diminished in retro-spect to the level of wild gambles, like the French invasion attempt of 1744 or the potentially French-backed Irish rebellion of 1797–8. In both cases, a plan made a domestic rising contingent on foreign military intervention that never materialised; but had the pieces fallen into place, as they did in 1660, 1688 and 1776, the historical landscape could have been transformed.

Implicit counterfactuals underpin all historical reconstructions of grand events, and only strongly purposeful ideologies condemn the open appraisal of alternatives as disreputable, inspired by impractical nostalgia. Yet the theoretical structure of nostalgia may be little more than an awareness of options not taken and potentialities never realised. Nostalgia has an emotional content too, sometimes securely grounded in the minutiae of past life, sometimes uncritically reliant on national or sectional myths. But whatever its emotional content, whether well- or ill-judged, the methodological significance of nostalgia suggests that popular understandings of history tend to be non-teleological.[110] It is with good reason, as Raphael Samuel reminds us, that the *bienpensant* instinctively reacts against popular attitudes to the past and seeks to denigrate them: however much popular nostalgia reflects an authentic empirical contact with the conditions of existence of past time, its unteleological structure robustly contradicts the thin-lipped commitments of the modern age.

Mankind has generally given little attention to counterfactuals. It is, of course, unprofitable to regret the might-have-been, whatever the logical status of such a stance:

> *Some natural tears they dropped, but wiped them soon;*
> *The world was all before them, where to choose*
> *Their place of rest, and providence their guide:*
> *They hand in hand with wandering steps and slow,*
> *Through Eden took their solitary way.*

Part of the reason for this mental block is psychological: a major decision once taken, a major counterfactual once actualised, has to be rationalised in retrospect as inevitable, as rational in the circumstances. Values are then adapted to outcomes to praise the new situation. A larger reason may, however, be methodological. W. B. Gallie offered one such account (perhaps over-complacent)

of how disruptive contingencies were absorbed and accommodated in historical explanations, an account which implied that
even an 'unparalleled, hope-shattering disaster' in the realm of
contingency did not entail the enforced choice of an alternative
counterfactual.[111]

Yet, examined more closely, the contingent and the counterfactual are only congruent at the outset of any historical enquiry.
Soon, they begin to pull in different directions. The counterfactual
assumes clearly identifiable alternative paths of development,
whose distinctness and coherence can be relied on as the historian
projects them into an unrealised future. An emphasis on contingency, by contrast, not only contends that the way in which
events unfold followed no such path, whether identified by the
merits of a case, by the good arguments or inner logic of principles
or institutions; it also entails that all counterfactual alternatives
would themselves have quickly branched out into an infinite
number of possibilities.[112] Mankind cannot greatly lament the path
not taken if that counterfactual is quickly lost, itself dividing into
a myriad of options determined by the kaleidoscope of contingency. These difficulties ought to be reasons for placing them in
the foreground of our enquiries; in fact, the need for consolation
overrides the desire for explanation. Historians impressed by the
force of contingency and their colleagues who stress counterfactuals can, after all, equally contend that, if Eve had not offered
Adam the apple, something else might have gone wrong anyway.

THREE

BRITISH IRELAND:

What if Home Rule had been enacted in 1912?

Alvin Jackson

In short, dear English reader, the Irish Protestant stands outside that English Mutual Admiration Society which you call the Union or the Empire. You may buy a common and not ineffective variety of Irish Protestant by delegating your powers to him, and in effect making him the oppressor and you his sorely bullied and bothered catspaw and military maintainer; but if you offer him nothing for his loyalty except the natural superiority of the English character, you will – well, try the experiment, and see what will happen!

GEORGE BERNARD SHAW, *John Bull's Other Island*

Home Rule was marketed by Gladstone as a patent cure for all the troubles of the Anglo-Irish relationship; and, since 1914, when the last of the three great Gladstonian measures of devolution was shelved, Home Rule has teased the consciences and (in some cases) the pride of British liberals. Home Rule, essentially a grant of limited self-government, was defined as a means of simultaneously satisfying Irish national aspirations, of binding Ireland to the empire, of correcting the sins of English conquest, and of ridding the congested imperial Parliament of its heroic but often prolix Irish members: as Winston Churchill remarked in the Commons in 1912, 'we think that the Irish have too much power in this country and not enough in their own'.[1] Moreover, Home Rule provided Gladstone (whose devolutionist convictions had been made public in December 1885) with a last great mission, and with a policy which (as with so many initiatives devised by this most intellectually subtle of politicians) served many purposes, both personal and political: Home Rule seemed to cast the complexities of late Victorian Liberalism inside a simple legislative format; Home Rule offered the chance of aligning a highly disparate party behind the leadership of its Grand Old Man.

The defeat of the two great measures of 1886 and 1893 robbed Gladstone of a Wagnerian climax to his political life, and left his followers confused and disoriented. The relegation of the third Home Rule measure in 1914 similarly robbed constitutional Nationalists of a crowning triumph, and appeared to create a political space for militant republicanism in the shape of the 1916 rebels and – after 1919 – the volunteers of the Irish Republican Army. Little wonder, then, that in the aftermath of the 1916 Rising, of the bloody Anglo-Irish war (of 1919–21) and of more or less sustained violence in Northern Ireland (especially between 1969 and 1994) the liberal conscience has turned to ponder the great counterfactual problem of modern Irish history: whether a successful Home Rule measure might have created a tranquil and unitary Irish state, and whether such a measure might have brought the simplification and betterment of Anglo-Irish relations. But such speculations are not merely the preserve of tortured Gladstonians: latter-day Tories, weighed by the burden of Northern Ireland, and embarrassed by the ferocious Unionism of their forebears in 1886, 1893 and 1912–14, turn apprehensively to the Liberal polemicists of this era, and to their arcadian vision of Ireland under Home Rule. This essay is a further contribution to the undead history of the Home Rule agitation.

The History of an Idea

At the end of the nineteenth century, when the Home Rule agitation came to prominence, Ireland was a constitutional anomaly.[2] The formal basis for the government of Ireland was the Act of Union (1800), a measure which abolished the medieval and semi-independent Irish Parliament and created a United Kingdom Parliament, with substantial Irish representation, at Westminster. But if (as Unionists came to allege) Home Rule was a constitutional halfway house, then this accusation might equally have been applied to the Act of Union – for the Union of Great Britain and Ireland effected in 1800 was as incomplete as the grants of legislative autonomy proposed by Gladstone in 1886 and by Asquith in 1912. Many vestiges of the pre-Union administration remained, and throughout the nineteenth century Ireland, though formally an integral element of the United Kingdom, was in practice quite distinct. Moreover, if the institutions of government were, in British terms, distinctive, then the mentality of the governing class, centred in Dublin Castle, was equally quixotic and colonial. Ireland was represented only at Westminster, and was governed (in theory) from London: but there was a lord lieutenant, or viceroy, in Dublin, appointed by the crown, and the vestiges of a distinct executive. Ireland had a separate Privy Council and a largely separate judiciary, headed by a lord chancellor and a lord chief justice; there were separate law officers, and even – after 1899 – something akin to a separate Irish minister for agriculture (the vice-president of the Department of Agriculture and Technical Instruction). At the heart of this administrative miasma was a concentration of senior civil servants, often Englishmen, generally decent if narrow officials, who brought a peculiarly provocative mixture of condescension and self-confidence to their postings. Irish government was thus an overlay of ancient, semi-autonomous institutions, the relics of its status as a separate kingdom, combined with the new institutions of Union: the whole composition was shaded by a vibrant imperialism.

The paradox of Irish government in the nineteenth century was that, though there was an elaborate array of institutions, and though ministers and officials were comparatively benign, and though – certainly at the end of the century – local officials and policemen were generally Irish Catholics, this administrative panoply was deeply unpopular. The Union, imperfect in terms of the institutions of government, proved to be an equally imperfect focus for popular political affections. The reasons for this may only briefly be summarised. First, the Union was driven on to the statute books in the aftermath of a bloody government victory in 1798 over republican rebels; it was designed in the first instance to serve the needs of British security, and to protect the existing propertied interest in Ireland. Though a long-standing political interest of its architect, William Pitt, the Union was made possible by British military supremacy.[3] Second, it was Pitt's original intention to combine the measure with a grant of complete civil equality for Catholics, but this politically essential sweetener was later dropped. The Catholic hierarchy, who had tentatively supported the Union proposal, given the likely prospect of concessions, felt themselves to be the victims of British perfidy: and the Catholic community generally, who might have been associated with the Union experiment from its inception, were instead largely excluded. The consequences of this alienation were far-reaching. From the late eighteenth century on, Catholic political and economic confidence was growing, bolstered by an upturn in the Irish economy, by some liberal Protestant endorsement, and by limited legislative concessions from the government (such as the re-enfranchisement of Catholic forty-shilling freeholders in 1793). Related to this general economic expansion was the rapid growth of the Irish population, and in particular the very rapid growth of the Catholic labouring class. This process of consolidation continued into the nineteenth century, and involved political victories such as Catholic 'emancipation' in 1829 (the achievement of more or less complete civil equality) and the disestablishment of the Anglican state church, the Church of Ireland, in 1869: indeed most of these victories were won at the expense of the old ascendancy interest, and in the teeth of its opposition. Even with this cursory survey, the weakness of the Union will be at once apparent: despite the intentions of Pitt, the measure effectively served British and ascendancy interests; and the emergent regime practically excluded the community which was simultaneously the most populous and the most dynamic and the most assertive.

This exclusion served to bolster the national sympathies of

Irish Catholics.[4] In no sense was the creation of a strident Catholic nationalism preordained, however. Although, with the benefit of hindsight, many nationalist writers saw continuities between Catholic Confederate protest in the 1640s, the Jacobite cause in the 1680s, the United Irish cause in the 1790s, and the varieties of nationalist protest in the nineteenth century, the reality of Catholic politics was considerably more complex than any vision of a national pageant.[5] If, as Elie Kedourie has famously argued, imperialism begets nationalism, then the circumstances of British rule in Ireland to some extent propagated a formidable coalition of national forces.[6] This need not have produced a popular republicanism (Irish republicanism almost certainly achieved a majority following only at the time of the War of Independence): many popular Irish politicians, from Daniel O'Connell, the masterbuilder of emancipation, through to John Redmond, the last leader of the Irish Parliamentary party, combined a desire for Irish self-government with loyalty to the British crown, or a commitment to Irish participation in the empire. But the failure of successive British governments to accommodate this distinctive (and otherwise highly successful) tradition of Irish patriotism-cum-loyalty lent credence to the demands of a more militant and thoroughgoing nationalist lobby. A vestigial British connection with Irish government was certainly possible from the point of view of these constitutional nationalists: that this connection failed was as much because of British policy in Ireland and indeed historical chance as the inexorable rise of a separatist republicanism.

Catholics were admitted to parliament and to most forms of government office in 1829; but while the Emancipation Act opened the door to Catholic advancement, it could not compel admission. Though there were some Smilesian success stories (Lord O'Hagan was the first Catholic Lord Chancellor of Ireland in modern times (1868–74), Lord Russell of Killowen was the first Catholic Lord Chief Justice of England (1894–1900)), on the whole there was a glass ceiling beyond which Catholics did not progress in the ranks of officialdom or in certain aspects of professional life. Though there was a vocal Irish Catholic representation at Westminster from an early stage, this was of course a minority interest, and possessed only an intermittent influence. The Union, therefore, served as a highly inadequate vehicle for Catholic social and political ambition.

The Catholic response to the inadequacies of the Union came increasingly in the form of calls for its modification or abandonment. O'Connell sought to raise an agitation demanding repeal of the Union, especially after 1840, when he created the Loyal National Repeal Association.[7] He garnered considerable popular Catholic support, but won few converts among the ranks of either northern Protestants or the British political elite. Though his emphasis was negative – upon repeal, rather than upon the type of government which might replace the Union – O'Connell may be regarded as an essential precursor of the Home Rule movement. He educated a large section of the Catholic poor (who were largely untouched by government, whatever its form) in the need for legislative independence; and he created a distinctive mixture of parliamentary pressure and popular protest which later Home Rulers would successfully mimic.

However, a specific call for 'Home Rule' was raised only after 1870, when a Protestant lawyer, Isaac Butt, created the Home Government Association from an unlikely mixture of disgruntled Tories and Catholic Liberals: when Butt's Home Rule party contested the general election of 1874, it captured the electoral base of the Irish Liberals, and emerged as the single largest Irish body at Westminster. The reasons for this dramatic electoral upset have preoccupied numerous Irish historians: popular sympathy with the fate of three revolutionary nationalists ('the Manchester Martyrs'), executed – many thought unjustly – for the murder of a police sergeant in 1867, developed into a national agitation which the Home Rulers were able to exploit; while the popular Catholic hopes invested in the government of W. E. Gladstone withered into disappointment after a timid Land Act (1870) and an abortive proposal for university reform (1873).[8] In addition Gladstone's assault on the Papacy in his pamphlet, *The Vatican Decrees*, alienated many of his Irish Catholic admirers. Home Rule therefore exploited popular Catholic exasperation at the apparent inadequacy of the British judicial system, as well as the failings of their most likely British sympathisers. Home Rule built upon popular sympathy with the thwarted revolutionary nationalists (as distinct from support for revolutionary nationalism, which remained a minority enthusiasm); it built upon the recognition (shared initially by Liberals and some Tories) that the opportunities for Irish gain from the British party system were highly limited.

Home Rule was also eventually fuelled by intense agrarian unrest. The movement had been launched in the early 1870s, against a background of relative agrarian prosperity; and to some extent this had determined both the character of the Home Rule party and the nature of its programme. Home Rule MPs were, initially, often landed ex-Liberals, and they pursued their constitutional cause in a genteel and gradualist manner. However, the advent of a new and authoritarian parliamentary leader in 1879–80, Charles Stewart Parnell, brought a more populist direction to the management of the party: Parnell harnessed the unrest which had been generated by the economic downturn of 1878–9, and – though himself a Protestant landlord – yoked together the Home Rule movement and the distress of the farming interest.[9] Parnell, in other words, had re-created the potent combination of forces which had driven the repeal movement in the early 1840s: popular agitation and a rigorous, urgent, vociferous parliamentary presence. The agrarian crisis was defused by good harvests and by a generous Land Act (passed by Gladstone in 1881), but the identification of the farmers with the Home Rule cause remained. By the mid-1880s, Parnell stood at the head both of a disciplined parliamentary party (numbering eighty-five members in November 1885), and a coherent local organisation, endorsed by the twin pillars of local Catholic society: the substantial farmers and the clergy.

Between 1870 and 1885 Butt and Parnell had resuscitated the popular campaign for the repeal of the Union which O'Connell had launched forty years earlier. But, if the battle for the hearts and minds of Catholic Ireland had been replayed and won, the Home Rulers still confronted the twin obstacles which had helped to break the earlier movement for repeal: the opposition of the British parties, and the more trenchant hostility of northern Protestants. The two areas of opposition were interrelated, a point which deserves some emphasis: it would have been virtually impossible for one of the main British political parties to oppose Home Rule effectively given the acquiescence – however sullen – of Ulster Protestants. The Home Rule movement never successfully either wooed or subjugated their northern opponents, and the Protestant attitude, which would prove crucial to the fate of the Home Rule movement, will presently receive some detailed consideration. If there is a danger in oversimplifying the politics of Irish Catholicism, or of supplying an over-determined analysis, then these pitfalls are also present in the interpretation of Irish Protestant politics in the nineteenth century. Irish Protestants were not automatically Unionist, any more than Irish Catholics were natural separatists. In the eighteenth century Irish Protestants had urged the case for legislative autonomy in the context of a prevailing connection with Britain and within a Protestant-dominated constitution; northern Presbyterians, though politically divided, had supplied enthusiastic recruits to the rebel armies of the 1798 rising. Economic prosperity under the Union, combined with the growth of a strong regional identity in Ulster and the spread of 'Britishness' – British royal and imperial imagery and attitudes – helped to suppress these earlier political attitudes: in addition, indeed crucially, the rise of a self-confident and popular Catholic nationalism appeared to create a variety of political and cultural challenges which Irish Protestants believed might only be overcome within the context of the Union. But to try to explain the evolution of late-nineteenth-century Protestant Unionism from late-eighteenth-century Protestant patriotism is perhaps to miss the point: many of the Irish patriotic notions of the eighteenth century continued to live on within the (apparently) coherent British Unionism of the Home Rule era. Indeed, the central paradox of Irish Unionism was that it was born as much out of a distrust of the British willingness to protect Irish Protestant interests as out of fear of Home Rule.[10] Fear of Catholic ascendancy and fear of economic victimisation appear to have played greater roles in sustaining Ulster Unionism than any abstract notion of national identity: certainly these were the emphases of Irish Unionist propaganda.

The opposition of Ulster Unionism will be reviewed in greater detail, and their political options in 1912–14 explored below. Neither O'Connell nor Parnell effectively addressed the problem of Ulster Unionism, and indeed both had only a passing acquaintance with northern politics: it was only at the end of his life, in 1891, that Parnell appears to have devoted serious consideration to the challenge proffered by northern Protestants.[11] However, Parnell's great advance over the achievement of O'Connell came with the breaking of the log-jam of British party politics: O'Connell had faced united British opposition to repeal, where Parnell's command of Irish popular opinion and of a strong parliamentary force helped to win Gladstone to the Home Rule cause. Gladstone's motives have been exhaustively researched: he certainly exaggerated Parnell's political genius and saw Parnellite Home Rule as a means – perhaps the only means – of sustaining a connection between Ireland and Britain.[12] He was also clearly convinced (through typically copious reading) of the historical case for the restitution of ancient wrongs, and for the re-establishment of the Irish Parliament.[13] There may, in addition, have been narrower party and leadership considerations: Home Rule may have been a means of consolidating his failing hold over a highly fissile Liberal movement.[14] Certainly Home Rule was a characteristically Gladstonian 'great issue' – an apparently simple political cry, highly charged with morality, and equally spiked with difficulty for his internal party challengers. Gladstone's political conversion was leaked to the press in December 1885, and in early 1886 he began to work quietly on the details of a Home Rule Bill (advised, it would seem, not by ministerial colleagues, but principally by two senior civil servants): he introduced the completed measure into the House of Commons in the spring of 1886.[15]

This initiative failed (the Bill was defeated on its second reading in the House of Commons in June 1886): but Gladstone's actions helped to determine the shape and some of the preoccupations of British parliamentary politics until 1921. His surprise endorsement of Home Rule precipitated the resignation of some Whig and radical ministerial colleagues: it also provoked an almost immediate hardening of the Tories' Unionist convictions. The short-term fall-out from Home Rule was therefore, paradoxically, Unionist in tendency, for the two great parties of the British state were more than ever bound to Irish subsidiary parties (this would have been to Gladstone's liking): the Liberals and Irish Parliamentary party forged an informal but lasting 'union of hearts', while the Tories pledged themselves with ever greater conviction to the Irish Unionists. But the party shake-down also brought the disruption of old political allegiances and friendships: the overall effect was akin to the aftermath of a civil war, where the combatants, traumatised by unfamiliar and brutal conflict, clung tenaciously to their new rallying call. Remarkably few of the dissident Liberal ministers retraced their steps across no man's land to the Gladstonian party (George Trevelyan was one): remarkably few Tories (even those who had flirted with the possibility of Parnellite support) showed anything other than a trenchant Unionism. Although a second Home Rule Bill was defeated in 1893, and although other issues achieved a momentary pre-eminence, Home Rule remained a touchstone of British party allegiance until the First World War and beyond. Gladstone retired in 1894, and died in 1898: but his imprint lingered upon the Liberal party. A new generation of Liberals remained unenthusiastically loyal to the legacy of Home Rule, and won elections in 1906, and twice in 1910, with the devolutionist commitment present, but buried, in their manifesto. The closely fought contest in December 1910 brought a renewed dependence upon Irish Nationalist votes: and the Liberal Prime Minister, H. H. Asquith, though he may have lacked the righteous convictions of the Grand

Old Man, did not lack his sense of party advantage – for a third Home Rule Bill, constructed along Gladstonian lines, was launched in the House of Commons in April 1912.

The Prospects for a Settlement

The third Home Rule Bill serves as a focus for the counterfactual arguments put forward in the remaining sections of this chapter. Some explanation for this choice (as opposed to the original Gladstonian measures of 1886 and 1893) may be appropriate, before the details of the Bill are outlined. Two suggestions, or premises, are offered: first, that the 1912 Bill, suitably presented, had a greater chance of success than its predecessors, and is therefore an intellectually more valuable focus for counterfactual speculation; and, second, that the range of counterfactual possibilities in the years before the First World War is greater and more intriguing than in either 1886 or 1893.

In 1912 and after, many Liberals looked back to the first Home Rule Bill, and speculated mournfully about the advantages which its successful passage would have brought.[16] In fact such speculation owed more to the intrinsic difficulties of Home Rule as an issue, and more to the problems (and increasing expense) caused by the government of Ireland in the intervening years, than to the rosy outlook for Home Rule in 1886. The first Home Rule Bill was decisively defeated in the House of Commons by a coalition of Conservatives and dissident Liberals. There is no doubt that, even had the divisions within Liberalism been settled (a highly unlikely prospect), the Bill would have fallen in the House of Lords. There was therefore an overwhelming parliamentary majority for the Unionist case. In addition, when, in July 1886, an election was held on the Home Rule issue, though Irish voters confirmed their support for the Parnellite party, British voters endorsed the Union. There remains the intriguing possibility that Home Rule might have been carried, had the Conservative party embraced the policy with tacit Liberal approval. This, though an apparently unlikely scenario, was in fact not quite as fantastic as appearances might suggest. In 1885, during the brief lifetime of the first Salisbury government, senior Conservative ministers (Lord Randolph Churchill, Lord Carnarvon) had flirted with the idea of some form of accommodation with Parnell: Parnell, famously, advised Irish voters in Britain to support Conservative candidates at the general election held in November–December 1885.[17] But the Tory enthusiasm for Home Rule and for Parnell was to prove more apparent than real. When, in December 1885, Gladstone held out the possibility of Liberal support for a Conservative measure of Home Rule, the offer was unhesitatingly rejected. Moreover, though some Tory ministers had toyed with the idea of cultivating Parnellite support in order to bolster a minority administration, Irish loyalists were simultaneously placated through honours and appointments. Lord Salisbury and his ministers appear to have been keeping their options open, in shoring up their minority regime.[18]

On the other hand, it has been persuasively argued that, had the second Home Rule Bill passed in 1893, 'a real possibility would have existed of a peaceful settlement of this issue'.[19] Ulster Unionists had not yet developed a paramilitary structure (as they were to do between 1910 and 1914, and especially in 1913–14); and even the rhetorical threat of armed resistance was still highly qualified, being contingent upon any coercion from Dublin of passive loyalist resistance. For their part, Irish Nationalists would probably have been so constrained by the financial terms of the Home Rule Bill that they would have had little choice other than to conciliate their Ulster Unionist opponents (eastern Ulster was the industrial power-house of the island). However, if the outlook in Ireland was as favourable in 1893 as it was ever likely to be in the Home Rule era, then the parliamentary and high-political prognosis remained distinctly bleak. It is true that Home Rule passed through the House of Commons, but it was sustained by only a small and unenthusiastic majority: on 9 September 1893 it was rejected (amid laughter) by 419 votes to 41 in the House of Lords. It is also true that an angry Gladstone proposed a dissolution of Parliament to his colleagues, and suggested an appeal to the electorate on the issue of the Lords' highhandedness. But Gladstone and his protégé John Morley were among the few Home Rule enthusiasts in the Liberal Cabinet; and their colleagues refused to sanction such a strategy. Moreover, not only was Gladstone an isolated zealot, he was also in his eighty-fourth year at the time of the second Home Rule Bill, and already experiencing 'a marked physical decline'.[20] It is also debatable whether, even allowing for the demands of a popular campaign on Gladstone's health, the Liberals would have won such a contest. Home Rule would have been presented to the British electorate by a doubtful combination of half-hearted Liberals and divided Nationalists.

There remains the last of the Gladstonian measures, the third Home Rule Bill of 1912. It is easy to see the prospects of this measure as being as bleak as those of its predecessors, but such a judgement (while giving a proper weight to the vehemence of Ulster Unionist opposition) may well involve interpreting 1912 in the light of the looming violence of mid-1914. By August 1914, on the eve of the Great War, Ulster Unionists had created a massive, armed paramilitary association, the Ulster Volunteer Force; they had also gone a considerable way to creating a provisional government for the North. They had, in addition, apparently tenacious support from their British Conservative allies. At no time was the chance of securing a peaceful and mutually satisfactory settlement so slight. The traditional judgement that Ireland was spared a civil war only by the German invasion of Belgium seems hard to fault.

And yet the outlook for Home Rule in 1912, though by no means uncomplicated, could not have been more different. While allowing due weight to the Ulster Unionist difficulty, the (by no means sanguine) Liberal civil servant Lord Welby deemed the prospects of Home Rule in early 1912 to be 'fairly favourable'.[21] Within the House of Commons the Liberals, the Irish party and Labour were united in their support; the House of Lords, the assassin of Home Rule in 1893, was now virtually disarmed, having lost its legislative veto through the Parliament Act of 1911. Outside Parliament there was still a Unionist majority in England, but this was offset by Home Rule sympathy in Scotland, Wales and of course Ireland. Moreover, English Unionism, in Welby's opinion, 'does not show any sign of vigorous or violent opposition as in 1886'.[22] The soundness of this judgement was in fact confirmed by the experience of British and Irish Unionist electioneers, who repeatedly encountered a more lively popular interest in land and social welfare issues than in the familiar plight of Irish loyalty. Otherwise sympathetic English Unionists were, by 1912, experiencing the Edwardian equivalent of donor fatigue: their concern for the likely fate of Irish Unionists under Home Rule was by now exhausted.

In defining the prospects of Home Rule in 1912, it is also important to gauge accurately the extent of Ulster Unionist resistance. It would be wrong to underplay the militancy of Ulster Unionism – even as early as 1912. In November 1910 a leading Ulster Unionist hawk, F. H. Crawford, wrote – apparently with the knowledge of other senior Unionists – to five munitions manufacturers, inviting quotations for 20,000 rifles and one million rounds of ammunition; the men of the ultra-loyalist Orange Order were beginning to learn simple drill movements by December 1910.[23] In April 1911 Colonel Robert Wallace, a veteran of the Boer War, and a leading Belfast Orangeman, confided that he had been 'trying to get my Districts in Belfast to take up a few simple movements – learning to form fours and reform two deep, and simple matters like that'.[24] But it was swiftly decided to postpone any large-scale purchase of weapons; and, though paramilitary drilling developed on a haphazard basis in 1911 and 1912, this was not centrally regulated until the creation of the Ulster Volunteer Force in January 1913. Thus, when the third Home Rule Bill was launched, in April 1912, Ulster Unionists had certainly demonstrated the seriousness of their concern; but they were as yet largely unarmed, and their military training (though already supervised by several distinguished veteran officers) was still relatively uncoordinated. There was certainly nothing like the fever-pitch of excitement and belligerence among the Unionist public which was reached in the summer of 1914.

Nor were the leaders either of British or Irish Unionism beyond the power of peaceful persuasion in 1912. The popular historical vision of Bonar Law, the British Unionist leader, and of Carson in these years depends largely on several histrionic displays of militancy (such as Bonar Law's angry endorsement of Ulster Unionist extremism at Blenheim Palace on 29 July 1912).[25] It would indeed be wrong to discount this anger: numerous public speeches from both men testify to its potency, as indeed do occasional private utterances (such as Carson's blunt declaration in a letter to James Craig written in July 1911 that he was 'not for a mere game of bluff, and unless men are prepared to make great sacrifices which they clearly understand, the talk of resistance is no use').[26] But such declarations, read out of context, do little to aid an appreciation of the complex political role which each of these senior Unionist statesmen occupied in the era of the third Home Rule Bill. Each was certainly angered by the successful alteration of the constitution achieved by the Liberals through the Parliament Act. Each was also fearful – rightly, as it transpired – that the new Home Rule proposal would contain as few concessions to northern Unionism as had its predecessors. But each was considerably more emollient and flexible in private than his public belligerence would lead one to expect.

Bonar Law had family connections in Protestant Ulster, and was highly sympathetic to the aspirations of this community. Yet it appears that in 1910, during the inter-party conference held to address the constitutional issues arising from the People's Budget, Bonar Law (along with F. E. Smith and other Tories) favoured a compromise involving concessions on the Home Rule question.[27] In 1911, when the Tory party divided into hardliners ('ditchers') and moderates ('hedgers') over the controversial Liberal Parliament Bill, Bonar Law was again in favour of the more conciliatory stance.[28] He was an ardent tariff reformer – tariff reform and Ulster were, he claimed, the two driving forces behind his political career – but he contrived to remain acceptable to both extreme tariff reformers ('confederates') and other, less zealous Unionists: in January 1913 he was persuaded to accept the relegation of the tariff question in the face of internal Tory opposition.[29] Equally, while his aggressive Unionism may have been partly a result of what Thomas Jones called 'primitive passion', there was also a more considered dimension.[30]

It has been argued persuasively that Bonar Law's particularly virulent defence of Unionism was a conscious and reasoned strategy designed to consolidate his own party leadership, and to extort a dissolution and general election from the Liberal government.[31] There is much to be said for this case, and indeed for the subsidiary argument which emphasises Bonar Law's hesitation when the stakes in the parliamentary game of brinkmanship were raised. In the context of mounting tension in Ulster (indeed Ireland as a whole) between October and December 1913, Bonar Law met the Liberal Prime Minister, Asquith, on three occasions in a discreet effort to establish the grounds for a peaceful settlement of the crisis. After the second of these meetings, on 6 November, it seemed probable that a deal would be struck on the basis of the exclusion from Home Rule of either four or six Ulster counties for a number of years; with the expiry of this period a plebiscite would be held within the excluded area to determine its future constitutional status. Bonar Law in fact appears to have misinterpreted Asquith's intentions (the guileful Prime Minister seems to have been less interested in a definite proposal than in assessing the minimum terms which the Opposition would accept). Nevertheless, Bonar Law's comment on this meeting is revealing: if the deal were accepted he saw that 'our best card for the election will have been lost'.[32] On the other hand, if a firm proposal were made 'I don't see how we could possibly take the responsibility for refusing'. Bonar Law, while alert to party advantage, had evidently some more statesmanlike instincts: indeed, party advantage and highmindedness coincided, for the Tories could not refuse a settlement which the English electorate might interpret as reasonable. Later actions – his refusal in 1914 to follow through extreme parliamentary strategies (such as amending the Army Bill to prevent the military coercion of

Ulster) – tend to confirm the presence of a more circumspect and amenable personality behind the prophet of apocalypse.[33]

A similar interpretation might be applied to Carson. At public meetings, at Craigavon, the grim Victorian home of his lieutenant, James Craig, and at the Balmoral showgrounds, a favoured venue for militant display, Carson roused and blessed the anger of his supporters. In private, behind closed doors at Westminster and in Belfast, he appears to have urged caution. Between December 1912 and May 1913 confidential police reports on private Unionist meetings chronicled several occasions when Carson had 'counselled peace and peaceful ways' on his leading followers.[34] In particular he seems to have been unenthusiastic about a general arming of the Ulster Unionists, a course of action which was being urged by some of his more hawkish lieutenants. When a mass importation of weapons was finally sanctioned, in January 1914, the decision appears to have been forced by the restlessness of certain elements within the Ulster Volunteer Force, and by the likelihood that – given the abortive negotiations with Asquith – the government were unlikely to offer serious concessions.[35] Certainly Carson, while he publicly celebrated militant loyalist coups (such as the Larne gunrunning of April 1914), appears to have been deeply concerned about the implications of such activity. By April 1914 he was frankly admitting his incapacity to control his own forces. In May 1914 his tentative exploration of a federal solution to the Home Rule impasse was brutally rejected by his own supporters. By the early summer of 1914 it seemed that the command of Ulster Unionism had been seized by the hawks within the Ulster Volunteer Force.[36]

By 1914 the likelihood of a peaceful settlement was slipping from the politicians' grasp. But, as will be clear, this was not because of any pathological cussedness on the part of Carson or Bonar Law. Both men, despite apocalyptic rhetoric, were essentially constitutional politicians; but both were in (partial) command of a volatile political following, and Carson in particular – who was profoundly fearful of civil war – was probably losing control over his own, increasingly militant support. This is not to mitigate his role in arousing Unionist passions (though here, again, the influence of any one politician, given the long history of loyalist unrest, may well be exaggerated): but it is to suggest that Carson and his British Conservative allies were open to compromise, and were probably in a position to deliver a compromise – but only in the earlier stages of the Home Rule crisis, and certainly not by the summer of 1914.

Could the Liberals and their allies in the Irish Parliamentary party have offered a deal, involving some form of Ulster exclusion, in the spring of 1912, at the start of the Home Rule crisis? If such a settlement was within the realm of practical politics, *should* it have been offered? It is important to remember that it was only in 1914, when both Unionist and Nationalist militancy were already far advanced, that any serious concessions were offered: but this should not obscure the chances of a peaceful settlement in 1912. Had some form of Ulster exclusion been contained within the Home Rule Bill, Irish Nationalists would undoubtedly have been angered; they viewed the island of Ireland as an indivisible whole, and were in any event inclined to dismiss the seriousness of Ulster Unionist protest. In addition, any form of exclusion would have placed the northern Catholic minority beyond the protection of the Home Rule executive. This might have mattered less in terms of practical politics had not one of John Redmond's most influential deputies, Joe Devlin, been a Belfast Catholic (Devlin was secretary of the United Irish League, the Nationalists' local party organisation).[37] But, viewed simply as a matter of political judgement, the Irish Parliamentary party would have done better to strike a deal in 1912, rather than to give way, inch by humiliating inch, between 1914 and 1916, when finally – in the middle of the war – Redmond accepted the temporary exclusion from Home Rule of six northern counties. Had the Liberal government demanded a slighter concession than this in 1912 (say four-county exclusion on a temporary basis), there would have been bitter Nationalist protest: but the Irish party would have been spared subsequent ignominy, and the electoral consequences of popular expectations which had been raised and crushed. In addition, Redmond would have had little choice but to accept the decision of the Liberals – for, while the government was dependent upon his party for support, he was dependent upon the government for Home Rule. The Irish Parliamentary party might have assisted the Tories in voting a partitionist Liberal government out of office, but this might well have brought either a Unionist majority in the House of Commons, or a Liberal government with an independent majority. Either outcome would have meant the relegation of Home Rule.

Much, then, hinged upon the state of Liberal ministerial opinion in late 1911 and early 1912: was exclusion regarded then as a practical proposition? To begin with a related issue, it is evident that some form of special treatment for north-east Ulster *ought* to have been seriously considered before the introduction of the Bill; this case had been made by several leading scholars of Edwardian Liberalism, and seems incontrovertible. As Patricia Jalland has argued, while Gladstone in 1886 might have been forgiven for underestimating the ferocity of Unionist opposition, Asquith (who had been in the House of Commons since 1886) had twenty-five years in which to observe the tenacity and fury of Ulster loyalism.[38] The resources of Unionism, emotional and institutional, had been grimly mobilised in 1904–5, in opposition to devolution, and again, in 1907, in opposition to the Irish Council Bill: in particular, the Ulster Unionist Council – which was the fulcrum of northern loyalist opposition to the third Home Rule Bill – had been founded in 1905, and was from the start quite clearly a powerful organisational tool. The appointment, in February 1910, of a formidably talented parliamentarian and lawyer, Carson, to head the Irish Unionist party in the Commons, was also a foretaste of the ferocious battles which lay ahead.

Asquith and other members of his Cabinet were in fact convinced of the probable need to deal separately with Ulster. The two leading proponents of some form of special treatment for the North were also the two most controversial and gifted members of the Cabinet, David Lloyd George and Winston

Churchill; they were joined by the less gifted and certainly less enthusiastic Chief Secretary for Ireland, Augustine Birrell. As early as August 1911 Birrell was privately toying with the notion of county option and temporary exclusion – a proposal which would be laid before the opposition parties (by Lloyd George) only in February 1914.[39] Birrell was directly acquainted, and on a day-to-day basis, with the powerful realities of Unionist intransigence, while Churchill (whose father, Lord Randolph, had been an outspoken advocate of Ulster) and Lloyd George (a Non-Conformist) had family and religious motives for their concern. Asquith affirmed in September 1913 that he had 'always thought (and said) that, in the end, we should probably have to make some sort of bargain about Ulster as the price of Home Rule' – but a combination of his rather vapid interest in the entire question along with a natural desire to identify with the majority case in any Cabinet discussion meant that in practice he was a highly uncertain exclusionist.[40] When, on 6 February 1912, Churchill and Lloyd George presented their Cabinet colleagues with a plan to exclude the Unionist counties of Ireland from Home Rule, they achieved some support – but were eventually voted down by a majority which included the Prime Minister.[41]

Nevertheless, the essential point should not be lost: that there was considerable support in the Liberal Cabinet for exclusion – even in February 1912, two months before the introduction of the Home Rule Bill. The Gladstonian purists were led by Lord Crewe and Lord Loreburn, and carried the day, but the exclusionists numbered, beyond those already mentioned, Haldane, Hobhouse and – for at least the first part of the cabinet debate – Asquith.[42] Given that Carson and Bonar Law were demonstrably not irrevocable militants, and given the presence of an exclusionist lobby within the Liberal Cabinet (a lobby which grew as the months passed), some form of constitutional settlement was clearly not beyond the bounds of credibility. In fact it is possible, on the basis of the evidence presented, to go further than this, and to suggest that the best chance for Home Rule – the Home Rule moment – came and went in the spring of 1912. The last sections of this essay are therefore devoted to considering the form of such a settlement, and its broader consequences.

Interpreting the Third Home Rule Bill

Before a description of the likely state of Ireland under Home Rule can be hazarded, the details of Asquith's measure, and the nature of the administrative devolution which it proposed, should be defined.[43] As will be evident from the earlier discussion, the Bill treated Ireland as a whole, though there were certainly numerous safeguards designed to address the more urgent Ulster Unionist fears. The initial clauses of the Bill dealt with the new, bicameral Irish legislature, and with its relationship to the imperial Parliament at Westminster. Although there was to be a vestigial Irish presence at Westminster (42 members as opposed to the existing 103), the focus of Irish parliamentary representation was to be shifted to a new House of Commons in Dublin, with 164 members elected for five years, and a nominated Senate, with 40 members. In addition provision was made for the creation of a responsible executive. It was calculated that the Unionists would probably win around 39 of the 164 seats in the Irish Commons, and perhaps 10 of the 42 Westminster seats; but (at least in the short term) they possessed another political resource in the Senate, which was initially to be nominated by the London government. Redmond, the Irish party leader, was certainly clear that the purpose of nomination was 'to secure inclusion from the first of valuable elements in the public life of Ireland which might be excluded by election on strictly party lines' – a comment which was probably directed to the southern Unionists, who were too thinly spread to exercise a significant electoral influence.[44]

The new body was to be subordinate to Westminster, and Asquith in fact emphasised 'the overriding force of Imperial legislation, which can at any time nullify, amend, or alter any Act of the Irish Parliament'.[45] Aside from this general assertion of imperial ascendancy, there were specific areas which were defined in the Bill as being beyond the authority of the new legislature:

these included the crown, the making of peace or war, the army and navy, foreign and colonial relations, honours, the coinage, trade marks and certain aspects of foreign trade and navigation. There were in addition areas, known as the 'reserved services', which were excluded from the Home Rule Bill on a provisional basis: these matters included land purchase, pensions, national insurance, tax collection, the Royal Irish Constabulary, and the regulation of the Post Office Savings Banks, Trustee Savings Banks and friendly societies. There was also an expansive prohibition on legislation which would discriminate either in favour of, or against, any form of religious practice. In particular the Parliament was prevented from legislating to 'make any religious belief or religious ceremony a condition of the validity of any marriage'.[46] Although much of the rest of the Bill was Gladstonian in origin, this restriction was a novelty, designed to address Protestant fears concerning the recent Papal decree, *Ne Temere*, and its effect on mixed marriages; as an emollient, it was however peculiarly ineffective. Aside from this range of permanent and provisional exclusions, and the particular ban on religious discrimination, there was a further brake on the Irish Parliament's freedom in the shape of the royal veto. The head of the Irish executive under the proposed Home Rule scheme, as indeed under the Union, was the lord lieutenant; and though this office was redefined along slightly more popular lines (it was now open to all religions, and was removed from the arena of British party politics), it was also empowered with both a suspensory authority over Irish legislation, and the right of veto – both to be exercised according to instructions supplied by London.

The financial clauses of the Bill were regarded by many contemporaries as a technical quagmire, and (in so far as they were fully understood by backbenchers) provoked rumbling disquiet. If an agreement on Home Rule had been achieved in early 1912, it almost certainly would have been on the basis of some form of special treatment of Ulster. This would have meant minor adjustments to some parts of the Bill (such as those which have already been outlined), but it also would have meant the collapse of the entire financial settlement, which was predicated on a unitary Irish state. It was no coincidence, therefore, that some of the more ardent opponents of exclusion within the Liberal Cabinet were also those who were most closely associated with the construction of the financial clauses of the Home Rule Bill (most conspicuously, Herbert Samuel).[47] A compromise on Ulster in 1912 would also have meant, therefore, a complete readjustment of the financial settlement. Accepting all of this, the financial aspect of the Bill is worth mentioning because it provides the best evidence available (however flawed) of some of the key principles upon which Home Rule would have been launched. And it is also the case, as will become clear, that many of the contemporary speculations concerning the future of Ireland emphasised the strengths and weaknesses (depending on party perspective) of Home Rule finance.

Under Samuel's elaborate proposal, all Irish revenue was to be paid into the imperial Exchequer. The operating cost of all the devolved services – a sum of around £6 million – would be returned to Ireland as the bulk of a 'Transferred Sum'; in addition a small surplus of (to begin with) £500,000 would be added to provide a margin of error for the new Irish administration. If the Irish government levied new taxes, the revenue from these would also be returned but the scope for new taxation was in fact highly limited. The new administration could impose new taxes, provided that they did not conflict with existing imperial taxation (a Joint Exchequer Board, controlled by the British government, would adjudicate on what did or did not constitute 'conflict'); and they could raise the existing taxes, but by no more than 10 per cent. Part of the levy still raised in Ireland by the imperial government consisted of land purchase annuities, paid by those farmers who had bought their holdings using government credit. Any arrears of these annuities would be charged to the new Irish government through a reduction of the Transferred Sum. As John Redmond commented bleakly, 'the whole revenue of Ireland is thus held in pawn for the security of payments under the Land Purchase Acts'.[48] Here was one issue which, in the opinion of contemporaries, held the potential for bitter future controversy between the new Home Rule administration and the imperial Parliament.

Another controversial aspect of these clauses, at least so far as Unionists were concerned, was the mechanism for furthering Irish financial autonomy. It will be evident that Samuel's legislative architecture concealed a miserable grant of financial devolution behind a grand façade, but he allowed for the possibility of further construction. If, in the verdict of the Joint Exchequer Board, Irish revenue met or exceeded Irish expenditure for three years in succession, then the Board could seek from Westminster fuller financial powers for the Home Rule Parliament. Irish Nationalists, who otherwise loathed Samuel's proposals, clung on to the hope of a later, and more generous revision. Irish Unionists, prophesying an economic apocalypse, based their jeremiads on the indefinite nature of the financial settlement.

The fate of the measure may be swiftly outlined. Asquith's strategy, which has since been much criticised, appears to have involved delaying an amendment on Ulster until the extent of opposition, and therefore the likely extent of concession, became more fully apparent.[49] Viewed from the relative serenity of Cavendish Square or of Sutton Courtney, and from the point of view of high-political gamesmanship, this was clearly a logical course of action – but of course it served to inflame an already highly volatile Ulster Unionism. In practice Asquith created immense difficulties for the Ulster Unionist leadership, and this may indeed have been part of his original calculation; but the price paid for this tactical squeeze was out of all proportion to any benefit obtained. In fact it was the financial proposals, rather than Ulster, which initially provoked the greatest ministerial concern and flexibility. In the aftermath of a Liberal backbench revolt, the government amended the Bill in committee so that the new Irish regime would have no power to reduce customs duties.[50] With the exception of the minor safeguards contained in the Bill (and regarded as not merely inadequate but also defective), no firm conciliatory proposal was offered to the Ulster Unionists until January 1914, when the Prime Minister's 'Suggestions' – a scheme of Home Rule-within-Home Rule – was placed on the table. Although an enhanced offer was put forward in March 1914 (a combination of temporary exclusion and county option), and incorporated within an Amending Bill in May, this still fell short of the Unionist demand for permanent exclusion. Moreover, by this time the extent of Ulster Unionist militancy was such that leaders like Carson and Craig had comparatively little room for manoeuvre – and proposals which might in 1912 have formed the basis for a successful negotiation could not now be countenanced. The antagonists were still deadlocked on 30 July 1914, by which time it was clear that a European war was looming. On the initiative of the Ulster Unionist leaders, and in the interests of at least the semblance of national unity, it was then agreed to postpone the Irish conflict. Asquith chose to exploit this party truce in order to place the Home Rule Bill on the statute book, albeit with an accompanying measure designed to suspend the establishment of an Irish parliament for the duration of the war.

Contemporaries, reading the details of the Bill, or viewing its tortuous progress through Parliament, extrapolated numerous visions of the nation's future.[51] The defining feature of these contemporary counterfactual arguments was partisanship: Unionists and Nationalists cherished their own distinctive, but often conflicting, views of Ireland under Home Rule. Occasionally these speculations were cast in either a satirical or dramatic form, but even with the most imaginative or outrageous literature there was often a kernel of political reality (or virtual reality). Frank Frankfort Moore, a highly prolific novelist of Irish Protestant descent, published a variety of work at the time of the third Home Rule Bill (*The Truth about Ulster* (1914); *The Ulsterman* (1914)), but his fullest commentary on Home Rule came with two satirical squibs published a generation earlier, at the time of the second Home Rule proposal.[52] In the comic *Diary of an Irish Cabinet Minister* (1893), Moore incorporated a number of loyalist prejudices into a pantomimic vision of an independent Irish government. The new regime is characterised by a rapacious attitude towards Ulster (a proposed hike in income tax is complemented by a retrospective tax on the profits from the Belfast shipbuilding industry), and by an abject surrender to clerical authority (the Catholic Archbishop of Dublin has a right of veto over all legislation, is consulted on official appointments and is in direct communication, through the novelty of the telephone, with the Cabinet chamber). Unionist institutions, such as Trinity College Dublin and the *Irish Times*, are suppressed. The economic background to the new administration is equally bleak, with a failed national loan, unpaid officials and a collapse in Irish stock. Moore's *The Viceroy Muldoon*, published a few weeks after *Diary of an Irish Cabinet Minister*, works from the same premise of a newly established Home Rule administration, and shares with the earlier work a range of assumptions about the new regime. In both works Ulster Unionists defy the Dublin government: in both they are treated as a resource to be mulcted (in the *Viceroy Muldoon* it is proposed to force 15/16ths of the taxation of Ireland on to the North). Clericalism is rampant in the regime envisioned in the *Viceroy*, and business is brought to a standstill through a combination of public and political anarchy and official improvidence. A low standard of political morality and of political debate is assumed in both satires, each of which concludes with set-piece punch-ups within the new Nationalist governing elite. In both tales it is assumed that the limitations of Home Rule will be initially swept aside by Nationalist ambition (in the *Viceroy* the Irish Parliament quickly acquires the right to nominate the lord lieutenant).

It would of course be wrong to place too great a burden of interpretation upon two outrageous satires (both works, for example, end with the triumphant re-establishment of the Union). But the comic success of these works rested in the fact that Moore worked from a series of popularly held Unionist assumptions concerning the clericalism, the rapacity and the violence of any future Home Rule administration. These assumptions were shared (as will become clear) even by the most solemn Unionist commentators on Home Rule.

Other writers, working from the premise that no settlement

would be reached, concentrated much more directly than Moore on the likely militancy of Ulster Unionists. At the time of the third Home Rule Bill at least two novelists speculated about the likely attitude of the North, and both – working from rather different political and national perspectives – detailed some of the broader, as well as some of the more personal, repercussions of Ulster Unionist militancy. These authors were George Birmingham, writing from a Liberal Protestant perspective in *The Red Hand of Ulster* (1912), and an English novelist, W. Douglas Newton, whose work *The North Afire* (1914) explored the same theme of civil war in Ulster. Both authors wrote before the outbreak of the European war in August 1914, and neither gave any serious consideration to the wider diplomatic context to British policy in Ireland. Both, however, deserve some attention, if only because their vision of Ulster with Home Rule but without the Great War, provides the theme for one of the counterfactual hypotheses explored in the last section of this essay.

George Birmingham, within the limits of a mildly comic and mildly satirical fantasy, predicted with remarkable clarity some of the actual forms of Unionist militant politics, as well as providing informed guesses about other likely developments. Joseph Conroy, an American millionaire of Irish extraction, and of Fenian sympathies, perceives that the potentially most disloyal and violent elements within Ireland are the Ulster Unionists, and he therefore chooses to fund their resistance to Home Rule (this – apparently unlikely – device in fact crisply foreshadowed the real, if grudging admiration of some militant republicans for the defiance of their northern loyalist contemporaries).[53] Conroy's Unionists fight a number of minor but successful engagements with the British army and (improbably) the Royal Navy, and secure a thoroughgoing grant of independence for all of the island. Douglas Newton, writing evidently without much first-hand knowledge of Ireland, and within the constraints of a rather florid romance, speculated not unconvincingly about the shape and personal repercussions of an Ulster Unionist rebellion. Comyns Loudoun, a British army officer, finds himself fighting a fellow officer and Unionist sympathiser in the course of the Ulster rising, while being otherwise distracted from his duty through his love for one of the rebel women. Birmingham's rebellion culminates in an Orange-toned Irish republic; Newton's rebellion flares briefly and bloodily, but is resolved after two weeks in a manner which is not detailed.

Birmingham's fantasy is of particular interest because it emphasises the complicated range of Unionist attitudes towards violence, and because it prophesies some of the likely political dynamics of any Ulster rebellion against Home Rule. The leaders of Unionist resistance, Lord and Lady Moyne (who bear a resemblance to Lord and Lady Londonderry) and the talented orator Babberly (who has some similarity to Carson) are nudged to the sidelines during the early stages of the rising by more militant forces, reliant upon American finance and upon German weapons (the actual loyalist militants used some funds from North America – though not of course from republican sources – and imported weapons from a private supplier in Germany).[54] Babberly, who combines in a Carsonian manner public belligerence and private moderation, highlights the possible effects of Ulster Unionist violence upon potential English support: 'I know that we shall sacrifice their friendship and alienate their sympathy if we resort to the argument of lawlessness and violence.'[55] In addition, the novel illustrates, in its paradoxical denouement, the highly constrained limits of Irish loyalism: the rebels prefer to dictate the terms of Irish independence rather than to return to the Union or to some form of Home Rule. Though this was a self-consciously comic and seemingly improbable finale, it reflects other, less ironic views of contemporary Irish Unionists, and their likely response to Home Rule. For example, the otherwise sober southern Unionist lawyer, A. W. Samuels, warned English observers in a prosy fashion that they 'may be well assured if they desert those in Ireland to whom they are in honour bound, then undoubtedly the bitterest opponents of England in the future, wherever their lot may be cast, will be those men and their descendants who shall have been so betrayed'.[56]

Newton's fantasy looks forward to the weeks following the passage of Home Rule. A bloody loyalist uprising is sparked by the killing of an Orangeman during a police raid. The new Ulster provisional government 'advises' Nationalists to leave their homes and property, while throughout Ulster the prevailing majority in a locality, whether Unionist or Nationalist, attacks the minority, inflicting casualties and destroying property. Sectarian resentment is compounded by a degree of economically inspired violence (such as the torching of factories by workers). British ministers, initially disoriented ('the Government had started weathercock whirlings as is the way with Governments with whom the essence of existence is the expending of wind'), finally agree on a declaration of martial law; and, after several bloody encounters between the crown forces and the insurgents, a form of compromise is settled.[57] This fantasy, though weak in certain details (Ulster is lavishly endowed with coal mines, and an Orange hero bears a Gaelic Irish Christian name), speculates rather convincingly concerning the development and local consequences of a loyalist revolt. The dilatory but ultimately effective response of the British government is in keeping with the combination of procrastination and swift, heedless action which characterised the Asquith administration; and the overall picture of a brief, bloody and pointless conflict is also plausible, in keeping with the unenthusiastic militancy of influential sections of the Unionist command, and the reluctance of the Liberal government to become embroiled in civil unrest.

Nationalist speculation, whether in historical or political polemic, or in fiction, tended to worry much less about the North than these English or Ulster Protestant commentators; and the apocalyptic themes which recurred in Unionist political rhetoric and literary fiction were generally absent from their Nationalist counterparts. There are, however, some points in common. One of the most revealing contemporary counterfactual speculations about Home Rule was offered by George Bernard Shaw in the 'Preface for Politicians' (1907) which he provided for the play *John Bull's Other Island*. Shaw, a Home Ruler, deemed a 'loyal'

Irishman to be 'unnatural' (in much the same way as the republican socialist James Connolly viewed Ulster Unionism as a form of false consciousness). Shaw instead emphasised the radical potential within Irish Protestantism.[58] He believed that Irish loyalism and Protestant social ascendancy were interdependent; and that with the end of 'English' rule in Ireland, and the end of the concomitant ascendancy class, so Irish loyalism would disappear. Shaw, writing before the elaboration of Ulster Unionist militancy, and as a Dublin Protestant, saw his co-religionists, not as sustained opponents of a Home Rule administration, but rather as potentially a most advanced and energetic presence within the new regime. Irish Protestant determination to influence national life would lead, in Shaw's vision, to an ever greater identification with 'the vanguard of Irish Nationalism and Democracy as against Romanism and Sacerdotalism'; and this Protestant interest would be aided by the votes of those Catholics anxious to advance national freedom, and throw off clerical supremacy.[59] While these hypotheses imposed upon northern Protestantism some of the preoccupations of its southern counterpart, and while the speculation as a whole owed much to Protestant national conceit, it is intriguing that Shaw should stress, in common with George Birmingham and others, the apparently very thin line separating trenchant Ulster loyalism and advanced Irish separatism. Both writers underline the fragility of any true unionism among the northern Protestant militants; and the vision of Ireland under Home Rule which each provides is coloured very largely by a dominant Protestant separatism.

Shaw's vision of Irish Catholicism under Home Rule is no less intriguing. Shaw saw the Union as an agent for clericalism, in so far as the church provided one of the key institutions around which popular Catholic political and religious resentments had gathered. The removal of the Union and the establishment of Home Rule would liberate Irish Catholics from servitude to Rome, freeing them to create their own Irish Gallican church: 'Home Rule will herald the day when the Vatican will go the way of Dublin Castle, and the island of saints assume the headship of her own church.'[60] Home Rule promised, according to Shaw, excited by the roller-coaster of his own paradoxes, to convert Orangemen into advanced separatists and pious Catholics into advanced Gallicans.

One final fictional vision of Home Rule may be offered, representative of separatist conviction. Terence MacSwiney, a Sinn Feiner, who was 'out' in the 1916 rising, and who died in prison in October 1920 after a seventy-four-day hunger-strike, published a play in 1914, *The Revolutionist*, which looked forward to the plight of separatists under an unsympathetic Home Rule administration.[61] The underlying premise of the drama, as with the other literary evidence which has been discussed, is the successful enactment of the third Home Rule Bill. The protagonist, Hugh O'Neill (a deliberate reference, presumably, to the late-sixteenth-century Gaelic lord and rebel), is confronted by bluster and timidity within his own advanced Nationalist circle, and with the intense hostility of influential figures within the Catholic Church: some of his personal intimates, in common with the rest of Nationalist Ireland, are softening in their attitude towards the empire. O'Neill is denounced from the altar as an atheistic revolutionary (he is in fact a sincere Catholic); he observes acquaintances compromising their political convictions in the interests of personal advancement; and, looming behind the action of the play, is the 'Empire Carnival', a popular entertainment, which, though designed ostensibly to celebrate the attainment of Home Rule, is luring good-hearted Nationalists along imperialist paths. O'Neill's fight for separatist principles is lonely and tragic; but his death, which comes after a ferocious proselytising campaign, is depicted as a beautiful and heroic culmination.

These literary visions of Ireland under Home Rule, though sometimes bizarre or even comic in their detail, were remarkably close to the speculations offered by ostensibly more sober commentators. The defining feature of these, as with the literary fantasies, was party affiliation, but some assumptions spanned the party divide. A Unionist satirist, such as Frankfort Moore, might look forward to the anarchic division within the Nationalist ranks after the passage of Home Rule, but this was only an exaggerated version of John Redmond's own prediction; Redmond looked forward (as did the agrarian radical, Michael Davitt) to the collapse of the Home Rule party, *'functus officio'*, after its goal had been attained.[62] In fact Redmond generally, and skilfully, turned the taunts of his opponents into political capital: when Unionists prophesied that Home Rule would destabilise the British constitution (the distinguished jurist, A. V. Dicey, claimed that 'Home Rule does not close a controversy – it opens a revolution'), Redmond accepted the general point, while claiming that Home Rule would precipitate a healthy revision in the form of a general federation of the United Kingdom.[63] Redmond, like the Unionists, accepted that aspects of the measure were highly unsatisfactory; like the Unionists, though working from a different perspective, he damned the financial provisions of the measure as, at best, provisional. It may also have been the case that, like the Unionists, he foresaw specific problems with the provision of the Bill which linked any default in the land purchase annuities with a reduction in the Transferred Sum.[64]

But, of course, the overall vision provided by Nationalist and Liberal commentators was of (in the words of the historian Richard Bagwell) a 'future Arcadia', and stood in contradistinction to the grim fantasies conjured up by Conservative and Unionist politicians.[65] Both Home Rulers and Unionists (albeit for different reasons) tended to emphasise the extent of the powers which were being devolved to the new Irish administration. But Redmond saw the Home Rule Bill as a final settlement of the historic quarrel between the English and the Irish (even though he accepted that some details were problematic), where Unionists saw merely a staging post to a much greater degree of autonomy. Some Liberal commentators envisaged the devolution of power to Dublin, and the reduction of Irish representation at Westminster, as 'the first step forward in the direction of Imperial efficiency', where Unionists saw only the probability of enhanced constitutional chaos ('the statement that the passing of the Home Rule Bill would relieve congestion at Westminster is palpably false', declared Carson's private secretary, Pembroke Wicks).[66] Redmond believed that the Bill heralded the establishment of a talented national assembly in Dublin (since Irish political skills were no longer being siphoned off in quantity to Westminster); Unionists foresaw the creation of an assembly of self-seeking and fratricidal mediocrities ('the scenes of Committee Room No. 15 are', claimed Dicey, 'a rehearsal of parliamentary life under Home Rule at Dublin').[67] Redmond saw the Bill as creating improved relations between Ireland and Britain, as well as between the Irish diaspora and the British. In particular, he argued, Britain would profit from improved relations with Irish America. Unionists believed, or at any rate argued, that the Home Rule Bill merely provided a forum for a fuller expression of national resentments, and that the British would pay dearly – especially in the event of war – for their light-headed optimism.[68]

Perhaps the single most complete Liberal or Home Rule vision of devolved government was provided by J. H. Morgan's edition, *The New Irish Constitution* (1912). Here the Bill was depicted as a perfect combination of generous devolution alongside judicious imperial restraint. Commentators acknowledged the existence of religious apprehensions, but (following the argument pursued in rather more flamboyant terms by Bernard Shaw) argued that 'full and free political life is the best, perhaps the only, solvent of intolerance'.[69] The notable Presbyterian Home Ruler, Revd J. B. Armour, turned conventional fears on their head by arguing (again with Shavian overtones) that Home Rule would benefit, and not destroy, Irish Protestantism, because it would free Protestantism from its damaging anti-democratic and anti-national associations: Home Rule gave 'Protestantism a chance of being judged on its own merits'.[70]

The writer on financial affairs Lord Welby was similarly dismissive of Unionist fears, arguing that Home Rule could not produce (as Unionists claimed) a viciously protectionist Irish government, because the English market for Irish goods was simply too important.[71] Unionist predictions of profligate admin-istration were also dismissed. One of the most perceptive Home

Rule commentators, Jonathan Pym, argued that the likely danger in the new Ireland came, not from excessive expenditure, but rather from excessive miserliness: 'the overwhelming peasant vote may render the administration unduly parsimonious, and so unwilling to place any additional burden on the owners of land that a kind of political stagnation may arise therefrom'.[72] This was far removed from Frankfort Moore's bitterly comic portrayal of a corrupt and spendthrift Home Rule government – but it was in fact a remarkably prescient forecast of the financial administration of the independent Ireland of the 1920s. The Unionist vision of an anarchic Ireland, where the old Royal Irish Constabulary would be humiliated and demoralised, was explored and dismissed elsewhere in the volume, where it was argued that the executive could not interfere with the legal process, and where the prediction was offered that agrarian disturbance would die out in the face of democratic institutions.[73]

Nationalists, dulled by years of loyalist bluster, dismissed the threat of Ulster Unionist violence as folly. Indeed, it was argued (again, with a skilful turning of the argument) that the very strength of Ulster Unionism within any Home Rule settlement would prevent persecution. Redmond predicted both that the Home Rule party would disintegrate after the successful attainment of its goal, and that Irish Unionists would have a strong representation within the Dublin House of Commons (roughly one-quarter of the seats); the combination of a splintered nationalist grouping and a strong Unionist bloc implied that Unionists would exercise an important influence within Home Rule Ireland.[74] In addition Nationalists believed that the third Home Rule Bill adequately reflected Unionist sensitivities: for example, as has been mentioned, the Irish parliament was not permitted, under the terms of the Bill, to legislate to the advantage, or to the detriment, of any form of religious conviction; and in particular it was not permitted to impose any religious condition on the validity of marriage. This last restriction (new to the Bill of 1912) was added in the light of the Papal *Ne Temere* decree on mixed marriages, and was designed to disarm some of the wilder loyalist predictions of an impending Catholic ascendancy.

Unionist commentators were less sanguine about their looming fate under Home Rule. Much of the Unionist vision of Ireland under Home Rule has already been outlined, but the Unionist case, as with the Nationalist, depended on offering a detailed forecast of the impending apocalypse. Unionists, whether the satirist Frankfort Moore or the sober ex-Solicitor-General for Ireland, J. H. M. Campbell, predicted anarchy. Moore's Home Rule parliamentarians sent a deputation to Tammany Hall to learn the arts of political management, while Campbell prophesied (without apparent irony) that after Home Rule 'politics in Ireland would be shaped after the model of Tammany Hall rather than that of St Stephen's'.[75] Dicey, Peter Kerr-Smiley (an influential Ulster Unionist MP) and others believed that the ruthlessness with which Nationalists pursued internal disputes would be applied more generally within a Home Rule parliament.[76]

Most Unionist writers and commentators predicted, not the fraternal harmony described by Redmond, but rather continuing friction between Ireland and Britain. Indeed, many believed that the Bill, with its complex array of checks and balances, was a seedbed for grievance and distrust. Pembroke Wicks argued that the combination of rights and restrictions with which the new Irish administration was burdened promised continual conflict with the imperial authorities; in particular the financial settlement, described earlier, was 'capable of producing only the minimum of revenue for the Irish Exchequer and the maximum of friction with the British Treasury'.[77] The Joint Exchequer Board, created as a peace-keeping mechanism, would – as a British-dominated institution – serve only as a further irritant for Irish Nationalism.

Unionists accepted that such continuing friction would destabilise the Home Rule settlement, and would help to inflame advanced separatist feeling within Ireland. No Unionist viewed Home Rule in Redmondite terms, that is as a final, or even lasting, constitutional arrangement ('our new constitution is not made to last', lamented Dicey).[78] Most saw the elaborate system of checks on Irish autonomy as being either (if the checks worked) a taunt to nationalist sentiment or (if they did not) practically worthless; Peter Kerr-Smiley, for example, dismissed the lord lieutenant's veto as 'a sham' and the right of judicial appeal to the British Privy Council as 'worthless'.[79] Several Unionist writers foresaw that tensions between Britain and Ireland would arise from the ongoing payment of the land purchase annuities. Some Unionists, like Richard Bagwell, shared the presumptions of Terence Mac-Swiney's *The Revolutionist* – and predicted that a moderate Home Rule administration would come under increasing pressure from advanced separatist feeling.[80] Many assumed that such feeling would be fired by Anglo-Irish tensions, and by the cancerous instability of Home Rule.

Political instability would affect the health of business. Frankfort Moore's satirical comment on the anarchic economic fall-out from Home Rule was not fundamentally different from the observations of some stolid northern Unionist businessmen. Moore predicted that the Home Rule parliament would impose penal taxation on northerners and upon northern business – and some less flippant Unionists feared that this would indeed be the case. Most informed comment, however, was centred less on the fear of immediate and brutal taxation than upon a more fundamental anxiety. If, as Unionists believed, Home Rule threatened political instability, then it also threatened the stock market and Irish credit. The Home Rule crises had been associated with a dip in Irish stock, and many Unionists feared that, were Home Rule to be enacted, this depreciation would be permanent. An able northern critic of the Bill, the Liberal Unionist businessman Thomas Sinclair, believed that Home Rule would seriously damage all forms of northern prosperity – industrial, commercial and agricultural; and he traced 'the root of the evil' to the financial instability of any future Irish administration.[81] The new Home Rule government, indebted and unstable, would fail to win credit in the international money market; and this would have damaging repercussions for the general prosperity. Sinclair's analysis, while sombre and measured, recalled Frankfort Moore's comic depiction of the Irish national £10 million loan, and the chaotic aftermath of its failure.[82]

But the instability of Home Rule, which these grim fantasies presumed, arose not merely from the pressure of advanced Nationalists, but also from the opposition of the Ulster Unionists themselves. Most serious Unionist comment between 1911 and 1914 assumed, at the very least, that there would be unrest in Ulster; many came to believe that civil war loomed. Peter Kerr-Smiley linked the likely financial instability of Home Rule Ireland to northern disturbance by arguing that the new administration would be burdened by exceptional policing costs.[83] Pembroke Wicks made the same connection in a rather different manner: Wicks prophesied that, if the Bill were forced into law, there would be 'civil war in Ulster and an end to public confidence, security and credit throughout the rest of Ireland'.[84] One of the most eerily prescient of these Unionist jeremiahs was Earl Percy, an army officer and son of the 7th Duke of Northumberland, who – writing in 1912 – was already utterly convinced of the impending European cataclysm, and who drew on his experience of South Africa to offer predictions of Irish politics. Percy's primary interest was in the general military disadvantages of Home Rule, but he toyed with two of the hypotheses which will be explored shortly, in the last section of this chapter: he imagined an Ireland under Home Rule, with Ulster excluded, and argued that there would be an irrevocable slide, as there had been in the Transvaal and Orange Free State, towards independence.[85] Unionists would be treated with the same asperity as had been applied to the British Uitlanders in southern Africa in the years before the Boer War. Alternatively, Percy worked with the notion of a unitary Ireland, governed by a Home Rule administration, and riven by at worst civil war, at best 'a condition where the rousing of old animosities, religious and otherwise, leads to internal disturbances of all kinds'.[86] Basing his judgement on the embryonic militancy in the North, Percy deemed an insurrection against any Home Rule administration to be 'highly probable'; and he was equally certain that troops would be required to quell unrest, and restore the authority of the Dublin regime.[87]

Part of Percy's vision of 'the march to Armageddon' came to life in August 1914. But the accuracy of his prophecies for Europe ensured that his fears of an Irish apocalypse were dispelled, at least for the moment. For, with the outbreak of the Great War, the paradoxical loyalist rebellion faded away, and the regiments of insurgents became battalions of king's men. None of the political futurologists, whether Nationalist or Unionist, speculated about the fate of Home Rule in the context of a European war: certainly none, not even Percy, dared to guess what the impact might be on Ireland of mass slaughter in the trenches. Percy was virtually alone in recognising the seriousness of the international situation, but not even he foresaw the profound political fall-out from the battles which he imagined on the horizon. Nevertheless, if speculations were made without allowance for the central event of European as well as Anglo-Irish history, then the seers accurately predicted some of the forces within, if not Home Rule Ireland, then at least the Dominion created in 1921, the Irish Free State: a Catholic and frugal polity, which hankered after fuller autonomy. And, given that the war, rather than Ulster, killed Gladstonian Home Rule, these partisan but acute and informed fantasies are the best guide which we have to the lost Liberal arcadia – an Ireland bound to Britain, but self-governing, an Ireland divided by religion and by culture, but united in patriotism.

Ireland under Home Rule

The available contemporary evidence for the likely shape of Irish government under Home Rule has been outlined and debated: the background to the Home Rule agitation has been sketched, the details of the third Home Rule Bill have been presented, and some of the rich array of contemporary speculation concerning Home Rule government has been excavated. It is now possible to draw together these different skeins to weave several counterfactual hypotheses: the first of these works with the assumption, already outlined, that a Home Rule settlement might well have been agreed in 1912; and the second toys with the premise that the European war was either delayed or averted, and that the Liberal government and the Ulster Unionists had directly to confront their own actions (rather than pirouette out of danger, as each did in August 1914).

Home Rule is agreed in 1912, and it is established on the basis of the temporary exclusion of six Ulster counties. The Cabinet meeting on 6 February 1912, at which Lloyd George and Churchill present their plans for Ulster exclusion, is divided, but the clamour for a pre-emptive offer grows, and Asquith, who has independently recognised the need for a deal, adds his weight to the exclusionist camp.[88] The Chief Secretary for Ireland, Birrell, aided perhaps by Lloyd George and Churchill, has to sell this proposal to Redmond and the Irish Parliamentary party; the semblance of a united and powerful ministerial front, allied with the temporary nature of the scheme, helps to overturn the deep-seated antipathy which the Irish leadership, and especially Devlin, the northern Nationalist leader, harbour towards any retreat from an all-Ireland polity.[89] However, the alternative to refusal is probably a dissolution, and perhaps a Unionist electoral victory.

A Home Rule Bill is therefore launched in April 1912 with a temporary partition scheme. The Conservatives and Ulster Unionists are – as Lloyd George has foreseen – wrong-footed and divided. The Conservative front bench is torn in several directions: influential southern Unionist sympathisers, like Lord Lansdowne, are bitterly unhappy with the Bill where more passionless figures such as Austen Chamberlain or Lord Hugh Cecil see the Liberal offer as a basis for negotiation, if not settlement.[90] Bonar Law's instincts are much more consensual than is widely understood, and he realises that his plans for an Ulster crusade in Britain are fundamentally undermined by the Liberal initiative. He may be able to rally the party on the basis of a call to defend embattled Ulster; but he will not be able to sway either the party or the country on the basis of squabbles over the minutiae of a partition deal. He is therefore prepared to work with the Liberals.

Bonar Law, however, needs the sanction of the Irish Unionist leadership. Here, again, the Liberal offer has had a profoundly divisive impact. Southern Unionists are appalled, as are the Ulster Unionists who live outside the excluded area. The Unionist leaders from the north-eastern heartland of the movement are more cautious, with some hawks – especially the Boer War veterans – unimpressed by Asquith's apparent generosity.[91] Carson, who fought Home Rule in 1886 and 1893, recognises the advance which Asquith has made on the Gladstonian formulation, and – as an acute political intelligence – he recognises the tactical difficulties which the offer creates for the Irish Unionist cause. Though distrustful, he is prepared to work with the Liberals. Carson takes advice from a number of Ulster lieutenants, but principally from James Craig, who throughout his career has reflected the concerns of his east Ulster political base. Since the Liberal offer protects this heartland, and since Craig, as an experienced campaigner in Britain and in the House of Common, recognises the likely difficulties of sustained opposition, he counsels in favour of a cautious acceptance.

A deal is struck on the basis of temporary exclusion, and the Bill passes into law. The new Irish Parliament meets, as specified within the terms of the new Home Rule Act, on the first Tuesday of September 1913.[92] Despite pressures and predictions, the unity of the former Irish party holds, and it emerges as the dominant force within both the new House of Commons in Dublin and the new Irish executive: John Redmond is the first Irish Prime Minister. There is a scattering of southern Unionist and Sinn Fein representation in the 164-seat Commons, but southern Unionists fare rather better in the new Senate, where the Lord Lieutenant allocates them a disproportionate number of the forty available seats. Some forms of minority constitutional Nationalism – such as the supporters of the centrist William O'Brien – also find a station in the Commons and the new Senate.

Will the new Irish administration create a Catholic and clericalist ascendancy, as the Unionist pundits of 1911–12 alleged? The Home Rule Act formally prohibits most forms of sectarian legislation, but there are certainly ways of circumventing this ban (some Unionists argued that the taxation regime of the Home Rule state would favour church institutions).[93] However, several leading Nationalists have Protestant family connections: Redmond, for example, has a Protestant mother and a Protestant wife.[94] Moreover, the new Parliament contains (as did the Irish Parliamentary party at Westminster) a comparatively large number of Protestants, who although widely recognised as political lightweights are likely to protest against any outrageous clericalism. But perhaps the strongest brake upon any sectarian ascendancy will come from the pressure created by the temporary partition arrangement; the new Irish administration will have every reason to demonstrate to the still hostile north the liberality of its intentions. There are undoubtedly strong sectarian forces in the new Parliament: Devlin's party organisation, the Ancient Order of Hibernians, is heavily represented.[95] But, equally, such forces are counterbalanced by a still influential centrist constitutional tradition, and by southern Unionists, as yet unscathed by the Great War. There is every reason to assume that, though Home Rule has been launched in the context of heightened sectarianism, the new Irish administration will be (at least initially) more sensitive to religious difference than the polities, the Irish Free State and Northern Ireland, actually created in 1920–1.

Relations between the new regime and the North remain highly volatile and highly intricate. Though a settlement has been reached on Home Rule, its temporary nature means that Ulster Unionists remain wary, and retain some of their defensive organisation (such as the nominal Ulster provisional government). Their attitude, and the fate of the temporary exclusion arrangement, are extremely difficult to predict. It is possible, however, that temporary partition will – as many Liberals prophesy – defuse the growing militancy within Ulster Unionism. It is, after all, difficult to sustain a credible defiance over six years, and with the possibility that the partition arrangement may be extended. Much depends upon the attitude of the new Home Rule executive. Redmond's sense of obligation to the Liberal government for the concession of Home Rule will lead him to support the British war effort in August 1914, and to encourage the recruitment of Irish volunteers to the British army.[96] In the context of a relatively settled constitution, Ulster Unionists will be impressed by this evidence of Redmond's 'loyalism'; and the broadly united Unionist–Nationalist attitude to the war may help to consolidate domestic political ties.[97] Temporary exclusion, combined with the war, will certainly bring the evaporation of British Unionist enthusiasm for Ulster, and especially if – as is probable – the new Home Rule administration proves its competence during the period of exclusion. Ulster Unionists will therefore be left with the alternatives of continuing the arrangement in the context of waning British sympathy, or of joining the new Home Rule polity. This last is not beyond the bounds of possibility: many Ulster Unionists in the much less propitious circumstances after 1920 (including, evidently, James Craig) believe that partition is a transient phenomenon – and the unity forged by the war may well act as a constitutional cement. However, whether these consensual attitudes and the political unity which they support will survive for long is quite another matter.[98]

But will the new Dublin administration prove to be competent, in the teeth of Ulster Unionist suspicion and British prejudice? The sharp political intelligence exercised by leading Nationalists such as Redmond, Devlin or John Dillon, allied to the discipline of office and the constraints imposed by the Home Rule Act, provide grounds for optimism. In addition, to look ahead, the politically less gifted and less experienced Free State ministers of the 1920s provide a highly competent, if unimaginative, administration to the newly independent Ireland. The constitutional Nationalists of the Home Rule administration have been long trained in the discipline of opposition, and they are unlikely to wield executive power in anything other than a highly circumspect manner.

The threat to constitutional stability lies less with the new rulers of Ireland than with the instrument of their authority, the Home Rule Act. Although the Act contains a number of checks and balances which may avert conflict with the North, it also contains the material for conflict with the British Parliament. Disputes may well arise from the distribution of powers outlined in the Act, or from the superior authority of the Westminster Parliament: the veto power of the lord lieutenant over Irish legislation will be a difficulty, as will ill-advised legislative interference from the British Parliament. Irish MPs at Westminster, though reduced in number, remain highly influential, and especially with (as in 1910) the two main British parties so evenly matched in parliamentary strength. This Irish leverage in London may well be used for further constitutional gain, and particularly if conflicts between the Home Rule and imperial administrations grow in frequency and severity.

Such conflict will also lend credence to the separatist or republican cause.[99] With every minor clash between Dublin and London constitutional nationalists will be angered, but they will also come under pressure from the vocal Sinn Fein minority to pursue an ever more independent line. In addition, as the unpopularity of the war grows, and as hostility towards the administration's pro-British stand deepens, support is delivered to the advanced nationalist cause. The Home Rule government may well be able to hold this at bay, but probably only by capturing at least some of the separatists' ground: after the armistice there will be demands for further constitutional concessions. These are likely to be granted, given the 50,000 Irish casualties which are sustained in the war.

The pursuit of this counterfactual speculation produces a vision of Ireland in the 1920s which in certain respects does not differ from the historical denouement: in both the historical and virtual-historical cases Ireland emerges as a dominion, loosely bound to the British empire. The inclusion or exclusion of Ulster has little bearing on this counterfactual fantasy. Few Ulster Unionists would have keenly supported the restoration of the Union after the 'betrayal' of Home Rule, and there are some grounds for supposing that, had the North joined a Dublin administration, Unionists would have been both influential members of the regime and interested in consolidating its powers. The presence of Ulster Unionists in Dublin would possibly, though by no means probably, have ensured a residual connection between Ireland and the British crown; but, even as it was, Ireland became a republic only in 1949.[100] However, it should again be emphasised that an independent Ireland with a strong Unionist representation need not have been – in the long term – a politically and culturally settled polity. There is, in fact, some justification for supposing the reverse.

It seems unlikely that, had Home Rule been enacted in 1912, there would have been an Anglo-Irish war; on the other hand, it is not improbable that advanced separatists would have staged a revolt against a Home Rule administration which seemed to be (in MacSwiney's metaphor) joining the Carnival of Empire. It is therefore unlikely that the revolutionary Nationalist tradition would have died in a Home Rule Ireland; but it is possible that, having a much less clear focus, it would have had less popular acceptance. Revolutionary Nationalists might well, however, have forced the Home Rule Parliament into a more defiantly nationalistic stance than would otherwise have been the case. Some ongoing form of civil unrest may have been unavoidable, but this would probably have arisen out of the Ulster issue rather than, as in 1922–3, between different forms of advanced nationalism.

This leads into another series of counterfactual speculations. The idea of a settlement in 1912 presumes that Ulster Unionist militancy would have been checked in its infancy, undermined by a combination of Liberal tractability and Conservative apathy. But for the moment these presumptions will be set aside. Returning to the historical record, there were no serious proposals for a settlement between the Liberal government and the Ulster Unionists until 1914, by which time northern militancy was fully formed. Sustained diplomacy from late 1913 until July 1914 demonstrated only the rigidity of the deadlock between the negotiating parties; and this tension was released only by the outbreak of the Great War. But what if there had been no war? Or, as is argued elsewhere in this volume, what if, while the rest of Europe marched to Armageddon, the United Kingdom had remained neutral? Would the Asquith government have bought the lives of British soldiers with the currency of an Irish civil war?

The prospect of a European war was certainly the mechanism by which the Unionist leaders and the Liberal ministers escaped from the Ulster crisis; and indeed it was thought at the time, and subsequently, that the larger war had averted a smaller and perhaps – at least from the narrow perspective of British constitutional stability – more damaging conflict. But these contemporary counterfactual assumptions deserve a fuller examination: would a civil war have been fought in Ulster in 1914 had there been no European conflagration? How would an Ulster civil war have altered the subsequent constitutional history of modern Ireland?

With the failure of the Buckingham Palace Conference in July 1914, Home Rule would have been enacted for the whole of Ireland. Asquith's Amending Bill, introduced in June 1914 and proposing temporary exclusion for Ulster, was by this stage widely seen as unsatisfactory, and was effectively lost. Assuming that there had been no party truce as a result of the European war, and assuming that British neutrality had been sustained, the machinery of the Home Rule Act would have ground into action, with elections for the new Irish House of Commons, and the gradual segregation of administrative functions between the new administration and London.

In the North of Ireland the enactment of Home Rule would have served as a signal for the Ulster provisional government, formed originally in 1911, to emerge from the shadows and operate as a rival executive. There had been plans (albeit sketchy) for an occasion such as this, and these would now have been put into operation: railway and communication lines would have been severed, arsenals and supply depots would have been seized, and the main roads into the North closed and guarded.[101] The UVF and its political masters had long recognised that the police force, the Royal Irish Constabulary, would present the most immediate opposition to the loyalist coup, and there were plans for the arrest and disarming of constables.[102] The machinery of Home Rule –

for example, the elections to the new House of Commons – would either have been ignored, or have been exploited for the benefit of the revolt. The elections in the North might have been used simply to provide an electoral mandate for the rebellion (Sinn Fein exploited British elections in 1918 and in 1921 for similar reasons). Almost certainly there would have been no immediate attempt by the government to suppress the coup. Asquith would have been fearful of converting (what was for the moment) peaceful defiance into a bloody rebellion, but he would also have been anxious to wait for a more propitious opportunity to intervene.[103]

The Ulster provisional government planned to seize and exercise control with the minimum of force (Carson was emphatic – for tactical as much as humanitarian reasons – that the Ulster Volunteers were not to fire the first shots); equally the British government was anxious to avoid, as far as possible, any bloody confrontation with the Unionist rebels.[104] But each had begun to plan for a civil war in Ireland at least as early as March 1914. It is probable that, while the Ulster Unionists were outlining the initial plans for their coup, hardliners within the government (such as Churchill and the War Minister, Seely) were debating the possibility of coercion.[105] The Ulster Unionists were now armed, having successfully (and illegally) imported 25,000 rifles and three million rounds of ammunition into the North in April 1914. In addition to these weapons, the Unionists had perhaps 12,000–15,000 rifles of different types and age: the total armament was calculated in July 1914 to be around 37,000 rifles, but this may well have been a slight underestimation.[106] Loyalists had been drilling since late 1910, and there were mass camps of instruction in 1913 and 1914 such as that at Baronscourt, County Tyrone, in October 1913.[107]

There would have been two distinct, but interrelated, forms of response to the loyalist coup. The Nationalists had a rival paramilitary force, the Irish Volunteers, which – inspired by advanced separatist feeling – was spreading rapidly in the spring of 1914, and especially in western Ulster, where there was a majority in favour of Home Rule. By May 1914, 129,000 Irish Volunteers had been recruited throughout Ireland, with 41,000 in Ulster. Badly armed, but enthusiastic, their commander – a former officer of the Connaught Rangers – declared in June that 'any government that attempts gerrymandering the nationalist counties out of Ireland must render an account to us'.[108] The government which had been seeking, in a half-hearted fashion, a 'gerrymander' had at its disposal the Royal Irish Constabulary as well as the troops of the Irish garrison. These, too, were potential, though by no means enthusiastic, opponents of the Ulster Unionists.[109]

It is highly probable that the enactment of Home Rule in 1914 would have stimulated a conflict between the UVF and the Irish Volunteers. In southern and western Ulster, and to a certain extent in Belfast, Unionists and Nationalists were marching for their respective causes, and displaying their armaments. Any attempt by the Ulster Volunteers to enact their plan of campaign – seizing strategically vital locations in the largely Nationalist South Down area, for example – would unquestionably have stimulated conflict.[110] It is probable that the Ulster Volunteers, with superior arms and (within the North, at any rate) superior numbers, would have temporarily fought off any Nationalist opposition, but at the politically very high price of causing bloodshed and sectarian unrest. The vague Unionist plans for the peaceful disarming of the local RIC men were, at best, highly ambitious. There is a fair probability that the process of disarmament would have brought conflict between the mainly Catholic policemen and the Protestant Volunteers. In both cases – bloody confrontation between either the police or the Irish Volunteers and the UVF – British support for the Unionist cause would have been jeopardised; and in particular it is difficult to see how Conservative endorsement of the Ulster Unionists could have been sustained after (say) a bloody sectarian affray or the assassination or wounding of members of the RIC.

Such episodes would have been publicly deplored by the Asquith government, and privately welcomed as a political bonanza. In addition they might well have served to simplify the attitude of the British army and navy towards the Ulster Unionist cause. This attitude had been temporarily (but only temporarily) defined by the 'incident' or 'mutiny' at the Curragh military camp, County Kildare, in March 1914 when a brigadier-general and sixty other officers had resigned rather than march north to impose Home Rule on Ulster.[111] But this military crisis had arisen, not from any coherent official attempt to coerce the Ulster Unionists, but rather as a result of bungling by the army commander, Sir Arthur Paget, and his garbled communication of relatively uncontroversial War Office orders. Precautionary troop deployments in Ulster were presented by Paget as a likely prelude to Armageddon, and he unilaterally offered his junior officers the option of resigning. From this episode it has often, understandably, been inferred that the army was irrevocably Unionist, and that it could not have been used against the Ulster Volunteer Force. Certainly as late as 4 July 1914 the Army Council acknowledged that there could be no military coercion of Ulster.[112] Equally, some stress has been laid upon similar attitudes within the ranks of the Royal Navy.[113] But it is all too easy to misinterpret this highly charged episode. It reveals, not a mutinous spirit among the army (no orders were disobeyed), but rather a broad Unionist sentiment, and a determination, if the option were available, of avoiding any bloody involvement in Ulster. But all the available evidence suggests that, had there been no option, army officers would have obeyed direct orders to march north in order to implement Home Rule: Brigadier-General Gough, the leading 'mutineer', stated unequivocally that 'if the GOC-in-C had ordered my brigade north to Belfast I should have gone without question'.[114]

The Curragh incident undoubtedly made the military imposition of Home Rule much more difficult than it would otherwise have been, but even so it is possible to exaggerate these difficulties. The passage of time clearly alleviated the burden of the Curragh; in particular the death in November 1914 of one of the most influential anti-coercionists, Field Marshal Lord Roberts, was a loss to Ulster Unionism. But, even more crucially, the Unionist sympathies of the officer cadre would have been tested to breaking point if, as has been argued, the Ulster Volunteers had become embroiled in the shooting of Catholic Irish Volunteers or police-men. In these circumstances, and given unambiguous orders from a less befuddled commander than Paget, it is highly unlikely that another 'mutiny' would have occurred.

Could the Ulster Volunteers have won a military victory?[115] The UVF would undoubtedly have scored isolated successes against both the Royal Irish Constabulary and the Irish Volun-teers. But, as has been argued, such successes would have been self-defeating, for they would have provided an opportunity for the government and the army to intervene; and in such a situation it is hard to see the possibility of either political or military gain. The UVF had large numbers (around 100,000), was heavily armed and had local knowledge. But it is probable that some of this number would have melted away as the prospect of a war came closer, and in addition the numbers of weapons, though impres-sive, obscured severe logistical difficulties. Some of the Unionist armoury was antique, and, while there were too many types of rifle, there were too few revolvers and – at the other end of the scale – too few machine-guns or field pieces for effective action. It appears that the amount of ammunition available to the UVF would scarcely have trained the force, let alone equipped it for a prolonged battle. It is therefore hard to doubt the judgement that 'in a full-scale military clash the UVF's weaponry would have created a logistical nightmare'.[116] These difficulties might have been overcome, and the local knowledge of the Volunteers might have been put to good use in a guerrilla conflict, but this was precisely the form of warfare which they had eschewed. The official preference was for 'a stand-up fight', and the training and organisation of the UVF indicate that they were in fact preparing for a conventional war.[117] There is little doubt that the UVF would have fought the British army as bravely as they fought the Germans on the Somme and at Messines; and, equally, there is little doubt that they would have been slaughtered in similar numbers. Neither the Unionist political leadership nor British public opinion would have permitted an extended bloodletting; and in all probability – as was suggested in the romance *The*

North Afire – a settlement would have been brokered after a few weeks of conflict.[118] Almost certainly this would have been along the lines of the mixture of temporary exclusion and county option which had been offered by Asquith and Lloyd George in the spring of 1914.

All the available evidence suggests that, had the army been embroiled in Ulster, the UVF would have suffered defeat. The terms of the settlement between the Liberal government and the Ulster Unionists can also be envisaged with some degree of certainty. It is much harder, however, to assess the long-term fall-out from such an episode. It is unlikely, on the basis of contemporary arguments, that the ferocious Unionism of the northern loyalists would have survived a humiliation at the hands of the United Kingdom government (even a Liberal government) and its army: Conservative sympathy in the light of British military casualties in Ulster would have been highly doubtful. It is possible that leaders such as Carson and Craig would have been repudiated in the wake of military failure, just as Redmond was rejected by Nationalist voters in the aftermath of a series of perceived political defeats. Some passive resistance of Home Rule would have been likely, again judging by the predictions of contemporary commentators.[119] Defeated on home territory, cut off from British sympathy, it is possible that northern Unionists might have trickled into a Home Rule parliament in Dublin in much the same grudging manner that northern Nationalists entered the Belfast Parliament and Fianna Fail entered Dáil Éireann in 1927. Whether the presence of such Unionists would have made for a successful multi-cultural democracy such as Switzerland, a workable, if unstable confederation such as Canada, or failure and schism, as with Czechoslovakia and Yugoslavia, is a moot point. Either way, it is unlikely that the relationship between Britain and Ireland would have been much better than was in reality the case. Unionists and Nationalists may well have been united only by their hostility towards British oppression.

Arcadia?

Home Rule failed, and the Irish wrested a form of independence from Britain through the war of 1919–21 and the Treaty of December 1921. The problem of Ulster was addressed through a partition scheme, launched in 1920 through the Government of Ireland Act. Anglo-Irish relations seemed permanently soured as a result of the circumstances in which the new Irish state was launched. Sectarian relations within Northern Ireland seemed permanently embittered as a result of the nature and extent of the partition settlement. Viewed with the luxury of hindsight Home Rule looked like a fleeting opportunity to create a settled Ireland and a fruitful diplomatic relationship between Dublin and London.

Yet there is a paradox inherent in the view that Home Rule might have averted the Northern Irish 'Troubles' – for much of the awkwardness of the Ulster problem arose, not out of the failure of Home Rule, but precisely because a Home Rule measure had been successfully imposed. The constitutional basis for the existence of Northern Ireland – the Government of Ireland Act – was a legislative mixture of partition and devolution, and, though it failed to satisfy southern Nationalist opinion, it was ruefully accepted by Ulster Unionists. The Act of 1920 created a Home Rule parliament and executive in Belfast, both of which lasted until the introduction of direct rule from London in 1972. Home Rule in Northern Ireland brought endemic financial difficulties (the economic relationship between Belfast and London was a recurrent source of acrimony, and had to be revised as early as 1924–5); it brought the domination of one political tradition, Unionism, and the marginalisation of another, the northern Nationalists. The irony of Unionists exercising power in a north-ern Home Rule administration has often been emphasised. But perhaps the true irony of the 1920 settlement was that through it Unionists brought to life many of their own most pessimistic predictions concerning Home Rule. The reality of Ulster under Stormont illustrates the virtual reality of Ireland under Home Rule.

And yet there was certainly nothing inevitable about the failure of the third Home Rule Bill as a piece of legislation. It has been shown how, in the spring of 1912, an opportunity for a settlement between the Liberal government and the Ulster Unionists was missed. Nor was partition inevitable, at least in the form of a permanent exclusion of the six northern counties from the Home Rule scheme. It has been suggested that there was a chance that Ulster Unionists might have at least temporarily reconciled themselves to a Dublin administration, particularly in the context of a united Irish commitment to the Allied war effort in 1914.

But arguing that Home Rule might have succeeded in parliamentary terms is very far from saying that it would have succeeded as a policy. And suggesting that the permanent partition of Ireland might have been avoided is far from proclaiming that a stable unitary Irish state might have emerged instead. Probably the only conditions upon which the Home Rule crisis might have been peaceably settled would have meant the temporary exclusion of four or six Ulster counties from Home Rule in 1912. At the most optimistic prognosis, these counties might have grudgingly accepted Home Rule after the expiry of the statutory term. But, even assuming that the reunification of Ireland could have been achieved without massive bloodshed, the state which would have emerged would have contained over one million reluctant and culturally distinctive citizens. And, given that the driving forces behind the emergence of Ireland as a mature and stable democracy included a shared Catholicism and a widely shared respect for Gaelic culture, the presence of a large, highly defensive northern Protestant community might have proved disastrous. The price paid by all the Irish for a unitary state might well have been higher than the price paid for partition: an unstable thirty-two-county Ireland, as opposed to an unstable six-county Northern Ireland.

In any event the failure of Home Rule did not mean the loss of British Ireland, because British Ireland had been lost long before the 1912–14 era. The consolidation of Irish national identity in the nineteenth century had been achieved partly on the basis of a conscious rejection of Britishness (as opposed to the complementary relationship between, for example, Scots national identity and Britishness). It is probable that Home Rule would have been swiftly redefined by an Irish parliament after 1914, just as dominion status was redefined in the 1920s; indeed it is probable that Home Rule would have served as a precursor to dominion status. It is likely that pressure from advanced separatists would have promoted a defensively nationalistic Home Rule administration in Dublin; and it is also likely that the terms of the Home Rule measure would have promoted rancour between the new administration and Westminster. This, added to the possibility that Ulster Unionists might have been subjected to military coercion, suggests that Home Rule, far from inaugurating a new and peaceful era in Anglo-Irish relations, might well have introduced a period of bloodshed and nagging international bitterness. If the victims of the 1916 rising and the Anglo-Irish war might have been spared, other lives would have been lost in the North, and with no mitigating political benefits. The vision of Home Rule as a pathway to arcadia is rooted more deeply in Gladstonian optimism and myopia than in the politics of 1914.

Home Rule, then, might have been enacted, but the political risks involved were great, and might well have been realised. The only terms upon which the measure might have been passed involved temporary, and possibly permanent, partition – with constitutional results broadly similar to those which exist today. Had Ulster Unionists been eased into a Home Rule Ireland, then it is just conceivable that a stable, pluralist democracy might have swiftly emerged. But it would have been a high-risk strategy, with every possibility that a short-term political triumph for Liberal statesmanship might have been bought at the price of a delayed apocalypse. Northern Ireland under the Union has been likened to Bosnia; but Ireland under Home Rule might well have proved to be not so much Britain's settled, democratic partner as her Yugoslavia.[120]

FOUR

THE KAISER'S EUROPEAN UNION:

What if Britain had 'stood aside' in August 1914?

Niall Ferguson

> There was no immediate cause for dreading catastrophe.
>
> SIR EDWARD GREY, *Fly Fishing*[1]

In Erskine Childers's highly successful novel *The Riddle of the Sands* (1903), Carruthers and Davies stumble across evidence of a German plan whereby 'multitudes of sea-going lighters, carrying full loads of soldiers ... should issue simultaneously in seven ordered fleets from seven shallow outlets and, under the escort of the Imperial navy, traverse the North Sea and throw themselves bodily upon English shores'.[2] This nightmare vision was far from unique in the years before 1914. Just such a German invasion was luridly portrayed three years later by the author William Le Queux in his best-selling *Invasion of 1910*, first serialised in Lord Northcliffe's Germanophobic *Daily Mail*. Earlier in his career as a 'scaremonger', Le Queux had been more preoccupied with the danger of Russian and French invasions. But (like Baden-Powell, the hero of Mafeking and founder of the Boy Scouts) he had acquired bogus 'plans' for a German invasion from a gang of forgers based in Belgium, and it was these which provided the inspiration for such titillating flights of fancy as 'The Battle of Royston' and 'The Siege of London'.[3] The final imaginative leap was taken by Saki (Hector Hugh Munro) in *When William Came: A Story of London under the Hohenzollerns* (1913), which depicts the aftermath of a lightning German victory.[4] Saki's hero, Murrey

Yeovil – 'bred and reared as a unit of a ruling race' – returns from darkest Asia to find a vanquished Britain 'incorporated within the Hohenzollern Empire ... as a Reichsland, a sort of Alsace Lorraine washed by the North Sea instead of the Rhine', with Berlin-style cafés in the 'Regentstrasse' and on-the-spot fines for walking on the grass in Hyde Park. Though Yeovil yearns to resist the Teutonic occupation, he finds himself deserted by his Tory contemporaries, who have fled (along with George V) to Delhi, leaving behind a despicable crew of collaborators, including Yeovil's own amoral wife Cecily, her bohemian friends, various petty bureaucrats and the 'ubiquitous' Jews.[5]

Was war between Britain and Germany inevitable in 1914? Certainly, few events in modern history have been subjected to more deterministic interpretations than the outbreak of the First World War. It was not only British popular novelists who saw it coming. In Germany too, there was a widespread assumption that war was unavoidable. The Reich Chancellor Bethmann Hollweg told his secretary at a critical moment in the July Crisis that he felt 'a force of fate stronger than the power of humans, hanging over Europe and our people'.[6] A few days later, once the war had actually begun, Bethmann Hollweg sketched what has since become one of the classic determinist explanations of the war: 'The imperialism, nationalism and economic materialism, which during the last generation determined the outlines of every nation's policy, set goals which could only be pursued at the cost of a general conflagration.'[7] A still greater fatalist was the Chief of the German General Staff, Helmuth von Moltke, who had been conscious of 'the Gorgon head of war grinning' at him as early as 1905.[8] 'War', he declared shortly after his resignation in September 1914, 'demonstrates how the epochs of civilisation follow one another in a progressive manner, how each nation has to fulfil its preordained role in the development of the world.'[9] Moltke's determinism was a mixture of fin-de-siècle mysticism and the 'Social Darwinism' popularised by writers like his former colleague Bernhardi[10] and also detectable in the later remarks of his Austrian opposite number Conrad.[11] But a similar conclusion could be based on very different ideological premises. As Wolf-gang Mommsen has shown, 'the topos of inevitable war' was as much a feature of the pre-war Left as the Right in Germany. Even if Marxist intellectuals like Hilferding and Kautsky – to say nothing of Lenin and Bukharin – failed to predict the war (until, of course, it had broken out), the Social Democrat leader August Bebel was by no means alone in anticipating, in December 1905, 'the twilight of the gods of the bourgeois world'.[12]

British politicians also sometimes used such apocalyptic language to explain the war – though it is not without significance that they tended to do so more in their memoirs than in their pre-war utterances. 'The nations slithered over the brink into the boiling cauldron of war,' wrote Lloyd George in a famous passage in his *War Memoirs*. Nor was this the only metaphor he employed to convey the vast, impersonal forces at work. The war was a 'cataclysm', a 'typhoon' beyond the control of the statesmen. As Big Ben struck 'the most fateful hour' on 4 August, it 'echoed in our ears like the hammer of destiny.... I felt like a man standing on a planet that had been suddenly wrenched from its orbit ... and was spinning wildly into the unknown.'[13] Winston Churchill used the same astronomical image in his *World Crisis*:

> One must think of the intercourse of nations in those days ... as prodigious organisations of forces ... which, like planetary bodies, could not approach each other in space without ... profound magnetic reactions. If they got too near the lightnings would begin to flash, and beyond a certain point they might be attracted altogether from the orbits ... they were [in] and draw each other into due collision.

A 'dangerous disease' was at work, 'the destiny of mighty races of men' at stake. 'There was a strange temper in the air.... National passions ... burned beneath the surface of every land.'[14] Like Churchill, the Foreign Secretary Sir Edward Grey recalled the same 'miserable and unwholesome atmosphere'. Like Lloyd

George, he too had the sensation of being 'swept into the cataract of war'.

The function of all these images of natural catastrophe is obvious enough. At a time when the Great War had come to be seen as the greatest calamity of modern times, they served to illustrate vividly the politicians' claim that it had been beyond their power to prevent it. Grey stated quite explicitly in his memoirs that the war had been 'inevitable'.[15] In fact, he had expressed this view as early as May 1915, when he admitted that 'one of his strongest feelings' during the July Crisis had been 'that he himself had no power to decide policy'.[16] 'I used to torture myself,' he admitted in April 1918, 'by questioning whether by foresight or wisdom I could have prevented the war, but I have come to think no human individual could have prevented it.'[17]

A few historians continue to favour the imagery of profound natural forces, propelling the great powers into the abyss.[18] Hobsbawm has likened the July Crisis to a 'thunderstorm'; Barnett has compared the British government to 'a man in a barrel going over Niagara Falls'.[19] Yet elsewhere – even in their memoirs – most of those concerned admitted that there had been at least some room for calculation, debate and decision before the British decision to go to war in August 1914. Two more precise reasons tended to be cited for British intervention: firstly, the belief that Britain had a moral and contractual obligation to defend the neutrality of Belgium. As Asquith put it, in the familiar language of the public school: 'It is impossible for people of our blood and history to stand by ... while a big bully sets to work to thrash and trample to the ground a victim who has given him no provocation.'[20] Lloyd George agreed: 'Had Germany respected the integrity of Belgium ... there would have been plenty of time for passions to exhaust their force.'[21] The argument that British intervention in the war was made inevitable by the violation of Belgian neutrality has been repeated by historians ever since. Forty years ago, A. J. P. Taylor wrote that 'the British fought for the independence of sovereign states'.[22] Most recently, Michael

Brock has argued that this was the crucial factor which persuaded a majority of the Asquith Cabinet to back intervention.[23]

However, of more importance – certainly to Grey and to Churchill – was a second argument that Britain 'could not, for our own safety and independence, allow France to be crushed as the result of aggressive action by Germany'.[24] According to Churchill, a 'continental tyrant' was aiming at 'the dominion of the world'.[25] In his memoirs, Grey made both points. 'Our coming into the war at once and united', he recalled, 'was due to the invasion of Belgium.'[26] 'My own instinctive feeling [however] was that ... we ought to go to the help of France.'[27] If Britain had stood aside, 'Germany ... would then [have been] supreme over all the Continent of Europe and Asia Minor, for the Turk would be with a victorious Germany.'[28] 'To stand aside would mean the domination of Germany; the subordination of France and Russia; the isolation of Britain; the hatred of her by both those who had feared and those who had wished for her intervention; and ultimately that Germany would wield the whole power of the Continent.'[29] According to K. M. Wilson, this self-interested argument was in fact more important than the fate of Belgium, emphasised by the government mainly to salve the consciences of wavering Cabinet ministers and to keep the Opposition out of office. More than anything else, the war was fought because it was in Britain's interests to defend France and Russia and prevent 'the consolidation of Europe under one potentially hostile regime'.[30] David French takes a similar view;[31] as do most recent syntheses,[32] as well as Paul Kennedy's suggestively titled *Rise of the Anglo-German Antagonism.*[33]

The idea that Germany posed a threat to Britain itself can hardly be dismissed as an *ex post facto* rationalisation. Between around 1900 and 1914, as the examples cited above show, the view was widely held that the German Reich intended to make some kind of military challenge to British power. Of course, books like Saki's are usually ridiculed by British historians as xenophobic 'scaremongering', mere propaganda in the radical right's campaign for conscription. (Indeed, they were ridiculed at the time by, among others, P. G. Wodehouse, who wrote a wonderful pastiche entitled *The Swoop, or How Clarence Saved England*, in which the country is simultaneously overrun not only by the Germans but by the Russians, the Swiss, the Chinese, Monaco, Morocco and 'the Mad Mullah'.) Yet it should not be forgotten that the idea of a German threat to Britain was taken quite seriously – even if depicted in less colourful forms – by senior officials at the British Foreign Office, including the Foreign Secretary himself.[34] Of the FO's contributions to the Germanophobe genre, perhaps the best known is the Senior Clerk Sir Eyre Crowe's memorandum of November 1907, which warned that Germany's desire to play 'on the world's stage a much larger and more dominant part than she finds allotted to herself under the present distribution of material power' might lead her 'to diminish the power of any rivals, to enhance her own [power] by extending her dominion, to hinder the cooperation of other states, and ultimately to break up and supplant the British Empire'.[35] Fundamental to Crowe's analysis was a historical parallel with the challenge which post-Revolutionary France had posed to Britain. As another FO Germanophobe, Sir Arthur Nicolson, put it in a letter to Grey in early 1909: 'The ultimate aims of Germany surely are, without doubt, to obtain the preponderance on the continent of Europe, and when she is strong enough, [to] enter on a contest with us for maritime supremacy.' The Foreign Office view was clear: Germany had a two-stage plan for world power: first, 'the hegemony of Europe'; then there would simply be 'no limits to the ambitions which might be indulged by Germany'.[36] Nor was this line of argument peculiar to the diplomats. When making the case for a continental expeditionary force, the General Staff employed the same analogy: 'It is a mistake', ran its 1909 memorandum to the Committee of Imperial Defence, 'to suppose that command of the sea must necessarily influence the immediate issue of a great land struggle. The battle of Trafalgar did not prevent Napoleon from winning the battles of Austerlitz and Jena and crushing Prussia and Austria.'[37] The argument was repeated two years later: domination of the continent 'would place at the disposal of the Power or Powers concerned a preponderance of naval and military force which would menace the importance of the United Kingdom and the integrity of the British Empire'. Even navalists like Viscount Esher sometimes took the same line. 'German prestige', Esher wrote in 1907, 'is more formidable to us than Napoleon at his *apogée*. Germany is going to contest with us the hegemony of the sea.... Therefore "L'Ennemi, c'est l'Allemagne".'[38] Without the navy, said Churchill, Europe would pass 'after one sudden convulsion ... into the iron grip of the Teuton and of all that the Teutonic system meant'. Lloyd George remembered the same argument: 'Our fleet was as much the sole guarantor of our independence ... as in the days of Napoleon.'[39] The Chief of the General Staff, Robertson, was thus only guilty of slight exaggeration when he wrote in December 1916 that 'Germany's ambition to establish an empire stretching across Europe and the North Sea and Baltic to the Black Sea and the Aegean and perhaps even to the Persian Gulf and Indian Ocean [had] been known for the last twenty years or more.'[40]

Not only did such influential contemporaries clearly believe in a German threat to Britain. The whole thrust of German historiography since Fritz Fischer published his seminal *Griff nach der Weltmacht* has been that they were right to do so. Even if they got the details wrong and exaggerated the likelihood of a German invasion, it seems, Saki and the other scaremongers were fundamentally correct that a Germany dominated by militaristic elites was planning an aggressive 'bid for world power' which made war inevitable.[41] Recent German writing has, albeit with some notable exceptions, tended to refine but not to revise Fischer's argument. A classic illustration of the teleological accounts which have resulted is Immanuel Geiss's recent synthesis, entitled (revealingly) *The Long Road to Catastrophe: The Prehistory of the First World War 1815–1914*, which argues, essentially, that the First World War was the inevitable consequence of German unification nearly half a century before.[42]

Yet it is hard not to feel a certain unease about the notion of a preordained war between Britain and Germany – if only because, eighty years on, the costs of the war seem to loom so much larger than its benefits. The loss of British life far exceeded the death toll of the Second World War, especially if one considers the figures for the British Empire as a whole: 908,371 deaths (more than a tenth of all those mobilised to fight) and total casualties of more than three million. Small wonder 'the Great War' continues to haunt the British imagination, inspiring modern writers of fiction like Pat Barker. Moreover, the financial costs of the war – which increased the national debt from £650 million to £7,435 million – burdened the subsequent, troubled decades with a crushing mortgage, gravely limiting politicians' room for manoeuvre in the depression. Britain entered the war 'the world's banker'; at the end it owed the United States some $5 billion.[43] In recent years, some social historians have sought to emphasise the 'progressive' side-effects of the war on the home front. They leave out of the account unquantifiable psychological wounds which blighted the subsequent lives of millions of survivors and dependants.

If all the sacrifices of the 'Great War' were supposed to prevent German hegemony in Europe, the achievement was short-lived. Within just twenty years, a far more serious German threat to Britain, and indeed the world, had emerged.[44] And, because of the costs of the first war, Britain was far worse placed to resist that threat. Quite apart from its own relative decline, its former allies in Europe were weaker too: France politically divided, Russia in the grip of Stalinism, Italy under fascism. It is therefore tempting to ask whether the four years of slaughter in the trenches were indeed as futile as they seemed to the poet Wilfred Owen and others. Certainly, Liberals like Lloyd George and Keynes – whose contributions to the British war effort had been second to none – came very quickly to believe that the defeat of Germany had been a waste of blood and treasure. If the policy of appeasement had any rationale, it might be said, then the war of 1914–18 can have had little, and vice versa.

Conscious of the underlying inconsistency of British policy, a few historians have questioned the notion of an inevitable Anglo-German war, arguing that British politicians in fact had more room for manoeuvre than they subsequently (and apologetically) claimed. However, the alternatives contemplated have tended to be variations on the theme of intervention. Writing in the thick of the Second World War, Liddell Hart argued that Germany could have been defeated in the First without embroiling Britain in a prolonged continental campaign if the British Expeditionary Force had been sent to Belgium rather than France, or if more troops had been made available for the Dardanelles invasion.[45] Essentially, this merely repeated two of the many arguments about strategy which had raged in political and military circles after 1914. Hobson, by contrast, has recently suggested that a bigger continental commitment *before* 1914 could have deterred the Germans from attacking France in the first place.[46] This too is a development of contemporary arguments. The French government always argued that a clear statement of British support for France at an early stage would have sufficed to deter Germany, a claim subsequently repeated by critics of Grey including Lloyd George and Lansdowne.[47] Grey's defenders, however, have with justice questioned whether the BEF was large enough to worry the German General Staff.[48] Hobson's solution to this problem is to imagine an increase in the size of the British army, making it a conscript army of between one and two million men on the continental model. As he rightly says, this could have been financed relatively easily by higher taxes or borrowing.[49] But such a counterfactual scenario is far removed from what contemporaries regarded as politically possible under a Liberal government.

There nevertheless remains a third possibility, which has been all but ignored by historians: that of British non-intervention.[50] Unlike Hobson's counterfactual, this was far from being politically unrealistic, a point which can be gleaned even from the memoirs of Asquith and Grey. Both men strongly emphasised that Britain had *not* been obliged to intervene by any kind of contractual obligation. In Asquith's words, 'We kept ourselves free to decide, when the occasion arose, whether we should or should not go to war.... There was no great military convention [with France]: we entered into communications which bound us to do no more than study possibilities.'[51] Nor did Grey make any secret of the political opposition to any 'precipitate attempt to force a decision', which had prevented him making any commitment to France in July.[52] If Grey's hands were tied, in other words, it was by his Cabinet colleagues, not by the force of destiny. He himself made clear in his memoirs that there *had* been a choice (even if he naturally insisted that his had been the right one):

> If we were to come in at all, let us be thankful that we did it at once – it was better so, better for our good name, better for a favourable result, than if we had tried to keep out and then found ourselves ... compelled to go in.... [Had we not come in] we should have been isolated; we should have had no friend in the world; no one would have hoped or feared anything from us, or thought our friendship worth having. We should have been discredited ... held to have played an inglorious part. We should have been hated.[53]

The neglect of the neutrality 'counterfactual' is a tribute to the persuasiveness of such emotive postwar apologies. Britain, we have come to accept, could not have 'stood aside' for both moral and strategic reasons. Yet a careful scrutiny of the contemporary documents – rather than the relentlessly deterministic memoir accounts – reveals how very near Britain came to doing just that. While it seems undeniable that a continental war between Austria, Germany, Russia and France was bound to break out in 1914, there was in truth nothing inevitable about the British decision to enter that war. Only by attempting to understand what would have happened had Britain stood aside can we be sure the right decision was made.

An Older Counterfactual: Anglo-German Entente

The story of the allegedly inexorable Anglo-German confrontation can be traced back to the crisis of confidence which beset the

British Empire at the turn of the century. Despite the intellectual vigour of Conservative and Liberal brands of 1890s imperialism, the Boer War dealt a profound blow to British morale. Rhetoric about 'national efficiency' and popular enthusiasm for militaristic 'leagues'[54] could not compensate for official and political anxieties about the costs of maintaining Britain's vast overseas *imperium*.[55] In fact, contemporaries tended to exaggerate the fiscal costs of the empire and to overlook the benefits of maintaining a vast international free-trade area. The real burden of defence averaged around 3.4 per cent of net national product between 1885 and 1913, including the cost of the Boer War. After 1905, the figure held steady at around 3–3.3 per cent – a remarkably low figure by post-1945 standards and less than the comparable figures for Russia, France and Germany.[56] But the *perception* of 'overstretch' – Balfour's hyperbolic claim that 'we were for all practical purposes at the present moment only a third-rate power'[57] – was what counted. Out of the increasingly complex institutional framework within which imperial strategy was made (and which the Committee of Imperial Defence and the new Imperial General Staff did little to streamline),[58] there emerged a consensus. Because it seemed financially and strategically impossible for Britain simultaneously to defend its empire and itself, isolation could no longer be afforded – and therefore diplomatic understandings had to be reached with Britain's imperial rivals.

At this point, it is worth asking once again an older counterfactual question which German liberals used endlessly to ponder: what if Britain had reached such an understanding, if not a formal alliance, with Germany? Despite some contemporary British anxieties about German commercial rivalry as German exporters began to challenge Britain in foreign markets and then to penetrate the British consumer market itself, the idea that economic rivalry precluded good diplomatic relations is a nonsense. Disputes about tariffs are only harbingers of war to the incurable economic determinist.[59] German economic success inspired admiration as much as animosity. Moreover, there were numerous overseas areas where German and British interests potentially coincided. In 1898 and 1900 Chamberlain argued for Anglo-German cooperation against Russia in China. There was serious though inconclusive discussion of an Anglo-German-Japanese 'triplice' in 1901. After much British grumbling, agreement was reached to give Germany Samoa in 1899. The period also saw cooperation between Britain and Germany over Portuguese Mozambique and Venezuela (in 1902). Even in the Ottoman Empire and the former Ottoman fiefdoms of Egypt and Morocco, there seemed to be opportunities for Anglo-German collaboration, though here opinion in London was more divided.[60] A priori, there is no obvious reason why an 'overstretched' power (as Britain perceived itself to be) and an 'under-stretched' power (as Germany perceived itself to be) should not have cooperated together comfortably on the international stage. It is simply untrue to say that 'the fundamental priorities of policy of each country were mutually exclusive'.[61]

Why then did the famous alliance discussions – which began between Chamberlain and the Germans Hatzfeldt and Eckardstein in March 1898 and continued intermittently until 1901 – come to nothing?[62] The traditional answer to this question is that the German Chancellor Bülow wished to keep a 'free hand', which meant in practice that he wished to build a navy capable of challenging Britain's maritime supremacy. It is certainly true that Bülow, perhaps exaggerating British decline even more than the British, was reluctant to conclude a formal alliance with England (though no more reluctant, as it transpired, than the British Prime Minister Lord Salisbury).[63] And one reason for this was undoubtedly the belief that an alliance with England might impede the German naval build-up.[64] Yet the notion that Anglo-German rapprochement was sunk by German Weltpolitik is misleading. Of equal importance at least was the petulant behaviour of Chamberlain, who allowed a diplomatic initiative which ought to have remained behind closed doors to become the stuff of speeches and editorials. Bülow's Reichstag speech of 11 December 1899 – in which he expressed his readiness and willingness 'on the basis of full reciprocity and mutual consideration to live with [England] in peace and harmony' – was interpreted by the intemperate

Chamberlain as 'the cold shoulder'. He later complained that he had 'burnt his fingers' by proposing the alliance.[65]

But this too is only part of the story. Of far more importance in explaining the failure of the Anglo-German alliance project was not German strength but German *weakness*. It was, after all, the British who killed off the alliance idea, as much as – if not more than – the Germans. And they did so not because Germany began to pose a threat to Britain, but, on the contrary, because they realised it did *not* pose a threat. The British response to the German naval programme illustrates this point well. In 1900, Selborne, the First Lord of the Admiralty, had gloomily told Hicks Beach that a 'formal alliance with Germany' was 'the only alternative to an ever-increasing Navy and ever-increasing Navy estimates'.[66] Yet by 1902 he had completely changed his view, having become 'convinced that the new German Navy is being built up from the point of view of a war with us'.[67] This realisation was disastrous for the Germans, who had always been well aware of their vulnerability while their navy was under construction. From the outset, Bülow had insisted on the need to operate carefully with regard to England 'like the caterpillar before it had grown into a butterfly'.[68] But the chrysalis had been all too transparent. By 1905, with the completion of the First Sea Lord 'Jackie' Fisher's initial naval reforms, the Director of Naval Intelligence could confidently describe as 'overwhelming' Britain's 'maritime preponderance' over Germany.[69] A sudden realisation of German vulnerability explains the panic about a pre-emptive British naval strike which gripped Berlin in 1904.[70]

The primary British concern had, of course, been to reduce rather than increase the likelihood of such expensive overseas conflicts. Despite German paranoia, these were in fact much more likely to be with powers which *already* had large empires and navies – rather than a power which merely aspired to have them. For this reason, it is not surprising that rather more fruitful diplomatic approaches ended up being made to France and Russia. As the Assistant Under-Secretary at the Foreign Office Bertie put it in November 1901, the best argument against an Anglo-German alliance was that if one were concluded 'we [should] never be on decent terms with France, our neighbour in Europe and in many parts of the world, or with Russia, whose frontiers are coterminous with ours or nearly so over a large portion of Asia'.[71] Salisbury and Selborne took a very similar view of the relative merits of France and Germany. German reluctance to support British policy in China in 1901 for fear of antagonising Russia merely confirmed the British view: for all its bluster, Germany was weak.[72]

The basis for improving relations with Russia was the conviction that a war with Russia over *any* imperial issue must be avoided. In quick succession, Britain indicated its readiness to appease Russia over Manchuria and Tibet, and to avoid unnecessary friction over the Black Sea Straits, Persia – even (to Curzon's dismay) over Afghanistan.[73] It is possible that this drive for good relations might have led to a formal understanding, as it did in the case of France, had it not been for Russia's defeat by Japan, with which Britain had concluded an alliance in 1902. It is a good indication of the rationale of British policy – appease the strong – that this alliance came to be seen as taking precedence over any agreement with Russia.[74] In the case of France, there was a similar list of imperial issues over which agreements could be reached: principally Indo-China, Morocco and Egypt.[75] There matters might well have rested had it not been for Chamberlain, who, still smarting from being jilted by the Germans, wished such colonial deals to form the basis of a fully fledged alliance.[76]

The Anglo-French 'Entente Cordiale' of 8 April 1904 amounted to colonial barter; but it proved to have three important implications. Firstly, it reinforced the tendency to improve relations with Russia: good relations with one implied good relations with the other.[77] Secondly, it further demoted the importance of good relations with Germany, as became evident during the First Moroccan Crisis.[78] Finally, and most importantly, it meant that military planners on both sides of the Channel began to think for the first time in terms of British naval and military support for France in the event of a war with Germany. The idea of using naval force to blockade Germany had been discussed before.

However, it was in 1905 that the idea of a naval division of responsibility was devised which would concentrate the French navy in the Mediterranean and the British navy in 'home waters'. At the same time, the General Staff began to think in terms of deploying an expeditionary force on the continent in support of France, precipitating a heated debate as to the relative merits of defending the Franco-German frontier with an expeditionary force or launching an amphibious invasion of North Germany.[79] It was in conjunction with the former strategy that the old question of Belgian neutrality came up,[80] though, as the former Permanent Under-Secretary Sanderson noted, the 1839 treaty was not 'a positive pledge ... to use material force for the maintenance of the guarantee [of neutrality] *in any circumstances and at whatever risk*'. That would, he added, be 'to read into it what no government can reasonably be expected to promise'.[81]

In short, Tory foreign policy was to conciliate those powers which appeared to pose the greatest threat to Britain's position, even at the expense of good relations with less important powers. The key point is that Germany (like Belgium) fell into the latter category; France and Russia into the former. The obvious exception to the rule might be said to have been Japan. But an alliance with Japan could be concluded without creating European complications, especially in view of Russian weakness after 1905. The same could not be said of an alliance with Germany. If the Tories had followed Chamberlain's initial strategy of concluding an alliance with Germany, the consequence would have been worsening imperial relations with France and Russia.

Would that have led one day to another kind of world war, with Britain on the side of Germany, fighting against its encirclement by – to adopt contemporary parlance – the Anglo-Saxons' traditional foes, the Latin and Slav Empires? It strikes us as fantastic. But at the time such a scenario was no more or less fantastic than the notion of British alliances with France and Russia, both of which had for years seemed impossible – 'foredoomed to failure', in Chamberlain's phrase. The task of diplomacy between 1900 and 1905 appeared to be to choose between these two options: some kind of rapprochement overseas with France and Russia, or the risk of a future war with one or both – a war which Britain would have had to fight not only in the Channel but in theatres as far afield as the Mediterranean, the Bosphorus, Egypt and Afghanistan.

Britain's War of Illusions

Such was the diplomatic legacy inherited by the Liberals following Balfour's resignation in December 1905. It is vital to emphasise that it in no way doomed Britain to fight the First World War. Certainly, it arranged Britain's diplomatic priorities *vis-à-vis* the other great powers in the order France, Russia, Germany (with Austria, Italy and Turkey trailing behind). But it did not irrevocably commit Britain to the defence of France, much less Russia, in the event of a German attack on one or both. It did not, in short, make war between Britain and Germany inevitable, as a few pessimists – notably Rosebery – feared.[82]

What is more, a Liberal government – particularly of the sort led by Campbell-Bannerman – seemed at first sight less likely to fall out with Germany or to fall in with France or Russia than its predecessor. Although attempts have been made to import the notion of 'the primacy of domestic politics' from German to British historiography, few observers in 1905 would have argued that the change of government increased the likelihood of war.[83] The non-conformist conscience, the Cobdenite belief in free trade and peace, the Gladstonian preference for international law to *Realpolitik*, as well as the Grand Old Man's aversion to excessive military spending and the historic dislike of a big army – these were just some of the Liberal traditions which seemed to imply a pacific policy, to which might be added the party's perennial, distracting preoccupations with Ireland and parliamentary reform.[84] To these, the 'New Liberalism' of the Edwardian period added a new concern with redistributive public finance and 'social' questions, as well as a variety of influential theories – such as Norman Angell's – about the economic irrationality of war.[85] If nothing else, the new government seemed likely to try (in Lloyd George's words) 'to reduce the gigantic expenditure on armaments built up by the recklessness of our predecessors'.[86]

The law of unintended consequences, however, is never more likely to operate than when a government is as fundamentally divided as the Liberal government by degrees became. As early as September 1905, Asquith, Grey and Haldane (who became War Minister) had agreed to act in concert as a 'Liberal Imperialist' or 'Liberal League' faction within the new administration, in order to counter the Radical tendencies feared by, among others, the King.[87] The appointment of Grey as Foreign Secretary was one of the faction's first and most important successes. Grey was certainly far from being an ardent imperialist. He was evidently familiar with the arguments of Angell about the illusory rationale of war.[88] He shared the Radical desire 'to pursue a European policy without keeping up a great army' and welcomed the support of the Gladstonians like John Morley when trying to rein in the Government of India. On the other hand, his enthusiasm for continuing and deepening the Entente with France and concluding a similar agreement with Russia was at odds with the aversion of the 'peace at any price' group within the Cabinet to continental entanglements. This fundamental division ought to have caused trouble sooner than it did. However, Asquith – who succeeded Campbell-Bannerman as Prime Minister in April 1908 – was adept at covering Grey's position.[89] It suited both men – not to mention the diplomats at the Foreign Office – to limit the direct influence of the Cabinet and Parliament over foreign policy. It was typical of Grey to complain, as he did in October 1906, about Liberal MPs having 'now acquired the art of asking questions and raising debates, and there is so much in foreign affairs which attracts attention and had much better be left alone'. When Cabinet colleagues pronounced on foreign affairs, Grey sought 'to convince them that there are such things as brick walls' against which they were merely 'run[ning] their own heads'.[90]

In this, he was unquestionably aided and abetted by the Opposition's tacit approval of his policy. It must always be remembered that the Liberals' majority was steadily whittled away between 1906 and 1914. At the last pre-war general election of December 1910, the Liberals and Tories had won 272 seats apiece, so that the government relied on 42 Labour MPs and 84 Irish Nationalists for its majority. Because the Conservatives won sixteen out of the twenty by-elections which followed, by July 1914 that majority had been reduced to just twelve. This helps explain the government's floundering over both the budget and Home Rule in that fateful month.[91] Under such circumstances, the influence of the Opposition was bound to increase. Had the Conservative leadership disagreed with Grey's policy, they could have made life as difficult for him as they made it for Lloyd George, with whose fiscal policy they disagreed, and Asquith, whose Irish policy they abhorred. But they did not. They believed that Grey was continuing their policy. As the Tory Chief Whip Balcarres put it in May 1912, his party had 'supported Grey for six years on the assumption that he continues the Anglo-French Entente which Lord Lansdowne established and the Anglo-Russian Entente Lord Lansdowne began'.[92] True, Balfour had to be careful not to offend the right of his party by appearing to 'love' the government too much.[93] Still, the fact remains that there was more agreement between Grey's faction of the Cabinet and the Opposition front bench than within the Cabinet itself. What this meant was that the detail of Grey's policy (and the Devil lay there) was not subjected to close enough parliamentary scrutiny. Moreover, where such scrutiny might have occurred – within the civil and military services – there reigned confusion. Despite the endeavours of Esher, the Committee of Imperial Defence declined in importance under the Liberals. In place of strategic planning, over which agreement between the Admiralty and the War Office seemed impossible, there developed a technocratic obsession with logistics as set down in the famous 'War Book' – the precision of which was matched only by its complete imprecision as to the objectives and economic implications of mobilisation.[94]

All of this in fact gave Grey far greater freedom of action than his memoirs subsequently suggested. Nor, it should be noted, was he a man unused to freedom, a point nicely illustrated by one of his less well-known pre-war publications. Fly-fishing – Grey's passion from childhood to blind old age – is not an occupation conducive to a deterministic cast of mind. In his book on the subject, published in 1899, he waxed lyrical about its uncertain, unpredictable pleasures. One passage in particular, in which he describes landing an 8-lb salmon, deserves quotation:

> There was no immediate cause for dreading catastrophe. But ...
> there came on me a grim consciousness that the whole affair
> must be very long, and that the most difficult part of all would
> be at the end, not in playing the fish, but in landing it.... It
> seemed as if any attempt to land the fish with [my] net would
> precipitate a catastrophe which I could not face. More than once
> I failed and each failure was horrible.... For myself, I know
> nothing which equals the excitement of having hooked an
> unexpectedly large fish on a small rod and fine tackle.[95]

It is with this Grey in mind – the excited, anxious fisherman on the riverbank, rather than the broken, disappointed self-apologist of the memoirs – that we should interpret British foreign policy between 1906 and 1914. At the risk of pushing the analogy too far, it might be said that much of the time – and especially in the July Crisis – Grey conducted himself exactly as he had on that occasion. He hoped he might land the fish, but knew the risk of 'catastrophe'. In neither case was the outcome a foregone conclusion.

In one sense, it must be said, the analogy is misleading. For, in his dealings with Russia and France, it was arguably Grey who was the fish others hooked and landed. In the case of Russia, Grey later maintained that he had effectively continued his predecessor's policy of detente, despite the distaste of the Radicals and the doubts of the War Office.[96] On closer inspection, however, Grey went significantly further than Lansdowne. This was partly because he could rely on backbench support for cuts in spending on the defence of India, and so could more easily override traditional 'North-West Frontier' sentiment.[97] In addition, he made substantial concessions to Russia over Persia. He even showed signs of favouring Russia's traditional ambitions in Turkey and the Balkans as a counterweight to Germany's growing influence. Such concessions may have encouraged the Russian Foreign Minister Sazonov to count on British support in the event of war. The decision in May 1914 to hold joint conversations on naval issues certainly did nothing to discourage him.[98]

It was much easier for a Liberal Foreign Secretary to pursue a Francophile policy than a Russophile policy, and Grey had signalled his intention to pursue the former even before taking office.[99] Again, it appeared that Tory policy was being continued. But again – as he himself admitted – Grey went significantly 'further than the late Government here were ever required to do'.[100] The military discussions between Britain and France which were initiated at the end of 1905 marked a new departure. Here, it has been argued, was Grey's gravest error – the moment at which he was effectively hooked by the French ambassador Paul Cambon. By allowing the military planners to discuss joint action not only at sea but also on land in the event of a Franco-German war, he implied a much stronger commitment to the defence of France than had hitherto been considered. Of vital importance was the General Staff's success in arguing for the immediate despatch of an expeditionary force of at least 100,000 men to France or Belgium in the event of a Franco-German war, on the grounds that naval operations alone would not prevent a successful German invasion of France.[101] It could be argued that these talks, and the subsequent development of British military planning, gave the Entente Cordiale what amounted to a secret military protocol. That was certainly what the hawks in the Foreign Office wanted. As early as January 1906, Bertie (now ambassador in Paris) was talking about giving 'more than diplomatic support' to defend French interests in Morocco, meaning an explicit 'promise of armed assistance'. This meant much more than was implied in the naval division of responsibility between Mediterranean and North Sea.[102] Indeed, it might even be suggested – to turn Fritz

Fischer on his head – that the CID meeting of 23 August 1911 (rather than the notorious meeting between the Kaiser and his military chiefs sixteen months later) was the real 'war council' which set the course for a war between Britain and Germany. Certainly, it appeared to mark a triumph for the General Staff's expeditionary force strategy over the Admiralty's envisaged combination of a close blockade and joint amphibious operations on the North German coast.[103] Outside the committee room, General Sir Henry Wilson, the Director of Military Operations, was energetic in selling the General Staff's strategy to Grey and other ministers, including – significantly – Lloyd George. Grey thus had a very clear idea of what he was promising when he gave Cambon a private assurance in early 1914 that 'no British government would refuse [France] military and naval assistance if she were unjustly threatened and attacked'.[104]

What made Grey shift in this way from the overseas ententes of his predecessors to a more or less explicit 'continental commitment' to France? The traditional answer is that Germany's *Weltpolitik* had come to be viewed in London as a growing threat to British interests in Africa, Asia and the Near East; and, more importantly, that Germany's naval construction constituted a serious challenge to British security. Yet, on close inspection, neither colonial issues nor naval issues were leading inevitably to an Anglo-German showdown before 1914. As Churchill later put it, 'We were no enemies to German colonial expansion.'[105] Indeed, an agreement between Britain and Germany which would have opened the way to increased German influence in the Portuguese colonies in southern Africa came close to being concluded.[106] Grey himself said in 1911 that it did not 'matter very much whether we ha[d] Germany or France as a neighbor in Africa'. he was eager to bring about a 'division' of the 'derelict' Portuguese colonies 'as soon as possible' 'in a pro-German spirit'.[107] Only his officials' reluctance to renege publicly on British commitments to Portugal made thirteen years before prevented a public deal; but the German blanks (notably M. M. Warburg & Co.) which had become involved evidently regarded this as a mere formality.[108] Even where Grey inclined to give French interests primacy – in Morocco – there was not a complete impasse with respect to Germany. In 1906, Grey had been willing to consider giving Germany a coaling station on the country's Atlantic coast.[109] It is true that the government took an aggressive line following the Agadir crisis, issuing a clear warning to Berlin against treating Britain 'as if she were of no account in the Cabinet of Nations'. But even Asquith had to admit that a Franco-German agreement involving territory and influence in non-British Africa had little to do with him. In any case, the German government backed down after Agadir; and when they then turned their attentions to Turkey, it was much harder for Grey to take an anti-German line without playing into the hands of the Russians with respect to the Straits.[110] Grey was pleased with the way the Germans acted during the Balkan wars of 1912/13 and was relatively unworried by the Liman von Sanders affair (the appointment of a German general as Instructor General to the Turkish army). Relations were further improved by Germany's conciliatory response to British concerns over the Berlin–Baghdad railway.[111] In this light, it was not unreasonable of the *Frankfurter Zeitung* to speak, as it did in October 1913, of 'rapprochement' between Britain and Germany and an 'end to the sterile years of mutual distrust'.[112] The FO view as late as 27 June 1914 – the eve of the Sarajevo assassination – was that the German government was 'in peaceful mood and . . . very anxious to be on good terms with 'England'. Even on 23 July, Lloyd George could be heard pronouncing Anglo-German relations 'much better' than they had been 'a few years ago'.[113]

Likewise, it is quite misleading to see the naval race as a 'cause' of the First World War. There were strong arguments on both sides for a naval agreement. Both governments were finding the political consequences of increasing naval expenditure difficult to live with. The Liberals had come in pledged to cut arms spending and could not easily sell increases in the naval estimates to their backbenchers and the radical press. At the same time, rising defence spending made the task of financing a more progressive social policy significantly harder. The German government was under even greater fiscal pressure. The rising cost of defence placed the Reich's federal system under intense strains which threatened to estrange the government from its traditional Conservative supporters and strengthen the Social Democrats' case for more progressive taxation at the national level.[114] So why was there no deal? The possibility surfaced on numerous occasions: in December 1907, when the Germans proposed a North Sea convention with Britain and France; in February 1908, when the Kaiser explicitly denied that Germany aimed 'to challenge British naval supremacy'; six months later, when he met the Permanent Secretary at the Foreign Office Sir Charles Hardinge at Kronberg; in March 1911, when the Kaiser called for 'a naval agreement tending to limit naval expenditure'; and, most famously, in February 1912, when Haldane travelled to Berlin, ostensibly 'about the business of a university committee', in reality to discuss the possibility of a naval, colonial and non-aggression agreement with Bethmann Hollweg, Tirpitz and the Kaiser.[115] The traditional answer is that the Germans refused to make concessions. Much blame for this has been heaped on Tirpitz and the Kaiser, who have been accused of torpedoing the Haldane mission by introducing a new naval increase on the eve of his arrival. In addition, it is argued the Germans were willing to discuss naval issues only after they had received an unconditional British pledge of neutrality in the event of a Franco-German war.[116] Yet this is only half the story. Asquith later claimed that the German formula of neutrality would 'have precluded us from coming to the help of France should Germany on any pretext attack her'. In fact, Bethmann Hollweg's draft stated:

> The high contracting powers ... will not either of them make any unprovoked attack upon the other or join in any combination or design against the other for the purpose of aggression.... If either ... becomes entangled in a war *in which it cannot be said to be aggressor*, the other will at least observe towards the power so entangled a benevolent neutrality.[117]

The most that Grey was willing to offer was a commitment not to 'make or join in any unprovoked attack upon Germany' because, in his words, 'the word neutrality ... would give the impression our hands were tied'.[118]

Similarly, the subsequent British claim that the naval escalation was the fault of the German side alone needs to be treated with scepticism. The Germans in fact offered real concessions during the Haldane mission; it was on the neutrality issue that the talks foundered, more than the naval issue.[119] And arguably it was the British position which was the more intransigent – not surprisingly, as it was based on unassailable strength. For despite the 'panic' of 1909, there was never much chance of the Germans being able to close the huge gap in naval capability.[120] Nor did the Admiralty ever doubt that its strategy of blockading Germany would be effective in the event of war. Indeed, there was a clear blueprint for naval war against Germany which was far more ruthless in conception than anything drafted by Tirpitz. In the first weeks of a war with Germany, as Fisher predicted in 1906, the Royal Navy would 'mop up' hundreds of German merchant ships around the world; and then impose a tight blockade without the slightest regard to the limits imposed by the London Convention agreed at the Hague Conference. So clear did the British superiority appear that senior naval figures including Fisher, Esher and Wilson found it hard to imagine Germany risking war against Britain.[121] Grey's view was accordingly uncompromising: any naval agreement could only be on the basis of 'permanent' British superiority.[122] In practice, as Churchill saw after his move to the Admiralty, the German government had been obliged to accept this by 1913. His concern as First Lord was to maintain the '60 per cent standard ... in relation not only to Germany but to the rest of the world'. 'Why', he asked bluntly, 'should it be supposed that we should not be able to defeat [Germany]? A study of the comparative fleet strength in the line of battle will be found reassuring.'[123] By 1914, as Churchill recalled, 'naval rivalry had ... ceased to be a cause of friction. ... We were proceeding inflexibly ..., it was certain we could not be overtaken.' Even Asquith later admitted that 'the competition in naval expenditure was not in itself a likely source of immediate danger. We had quite determined to maintain our necessary predominance at sea and we were well able to make that determination effective.'[124]

It is therefore not difficult to see why Bethmann Hollweg's proposed deal – accepting British naval supremacy in return for continental neutrality – was rejected out of hand by Grey: quite simply, Britain could have the former without giving the latter. What is harder to understand is Grey's belief that almost *any* expression of Anglo-German rapprochement was out of the question. Why, if Germany posed neither a colonial nor a naval threat to Britain, was Grey so relentlessly anti-German? The answer is simply that, even more than his Tory predecessors, Grey cared more about good relations with France and Russia – with the difference, as we have seen, that he was willing to do more to conciliate them (and therefore less to conciliate Germany). 'Nothing we do in our relations with Germany', he had declared in October 1905, 'is in any way to impair our existing good relations with France.' 'The danger of speaking civil words in Berlin', he wrote the following January, 'is that they may be ... interpreted in France as implying that we shall be lukewarm in our support of the entente.'[125] He made the point unambiguously to his ambassador in Berlin, Edward Goschen, in April 1910: 'We cannot enter into a political understanding with Germany which would separate us from Russia and France.'[126] However, when Grey said that any understanding with Germany had to be 'consistent with the preservation of [our existing] relations and friendships with other powers', he was effectively ruling out *any* meaningful understanding.[127] In this he was at one with senior Foreign Office officials like the Permanent Under-Secretary Nicolson, who opposed the idea of an agreement with Germany in 1912 mainly because it would 'seriously impair our relations [with France] – and such a result would at once react on our relations with Russia'.[128]

On close inspection, Grey's reasoning was deeply flawed. Firstly, his notion that bad relations with France and Russia might actually have led to war was preposterous. There was a big difference in this respect between his situation and that of his Tory predecessors. At the time, Grey himself acknowledged that Russia's recovery from the ravages of defeat and revolution would take a decade. Nor did he see France as a threat: as he put it to President Roosevelt in 1906, France was 'peaceful and neither aggressive nor restless'.[129] The original point of the ententes had been to settle overseas differences with France and Russia. This having been done, the chances of war between Britain and either power were remote. It was simply fantastic for Grey to suggest to the editor of the *Manchester Guardian* C. P. Scott, as he did in September 1912, 'that if France is not supported against Germany she would join with her and the rest of Europe in an attack upon us'.[130] Only slightly less chimerical was the fear that France or Russia might 'desert to the Central Powers'.[131] This was a constant Foreign Office preoccupation. As early as 1905, Grey feared 'losing France and not gaining Germany, who won't want us if she can detach France from us'. If Britain did not respond to French overtures over Algeciras, warned Bertie, 'We shall ... be looked upon as traitors by the French and ... be despised by the Germans.' Typically, Nicolson argued for a formal alliance with France and Russia 'to deter Russia from moving towards Berlin ... [and] prevent [France] from deserting to the Central Powers'. Obsessively, Grey and his officials dreaded losing their 'value as friends' and ending up 'standing *alone*' – 'without friends'. Their recurrent nightmare was that Russia or France would succumb to 'the Teuton embrace'. For this reason, they tended to see all German policy as aimed at 'smashing ... the Triple Alliance'.[132] Characteristically, Grey reasoned that 'if ... by some misfortune or blunder our Entente with France is to be broken up, France will have to make her own terms with Germany. And Germany will again be in a position to keep us on bad terms with France and Russia, and to make herself predominant upon the Continent. Then, sooner or later, there will be a war between us and Germany.'[133] Yet, in his determination to preserve the Entente with France, Grey was willing to make military commitments which made war with Germany *more* rather than less likely, sooner rather than later. By a completely circular process of reasoning, he wished to commit Britain to war with Germany – because otherwise there might be war with Germany.

The strongest justification for all of this, of course, was that Germany had megalomaniac ambitions which posed a threat not only to France by to Britain itself. As we have seen, this view was widely held by Conservative journalists and Germanophobe diplomats. Yet it is a striking fact that their alarmist claims were at odds with much of the intelligence the Foreign Office actually received from Berlin before the war. This is a point which has hitherto been overlooked by historians. True, there was little in the way of good military intelligence on Germany before 1914 in the absence of a modern espionage network.[134] But the reports from British diplomats and consuls in Germany were of a high quality. A far better analysis than Crowe's of 1907 was Churchill's of November 1909. Churchill was scarcely a Germanophile. But he argued – evidently on the basis of such intelligence – that 'the increasing difficulties of getting money' were 'becoming terribly effective' as 'checks upon German naval expansion':

> The overflowing expenditure of the German Empire strains and threatens every dyke by which the social and political unity of Germany is maintained.... The heavy duties upon food-stuffs, from which the main proportion of the customs revenue is raised, have produced a deep cleavage between the agrarians and the industrial[ist]s ... The field of direct taxation is already largely occupied by the State and local systems. The prospective inroad by the universal suffrage Parliament of the Empire upon this depleted field unites the propertied classes ... in a common apprehension ... On the other hand, the new or increased taxation on every form of popular indulgence powerfully strengthens the parties of the Left, who are themselves the opponents of expenditure on armaments and much else besides. Meanwhile the German Imperial debt has more than doubled in the last thirteen years of unbroken peace ... The credit of the

German Empire has fallen to the level of that of Italy. . . . These circumstances force the conclusion that a period of severe internal strain approaches in Germany.[135]

Nor was Churchill alone in discerning Germany's financial weakness. As early as April 1908, Grey himself had 'pointed out that finance might in the course of the next few years prove a very serious difficulty to Germany and exercise a restraining influence on her'. The German ambassador Metternich actually drew his attention to domestic political 'resistance' to naval expenditure the following year.[136] Goschen too commented on Germany's fiscal problems in 1911 and was sceptical of the Kaiser's protestations to the contrary.[137] At the time of the controversial 1913 Army Bill, he noted that 'each class would . . . be glad to see the financial burden thrust onto shoulders other than its own'.[138] In March 1914, Nicolson went so far as to predict that 'unless Germany is prepared to make still further financial sacrifices for military purposes, the days of her hegemony in Europe [sic] will be numbered'.[139] There was also a strong awareness of the vulnerability of Germany's alliances with Austria and Italy. In short, British observers admitted that Germany was weak, not strong, and that it was financially and politically incapable of winning a naval arms race against Britain, or a land arms race against France and Russia. The only danger Churchill discerned was that the German government, rather than try to 'soothe the internal situation', might 'find an escape from it in external adventure'. Grey himself twice commented in July 1914 on the logic, from a German point of view, of a pre-emptive strike against Russia and France, before the military balance deteriorated any further.

The truth is that whereas formerly the German government had aggressive intentions . . . they are now genuinely alarmed at the military preparations in Russia, the prospective increase in her military forces and particularly at the intended construction, at the insistence of the French government and with French money, of strategic railways to converge on the German fron-

tier. . . . Germany was not afraid, because she believed her army
to be invulnerable, but she was afraid that in a few years hence
she might be afraid. . . . Germany was afraid of the future.[140]

Why then did he and the most senior officials in the Foreign
Office and the General Staff nevertheless conjure up a German
design for Napoleonic power, posing a direct threat to Britain?
The possibility arises that they were exaggerating – if not fabricat-
ing – such a threat in order to justify the military commitment to
France they favoured. In other words, precisely *because* they
wished to align Britain with France and Russia, it was necessary
to impute grandiose plans for European domination to the
Germans.

Germany's Bid for European Union

This brings us to the crucial question: what *were* Germany's 'war
aims' in 1914? According to Fritz Fischer, of course, they were
every bit as radical as the British Germanophobes feared. The war
was an attempt 'to realise Germany's political ambitions, which
may be summed up as German hegemony over Europe' through
annexations of French, Belgian and possibly Russian territory, the
creation of a Central European customs union and the creation of
new Polish and Baltic states directly or indirectly under German
control. In addition, Germany was to acquire new territory in
Africa, so that its colonial possessions could be consolidated as a
continuous Central African area. There was also to be a concerted
effort to break up the British and Russian empires through
fomenting revolutions.[141] Yet there is a fundamental flaw in
Fischer's reasoning which too many historians have let pass. It
is the assumption, typical of determinist historiography, that
Germany's aims as stated after the war had begun were the same
as German aims beforehand.[142] Thus Bethmann Hollweg's 'September Programme' – 'provisional notes for the direction of our
policy' for a separate peace with France, drafted on the assumption
of a swift German victory in the west – is portrayed as the first

open statement of aims which had existed before the outbreak of war.[143] If this were true, then the argument that war was avoidable would collapse; for it is clear that no British government could have accepted the territorial and political terms which the September Programme proposed for France and Belgium,[144] as these would indeed have realised the 'Napoleonic nightmare' by giving Germany control of the Belgian coast. Yet the inescapable fact is that no evidence has ever been found by Fischer and his pupils that these objectives existed *before* Britain's entry into the war. It is possible that they were never committed to paper, or that the relevant documents were destroyed or lost, and that those involved subsequently lied rather than concede legitimacy to the 'war guilt' clause of the Versailles Treaty. But it seems unlikely. All that Fischer can produce are the pre-war pipedreams of a few pan-Germans and businessmen (notably Walther Rathenau), none of which had any official status, as well as the occasional bellicose utterances of the Kaiser, an individual whose influence over policy was neither consistent nor as great as he himself believed.[145]

To grasp Germany's pre-war objectives, it is necessary first to realise how right Churchill had been about the weakness of Germany's position. For primarily financial reasons, it had indeed lost the naval arms race against Britain, and it was losing the land arms race against Russia and France. It also had good reason to fear for the reliability of its principal ally Austria, and little reason to have confidence in such other powers as it had been wooing (notably Italy and Turkey). By contrast, the strength of the Triple Entente seemed to be confirmed by the rumours of Anglo-Russian naval talks. In these circumstances, the long-held belief of the Chief of the General Staff, Moltke, that some kind of pre-emptive military strike against Russia and France might be preferable to continuing military decline, had begun to win influential converts even before the Sarajevo assassination. In the first instance, to be sure, Bethmann Hollweg's objective in July 1914 was to score a diplomatic success. His hope was that a swift Austrian military strike against Serbia would cement the Dual Alliance and split the Triple Entente, because he doubted that Britain would be willing to support a Russian intervention on behalf of Serbia.[146] But from the outset he was sanguine about the possibility of a war against Russia and France. Provided Russia could be made to appear the aggressor, he was ready for continental war, calculating that under those circumstances Britain would not intervene – or at least not 'immediately'.[147]

The critical point is that, had Britain not intervened immediately, Germany's war aims would have been significantly different from those set out in the September Programme. Bethmann Hollweg's statement to Goschen of 29 July 1914 shows clearly that he was prepared to guarantee the territorial integrity of both France and Belgium (as well as Holland) in return for British neutrality.[148] Had Britain in fact stayed out, it would have been madness to have reneged on such a bargain. So Germany's aims would almost certainly not have included the territorial changes envisaged in the September Programme (except perhaps those relating to Luxemburg, in which Britain had no interest); and they certainly would not have included the proposals for German control of the Belgian coast, which no British government could have tolerated. The most that would have remained, then, would have been the following proposals:

1. *France.* . . . A war indemnity to be paid in instalments; it must be high enough to prevent France from spending any considerable sums on armaments in the next 15–20 years. Furthermore: a commercial treaty which makes France economically dependent on Germany [and] secures the French market for our exports . . . This treaty must secure for us financial and industrial freedom of movement in France in such fashion that German enterprises can no longer receive different treatment from French.

2. . . . We must create a *central European economic association* through common customs treaties, to include France, Belgium, Holland, Denmark, Austria–Hungary, Poland, and perhaps Italy, Sweden and Norway. This association will not have any common constitutional supreme authority and all its members

will be formally equal, but in practice will be under German leadership and must stabilise Germany's economic dominance over *Mitteleuropa*.

[3.] *The question of colonial acquisitions*, where the first aim is the creation of a continuous Central African colonial empire, will be considered later, as will that of the aims realised *vis-à-vis* Russia. . . .

4. *Holland*. It will have to be considered by what means and methods Holland can be brought into closer relationship with the German Empire. In view of the Dutch character, this closer relationship must leave them free of any feeling of compulsion, must alter nothing in the Dutch way of life, and must also subject them to no new military obligations. Holland, then, must be left independent in externals, but be made internally dependent on us. Possibly one might consider an offensive and defensive alliance, to cover the colonies; in any case a close customs association . . .[149]

To these points – in effect, the September Programme without annexations from France and Belgium – should be added the detailed plans subsequently drawn up to 'thrust [Russia] back as far as possible from Germany's eastern frontier and [break] her domination over the non-Russian vassal peoples'. These envisaged the creation of a new Polish state (joined to Habsburg Galicia) and the cession of the Baltic provinces (which would either be independent, incorporated in the new Poland or annexed by Germany itself).[150] Even this edited version of the September Programme probably exaggerates the pre-war aims of the German leadership. Bülow, of course, was no longer Chancellor; but his comments to the Crown Prince in 1908 were not so different from Bethmann Hollweg's view that war would strengthen the political left and weaken the Reich internally:

No war in Europe can bring us much. There would be nothing for us to gain in the conquest of fresh Slav or French territory. If we annex small countries to the Empire we shall only strengthen those centrifugal elements which, alas, are never wanting in Germany.... A war, lightly provoked, even if it were fought successfully, would have a bad effect on the country.... Every great war is followed by a period of liberalism.[151]

Would the limited war aims outlined above have posed a direct threat to British interests? Did they imply a Napoleonic strategy? Hardly. All that the economic clauses of the September Programme implied was the creation, some eighty years early, of a German-dominated European customs union not so very different from the one which exists today – the European Union. Indeed, many of the official statements on the subject have a striking contemporary resonance, for example Hans Delbrück's 'It is only a Europe which forms a single customs unit that can meet with sufficient power the over-mighty productive resources of the transatlantic world'; or Gustav Müller's enthusiastic call for a 'United States of Europe' (a phrase used before the war by the Kaiser) 'including Switzerland, The Netherlands, the Scandinavian states, Belgium, France, even Spain and Portugal and, via Austria–Hungary, also Rumania, Bulgaria and Turkey'; or Baron Ludwig von Falkenhausen's aspiration 'to match the great, closed economic bodies of the United States, the British and the Russian Empires with an equally solid economic bloc representing all European states ... under German leadership, with the twofold purpose: (1) of assuring the members of this whole, particularly Germany, mastery of the European market, and (2) of being able to lead the entire economic strength of allied Europe into the field, as a unified force, in the struggle with those world powers over the conditions of the admission of each to the markets of the other'.[152] The difference is that in 1914 Britain would not have become a member of the Kaiser's 'EU'. On the contrary, with its maritime empire intact, Britain would have remained a superpower in its own right.

Of course, it was not to be: the bid for British neutrality was, as we know, rejected. Yet German historians have been too quick to dismiss Bethmann Hollweg's proposal as wild miscalculation;

or even to argue that the Germans themselves did not expect to secure British neutrality. The documentary record does not bear this out. On the contrary, it shows that Bethmann Hollweg's hopes of British non-intervention were far from unreasonable. He can be forgiven for not anticipating that, at the very last minute, the arguments of Grey and Crowe would prevail over the numerically stronger non-interventionists.

The Continental Non-Commitment

For it would be quite wrong to conclude that British pre-war military planning on the assumption of intervention in a Franco-German war actually made war inevitable. The majority of Cabinet members (to say nothing of Parliament) had at first been kept in ignorance of the discussions with the French. As Sanderson put it to Cambon, the notion of a military commitment to France 'gave rise to divergences of opinion' – 'anything of a more definite nature would have been at once rejected by the Cabinet'. Extra-ordinarily, even the Prime Minister Campbell-Bannerman was initially kept in the dark. When he was told, he expressed his anxiety that 'the stress laid upon joint preparations ... comes very close to an honourable undertaking'. Haldane accordingly had to make it 'clear' to the Chief of the General Staff, Lyttleton, 'that we were to be in no way committed by the fact of having entered into communications'.[153] Under these circumstances, it was quite impossible for Grey to take the step towards a formal alliance with France favoured by the Foreign Office hawks Mallet, Nicolson and Crowe.[154] As the more cautious Permanent Secretary Hardinge emphasised in his testimony before the CID sub-committee meeting of March 1909, 'We had given *no* assurance that we would help [the French] on land, and ... the only grounds upon which the French could base any hopes of military assistance were the *semi-official* conversations which had taken place between the French military attaché and our General Staff.' Accordingly, the sub-committee concluded that 'in the event of an attack on France by Germany, the expedient of sending a military force abroad, or of relying on naval means only, is *a matter of policy that can only be determined, when the occasion arises, by the Government of the day'*.[155] The option of military intervention was merely being considered (and its logistical implications explored), just as the option of nuclear retaliation in the event of a Soviet attack on Western Europe was considered by the US during the Cold War. In both cases the same distinction must be made: simply because plans for war were drawn up, war was not inevitable. Even the Germanophobe Eyre Crowe had to concede, as he did in February 1911, 'the fundamental fact ... that the Entente is not an alliance. For purposes of ultimate emergencies it may be found to have no substance at all. For an Entente is nothing more than a frame of mind, a view of general policy which is shared by the governments of two countries, but which may be, or become, so vague as to lose all content.'[156]

It was the Cabinet, not Grey, which would make the final decision; and the government as a whole was, in Grey's words, 'quite free'.[157] As far as the Lord Chancellor Loreburn was concerned, intervention in 'a purely French quarrel' was therefore inconceivable, because it could only be done with 'a majority largely composed of Conservatives and with a very large number of the Ministerial side against you.... This would mean that the present Government could not carry on.'[158] In November 1911, Grey was comprehensively outvoted in the Cabinet (by fifteen to five) over two resolutions expressly repudiating any military commitment to France.[159] The issue came up again in November 1912, when the Radicals in the Cabinet, backed up by the navalists Hankey and Esher, succeeded in forcing Grey to deny in the House of Commons that any secret and binding military commitment to France had been given. Haldane felt that he had emerged from the decisive Cabinet session 'unhampered in any material point', but that was not the way Asquith summarised the Cabinet's conclusion to the King: 'No communications should take place between the General Staff and the Staffs of other countries which can, directly or indirectly, commit this country to military or naval intervention.... Such communications, if they related to concerted action by land or sea, should not be entered into without the previous approval of the Cabinet.'[160] Small wonder the French military attaché in Berlin concluded that, in a war with Germany, 'England will be but of very little assistance to us'. Crowe continued to press 'to render our general understanding with France both wider and more definite', but the opponents of alliance were in the ascendant.[161] Nothing illustrates this more clearly than Churchill's notes of 1912 on the naval division of responsibility which concentrated the French navy in the Mediterranean and the British fleet in home waters. These dispositions, Churchill stated, had been 'made independently because they are the best which the separate interests of each country suggests [*sic*]. . . . They do not arise from any naval agreement or convention. . . . *Nothing in the naval or military arrangements ought to have the effect of exposing us . . . if, when the time comes, we decide to stand out.*'[162]

With Harcourt and Esher publicly and privately hammering home the point, Grey had no option but to tell Cambon that there was no 'engagement that commits either Government . . . to cooperate in war'.[163] The Anglo-Russian naval talks implied still less of a commitment. Indeed, there was growing unease in London about the Russian appetite for unreciprocated concessions in the Near East.[164] As Grey told Cambon in May 1914, 'We could not enter into any military engagement, even of the most hypothetical kind, with Russia.' On 11 June 1914 – just days before the Sarajevo assassination – he had to repeat his assurance to the Commons that 'if war arose between the European Powers, there were no unpublished agreements which would restrict or hamper the freedom of the Government or . . . Parliament to decide whether or not Great Britain should participate in a war'.[165]

Thus the sole plausible justification for Grey's strategy – that it would deter a German attack on France – fell away. 'An Entente between Russia, France and ourselves would be absolutely secure,' he had said shortly after becoming Foreign Secretary. 'If it is necessary to check Germany it could be done.'[166] That had been the basis for his, Haldane's and even the King's statements to various German representatives in 1912 that Britain could 'under no circumstance tolerate France being crushed'.[167] These statements have often been seen by historians as categorical commitments which the Germans ignored at their peril. But the truth, as the German government could hardly fail to realise, was that the Entente was not as 'absolutely secure' as Grey had intended. Indeed, he had been forced by his Cabinet colleagues to disavow publicly the idea of a defensive alliance with France and Russia. All that remained to console the French in the event of a German attack was Grey's *private* undertaking as a Wykehamist, a Balliol man and a gentleman. But that would mean British intervention only if Grey could convert the majority of the Cabinet to his standpoint, something he had wholly failed to do in 1911. If he could not, he and possibly the whole Government would resign – hardly a cause for German trepidation. Is it therefore so surprising that Bethmann Hollweg was willing to take his gamble? If the *Manchester Guardian* could confidently state – as it did in July 1914 – that there was 'no danger of [Britain] being dragged into the conflict [between Austria and Serbia] by treaties of alliance'; if Asquith himself could see 'no reason why we should be more than spectators' as late as 24 July – why should Bethmann Hollweg have thought otherwise?[168] On balance, the uncertainty about Britain's position probably made a continental war more rather than less likely, by encouraging the Germans to consider a pre-emptive strike.[169] But it certainly did not make *British* intervention in such a war inevitable – quite the reverse, as the events of July 1914 were to show.

When, in the wake of the Sarajevo assassination, it became clear in London that the Austrian government intended demanding 'some compensation in the sense of some humiliation for Serbia', Grey's first reaction was to worry about how Russia might react. Seeing the possibility of a confrontation between Austria and Russia, he sought to exert indirect pressure via Berlin to temper any Austrian reprisals, hoping to repeat the success of his Balkan diplomacy of the previous year.[170] At first, Grey urged Austria and Russia to 'discuss things together' in the hope that terms could be devised for the Serbs which both sides would find acceptable, but this was dismissed by the French President Poincaré, who happened to be in St Petersburg. Doubting his ability to exercise a moderating influence over Russia, and suspecting that the German government might actually be 'egging on' the Austrians, Grey changed tack, warning the German ambassador Lichnowsky that Russia would stand by Serbia, prophesying a second 1848 revolution in the event of a continental war and suggesting mediation between Austria and Russia by the four other powers (Britain, Germany, France and Italy).[171]

From the outset, Grey was extremely reluctant to give any indication of how Britain might respond to an escalation of the conflict. He knew that if Austria pressed extreme demands on Belgrade with German backing, and Russia mobilised in defence of Serbia, then France might well become involved – such was the nature of the Franco-Russian entente and German military strategy. The whole strategy of the ententes with France and Russia had been to deter such a Franco-German war. However, Grey also feared that too strong a signal of support for France and Russia – such as Crowe and Nicolson predictably urged – might encourage the Russians to risk war. He found himself in a cleft stick: how to deter the Dual Alliance without encouraging the Dual Entente.[172] The impression he gave, unfortunately, was exactly the opposite of what he hoped to achieve: by Sunday 26 July, the French thought they could count on Britain, while the Germans felt 'sure' of English neutrality. As Jagow put it to Cambon: 'You have your information. We have ours'; unfortunately, the source was identical in each case.[173] The German government continued undeterred, feigning interest in Grey's proposals for mediation, which it had no intention of pursuing.[174]

To be fair to Grey, his tactic of studied ambiguity very nearly paid off. So exposed did the Serbian government feel itself to be that – despite Grey's dismay at its 'formidable' terms – it all but accepted the Austrian ultimatum, seeking only the most limited modifications to it.[175] Moreover, to the dismay of both Bethmann Hollweg and Moltke, who had been urging the Austrians not to take Grey's mediation proposal seriously, the Kaiser hailed the Serbian reply as a diplomatic triumph, urging Vienna simply to 'Halt in Belgrade' – that is, to occupy the Serbian capital temporarily (much as Prussia had occupied Paris in 1870) to ensure the implementation of the Austrian demands. This compounded the confusion which Jagow had created by stating that Germany would *not* act if Russia mobilised only in the south (that is, against Austria but not Germany).[176] At the same time, the Russian Foreign Minister Sazonov unexpectedly changed his mind about the possibility of bilateral talks between Austria and Russia, an idea Grey immediately returned to when it became clear that the German government did not really favour his scheme for a four-power conference.[177] For a moment, it seemed that the continental war might be averted. Unfortunately for Grey, however, there was already an unbridgeable gulf between Berlin and St Petersburg. On the one hand, Sazonov had no intention of accepting the occupation of Belgrade by Austria, which would have represented in his eyes a serious reverse for Russian influence in the Balkans.[178] On the other, Bethmann Hollweg had no intention of treating the terms of the Austrian ultimatum as in any way negotiable.[179]

At this stage, military logic began to supersede diplomatic calculation. Even before the Austrian bombardment of Belgrade began, Sazonov and his military colleagues issued orders for partial mobilisation, which they then desperately tried to turn into full mobilisation on being warned that Germany in fact intended to mobilise even in the case of partial Russian mobilisation.[180] This was precisely the pretext the Germans wanted to launch their own mobilisation against not only Russia but also France.[181] The idea of Austro-Russian talks was forgotten in a bizarre 'reverse race', in which, for the sake of domestic opinion, Germany tried to get Russia to mobilise first and vice versa. Continental war was now surely unavoidable. Even when Bethmann Hollweg, grasping at last that Britain might intervene immediately in response to an attack on France, sought to force the Austrians to the negotiating table, they refused to suspend their military operations.[182] Royal appeals from London to St Petersburg to halt mobilisation were equally futile, as the Chief of the Russian General Staff Yanush-kevich had (in his own words) 'smashed his telephone' in order to prevent a second cancellation by the Tsar.[183] And, if Russia continued to mobilise, the Germans insisted they had no option but to do the same. That meant the invasion of Belgium and France.[184] In short, what Taylor called 'war by timetable' had become unavoidable the moment Russia decided on even partial mobilisation – that is, war by timetable between the continental powers. What still nevertheless remained avoidable – contrary to the memoir literature and so much determinist historiography – was Britain's involvement.

Not surprisingly, it was at this point that the French and Russian governments began seriously pressing Grey to make Britain's position clear.[185] The French argued that if Grey were to 'announce that in the event of a conflict between Germany and France ... England would come to the aid of France, there would be no war'.[186] But Grey, who had been trying for some days to intimate this to Lichnowsky, knew that he alone could not make such a commitment to France. True, he already had the hawks at the Foreign Office behind him arguing that a 'moral bond' had been 'forged' by the Entente, the repudiation of which would 'expose our good name to grave criticism'.[187] But, as had been made perfectly clear in 1912, he could not act without the support of his Cabinet colleagues and his party – to say nothing of that nebulous and frequently invoked entity 'public opinion'. And it was far from clear that he could rely on any of these to back a public military commitment to France. As we have seen, there was a substantial body of Liberal politicians and journalists who strongly opposed such a commitment.[188] Their arguments were now underlined by the acute financial crisis which the threat of war had unleashed in the City of London.[189] On 30 July, twenty-two Liberal members of the backbench Foreign Affairs Committee intimated through Arthur Ponsonby that 'any decision in favour of participation in a European war would meet not only with the strongest disapproval but with the actual withdrawal of support from the Government'.[190] The Cabinet too proved as divided as it had been in 1912, and, as then, the proponents of a declaration in support of France were in the minority. It was therefore decided simply to decide nothing, 'for (as the President of the Local Government Board Herbert Samuel put it) if both sides do not know what we shall do, both will be the less willing to run risks'.[191]

The most Grey could do was once again to tell Lichnowsky *privately* – 'to spare himself later the reproach of bad faith' – that 'if [Germany] and France should be involved, then ... the British government would ... find itself forced to make up its mind quickly. In that event, it would not be practicable to stand aside and wait for any length of time.'[192] That this impressed Bethmann Hollweg where Grey's previous statements had not can be explained by the fact that, for the first time, Grey implied that any British action in defence of France would be swift.[193] An equally deep impression was made in London by Bethmann Hollweg's bid for British neutrality – which he made just before he heard Grey's warning to Lichnowsky – principally because it made Germany's intention to attack France so blatantly obvious.[194] But, although it was sharply rebuffed, even this did not prompt a commitment to intervene, and Churchill's limited naval preparations of 30 July certainly did not have the same significance as the continental armies' mobilisation orders.[195] On the contrary: having issued his private warning, Grey took a markedly *softer* official line with Germany, in a last bid to revive the idea of four-power mediation.[196] Indeed, on the morning of 31 July Grey went so far as to say to Lichnowsky:

> If Germany could get any reasonable proposal put forward which made it clear that Germany and Austria were still striving to preserve European peace, and that Russia and France would be unreasonable if they rejected it, I would support it ... and go the length of saying that if Russia and France would not accept it, His Majesty's Government would have nothing more to do with the consequences.

The 'reasonable proposal' Grey had in mind was that 'Germany would agree not to attack France if France remained neutral [or kept its troops on its own territory] in the event of a war between Russia and Germany.'[197] Even the pessimistic Lichnowsky began to think on hearing this that 'in a possible war, England might adopt a waiting attitude'.[198] Reactions in Paris were correspondingly bleak. On the evening of 1 August, Grey told Cambon baldly:

> If France could not take advantage of this position [i.e., proposal], it was because she was bound by an alliance to which we were not parties, and of which we did not know the terms.... France must take her own decision at this moment without reckoning on an assistance that we were not now in a position to promise.... We could not propose to Parliament at this moment to send an expeditionary military force to the Continent ... unless our interests and obligations were deeply and desperately involved.[199]

A private warning to Lichnowsky was not, as Grey explained to Cambon, 'the same thing as ... an engagement to France'.[200]

Grey's conduct in these crucial days faithfully reflected the acute divisions within Asquith's Cabinet. The nineteen men who met on 31 July were divided into three unequal groups: those who, in common with the bulk of the party, favoured an immediate declaration of neutrality (including Morley, Burns, Simon, Beauchamp and Hobhouse), those who were in favour of intervention (Grey and Churchill only) and those who had not made up their minds (notably Crewe, McKenna, Haldane and Samuel, but probably also Lloyd George and Harcourt, as well, of course, as Asquith himself).[201] Morley argued forcefully against intervention on the side of Russia, and it seemed clear that the majority was inclining to his view. However, Grey's threat to resign if 'an out-and-out uncompromising policy of non-intervention' were adopted sufficed to maintain the stalemate.[202] The Cabinet agreed that 'British opinion would not now enable us to support France ... – we could say nothing to commit ourselves'.[203] Nor was the deadlock really broken when, on the night of 1 August, Churchill was able to persuade Asquith to let him mobilise the navy on the news of the German ultimatum to Russia.[204] This merely prompted Morley and Simon to threaten resignation at the next morning's meeting and the majority once again to close ranks against Grey's repeated pleas for a clear declaration. The most that could be agreed in the first session of that crucial Sunday was that 'if the German fleet comes into the Channel or through the North Sea to undertake hostile operations against the French coasts or shipping, the British fleet will give all the protection in its power'.[205] Even this – which was far from being a declaration of war, given that such German naval action was highly unlikely – was too much for Burns, the President of the Board of Trade, who resigned. As Samuel noted, 'Had the matter come to an issue, Asquith would have stood by Grey ... and three others would have remained. I think the rest of us would have resigned.'[206] At lunch at Beauchamp's that day, seven ministers, among them Lloyd George, expressed reservations about even the limited naval measures.[207] Had they realised that Grey had already surreptitiously withdrawn his proposal to Lichnowsky for French neutrality in a Russo-German war, and that Lichnowsky had been reduced to tears at Asquith's breakfast table that morning, they might have acted on those reservations.[208] As it was, Morley, Simon and Beauchamp now joined Burns in offering their resignations, following the commitment to Belgium which Grey had been able to secure that evening only by himself threatening to resign. A junior minister, Charles Trevelyan, also went.

The War against the Tories

Why then did the government not fall? The immediate answer is, as Asquith recorded in his diary, that Lloyd George, Samuel and Pease appealed to the resigners 'not to go, or at least to delay it', whereupon 'they agreed to say nothing today and sit in their accustomed places in the House'.[209] But why did these erstwhile waverers set their faces against resignation at this decisive moment? The traditional answer can be expressed in a single word: Belgium.

Certainly, it had long been recognised in the Foreign Office that the decision to intervene on behalf of France 'would be more easily arrived at if German aggressiveness ... entailed a violation of the neutrality of Belgium, which Great Britain has guaranteed to maintain' under two treaties dating back to 1839.[210] And certainly, with hindsight, Lloyd George and others cited the violation of Belgian neutrality as the single most important reason for swinging them – and 'public opinion' – in favour of war.[211] At first sight, the point seems irrefutable. On 6 August 1914, Britain's 'solemn international obligation' to uphold Belgian neutrality in the name of law and honour, and 'to vindicate the principle ... that small nations are not to be crushed', provided the two central themes of Asquith's 'What are we fighting for?' speech to the Commons.[212] It was also the keynote of Lloyd George's successful Welsh recruitment drive.[213] And if subsequent memoirs by combatants like Graves and Sassoon are any guide (to say nothing of the *Punch* cartoons of the day), the Belgian issue struck a chord.[214] Nevertheless there are reasons for scepticism. As we have seen, the Foreign Office view in 1905 had been that the 1839 treaty did not bind Britain to uphold Belgium's neutrality 'in any circumstances and at whatever risk'. When the issue had come up in 1912, none other than Lloyd George had expressed the concern that, in the event of war, Belgium should 'either be entirely friendly to this country ... or ... definitely hostile', as neutrality would undermine the British blockade strategy.[215] Significantly, when the issue was raised in Cabinet on 29 July, it was decided to base any response to a German invasion of Belgium on 'policy' rather than 'legal obligation'.[216] The government's line was therefore to warn the Germans obliquely by stating that a violation of Belgium might cause British public opinion to 'veer round'. Thus Grey was able to respond to German prevarication on the subject with a unanimous Cabinet warning that 'if there were a violation of Belgian neutrality ... it would be extremely hard to restrain public feeling'.[217] But that did not commit the government itself. This is not so surprising, as a number of ministers were in fact rather keen to welch on the Belgian guarantee.

Lloyd George was one of those who, as Beaverbrook recalled, tried to argue that the Germans would 'pass only through the furthest southern corner' and that this would imply 'a small infraction of neutrality. "You see," he would say [pointing to a map], "it is only a little bit, and the Germans will pay for any damage they do."'[218] It was widely (though wrongly) expected, in any case, that the Belgians would not call for British assistance, but would simply issue a formal protest in the event of a German passage through the Ardennes. The German bid for British neutrality on 30 July had very clearly implied an incursion into Belgium; but even on the morning of 2 August, after Jagow had clearly refused to guarantee Belgian neutrality, Lloyd George, Harcourt, Beauchamp, Simon, Runciman and Pease agreed that they could contemplate war only in the event of 'the invasion *wholesale* of Belgium'. Charles Trevelyan took the same view.[219] Hence the careful wording of the Cabinet's resolution that evening, communicated by Crewe to the King, that 'a *substantial* violation of the neutrality of [Belgium] would place us in the situation contemplated as possible by Mr Gladstone in 1870, when interference was held to compel us to take action'.[220] When news of the German ultimatum to Belgium reached Asquith on the morning of 3 August, he was therefore profoundly relieved. Moltke's demand for unimpeded passage through the *whole* of Belgium, the subsequent appeal of King Albert to George V and the German invasion the next day distinctly 'simplified matters', in Asquith's words, because it allowed both Simon and Beauchamp to withdraw their resignations.[221] The last-minute attempts by Moltke and Lichnowsky to guarantee the postwar integrity of Belgium were therefore futile.[222] When Bethmann Hollweg lamented to Goschen that 'England should fall upon them for the sake of the neutrality of Belgium' – 'just for a scrap of paper' – he was missing the point. By going for the whole of Belgium, Moltke had unwittingly saved the Liberal government.

Yet, as Wilson has argued, it was not so much the German threat to Belgium which swung the Cabinet behind intervention as the German threat to *Britain* which Grey and the hawks had always insisted would arise if France fell. This can be inferred from Asquith's note to Venetia Stanley of 2 August in which he set down the six principles by which he was guided: only the sixth referred to Britain's 'obligations to Belgium to prevent her being utilised and absorbed by Germany'. The fourth and fifth were more important, stating as they did that, while Britain was under no obligation to assist France, 'It is against British interests that France should be wiped out as a Great Power' and 'We cannot allow Germany to use the Channel as a hostile base.'[223] Likewise, the main argument of Grey's famous speech to the Commons of 3 August – delivered before the news of the German ultimatum to Belgium – was that 'if France is beaten in a struggle of life and death ... I do not believe that ... we should be in a position to use our force decisively to ... prevent the whole of the West of Europe opposite to us ... falling under the domination of a single Power'.[224] The strategic risks of non-intervention – isolation, friendlessness – outweighed the risks of intervention. As Grey put it in a private conversation the next day: 'It will not end with Belgium. Next will come Holland, and after Holland, Denmark. ... England['s] ... position would be gone if Germany were thus permitted to dominate Europe.' 'German policy', he told the Cabinet, was 'that of the great European aggressor, as bad as Napoleon'. That this argument also won over waverers like Harcourt seems clear.[225] Morley was thus not far wrong when he said that Belgium had furnished a 'plea ... for intervention on behalf of France'.[226]

There was, however, another and arguably even more important reason why Britain went to war at 11 p.m. on 4 August 1914. Throughout the days of 31 July–3 August, one thing above all maintained Cabinet unity: the fear of letting in the Tories.[227] As early as 31 July, Churchill secretly asked Bonar Law via F. E. Smith whether, in the event of up to eight resignations, 'the Opposition [would] be prepared to come to the rescue of the Government ... by forming a Coalition to fill up the vacant offices'.[228] Bonar Law declined to respond, but, after consultation with Balfour, Lansdowne and Long, sent a letter to Asquith making clear the Tory view that it would be 'fatal ... to hesitate in supporting France and Russia at this present juncture'. The 'unhesitating support' offered by Bonar Law 'in any measures [the government] may consider necessary for that object' was nothing less than a veiled threat that Conservatives would be willing to step into Liberal shoes if the government could not agree on such measures.[229] After years of bellicose criticism from the Tory press, and especially the Northcliffe-owned papers, this was the one thing calculated to harden Asquith's resolve. Resignation, he told the Cabinet, might seem the ordinary course for a government so divided. But, he went on, 'the National situation is far from ordinary, and I cannot persuade myself that the other party is led by men, or contains men, capable of dealing with it'.[230] Samuel and Pease immediately grasped the point, telling Burns: 'For the majority of the Cabinet now to leave meant a ministry which was a war one and that was the last thing he wanted.' 'The alternative government', as Pease put it, 'must be one much less anxious for peace than ourselves.' He said the same to Trevelyan three days later, by which time Simon and Runciman had taken up the refrain.[231]

At first sight, the fact that the Conservatives were more eager than the Liberals for war might seem to strengthen the determinist case: if Asquith had fallen, then Bonar Law would have gone to war just the same. But would it have been just the same? Let us suppose Lloyd George – defeated on his most recent Finance Bill, beset by financial panic, assailed by pacifist editorials in the *Guardian* and the *British Weekly* – had deserted Grey at the critical Cabinet meeting. Grey would certainly have resigned; Churchill would have rushed off to join Bonar Law. Would Asquith have been able to hang on with his slender majority already strained to breaking point by Irish Home Rule? It seems unlikely. But how quickly could a Conservative government have been formed? The last change of government had been a protracted affair: Balfour's administration had shown the first signs of disintegrating over tariff reform as early as 1903, had actually been defeated in the Commons on 20 July 1905, had lost the confidence of the Chamberlainites in November 1905 and had finally resigned on 4 December. The general election which confirmed the strength of Liberal support in the country was not over until 7 February 1906. It is conceivable that matters would have moved more swiftly had Asquith been forced to resign in early August 1914. Certainly Churchill's plan for a coalition was designed to prevent any delay in intervention. But would a declaration of war on Germany have been possible under such circumstances before a general election? Much would have depended on the King, who, like his cousins in Berlin and St Petersburg, had shown little enthusiasm for war once he looked over the edge of the abyss.[232] It seems reasonable to assume that a change of government would have delayed the despatch of the British Expeditionary Force by at least a week.

Even with the government unchanged, the despatch of the BEF was not a foregone conclusion and did not go according to the plans which had been worked out by Wilson in consultation with the French General Staff.[233] This was because, as we have seen, a clear decision in favour of the continental commitment had never actually been made, so that all the old arguments against it immediately resurfaced when war broke out. The navalists insisted, as they had always insisted, that sea power alone could decide the war.[234] They also tended to favour keeping part or all of the army at home to preserve social peace and fend off any invasion. Others worried that even six divisions (plus one cavalry division) were too few to make a decisive contribution: the Kaiser was not alone in doubting whether 'the few divisions [Britain] could put into the field could make [an] appreciable difference'.[235] There were also conflicting views about where an expeditionary force should be sent, and how far it should be placed under

French command.[236] The decision to send just four divisions and a cavalry division to Amiens rather than (as Wilson had always intended) Maubeuge was the result of two days of haggling.[237]

Did it – as its proponents claimed and subsequent apologists have argued – make a decisive difference to the outcome of the war?[238] It is sometimes argued that the Schlieffen Plan would have failed anyway even without the BEF, such were the flaws Moltke had introduced into it.[239] Perhaps the French could have halted the German offensive unassisted, had they themselves not attempted to launch their own offensive rather than concentrating on defence. But they did not; and, even allowing for German errors, it seems likely that, despite the initial chaotic retreats and the failure of the feint at Ostend, the presence of British troops at Le Cateau on 26 August and at the Marne (6–9 September) *did* significantly reduce the chances of German victory.[240] Unfortunately, what it could not do was to bring about a German defeat. After the fall of Antwerp and the first battle of Ypres (20 October–22 November), the bloody stalemate that was to endure for four years on the Western Front had been established.

A War without the BEF

If the BEF had never been sent, there is no question that the Germans would have won the war. Even if they had been checked at the Marne, they would almost certainly have succeeded in overwhelming the French defences within a matter of months in the absence of the substantial British reinforcements which Kitchener had resolved to recruit as early as 10 August.[241] And even if the BEF *had* arrived, but a week later or in a different location as a result of a political crisis in London, Moltke might still have repeated the triumph of his forebear. At the very least, he would have been less inclined to retreat to the Aisne. Then what? Doubtless the arguments for British intervention to check German ambitions would have continued – especially with Bonar Law as Prime Minister. But only intervention of a very different kind would have been conceivable. The expeditionary force would have been rendered obsolete by French defeat; had it been sent, a Dunkirk-like evacuation would probably have been necessary. The navalists' old schemes for landings on the German coast would also have been consigned to the rubbish bin. With hindsight, it seems more likely that some version of the Dardanelles invasion would have emerged as the most credible use of the army (especially if Churchill had remained at the Admiralty, as he almost certainly would have). Besides that hazardous enterprise – which might, of course, have fared better if the full BEF had been available – the most Britain could have done would have been to use its naval power to wage the kind of naval war against Germany which Fisher had always advocated: rounding up German merchant vessels, harassing neutrals trading with the enemy and confiscating German overseas assets.

Such a dual strategy would certainly have been an irritant to Berlin. But it would not have won the war. For the evidence is strong that the blockade did not starve Germany into submission, as its advocates had hoped it would.[242] Nor would a victory over Turkey have significantly weakened the position of a Germany which had won in the west, though it would certainly have benefited the Russians, by realising their historic designs on Constantinople.[243] Without the war of attrition on the Western Front, Britain's manpower, its economy and its vastly superior financial resources could not have been brought to bear on Germany sufficiently to ensure victory. A far more likely outcome would have been a diplomatic compromise (of the sort which Kitchener and later Lansdowne actually advocated), whereby Britain ended hostilities in return for German guarantees of Belgian integrity and neutrality and some kind of division of spoils in the Ottoman Empire. That, after all, had been Bethmann Hollweg's objective all along. With France beaten and the German offer to restore Belgium to the status quo ante still on the table, it is hard to see how any British government could have justified continuing a maritime and perhaps Middle Eastern war of unforeseeable duration. For what? It is possible to imagine embittered Liberals still calling, as they did, for a war against Germany's 'military caste', though the argument cut little ice with Haig and would have been hard to sustain if, as seems probable, Bethmann Hollweg had continued his policy of collaboration with the Social Democrats which had begun with the 1913 tax bill and borne fruit with the vote for war credits.[244] But a war to preserve Russian control over Poland and the Baltic states? To hand Constantinople to the Tsar? Although Grey at times seemed ready to fight such a war, he would surely have been overruled by those like the Chief of the General Staff Robertson, who could still argue in August 1916 for the preservation of 'a strong ... Teutonic ... Central European power' as a check against Russia.[245]

In the final analysis, then, the historian is bound to ask if acceptance of a German victory on the continent would have been as damaging to British interests as Grey and the other Germanophobes claimed at the time, and as a generation of Fischerite historians have subsequently accepted. The answer suggested here is that it would not have been. Eyre Crowe's question had always been: 'Should the war come, and England stand aside ... [and] Germany and Austria win, crush France and humiliate Russia, what will then be the position of a friendless England?'[246] The historian's answer is: better than that of an exhausted England in 1919. A fresh assessment of Germany's pre-war war aims reveals that, had Britain stood aside – even for a matter of weeks – continental Europe would have been transformed into something not unlike the European Union we know today – but without the massive contraction in British overseas power entailed by the fighting of two world wars. Perhaps too the complete collapse of Russia into the horrors of civil war and Bolshevism might have been averted: though there would still have been formidable problems of rural and urban unrest, a properly constitutional monarchy (following Nicholas II's abdication) or a parliamentary republic would have stood more chance of success after a shorter war. And there certainly would not have been that great incursion of American financial and military power into European affairs which effectively marked the end of British financial predominance in the world. True, there might still have been fascism in

Europe in the 1920s; but it would have been in France rather than Germany that radical nationalists would have sounded most persuasive. It may even be that, in the absence of a world war's stresses and strains, the inflations and deflations of the early 1920s and early 1930s would not have been so severe. With the Kaiser triumphant, Hitler could have lived out his life as a failed artist and a fulfilled soldier in a German-dominated Central Europe about which he could have found little to complain.

Immanuel Geiss, in an article published in 1990, argued:

> There was nothing wrong with the conclusion that Germany and continental Europe west of Russia would only be able to hold their own if Europe pulled together. And a united Europe would fall almost automatically under the leadership of the strongest power – Germany.... [But] German leadership over a united Europe in order to brave the coming giant economic and political power blocs would have to overcome the imagined reluctance [sic] of Europeans to domination by any one of their peers. Germany would have to persuade Europe to accept German leadership ... to make crystal clear that the overall interest of Europe would coincide with the enlightened self-interest of Germany ... in order to achieve in the years after 1900 something like the position of the Federal Republic today.[247]

Though his assumptions perhaps unconsciously reflect the hubris of the post-reunification era, in one sense he is absolutely right: it would have been infinitely preferable if Germany could have achieved its hegemonic position on the continent without two world wars. But it was not only Germany's fault that this did not happen. True, it was Germany which forced the continental war of 1914 upon an unwilling France (and a not so unwilling Russia). But it was – as the Kaiser rightly said – the British government which ultimately decided to turn the continental war into a world war, a conflict which lasted twice as long as and cost many more lives than Germany's first 'bid for European Union' would have, if it had only gone according to plan. By fighting Germany in 1914, Asquith, Grey and their colleagues helped ensure that, when Germany did finally achieve predominance on the continent, Britain was no longer strong enough to provide a check to it.

FIVE

HITLER'S ENGLAND:

What if Germany had invaded Britain in May 1940?

Andrew Roberts

Finally when it was plain, even to Sir Joseph, that in the space of a few days England had lost both the entire stores and equipment of her regular army and her only ally; that the enemy were less than 25 miles from her shores; that there were only a few battalions of fully armed, fully trained troops in the country; that she was committed to a war in the Mediterranean with a numerically superior enemy; that her cities lay open to air attack from fields closer to home than the extremities of her own islands; that her sea-routes were threatened from a dozen new bases, Sir Joseph said: 'Seen in the proper perspective I regard this as a great and tangible success.... The war has entered a new and glorious phase.'

EVELYN WAUGH, *Put Out More Flags*

Jackboots goose-stepping through London: a column of Wehrmacht soldiers marching down the Mall towards Buckingham Palace. Such images are familiar enough from film and fiction.[1] But how close in reality did a German invasion and occupation of Britain actually come? Fifty years after the defeat of Nazism, we tend to take it for granted that Britain was bound to fight against Hitler in 1939 – to fight and, despite the overwhelming odds the country faced in the *annus mirabilis* of 1940, ultimately to win. Throughout all 1995's celebrations of VE Day, the possibility that it might have turned out differently was scarcely mentioned. On the contrary: the Allied victory in the war was remembered as not only just and right – but also inevitable.

Yet few events in history, particularly in the military and diplomatic spheres, can really be described as inevitable. When we go back to the early 1930s, and consider the options open to Britain as the European political situation deteriorated, we can see that, of all of them, a declaration of war against Germany over Poland in 1939 (to say nothing of five long years of 'blood, toil, tears and sweat' under the leadership of Winston Churchill) was among the least likely. The road to war in 1939 was twisted and tortuous. We need only to imagine how one or two things might have turned out otherwise – not always important things either – to see how easily events might have taken a radically different course.

Hitler's adjutant Fritz Wiedemann claimed that Lord Halifax – Neville Chamberlain's envoy to Hitler in 1937 and his Foreign Secretary at the time of the Munich agreement – once said that he 'would like to see as the culmination of my work the Führer entering London at the side of the English king amid the acclamation of the English people'.[2] Of course, we know that Halifax began to question the policy of appeasement even as the Munich agreement was signed – and it was he who advised committing Britain to the defence of Poland in 1939. But he remained deeply pessimistic about the prospect of a war with Germany if this attempt at deterrence failed; and, when the war was going badly in May 1940, was one of a number of influential voices who advocated negotiating some kind of peace with Hitler. We know also that Churchill rejected those arguments, despite Britain's impending isolation as France crumbled. And we know too that Britain was able to hold out and ultimately – once the Soviet Union and the United States had joined the fight against Germany – to win the war. But these outcomes were anything but predestined.

An Older Counterfactual: Non-Appeasement

Of course, the question 'what if?' has been asked many times about the events which led up to the outbreak of the Second World War. But, until relatively recently, historians have tended to ask whether more could have been done sooner to prevent Hitler's rise to power, or to undermine his position once he was there. What if Britain had stood up to the Third Reich earlier? – that has been the traditional basis for counterfactual arguments about Britain and Hitler. It was, of course, a question originally posed by Churchill himself. As he later wrote: 'If the risks of war which were run by France and Britain at the last moment had been boldly faced in good time and plain declarations had been made and meant, how different would our prospects have been today.' For Churchill, the Second World War had been 'the unnecessary war'. He and others believed that a strong signal of determination by France, Britain and the Soviet Union to resist German aggression in Czechoslovakia might have given enough encouragement to Hitler's critics within the German military establishment to bring about, if not his downfall, then at least a change of policy. As he argued: 'If the Allies had resisted Hitler strongly in his earlier stages ... the chance would have been given to the sane elements in German life, which were very powerful – especially in the High Command – to save Germany from the maniacal system into the grip of which she was falling.'

What if, instead of concentrating on her air defences, the British governments of the 1930s had built up a serious land force capable of resisting, if not deterring, a German invasion of France? What if Britain and France had resisted the German remilitarisation of the Rhineland in 1936? Hitler himself admitted: 'If France had marched into the Rhineland' – which had actually happened in the early 1920s – 'we would have had to withdraw with our tails between our legs.'[3] What if, despite the known weakness of Britain's military capability, the government had indeed issued a clear signal – even if it was a bluff – of Britain's intention to defend Czechoslovakia if it was attacked? What if Britain and

France had persuaded Stalin to join them against Germany in 1939, instead of leaving him to succumb to the advances of Ribbentrop? These are among the acceptable counterfactual questions historians have for years asked about the 1930s. And yet the alternative scenarios envisaged are in fact far less plausible than the much less pleasant alternative – of a German victory over Britain.

Britain after the First World War was a shadow of the proud empire which had gone to war in 1914. Economically, the country struggled to turn back the clock to pre-war days, saddled with the huge debt incurred during the war and an economic obsession with restoring the pound's lost value. From 1920 onwards, unemployment on an unprecedented scale was the recurrent affliction which condemned hundreds of thousands – and soon, for the first time, millions – to inactivity. In the wake of the Wall Street Crash of 1929 and the European financial crisis of 1931, capitalism itself appeared to be entering its death throes. This had two immediate political consequences which had profound implications for British foreign policy. First, the costs of social security rose as they had never before, growing far more rapidly than the sluggish economy. Secondly – and consequently – the money available for defence became more limited than it had been for over a hundred years. Between 1920 and 1938, British defence spending was consistently less than 5 per cent of national income per annum – less than at any time before or since; and this at a time when Britain's imperial commitments had almost reached their maximum historic extent. As far as the Treasury was concerned, priority had to be given to the traditional pre-war policies of a strong currency and balanced budgets. In view of the enormous burden of debt run up during the war, and the persistent unemployment caused by the policy of deflation, this drastically reduced the amount of money available for defence. Yet the running down of British security worried only a few hawkish figures like Churchill, the former First Lord of the Admiralty during the First World War. And, unfortunately, he and his associates did not enjoy much popular support. During the Great

War, Churchill had won for himself the reputation of a war-monger and, after the fiasco of Gallipoli, a bungler. Nor was that the only stain on his reputation. He was extremely unpopular with Labour because of his perceived hostility to the trade unions and the Russian Revolution. The Liberals thought him a block-head for his mismanagement of the economy as Chancellor in the 1920s, where, incidentally, he too had cut defence spending. And he also managed to make himself deeply unpopular with his own party during the 1930s by opposing the policy of political reform in India and then by espousing the cause of Edward VIII and Mrs Simpson.[4]

The majority of voters had had enough of war. It was not just the Communist Party – and its young recruits like Burgess, Philby, Maclean and Blunt at Cambridge – who were doctrinally opposed to all 'imperialist' war (until such times as Moscow changed its line). Nor was it just the Labour party which adopted a pacifist position summed up by its leader George Lansbury's pledge 'to close every recruiting station, disband the army and disarm the Air Force' – in short to 'abolish the whole dreadful equipment of war'. Liberals like John Maynard Keynes and even the former wartime Prime Minister Lloyd George now regarded the Great War as having been a waste of young lives: the result of diplomatic blundering in 1914 which had done nothing to dimin-ish Germany's claim to European predominance and everything to aggrieve the German people. A great many Conservatives shared that sneaking sympathy with postwar Germany which was in many ways the foundation of appeasement.

To a great extent, the desire to avoid war was understandable. The apparently futile slaughter in the trenches had provoked a deep-rooted reaction against the whole idea that it was noble to die for one's country – once the motto of a generation of brave (and short-lived) public-school-educated officers. In addition, there was a fear that technological advances would make any new war far more costly in terms of civilian lives than the First World War had been. 'The bomber will always get through,' prophesied the Prime Minister Baldwin. Churchill himself predicted that

40,000 Londoners would be killed or injured in the first week as a result of intensive aerial bombardment.[5] The ideal of the American President Woodrow Wilson – that diplomacy should cease to be a matter of secret treaties and alliance, and should become the preserve of a new League of Nations – was an attractive one, as the ten million votes cast in the so-called Peace Ballot of 1934–5 revealed. Well-intentioned clergymen like Archbishops Temple of York and Lang of Canterbury were not the only ones to embrace the attractive but impracticable principle of 'collective security'. It was in the debating chamber of the Oxford Union in 1933 that perhaps the most famous demonstration of such feelings took place – striking in that it was a demonstration by traditionally conservative Oxford men. Arguing for the motion 'That this House refuses in any circumstances to fight for King and Country', Cyril Joad warned his audience: 'Bombers would be over Britain within twenty minutes of the declaration of war with a western European power. And a single bomb can poison every living thing in an area of three-quarters of a square mile.' When the tellers tallied up the votes, the result was as clear as it was sensational: 275 votes for to 153 against. Churchill called it an 'abject, squalid, shameless avowal ... a very disquieting and disgusting symptom'. But his son Randolph's attempts to have the motion erased from the union's minutes were defeated.[6]

The combination of financial tightness and popular pacifism explains better than almost anything else the external weakness which characterised most of Neville Chamberlain's ill-starred premiership. Under those circumstances, there seemed much to be said for a policy of appeasing a Germany which many people – influenced by Keynes – believed had been treated too harshly by the Peace of Versailles in 1919. Appeasement meant, in practice, granting Germany's supposedly legitimate claims, in order to avert (or, at best, postpone) war. Paramount among these was the claim to 'self-determination', a term much used at the Versailles peace conference to justify independence for Poland, Czechoslovakia and other Central European countries; but deliberately not applied to Germany, which in fact had to give up around 10 per cent of its territory to its neighbours. The problem was that if all the Germans in Europe were united in a single Reich, the result would be bigger in extent than the Reich of 1914 – because such an entity would also include Austria, as well as parts of Czechoslovakia, Poland and Lithuania. This was the fundamental flaw in the policy of appeasement: Germany's 'back yard' – a phrase used to justify the remilitarisation of the Rhineland – was much too big for the peace of Europe. Until disastrously late in the day, the advocates of appeasement – in particular, Halifax and the British ambassador in Berlin Nevile Henderson – failed to grasp this.

Halifax himself expressed the views of many aristocratic conservatives when he said about the Germans: 'Nationalism, Racialism is a powerful force. But I can't feel that it's either unnatural or immoral! . . . I cannot myself doubt that these fellows are genuine haters of Communism etc.! And I dare say if we were in their position we might feel the same!' This rather patronising attitude – Halifax momentarily mistook Hitler for a footman when they first met and nearly handed him his coat – was characteristic. When the Führer told the former Viceroy how to deal with Indian nationalism ('Shoot Gandhi'), Halifax 'gazed at [him] with a mixture of astonishment, repugnance and compassion'. Similarly, Goering struck him as 'a great schoolboy'. He could not help but 'rather like . . . the little man' Goebbels. Yet in telling Hitler that 'Danzig, Austria and Czechoslovakia' were 'questions [which] fall into the category of possible alterations in the European order which might be destined to come about with the passage of time', Halifax handed him more than just a coat. He seemed to be handing him Central Europe.[7]

Of course, the strategy of appeasement was far from being an irrational policy in 1938, when Britain was militarily unready for a war which Germany seemed all too eager to fight. Hitler actually felt outmanoeuvred by Chamberlain, whose diplomatic efforts effectively denied him the war against Czechoslovakia he wanted and had been planning for since the spring of 1938. In the most recently published sections of his diaries, Goebbels described Chamberlain as an 'ice cold' 'English fox', frustrating Hitler's desire for a short, sharp war with the Czechs by one ploy after another. Evidently, Chamberlain's sometimes melodramatic diplomacy at Berchtesgaden succeeded in persuading the Germans that he was not bluffing about the risk of British intervention: 'Things go so far', wrote Goebbels, 'that Chamberlain suddenly goes to get up and leave as if he has done his duty, there is no point continuing and he can wash his hands innocently.' On 28 September, Hitler was prompted to ask Chamberlain's aide Sir Horace Wilson 'straight out if England wants world war', from which it might be inferred that he feared Chamberlain might. Goebbels, who six days before had been confident that 'London is immeasurably frightened of force', was obliged to conclude that 'we have no peg for a war.... One cannot run the risk of a world war over amendments.'[8]

What if, instead of pressing for the fateful four-power conference at Munich, Chamberlain had confined himself to making an explicit guarantee to defend Czechoslovakia if it was attacked? We know that at its meeting of 30 August 1938 the Cabinet had agreed unanimously that 'if Hitler went into Czechoslovakia we should declare war on him'; but that Chamberlain had insisted on keeping this commitment secret, as he did not wish to 'utter a threat to Herr Hitler'. What if he had? Would that, as has often been suggested, have been the signal for a military coup against Hitler? It seems extremely unlikely – not least because the key figure, the Chief of Staff Ludwig Beck, had already resigned some days before the crucial Cabinet meeting (a fact not announced until the day after the Cabinet met). In any case, Chamberlain was dubious about the idea of overthrowing Hitler.[9] 'Who will guarantee that Germany will not become Bolshevik afterwards?' he asked the French General Gamelin on the eve of the Munich conference.

Today, we remember Munich as a gross betrayal of the Czechs – which it was. To avert war, Chamberlain effectively forced them to surrender not only the Sudetenland, but also their ability to defend themselves. Yet at the time Hitler saw this as a defeat, not a victory for his policy: he had wanted a quick, violent solution, not a diplomatic compromise. He stormed back to Berlin, furious at the signs of popular enthusiasm for peace in Germany, and ordering a new propaganda campaign to prepare the German *Volk* for war. Chamberlain, by contrast, was fêted as a hero when he flew back to Britain. Indeed, his popularity at the time of Munich was such that if he had called a general election – as some of his closest advisers were urging – there can be little doubt that he would have won a larger landslide victory than even those of 1931 and 1935.

Of course, his achievement at Munich turned out to be ephemeral. On 15 March 1939, Hitler simply tore up the guarantees he had give to the rump Czech state, and unilaterally invaded. This has often been seen as the moment at which war became inevitable. Yet there were still strong voices raised for carrying on with appeasement thereafter. There was nothing inevitable about the guarantee given to Poland at the beginning of April. Indeed, Chamberlain's first reaction to the occupation of Prague was to hope for the 'possibility of easing the tension and getting back to normal relations with the dictators'. Poland was not a popular cause in Britain until the war had actually broken out and the Ministry of Information made it one. Lloyd George and many socialists were highly critical of General Beck's anti-Semitic and undemocratic government, and believed that it was only getting its just deserts for the way it had grabbed Teschen from Czechoslovakia during the Munich crisis. Indeed, Lloyd George remarked that giving Poland independence was like giving a monkey a fine pocket watch. Had Hitler replayed the Sudetenland gambit – stressing Germany's claim to Danzig and the 'Polish corridor' through Prussia on the basis of self-determination – there would have been little in the way of a popular *casus belli*. After all, 80 per cent of the inhabitants of Danzig said they wished to accede to Germany.

The key figure in the decision to commit Britain to the defence of Poland was in fact a repentant Halifax. Had he not succeeded in overruling the powerful combination of Chamberlain, Wilson, Sir John Simon, Sir Samuel Hoare, R. A. Butler, Joseph Ball and others, the Polish Guarantee could not have been made. As it was, it took place without consultation and in an atmosphere of panic created by totally unfounded rumours of an imminent German invasion of Poland and Romania. Halifax's argument gained vital strength from the constant supply of information, both overt and secret, reaching Britain about the true intentions of Nazi Germany. The so-called *Kristallnacht* of November 1938 – in effect, a state-sponsored pogrom initiated by Hitler and organised by Goebbels – had further revealed the true face of Nazi Germany as far as racial policy was concerned. Now the fall of Prague, and the seizure of Memel from Lithuania, revealed how wrong Halifax had been in arguing, as he had a year before, that Hitler did not 'lust for conquest on a Napoleonic scale'. Hitler could hardly claim that his seizure of the rump of Czechoslovakia represented a victory for ethnic self-determination. It was this belated realisation – this sense of having been duped – which led to the revolt against appeasement on both sides of the House of Commons. Under these circumstances, could Chamberlain have backed down once again over Poland as he had over Czechoslovakia? Probably not.

Nevertheless, it is important to note that Hitler expected him to. On 22 August, he told his commanders at the Obersalzberg: 'England does not want the conflict to break out for two or three years.'[10] And Ribbentrop's master-stroke – the Nazi–Soviet Pact, signed the next day in Moscow – seemed only to strengthen his hand. How could Britain possibly threaten intervention over Poland when Hitler had Stalin on his side? Although Hitler does seem to have wavered momentarily, postponing his invasion of Poland scheduled for 26 August, within four days he had swung back to bellicosity ('The English believe Germany is weak. They will see they are deceiving themselves'); and the next day he overruled Goering and Goebbels, despite their 'scepticism' about English non-intervention: 'The Führer does not believe England will intervene.'[11]

Hitler was wrong, of course, but the fact that he could think in this way on the very eve of the war shows how unrealistic it is to imagine a harder-line British policy somehow averting war and perhaps even toppling him. In fact, a far more plausible counter-factual is of British policy going even further than appeasement to conciliate Germany and avoid war, oblivious to the fact that Nazism had an internal dynamic to its foreign policy, requiring sustained expansion.

Peaceful Coexistence: The Charmley Counterfactual

The possibility of a formal understanding, if not an alliance, with Germany was seriously discussed on numerous occasions during the 1930s. Hitler frequently expressed his desire for such a deal with Britain, beginning even before *Mein Kampf*.[12] From November 1933, he sought some kind of naval agreement with Britain, and secured one in June 1935. 'An Anglo-German combination', he noted at the time, 'would be stronger than all the other powers.'[13] Such ideas resurfaced four years later when Hitler started to feel nervous about British intervention on the eve of his invasion of Poland. He had 'always wanted German–British understanding', he assured Henderson on 25 August 1939.[14]

There was no shortage of people in 1930s Britain who would have viewed a British accommodation with Hitler positively, if not with enthusiasm. This feeling extended far beyond the lunatic fringe of anti-Semites like William Joyce ('Lord Haw-Haw'), Henry Hamilton Beamish and Arnold Leese, some of whom would actually end up on the German side during the war. Notoriously, there was also the British Union of Fascists of Sir Oswald Mosley, the one-time Labour party darling, who had followed Mussolini down the fascist road. But there were other, far less radical Germanophiles. There were imperialists who saw Germany threatening no part of the empire, conservatives and Catholics who saw Germany as a bulwark against atheistic Russian Bolshevism, press barons who admired the rhetoric of the dictators, and businessmen who thought appeasement good for trade.[15] Perhaps most interestingly, a significant proportion of the British aristocracy had strong pro-German and sometimes even pro-Nazi leanings. In his early months as ambassador in London, for example, Ribbentrop won over Anglo-German aristocrats like the Earl of Athlone, Germanophiles like Lord Lothian and socialites like Lady Cunard. Lothian, not untypically, described Nazi anti-Semitism as 'largely the reflex of the external persecution to which Germans have been subjected since the war'. Similarly, when Lord Derby heard that Goering planned to visit Britain he invited him to stay at Knowsley Hall to watch the Grand National. The Marquess of Londonderry and Lords Allen of Hurtwood and Stamp were all impressed favourably by Hitler when they met him.[16]

One very well-born Englishman in particular could have made a very substantial contribution to Anglo-German rapprochement had he not given up his position of influence for the sake of love – or for the sake of the then Prime Minister Stanley Baldwin's rather Victorian notion of public attitudes towards divorce. King Edward VIII not only loved Mrs Simpson, he also admired Hitler. While still Prince of Wales, he was authoritatively described as being 'quite pro-Hitler' and was reported to have declared that: 'It was no business of ours to interfere in Germany's internal affairs either on Jews or anything else.... Dictators were very popular these days and we might want one in England before long.' In 1935 his father, George V, had to rebuke him for a notably pro-German speech. A year later, Edward succeeded to the throne and almost immediately tried to persuade the then Foreign Secretary, Anthony Eden, not to oppose the German remilitarisation of the Rhineland. In response to an appeal from the German ambassador, he 'sent for the PM' – Baldwin – and, according to one version, 'gave him a piece of my mind. I told the old so-and-so that I would abdicate if he made war. Then there was a frightful scene. But you needn't worry. There won't be a war.' When Ribbentrop took over as ambassador, the German embassy also took pains to cultivate Mrs Simpson.[17]

What if Stanley Baldwin had not prevailed upon Edward to abdicate? There were alternatives: a morganatic marriage, as proposed by the newspaper magnate Beaverbrook, for example, which would have allowed Mrs Simpson to marry Edward without acquiring the formal status of royalty. Or he could have opted for the throne and sacrificed love. The question may seem irrelevant to the history of the Second World War; but it is a crucial one because of the key role played by the King in May 1940, following Chamberlain's humiliation in the House of Commons in the wake of the Norwegian fiasco. George VI, Edward's brother and reluctant substitute on the throne, was a committed appeaser who did not want Chamberlain to resign, and favoured Halifax over Churchill as his successor. But he did little more than accept grudgingly Halifax's decision to step aside. Would Edward VIII have acted differently? Just possibly, he might have been more committed to Churchill, who had leapt somewhat quixotically to his defence during the Abdication Crisis. But when confronted with the possibility of war with Germany, his pro-German leanings might well have counted for more.

For the possibility of peace with Germany did not end with the declaration of war over Poland in September 1939. Hitler was dismayed by the British declaration of war, telling Alfred Rosenberg that he 'couldn't grasp' what Chamberlain was 'really after'. 'Even if England secured a victory,' he pointed out, 'the real victors would be the United States, Japan and Russia.'[18] On 6 October, he therefore renewed his offer of peace, though once again it was spurned by Chamberlain. But as late as 1940 Goebbels's Propaganda Ministry continued to press this idea: 'Sooner or later the racially valuable Germanic element in Britain would have to be brought in to join Germany in the future secular struggles of the white race against the yellow race, or the Germanic race against Bolshevism.'[19] Hitler wanted, as he said in May 1940, 'to sound out England on dividing the world.' A month later, he spoke of the possibility of a 'reasonable peace agreement' with Britain. Time and again, Hitler expressed regret that he was fighting Britain, because (in Ribbentrop's words) he doubted 'the desirability of demolishing the British Empire'.[20] As he told Halder in July, six days before his final peace offer, he 'did not like' war with Britain: 'The reason is that if we crush England's military power, the British Empire will collapse. That is of no use to Germany ... [but] would benefit only Japan, America and others.'[21]

In recent years, revisionist historians such as John Charmley have argued that this analysis was all too prescient. Britain's victory in 1945 was, they argue, a Pyrrhic one. So another possibility needs to be addressed. What if the war had gone ahead in 1939, but Britain had subsequently sought peace with Germany? The idea is that Germany would then have spent itself fighting against Soviet Russia, leaving the British Empire intact, the Conservatives in power and the British economy unimpaired. According to Charmley, opening negotiations through Mussolini in the summer of 1940, after the defeat of France, would have made sense to many people, not least Halifax and Butler.[22] In his view, we should not accept without question Churchill's argument that any terms from Hitler would necessarily have been 'Carthaginian'. Before becoming Prime Minister, even Churchill himself had urged Chamberlain 'not [to] close the door upon any genuine peace offer' from Germany. And when the War Cabinet met to discuss the question of seeking a negotiated peace on 26 May, he could not deny the attractions of such a course, with Britain's strategic and economic positions both so parlous. Of particular concern to Churchill was the lack of tangible support from the United States, which he already saw as the key to victory over Germany. He even went so far as to remark: 'If we could get out of this jam by giving up Malta and Gibraltar and some African colonies I would jump at it.' Of course, he added that it was 'incredible that Hitler would consent to any terms that we would accept' – a point he reiterated two days later: 'The Germans would demand our Fleet ... our naval bases, and much else. We should become a slave state.'[23] But the drift of Charmley's argument is that this was self-serving; Churchill knew that his position as Prime Minister depended on maintaining the 'victory at all costs'/ 'conquer or die' line. Alan Clark has also rejected this distinction as 'a lethal concept'.[24] According to Clark, a deal could have been made with Germany as late as the spring of 1941, with the Battle of Britain won and Italy defeated in Africa. Hitler wanted to secure his flank before he turned on Russia. Hess flew to Britain in an attempt to broker a deal; but his mission was hushed up by Churchill.

It is not inconceivable that a government led by someone other than Churchill might have made a separate peace with Germany, leaving Hitler free to fight Stalin. A German war directed solely against the Soviet Union would have attracted at least some support on the British right. After all, many Conservatives had all along regarded Communism as a bigger threat than fascism. Support for the Finns' struggle against Stalin was widespread in 1940. It is not impossible to imagine a Legion of St George (perhaps commanded by John Amery) fighting against Communism and serving under German command rather as the Spanish and French fascists did on the Eastern Front. Even within the government, despite the new-found Russophilia of Churchill and some of his close supporters, there were those who favoured a strategy of pitting Hitler against Stalin. As late as 1942, a Tory minister, John Moore-Brabazon, had to resign for saying openly what a number of people thought privately – that a struggle between Nazi Germany and Stalin's Russia 'suited us'. It was the same stance as Henry Kissinger took during the Iran–Iraq War: 'A pity they both can't lose' – the revisionist argument in a nutshell.

But what would have been the result when, as would inevitably have happened sooner or later, one side or the other finally won? If it had not been for the distraction of the war in the Mediterranean, where Mussolini's botched invasion of Greece allowed British forces to attack the Italians in Libya, the victor might well have been Germany. The German intervention in the Mediterranean, which necessitated not only sending troops to Libya but also taking over Bulgaria, Yugoslavia, Greece and Crete, delayed the launch of Operation Barbarossa against Stalin by a crucial month. Had Hitler secured some kind of agreement with Britain, however, he could have avoided the Mediterranean distraction and attacked the Soviet Union on schedule. He could also have deployed his entire army, navy and air force solely against

Russia. With no hope of a Second Front in the West, no convoys and no allies whatever, Russia's much purged Red Army – which could not even smash puny Finland – might well have been defeated and driven back behind the Urals. As it was, the Wehrmacht took most of Stalingrad, besieged Leningrad and reached Moscow's outlying metro stations. A victory in European Russia would certainly have been more likely if, as the revisionists suggest, Britain had sought an accommodation with Germany in 1940 of 1941. And, as Michael Burleigh argues in the next chapter, it would have left Britain in a position of parlous weakness.

A Still Worse Scenario: The Invasion of Britain

A central assumption of the Charmley–Clark thesis is that Hitler's peace offers to Britain were sincere – or at the very least that they could be publicly treated as such. However, in assessing Hitler's supposed Anglophilia, we have to distinguish between casual reflections based on Hitler's theory that there was a racial affinity between the Anglo-Saxons and the Germans, and the *Realpolitik* of Hitlerian strategy, which from 1936, if not earlier, always implied the subordination of Britain to German power. Encouraged by a disillusioned Ribbentrop to regard Britain as a decadent and declining power, Hitler had in fact come to the conclusion by late 1936 that 'even an honest German–English rapprochement could offer Germany no concrete, positive advantages', and that Germany therefore had 'no interest in coming to an understanding with England'.[25] As he put it at a meeting with his military chiefs in November 1937 (recorded in the infamous 'Hossbach Memorandum'), Britain (along with France) was a 'hate-inspired antagonist' whose empire 'could not in the long run be maintained by power politics'.[26] It was a view constantly reinforced by Ribbentrop, who saw England as 'our most dangerous opponent'.[27]

In planning his invasions of Austria, Czechoslovakia and Poland, Hitler swung between confidence that Britain was too weak to intervene and a conviction that Germany would withstand such an intervention. Talking to the army commanders in

May 1939, he expressed his 'doubt whether a peaceful settlement with England is possible. It is necessary to prepare for a show-down. England sees in our development the establishment of a hegemony which would weaken England. Therefore England is our enemy and the showdown with England is a matter of life and death.'[28] Nothing is more indicative of Hitler's true attitude towards England than his 'Z plan' naval directive of 27 January 1939, for a fleet which by 1944–6 would be capable of challenging any power on the high seas – that is, Britain or the United States. John Keegan has posed a further naval counterfactual: 'Had Germany deployed at the outset of the war the force of 300 U-boats which Dönitz had advised Hitler was necessary to win the Battle of the Atlantic, Britain would surely have collapsed as a combatant long before events in the Pacific War brought about the United States' entry.'[29] With only half its food consumption met from domestic resources, and all its oil, rubber and non-ferrous metals imported, Britain could have been brought to its knees by a submarine blockade.

It is true that Hitler was thrown by the British declaration of war; but it would be wrong therefore to regard his subsequent offers of peace as sincere. As he told von Brauchitsch and Halder two days after his offer of peace in October 1939: 'The German war aim ... must consist of the final military defeat of the West.... This fundamental aim must be adjusted from time to time for propaganda purposes.... [But] this does not alter the war aim itself ... [which is] the complete annihilation of the French and British forces.'[30] Even the decision to attack Russia had an anti-British objective: as he put it on 31 July 1940, only twelve days after offering peace with Britain: *Russia is the factor on which Britain is relying the most.... With Russia shattered, Britain's last hope would be shattered.*'[31] The fact that Hitler repeatedly changed his tactics, mingling racial goals of *Lebensraum* with his own version of grand strategy, has tended to confuse historians as to his ultimate intentions. The simple reality is that from 1936, if not earlier, Hitler regarded final confrontation as inevitable, even if it was regrettable on racial grounds, and came five years too early. The idea that a peace could have been struck with 'That Man', as Churchill called him, which would have preserved the British Empire and Conservative power is fanciful. Had Britain not fought over Poland; had Britain sought to make peace in May 1940 or before Barbarossa; had Britain been brought to its knees by the force of 300 U-boats which Admiral Dönitz had recommended – whichever alternative scenario one considers, the consequence would have been the same: subordination to the Third Reich.

Churchill was therefore right. When, on Wednesday 5 October 1938, he swam against the tide of popular euphoria by denouncing the Munich agreement in the House of Commons, he put his finger on the essential truth:

> [T]here can never be friendship between the British democracy and the Nazi Power, that Power which spurns Christian ethics, which cheers its onward course by a barbarous paganism, which vaunts the spirit of aggression and conquest, which derives strength and perverted pleasure from persecution, and uses, as we have seen, with pitiless brutality the threat of murderous force. That Power cannot ever be the trusted friend of British democracy. What I find unendurable is the sense of our country falling into the power, into the orbit and influence of Nazi Germany and of our existence becoming dependent upon their good will or pleasure.[32]

Yet Churchill was not contemplating the worst possible scenario when he spoke of Britain falling into Germany's 'power, orbit and influence'. There was another still worse possibility which also needs to be considered: an outright German invasion and occupation of Britain.

On Friday 24 May 1940, General Heinz Guderian's 1st Panzer Division reached the Aa canalized river south of Gravelines in France, and in fierce fighting secured bridgeheads across it. They were only ten miles away from 400,000 exhausted Allied soldiers pinned down on the Flanders beaches. Then, just as the greatest tank commander prepared the greatest mechanised unit for the greatest military coup of the twentieth century, he received an order to halt. Despite his protestations, three days later the order was still in force. In the meantime the perimeter was fortified and over the next nine days 338,226 Allied troops were evacuated to Britain in Operation Dynamo.

Guderian always believed that Hitler's order – issued despite Chief of Staff General Franz Halder's and Field Marshal Walther von Brauchitsch's opposition – was 'a mistake pregnant with consequence, for only a capture of the BEF . . . could have created the conditions necessary for a successful German invasion of Great Britain'.[33] Historians have long debated the reasons it was issued, but they have rarely asked what would have happened if the BEF *had* been captured wholesale; or if, during Dynamo, the 1,400-yard-long, 5-foot-wide wooden pier at the East Mole, down which a quarter of a million Allied troops walked to safety, had been destroyed by the Stukas which spent over a week trying to hit it.[34]

Grand Admiral Erich Raeder first discussed invading Britain with Hitler on 21 May 1940, having already instructed his staff to investigate the possibility on 15 November the previous year.[35] Hitler was unenthusiastic, and by the time of their next talk on the subject, on 20 June, he seemed more interested in discussing resettling Jews on Madagascar. By that time the vital moment had passed and although Hitler was to issue Führer Directive No. 16, entitled 'Preparations for a Landing Operation against England' on 16 July 1940, the ideal time to strike had passed.[36] The target date of 15 September set by Hitler at the end of July was contingent on the destruction of Britain's naval and air defences, which it proved impossible to achieve. The invasion was postponed three times and by December 1940 preparations for it had become mere 'camouflage' for the planned attack on the Soviet Union (which Hitler saw as less risky than a cross-Channel invasion).[37] But what if Hitler had been planning Operation Sealion for years at the Armed Forces High Command (OKW) level rather than just as a half-hearted, last-minute initiative by the

Naval Staff? What if the vast amount of shipping – 1,722 barges, 471 tugs, 1,161 motor boats and 155 transport vessels were estimated as being needed – had already been earmarked and were sailing towards the Maas and Scheldt estuaries in late May? What if the plan of General Erhard Milch of the Luftwaffe to drop 5,000 parachutists on the seven vital RAF sectors in south-east England with a mission to rip out the heart of Fighter Command had been adopted rather than rejected by Goering? What if London, rather than Paris, had been Hitler's goal?[38]

Most of the many historical and literary analyses of German invasions of the British Isles assume one coming in August or September 1940 or even later. But a German arrival in late May 1940 would have faced, not the recently returned BEF, but the minimal forces left behind.[39] The 483,924 First World War Springfield rifles which equipped the Home Guard did not arrive from America until August 1940, and many of the 18,000 pillboxes constructed across southern England did not have their concrete foundations put down until mid-June.[40] South of London at that time there were only forty-eight field guns, and fifty-four two-pounder anti-tank guns. As General Günther Blumentritt of the OKW was to lament after the war, 'We might, had the plans been ready, have crossed to England with strong forces after the Dunkirk operation.' Instead, in Halder's words, the invasion was 'a thought [Hitler] had hitherto avoided'.[41]

If the initial thirteen crack German divisions had forced their way ashore across a broad front on the English south coast, they would, it is true, have had 1,495 tons of First World War surplus mustard gas dropped on them from low-flying aircraft. But this was an eventuality for which they were nevertheless prepared and trained.[42] If they had managed to cross the twenty-two miles of English Channel it is doubtful that any artificial or natural obstacles – such as the Rye–Hythe Royal Military Canal – would have long impeded their drive north. According to Field Marshal Gerd von Runstedt's 'Forecast of Early Fighting on English Soil', issued on 14 September 1940, 'small but complete Panzer units will be included at an early stage in the first assault'.[43] Had the

RAF not had the advantage of the recently deployed radar, or had the Luftwaffe's codes not been cracked – or had General Kurt Student, the Commander-in-Chief of airborne troops, managed to neutralise the key sectors of Dowding's Fighter Command – the war in the air too might well have gone differently.

In fact, it was not until 20 July that General Alan Brooke took over General Ironside's command as Commander-in-Chief Home Forces. He immediately moved the few tanks he had closer to the coast. An attack in late May, however, would have found much of the British armour defending a makeshift defence line far further back inland, effectively conceding the bridgeheads on the south coast. The Germans themselves – for all their generals' postwar protestations that Sealion was, as von Runstedt told his captors in 1945, 'a sort of game because it was obvious that no invasion was possible' – were hoping to reach Ashford in Kent at an early stage in the engagement.[44] Although they were expecting fierce resistance at the beachheads by mid-September, the Germans might have been pleasantly surprised had they attacked in May. As the official historian of Britain's defences, Basil Collier, points out: 'The vital sector from Sheppey to Rye was manned by 1st London Division with 23 field guns, no anti-tank guns, no armoured cars, no armoured fighting vehicles and about one-sixth of the anti-tank rifles to which it was entitled.'[45] Those places which were well defended, such as the six-inch gun emplacements at Shoeburyness, could have been bypassed as easily as was the Maginot line.

Would the Luftwaffe and German navy have been able to neutralise the Royal Navy for the crucial twelve hours necessary to transport the first wave across the Channel? With a gamble of this nature, the Germans would have had to commit virtually their entire naval forces to the operation. On the other hand, a very short period of time – half a day – would have sufficed to get the invasion force across. Moreover, it is important to remember that nine out of the fifty destroyers taking part in Operation Dynamo had been sunk and twenty-three damaged. In June 1940 the Royal Navy had only sixty-eight operational destroyers –

against a 1919 total of 433. It is certainly not impossible to see how the first successful invasion of Britain for 874 years might have been effected.

The Collaboration Counterfactual

What would occupation have meant? In the next chapter, Michael Burleigh deals separately with the horrendous implications of a German victory in Eastern Europe. It is clear that the experience of Western Europe – a more appropriate model for Britain – was very different. In France, The Netherlands and other parts of occupied Western Europe, racial policy did not become paramount in the way that it did on the Eastern Front, with the exception that Jews were sent eastwards to the extermination camps irrespective of their nationality. Otherwise, the model of exploitation in Western Europe was more economic than racially based. France in particular was run as a kind of milch cow for the German war effort, with many thousands of French POWs being held as working hostages in Germany to provide labour and guarantee the good behaviour of the Vichy regime.

It has recently become fashionable to argue that the response of the British people to invasion and occupation would have been no different from that of the French, Czechs or Luxemburgers. It is an issue which, of course, goes to the heart of British national self-perception. In her book on the wartime Channel Islands, published in 1995, the *Guardian* journalist Madeleine Bunting argues that because 'the islanders compromised, collaborated and fraternised just as people did throughout occupied Europe' it follows that their experience 'directly challenges the belief that the Second World War proved that [Britons] were inherently different from the rest of Europe'. She believes the Channel Islands experience between 1940 and 1945 weakens the hold of 'the myth of the distinctiveness of the British character from that of continental Europeans'. In the light of her research, the 'narrow, nationalistic understanding of the war' needs to be replaced with 'a recognition of the common European history of those tumultuous years'.[46] Reviewing her book, the playwright John Mortimer described the Islands as 'the ideal testing ground for the British character and British virtues under stress'. He concluded that 'the British were put to the test and behaved no better or much worse than many people in Europe'.[47] Even the journalist Anne Applebaum, writing in the conservative *Spectator*, has argued that 'in the event of Nazi occupation, Britons would have behaved no better and no worse than other defeated peoples'.[48] Other authors have imagined a Britain in which 'slowly a relationship of sorts began to develop between the British people and members of the German armed forces ... and many a child in hospital was given presents by a Father Christmas with an unfamiliar accent'.[49] Another historian believes that 'great numbers of ordinary decent Britons would have begun to cooperate with the Germans in putting down the Resistance just to bring about a sort of peace'.[50]

All these commentators have failed to appreciate the profound differences between the situation of the Channel Islands and that of mainland Britain. Firstly, the Islands had been ordered by the War Office *not* to resist the invader as their strategic importance was minimal; whereas in Britain Churchill was exhorting the people to 'fight on the beaches' on 4 June. St Helier could hardly, as Churchill said of London, have swallowed an entire German army. Secondly, the Islands had been evacuated of one-third of their population, including all their able-bodied men of military age (10,000 of whom served with distinction in the war). The 60,000 who were left were guarded by no less than 37,000 Germans – a ratio which, if translated to mainland Britain, would have required the Nazis to station thirty million troops! Thirdly, the Channel Islanders cannot be equated with the British as a whole, for all the Surrey-like nature of their architecture. Guernseymen still call Jerseymen 'crapauds' and in 1939 Norman French, the Islands' original patois, was still widely spoken.[51] At 0.1 per cent of the mainland population, the Islands anyhow represent too statistically insignificant a sample to be of any meaningful use as a political barometer for the rest of the United Kingdom. The geography and society of the Islands also precluded useful resistance. Flat, densely populated, with a higher proportion of Germans per square mile during the war than Germany itself, with no political parties, trade unions or obvious centres for resistance, the Islands cannot provide any indication as to how the East End of London, the mining valleys of South Wales, the factories of the North-east or the slums of Glasgow would have reacted to the advent of the Nazi jackboot. Even Bunting acknowledges that 'the islands had no tradition of opposing authority. They were rigidly hierarchical, conformist societies'.[52]

In fact, the evidence suggests that if the Germans had landed in Britain, though they might well have won the set-piece military engagements through sheer superiority of weaponry and battle-field tactics, they would have then been faced with the implacable, visceral enmity of a nation in arms – albeit fairly makeshift ones. To conquer a country, infantry have to occupy the towns and cities. An army confined to its tanks and camps is not necessarily victorious. From what we know about what happened in Britain in May 1940 it is clear that any German invasion, however ruthless, would have faced an extremely difficult task.

On 14 May, Anthony Eden, the War Minister, went on the wireless to call for 'large numbers of men ... between the ages of seventeen and sixty-five to come forward now and offer their services' as Local Defence Volunteers. Even before he finished speaking, police stations across the land were inundated with calls. The next morning vast but orderly queues formed and within twenty-four hours a quarter of a million Britons had volunteered. By the end of May the War Office – which had only expected 150,000 recruits – was having to deal with 400,000, with no sign of the numbers tailing off. By the end of June no fewer than 1,456,000 men had volunteered to fight the expected invader.[53] Over a third of them were First World War veterans.

To be sure, they were ill equipped. Often without waiting for instructions from higher authority, LDV units immediately began patrols, armed with farm implements, shotguns and homemade weapons. Only one in six men received a rifle. It was, of course, at this period in 1940 that Noël Coward wrote the Home Guard's lament:

> *Could you please oblige us with a Bren Gun?*
> *Or failing that a hand grenade would do,*
> *We've got some ammunition*
> *In a rather damp condition,*
> *And Major Huss*
> *Has an arquebus*
> *That was used at Waterloo.*
> *With the vicar's stirrup pump, a pitchfork and a spade,*
> *It's rather hard to guard an aerodrome,*
> *So if you can't oblige us with the Bren Gun*
> *The Home Guard might as well go home.*[54]

But, as was shown in the Spanish Civil War and the Warsaw Uprising, a population unconventionally armed can be a highly effective guerrilla insurgency force. In June, Ministry of Information posters on the Isle of Wight made it clear that the government intended to encourage every form of resistance: 'The people of these islands will offer a united opposition to an invader and every citizen will regard it as his duty to hinder and frustrate the enemy and help our own forces by every means that ingenuity can devise and common sense suggest.' The 'Stand Fast' leaflet also distributed at that time even had to discourage the overzealous: 'Civilians should not set out to make independent attacks on military formations.'[55]

It would have been in the built-up areas that resistance would have been most effective. A recent 'post-revisionist' historian of wartime London has described how 'the population as a whole endured the blitz with dignity, courage, resolution and astonishingly good humour'.[56] Tom Harrison of the Mass-Observation movement, who almost made a career out of exploding wartime myths, nevertheless also believed that in the Blitz, 'the final achievement of so many Britons was enormous enough. Maybe monumental is not putting it too high. They did not let the soldiers or leaders down.'[57] There is no reason to suppose that they would have reacted to invasion and occupation any differently than to nightly bombing – indeed the vigour of their response was likely to have been all the greater. The aerial bombardment of London did not begin until September 1940, so morale would have been far higher than it was in Germany in May 1945 when German resistance finally collapsed after four years of bombing and one year of devastating Thousand Bomber raids.

For all his talk of dying in Downing Street, or in the Citadel bunker in Whitehall on the corner of the Mall and Horse Guards, Churchill himself would probably have met his end in the more prosaic Neasden. The 'Paddock' bunker on the northern heights of London, camouflaged to look like part of Gladstone Park, housed an underground city accommodating the War Cabinet and 200 staff. It was from the broadcasting studio there that Churchill would have rallied the capital's resistance. As one newspaper put it when the place was opened to journalists in 1995, 'Paddock would have seen Churchill's last stand. The extinction of the British Empire could have taken place here – as German tanks advanced up Dollis Hill Lane to overwhelm the defenders of the municipal putting green.'[58] As Churchill wrote after the war, 'The massacre on both sides would have been grim and great ... I intended to use the slogan "You can always take one with you".'

The Channel Islands, of course, do not provide the only possible basis for an argument by analogy about British behaviour under German occupation. In some ways, a comparison with France has more to commend it. Yet those who point to Vichy France as a model for what would have taken place here fail to appreciate the many and profound differences between the British national condition in 1940 and that of France. The Third Republic was far less able to command the allegiance of its citizens than the King-Emperor and Queen Elizabeth. Between 1924 and 1940 France saw thirty-five ministries come and go, Britain only five. On 6 February 1934, when the most contentious political issue in

London was the introduction of driving tests, Paris saw fifteen people killed and over 2,000 injured in street fighting around the Place de la Concorde. The polarisation of French society and politics – at a time when in Britain Communists and fascists regularly lost their deposits – meant that in the 1936 elections 37.3 per cent voted for the left-wing Popular Front and 35.9 per cent for neo-fascist parties. No one in British politics said of Leslie Hore Belisha, as Charles Maurras of Action Française said of Léon Blum, that the Jewish minister 'must be shot – but in the back'.[59] Corruption, party rancour, demagoguery, anti-parliamentary leagues, anti-Semitism and a widespread opposition to the constitution itself were features of French politics in the 1930s in a way that they simply were not in Britain. In France, where the half-century-old divisions over the Dreyfus affair had yet to heal, a united national effort against Nazism was impossible. On 9 July 1940, André Gide wrote in his diary: 'If German rule were to bring us affluence, nine out of ten Frenchmen would accept it, three or four with a smile.'[60]

Yet at exactly the same time Harold Nicolson was writing to his wife that he would be bringing a suicide pill ('a bare bodkin') down to Sissinghurst rather than live under the Nazi heel: 'I am not in the least afraid of a sudden and honourable death.'[61] Although pacifism had been widespread in Britain in the mid-1930s, it had almost completely evaporated as a serious political force by the outbreak of war, as attested by the ill-attended meetings held during the Phoney War and the lack of pacifist sentiment within the Labour party. In any case, British pacifism was actuated by religious and moral principles, whereas in France refusal to serve often had nihilistic, amoral overtones. 'Die for Danzig?' was a popular headline in Paris in the summer of 1939. No British commentator could ever have written, as Roger Martin du Gard did in September 1936: 'Anything rather than war! Anything! ... Even Fascism in France: Nothing, no trial, no servitude can be compared to war: Anything, Hitler rather than war!'[62] In terms of political corruption, Britain had no equivalents of the Stavisky, Hanau, Oustria or Aérospatiale affairs.[63] France, already twice invaded by Prussia in 1870 and 1914, and having suffered heavier casualties than Britain in the Great War, even had advertisements for houses which boasted that they were 'far from invasion routes'.

It is true that the foremost focus for loyalty, and ultimate guarantor of the state's legitimacy, the royal family, might have been forced by military circumstances to leave the country. Just as the BBC had Wood Norton Hall in Worcestershire as its refuge if Broadcasting House fell, so the royal family had earmarked four stately homes – principally the Earl of Beauchamp's Madresfield Court, near Worcester – as their refuges should Windsor prove uninhabitable.[64] From there it was assumed that they would have gone to Liverpool and thence to Canada to continue imperial resistance. The Crown Jewels, which had been taken to Windsor Castle wrapped up in newspaper in 1939, would have been unwrapped in Ottawa as symbols of King George VI's continued legitimacy. A little-known footnote to the royal evacuation story might cast some doubt, however, on whether Ottawa or Government House, Bermuda, would have been their ultimate haven. On 25 May 1940, President Roosevelt heard from his Secretary of State, Cordell Hull, that the arrival of the King and Queen in Canada:

> would have an adverse political effect on the United States. They agreed that it would be used by political opponents of the Administration to accuse the President of establishing monarchy on the North American continent. They further agreed in suggesting that the King might take refuge at, say, Bermuda, without arousing republican sentiment in the U.S.[65]

Roosevelt went so far as to mention this to Lord Lothian, the British ambassador in Washington. Although it aroused Churchill's ire at the time, American support for an eventual liberation of mainland Britain was so crucial that in the event, if the administration had insisted, the royal family might well have wound up in Bermuda, Delhi, Canberra or Auckland instead. It is worth noting that the Americans had no such reservations about the Bank of England's gold and securities being transported to Canada. They started leaving Greenock on HMS *Emerald* on 24 June and over the next three months all Britain's tangible wealth in specie was stored in a sixty-foot-square, eleven-foot-high vault three storeys under the Montreal office of the Sun Life Assurance Company of Canada, where it was guarded by two dozen Mounties.[66]

The British resistance in metropolitan Britain would have been spearheaded by Colonel Colin Gubbins, later of the Special Operations Executive. One of the war's unsung heroes, Gubbins was organising the Auxiliary Units in May 1940. He would have been Britain's Jean Moulin, as his was the 'left-behind' organisation intended to form the nucleus of the national resistance effort. Based at Coleshill House, near Highworth, Swindon, the 3,524 men and women were trained in explosives, ambushes, guerrilla tactics and short-wave communications. From their well-stocked hideouts in woods, cellars and even deserted badger sets, their patrols of three to five people would have emerged at night to harass the enemy behind his lines.[67] Judging by the German occupation record in the rest of Europe, the Auxiliary Units – and perhaps millions of untrained supporters – would have suffered grievously. Savage reprisals against hostages would have been the norm. Hitler would already have had a quarter of a million hostages in continental POW camps after the fall of Dunkirk. Local dignitaries – mayors, county councillors, squires, rotary chairmen – would also have been taken to ensure good conduct by the rest of the populace, and shot on a ratio of ten to every German soldier killed. As Churchill said: 'They would have used terror, and we were prepared to go to all lengths.'[68]

Undoubtedly, the threat of reprisals might have altered some people's perceptions of the wisdom of continued resistance. This would have become more marked when villages like Shamley Green in Surrey met the same fate as Czechoslovakia's Lidice or France's Oradour-sur-Glane. Sir Will Spens, the Regional Commissioner for Civil Defence for the Eastern Region and a former

Vice-Chancellor of Cambridge University, felt that once the Germans were victorious his first responsibility would have to be to the welfare of his civilian population. He threatened Gubbins's Chief of Staff, Peter Wilkinson, that he would 'arrest any [Auxiliary Unit] member found operating in his area'.[69]

Field Marshal von Brauchitsch, the Army Group Commander earmarked to rule Britain, signed the 'Orders Concerning the Organisation and Function of Military Government in England' on 9 September 1940. All firearms and radio sets were to be handed in within twenty-four hours of the British surrender, hostages would be taken to ensure good conduct, placard-posters would be liable to immediate execution and, most draconian of all, 'the able-bodied male population between the ages of seventeen and forty-five will, unless the local situation calls for an exceptional ruling, be interned and dispatched to the continent with a minimum of delay'.[70] Albert Speer would thus have been presented with a vast extra labour force for his construction projects. The officials of the Defence Economic Command would also have stripped the country of raw materials and strategic equipment. Strikers, demonstrators and anyone possessing firearms were to be summarily dealt with by military courts. As long as the war continued, this would have meant hunger and hardship; the worse conditions got, the French experience suggests, the greater support there would have been for resistance.

For the 430,000 British Jews, worse would have lain in store: the inevitable prospect of 'resettlement East' – that is, transportation to Polish extermination camps. Considering the length of journeys Jews from Crete and Southern France were forced to undergo to get to Auschwitz, it is unlikely that Himmler would have built gas chambers on mainland Britain. Madeleine Bunting assumes that the British people and police would have cooperated in the rounding up of Jews, or at least looked the other way.[71] This ignores the fact that the British did not blame the Jews for the war or their social troubles in the same way that so many Frenchmen did. The relatively small size of the British Union of Fascists (which had only forty full-time staff members in late 1937 and never won a parliamentary seat) would also suggest that anti-Semitism was less widespread than in France. It is instructive that, despite the best efforts of MI5 and Special Branch to locate one, and even in some cases to conjure one up, there was no Nazi Fifth Column in wartime Britain.[72] Examples of Britons protecting Jews – as working people did against Mosley's thugs in the East End – would surely have outnumbered the cases of those denouncing them. Jews would have been identified as among the most committed anti-Nazis in the national resistance effort, and appreciated as such, rather as the Free Polish and Free Czech forces were during the Battle of Britain.

On 1 August 1940, Goering ordered Reinhard Heydrich of the Reich Central Security Office (RSHA) to 'commence activities simultaneously with the military invasion in order to seize and combat effectively the numerous important organisations and societies in England which are hostile to Germany'. These were to include trade unions, masonic lodges, public schools, the Church of England and even the Boy Scout movement. Six *Einsatzkommandos* were to be set up to coordinate the liquidation of Germany's political enemies. These were to be in London, Bristol, Birmingham, Liverpool, Manchester and Edinburgh (or Glasgow if the Forth Bridge had been destroyed). The SS colonel whom Heydrich appointed as SS and Higher Police Leader to oversee the operation was Dr Franz-Alfred Six, former dean of Berlin University's economics faculty. In the event, Six ended up in Smolensk rather than London, where he was responsible for the massacre of numerous Soviet commissars, crimes for which he was subsequently sentenced to twenty years in prison.[73] To help Six identify individuals as well as organisations, the RHSA drew up a list of 2,820 names and addresses for people who were to be taken into 'protective custody'. This *Sonderfahndungsliste GB* – the 'Special Search List' or 'Black Book' – was a rushed job: Sigmund Freud had died in September 1939, for example, and Lytton Strachey in 1932. Nevertheless, it shows who the Nazis considered were their potential enemies, not just in politics but in the cultural and literary worlds as well. In addition to obvious political figures – including Churchill, Eden, Masaryk, Beneš and de Gaulle – the list named H. G. Wells, Virginia Woolf, Aldous Huxley (who had been living in America since 1936), J. B. Priestley, C. P. Snow and Stephen Spender, as well as the émigré art historian Fritz Saxl and the left-wing publisher Victor Gollancz.[74] When Rebecca West discovered that she and Noël Coward were on the list she telegraphed: 'My dear, the people we should have been seen dead with!' It was perhaps optimistic to expect 'Churchill, Winston Spencer, Ministerpräsident' to be waiting patiently at 'Chartwell Manor, Westerham, Kent' to be arrested, but the list gives a good indication of how thoroughly the Nazis intended to purge the upper echelons of British public life. Those who advocated peace with Germany were conspicuously absent from the list, including prominent individuals such as George Bernard Shaw (who had written in the *New Statesmen* on 7 October 1939: 'Our business is to make peace with him') and David Lloyd George (who had declared in 1936: 'He is indeed a great man. Führer is the proper name for him, for he is a born leader – yes, a statesman').[75]

The game of attempting to identify who would actually have collaborated with the Germans has been described by Sir Isaiah Berlin as 'the most vicious an Englishman can play'.[76] Although the administration of the country could have been undertaken by the usual pathetic collection of fascist fanatics, passed-over civil servants and ambitious malcontents, some nationally recognisable figureheads would have been essential in establishing the quisling state's political legitimacy in the eyes of the populace. As we have seen, the man best placed to achieve this would have been the Duke of Windsor, who privately opposed the war in 1939 and even in December 1940 was telling American journalists off the record that Britain should come to terms with Hitler to prevent the otherwise inevitable triumph of Bolshevism. Recent, sensationalist accounts of the Duke's remarks and actions in the summer of 1940 have given an exaggerated impression of his complicity with the Nazis. All serious historians of the period are agreed that, for all his vanity and naivety, he did nothing treacherous.[77] But what he might have done if England had fallen is another question. Had Ribbentrop flatteringly presented the Duke, who was in the South of France in late May – and more pertinently perhaps the Duchess in her role as Lady Macbeth – with the opportunity of returning to a vacant throne as the binder of the nation's wounds, they might easily have accepted. The Duke could have justified his decision as an attempt to keep the British Empire – which Hitler consistently proclaimed he felt no antipathy towards – together and functioning as a viable world force. The restored Duke's regime would, of course, have depended upon renunciation of the four-year-old Instrument of Abdication. The full force of Goebbels' propaganda machine – run, perhaps, by William Joyce ('Lord Haw-Haw') as Director-General of the BBC – would have been directed towards altering British perceptions of the Abdication. We know roughly the line that would have been taken, because in September 1940 Joyce published his political testament *Twilight over England*. In it he wrote:

> It is interesting to see how the sacred constitution and all the principles of popular representation can be scuppered in a few hours at the instigation of a couple of hardened schemers like Baldwin and the Archbishop of Canterbury.... Edward was hustled off the throne in a weekend.... There is no question upon which any people has more right to be consulted than the identity of the King or President.... Yet nobody consulted the English people before getting rid of their King.[78]

Thus Edward VIII's return to the throne would have been represented as a democratic initiative.

Through the bewilderment, demoralisation and despair attendant upon a British defeat, some collaborators would doubtless have emerged with broadly patriotic (if misguided) motives. In his novel *A Question of Loyalties*, the writer Allan Massie portrayed some of the Vichy leaders, at least at the beginning, as motivated primarily by a desire to protect their defeated people, once the German victory had become a *fait accompli*.[79] 'The King's government', it would have been argued in Britain, 'must be carried on,' and precedents from 1688 and even the Wars of the Roses would doubtless have been invoked to legitimise the new regime. Candidates for the role of the British Pétain usually include Lloyd George, Sir Oswald Mosley, Sir Samuel Hoare – none of whom featured in the RHSA's 'Black Book' – and Lord Halifax, who did. Lloyd George was, like Pétain, a Great War hero; he was also a former Prime Minister. Hitler believed he could work with him, telling Martin Bormann in January 1942, 'If Lloyd George had the necessary power, he would certainly have been the architect of a German–English understanding.'[80] The Germans knew he was sceptical about the war, and he would have undoubtedly have been their first choice. 'If the chances are against,' Lloyd George had told Harold Nicolson on the outbreak of war, 'then we should certainly make peace at the earliest opportunity.'[81] He said as much again in the House of Commons on 3 October 1939. By August 1940, Beaverbrook believed that 'the public are divided into two camps; there are the people who think Winston should bring him in and other people who think Hitler will put him in'.[82] Lloyd George himself, who in October 1940 told his secretary, 'I shall wait until Winston is bust,' might well have persuaded himself that it was his duty to return to power in order to vitiate the worst aspects of German direct rule.[83]

By contrast, it is doubtful that, even if he had been prepared to serve (which is unlikely considering his orders of 9 May 1940 to fight 'until the foreigner was driven from our soil'), Mosley would have been chosen to govern Britain.[84] The BUF's dismal political record in peacetime would have left any Blackshirt ministry far too transparently a puppet government and, as was shown in France, the Germans wanted legitimacy, however bogus, above all. Always more an admirer of Mussolini than Hitler, Mosley's stock was not particularly high with the Germans by the outbreak of war. In December 1940, in his cross-examination of Mosley, Norman Birkett KC accepted that he could 'entirely dismiss' any suggestion that Mosley was a traitor who would have taken up arms and fought on the Germans' side had they landed.[85]

In any case, Mosley himself, who was interned on 22 May 1940, might well have been found hanged in his Brixton jail cell by the time the Germans arrived, such was his unpopularity as a result of his pre-war activities, his arrest and the sustained campaign against him in the press.

The extremely vain Sir Samuel Hoare, formerly a leading appeaser, but by late May British ambassador in Madrid, was also someone Hitler hoped might replace Churchill as Prime Minister.[86] He would have been flattered by an approach. R. A. Butler, the Under-Secretary at the Foreign Office, was another politician for whom *Realpolitik* mattered more than emotion. He told the Swedish envoy, Byorn Prytz, on 17 June that his 'official attitude will for the present be that the war should continue, but he must be certain that no opportunity should be missed of compromise if reasonable conditions could be agreed and no diehards would be allowed to stand in the way'.[87] Butler was the master of compromise who saw politics as 'the art of the possible', and was suspicious of conviction politicians like Churchill. He further told Prytz that 'common sense and not bravado' must govern the actions of the government in its dealings with Germany. When asked about just such a Vichy Britain situation, his friend and colleague Enoch Powell said, elliptically, 'Rab was an administrator.'[88] As keen on appeasement as Chamberlain himself, Butler might well have felt that it was his patriotic duty to do what he could to relieve the anguish of the British people by establishing a viable *modus operandi* with the conquerors.

Halifax, on the other hand, would probably have been the man chosen by Churchill to accompany the King and Queen (whom he knew well) to Canada to organise continued extra-metropolitan resistance. As a former Under-Secretary at the Colonial Office, Viceroy of India and now Foreign Secretary since early 1938, Halifax had a wide knowledge of the empire and personal knowledge of those colonial politicians with whom a Free British government would have had to deal. If he could have been persuaded to leave his beloved Yorkshire he would probably have become Prime Minister of the government-in-exile. The support he had enjoyed across the political spectrum in early May, when he ceded the premiership to Churchill, would have reverted back to him had Churchill perished. The only other potential leader, Neville Chamberlain, was dying of cancer. He was incapacitated by October and dead by November.

Had the Germans adopted the same policy as they did in France, occupying the industrialised, highly populated part of the country and the national capital themselves, and choosing a country spa town as the capital of the puppet regime, Britain's Vichy could well have been Harrogate. The vast Victorian hotels, such as the Cairn, Crown, Majestic, Old Swan, Granby and Imperial, might have housed the ministries of Agriculture, Health, Transport and Interior. Foreign and defence policy would have been run from London by Brauchitsch or whoever else Hitler created General Governor or Reich Protektor. Whereas the French Republic finally dissolved itself in a converted cinema, the rump House of Commons would at least have had the Royal Baths Assembly Rooms.

An important consideration for any British politician taking over either the 'Vichy' government or the Canadian government-in-exile would have been the status of the empire. Despite Hitler's 1937 offer to 'guarantee' it, and his positive allusions to it in his peace offer speech of 6 October 1939, it is unlikely that the empire could have been maintained under any meaningful British control for long. Had Hitler turned his attentions towards the United States after defeating Russia, Britain's Caribbean bases would have been invaluable forward ports for the German navy. The British Empire, as was the case with the French, would also have been the most likely area of conflict between the two British governments. If both the Harrogate (Vichy) government and the Ottawa (Free British) government had laid claim to India and other British possessions, friction would inevitably have arisen, as it did between the Vichyites and Free French in Africa from 1940 to 1942. Setting Briton against Briton would have been the ultimate victory for the Nazis.

It is easier to predict the explanation which Goebbels would have presented to the British people for their catastrophe. He would have encouraged them to blame their defeat on the Jews, socialists, vacillating democratic 'Old Gang' politicians, Churchillian warmongers, arms-manufacturing Yankee capitalists, foreign financiers and so on. He would also have argued that the royal family and Halifax had taken a cowardly escape route. (One can almost hear Lord Haw-Haw's nasal sneers at their 'chicken-run'.) But a new hope would also have been offered; as Joyce put it in his book, 'The defeat of England will be her victory.' Joseph Chamberlain's talk of an Anglo-German alliance at the turn of the century would have been resuscitated and 'successfully' negotiated between Lloyd George and Hitler. The Germans and British would have been portrayed as natural Aryan allies against Bolshevik Slavs and capitalist Americans. The medium Goebbels would have chosen to disseminate his message, besides the wireless, was known elsewhere in occupied Europe as the 'reptile' press. In Occupied Poland the General Government ran eight (fairly identical) dailies in different cities, as well as six periodicals. These were written by Germans who had lived in Poland before the war, aided by about 120 Poles. A score of politically neutral professional magazines, covering subjects as varied as midwifery and poultry-breeding, were also tolerated.[89]

The British 'reptile' press, like the Polish, would have subtly changed its tune had the Germans begun to suffer the same reverses on the Eastern Front as they did in 1943. The emphasis would have begun to shift away from the glories of German arms and culture towards the common 'pan-European struggle against Bolshevism'. The emphasis which Vichy propagandists placed on a common European future as the catalyst by which honour and self-respect could be restored would have been repeated word for word in Britain. 'Instead of maintaining European rivalries', Hitler told Martin Bormann, 'Britain ought to do her utmost to bring about a unification of Europe. Allied to a United Europe, she would then still retain the chance of being able to play the part of arbiter in world affairs.' In 1942, Dr Walther Funk, the Reich Economics Minister and President of the Reichsbank, wrote the first chapter of a book entitled *Europäische Wirtschaftsgesellschaft* (European Economic Society) in which he called for a European single currency. Other chapters set out the Nazi blueprint for a common agricultural policy, an exchange rate mechanism, a single market and a central bank. Dr Anton Reithinger of the chemical giant IG-Farben wrote a chapter entitled 'The New Europe and its Common Aspects'.[90] New European Order aspirations would have been sedulously fostered by Nazi propaganda, partly to make British defeat more palatable, partly as a figleaf for the nakedness of German *imperium*, and partly as a way to promote anti-Slav and anti-American sentiment.

Regional independence movements would also have been encouraged to weaken the influence of London. 'Radio Caledonia' broadcast from Belgium in the summer of 1940, inciting Welsh and Scottish nationalists to rise up against their English oppressors. Goebbels would have promoted anything that might weaken the sense of British national identity in the defeated people. In 1941 Hitler said, 'Our policy towards the nations inhabiting the vast expanse of Russia must be to encourage every form of discord and division.' What went for the Soviet Union would certainly have applied to the Celtic fringe of Britain. Such propaganda is unlikely to have deceived many Scots, however. One Highlander on the beaches of Dunkirk was overheard telling a comrade: 'If the English surrender too, it's going to be a long war!'[91] On the other hand, anyone believing that the independence of the Irish Free State would have been respected by the Nazis once the United Kingdom had fallen would soon have come in for a rude shock.

Another method by which the Nazis hoped to strip the British of their sense of national identity was architectural, an aspect of the New Order which deeply interested Hitler. As is well known, he spent many hours planning massive reconstruction programmes for Berlin and other German cities to be implemented once the war was won. The converse of this policy was architectural despoliation for the cities conquered by the Germans. In its memorandum 'Plans for England', Department III of the RHSA envisaged a symbolic architectural humiliation. 'The Nelson Column represents for England a symbol of British naval might and world domination,' stated the report. 'It would be an impressive way of underlining the German victory if the Nelson Column were to be transferred to Berlin.'[92] Long lists of British art treasures to be looted were drawn up and there can be little doubt that – had the British not been able to evacuate the National Gallery paintings from the North Wales mineshaft, where they were stored, safely to Canada – Goering would have denuded the country of its greatest works of art as he did across the rest of Europe. The Nazis also planned to return the Elgin Marbles to Greece.[93]

Never Surrender?

The eventual liberation of Britain is, of course, taken for granted in almost all of the books, films and plays which deal with the subject. Either through exhaustion on the Eastern Front, the American atomic bomb or Nazi economic overstretch and collapse, it is always assumed that a Nazi Britain would have eventually been freed, usually with New World help. This is the least likely part of the whole scenario, however. As we have seen, America came into the struggle in Europe only once Hitler had declared war on *her*. It is wishful thinking that she would have entered the war out of a sentimental attachment to the (at that time virtually non-existent) Special Relationship. And if the Royal Navy had fallen into German hands, or more likely been crippled or sunk, the United States would have had to face the combined German, Japanese, Vichy and possibly Italian fleets alone. Churchill refused to promise Roosevelt that the Royal Navy would sail to Canada in the event of a German invasion.[94] Again, as we have seen, Hitler would have been able to invade Russia in his own time, without wasting crucial weeks on Yugoslavia and south-eastern Europe. America, even supposing she had wished to antagonise Nazi Germany while occupied with Japan in the Pacific, could not have supplied the English resistance on anything like the scale that Britain supplied the French and the Dutch. The sheer width of the Atlantic compared with the Channel would have seen to that. (When the US and Britain supplied the Soviet Union during the war, they had access to friendly Russian-held ports; there would have been no equivalent in an occupied Britain.) It is also worth bearing in mind that a large number of the scientists who later built the atomic bomb were resident in Britain in May 1940, and would have been captured in the event of a successful German invasion. If Hitler had himself developed a nuclear capacity, possibly in the late 1940s, a terrifying new factor would have entered the equation.

Thus when Guderian wrote in his memoirs that Hitler's halt order of 24 May had 'results which were to have a most disastrous influence on the whole future of the war' he was very probably right.[95] Everything would have depended on whether the Nazis would have been militarily able to hold down Britain by brute force. To gauge the answer one must remember the spirit abroad in this country during those vital months. As the author Margery Allingham wrote in 1941:

In those weeks in May and June [1940], I think 99 per cent of English folk found their souls, and whatever else it may have been it was a glorious and triumphant experience. If you have lived your life's span without a passionate belief in anything, the bald discovery that you would honestly and in cold blood rather die when it came to it than be bossed about by a Nazi, then that is something to have lived for.[96]

However, Colonel Gubbins's Chief of Staff, Peter Wilkinson, may have been more realistic when in late May 1940 he gave the following orders to one of his officers, Douglas Dodds-Parker:

If the United Kingdom is to be overrun, keep outside the ring. Go to South Africa, Australia, Canada. Keep going, and stay in touch with Auxiliary Units in the UK. Remember, it took the Greeks only six hundred years to get free of the Turks.[97]

SIX

NAZI EUROPE:

What if Nazi Germany had defeated the Soviet Union?

Michael Burleigh

What a task awaits us! We have a hundred years of joyful satisfaction before us.

ADOLF HITLER

Operation Barbarossa began in the small hours of 22 June 1941 with the roar of 6,000 guns. By late morning, the Luftwaffe had destroyed 890 Russian aircraft, 668 of which were caught on the ground. By 12 July some 6,857 Russian aircraft had been put out of commission, with the loss of 550 German aeroplanes.[1] Over three million German and Axis troops, including Finns, Romanians, Hungarians, Italians and Slovaks, divided into three Army Groups, North, Centre and South, crossed the frontier in the direction of respectively Leningrad, Moscow and the Ukraine. The fundamental intention was to annihilate the Red Army west of the Dvina–Dnieper line. Their advance was so swift that as early as 3 July Franz Halder, the Chief of General Staff, noted in his diary that 'the Russian campaign has been won in the space of two weeks'. He then turned his mind to the matter of denying the Russians the economic resources for future recovery; the ongoing irritant of Britain; and a possible thrust through the Caucasus to Iran.[2] This confidence was reflected in armaments policy. On 14 July 1941, Hitler decreed a shift in priorities away from the army and in favour of the navy and Luftwaffe.[3]

As is well known, Halder's optimistic assessment was gradually belied by events on the ground. Maps showing roads failed to correspond with the reality of tracks that in the heat generated clouds of dust, or else, following rainfall, mired vehicles in mud. The panzer and motorised infantry may have chugged and clanked ahead regardless of mechanical fatigue, but the infantry and horse-drawn supplies lagged increasingly far behind.[4] Heavily laden infantrymen marched across a monotonous landscape where the incomprehensible distances made them by turns angry and despondent and where flies and stinging insects unerringly homed in on their sweat. Nor did the vast numbers of Russians taken captive – for example, 300,000 at Smolensk, 650,000 at Kiev, 650,000 at Vyazma and Bryansk (most of whom would perish in desolate conditions) – seem to entail a slackening of enemy resolve. Indeed, the Soviets seemed to find new troops with ease, whether from Siberia or in the shape of hastily improvised citizen militias.[5] Stalin's Order Number 270 stiffened the resolve of would-be deserters by sanctioning the arrest of their families; at the very least, the relatives of soldiers who surrendered were to be deprived of all state assistance. Generals such as Pavlov whom Stalin blamed for his own mistakes were shot. Civilian productive capacities were rapidly converted for military purposes, with bicycle factories soon producing flamethrowers, while vast plants and their workforces were dismantled and evacuated to the Urals, western Siberia, Kazakhstan and Central Asia. For example, in late December 1941, the Zaporozhstal steel works in the Ukraine was relocated to near Chelyabinsk in the Urals in the space of six weeks, despite the fact that the ground had to be heated up before foundations could be laid, or that cement froze in temperatures of −45 degrees centigrade.[6] The consequences for the Germans of this massive effort have been aptly described as 'an economic Stalingrad'.[7]

Soviet resistance was compounded by German miscalculation. In late July, and against the advice of those generals who wished to concentrate offensive operations upon Moscow, Hitler halted Army Group Centre at Smolensk, diverting its flanking armour to the assault on Leningrad and a drive to the Donets Basin and

Caucasus in the south. By 11 August, a less confident Halder noted the disturbing existence of Russian divisions the Germans had somehow failed to count, divisions 'not armed and equipped according to our standards ... but there they are, and if we smash a dozen of them, the Russians simply put up another dozen'.[8] Operation Typhoon, the resumption of Army Group Centre's push on Moscow, commenced in October, perilously close to the onset of winter. By early December temperatures fell to below −30 degrees centigrade so that grease and oils congealed and the ground hardened. Inadequately clothed soldiers stuffed newspaper or propaganda leaflets into their overalls and huddled miserably around fires which consumed precious stocks of gasoline. Axes glanced off frozen horse meat. Hitler refused to countenance the notion of tactical withdrawal, sarcastically asking a general who advocated such a strategy: 'Sir, where in God's name do you propose to go back to, how far do you want to go back? ... Do you want to go back 50 kilometres; do you think it is less cold there?'[9] After coming so close to Moscow, in late December exhausted and panic-stricken German troops, pursued by fresh Siberian divisions wearing winter-quilted overalls and equipped with tommy-guns, finished up 280 kilometres away from the Soviet capital. The Blitzkrieg strategy of destroying the Russians before the onset of winter had failed; a long war of attrition ensued. Speaking to Bormann on 19 February, Hitler observed: 'I've always detested snow, Bormann, you know. I've always hated it. Now I know why. It was a presentiment.'[10]

Having blunted Soviet winter offensives by ordering fanatical resistance, Hitler scaled down his ambitions for the 1942 summer campaign (Operation Blue), aiming to make one major push towards the oilfields of the south. He realised that he needed the natural resources of this region in order to make the transition from the failed Blitzkrieg to what was becoming a long war of attrition against a global coalition of the major powers. As he said: 'If I don't get the oil in Maikop and Grozny, I'll have to liquidate this war.'[11] Hitler again fatefully interfered in the disposition of his forces, by dividing them between different objectives – that is, the oil in the south and a final showdown with Soviet reserves west of the Volga. He followed Stalin in transforming the battle for Stalingrad into a real and symbolic contest of wills. Every pile of charred bricks and each level of gutted buildings had to be contested with cannon, grenades, flamethrowers and sniperfire. The Central Station was taken and retaken by the two sides fifteen times in three days. While Paulus's troops tried to clear the Russian defenders out of the rubble, the Soviet pincers closed around them at a depth that made relief impossible, and which, following the Luftwaffe's failure to supply the pocket from the air, eventuated in the surrender of Paulus and 90,000 men.[12] After Stalingrad, Hitler's Finnish, Hungarian and Romanian allies began to urge a compromise peace. But on 4 July 1943 he again went on to the offensive, this time on a comparatively restricted 150 kilometres front to pinch out the Kursk salient. What developed into the largest tank battle of the Second World War resulted in the strategic initiative passing to the Soviets, who thenceforth dictated the pace of events.

As both a final reckoning between two antagonistic ideological systems and a politico-biological crusade against Jews and Slavic 'Untermenschen', the German invasion of the Soviet Union had a fundamentally different character from the campaigns in the West. This can be demonstrated by the fact that whereas 3.5 per cent of Western Allied prisoners of war died in German captivity between 1939 and 1945, 31.6 per cent, or one million Germans, died in Soviet captivity and a staggering 57 per cent or 3,300,000 Russians died either in, or *en route* to, poorly improvised German camps or directly at the hands of SD or Wehrmacht executioners, the majority before the summer of 1942.[13] Hitler set the tone, as in his address on 30 March to about 250 generals: 'We must get away from the standpoint of soldierly comradeship. The Communist is from first to last no comrade. It is a war of extermination. . . . The struggle will be very different from that in the west. In the east toughness now means mildness in the future.'[14] Directives and guidelines, suffused with Nazi ideology, notably the decree on military justice of 13 May 1941 and the infamous Commissar

Order of 6 June, issued by senior army commanders before the invasion, served to blur the line between conventional and racial–ideological warfare, converting the Wehrmacht into a more or less willing accomplice in the depredations of the SS and its multifarious police cohorts.[15]

They also prove that military criminality was premeditated. The predetermined ideological character of the war and the creeping conversion of the military into political soldiers resulted not just in the systematic mass murder of 2.2 million Jewish people in the areas behind German lines, but also in the slaughter of 'gypsies', people in psychiatric asylums and, because of a latitudinarian use of concepts such as 'agents', 'bandits', 'partisans', 'saboteurs', 'spies' or 'resisters', the entire populations of villages, who were shot, hanged from telegraph poles or incinerated in barns and churches. Hitler's observation that the activities of partisans 'gives us the chance to exterminate whoever turns against us' was a characteristic half-truth: the victims could easily be people who had 'turned against' no one. As SS General Erich von dem Bach-Zelewski subsequently acknowledged:

> The fight against partisans was gradually used as an excuse to carry out other measures, such as the extermination of the Jews and gypsies, the systematic reduction of the Slavic people by some 30,000,000 souls (in order to ensure the supremacy of the German people) and the terrorisation of civilians by shooting and looting.[16]

When one militiaman was shot in Pinsk, 4,500 Jews were murdered in line with the formula: 'where there are partisans, the Jew is there too, and where there is the Jew, there are also partisans'.[17] The more reflective German officers began to worry about what one dubbed 'the 6,000/480 problem' – that is, the mystery of why only 480 rifles had been recovered from 6,000 dead 'partisans'.[18] That there were partisans at all was as much the product of heavy-handed German occupation policies as of Stalin's belated attempts to maintain a presence in areas overrun by the enemy. For most of the partisans, beyond a small dedicated core, remaining a 'volunteer' (the preferred euphemism for draftees whose families were often murdered in the event of desertion) was a marginally lesser evil than living under German occupation.

'What if' scenarios for the 'thousand-year Reich' have fitfully excited writers of popular fiction, military history buffs and a few professional historians. Writers such as Len Deighton, Robert Harris and most recently the American politician Newt Gingrich have (with varying degrees of historical accuracy) used the Third Reich as a backdrop for popular thrillers.[19] Others, most recently Ralph Giordano, offer less speculative accounts of what would have happened 'if Hitler had won the war'. However, such writers invariably overlook the fact that in a system of competing Nazi agencies, representing a plurality of ideological tendencies, there could have been more than one possible outcome.[20] Moreover, much of this work reflects latent (Anglo-American or German) anxieties about the economic and political power of the recently unified Federal Republic, where its implications are deeply resented. By contrast, the military historians, most of whose contributions to this field are severely 'operational', merely shuffle armies around in the comfort of their studies.[21] In a qualitatively different class, professional historians such as Jochen Thies have concentrated upon the symbolic expressions of Nazi megalomania, deducing plans for 'world domination' from the architectural plans for the postwar period, or have explored the Nazis' plans for a pseudo-European union or a single currency.[22]

In the case of the Eastern Front, however, the vast quantity of surviving documentation relating to the immediate and long-term future makes it otiose to imagine hypothetical scenarios. For over three years the Germans fought over and occupied vast areas of the Soviet Union behind a front that at some points was 2,000 kilometres deep. We can thus see very clearly how a victorious Germany would have dealt with the territories of a dismembered Soviet Union. Plans survive in profusion. All we need to imagine to construct a credible counterfactual is a military victory.

Rosenberg's Counterfactual

How would matters have been if, following the advice of his generals, Hitler had managed to capture Moscow before the onset of winter in 1941 in the manner imagined – Operation Wotan – by the military historian James Lucas?[23] Let us suppose, in a single venture into the fantastic, that some accident befell Stalin and the Stavka leadership before or during their flight from the beleaguered capital, and that this resulted in the collapse of the Red Army's will to offer organised resistance. Reading between the lines of the brief account above of what actually happened, one can easily perceive some of the alternative strategies for domination that could have been pursued in the occupied Soviet Union, if the combination of crude Nazi racial dogmas as espoused by Hitler and military–economic necessity had not been the order of the day. The occupiers could have exploited separatist sentiments, installing a series of puppet regimes (under the control of German governors) in the Baltic, Belorussia, the Caucasus and the Ukraine. The Bolshevik edifice could have been undermined by decollectivisation and the reprivatisation of property, the restoration of religious freedom and so forth. It is unlikely, given the terrain and the existence of trans-Urals weapons plants, that resistance would have ceased, but this would have been counterbalanced by large numbers of collaborators who would have decided that the Bolshevik game was up.

That such a strategy might have worked is clear. In L'vov, western Ukrainian nationalists under Bandera staged an anti-Soviet revolt (and pogroms) before the German invaders arrived. Throughout the occupied territories, there was significant collaboration by the indigenous populations. About one million Russians had varying degrees of involvement with the German armed forces, the majority being unarmed auxiliaries or 'Hiwis' after their German acronym, but there were also more than a quarter of a million armed military collaborators including the Kaminski Brigade, which helped suppress the 1944 Warsaw Uprising, Vlasov's Russian Liberation Army, and various Cossack,

Kalmyk or Tatar formations who are less well known today than their Baltic or Ukrainian SS equivalents. Some nationalities were better represented in the Wehrmacht than in the Red Army.[24] As post-Soviet Russian historians are now revealing, former Communists, as amoral adepts at control, police work and terror, were not absent from the ranks of those who assisted the occupier.

Thus those with a more reflective understanding of political warfare, for example in the Wehrmacht Propaganda branch, cautioned against alienating the Great Russian population through flirtations with excitable émigré separatists. Rather, the object should be to drive a wedge between the Kremlin and the Russian population with the slogan 'Liberation, not Conquest'.[25] From a different perspective, Hitler's Minister for the Occupied Eastern Territories, Alfred Rosenberg, shared his Führer's rampant Russophobia, but combined this with an appreciation of the differences between, and the strategic utility of, other national groups. He envisaged a protectorate over Lithuania, Latvia, Estonia and Belorussia; an expanded Ukraine; a Caucasian federation; and – surrounded by this *cordon sanitaire* – a revived, and greatly reduced, 'Muscovy' whose dynamics would be redirected towards Asia. Plans for Reichskommissariats in the Caucasus or Muscovy were drafted. Rosenberg and his circle of Eastern experts even had fitful fantasies about a Crimean Muftiate or a vast 'pan-Turanic' bloc carved out of former Soviet Central Asia with appropriate adjustments to the depiction of Tatars and Turks (the classic 'Untermenschen') of German propaganda.

It was in this part of the former Soviet Union – to be precise, in the Northern Caucasus – that German occupation policy most successfully sought to reap dividends of concessions to the indigenous population. The non-Slavic character of the people; the fact that Chechens and Karachai threw off the Soviet yoke before the Germans came; the need to make a favourable impression on neighbouring Turkey; and the fact that the army remained in control – all this resulted in a distinctly conciliatory approach, as the tone of the following military directives makes clear:

1. To treat the population of the Caucasus as friends. . . .
2. To lay no obstacles in the path of the Mountaineers striving to abolish the collective state farms.
3. To permit the reopening of places of worship of all denominations.
4. To respect private property and pay for requisitioned goods.
5. To win the confidence of the people by model conduct.
6. To give reasons for all harsh measures affecting the population.
7. To respect especially the honour of the women of the Caucasus.[26]

The German authorities recognised a Karachai National Committee and entrusted it with former Soviet state enterprises and forests. The Muslim Balkars welcomed German visitors to the Kurman ceremonies, presenting them with horses in return for Korans and weapons. When the SD geared themselves up to murder the Tats, or Mountain Jews, the local committee interceded with the military, who told the SD to desist. Herds were reprivatised and the conscription of labour was minimal. In return, large numbers of the inhabitants fought on the German side, with Hitler declaring 'I consider only the Muslims to be reliable.' Along with an estimated three and a half million other people whom the Soviets deported to Kazakhstan and Central Asia, they would pay a terrible price for this during and after the war.[27]

Hitler's Vision

The problem was that these suggestions for a strategy of cooperation with national minorities came from quarters that lacked political weight. By contrast, it is clear from statements made by Hitler himself that this was in fact *politically* the least likely of all the possible outcomes of a German military victory. Judging from his *Table Talk*, the record of his idiosyncratic observations on an Aryan Jesus, the vegetarianism of Caesar's legions, prehistoric dogs and such *obiter dicta* as 'Tarts adore poachers', Hitler was simultaneously attracted and repelled by 'the East'. Impervious to the ironies involved, he called Russia a 'desert'; his own battles would supply the country with a past.[28] Vast roads built on ridges so that the wind would sweep them clear of snow would pass through German towns and settlements.[29] The Crimea would become a German Riviera.

Characteristically, he was much clearer about the negative sides of his vision, namely the desire to subject the 'natives' to a particularly barbaric and crude version of colonial rule, so inhumane that it seems like something he had read in a rather lurid book. His preferred, and egregious, analogy was with British rule in India: 'Our role in Russia will be analogous to that of England in India ... The Russian space is our India. Like the English, we shall rule this empire with a handful of men.'[30] He envisaged settling 'the space' with German peasant–soldiers, that is, veterans of twelve years' military service, although there was room too in the Baltic for Danish, Dutch, Norwegian and Swedish settlers – the latter, in a characteristically irrelevant and quirky qualification, 'by special arrangement'. The German colonists would enjoy large farms, officialdom handsome quarters and the regional governors 'palaces'. German colonial society would be a literal and metaphorical 'fortress', closed to outsiders, since 'the least of our stable-lads must be superior to any native'. The latter were 'a mass of born slaves, who feel the need of a master'. Outsiders (that is, Germans) had introduced the notion of organised society to peoples who would otherwise behave in the antisocial manner of 'rabbits'.[31] Health and hygiene were to be things of the past: 'No vaccination for the Russians, and no soap to get the dirt off them. ... But let them have all the spirits and tobacco they want.'[32] With characteristic callousness, he said on 17 October 1941:

> We're not going to play at children's nurses; we're absolutely without obligations as far as these people are concerned. To struggle against the hovels, chase away the fleas, provide German teachers, bring out newspapers – very little of that for us! ...

For the rest, let them know just enough to understand our highway signs, so that they won't get themselves run over by our vehicles![33]

If the Russians rebelled, 'we shall only have to drop a few bombs on their cities, and the affair will be liquidated'.[34] Economic intercourse was to be of the most exploitative kind:

At harvest time we will set up markets at all the centres of any importance. There we will buy up all the cereals and fruit, and sell the more trashy products of our own manufacture.... Our agricultural machinery factories, our transport companies, our manufacturers of household goods and so forth will find there an enormous market for their goods. It will also be a splendid market for cheap cotton goods – the more brightly coloured the better. Why should we thwart the longing of these people for bright colours?[35]

The Ukrainians were to be tantalised with scarves, beads 'and everything that colonial peoples like'.[36]

Sentiments like these – mostly shared by his generals – set the tone of German occupation policy in Russia, thwarting any prospect of capitalising on the widespread unpopularity of the Bolshevik regime, particularly in areas seized by Stalin under the terms of the 1939 Nazi–Soviet Pact, or of exploiting the deep ethnic and religious fissures latent within the Soviet empire. Hitler was simply unwilling to set aside their ideological imperatives in the interests of winning local support. His sense of German racial superiority effectively precluded any concessions to national autonomy – except in areas which the Nazis did not wish to settle or where policy was pitched at a wider Muslim or Turkic audience.

This had direct political consequences for Rosenberg and his supporters. Powerless even to determine senior appointments within his vast and largely notional fiefdom, Rosenberg had to suffer the appointment as Reichskommissar in the Ukraine of

Erich Koch, who rivalled Hitler in his contempt for Slavic helots, and Hinrich Lohse as Reichskommissar of Ostland, who not surprisingly resisted all attempts by Rosenberg to grant the three Baltic states some measure of severely limited autonomy. In practice, separatism – or more accurately the redrawing of political geography – took place strictly under German auspices and did not permit any element of self-determination.[37] The febrile desire of sundry fascist, nationalist or religious émigrés to turn the German invasion to their own advantage mostly came to nothing. They were cultivated, dropped and in some cases imprisoned and murdered – the same fate that many of them would subsequently meet at the hands of a vengeful NKVD (in Stefan Bandera's case, in 1950s Munich where he was working for Radio Free Europe).[38]

Himmler's Counterfactual

It was not only Hitler who opposed Rosenberg's policy, however. Both he and Lohse found their local powers contested by the economic agencies of the Reich which operated independently of Rosenberg's ministry in Berlin and, more importantly, by Himmler's Higher SS and Police Leaders.[39]

Economic and military necessity stalled any attempts to reform the Bolshevik socio-economic order in ways appealing to the local population. As we saw above, Hitler's conception of future Germano-Russian economic relations was based upon crude exploitation. Practical concerns also ensured that there was no more than cosmetic tinkering with the institution of collective farming. Decollectivisation, with all its attendant dislocation, would have vastly complicated the military's capacity to secure food supplies. It was much easier for the SS to convert *kolkhoz* into landed estates than to mess around later 'rationalising' small farms recently returned to their owners. As Backe, the responsible State Secretary for agriculture, remarked, if the Bolsheviks had not established collective farms, the Germans would have had to invent them. German propaganda posters announced 'The end of the *kolkhoz*! The free peasant on his own land!', and depicted German soldiers using rifle-butts to shove the burden of vodka-swilling bureaucrats from the shoulders of Russian peasants. The reality was otherwise. Rosenberg's Agrarian Decree of 15 February 1942 may have set up 'communal economies' based upon individual farms, but the semi-feudal 'work-days' and tithe-like delivery obligations were not dissimilar to the hated Soviet system.[40] In the industrial economy, the struggle for ownership was an all-German affair involving various agencies and the private sector, with firms such as Flick, Krupp and Mannesmann acting as 'foster-parents' to Soviet firms in their sector.

It is interesting to speculate what might have happened if such economic exploitation had been remotely as successful as German policy in Western Europe (especially France). Yet the fact remains that it was not. This was primarily due to the fact that policy in the occupied territories was increasingly determined by that most sinister of the Nazi Diadochi: the Reichsführer-SS Heinrich Himmler, whose priorities were racial rather than economic. Indeed, it may be that Himmler's plans for Eastern Europe give us the most reliable picture of how the Germans would have ruled if they had won the war.

Himmler believed that the East 'belonged to' the SS, which would assume control of the deportation, repatriation and extermination of entire populations.[41] This ascendancy began long before Barbarossa, in the context of occupied Poland. Already on 24 October 1939, shortly after he had secured the title of Reich Commissar for the Strengthening of Ethnic Germandom (RKFDV), Himmler addressed SS leaders in Posen on the subject of German settlement in Poland.[42] Each settlement was to consist of a leading nucleus of soldier–farmers (drawn from the ranks of the SS), surrounded by the farms of settlers from the 'old Reich', and then an outer ring of ethnic Germans. The Poles would be their farmhands and labourers. With characteristic pedantry, the Reichsführer specified the thickness of the brick farmhouse walls; insisted on the installation of baths and showers in the cellars 'for the farmer who returns sweatily from the fields'; and the prohibi-tion of 'kitsch and urban clutter' in the farmhouse interiors, which were to be 'neither luxurious nor primitive'.[43]

In May 1940, Himmler outlined the fate of the indigenous Polish population in a key memorandum entitled 'Some Thoughts on the Treatment of Alien Populations in the East'. Poland was to be dissolved into its real, or imagined, constituent ethnic parts. Those deemed unfit for regermanisation – that is, those 'fished out' of 'this mishmash' – were to be relegated to the status of helots, provided, he ominously and sententiously mused, 'one rejects the Bolshevik method of physically exterminating a people as fundamentally unGerman and impossible'. The helots were to receive a rudimentary education, namely 'simple arithmetic up to 500 at the most, how to write one's name, and to teach that it is God's commandment to be obedient to the Germans and to be honest, hard-working and well behaved. I consider it unnecessary to teach reading.' This 'inferior remnant' would exist in the General Government as a leaderless labouring class supplying Germany with the manpower for major capital projects such as quarries, public buildings and roads.[44] On 24 June 1940, Himmler addressed himself to the problem of Polish rural labour. The Poles would be used to create towns, villages and infrastructural improvements, after which '7/8ths' of them would be deported to the General Government. There they would constitute a seasonal reserve army of labour brought in to work in quarries or at harvest time. There was to be no fraternisation between Germans and Poles, between whom 'there was no more of a connection than between us and the negroes'. Poles who had sexual relations with German women would 'suffer the noose'; German men and women who consorted with Poles would be sent to concentration camps.[45] Himmler's RKFDV planning staff, notably Professor Konrad Meyer, an ambitious thirty-nine-year-old agronomist and SS-Oberführer, converted these random thoughts into coldly technocratic schemes such as his February 1940 'Planning Funda-mentals for the Reconstruction of the Eastern Territories', which envisaged deporting 'Zug um Zug' (without delay) 3.4 million

Poles and all Jews.[46] Meyer was merely the most prominent participant in what amounted to a Gadarene stampede by more or less cranky academics to provide the SS with their expertise in everything from ethnic relations, race biology or types of plants suited to cold climates.[47] Apparently, Himmler regarded talking to such people as a form of late-night relaxation after his taxing daytime duties.[48]

Speaking in Madrid on 22 October 1940, Himmler announced that in Poland resettlement was taking place 'on the basis of the latest findings of research and will bring revolutionary results'. A 'Generalplan' existed for the total refashioning of 200,000 square kilometres of territory which would be implemented in the first half of 1941.[49] Actually, a 'general plan' probably did not exist at this stage, but the concept was a useful one to tout around if one's intention was to steal a march on rivals in the business of moving entire populations. And moved they were. By the end of 1940, some 261,517 Poles had been expelled from the Warthegau, 17,413 from Upper Silesia, 31,000 from Danzig–West Prussia, and 15,000 from Zichenau, in sum nearly 325,000 people. Only the transport priority accorded Barbarossa prevented further massive deportations in 1941. As it was, a further 400,000 Poles were shuffled around in the incorporated territories to make room for ethnic German repatriates before 1945. Over the demarcation line, the Russians did likewise.

The invasion of the Soviet Union provided Himmler with a vastly expanded potential field of activity. To this end, within two days of the invasion he gave Professor Meyer three weeks to supply him with a sketch of the broad outlines of future German settlement policy in the augmented occupied territories. Even within the SS, planning was a congested field. Thus in his inaugural address on 2 October 1941 to senior members of the occupation regime in Prague, Reinhard Heydrich, the new Reichsprotektor of Bohemia–Moravia, outlined his plans for the settlement of the East. These were based upon two separate moral universes. In the first, Germans would treat cognate peoples such as the Dutch, Flemings and Scandinavians with relative decency. Beyond in the

East, a German military elite would preside over 'helots' – 'if I may put it drastically' – who would be the workforce for major projects. A form of human polderisation would ensue. An outer wall of soldier–farmers would keep out the human 'storm flood of Asia for all time'. Behind this primary line of defence, an expanding ring of subsidiary 'dams', commencing in Danzig–West Prussia and the Warthegau, would ensure German settlement of one 'space' after another.[50]

In late 1941, the Reich Main Security Office (RSHA) of the SS drew up its own version of a 'Generalplan Ost', whose contents can be inferred from a critical commentary dated April 1942 by Dr Erhard Wetzel, the desk officer for racial policy in Rosenberg's Ministry for the Occupied Eastern Territories. The plan would have taken thirty years to realise from the end of the war. It dealt with Poland, the Baltic states, White Russia, parts of the Ukraine, and 'Ingermanland' (the region around Leningrad) and the 'Gothengau' (the Crimea). Its SS authors envisaged up to ten million Germans settling in the occupied East; with thirty-one million of the forty-five million indigenous inhabitants of these areas being deported to western Siberia. Here Wetzel punctiliously corrected the SS's arithmetic. Their original figure of forty-five million indigenous people appeared to include five to six million Jews who would have been 'got rid of' before the evacuation. Moreover, allowing for such factors as the birthrate, the native population would in fact have been sixty to sixty-five million people, of whom forty-six to fifty-one million would be 'resettled'. The plan envisaged deporting different percentages of the various populations who were its object. Thus '80 to 85 per cent' of the Poles (or twenty to twenty-four million people) were to be 'evacuated'. Wetzel did not like the idea of creating a Greater Poland in exile, especially since the Poles' presence would antagonise the inhabitants of Siberia whom he wished to cultivate against the Greater Russians. Pondering what to do with the Poles – since 'it is taken for granted that one cannot liquidate the Poles like the Jews' – Wetzel suggested the alternative strategy of 'encouraging' the emigration of their intellectual classes to southern Brazil in return for the repatriation of ethnic Germans. The Polish lower classes could go to Siberia, which after other nationalities had been 'pumped in' would constitute a denatured, 'Americanised' hodge-podge distinct from the neighbouring Russians. Sixty-five per cent of the Ukrainians and 75 per cent of White Ruthenians were to accompany the Poles eastwards. Censoriously, Wetzel remarked that the RSHA plan had nothing to say about the Russians. By contrast, he had a great deal to offer in the way of detailed advice about how to curb the fecundity of the Russian population, which he regarded as the potential cause of future wars. Apart from factories mass-producing prophylactics, he suggested the retraining of midwives as abortionists and deliberate under-training of paediatricians; voluntary sterilisation; and the cessation of all public health measures designed to diminish infant mortality. He concluded his commentary with some observations about how some climates in the area covered by the plan were unsuited to 'nordic–falian' settlers, suggesting that the planting of woods in the Ukrainian steppe would render it more suitable.[51]

The obvious statistical errors and logistical deficiencies in the RSHA plan ensured that Himmler (who would have to present the case to Hitler) entrusted the task to the more expert Meyer. In May 1942, Meyer delivered the memorandum 'Generalplan Ost: Legal, Economic and Spatial Foundations for Development in the East'. The plan, which exists only in summarised form, envisaged the creation of three vast 'marcher settlements' (Ingermanland, Memel–Narew and Gothengau) which would consist of 50 per cent German colonists, linked to the Reich at 100 kilometre intervals by thirty-six 'settlement strongpoints' whose inhabitants would be 25 per cent German. The plan would take twenty-five years to implement, would involve five million German settlers and would cost 66 billion Reichsmarks. The writ of the Ministry for the Occupied Eastern Territories would not run in the 'marcher settlements', latter-day fiefdoms held by the SS. Himmler expressed himself pleased with the overall thrust of the plan, although he wanted the time-scale shortened to twenty years, integration of areas like Alsace and Lorraine or Bohemia–

Moravia into the plan, and the more rapid Germanisation of the General Government, Estonia and Latvia. Meyer was set to work on a 'general settlement plan' incorporating these revised features.[52]

These plans were dismissed by earlier historians as the musings of desk-bound academic fantasists, but many German historians now argue that they were meant in earnest. Nazi practice in the Zamosc district in the south-east of the General Government tends to support the revised view. In July 1941 Himmler ordered Odilo Globocnik, the local SS and Police Leader in Lublin, to begin the 'Germanisation' of this area. There were several reasons why Himmler alighted on this district, apart from the fact that in Globocnik, the organising mind behind the 'Aktion Reinhard' extermination camps, he had an efficient and willing tool. First, Zamosc could function both as a gateway to the Ukraine and Black Sea areas and as the first link in a chain of German settlements stretching from the Baltic to Transylvania. The soil was rich, there was a significant ethnic German presence, and tensions between Poles and Ukrainians would facilitate a policy of dividing and ruling the 'natives'. Secondly, the town of Lublin was a vital crossroads and supply point for Waffen-SS troops *en route* to south-east Russia. Plans for the development of an SS-town included barracks for three Waffen-SS regiments and various SS-controlled factories which would be built and run by labour from nearby Majdanek concentration camp.[53]

In November 1941 Globocnik undertook an experimental resettlement of the populations of eight villages to test the feasibility of what was to come. The situation on the Eastern Front forced a postponement of the main action, which recommenced in November 1942. That autumn, the SS worked out the criteria for 'selecting' the population. There were four categories: Groups I and II consisted of the 5 per cent of the population deemed to be of German ancestry. Group III consisted of fourteen- to sixty-year-old Poles who were to be deported as forced labour to the Reich, while their 'unemployable appendage' of young or elderly relatives were to be concentrated in villages recently vacated by the Jews, where they would slowly die. Group IV (which included 21 per cent of the population of Zamosc) were to be sent direct to Auschwitz. The Ukrainians were to be concentrated in Hrubieszow county, before being redistributed around the new German settlements as a sort of human shock-absorber for the anticipated resentments of the residual Polish population.[54] The Zamosc resettlements also served a final purpose. Trains taking Group III forced labour from Zamosc to Berlin in the winter of 1943 were reloaded there with so-called 'armaments Jews' and their dependants who were then shipped to Auschwitz and killed. The trains then went back to Zamosc where they picked up Group IV Poles, bringing them in turn to the extermination camp. Only the incoming ethnic German settlers were spared a journey in the same cattle trucks since they were transported in regular passenger trains.[55]

Between 28 November 1942 and August 1943 over 100,000 Poles were driven from over 300 villages in two major sweeps. Villages were surrounded at first light, with the inhabitants being given a few minutes to pack. Word of this practice quickly spread, causing mass panic and flight, so that in the first sweep the Germans 'only' picked up under a third of the inhabitants, many of them old or sick or women and children. Some 4,500 children were separated from their parents and sent to Germany for adoption. Younger men and women fled to the woods and joined the partisans, which meant that, when the second major sweep took place in the summer of 1943, it assumed the characteristics of a 'pacification' campaign – that is, the destruction of entire villages and the murder of their inhabitants. Flawed in execution it might have been, nonetheless the deportations in Zamosc demonstrated that the 'ethnic cleansing' of a large area was feasible.

And Tomorrow, the World?

The deteriorating course of the war put a stop to the planning activities of Professor Meyer in the spring of 1943, although

Himmler continued to fantasise about settlements in the East long after the Red Army had crossed the frontiers of East Prussia. Ultimately, as we know, the moral and material might of the Allies prevented the realisation of the nightmarish scenarios of the SS. The expulsion and flight of millions of ethnic Germans from eastern Europe and the division of Germany for forty-five years ensued. But it is important to remember that German victory on the Eastern Front would have had wider consequences than those affecting the population of the Soviet empire.

Historians have long debated whether Hitler's final goal was simply the conquest of 'living space' in Eastern Europe or whether this was 'merely' the prerequisite for world domination (implying an ultimate conflict with Britain and America). Some historians, notably Hugh Trevor-Roper and Eberhard Jäckel, insist that Hitler was a 'continentalist', with his final objective consisting of the acquisition of *Lebensraum* in the East and the resolution of the 'Jewish Question'. Others, notably Günther Moltmann, Milan Hauner and Meier Michaelis, have insisted that Hitler's ambitions were 'globalist'.[56] In fact, the two positions are not mutually exclusive, but rather reflect different emphases. The continentalists point to the frequency with which Hitler dilated upon the East, relegating his more expansive remarks to the world of fantasy; the globalists piece together his more random utterances about colonies or a war with America and take them seriously. Some historians, for example Andreas Hillgruber, have systematised Hitler's statements into a 'programme' for aggression:

> After the creation of a European continental empire buttressed by the conquest of Russia, a second stage of imperial expansion was to follow with the acquisition of complementary territory in Central Africa and a system of bases to support a strong surface fleet in the Atlantic and the Indian Ocean. Germany, in alliance with Japan and if possible also Britain, would in the first place isolate the USA and confine it to the Western hemisphere. Then, in the next generation, there would be a 'battle of the

continents' in which the 'Germanic empire of the German nation' would fight America for world supremacy.

Subsequent research, while not endorsing the notion of a 'programme', does appear to confirm that Hitler's aims were global. It has drawn attention to Hermann Rauschning's liberal, rather than literal, accounts of Hitler's conversation in 1933–4, accounts originally designed, of course, to deter fellow conservatives from their *liaison dangereuse* with Nazism. In this period shortly after the 'seizure of power', Hitler announced his intention of 'creating a new Germany' in Brazil and taking over the Dutch colonial empire, Central Africa and 'the whole of New Guinea'. The allegedly dominant Anglo-Saxon influence in North America would be subverted 'as a preliminary step towards incorporating the United States into the German World Empire'. These objectives were accompanied by quasi-messianic declarations of intent about 'recasting the world', or the 'liberation' of mankind from the restraints of intellect, freedom and morality.

Hitler and his associates returned to these themes during the first flush of victory. In 1940 Ribbentrop and officials in the Foreign Ministry were thinking of augmenting the 'Greater European economic sphere' with a 'supplementary colonial area' carved from British and French West Africa, French Equatorial Africa, the Belgian Congo, Uganda, Kenya, Zanzibar and Northern Rhodesia, with Madagascar acquired for the purpose of 'resettling' the Jews. The Racial Political Office of the NSDAP began detailed planning for the creation of colonial regimes in Africa and for the regulation of relations between whites and blacks. Back in Europe, neutrality, benevolent or otherwise, was no guarantee against attack. Operation Tannenbaum was designed to conquer Switzerland, which was to be divided between its neighbours; Operation Polar Fox would secure the iron ore reserves of Sweden; while Operations Isabella and Felix would secure respectively Portugal and Gibraltar, in the latter case with or without the consent of Franco.

In the aftermath of a victory on the Eastern Front, Hitler would have been in a position to dictate terms to Britain. If the government had once again rejected his offers of peaceful coexistence, then the resources of the occupied East would have been deployed in a sustained air war against Britain, a war which, if won, could have resulted in the eventual activation of Operation Sealion (see the previous chapter). The war would then probably have extended into the late 1940s. Only a Russian recovery behind the Urals and an American intervention with atomic weapons would have averted the consolidation of Nazi rule throughout the continent of Europe and the conquered regions of the Soviet Union – and neither of these would have been guaranteed if Britain had been defeated.[57] Indeed, they would have been positively unlikely if Hitler had made more effective use of his alliance with Japan, which formally joined the German–Italian axis in September 1940, against the Soviet Union or against the British Empire. Hitler could, for example, have agreed to concentrate on driving the British out of Egypt and the Middle East, leaving Japan to direct its military efforts against the British in Singapore and India. Alternatively, he could have coordinated the German and Japanese attacks on the Soviet Union. Either way, there would have been a pincer effect which would have been very hard to defeat. And, of course, the Americans would have still been on the sidelines, because Pearl Harbor would not have been attacked.

Instead, of course, the Japanese were allowed to conclude a neutrality agreement with Stalin just two and a half months before Barbarossa was launched, and were actually encouraged by Hitler to attack the United States in November 1941. The next month, on 6 December the Russian counter-offensive was launched; and, two days later, the Japanese attacked Pearl Harbor, bringing the Americans into the war. To compound the mistake, Hitler declared war on the US on 11 December. This decision has often been seen as a short-sighted and fatal mistake. Yet Hitler seems to have envisaged confrontation with the United States from a relatively early stage. For some time, he persisted in the delusion that Britain would accept German leadership in a 'revitalised'

Europe, turning with Germany upon the USA: 'I shall no longer be there to see it, but I rejoice on behalf of the German people at the idea that one day we will see England and Germany marching together against America.' But, in the event that neither the prospect of an alliance with Britain nor an economic blockade would bring the USA to its knees, he seems to have been willing to contemplate transatlantic aggression. He toyed with the idea of air-strikes against America from bases in the Azores and Canary Islands, commissioning the development of Messerschmitt four-engine bombers, capable of delivering eight-ton payloads at a range of 11,000–15,000 kilometres. Similar ambitions were also apparent in his special 'Z plan' naval directive of 27 January 1939, for a fleet which by 1944–6 would be capable of challenging any power on the high seas from its vast base at Trondheim. The 800 ships were to include 100,000-ton battleships with a length of over 300 metres and guns of 53 cm calibre.

In sum, there is some evidence that Hitler's objectives were almost without limit. Nor was his planning hampered by questions of cost, human or otherwise, for war in his eyes had a positive, regenerative value for the 'health' of the race and nation. As he said, 'We may have a hundred years of struggle before us; if so, all the better – it will prevent us from going to sleep.'

How long would a Nazi empire have endured if Hitler had been successful in at least one part of his programme, the defeat of the Soviet Union? A hundred years, as he himself envisaged? Certainly, that was the assumption on which he based his grandiose projects for the reconstruction of postwar German cities. Hitler, the failed architecture student and small-town bohemian, was obsessed with architectural planning. During the last weeks of the war, with Soviet soldiers scuttling through the debris of Berlin, he spent much of his time reshuffling architectural models in the glare of spotlights positioned to simulate sunlight. The main purpose of Hitler's architecture was to overawe through excesses of scale and to give his regime the aura of power and permanence by reducing human beings to the scale of Lilliputians. Hitler made his views on the function of architecture quite clear when he remarked in 1941, 'Those who enter the Reich Chancellery should feel that they stand before the lords of the world.' He gave this a characteristically barbaric twist with regard to the surviving population of conquered Russia: '. . . once a year, a troop of Kirghiz will be led through the Reich capital in order that they may fill their minds with the power and the grandeur of its stone monuments.'[58]

This need to overawe was accompanied with an obsession with scale which bordered on the infantile. Musing with Himmler in 1941, Hitler remarked:

> Nothing will be too good for the beautification of Berlin. . . . One will arrive there along wide avenues containing the Triumphal Arch, the Pantheon of the Army, the Square of the People – things to take your breath away! It's only thus that we shall succeed in eclipsing our only rival in the world, Rome. Let it be built on such a scale that St Peter's and its Square will seem like toys in comparison![59]

Similar competitive gigantomania was evident in his plans for the redevelopment of Hamburg. These included plans for a massive suspension bridge across the Elbe, with pylons soaring to 180 metres. He explained the project to his army commanders as follows:

> You will perhaps ask: Why don't you build a tunnel? I don't consider a tunnel useful. But even if I did, I would still have the largest bridge in the world erected in Hamburg, so that any German coming from abroad or who has the opportunity to compare Germany with other countries must say to himself: 'What is so extraordinary about America and its bridges? We can do the same.' That is why I am having skyscrapers built which will be just as 'impressive' as the American ones.

The skyscrapers included a new NSDAP Regional Headquarters, designed to relegate the Empire State Building in the league table of tallest buildings. (Some idea of the scale is conveyed by the fact that due to the poor sub-soil, the structure had to be reduced by 250 metres.) Modernity, megalomania and vulgarity were to be conjoined in a gigantic neon swastika on top of the building, which would guide vessels at night into the Elbe.

The largest buildings were inevitably reserved for Berlin, which in 1950, once building work was complete, would have been rechristened 'Germania'.[60] The city was to be rebuilt around a vast axial grid, whose avenues would be over a hundred metres wide. Emerging from railway terminals larger than Grand Central Station, the visitor would be confronted by wide vistas and enormous marble-clad buildings. A triumphal arch, double the height and breadth of Napoleon's Arc de Triomphe, would be inscribed with the names of the fallen, while defunct enemy weaponry would be displayed on plinths erected for the purpose. Passing the new 'Führer Palace', equipped with a dining hall for thousands and a private theatre, the visitor would arrive at the great Hall, billed as the largest assembly hall in the world. With a capacity of a quarter of a million, the light in the cupola could alone encircle the dome of the Pantheon, the condensation thus raising the problem of interior rainfalls. Above, some 290 metres from the ground, a lantern supported an eagle perched at first upon a swastika, and then in the revised version, upon the globe.[61] These buildings, and the parade grounds that went with them, were to be the stage for the choreography of millions, marching, singing, acclaiming seas of people, beneath the glacial shafts of a hundred searchlights. And they were intended to last. As Hitler once remarked: 'Granite will ensure that our monuments will last for ever. In ten thousand years they'll be still standing, just as they are, unless meanwhile the sea has again covered our plains.' The materials were to come from a new generation of concentration camps, established by the SS in the vicinity of stone quarries.

Beyond Germany, architectural planning became a matter of Wilhelm Kreis's monuments to the dead which were to punctuate the landscape from Africa to the plains of Russia. More importantly, the regime planned major changes to Europe's infrastructure. Canals would bring the grain and petroleum of Russia along the Danube, and three-lane motorways would enable German tourists to speed along in their Volkswagens from Calais to Warsaw or Klagenfurt to Trondheim. In early 1942, Hitler and his chief engineer, Fritz Todt, began plans for a four-metre-gauge railway, which would convey double-decker trains at 190 kilometres an hour to the Caspian Sea and the Urals. Some time after the defeats at Stalingrad and Kursk, Hitler was still designing saloon and dining cars to take ethnic German settlers to and fro in Russia.

Of course, historians who stress the chaotic and ultimately self-destructive character of the Third Reich would have us believe that all such plans were mere fantasy: the Third Reich was preprogrammed to collapse in 1945. What remains unclear, however, is how far their assumptions of an inevitable Nazi defeat are based on a realistic assessment of what could have happened – and how far on mere wishful and teleological thinking. Certainly, many aspects of Nazi planning appear so bizarre to us that it is hard to imagine their ever having been realised. But not all. While Himmler planned his ethnic revolution and Hitler built his architectural models, other agencies were mapping out futures for ordinary Germans which were far from unrealistic in their conception. Robert Ley's mammoth German Labour Front apparatus (DAF) was the socially 'progressive' arm of a regime better known for repression and terror. Through its subordinate 'Beauty of Labour' and 'Strength through Joy' organisations it endeavoured to bring improved conditions, cheap holidays, sport and a greater sense of worth to the 'German worker', and hence to boost his or her productivity while breaking down traditional class solidarities. Even the exiled SPD leadership was forced to acknowledge the efficacy of these policies, lamenting the 'petit bourgeois inclinations' evinced by sections of its erstwhile constituency. During the first years of the war, the DAF's Scientific Labour Institute made detailed plans for the provision of comprehensive health, insurance and pension coverage, thus simultaneously generating and responding to expectations of a postwar reward for present deprivation. Interpreting a specific mandate to improve public housing – a field hitherto neglected in favour of monumental building – as a general commission for welfare reform, Ley and his staff made proposals which bear some superficial similarities to the Beveridge Report. For example, there was to be a new national pensions scheme whereby the over sixty-fives would receive 60 per cent of their average earnings over the last decade of employment. These plans were augmented with a child benefit scheme and measures to reform health provision.[62]

Only a closer examination of these schemes reveals that the benefits were contingent upon past 'performance', and that whole categories of people were to be excluded from any provision whatsoever on the grounds of race or 'asocial' behaviour. The projected health-care reforms, including the provision of public clinics, factory physicians and affordable spas and sanatoria, also concealed a collectivist and mechanical view of human beings as epitomised in the chilling slogan 'Your health does not belong to you', or in the objective of 'periodically overhauling' the German population in the same way as 'one services an engine'. This would have been a welfare state only for those Germans who were not imprisoned, sterilised or murdered as 'ballast existences', 'asocials' or racial 'aliens'.[63] Perhaps it is this aspect of the counterfactual of a German victory which is most chilling of all – precisely because in its superficial 'modernity' it is so easy to imagine it coming true.

SEVEN

STALIN'S WAR OR PEACE:
What if the Cold War had been avoided?

Jonathan Haslam

> If there hadn't been any Yalta conference at all, the result would
> have been much the same. I think history would have fulfilled
> itself, Yalta or no Yalta.
>
> GLADWYN JEBB[1]

What does it mean to say that 'history would have fulfilled itself'?
Why would the result have been 'much the same'? *Could* anything
else have happened in 1945 or soon thereafter?

It is as well to confess at the outset that the author is a
convinced sceptic as to the value of such questions. One dubious
instance is where the historian arbitrarily selects a single favourite
variable, alters its weight or true composition, but holds all other
variables from the same equation constant. Very often this means
choosing one historical figure who lost and replaying the game by
tying the hands of others, reducing the significance of larger but
material historical forces, and then arranging that figure's victory
with happy consequences all round. In the Western historiography
of the Soviet Union, there has been no shortage of such wishful
thinking. Moshe Lewin, a self-professed Marxist of anti-Stalinist
beliefs, believed that Bukharin would have avoided the forced
collectivisation of agriculture in the Soviet Union, yet secured
industrialisation and assured the future of socialism.[2] The more
orthodox Marxist view, of course, is that the success or failure of
a particular figure is to be explained as the result of a conjunction

of larger circumstances, not as an independent variable in its own right. The danger is that the attachment of the historian to a particular figure – very often matched by deep dislike of that figure's leading rival – blinds him to what else is driving events. A more serious objection to counterfactualism, however, was raised by the Italian historian and philosopher of history Benedetto Croce.[3] As he suggested, it is hard to justify jumping into the stream of history arbitrarily at a point of one's choosing and at that point rearranging events, dismissing the effect of the past on the present. Why not another section upstream or downstream?

In order to allow at least in part for Croce's misgivings, the choice of counterfactual must be made as consciously, as cautiously and as open-mindedly as possible. Perhaps also the way forward is to intervene at more than one point and take more than one variable at any given point to present various possible outcomes that may highlight the role of any one factor in the equation. Let us therefore take three counterfactual questions that will attack the issue of the origins of the Cold War from diverse directions:

1. What if the United States had not possessed the atomic bomb?
2. What if Soviet intelligence had not successfully penetrated the upper reaches of state in Britain and the USA?
3. What if Stalin had limited Soviet expansion to the kind of spheres of influence familiar to the democracies?

The first question explores the impact of the atomic bomb on relations between Moscow and the West. It has been suggested that the bomb was dropped not to defeat the Japanese but to intimidate the Russians.[4] This raises the key issue whether the pattern of confrontation between the Russians and the democracies was set by US or by Soviet policy. The 'revisionist' school of historiography in the United States has never been in any doubt that 'Truman's early 1945 strategy toward the Soviet Union flowed in significant part from a belief that the atomic bomb, once tested, would strengthen the U.S. diplomatic position';[5] that 'far from following his predecessor's policy of cooperation, shortly after taking office Truman launched a powerful foreign policy initiative aimed at reducing or eliminating Soviet influence from Europe';[6] and that 'Stalin's approach seems to have been cautiously moderate' through 1945.[7]

The second question deals with the crucial issue of espionage. The list of spies the Russians possessed in the higher echelons of government in Britain is well known. Equally well known is the fact that the Russians employed spies who gave them critical information on the progress of experiments leading to the creation of the atomic bomb. And the US government has released documents which show the enormous extent of that atomic espionage.[8] What if the Russians had had no knowledge of the bomb before August 1945; what if they had had no knowledge of Western reactions to their expansionist moves against the democracies: would Stalin have taken such risks?

During the war there were advocates of the division of Europe into Russian and Western spheres of influence, in the Soviet Union, in Britain and in the United States. These advocates – Maxim Litvinov, E. H. Carr and Walter Lippmann – all envisaged a relatively benign system of spheres of influence of the traditional variety, according to which the internal politics and socio-economic structures of these countries would be allowed to function without undue interference from the neighbouring Great Power except where the conduct of defence and foreign policies was concerned. This was not how Stalin envisaged a sphere of influence. To him it ultimately entailed all but total control, and the implications of that interpretation and its implementation in Eastern and Central Europe provoked conflict with the West. What if he had chosen the course recommended by Litvinov, Carr and Lippmann? Could the Cold War have thereby been averted?

These are the questions we wish to consider. Before we proceed, however, the reader should be made aware of certain problems with regard to the sources upon which any interpretation of the origins of the Cold War have to be based. The first waves of writing were based exclusively on documents from the

US National Archives because the US government was the first to declassify its holdings. More recently the British and the French have declassified the larger part of their archives relating to the 1940s. But the Soviet Union resolutely refused to do so, except for marginal access by official historians. As a result the historiography is necessarily one-sided. Throughout, the historians of US diplomacy and British and French foreign policy have had to limit themselves to drawing uncertain conclusions about the motives for Soviet behaviour. It is this, as much as anything, which explains the chasm yawning between the more conservative historians and the 'revisionists' – since there was no way of determining the reasoning behind Soviet foreign policy but through inference, ideological preference supplanted judgement based on documentary evidence.

The collapse of the Soviet Union in 1991 facilitated the opening of certain hitherto secret archives in Moscow. In 1992 the Russian Ministry of External Affairs agreed upon the release of documents to researchers, and since that time a mass of material from 1945 to 1955 has become available.[9] However, due to resistance from the operational departments of the Ministry, the most important documents – the ciphered telegrams which form the bulk of the diplomatic correspondence between ambassadors and the Ministry – have been debarred from declassification. Furthermore, the other responsible archives in foreign affairs – the RTsKhIDNI (which contains the archives of the International Department of the Central Committee), the Ministry of Defence, the KGB and the Presidential Archive (which holds Politburo papers on foreign affairs) – have all denied researchers access to their holdings for the period under discussion. Thus anyone currently analysing the development of Soviet foreign policy for the origins of the Cold War is deprived of the Russian equivalent of what can be found in the US, British and French archives. All is not entirely lost, however. Diligent research using the holdings now available from the Foreign Ministry – diplomatic letters, memoranda, ambassadorial diaries and annual reports – in combination with work in Western archives can still yield findings of significance. But we are here talking of research now under way, with only incomplete results so far available.

Within these limitations, therefore, let us address the questions asked above.

What if the United States had not had the Atomic Bomb?

Although the bulk of the evidence demonstrates that the US administration under Truman decided to use the bomb against Japan primarily to forestall a full-scale and bloody invasion of Japan by the Allies, there is sufficient evidence to suggest that the Americans also hoped that a by-product of the use of the bomb would be to moderate Russian behaviour.[10] Since the entrance of Soviet troops into Romania and Bulgaria in 1944, followed by Poland and the remainder of East-Central Europe in 1945, it had become apparent to Western leaders that the Russians were not interested in fully fledged cooperation at the close of hostilities in the Pacific; more than that, some believed they were moving beyond the establishment of a legitimate sphere of influence and on to a path of resolute expansion.

Before the bomb was dropped, Truman took Stalin aside at the Postdam conference and warned him about a new deadly weapon that they would use against the Japanese. Stalin famously showed no reaction. But in private Foreign Minister Molotov said: 'They are raising the stakes.' Stalin smiled and replied: 'Let them. Today we must talk to Kurchatov [the head of the Soviet programme] about speeding up our own work.'[11] The bomb thus had an identifiable effect on Stalin and his entourage. Stalin was evidently concerned that the United States should not sustain a monopoly of this new weapons system. However, it was not so much use of the bomb against the Japanese as the successful detonation of the bomb that prompted Stalin to speed up development. Restraint on Truman's part would therefore have had no signal effect on the pace of the Soviet programme.

The proponents of the argument that the bomb had a decisive effect for the worse on East–West relations go much further than this. They argue that the United States used possession of the bomb to intimidate the Russians and succeeded instead only in precipitating the Cold War by frightening them into raising barriers against Western influence and striking out against those whom the West sought to defend.

But, if the bomb had not existed, would East–West relations have taken a different course? The assumption that weapons systems were the root cause of conflict in the Cold War became fashionable with those who advocated nuclear disarmament.[12] This assumption is in essence no different from the belief before and after 1914 that the arms race between the Great Powers explained the origins of the First World War. To prove or disprove the point we need to look at what evidence there is of Soviet attitudes to the bomb, because the proponents of the centrality of the bomb in further developments imply that Soviet policy was purely reactive and that the Russians were responding to fear generated by the United States.

In fact, Soviet attitudes were characterised more by self-confidence than by fear. There are clear indications that Stalin did not consider the atomic bomb decisive in war and therefore decisive as a bargaining counter in diplomatic negotiation. Indeed, he was to a degree contemptuous of the United States because in his view it did not possess the will to greatness essential to global supremacy.

The first piece of evidence is a statement by Deputy Commissar Maxim Litvinov, who disagreed so fundamentally with the new thrust of Soviet policy that he broke all the rules by granting indiscreet unattributable briefings to Western journalists and diplomats alike. In June 1946 the American journalist Hottelet asked Litvinov about the US atomic monopoly and the Soviet attitude to the international control of atomic energy. Litvinov 'said that Russia would not agree to atomic control, that it did not attach undue importance to the bomb and that it would not necessarily be afraid of atomic war'. He added that the leadership banked on the belief that the country's 'immense area and manpower, resources and dispersed industry safeguarded it to a large extent'.[13] In September Stalin himself told Werth of the *Sunday Times* that he did 'not consider the atomic bomb such a serious force that some political figures are inclined to. Atomic bombs are designed to terrify those with weak nerves, but they cannot decide the outcome of war since there are simply not enough atomic bombs.'[14] This was later repeated by Molotov in his recollections recorded by Chuyev: 'And they [the Americans] understood that they were for the time being in no condition to unleash a war; they had all in all one or two bombs'.[15] This was an unusual assertion by Stalin since it acknowledged the secrets of the American nuclear stockpile (or, rather, the absence of one) accessible to Soviet intelligence (for more on this, see below). There was doubtless an element of bravado in all this. If the Americans had any intention of blackmailing the Russians through the threat of atomic bombs, it was essential to convince them that the threat would carry little weight. But Litvinov was not acting under Stalin's orders; quite the contrary, he was seen as having betrayed the country, as Molotov subsequently testified. 'Litvinov was completely hostile to us,' he recalled. 'We intercepted the record of his conversations with an American correspondent ... Total betrayal.'[16]

The calm assessment of the bomb, as Litvinov had already indicated, reflected a view of warfare based on Russia's inherent strengths and the West's evident weakness. If the West were unwilling to send land forces into Russia to defeat Soviet forces and occupy the country, it could not make the ultimate threat a reality; and if it could not do that, why should the Russians take any of these threats seriously? In an interview with Elliott Roosevelt on 21 December 1946 Stalin expressed the confident opinion that he did

> not see anything frightening in the sense of a breach of the peace or a military conflict. Not one of the Great Powers, even if its government wanted to, could at the present time put up a big army for a struggle against another allied Power, another Great Power, because at the present time no one can fight without his

people, and the people do not want to fight. The people are weary of war.... I suggest that the threat of a new war is unreal.[17]

For final confirmation, which came after the Russians detonated their first atomic device at the end of August 1949, consider Stalin's comments, made in July 1952 with the Korean War still in progress, to the pro-Soviet Italian socialist Nenni: 'Certainly,' he said, 'there are those in the United States who talk of war, but without being in a position to undertake one; America has the technical but not the human potential for war; it has the air force, it has the atomic bomb but where is it going to find the soldiers needed to launch a third war?' He added: 'It is not enough for America to destroy Moscow, just as it is not enough for us to destroy New York. Armies are required to occupy Moscow and to occupy New York.'[18] Finally, former US Secretary of State Byrnes acknowledged in reference to the bomb that the Russians 'don't scare'.[19]

The Marshall Plan for European reconstruction – which represented the first clear indication that the United States meant business in containing Soviet expansionism in Europe – came into being in July 1947. The Soviet reaction was, at least publicly, somewhat hysterical and Stalin pushed the East European Communist Parties into the creation of the Communist Information Bureau (Cominform) to enforce conformity that September. In addition a wave of strikes and militant demonstrations hit the streets of Western Europe. Yet as late as November Soviet leaders reassured the Italian socialist Nenni that they did not consider war 'imminent or near. The United States is not in a position to provoke one. It is conducting a cold war, of nerves, with the aim of "blackmail". The Soviet Union will not allow itself to be intimidated and will persist in its policy.'[20] And one Soviet diplomat said of the Americans in France: 'in a few years they will be chucked out of here' ('ils seront fichus d'ici quelques années').[21]

The confident Soviet assessments of the threat posed by nuclear weapons – which most certainly changed to a more sober appreciation after the death of Stalin – were matched by similar expressions of self-confidence generally. This sense of relative invulnerability will seem barely credible to many today given our knowledge of the devastation wrought on Russia by Axis forces and the loss of some twenty-eight million lives in the war. But the calculation of the balance of power made in Moscow rested not least upon the presumed superiority of the socialist means of production over those of capitalism and upon the view that the United States lacked the will to war. Moreover, if the US were engulfed in a new depression – which many in Moscow fully expected – then that will would be undermined still further to the point where Washington would in all probability retreat into isolation as it had done after 1929.

What emerges is not that Stalin and his subordinates had no fears of the United States – though they feared the United States far less than the democracies hoped and believed – but that any such fears were severely curtailed by the assessment that the most significant weapon in the American arsenal was of very limited value, that there were structural problems in the capitalist world economy that would inevitably cause a further collapse, that US relations with the British Empire in decline were uneasy at the best of times and that the Americans ultimately did not have the kind of resolution Stalin saw in Churchill's eyes. Although apparently reckless in alienating the Western Powers – in crushing anti-Communist opposition in East-Central Europe, in sustaining massive forces in the Eastern zone of Germany, in making territorial demands on Turkey (1945), in attempting to sustain a Communist regime in Northern Iran (1945–6), in taking over Czechoslovakia (1948) and in launching a blockade of West Berlin – Stalin was in reality taking only calculated risks. His was a policy of bluff.

What if Western Intelligence had not been Penetrated?

Stalin's relatively sanguine assessment of the limits of American military potential was partly the result of his understanding of the less than overwhelming nature of nuclear weapons but partly also derived from intelligence assessments. These gave him knowledge of the absence of a nuclear stockpile, and of the fact that the B-29 aircraft which were flown to Britain in the summer of 1948 to bolster the military posture of the West were not genuinely nuclear-capable. This brings us to one of the most publicised stories of the Cold War. What would have been different had Stalin possessed no such information? Would he have acted more cautiously, even assuming his reservations considering the effectiveness of the bomb?

The answer depends upon how one reads the motivation for Soviet expansionism after the end of the war. As it is usually presented, we are faced with two alternatives: either Stalin was embarking on a conscious path of expansion at the risk of war or he was acting defensively in keeping his likely adversaries at bay. Litvinov, who may be taken as the most accurate contemporary analyst of Stalin's and Molotov's policy because he saw it emerge from within, interpreted it as a mixture of both, but a mixture explosive enough to cause a war if pre-emptive action were not taken to remedy the situation. Litvinov told Hottelet that the Soviet Union had returned to 'the outmoded concept of security in terms of territory – the more you've got the safer you are' and that if the democracies gave way under pressure, 'It would lead to the West being faced, after a more or less short time, with the next series of demands.' And as to what lay behind this policy: 'As far as I am concerned,' he said, 'the root cause is the ideological conception prevailing here that conflict between the Communist and capitalist worlds is inevitable.' This was said in June 1946.[22] When in further conversations along similar lines Roberts, the British deputy head of mission, suggested that the Kremlin could not want war, 'Litvinov has agreed but has usually added: "Neither did Hitler, but events become too strong for those who should control them, if they set the wrong course." '[23] This seems convincing enough. However, what really counts is how essential Stalin deemed that expansion to be, whether for defensive or offensive purposes. Every indication is that the atomic bomb made no appreciable impact either way. Stalin was set on a course of action that was fixed before the bomb appeared on the scene. The momentary concern in July and August of 1945 when the weapon was tested and then dropped on the Japanese gave way to resolute defiance, if not indifference.

But how much of Stalin's sang-froid can be attributed to the fact that he had intimate knowledge of not only Western capabilities but also their intentions? The access the Russians had is very striking. To give just one instance: in the archives of the Comintern you can find such items as a report from Fitin, head of the First Directorate (foreign intelligence) of the NKGB, to General Secretary of the Comintern Dimitrov, giving the details of the names and addresses of British Communists whom the Special Branch of Scotland Yard intended to watch in the coming weeks. More important for our purposes is the group of five spies: Philby, Burgess, Maclean, Blunt and Cairncross. Between them they had access to all the key secrets of state in foreign, defence and intelligence policies. In the British section, department three of the First Directorate of the NKGB (forerunner of the KGB), throughout the war the focus was on 'atomic research, the war economy and Britain's relations with other countries',[24] not necessarily always in that order of importance. Philby worked in the Secret Intelligence Service (SIS), reaching the level of deputy head; Burgess's various appointments included a brief period in the Ministry of Information and at the Foreign Office (latterly as secretary to Minister of State McNeil); Maclean was also in the Foreign Office (since 1935) and ultimately defected having become head of the American Department; Blunt worked in MI5; and Cairncross in the Cabinet Office, the Code and Cypher School and later the Treasury. Philby, Burgess and Maclean also served at one time or another in the British embassy in Washington during the early Cold War.[25] What happened to such information is described by Yuri Modin:

> The information from London mostly reached Moscow in the form of coded telegrams. At that time our secret service department number one worked hand in glove with the Politburo,

which meant Stalin, Molotov and Beria. Our reports seldom reached the lower echelons of the Foreign Affairs Commissariat. The truth was that Molotov was in sole charge of the information we provided, and he did what he liked with it.[26]

Through these channels the Kremlin 'knew absolutely everything about the technical and political aspects of atomic bomb development'.[27]

They, of course, knew a good deal more than that. In October Philby was appointed head of the anti-Communist branch – Section 9 – of SIS. NKGB headquarters considered this an achievement 'hard to overestimate'.[28] Indeed, in February 1945 Philby reported that the head of SIS, Menzies, had sent a directive 'regarding the development of active work by "The Hotel" [SIS] against Soviet institutions on territory taken by the Red Army'.[29] No less important was secret political intelligence. During the Allied conferences from 1945 to 1949, Molotov knew what the Allies were saying about Soviet policy behind his back. We know that when Secretary of State Marshall announced his plan for European recovery in June 1947, Molotov felt strongly that the Soviet Union should take up the offer and that as a result he led a delegation to Paris to negotiate Moscow's participation.[30] But, after only a short time, they walked out, dragging the East Europeans along with them. Information had come in about Foreign Secretary Bevin's discussions with Clayton, the US Secretary to the Treasury, to the effect that the West would use the Plan to extract necessary political concessions from the Russians in Eastern Europe.[31] We also know that when he first arrived in Paris Molotov is reported to have flown into a rage because there were no 'documents' (that is, British and American secret communications) – only to be told that neither London nor Washington had yet heard from their delegations in Paris![32]

Yet receiving intelligence information and making correct use of it are two entirely distinct things. What appears to have occurred is that Stalin and Molotov believed all the information that reinforced their own predisposition to mistrust their allies and disbelieved or discounted the information that tended to show the intentions of the British and Americans in a better light. It also meant that, where Stalin and Molotov came to a basic premise about a subject, the NKGB was pestered constantly for information to support and illustrate that premise. One crucial instance is that of the degree of conflict between the British and the Americans. Former ambassador to Britain Maisky appears to have convinced the leadership that the prevailing antagonism in the postwar world would be between the British Empire and the United States. Of course, once relations between Moscow and its allies began seriously to deteriorate, the Kremlin had to revise this basic assumption. But it seems it never underwent a fundamental revision and the expectation remained that sooner or later the British and Americans would fall out. This reinforced Russian reluctance to accept that a solid Western bloc was coming into being and that only through timely concessions could the Russians avoid cementing that bloc against their interests. 'As usual,' Modin recalls, 'the Centre was very interested by [sic] the Anglo-American relationship, and by the various difficulties that might arise between Britain and the United States.'[33] The extraordinary focus on the atomic bomb project naturally encouraged such expectations. The Americans absorbed British expertise then denied Britain the benefits of the programme. 'We also knew', Modin recalls, 'that the Americans fully intended to deceive the British every step of the way. In the certainty that they were substantially behind the British in terms of research, their strategy was to use the expertise of their allies ... and then to jettison them once they had caught up. And this, of course, is exactly what they did.'[34]

Would absence of such information have made Stalin more cautious and have averted the Cold War? In answer to our first question we concluded that Stalin was set on the course he ultimately pursued, that he did not sufficiently fear the United States to justify deviating from that path, but that his decisions were based on calculated risks rather than the rash, intuitive risks that his successor Khrushchev was later to take. If that is correct, and the evidence thus far available suggests that it is, then intelligence information formed a crucial basis for those calculations: hence Molotov's positive addiction to it and total reliance upon it. The inside historians of Soviet intelligence cite at least one instance in which Stalin drew back after hearing from intelligence sources what position the United States was about to adopt. This concerned Soviet demands on Turkey for territory which were made in 1945 and once again issued in 1947.[35] It is entirely possible, though the proof has not yet been presented from the same files, that Stalin eventually backed down over West Berlin in 1949 having finally convinced himself through direct access to Western official thinking that he was not about to have his way in successfully cutting off all access from the democracies to this island of freedom in the midst of the Russian occupation zone. Thus, where the West showed every resolution to stand firm in their internal discussions, Stalin's knowledge of that fact through intelligence would lead him to caution; where, however, that same access made him silent witness to internal dissent or conflict between Britain and the United States, it seems plausible to conclude that this encouraged him to remain defiant. If Stalin had known none of this, everything would have depended on the degree to which the democracies held to a firm position, such as Litvinov had advocated, and the degree to which Stalin believed in their firmness.[36]

What if Stalin had accepted the Western definition of 'Influence'?

But are we necessarily right in assuming that Stalin had fixed his course of action much earlier in the game than the West ever realised? Stalin had long adopted a method of decision-making which, contrary to totalitarian theorists and simplistic biographers, included rather than precluded the discussion of alternative avenues of advance.[37] We know that in relation to both postwar Europe and the postwar Far East, Stalin had plans drawn up from varying perspectives. One of these was put together by a committee under Litvinov and this advocated what amounted to an

Anglo-Soviet condominium in postwar Europe, but based on the kind of spheres of influence familiar to the democracies rather than the kind Stalin ultimately adopted. What if Stalin had followed Litvinov's model rather than the form he finally decided upon? Could the Cold War have been avoided?

It may be put down to naivety, but not until the Red Army had liberated the territories of East-Central Europe did the Western Powers fully understand that what Stalin meant by a sphere of influence was in fact closer to what would commonly have been called colonisation. The accepted idea of what constituted a sphere of influence or interest was the Monroe Doctrine that governed US dominance in the Americas: powers external to the region would be forcefully prevented from interfering in the internal affairs of the region but, allowing for occasional and temporary armed intervention by the United States, these countries would largely be able to govern themselves according to their own priorities. The same principle had governed the status of the Low Countries in relation to Britain, which saw its security dependent upon the insulation of these states from direct external interference and which went to war in 1794 and 1914 in part to assert that vital principle. This minimalist approach to the maintenance of national security was more easily adopted by Great Powers with no recent experience of invasion than by a Power that had just undergone the horrors of Nazi occupation. Nonetheless the democracies assumed that Moscow would see its allies as a significant, if not the main, guarantor of its security in Europe after the common defeat of Germany.

It is often suggested that the real reason for the failure of the Russians and the West to agree upon a commonly accepted division into spheres of influence was US President Roosevelt's steadfast refusal to commit himself. Yet the one agreement reached, between Churchill and Stalin in October 1944, was implemented by the Russians in the manner of colonisation rather than in the manner expected by the British. And it was as much Soviet procedures as Soviet ambitions that unnerved the democracies. There is thus little basis for assuming that had Roosevelt been more forthcoming on this question the Russians would have been more obliging.

But what if Stalin had conformed to Western expectation? Before one dismisses such a turn of events as impossible, it is worth reflecting on Stalin's known pragmatism in foreign policy matters hitherto, and on the fact that a commission set up under his authority did recommend this very option. To essentialists like the American political scientist R. C. Tucker, the outcome was predetermined by the very nature of Stalin's personality. But, if one could deduce Stalin's foreign policy entirely from his personality, how is one to explain that in the 1930s he switched from one policy to another policy completely at odds with his first choice? It would be prudent to assume that, for all Stalin's known paranoid tendencies, there was nonetheless a streak of pragmatism within his make-up that to a certain extent allowed for the effective influence of others on the options chosen.

In the West the proposals for spheres of influence in their traditional form were made by Walter Lippmann (in the United States) and E. H. Carr (in Britain). The most explicit advocacy of this approach appeared in an editorial in *The Times* on 10 March 1944. Here Carr argued that 'there can be no security in Western Europe unless there is also security in Eastern Europe, and security in Eastern Europe is unattainable unless it is buttressed by the military power of Russia'. He went on: 'A case so clear and cogent for close cooperation between Britain and Russia after the war cannot fail to carry conviction to any open and impartial mind.' More specifically, he continued: there should be 'ungrudging and unqualified agreement' between London and Moscow on the assumption that: 'If Britain's frontier is on the Rhine, it might just as pertinently be said – though it has not in fact been said – that Russia's frontier is on the Oder, and in the same sense.'

The launching of such a controversial *ballon d'essai* naturally had its impact in Moscow. It was no accident that only a matter of weeks later, on 31 March 1944, a committee on the preparation of the peace treaties and postwar construction was convened under the chairmanship of Deputy Commissar for Foreign Affairs Litvinov.[38] On 4 August, well before its proceedings closed on 21 September, he began composing his findings, which he presented on 15 November. Since his removal as Commissar in May 1939, and despite his resurrection as ambassador to the United States after Pearl Harbor had brought the Americans into the European war, Litvinov was regarded with both mistrust and respect by Stalin. If he decided on the need for closer relations with the democracies, Stalin would need Litvinov again; hence his survival while others with no heretical views at all were mercilessly consigned to the police, the camps or the firing squad. For Litvinov had originally been dismissed for trusting the democracies. This was not something of which Molotov could ever be accused. Stalin's reluctance to rule out any option, however remote, in international relations prompted him to set up the Litvinov committee. True, its relatively low status was evident from the fact that it had access to no classified material, only foreign press cuttings. Nonetheless the application of Litvinov's trenchant intelligence and enormous experience of over twenty years at the helm of Soviet foreign policy counted for something. Litvinov explained the long-standing antagonism between Russia and Britain in terms of imperial disputes on the Asian periphery rather than ideological differences. In other words the conflicts of interest were not irredeemable but negotiable. As far as he was concerned this applied to the Soviet period as much as that of the tsars. This had been his consistently held view at least since 1920. Indeed it was this non-ideological approach to foreign affairs that set him at odds with mainstream Soviet thinking. Had not the collapse of Litvinov's collective security policy in the 1930s underscored the existence of an unbridgeable ideological divide? Yet Litvinov hoped a lasting structure could be built on the temporary coalescence of interests forged in the alliance against Hitler's Germany. Seeing the greatest danger in a postwar confrontation between London and Moscow, Litvinov argued that an agreement should be reached which amounted to an Anglo-Soviet condominium over Europe.

It is clear that what Litvinov meant by a sphere of influence was the same as what was meant in the English-speaking world, because he cited both Lippmann and *The Times* (Carr) as evidence of a willingness to move in this direction on the part of the Allied governments. 'Such an agreement can be achieved', he wrote,

> only on the basis of some kind of delimitation of spheres of security in Europe on the principle of working together as closely as possible as good neighbours. As its maximum sphere of interests, the Soviet Union can consider Finland, Sweden, Poland, Hungary, Czechoslovakia, Romania, the Slavic countries of the Balkan peninsula, and Turkey equally. In the English sphere Holland, Belgium, France, Spain, Portugal and Greece can undoubtedly be included.

He also envisaged an accommodation with British interests (to British advantage) in Iran, Afghanistan and Sinkiang (China).[39]

This pattern fitted that proposed by Carr in the editorial pages of *The Times*. Yet that august and usually authoritative mouthpiece of British foreign policy did not, under Carr's direction, any longer represent the establishment consensus. In fact the democracies were reluctant to move in this direction. The Americans, tied by a political system that required Congressional involvement in major foreign policy decisions, resolutely abstained from such practices, though the British seemed to be moving in Litvinov's direction when Churchill visited Moscow in October 1944. By then, however, Stalin had already sent his forces into Romania and Bulgaria and the die was cast. Litvinov, in later conversation, gave to understand that he believed a genuine opportunity had been lost; the idea being that had the democracies acted earlier – most probably when the Soviet Union was weaker – a deal could have been struck.

Had Stalin and Molotov chosen such an option, rather than the course they chose of imposing their own system on the countries they liberated and occupied, would the Cold War have been avoidable? The decision to allow the other states of Eastern

Europe to go their own way in respect of domestic policy would most certainly have assured the democracies that it was not the intention of the Soviet regime to expand Communism on the point of the bayonet. This would have confirmed Carr's claim that such revolutionary ambitions had withered on the vine by the close of the war. And it was most certainly the fear that the Russians would sponsor Communist revolutions in Central and Western Europe which worried the West (as in the 1920s), particularly because of the significant destruction of physical capital plus widespread social and economic dislocation consequent upon the war. Would not social unrest find fertile soil in such conditions, and could not social unrest result in revolution as in Greece? The sizeable vote for the Communist parties in France and Italy gave a clear indication of the trend of opinion in Western Europe, as did the election of a Labour government in Britain. In these circumstances reassurance on the issue of revolution was blatantly denied by the sovietisation of territories occupied by the Red Army.

It would not all have been plain sailing, however. It is striking that Litvinov's recommendations omit Germany, which was the subject of another committee's brief – that of Voroshilov.[40] And in many respects Germany was a crucial focal point of difference between East and West. Stalin was determined that the fate of Germany should not be decided by the democracies without Soviet veto. It was also the case that if not Stalin then other members of his entourage still nurtured the old hopes of the decade after the October Revolution to take the red banner as far as Berlin. The only means of ensuring that Moscow retained a decisive role in the fate of Germany was to maintain military occupation, and how could that occupation be assured without secure lines of communication through Poland? And how could those lines be secured if the Poles were allowed to elect governments or were left free to have military *coups d'état* which would most likely bring to power men unalterably hostile to Soviet interests?

It seems certain that, regardless of the sovietisation of Eastern

Europe, differences would have arisen over Germany between the Allies. Indeed, this would have been the case whether Russia was run by Stalin or the tsars. But, that said, the key point surely is that the sovietisation of Eastern Europe was *not* merely a natural geopolitical response to a long-term security challenge. However hard some tried – and both Carr and Litvinov in their own way did so as an article of faith – one simply could not remove the ideological factor from international relations and substitute for it the mechanistic philosophy of the balance of power characteristic of the eighteenth century and the latter half of the nineteenth. In this sense perhaps the Cold War was inevitable – just as Gladwyn Jebb suggested.

EIGHT

CAMELOT CONTINUED:

What if John F. Kennedy had lived?

Diane Kunz

> Don't let it be forgot
> That once there was a spot
> For one brief shining moment
> That was known as Camelot
> *Camelot*

The Cold War is over and the statues of Marx and Lenin have fallen to the ground – but John F. Kennedy's image, though tarnished, remains fundamentally intact. In the years after his death, a legend of Camelot on the Potomac took root. According to this myth, propagated in large part by the Kennedy family and court, John F. Kennedy was a kind of King Arthur in modern dress. His advisers were modern Knights of the Round Table and Jacqueline Kennedy his noble Guinevere. More recently, it has become clear that Kennedy's private life was anything but Arthurian. But his reputation as a *public* figure – as a great President gunned down in his prime – has been subjected to far less scrutiny.

Not surprisingly, no aspect of the Kennedy legend has proved more durable than the notion that, had he lived, the United States would never have become mired in the Vietnam conflict. That faraway war in a country of which Americans knew next to nothing gravely weakened the power of the Democratic party while making many Americans question the value of democracy. Not only was it the first war that the United States clearly lost. In addition, the shameful aspects of the American role in the conflict and the ignominious departure from Saigon (Ho Chi Minh City) of the last remaining American personnel in the spring of 1975 gave rise to a vociferous anti-establishment movement, deeply dividing American society. How nice it would be to believe that the Vietnam débâcle was not the result of ill-timed and ill-conceived American ideas but rather the fault of one man: Lee Harvey Oswald.

This myth has respectable sponsors. Former presidential advisers such as McGeorge Bundy and Robert McNamara, for example, (as recently as 1993 and 1995) have speculated that Kennedy would have ended the American military commitment after the 1964 presidential elections.[1] Less respectably but more influentially, the film-maker Oliver Stone has suggested in the movie *JFK* that because Kennedy was about to order the United States to pull out of Vietnam a dark conspiracy of munitions-makers and military officers – perhaps with Lyndon Johnson's support – arranged to have him killed.[2]

The Kennedy myth has a domestic component too, inspired by the persistent racial divisions within American society. This is that Kennedy, together with his brother Robert, had a unique empathy with African-Americans. After all, did not Jack preside over the beginning of the civil rights revolution? With memories of the inspiring March on Washington of August 1963 still vibrant, Americans of all races continue to carry a torch for both Kennedys. Had Jack lived, so the argument runs, the second American reconstruction of the South might have come to fruition without the bloodshed and racial division of the past thirty years.

Fairy stories are necessary for children. Historians ought to know better. In fact, John F. Kennedy was a mediocre president. Had he obtained a second term, federal civil rights policy during the 1960s would have been substantially less productive and US actions in Vietnam no different from what actually occurred. His tragic assassination was not a tragedy for the course of American history.

The Origins of a Myth

John Fitzgerald Kennedy was born on 29 May 1917. His name reflected his dual Irish heritage. His mother's father and his namesake John Fitzgerald had been among the first generation of Irish politicians to wrest political office from the Yankee WASP elite. Honey Fitz was mayor of Boston, the most Irish city in the world, from 1906 to 1908 and again between 1910 and 1914. A politician down to his core, he was driven from public life by a scandalous relationship with a twenty-three-year-old cigarette girl named Toodles.[3] His daughter Rose was educated to be at home in the Catholic woman's world of domesticity and devotion.

The Kennedys occupied a lower rung of Boston's immigrant Irish social ladder. Patrick Kennedy was the son of a saloon keeper, who became a local politician and power broker. True, his son Joseph P. Kennedy obtained admission to Harvard, the oldest university in the United States. But Kennedy's Cambridge years followed a different path from that enjoyed by WASP scions such as Theodore or Franklin Roosevelt. The elite clubs that loomed so large in both Roosevelts' remembrances of their bright college years barred their doors to the likes of Joe Kennedy: Irish Catholics were not welcome in those exclusive precincts. Both Roosevelts had politics firmly at the centre of their ambitions at an early age. By contrast, Kennedy – though his father and father-in-law were politicians – intended to make serious money. His trajectory during two decades after his graduation in 1912 was financially if not socially upward: banker, steel man, movie mogul, bootlegger and stock-market speculator. Having the sense to sell most of his Wall Street holdings in the spring and summer of 1929, he escaped the crash unscathed with a spectacular fortune that he hoped would buy him social respectability and national political power. During the 1920s Joe had thumbed his nose at Boston and New York society. He now backed Franklin Roosevelt for the 1932 Democratic presidential nomination, expecting a serious *quid pro quo*. As chairman of the newly established Securities and Exchange Commission Joe, poacher turned policeman, enforced regulations prohibiting others from making money in the under-hand ways he himself had employed. Although disappointed by his next job as chairman of the Maritime Commission, Kennedy nevertheless made the most of his continuing role on the political stage. His success at bureaucratic re-engineering, coupled with his understanding that what you did was less important than what people thought you did, brought him steady publicity.

Eager to reward Kennedy for a job well done (and get him far away from Washington), Roosevelt appointed Joe ambassador to Great Britain in 1938. Having grown up with WASP prejudices against shanty Irish ringing in his ears, Kennedy relished becoming the first Irish-American ambassador to the Court of St James. With him to London came Rose and their nine children. The eldest, Joe Jr, bore lightly the strains of being his father's chosen vehicle for the next level of achievement – Joe Jr would enter politics and nothing would stop his rise to the top. Jack, a sickly version of his elder brother, became the family clown. But all the Kennedy children were raised with the same principles: winning isn't everything, it's the only thing; anything is permissible to succeed; have no idols except for the family – the Kennedy family, that is. Why the family should want political power was not discussed; it was accepted that power was its own reward. Indicative of the prevailing attitude was Jack's observation in 1960 that Eleanor Roosevelt (widow of Franklin) disliked him because 'She hated my father and she can't stand it that his children turned out so much better than hers.' It never occurred to him that Eleanor Roosevelt might dislike him on principled political grounds.[4] No doubt, worship of the family is a virtuous secondary good. But democratic rule is based on a devotion to ideas not siblings. Though they portrayed themselves as the inheritors of Washington, Jefferson and Roosevelt, the Kennedys proved to be more akin to the Medici.

Jack's career reflected his upbringing. The wartime death of his brother Joe left him the heir apparent. Stepping into Joe's shoes, he followed his father's programme, successfully running for Congress in 1946, for Senator in 1952 and for President in

1960. Rumours still persist that the Kennedy forces 'stole' the election. Richard Daley, Chicago mayor and boss of the formidable Cook County Democratic machine, allegedly held back Chicago's heavily Democratic votes until the downstate Illinois Republican numbers had been tallied. In the event, Chicago's Kennedy votes swung the state for the Democratic nominee. That the Texas returns gave that state narrowly to the Kennedy–Johnson ticket did not go unnoticed either; allies of vice-presidential candidate Lyndon Johnson controlled its electoral machinery too. But outwardly each campaign was a family effort, featuring Rose's teas for Democratic women, brother Bobby's generalship and, most importantly, Joe's money. Like father, like son: Jack's passions were about evenly divided between the chase for office and the chase for women. Joe's conquests ranged from the famous, such as movie star Gloria Swanson, to his sons' and daughters' less celebrated friends. His son ranged still wider, carrying on with Marilyn Monroe, alleged Nazi and East German spies, Mafia molls, the wives of his friends and the friends of his wife.

The Second Emancipation

The Kennedy years coincided with the apogee of the civil rights movement, the push by African-Americans for the legal and constitutional rights that had been denied them most egregiously in the South since the American Civil War a century before. The 1954 *Brown v. Board of Education* decision by the Supreme Court outlawing segregated facilities had spawned a revolution and counter-revolution in the Southern American states. Emboldened by the decision, African-Americans organised as never before to dismantle the dual-system apartheid of schools, parks, buses, housing and public facilities that characterised the United States below the Mason–Dixon line. At the same time, Southern whites closed ranks, determined to enforce 'our way of life' against all challenges. In 1957 President Dwight Eisenhower, who personally wished that the Supreme Court had not overturned state-sponsored segregation, reluctantly sent federal troops to Little Rock, Arkansas, to enforce the peace during the integration of its Central High School.[5] Kennedy, then a Senator, criticised the President for sending these soldiers. The photographs of federal troops pointing rifles at angry mothers and fathers provided a propaganda feast for the Soviet Union.[6]

During the 1960 campaign the Kennedy people did their best to keep civil rights from becoming an issue. But on 19 October local policemen arrested the Revd Martin Luther King Jr, soon to become the most prominent individual in the movement, while he was attempting to desegregate Rich's department store in Atlanta. Other demonstrators were released on bail but six days later the judge sentenced King to four months in jail. Hard evidence supported widespread fears that King would be killed while incarcerated. Vice-President and Republican presidential nominee Richard Nixon believed that King was 'getting a bum rap' but, bowing to legal niceties, he refused to intervene. Robert Kennedy, serving as his brother's campaign manager, made that effort while Jack called Mrs King to reassure her. As a result, King, who had voted Republican in 1956, and his father, the Revd Martin Luther King Sr, who had endorsed Nixon, both switched sides. The senior Revd King announced, 'I've got a suitcase of votes, and I'm going to take them to Mr Kennedy and dump them in his lap.' Nixon had counted on significant support from African-Americans still grateful to the party of Lincoln; his hopes now vanished.[7]

Kennedy's inaugural address, given on an unusually cold 20 January, summoned Americans to 'bear the burden of a long twilight struggle', to 'ask not what your country can do for you – ask what you can do for your country'.[8] Although Martin Luther King did not receive an invitation to the inaugural ceremonies, millions of his followers took Kennedy's soaring words as a call to action. In the spring of 1961 members of the Congress of Racial Equality (CORE) began the so-called 'Freedom Rides'. Their goal was to test the enforcement of the Supreme Court's December 1960 ruling which declared unconstitutional the segregation of facilities serving interstate travellers. When they reached Rock

Hill, South Carolina, a mob of whites severely beat a fifty-five-year-old white Freedom Rider. Then, in Anniston, Alabama, all hell broke loose. A group of whites ambushed two buses, setting upon the Riders as they desperately sought to escape the fire-bombed vehicles. Pictures of these outrages flashing around the world on 15 May presented Kennedy with his first civil rights crisis. He was angry at his lack of control over the Freedom Riders and furious that they had created an opportunity for a Communist propaganda coup. As Kennedy and his brother Robert, now US Attorney-General, conferred they drew two conclusions: that 'this whole thing and the people behind it were a giant pain in the ass' and that, albeit reluctantly, the federal government had to take the side of the Riders.[9] As was his wont, Kennedy tried to steer a middle course between the two extremes as he saw them – the one embodied by civil rights demonstrators and the other exemplified by the civil rights deniers. Most of all the President wanted to avoid any confrontation over the issue – with African-Americans or white Southerners.

Political imperatives only increased Kennedy's reluctance to intervene in this issue. The most powerful members of Congress were Southern Democrats who, because of the South's entrenched one-party system, had amassed the seniority to control powerful Congressional committees. These so-called Dixiecrats had the power to block any legislation Kennedy sought. His reaction was not to argue but to buy them off. For example, Kennedy appointed to the federal courts in Alabama the rigid segregationist lawyers suggested by Southern senators.[10] The one thing the President wanted to avoid was a call to principle. Believing that the nation was not yet ready to deal with the agenda formulated by Civil Rights leaders, Kennedy hoped that blacks would take a forbearing, low-key approach.[11] African-Americans, understandably impatient after a century of waiting for equal rights, declined to fit into the President's agenda, forcing Kennedy repeatedly to confront civil rights crises. In 1962 the issue was the attempt by air force veteran James Meredith to integrate the University of Mississippi. The following year volunteers sought to integrate the

University of Alabama. In both cases the President initially pandered to grandstanding segregationist governors, Ross Barnett of Mississippi and George Wallace of Alabama, rather than send in federal troops. He bobbed and weaved, attempting to avoid a presidential call to the people of the sort other chief executives had given. Without principles himself, he could not invoke them for America.

But the civil rights issue would not go away. As the Kennedy brothers pondered their options – most importantly the question of whether the administration should seek Congressional approval of a new federal Civil Rights Bill – they used a surprising system of information gathering. The head of the FBI, J. Edgar Hoover, supposedly investigating Communist influence on the civil rights movement, had tapped the phone lines of King's lawyer and counsellor, Stanley Levison. When Hoover first proposed this step to the Attorney-General, his nominal superior, Robert could only assent: the FBI Director's evidence of Jack's sexual activities had made both the President and Attorney-General his prisoners. Although the Kennedy brothers did not use their knowledge about King's sex life (he shared Kennedy's proclivities), the information they obtained increased their reluctance to deal with King.[12] In the end, it took George Wallace, the theatrical Governor of Alabama, to force Kennedy to make the televised address on civil rights he had long avoided. The President had to respond in kind to Wallace's stance in the schoolhouse door of the University of Alabama at Tuscaloosa on nationwide television. His eighteen-minute address on 21 May 1963, invoking the spirit of Lincoln, finally gave the principled call white Americans could not ignore. One week later Kennedy asked Congress to pass a civil rights law that provided for desegregated public housing and included federal enforcement provisions. The price was immediately made clear: on 22 June the administration's anodyne funding Bill for the Area Redevelopment Act was defeated in the House of Representatives by a margin of 209–204. The difference was made by nineteen Southern Democrats and twenty Republicans who voted against the Bill after Kennedy's civil rights speech.[13]

In fact, the legislation that Kennedy had requested languished in Congress, becoming law only in July 1964. Only Kennedy's death made its passage possible. For the assassination removed from office a president who at heart was not committed to civil rights, substituting one who was. Johnson, from an impoverished Texas family, had a gut-level commitment to poor people of whatever race. It was he who believed in the principles which the Civil Rights Act of 1964 and the Voting Rights Act of 1965 embodied. Moreover, Johnson had the legislative skill to obtain passage of these Acts. Johnson was not naive. He knew that his legislation would cost the Democratic party the 'solid South' – its complete domination of that part of the United States. Yet he exerted all his skill to turn Kennedy's original civil rights proposal into the 1964 Act. Johnson, arguably the most talented senator of his generation, alternately cajoled and strong-armed senators, beating down a filibuster that lasted eighty days. Aided by the large majority he had racked up in the 1964 presidental election, he persevered. During that campaign, Johnson had launched the War on Poverty designed to banish want and deprivation 'by opening to everyone the opportunity to live in decency and dignity'.[14] The next year he obtained from Congress the legislation that transformed an agenda into reality. At the same time he introduced and achieved passage of the Voting Rights Act. The President from Texas empathised with the underprivileged of America as the rich boy John Kennedy never could do. The consequent revolution, redistributive of rights and riches, was possible only with a president who had experienced poverty and discrimination himself and was willing to pay a stiff political price for their amelioration.

Kennedy would never have put his future on the line for civil rights as Johnson did. As we shall see, he would almost certainly have faced a tougher fight in 1964 than Johnson. And, even if he had emerged victorious, he would not have spent political points in the profligate manner Johnson did to achieve his civil rights programme. Splitting the difference between the options on offer, Kennedy's habitual *modus operandi*, would have denied African-

Americans the legal, moral and economic support that made possible the massive changes in American society during the 1960s.

America's Longest War

The American involvement in Vietnam began in 1945 when Washington decided not to oppose British on-the-ground decisions favouring French imperial dominance over Indo-China.[15] It ended thirty years later when the last remaining Americans in Saigon ignominiously fled as Communist forces overwhelmed the city.

This conflict was the third American–Communist confrontation of the Cold War to take place in Asia. In 1949 Mao Zedong had succeeded in capturing control over China. Many Americans had long believed in a special relationship between the United States and China. Indeed, Franklin Roosevelt had elevated China to the status of the Soviet Union, Britain and the United States as one of the 'Four Policemen' which would govern the postwar world. The question of 'who lost China?' would haunt the Democratic party for the next twenty years. Then, in 1950, another American confrontation on the Asian mainland began. The decision by Communist North Korea to invade the South placed the Truman administration at war in a conflict few Americans had envisaged. In the process of fighting to a bloody stalemate the United States decided to grant significant aid to France, whose battle to retain control over Indo-china had grown progressively more difficult. The death of 50,000 Americans to restore only the Korean status quo ante was another black mark for Democratic administrations; Truman's brave words about a rollback of Communist forces dissolved in the Chinese onslaught that followed General Douglas MacArthur's drive to the north.

The Geneva Conference of 1954, co-chaired by Britain and the Soviet Union, designated Laos an independent, neutralist monarchy. Chronic civil war among the Communist Pathet Lao faction, a neutralist group and a pro-American military cadre bedevilled the country thereafter. The Geneva Conference also attempted to carve a settlement of the Vietnam conflict. France renounced control over the country. The Vietminh, led by Ho Chi Minh, who had defeated the imperialist forces, were given temporary control over the northern half of the nation. The southern half of Vietnam rejected the leadership of the Emperor of Annam province, Bao Dai, in favour of a republic, proclaimed on 26 October 1955, with Ngo Dinh Diem at its head. The Geneva accords called for all-Vietnam elections to be held in the summer of 1956. Understanding that Ho's popularity as a nationalist leader and the larger population of the North ensured a Communist victory, Eisenhower and Secretary of State John Foster Dulles encouraged Diem to cancel the elections.[16] Eisenhower avoided sending American fighting soldiers to Vietnam; but the American government during his term of office assumed the French responsibilities for training the Vietnamese army as well as funding Vietnamese needs. By 1961 Diem's government ranked fifth among all recipients of American foreign aid; the US mission in South Vietnam was the largest in the world. Part of the funding went to assist the resettlement of refugees. With American encouragement almost 1,000,000 North Vietnamese fled to the South. These overwhelmingly Catholic exiles supported their co-religionist Diem. In return he favoured them over the indigenous Buddhist majority.[17]

Diem also appealed to the American Catholic community and the 'China-lobby' which had kept American support for the former Nationalist Chinese leader Chiang Kai-shek at fever pitch since his flight to Taiwan in 1949. Significantly, Jack Kennedy was one of the organisers of the American Friends of Vietnam, explaining in 1956 that 'Vietnam represents the cornerstone of the Free World in South-east Asia, the keystone to the arch, the finger in the dike'. The son of an official at the imperial court at Hué, Diem shared the Kennedys' paramount belief in family. His paranoid, drug-addicted brother Ngo Dinh Nhu had charge of internal security, including the feared national police force; another brother, Ngo Dinh Thuc, was the Catholic Archbishop of Hué; while a third brother, Ngo Dinh Luyen, was ambassador to Great Britain. His sister-in-law Madame Nhu, much to the regret of the Americans, became a leading spokesperson for the regime. Her father, Tran Van Choung, became South Vietnam's Ambassador to Washington.[18]

The prevailing anti-Communist consensus of the 1950s obliged putative Democratic candidates to fight over the right side of the foreign policy spectrum in their race for the presidency. Kennedy was an ardent critic of Eisenhower's foreign and defence policies. The young Massachusetts Senator argued that the aged General-turned-President had permitted American prestige to decline and its defences to weaken. As a result, Kennedy claimed, the Soviet Union stood poised to triumph in the Cold War. At the same time Kennedy used his televised debates against Nixon to criticise the Eisenhower administration for taking a weak stance against the Chinese Communists on the Quemoy and Matsu islands and for abandoning Cuba to the Communists. Kennedy's inaugural address reflected this martial attitude:

> Let every nation know, whether it wishes us well or ill, that we shall pay any price, bear any burden, meet any hardship, support any friend, oppose any foe, to assure the survival and success of liberty. This much we pledge – and more.

Once elected Kennedy learnt that the Eisenhower administration did have a plan against Castro – a Central Intelligence Agency-sponsored coup. Much to his later regret, Kennedy made the plan his own. The failure of the Bay of Pigs operation, launched on 17 April 1961, proved the worst defeat of the Kennedy administration. The United States and its leader appeared both incompetent and impotent. Six months later the Berlin crisis seemed to give further evidence of American debility. The decision by Soviet Communist Party First Secretary Nikita Khrushchev and East German leader Walter Ulbricht to construct a wall around West Berlin posed an apparently unanswerable challenge to the Western alliance. Apparently Khrushchev, having sized up his opponent at the Vienna summit, had found him wanting. Historians have now concluded that the building of the wall actually signalled a Soviet acknowledgement of American strength; at the time it symbolised American weakness, as did Kennedy's decision to accept a negotiated cease-fire in Laos.

The Laotian settlement had made the position of Vietnam more vulnerable at the same time as it became more valuable to the United States in its struggle against international Communism. At their final meeting on 19 January 1961 Eisenhower informed Kennedy that the situation in Laos had deteriorated to the point of crisis.[19] But as Kennedy told his officials, 'If we have to fight in South-east Asia, let's fight in Vietnam.'[20] Conditions in the South had steadily deteriorated since 1959, when the Communist guerrilla forces there, the Vietcong, had received the permission of the Ho Chi Minh government to step up their campaign against Diem's regime. In 1960 the North Vietnamese party Congress reaffirmed this decision. Two months later a military uprising shook Saigon.[21] Diem's decisions eased the way for the Vietcong's insurgency. His system of enforcing control over the peasants won the Vietcong converts rapidly while his 'autocratic methods and lack of communication' alienated even those willing to support anti-Communist efforts.[22] Diem had imported Northern officials to run the countryside; they quickly reduced peasants to the same quasi-serf status they had loathed under the French. With the Vietcong willing to use less gentle methods of persuasion when propaganda failed, the Saigon government's control over the countryside rapidly diminished.

Panicking Kennedy administration officials devised a two-step response. Accused of being soft on Communism by no less an authority than *Time* magazine, the President knew that he had to draw a line in the sand in Vietnam, a country which was important not so much for its own sake but because the United States could not afford another defeat in the struggle against international Communism. The President created a Task Force on Vietnam and sent Vice-President Lyndon Johnson to South Vietnam. The Task Force report, delivered on 3 May 1961, recommended that the US government 'undertake military security arrangements which establish beyond doubt our intention to stand behind Viet Nam's resistance to Communist aggression ...'. At the same time the Task Force report urged a crash effort to bolster the economic and political viability of Diem's administration.[23] One week later Kennedy approved National Security Action Memorandum No. 52, embodying many of the ideas of the Task Force report. Reiterating that the American objective was to prevent Communist domination in South Vietnam by 'a series of mutually supporting actions of a military, political, economic, psychological and government character', it directed that the Defense Department make a 'full examination' of the size and composition of forces which would be desirable in the case of a possible commitment of U.S. forces to Vietnam'. At the same time Washington would 'seek to increase the confidence of President Diem and his government in the United States'. Crucial to this effort was Johnson's trip.[24] The Vice-President, decidedly not part of the Kennedy inner circle, arrived in Vietnam on 11 May for a thirty-six hour visit. In company with most visiting dignitaries, Johnson could barely get a word in edgewise as Diem, in a windy monologue, explored the history and trials and tribulations of South Vietnam. The bottom line was that America's ally proved far less interested in Washington's ideas than in increased American aid. Although he publicly lauded him in Saigon as the Winston Churchill of Vietnam, Johnson had no illusions about the Vietnamese leader. During the plane ride out of Saigon, a reporter asked the Vice-President if he really meant what he said. 'Shit, Diem's the only boy we got out there,' replied Johnson.[25] His report expressed support for the regime while stressing the need for the United States to aid South Vietnam's creation of an extensive network of military and economic reforms.[26]

The recommendations of spring became the policies of summer; but key American officials, alarmed by the deteriorating position of free world forces around the world, pushed for more sooner. On 19 July, successful Vietcong terrorist activities in the South led William Bundy, Assistant Secretary of State for Far

Eastern Affairs, to recommend to General Lyman Lemnitzer, the chairman of the Joint Chiefs of Staff, that he begin 'evaluating military measures which the U.S. might institute in reprisal against North Vietnam'.[27] As Robert Komer, a member of the National Security Council Staff, advised his colleague Walt Rostow, 'After Laos, and with Berlin on the horizon, we cannot afford to go less than all-out in cleaning up South Vietnam.'[28]

However, the advisers' unanimous agreement on the goal hid their disagreement about appropriate tactics. His search for a solution led Kennedy to send in October a special fact-finding mission to Vietnam headed by General Maxwell Taylor, featuring Rostow and counter-terrorist expert Edward Lansdale. Among other things, the President ordered Taylor to 'evaluate what could be accomplished by the introduction of SEATO [South-East Asia Treaty Organisation] or United States forces into Vietnam'.[29] The resulting report, delivered to the President on 3 November, represented a sharply escalated American commitment wrapped in optimistic ribbons. The Presidential emissaries were convinced that they had seen one of 'Khrushchev's "wars of liberation"' in action. Believing that the situation was 'serious' but 'by no means hopeless', the report recommended 'a shift in the American relations to the Vietnamese effort from advice to limited partnership ... at all levels Americans must as friends and partners – not as arms-length advisers – show them how the job might be done'.[30] During the next twelve days the President and his senior aides and officials debated the future of American policy in Vietnam. Taylor wanted American soldiers deployed in Vietnam, an option Rostow also endorsed.[31] Defense Secretary McNamara revealed himself to be one of the hardliners in the administration, arguing that 'the fall of South Vietnam to Communism would lead to the fairly rapid extension of Communist control in the rest of the mainland South-east Asia right down to Indonesia'. In urging an enlarged American commitment, however, the Defense Secretary also told the President that 'the ultimate possible extent of our military commitment must be faced. . . . I believe we can assume that the maximum US forces required on the ground will not exceed (6–8) divisions, or about (220,000) men . . . . '[32]

As was his habit, Kennedy reflected on the range of available options to various visitors, including Indian Prime Minister Jawaharlal Nehru, who came to the White House on 7 November. The President convened the crucial meeting of the National Security Council eight days later. It was obvious that he retained doubts about the American commitment to South Vietnam, stating 'that he could even make a rather strong case against intervening in an area 10,000 miles away against 16,000 guerrillas with a native army of 200,000, where millions have been spent with no success'. Kennedy also asked General Lemnitzer how he could justify an expanded military commitment in Vietnam while a Communist government remained in Cuba. Lemnitzer 'hastened to add that the Joint Chiefs of Staff feel that even at this point the United States should go into Cuba'.[33] But it was at least partly because the United States was *not* going into Cuba that Kennedy, on 22 November 1961, approved NSAM-111. After receiving an opinion from the State Department's legal adviser that international law allowed the United States to send troops to Vietnam, Kennedy granted some but not all of the Taylor Report's requests for additional American soldiers. At the same time he authorised increased American logistical support for ARVN (Army of the Republic of South Vietnam) forces as well as personnel and equipment to improve the 'military–political Intelligence system' and such economic aid 'as may be required to permit the GVN' (South Vietnam government) to pursue a 'vigorous flood relief and rehabilitation program'.[34] The President had rejected the two extremes, a negotiated settlement or immediate deployment of US combat troops. Instead, in keeping with his usual practice, he had chosen the middle course, transforming the American presence from an advisory role into a joint venture. In so doing, he had Americanised the war, casting in stone the US commitment to the conflict. In the future the debate would not be over whether Washington should let down its ally. American officials would be forced to wrestle with the question: should the United States itself admit defeat in its challenge to a Communist insurgency? A turning point had come: Kennedy had crossed a Rubicon from beyond which neither he nor his successors could return unscathed.

American advisers streamed into Vietnam, their number trebling from 3,205 in December 1961 to over 9,000 one year later. An expanded counter-insurgency programme, Project Beefup, began with the arrival of armoured personnel carriers and over 300 military aircraft made in America.[35] But neither American men nor material made the difference. By the end of 1962 the Vietcong had regained the initiative. The best the President could report at his 12 December news conference was: 'We don't see the end of the tunnel, but I must say I don't think it is darker than it was a year ago, and in some ways lighter.'[36] Given that the Cuban missile crisis had wiped out any chance of the United States eliminating the Communist Fidel Castro from his base ninety-one miles from the American shore, these words were grim tidings. Shortly after this, the battle of Ap Bac on 2 January 1963 destroyed any remaining American illusions. For years high-ranking US military men had maintained that if the Vietcong forswore their guerrilla tactics in favour of a set-piece battle, the ARVN forces would triumph. In granting this wish, the Vietcong decisively proved their mettle. Called in by American adviser John Paul Vann, more than 1,200 of South Vietnam's best troops, ferried by waves of American helicopters, came to the village of Ap Tan Thoi to capture a Vietcong radio transmitter. Three American advisers died that day, as did sixty-one ARVN men. But the Vietcong, having downed five American helicopters and hit nine others, escaped the trap with their transmitter intact. Worse, the ARVN general refused to order his men to attack. As *New York Times* reporter David Halberstram wrote, US officials in Saigon were bewildered by this turn of events.[37]

Increasingly Americans found their explanation in the failure of the Diem government. Diem had decided that his government could not bear the political cost which would follow if ARVN commanders listened to American advisers and began intensive, higher-casualty missions against the Vietcong. The South Vietnam leader instead ordered his field commanders to avoid extended confrontation. The result was the rout at Ap Bac.[38] Moreover, having paid lip-service to American requests for political, social and economic reforms, during 1962 Diem instead embarked on a crackdown against his critics. Counselled by his secretive and increasingly demented brother Nhu, Diem expelled reporters from CBS and NBC and banned the sale of *Newsweek*. His actions exposed the frustrations and futility of dealing with such an ally. Throughout the Cold War the United States often had the ill-luck to have extremely venal allies while the Communist system nurtured surrogates whose sins could better be described as mortal. In the eyes of God, mortal transgressions are far worse; but joint operations are easier with committed, ideological murderers than with corrupt, avaricious surrogates.

The domestic politics of South Vietnam took a decided turn for the worse in May 1963. The long-standing hostility between Diem's minority Catholic government and the resentful Buddhist majority constituting some 80 per cent of the population erupted into open confrontation on 8 May. A celebration of the Buddha's birthday turned into a bloody riot as South Vietnamese police used tear-gas, clubs and gunfire to stop Buddhists attempting to fly religious flags. American officials reported the deaths of six children and two adults.[39] Police repression only ignited further demonstrations. While the Buddhists sought only the same religious freedom given to Catholics, Diem insisted that 'the NLF and the Vietcong are exploiting the situation' and refused concessions.[40] The culmination came on 11 June when a seventy-three-year-old Buddhist monk, Trich Quang Duc, immolated himself at a busy Saigon crossroads.[41] Suddenly the local clash had become an American crisis. Kennedy himself believed that 'no news picture in history has generated as much emotion around the world'. Even worse, from Washington's point of view, was Diem's refusal to follow American advice and make concessions to the protesters. Negotiations with the Buddhists came to naught and another monk burnt himself. Madame Ngo Dinh Nhu responded by telling CBS News on 1 August that the Buddhists had merely 'barbecued a bonze [monk] with imported gasoline'. The State Department instructed US ambassador Frederick Nolting to advise Diem to get his sister-in-law out of the country as White House staffers lost any hope that the current South Vietnam government could make the changes American advisers thought were necessary to win the war.[42]

The American solution was obvious: another government. As the State Department had concluded that 'We do not know whether Diem really will do the things he must if his regime is to survive,' Washington moved to cut its ties with the family it had long succoured.[43] American diplomats informed South Vietnam's Vice-President Nguyen Ngoc Tho that the United States would support him if Diem lost power. The President played his part, signing NSAM-249 which adopted once again a middle-of-the-road position. Rejecting an American departure or an all-out military campaign, it merely recommended increased military assistance and more advisers.[44] Kennedy also selected the hardline Republican Henry Cabot Lodge II to be American ambassador and the President's personal emissary, telling him at their meeting on 15 August that 'apparently the Diem government was entering a terminal phase'.[45] Kennedy's decisions made his prediction reality. Diem's regime had, of course, long been plagued by abortive coups. But, when in August the most serious bid failed as the South Vietnamese generals lost their nerve, Lodge had approved the coup in advance.

Attempting to make sense out of chaotic reports from the field, Kennedy sent two investigative missions to South Vietnam in September. The second one featured a return by Taylor, now chairman of the Joint Chiefs of Staff, accompanied this time by Defence Secretary McNamara. They returned in optimistic spirits, telling the President that the American advisers, now numbering 16,000, might actually be withdrawn in 1965 if things went well. Taylor and McNamara also recommended withdrawing a 1,000-men construction battalion by the end of the year.[46] On

11 October Kennedy approved the implementation of the McNamara–Taylor recommendations but directed that no public announcement of the troop withdrawal be made.[47] American relations with Diem continued to deteriorate, however. Nhu now publicly attacked the United States, stating that American aid reductions had 'initiated a process of disintegration in Vietnam'. Persistent rumours reached Washington that Nhu was talking to the Communists. The ARVN generals once more approached American officials, seeking to ascertain the American reaction if they staged a coup. Meanwhile, in South Vietnam, Lodge, who viewed himself as a proconsul rather than presidential envoy, orchestrated US support for the ARVN dissidents, keeping the President informed by a series of private cables. As October ended Kennedy's main preoccupation was to preserve 'control and cut-out' – the ability to retain command over the coup without sacrificing deniability should things go badly.[48] Finally, on 1 November, All Saints Day, the expected happened. ARVN officers, following their American-edited script, took over the Saigon government. What was not in the script was their execution of Diem and Nhu, unconvincingly portrayed as suicide. Those deaths haunted the President, particularly once he learnt that the United States probably could have saved their lives.[49] Yet in a speech prepared for delivery on the afternoon of 22 November 1963 the President intended to warn Americans that they 'dare not weary of the task' of supporting South Vietnam, no matter how 'risky and costly' that decision might be.[50]

What if Kennedy had Lived?

When Kennedy died that same day, he left behind a country determined to worship at the grave of a President whom, in truth, it had not particularly respected in life. The mythologising of JFK was given every encouragement by the Kennedy family, who were determined to use Jack's death to further the career of his brother. Although Robert in fact remained a supporter of the war for some time after his brother's death, the Kennedy publicity machine began obfuscating his track record as soon as it became clear in early 1968 that President Lyndon Johnson's escalation of the war made him vulnerable to a primary challenge. By the time of Robert's assassination that June, the myth was well established that Jack Kennedy would have withdrawn from Vietnam if only he had lived.

Yet, as we have seen, serious historical evidence for such arguments is scant. Much has been made, for example, of Kennedy's September 1963 interview with Walter Cronkite, America's most respected television journalist (specially arranged to mark the transition of the networks to thirty-minute nightly news broadcasts). Determined to use the interview to pressure Diem and his brother, Kennedy explained that, 'In the final analysis it is their war. They are the ones who have to win it or lose it.' The President then explicitly told Diem on nationwide American television how he should conduct his country's internal affairs: stop the repressive anti-Buddhist actions, change policy and personnel or forfeit American support. Similarly, on 14 November, at his last press conference, the President defined 'our object' as 'to bring Americans home [and] permit the South Vietnamese to maintain themselves as a free and independent country'.[51] Only two months before, however, he had told another evening news broadcast that 'we should not withdraw'. This was in fact more consistent with the policy he was actually pursuing. Such contradictory utterances simply convey Kennedy's dismay at the choices he faced: the same alternatives which had faced Eisenhower earlier and which were to face Johnson and Nixon thereafter. In all four cases, the President of the moment found it impossible to pull out and nakedly abandon South Vietnam.

In dying, Kennedy handed Johnson a poisoned chalice. The coup leaders had proved themselves more inept than Diem; on 29 January a second coup, supported by the Central Intelligence Agency, deposed the initial rebels. Taylor prodded McNamara to 'put aside many of the self-imposed restrictions which now limit our efforts and undertake bolder actions which may embody greater risks'.[52] Aware at every juncture of the possible downside of increased American efforts, Johnson nevertheless found himself sucked into the expansion of the war that he dreaded. The fear of an American domestic backlash if the war were lost combined with a fervent belief in the domino theory led him inexorably towards escalation: in 1964 the President obtained from Congress the Tonkin Gulf Resolution granting unlimited war-making powers; in 1965 the first American combat troops arrived; by 1967 American forces exceeded half a million.

Yet, had he lived, Jack Kennedy would have found himself drinking from exactly the same poisoned chalice. He was the one who had made the two decisions which Americanised the war. In 1961 he had increased drastically the American men and material flowing to South Vietnam, thereby turning an advisory relationship into a partnership. His determination two years later actively to encourage the overthrow of the Diem government had signified the depth of the American involvement and ensured its extension. The crime for which Diem paid with his life was his failure to follow the US prescription for winning the war – a war which Kennedy could not afford to lose. Diem's death over-determined the American commitment to South Vietnam: with blood on his hands, Kennedy could not have walked away from the conflict, and a decision to stay in 1963 implied inevitable escalation. As a marginal president determined to secure his own and his brother's political future, Kennedy would never have dared take the step that even Richard Nixon – who made a volte-face on every other decision – could not take.

This brings us to an important counterfactual question which proponents of the Kennedy myth seldom ask: would Kennedy have won the 1964 presidential election if he had lived to fight it? The answer is probably yes (albeit with a smaller majority than Johnson won) – but only if he had maintained his commitment to Vietnam. For anti-Communism was a pervasive fact of domestic politics in the 1960s: it was in the air politicians breathed. It is easily forgotten that, as late as 1968, with 36,000 Americans dead and anti-war demonstrations raging on and off university campuses, half of Americans polled still thought that the United States should increase its effort in Vietnam. Four years earlier, Kennedy would almost certainly have faced Barry Goldwater, the standard-bearer of the right wing of the Republican party. (Nixon had ruled himself out by the tantrum he threw following his defeat in the 1962 California gubernatorial race; and the leading Eastern establishment candidate Nelson Rockefeller had become politically unacceptable to the Republican rank and file after his divorce and hasty remarriage.) With Goldwater watching eagerly for any sign of softness on Communism, Kennedy would have been obliged to reaffirm his commitment whether he liked it or not.

Even after a 1964 election victory, it seems unlikely that Kennedy would have lessened American support for South Vietnam. Having made the same decisions as Johnson actually did in that election year (decisions made on the advice of Kennedy's men), he would have faced the identical pressures his successor did in 1965. Inevitably, like Johnson, he would have taken the middle road at every juncture. He would have refused to escalate to the extent the military men requested, but would not have sought a negotiated peace treaty. Under his leadership, combat troops would have followed as surely as they did in the Johnson presidency. If anything, his commitment would have been even greater. For Kennedy's personal inclination was to be a foreign policy president: compared with Johnson, his lack of success in realising a domestic agenda made international success indispensable. For the sake of his place in history (not to mention his brother's political career), he could never have risked the political ramifications of a decision to withdraw from Vietnam.

That Kennedy occasionally pondered the arguments against the idea of sending US combat troops to Vietnam is poor evidence for the proposition that he would have never taken such a step. Like many high-ranking officials, the President used the stream of people in and out of his office as sounding-boards for different strategies. As a result, Kennedy statements can be found supporting the entire spectrum of possible American decisions. But the fact is that, once the Vietnam conflict had intensified, he too would have seen no easy way out. He of all people could not have renounced the prevailing American belief that the United States had to wage the Cold War – as it was a belief which he himself had nurtured. In short, it would have been All the Way with JFK too.

As the poem says, John F. Kennedy's term in office was certainly brief; but shining it was not. Nor would it have been otherwise had he lived to serve a second term. There would have been no early withdrawal from Vietnam. There might well have been no Great Society.

The former Communist world has lost its idols. It is now time for Americans to relinquish one of theirs.

NINE

1989 WITHOUT GORBACHEV:

What if Communism had not collapsed?

Mark Almond

> The great of this world are often blamed
> for not doing what they could have done.
> They can reply: Just think of all the evil
> that we could have done and have not done.
> GEORG CHRISTOPH LICHTENBERG

The collapse of Communism is now history. Already it seems inevitable. But it is worth remembering that no major event in modern history was less predicted by the experts than the fall of the Berlin Wall in 1989 or the hauling down of the red flag for the last time from the Kremlin in 1991. The rubble left behind by great revolutions and the collapse of great empires is always impressive and its very scale makes it tempting to look for fundamental, long-term causes. However, looking for the deep roots of historical change is the *déformation professionelle* of historians. Sometimes what happened did not have to be; or, to put it another way, it only became inevitable very late in the day.

The dramatic events of the autumn of 1989 are still too close for us to have a proper perspective, but it is already becoming clear that the Western myth of its inevitable victory over a monolithic, inefficient and oppressive Communism is untenable. Ironically, the very structural and economic determinist arguments which were pooh-poohed by Western advocates when Marxists tried to prove the inexorable logic of the rise of their system are now trotted out to demonstrate that the triumph of the West was preprogrammed. Would that it were so, and that all future rivals were equally doomed by internal contradictions to humiliating failure; but this notion is too self-serving to be convincing. In any case, since the 'End of History' was confidently announced by Francis Fukuyama in 1989, that capricious goddess has given our self-satisfaction a few well-placed digs in the ribs. Who is now so confident that democracy has won after all? To many observers at the time, the suddenness, the apparent completeness of the collapse of the East European regimes in 1989 seemed to confirm that some widespread canker had eaten away at the vital organs of the Communist system, leaving it moribund. A popular eye-witness account asks, 'For what, after all, happened?' And gives the answer:

> A few thousand, then tens of thousands, then hundreds of thousands went onto the streets. They spoke a few words. 'Resign!' they said. 'No more shall we be slaves!' 'Free elections!' 'Freedom!' And the walls of Jericho fell. And with the walls the communist parties simply crumbled . . .[1]

Yet much the same had already happened several times before: in East Germany in 1953, in Hungary in 1956, in Czechoslovakia in 1968, and then in Poland in 1980. An all-powerful Communist apparatus lost its authority overnight. But, each time the tanks rolled, the crowds were dispersed and Humpty-Dumpty was put back together again. Even in June 1989, in China, Deng Xiaoping was able to show that 'a million is not a large number' when his forces shot down mass demonstrations in Peking and a few other cities.

Popular discontent does not explain the collapse of Communism. It had always been there, only bottled up. The question is why the cork was released and why it was not promptly reinserted in the bottle when public protest began. The People may make sympathetic characters in history, but in practice in 1989 (as so often, not least in revolutions) they were merely charming stage-extras, whose antics distracted historians and other observers from the real action. After all, if the events in Central Europe in 1989 often reminded observers of the short-lived 'springtime of the peoples' in 1848, why was 1849 so completely unimaginable? In many ways, the return to power of the former Communist parties in the second set of free elections across Central and Eastern Europe in the early 1990s suggests that a slow-motion – and largely non-violent – 1849 has been taking place in any case. The People weary of political involvement very quickly. The absence of organisation in the revolutions of 1989 is striking – only Solidarity in Poland was an exception to the rule that local dissidents had no levers to move society. Most dissidents were better known to readers of the *New York Review of Books* than to the man on the Prague metro or the Leipzig tram.

The real question about 1989 is why did the Communist regimes' battalions of secret policemen, soldiers and workers' militias fail to fire a shot? What went wrong with the party's 'sword and shield' this time? More important still, why did the Kremlin renounce its empire so passively and open the way for its rival of decades, NATO, to advance its socio-economic system and probably its military power into the region? Why did the Soviet elite let Central Europe go? Even in 1989, the force required to stifle popular protest would not have been so great. After all, General Jaruzelski's most potent weapon in 1981 against Solidarity had been water-cannon. Eight years later the disgruntled in East Germany lacked weapons to reply to any assault on the demonstrations which spread across the country.

This leads us back to a more basic question: Was the process of reform started by Gorbachev in 1985 really necessary? Could an alternative Soviet leadership have adopted fundamentally different policies in the mid-1980s, or was there no way out? Only a very crude determinism would insist that Gorbachev happened because Gorbachev had to happen. Even a different approach by Gorbachev himself could have had significantly different results. More than a decade after the start of *glasnost* and *perestroika* it is very difficult to recall how different the academic and establishment consensus was about the Soviet system before Gorbachev's lifting of the veil of censorship confronted Western scholars and analysts with their own delusions and self-censorship about the Soviet Union's social problems and incapacity to meet consumer demands. Yet if Gorbachev had been the cynical manipulator of public opinion that some Westerners at first feared – before meeting Gorbachev, Chancellor Kohl compared his skills as a propagandist with those of Goebbels – those local problems could well have remained disguised from most policy- and opinion-makers in the West. The very fact that ardent Reaganite Cold Warriors drew attention to them disqualified their importance in the eyes of 'reasonable' scholars and statesmen. By contrast, experts like Severyn Bialer had assured a mass readership in *Time* magazine in 1980 that the Soviet Union was the first state to be able to supply 'guns and butter' simultaneously, elevating the standard of living and achieving military parity with the West.[2] In 1984, with all his authority as an economist, J. Kenneth Galbraith assured the West that labour productivity per person was higher in the USSR than in America. A year later, the sociologist David Lane argued:

> If legitimacy is viewed in terms of psychological commitment on the part of the citizen ..., then the Soviet system is as 'legitimate' as Western ones. It has to be understood from the standpoint of its own history, culture and traditions. 'Real' democracy does not exist in the real world. Support for the Soviet regime has increased. It is no longer held together by coercion ... One should not expect very radical change from Gorbachev or any Soviet leader ... It is a united government: decisions are not questioned – in public ... It is an accepted government: its process and structures are legitimate in the sense of being 'taken for granted by the masses'. *Organized political dissent has little public salience: it is comparable to that of the communists in Britain or the USA.*[3]

As late as 1990, the distinguished US Sovietologist Jerry Hough could dismiss the notion of 'the Soviet Union becoming ungovernable'. This was, he argued, merely:

> a judgement which reflected the novelty of the political developments of 1989, not a sober assessment of the evidence ... Least of all should it have been assumed that the country was about to fly apart. Americans have had little experience with ethnic unrest based on linguistic demands, and they have grossly overreacted to what they have seen in the Soviet Union.... From a comparative perspective the Soviet Union looks like one of the more stable multinational countries ... The turmoil of 1989 served Gorbachev well.... The turmoil also served Gorbachev well economically.[4]

The point of quoting such sentiments is not that they were insightful – they were not – but that they represented a common operating code of those supposedly in the know in the West.

One answer to the question why the Communists failed to crack down is that the party had lost its own sense of legitimacy. This is indeed true, but who had disillusioned the party members? Certainly not the few cowed dissidents. Nor was it novel for the bulk of the party's millions of members to be careerists and sunshine Communists: they were always that way, in Central Europe at least. No, it was the high priest of Communism who was to blame (or praise) for paralysing the Communists' will to assert their power. Gorbachev's *glasnost* and *perestroika* caused the collapse of Communism. As is evident elsewhere around the world where other Communist leaders were not naive enough to try to reinvigorate the revolution like Gorbachev, the *nomenklatura* state survives. Of course, in Cuba or North Korea, the people are impoverished and not a few are desperate enough to risk fleeing abroad despite trigger-happy border-guards and sharks; but that has not shaken the system. For poverty and immobility are its secrets of survival, not the causes of its downfall. The real mystery is why Gorbachev threw away a patent on power tried and tested in so many different states across the globe.

The End of Ideology – and of the Ideologists

At one level, it is clear that Gorbachev's actions led the bulk of the Communist party to lose faith in itself; but the use of religious analogies to explain why the Communists gave up the ghost is misleading. The Communist party after all was not a hippy cult based on a charismatic leader appealing to a few psychologically vulnerable types. It was a bureaucracy of millions of mediocrities, many of them armed. Nevertheless, even the most self-interested clique needs some ideological cement to hold it together, however cynical the calculations of interest underlying it may be.

Endorsing the end of ideology was Gorbachev's big mistake. So long as this was a Western slogan promoting the ideological disarmament of Western intellectuals, talk about 'convergence' was very useful to the Kremlin, but actually to promote it was suicidal. Yet Gorbachev made it a keynote of his rhetoric. Noting the recent seventieth anniversary of the Bolshevik Revolution and the forthcoming celebrations of 200 years since the storming of the Bastille, he told the UN in December 1988:

> To a large extent, those two revolutions shaped the way of thinking that is still prevalent in social consciousness.... But today we face a different world, for which we must set a different road to the future.... We have entered an era when progress will be shaped by *universal human interests....* World politics too should be guided by universal human values.[5]

In fact, insulation from Western contacts was essential to the stability of the system. Believing that it had to compete on Western terms and yet trying to retain something of its manipulative past, Gorbachev and the KGB blundered into a series of disastrous moves which upset the stability of stagnation without offering any prospects of real gain. Lenin of course had often argued that retreat to a better position was the best route to follow for revolutionaries under pressure, but the pressure on Gorbachev was increasingly self-inflicted. Apathy, such as was commonplace in the USSR, may be frustrating for a government – but it is rarely fatal.

Nobody should doubt that the real impetus for change in 1989 came from within the system, especially from the secret police. Gorbachev's connections with the KGB are well documented and his favoured reformers throughout Eastern Europe were linked either directly to it or indirectly via their countries' own security police. Iliescu in Romania, for instance, had apparently been recruited by the KGB during his years of study in Moscow in the 1950s, though he vehemently denies meeting Gorbachev then. Another reform Communist leader who knew Gorbachev in those days was Hans Modrow, the last Communist Prime Minister of the German Democratic Republic and a close friend of Markus Wolf, the Stasi's shadowy reformer-in-chief. Moreover, it is now clear that the key events in Prague on 17 November 1989 involved a classic *Provokation*. Since the dissidents were not capable of stirring up the necessary discontent to persuade the party's leaders to change, the secret police (StB) had to organise the protest itself. Of course, the many students who took part in the demonstration (recalling an anti-Nazi protest fifty years earlier) were moved to take part by the events in neighbouring East Germany. But the key event, the so-called 'Massacre', was staged. The dead student, Martin Schmid, turned out to be alive and well and a serving undercover officer of the StB. His 'beating to death' was the spark for further mass protests and the downfall of the hardliners in Prague.

Multi-party democracy, however, is difficult to manipulate. That is why Stalin had preferred 'people's democracy', in which all the parties accepted the 'leading role' of the Communists, even where nominally separate parties existed as they did in Poland and East Germany. In 1989, however, these 'front parties' came to life like Pinocchio when suddenly they were given a real role to play.

Indeed, in conditions of multi-party elections their previously supine leaders had every reason to play an independent role to distance themselves from the unpopular Communists. From the first multi-candidate elections in the Soviet Union itself in March 1989, via the Polish elections in June, to the next year's flurry of contested polls, the same phenomenon was repeated. Everywhere they were allowed, people took the opportunity to vote against the Communists. A few years later, they might be disillusioned with the failure of the non-Communists to solve their problems; but in the first flush of freedom, even when granted from above, they liked to deliver a negative verdict on decades of undemocratic rule.

By mid-autumn 1989 it was already clear that the mere removal of Honecker and his closest associates would not calm East Germans' newly aroused civic courage. The scale of demonstrations grew across the country as the regime made concession after concession. Far from introducing a viable reform-Communist regime, the fall of Honecker emboldened the people for a final push to open the Wall and abolish the state altogether. As the process of reform threatened to unravel the schemes of the Wolf–Modrow group to implement a pseudo-democratisation, Modrow looked around for ways to bring to the front rank of the political process other reform-Communists with Stasi links. The lawyer and informer Gregor Gysi was one of them. On 21 November 1989 Modrow told Stasi leaders: 'Gysi belongs to the smart brains [*klugen Köpfen*], who are waiting to be mobilised.'[6]

Unfortunately, the 'smart brains' bit off more than they could chew, at least in East Germany. Once the regime faltered and started to play at real politics, then all the powers of simulation and manipulation routinely used by Communists lost their force, not least because Gorbachev and Wolf underestimated the dual attraction of nationalism and the Deutsche Mark to East Germans. Too clever for their own good, the would-be manipulators of democratisation were overtaken by events. A shrewd old fox like Brezhnev would never have been naive or overconfident enough to think that the KGB's experts could let the people off the leash and still keep them dancing to its tune. It takes a very special kind of political cleverness to juggle with the fate of empires – and then drop all the balls.

To be fair to Gorbachev, much of his miscalculation was due to his limited contacts with reality. Kept insulated from Soviet reality by the protocol and privilege surrounding the high priest of the *nomenklatura* (which his palatial dacha at Foros on the Crimea symbolised), his contacts with Western leaders can hardly have encouraged much self-doubt. Lauded and lionised by them, Gorbachev believed his own propaganda – a mistake which his predecessors (so often dismissed as senile over-promoted peasants) never made. After generations of dullard apparatchiks had safely guided the Soviet Union to super-power status, it was the bright-eyed Gorbachev who grabbed the steering-wheel and headed straight for the rocks.

The Politics of Economic Crisis

Part of the explanation thus seems to have been Gorbachev's own idealism. But no pure idealist ever rose to the top of the Politburo. Gorbachev's oft-proclaimed Soviet patriotism was not just an expression of genuine socialist commitment but also a reflection of his belief that the USSR had to continue to play a super-power role. It was his wishful thinking that the Soviet Union could compete with the USA in technological prowess that led him to change the tried-and-trusted structures of domestic power inherited from Stalin. Contrary to Western Marxoid academics who insist on the primacy of domestic policy as the basic factor in politics, it was the Kremlin elite's obsession with international status which led Gorbachev to decry stagnation at home as a threat to the system. He was supported by a gamut of advisers and experts from the KGB who had access to secret intelligence about how advanced the West was in its technological lead over the USSR, but who failed to see that it would be decades before any conceivable US government might seek to use its power directly against the Soviet Union. On the contrary, the West was happy to see the Soviet Union and its system survive in a non-threatening form.

Ironically, by breaking with stagnation, Gorbachev threw away the Soviet Union's best chance of shifting the balance of power decisively to its advantage while doing little or nothing active itself. His fevered efforts to reform the Soviet economy actually disrupted and distorted its structure and made matters much worse than the legacy inherited from Brezhnevism.[7]

Was even the GDR bankrupt in 1989? The short answer is 'Yes'; but only from a capitalist perspective. Of course, in a profit-and-loss sense, East Germany had been going down the drain for years. Its efforts to obtain hard currency to service its Western debts were becoming ever more frantic, but the real pressure to satisfy the Western bankers came not from the gnomes of Zurich or the Dresdner Bank, but from the Kremlin. East Germany had little difficulty raising fresh loans from the West.[8] Keynes famously noted that if a debtor owed a bank one thousand pounds and fell into difficulties repaying, the debtor had a problem. But if the debtor owed the bank a million pounds and could not pay, then it was the bank which needed to worry. Imagine if East Berlin had adopted a 'can't pay, won't pay' attitude to its hard currency debt: would the Western banks have sent in the bailiffs? Rescheduling and new loans would of course have been the likely response, or at worst a writing-off of the debts. In fact, it was from the East that economic pressure was felt. Gorbachev wanted to stop the decades of generous subsidy to the Soviet Union's 'little brothers'. After the first OPEC oil-price shock in 1973, the Soviet Union had adjusted its energy prices to the East bloc but still left them paying well below world prices.[9] The difficulties which the East European states faced adjusting to these price increases were negligible compared with those likely to result from full market pricing for inter-bloc trade. The collapse of much industry and other sectors of the economy across the ex-Communist bloc after 1989 illustrates much of what would have happened to these economies under Gorbachev's proposed reforms if they had been carried through.

Poland and Hungary stand out from the other Warsaw Pact states because they had already attempted several liberalising economic reforms before 1989. After 1989, their paths diverged quite markedly. Poland pursued the most radical form of shock therapy (even if it was less all-encompassing than many of its admirers admitted or noticed), while Hungary remained relatively slow to privatise. Before the election of the Solidarity-led government in the summer of 1989, Poland's economy had remained obdurately resistant to stimuli, though Jaruzelski and his ministers offered various incentives to cooperative and *de facto* small-scale private enterprise. Clearly political reform was needed to unleash Polish entrepreneurship, though those who were the first to jump into the market tended to be Communists with accumulated black-market capital and good connections. As Lech Walesa told an audience in Buffalo, USA, on 23 October 1994:

> The communists are the best capitalists today and they will defend capitalism like nobody before. We, of course, do not like it, it is a bit immoral, because now these particular people should be building capitalism and stand in the avant garde. But they are more efficient and more active. We cannot stop them, we must survive this.[10]

The massive indebtedness of Hungary did not, however, disappear with the election of a non-Communist government in 1990. Nor yet did it vanish with the return to power of the Hungarian reform-Communists in 1994. A *per capita* burden greater than that of Mexico still weighs down on the Hungarian economy, making privatisation of the few profitable parts of the state sector difficult for a government anxious to service the debt above all else. Nevertheless, Hungary has survived.

The markets expected the Soviet Union to survive too. Although the market in capitalism cannot be resisted, it can and does make mistakes. Unfortunately, to misquote Radek on the party's claim to infallibility, it is always more profitable to be wrong with the market than right against it. Certainly, as late as

1988, the Kremlin's first issue of Eurobonds (to mature at a tight 5 per cent ten years later) was oversubscribed by the world's capitalists. The Swiss regulators waived the normal requirement for a state issuing bonds to reveal its debt obligations and foreign exchange reserves, so confident were they of their new business partner.[11] It was the Soviet leadership which precipitated the crisis of confidence among Western lenders and potential aid-donors by unleashing destabilising political change.

Gorbachev and his Prime Minister Ryzhkov had insisted that the Comecon states move from a situation in which they were subsidised by cheap energy and raw material imports from the Soviet Union to a hard-currency settlement system for transactions between the fraternal states. Until July 1989, the other members of Comecon had taken advantage of the mysteries of payments through the transferable rouble system to avoid or conjure away unpleasant trade imbalances. Then with breakneck speed, the Soviet leaders decided to force through the replacement of the transferable rouble with the dollar as the currency of accounting between Comecon members. The speed and brutality of the changeover threatened economic catastrophe for the Warsaw Pact states. In practice, their political systems collapsed before the full impact of the market transitions demanded by the Kremlin became apparent. They were to be borne by the newly elected democratic governments.

Was this necessary? Again from a crude market point of view, naturally it made sense. Subsidising the fraternal republics had depressed the standard of living of the Soviet people. But its purpose was after all not social, nor even economic, but political. The East European states had been tied to the Soviet Union by virtue of their economic dependence as well as its military dominance. Their poverty was in fact a function of the viability of Soviet dominance. If the fraternal republics became market-orientated states paying world prices for their raw materials and fuel, there was no obvious reason why they should buy them from the Soviet Union. Many economic reasons suggested a reorientation to Western suppliers.

Attempts to reform the economics of the Soviet bloc were thus deeply destabilising to its political existence. Gorbachev resented the resistance of the old Soviet stooges in Eastern Europe to his changes, though in fact Honecker and Ceausescu showed more wisdom than the upstart from Stavropol about what kept Communism in being. Gorbachev, needless to say, was offended by the presumption of the leaders of the little fraternal states, that because they had been active Communists since he was in short trousers, they knew best. Ironically, Gorbachev was most dogmatic about asserting his rights as the lineal heir of Lenin and Stalin and the true interpreter of Marxism–Leninism only when he was bulldozing their heritage.

By August 1991 Gorbachev's clique had encouraged such a disintegration of authority that when some of his comrades tried to call a halt to the slide to chaos it was too late. Gorbachev's own naivety was revealed by his behaviour on his return from captivity. Instead of trying to rescue his own position from the wreckage by a cynical attack on the prostrate Communist party as many expected, the Louis XVI of Soviet Communism still talked about the party's role in regenerating society. His embarrassing comments were proof of how out of touch with reality he was. Only in the West was he taken seriously.

Perestroika accelerated the decay of the Soviet Union's infrastructure. Far from enhancing the Soviet economy's ability to compete in high-tech goods, the effect of Gorbachev's 'katastroika' was to undermine even those areas of the economy in which the Soviet state could still muddle along in its own way. The energy and raw-material base of the old Soviet economy has been woefully mismanaged, squandered and simply stolen since 1985. The rupture of oil and natural gas pipelines – with concomitant human and ecological casualties – has become commonplace in recent years. Even the old Soviet system was not so careless. (It is true that Stalin was indifferent to the human cost of his projects, but he did not like waste of material resources. Only with the decay of discipline did the neglect of infrastructure take on catastrophic proportions.)

Particularly since 1991, the exploitation of the Soviet Union's stockpile of raw materials (such as non-ferrous metals) and its oil and natural gas resources has taken on a frenzied character as erstwhile state managers line their pockets and pay off their political masters in an unprecedented spree of asset-stripping. The effect has been to drive down world market prices for these goods further and to undermine the state's viability, as the same new capitalist entrepreneurs have little time for filing tax returns. The unsteady tax base of the new post-Soviet states must call into question their viability especially as these assets are irreplaceable. Although it is commonplace to compare the current phase of asset-stripping capitalism in the ex-Soviet Union with the so-called 'robber baron' period in the USA a century ago, in fact a stark contrast exists between today's bargain basement sale of the ex-Soviet Union's assets and the ruthless construction of pipelines, railroads and steel mills by the Rockefellers and Carnegies of the late nineteenth century. In effect, many post-Soviet traders in raw materials are busy sawing off the economic branch upon which they are sitting.

Perestroika and 'shock therapy' have so far only destroyed the asset-base and infrastructure of the Soviet Union. Whether they have produced much material benefit for the population remains debatable. But, unlike the economy of poverty produced by the Stalinist economic model, the reformed version does not even produce the sinews of power. Stagnation may not be a desirable model, but it served the Soviet Union better than *perestroika*. In retrospect, its mortality was exaggerated. As a system for producing the wherewithal of political and military power it still served. Certainly, its long-term ability to compete with the West at the high-tech end of weaponry was questionable; but the West was not likely to test the defences of the USSR even in the medium term. In any case, a state-controlled export of raw materials and fuel would have provided the funds for the continuation of the Soviet Union's traditional practice of illicit purchase of technology, as well as consumer goodies for the *nomenklatura*. If $17 billion can nowadays flow out annually into Western bank accounts and real estate never to return, a less dramatic sell-off of moveable assets could have funded a lot of stabilising measures inside the USSR.

Far from objective economic criteria forcing the collapse of the Soviet Union, it was the false intellectual analysis and expectations of the Soviet elite which were responsible. No doubt Gorbymania in the West encouraged hubris on the part of the General Secretary: if the capitalists were so impressed surely the *muzhiki* down on the collective farm would be won over too!

How would the West have reacted to a Crackdown?

The West's subsequent relations with China after the Tiananmen Square events in 1989 or the West's reactions to the collapse of Yugoslavia and the Russian invasion of Chechnya suggest that the preservation of the Soviet bloc would not have caused too much regret among the bulk of the political establishment in Europe or America.

As President Bush showed in his infamous 'Chicken Kiev' speech to the Ukrainian Supreme Soviet in the summer of 1991, the United States did not want the Soviet empire to disappear. Referring to the 'Soviet nation', to the bemusement of even Communist Ukrainian deputies, Bush intoned against the threat posed to Gorbachev's empire by 'suicidal nationalism'. At the same time of course, his Secretary of State, James Baker III, was regularly announcing that the USA would never recognise secessionist Slovenia or Croatia. Bush, it might be said, was the Metternich of the end of Communism. Like his predecessor in the nineteenth century, he struggled manfully to preserve an old order under democratic and nationalist assault and, like Metternich, he failed.[12]

Early in his presidency, Bush made clear that gunning down anti-Communist demonstrators would not affect his international policy. He sent two of his closest advisers, Lawrence Eagleburger and Brent Scowcroft, to Beijing in July 1989 to reassure the Communist gerontocrats that the disorders in Tiananmen Square need not damage US–Chinese trade and security relations. (Eagle-burger and Scowcroft were also two of the loudest voices backing Belgrade's 'federal' case in the Yugoslav conflict.) Since then, Bush's successor, Clinton, has ended the hypocrisy of linking China's Most Favoured Nation-status to its human rights record. Now China is free to flood US markets with goods from its own *gulag* without the annual pretence that it might lose this right. If elderly Chinese mass murderers could get away with their well-publicised actions in June 1989, would the West really have taken mortal offence at a few bullets whistling around East Berlin or Leipzig? (As an example of the complicity between the White House and hardliners, it is worth recalling that, when Iraq seized Kuwait in August 1990, Bush expected Chinese support for UN sanctions 'since he had tempered his criticism of the previous year's slaughter of students in Tiananmen Square'.)[13]

Apart from Thatcher's Britain – and policy changed under Major – Bush's European allies were equally prepared to see the Cold War order maintained across Europe. In October 1989, Kohl's supposedly closest ally, François Mitterrand, was still insisting: 'Those who talk about German reunification understand nothing. The Soviet Union would never accept that. That would be the death of the Warsaw Pact. Can you imagine that? The GDR is Prussia. It will never accept the yoke of Bavaria.' Even after Kohl's cautious opening to reunification on 27 November, eighteen days after the opening of the Wall, the French President still looked to the Kremlin to halt the tide of German unity: 'Gorbachev will be furious. He won't accept that. Impossible! I don't need to oppose it myself, the Soviets will do it for me. They will never accept a great Germany . . .'[14] Mitterrand was equally hostile to Gorbachev's opponents. His regime was still reluctant to receive Yeltsin in April 1991. The President of the Russian Federation was subject to a dressing-down by Jean-Pierre Cot when he visited the European Parliament, whose President, Baron Crespo, assured him, 'we prefer Gorbachev'. This was of course shortly after the massacre of unarmed Lithuanians at the television tower in Vilnius, and not so long after Soviet troops killed scores of people in Baku. At the time of the anti-Gorbachev coup in August 1991, Mitterrand assured French television viewers, 'The putsch has succeeded in its first phase.' He went on to refer to the 'new Soviet authorities'.[15] (Of course, later on, when Yeltsin was the boss sending in the tanks to attack the Russian Parliament or Chechnya, he became the object of Western concern, anxious that moralising reactions should not weaken his position.)

Alongside Mitterrand, other European heads of government would have been only too happy to see the Soviet Union hinder German reunification by force if necessary. For instance, the Italian Prime Minister, Giulio Andreotti, was opposed to reunification and advocated using tanks on the streets ('sometimes they are necessary') to crush anti-Soviet demonstrations in Vilnius and elsewhere – as might have been expected from a proud honorary doctor of Beijing University and an alleged 'man of honour'. Only Margaret Thatcher showed any democratic principles, regretting reunification but welcoming the fall of the Wall and the tyranny which it symbolised.[16]

Chancellor Kohl would have found a Tiananmen Square-style massacre on his doorstep awkward to handle, but no doubt his opponents would have been hamstrung by the propaganda argument that the East German demonstrators were endangering detente and awakening neo-Nazi nostalgia for a reunited Germany. Kohl would have made do with bluster before trying to rebuild his fences with the East. Certainly, the Social Democrats and the West German intellectual elite would have backed any attempt to leave the Leipzig demonstrators to bury their own dead while the sacred rites of renewed detente went on. After all, the West German Social Democrats refused to support an attempt by East Germans to form their own (illegal) Social Democratic party as late as 1989. Instead they carefully cultivated their round of joint papers and conferences with the 'comrades' in East Berlin.

In West Germany, no serious political force agitated for reunification. The Greens were against it. The Social Democrats no longer even paid lip-service to the ideal. The Free Democrats ignored the question. Their coalition partners, the Christian

Democrats, prided themselves on their scoop in enticing Erich Honecker to visit the Federal Republic in September 1987, something which Brandt and Schmidt had never managed, or dared, to do. Even Axel Springer's newspaper, *Die Welt*, gave up its lonely refusal to recognise the existence of the German Democratic Republic – with impeccable timing – in the summer of 1989, when it finally dropped the obligatory inverted commas which had always surrounded any mention of the 'DDR' (German Democratic Republic) before. Whoever was working for German reunification, it was not the West.[17]

Apart from anything else, West Germany was a thoroughly 'penetrated' society. Agents of Markus Wolf's Stasi intelligence were everywhere in Bonn, but also in key centres of West German economy and culture. From secretaries in the Chancellor's official bungalow to opinion-makers in the media, the Stasi had its eyes, ears and, when necessary, lips. It would take a book as long as the Bonn telephone directory to list all of the *Stasi*'s contacts in the Federal Republic, but a few are worth recalling. A bug had been placed in the bedside telephone of Manfred Wörner, West German Defence Minister, then NATO Secretary-General. At the beginning of the 1980s, West German politics was rocked by the Flick scandal when it was discovered that hosts of leading German politicians across the spectrum had been receiving cash payments from the Flick concern; a central figure in the distribution of this cash was Adolf Kanter, a CDU member who also worked for the Stasi.[18]

As late as September 1989, Willy Brandt was dismissive of reunification as the 'Lebenslüge' ('living lie') of the Federal Republic. In January 1989, the new mayor of West Berlin, Walter Momper, announced that the question of reunification was dead. In private conversations with East German officials, Momper argued that the most objectionable aspect of the Wall for West Berliners was the regulation forbidding them to bring their pet dogs with them on a visit to the 'capital city of the German Democratic Republic'. Ever obliging, Comrade Honecker changed the rules to remove this egregiously offensive aspect of his 'anti-fascist protection barrier'. A month later, the last victim of the Wall, Chris Gueffroy, was shot down – like a dog – by Honecker's border-guards.[19]

Ingrained anti-Polish feelings among the Germans were commonplace on left as well as right. Brandt refused to meet Walesa in 1985 (though he invited the Communist Polish Premier, Rakowski, to his birthday party). Germany's Chancellor Kohl was thoroughly antagonistic towards any kind of popular Polish movement which might challenge the stability which had allowed West Germans to grow fat in security. Kohl told Mitterrand, in March 1985: 'We will have to help Jaruzelski. Anything that came after him would be worse. The Poles have always had eyes bigger than their stomachs and ambitions beyond their means.'[20]

If it is true that already in 1987 Gorbachev and Shevardnadze were envisaging reunification on the grounds that 'without the resolution of the German question' no normal relations could be created in Europe, then Gorbachev was actually opening a door which the vast majority of the West German establishment wished to leave firmly shut.[21] Although Kohl was happy to grab unity in 1990 when it was offered on a plate by Gorbachev, even he had long since reconciled himself to its unachievability.

As a politician Kohl lays great emphasis on personal empathy and contact with his negotiating partners. Apart from his physical bulk he is quite unlike the first unifier of Germany: Bismarck would never have shared Kohl's petit-bourgeois sentimentality about foreign statesmen. It is impossible to imagine a Bismarck (or an Adenauer) reacting with unfeigned personal sympathy to a foreign leader's domestic crisis as Kohl did after Yeltsin unleashed his armed forces against Chechnya in December 1994. Then Kohl told the Bundestag: 'I'm proud that I was able to build a friendly relationship with Yeltsin. *What a pitiful sort of man I would be if one of my friends had difficulties and I refused to support him....* Even if Yeltsin has made mistakes, I will not write him off now.'[22] Would the 'Gorby' who aroused so much West German hysteria during his visit in June 1989 have been completely decried if Honecker's troops had beaten down the opposition a few months later? Surely Gorbachev could have arranged to be 'asleep' then, as he was whenever Soviet troops clamped down in his own empire? (It is odd that Ronald Reagan's somnolence during moments of crisis was taken as a sign of unfitness for office, but Gorbachev's jet-lag on 9 April 1989, when his special forces were killing people in Tbilisi, was yet further proof of his saintliness.) And, if Gorbachev had found himself in 'difficulties' with recalcitrant subjects, would Kohl have denied him the support he lent when Boris Yeltsin sent in the tanks and strategic bombers in December 1994? It is only necessary to recall the reaction of joy elsewhere in the West when Yeltsin unleashed a ferocious bombardment against his elected, if left-wing, rivals in the Russian Parliament in October 1993. Immediately after the bombardment, Clinton telephoned Yeltsin and gushed: 'You get stronger and better.'[23]

Russians themselves noted the rapidity with which Westerners took up the idea that only authoritarian reform could work in their sort of society. When the farcical coup against Gorbachev took place in August 1991, the Russian deputy, Galina Starovoitova, was in Britain. As she noted, 'The reaction of Mitterrand and Kohl and of the entire West on the first day was very temporizing. And I was told at the beginning of the coup – but not by Mrs Thatcher – that we should wait and see if the Soviet people accepted this junta.' Staravoitova got the impression that Western leaders could not imagine a democratised Russia, let alone a disintegrated USSR:

> They also desire a strong hand for us. Western businessmen and politicians bring up the example of the Chinese events: Yes, they say, the Chinese leaders suppressed democracy with tanks, but their economy is now developing normally, and that will almost automatically lead to democracy. The West, they claim, needs stability. It is afraid of the collapse of the [Soviet] empire.[24]

With the exception of Reagan and Thatcher, the Western political establishment was not composed of ideological anti-

Communists. Quite the contrary. By 1989, Reagan was out of office. Without Gorbachev's sympathetic handling of her pre-election visit to Moscow in 1987, perhaps Mrs Thatcher would also not have survived until 1990. She might have given way to Neil Kinnock, who was still anxious to deal 'secretly if necessary' with Egon Krenz, Erich Honecker's successor as Communist leader in East Germany, in November 1989, or some more emollient classic Conservative from the Chamberlainesque wing of the Tory party (as happened later).[25]

The Final Oil Shock

A key component in the Soviet crisis was the collapse in oil prices. Gorbachev's foreign policy soothed nerves and encouraged a fall in oil prices. In turn, however, the USSR's oil revenues slumped. This was the opposite policy to what Soviet Great Power interests required – and ignored the possibilities offered by the circumstances of the late 1980s.

Consider the following scenario: What if Saddam Hussein had invaded Kuwait in 1990 with the tacit consent of a nuclear-armed and still hawkish Kremlin? It was difficult enough to get General Colin Powell to support a conventional war against Iraq when Gorbachev backed UN sanctions against Baghdad. Would Washington have risked nuclear war to save the Al-Sabah dynasty from enforced retirement to its villas in the West?[26] Even if the United States had sustained its military spending after Reagan's second term came to an end in 1988, would Bush (or Dukakis) have risked nuclear holocaust to stop Saddam exercising control over the lion's share of Mid-Eastern oil reserves? It is highly unlikely. Remember how close was the actual Senate vote to endorse Operation Desert Storm in January 1991. Under less favourable strategic conditions, prophets of doom like Senator Edward Kennedy would surely have carried at least the three more votes necessary to stick with sanctions.[27] What would Saddam's strategic arsenal of nuclear and biochemical weapons have consisted of by now if that had been US policy?

Even this prognosis may understate the implications of such an alternative scenario. What if eight years of trillion-dollar deficits under Reagan had not produced a major shift in Soviet policy towards disarmament? In fact, the Soviet military–industrial complex could have trundled along for the rest of the 1980s wasting resources on tanks and SS-20s – as we have seen, the post-Soviet capital outflows suggest that ample raw materials were still available, which have since been converted into cash in Western bank accounts. It seems hardly credible that the US public would have endorsed Bush or another Republican as the successor to Reagan if both federal and trade deficits were spiralling upwards without any geopolitical gains to offset them in public opinion terms. Perhaps by mid-summer 1990, the US military would have been well into a post-Reagan round of defence cuts. It could not have risked moving large numbers of troops, tanks and aircraft from West Germany to the Gulf (as it did in 1990) because of the continuing Soviet threat. In all probability, the US military would not have had the reserves to fight Saddam and guard NATO simultaneously. The arguments against Israeli involvement would have been at least as powerful as they were in reality in 1991. Who would have wanted to risk a general war against the Arabs too?

The Gulf War could have been spun out. The resulting high energy prices would have stabilised the Soviet economy. Quite probably some Western oil companies would have come cap in hand to the Kremlin to let them set up joint ventures in the Caspian or Kazakhstan to exploit the Soviet Union's fabled reserves of oil and natural gas. To avoid Saddam's stranglehold on Middle Eastern oil, the West might have had to pay generous Danegeld to Moscow for its supplies – and even to provide the pipeline technology. After all, despite American protests as a result of the declaration of martial law in Poland in 1981, the Germans had locked themselves into deals to import natural gas from Siberia via Poland along a pipeline laid by Komsomol volunteers and other less willing labour. Why shouldn't oil have come the same way? Who would have refused such a chance to build cooperation in Europe and sidestep the tensions in the Middle East?[28]

Naturally, ordinary Soviet citizens would have been badly off, even worse off with life expectancy declining. But reform since 1985 or 1991 has hardly benefited them and they show little sign of revolting. Higher revenues would at least have enabled the Kremlin to satisfy the yearning for Western consumer goods of the elite. The several million members of the *nomenklatura* could have received access to brand-new videos, microwaves and cars from the West. They could even have received a few more stylish clothes. Better brands of alcohol – which the puritanical Gorbachev tried to ban altogether from party receptions – could have graced every state dacha in the Socialist Commonwealth. In fact, a neo-Stalinist regime would have been more viable economically precisely *because* of the increased tension around the world which its existence would have fostered. Oil, gas and gold prices would have soared, bolstering the USSR's foreign exchange revenues. In turn, economic and technical espionage as well as subsidies to the fraternal states would have been easier to fund.[29]

Gorbachev's belief that a relaxation in tension was in the Soviet Union's interest was profoundly misplaced. Only the 'two camps' division of the world provided the kind of global scenario in which such a strange animal as the Soviet economy could function. Once the external pressures – self-generated as they may have been – were removed, the Soviet metabolism was fatally infected.

Gorbachev went further and actually relaxed the pressure on the Western elite at a time in the mid-1980s when unilateralism was rampant among Western opinion-makers and in universities. The next generation of the Western establishment was subject to daily doses of anti-Reaganite and anti-Thatcherite thinking. The long march through the institutions of post-1960s pacifism and fellow travelling combined with nuclear panic was just about to reach its goal. It was only the surprising and total collapse of Communism under the impact of internal changes which brought much of the Western intelligentsia to admit that the Right had been correct in much of its analysis of 'real existing socialism'. Had the Wall stayed up, much of the Western elite would have remained oblivious to Communism's failings, moral as much as material, for at least another generation.

The survival of Soviet Communism into the 1990s would have coincided with renewed economic downturn in the West at the end of the 1980s as well as a possible triumph of Saddam Hussein during those years. Western success in reality was predicated on the Soviet system's sudden impotence and then demise. Had the Soviet Union preserved the façade of power which had so fascinated and beguiled Western policy-makers for so long, what mischief could the Kremlin not have worked in that time – and who can be confident that it would not have succeeded?

The disappearance of a corrupt and brutal system which stultified the lives of hundreds of millions is a cause of rejoicing. But its collapse was not foreordained by the hidden hand which controls history's economic forces. It was a much closer run thing than the textbooks allow. No doubt it is better that Communism's hold over much of the world is gone; but had it turned nasty, even as late as in Leipzig in October 1989, at least one group would have rejoiced in the West. If the Soviet system had survived, sundry Sovietologists and historians would have been able to say, for once truthfully: 'We told you so.'

AFTERWORD:

A Virtual History, 1646–1996

Niall Ferguson

As we approach the 300th anniversary of the accession of James III in September 1701, it is all too easy to be complacent about the subsequent course of modern history. Viewing the past, as we do, through the distorting lens of hindsight, we are often tempted to assume that there was something inevitable about the Stuarts' success in withstanding the religious and political storms which caused so much upheaval in the rest of Europe during the seventeenth century. The world we know today may be said to owe much to James III, and perhaps more to his grandfather Charles I. But it is the great error of historical determinisn to imagine that their achievements were in any sense predestined. We should never underestimate the role of contingency, of chance – of what the mathematicians call 'stochastic behaviour'.

If, for example, we look back further, to the victory of James's grandfather Charles I over the Scottish Covenanters at the battle of Duns Law in June 1639, we can see clearly the contingent nature of the Stuart triumph. With the benefit of hindsight and historical research, we know that Charles's army was larger and better funded than the Scottish forces which faced it across the Tweed. And we know that the King's victory at Duns Law dealt a death blow not only to the Covenanters but to the Scottish Parliament and Kirk. Yet none of this was as clear to Charles's commanders as it is to us now. The Earl of Holland, as John Adamson points out, was strongly tempted to retreat when first confronted by the Scottish forces under Leslie.

Of course, there are those historians who see no point in asking counterfactual questions. But let us venture to do so. What if Charles *had* backed down at the critical moment and sought some kind of settlement with the Scots? Under these circumstances, it seems clear that he would very quickly have found himself in the most acute political crisis to face the crown in over a century. Not only would he have been at the mercy of a militant kirk and a recalcitrant Edinburgh parliament. He would also have played directly into the hands of his opponents in England and Ireland.

With the benefit of hindsight we know, of course, that most of the old Puritans who had caused so much trouble in the reign of Charles's father were to die out in the course of the 1640s. We know that the judges who had opposed Charles's financial policies in the 1630s were also in their seventies. But had Charles returned to England without a victory in 1639 – and had he (as it seems reasonable to assume) demoted those who had been responsible for the expedition – there might yet have been time for one last offensive by that ageing generation. Fears of a 'Popish plot' were much exaggerated, as we know, and soon faded as the Thirty Years' War drew to its close in 1648. But such fears were at their peak in 1639–40 – a time when a Catholic victory on the continent still seemed a real possibility. Moreover, the lawyers who had opposed Charles over his raising of ship money would have seized the opportunity of a retreat from Scotland to reiterate their arguments against the raising of revenue without parliamentary consent. Even if not a single shot had been fired, the expedition to Scotland would still have cost more than the Exchequer had anticipated. True, if Charles had still been able to rely on the City of London to advance him the additional costs of his abortive expedition, there would have been only limited cause for anxiety. Then again, failure in Scotland might also have precipitated a crisis in Charles's relations with the City. That would have left him with only one option: to recall Parliament and abandon Personal Rule.

For anyone who subscribes to a determinist theory of history, it is almost impossible to imagine what the consequences of such a climb-down might have been. We are so used to the idea of the Stuart victory over the forces of Puritanism and Coke's legal conservatism that any other outcome seems inconceivable. Yet it was far from being inevitable that Charles would emerge from the Scottish crisis victorious and go on to reign for a further twenty years, presiding over that era of tolerance at home and peace abroad which we have come to associate with his name. On the contrary, failure in Scotland might have precipitated a similar crisis of governance in Ireland. It has even been suggested by some writers that, under those circumstances, a fully fledged parliamentary revolt might have broken out against his rule in the 1640s; and that this might have led Britain into just the kind of bloody civil war which had racked Europe in the preceding decades. Had the opponents of Personal Rule managed to recover a forum for their grievances in the form of a parliament, it is certainly clear which of Charles's ministers would have been their first targets: Archbishop Laud and the Earl of Strafford. It is even conceivable that the incompatibility of royal and parliamentary objectives could have led to outright rebellion.

The consequences of what has sometimes misleadingly been called 'Stuart absolutism' have been debated often enough. Critics of the regime – especially the more backward-looking Puritan settlers in North America – alleged that the relative decline of the Westminster Parliament marked the end of 'liberty' in England, just as they never tired of predicting, quite wrongly, that Laud would one day reintroduce 'Popery' to the established church. However, it was precisely the decline of the rigid doctrine of the sovereignty of the crown-in-parliament that enabled the Stuarts to deal as effectively as they did with the problems of political 'overstretch' which inevitably arose as their territories expanded in the course of the eighteenth century. The Stuart polity – not unlike its Habsburg counterpart – was, in fact, a far less centralised system than that which developed under Louis XIV in France. Indeed, for all the fears of the older generation in the 1640s, Charles's son was content to see an increased role for the parliaments of London, Edinburgh and Dublin after his accession.

Yet precisely the *non*-absolutist nature of Stuart rule gave it a certain resilience and flexibility. The so-called 'Restoration' of parliaments in 1660 did not, after all, mean a return to the fraught days of James I's reign, when the English House of Commons had been crowded with aggressive Puritans seeking to check the royal prerogative. By the 1660s, a new generation was represented in Parliament, for whom those days lay in the remote past. And where there was dissent on the periphery of Charles's empire – dissent which might, under different circumstances, have boiled over into open warfare – this was contained by a judicious mixture of concessions and coercion. In Scotland, where antagonism between Lowland Calvinists and Highland Catholics at times verged on civil war, James II followed his father's example in delegating considerable power to the nobles who dominated the Scottish Parliament. When the Covenanters nevertheless sought to revive their 'old cause', his grandson Charles Edward decisively quashed them at Culloden in 1745 – with the enthusiastic support of the Highland clans who continued to adhere to the Catholic faith. Ireland was left even more to its own devices, despite similar tensions between the Protestant settlers of Ulster and the majority Catholic population of the rest of the island who, like the Scottish clans, benefited from the latitudinarian religious policies which had prevailed since the 1640s.

It was in America, however, that Stuart policies enjoyed perhaps their greatest success. A few radicals (influenced mainly by French ideas of natural law) may have expressed criticism of the continuing allegiance of the rapidly growing colonies to a remote British crown. But many Americans agreed with Lord Mansfield's view that the colonies should stand in relation to Great Britain just 'as Scotland stood towards England'. In the words of Daniel Leonard, talk of rebellion against the King was 'more disgraceful to the annals of America than that of witchcraft'. The continued French threat from Canada – confirmed by the Peace of Paris in 1763, following Wolfe's defeat at Quebec –

ensured that American and British interests continued to coincide with respect to foreign policy and security. And in any case, as Benjamin Franklin observed in 1760, there was more disagreement between the fourteen colonies themselves than with distant London – hence the failure of proposals for a union of the colonies within the empire in 1754.

True, there was considerable friction in the wake of the Seven Years' War over taxation, focusing principally on the Stamp Act and the Townshend duties of 1767. But on 1 May 1769 the Cabinet voted by a narrow majority to repeal them all in response to colonial protests, including the especially unpopular tea duty. This, as Jonathan Clark argues, seemed to prove the truth of the doctrine of 'virtual representation', which held that (in the words of Thomas Whately) MPs represented not only their own constituents but 'all the commons of *Great Britain*' as well – including the American colonies.

At the same time, the government in London saw the need to take a harder line when irreconcilable advocates of secession from Great Britain took up arms in 1776. Howe's defeat of Washington's army at Long Island and the Delaware River, Burgoyne's victory over the rebels at Saratoga, and the final victory after Washington's ill-judged attack on New York ensured that what threatened to escalate into civil war was nipped in the bud.

But what if the government had pursued a different line? What if it had insisted on some, if not all, of the unpopular taxes of the 1760s. Some historians have gone so far as to suggest that a full-scale war for American independence might have broken out of the sort which had freed the Dutch United Provinces from Habsburg rule nearly two centuries before. And what if the British had been less resolute and less successful in quelling rebellion? It may seem fantastic to imagine that Charles III (1766–88) might have forfeited his American colonies – but, as Clark shows, this was far from being an impossible outcome.

Of course, the sheer geographical extent of Stuart power in the 1780s could not disguise its relative financial weakness: part of the price of consent in the British Isles and North America was, after all, low taxation. Indeed, it can be argued that it was for precisely this reason that it had proved impossible for the Stuarts to defeat completely the French challenge in North America. This and other French successes overseas did much to consolidate the power of the Bourbon monarchy. The financial reforms of the reign of Louis XVI, implemented by Necker, ended the era of administrative decay which had threatened to undermine the monarchy's power relative not only to the *parlements* – which had effectively vanished by the 1770s – but to the Paris mob as well. As in England, the mob was a very visible part of public life in the 1780s and 1790s, and at times of food shortage threatened to wreak havoc. But without some kind of institutional focus for opposition to royal power, even of the limited sort which the British parliaments still provided, it could do little but riot for cheaper bread, albeit in the name of 'liberty'. The same pattern of relatively inarticulate urban protest was to recur in 1830 and – throughout the continent – in 1848. However, rising living standards as a consequence of increasing industrialisation in northern and central France as well as rapidly growing trans-atlantic trade with Canada and Louisiana tended to diminish popular political protest in the second half of the century. In view of the economic developments of the nineteenth century, it seems idle to speculate about what a successful popular rebellion against either the Bourbons or the Stuarts might have achieved in the 1790s.

In any case, contemporaries were more impressed by the extent of religious revival than by inchoate urban bread riots. In England, this took the form of a relatively conservative Methodism. In Ireland, Poland and northern Scotland, there were significant but relatively unremarkable revivals of Catholic piety. But France and Spain experienced sporadic outbreaks of violent iconoclasm (a pattern which repeated itself in Russia in 1905 and 1915–16); while in Central Europe the millenarian Jewish prophet Karl Marx attracted a considerable number of followers, by no means all of them Jews, with his predictions of an impending apocalypse. Marx was of course arrested by the Mainz authorities in 1847 and spent most of his life in prison. Few of his writings survived the strict censorship of the period. Yet he indirectly influenced a host of Orthodox imitators in Russia, notably the priest Vladimir Ulyanov, whose brother was executed for his part in the abortive assassination attempt against Alexander II in 1881. If successful, it is worth noting, that could have postponed the creation of a representative assembly in Russia, the Duma, for a generation by putting Alexander's reactionary son on the throne. Revisionist historians are fond of arguing that in fact material 'class' divisions played a more important part in such popular movements; but it is hard to see how the leading role of well-educated and relatively prosperous figures like Marx and Ulyanov can be explained in such terms.

Faced with the twin threats of food riots and religious cults, the monarchical states of Europe responded in two ways. Firstly, they sought to create more sophisticated and efficient forms of policing and administration. Secondly, they sought (as in the past) to export domestic problems by encouraging emigration.

However, the former strategy often implied a greater degree of centralisation than had hitherto existed. The resulting opposition to centralisation gave the age its distinctive political language. On the one hand, 'unitarists' and 'federalists' supported the drive for more efficient government, arguing not only for centrally controlled police forces and bureaucracies, but also for centralised revenue-raising agencies and banking systems – even, in some cases, common currencies. On the other hand, so-called 'particularists' or 'states' righters' sought to defend what they saw as their traditional 'liberties'. (Those few enthusiasts for French philosophy who sought to define their positions as 'liberal' or 'conservative' soon came to sound quaintly old-fashioned.) The classic confrontation between the centralisers and the particularists came in British America, between the centralists who wished (for primarily religious reasons) to see the abolition of slavery throughout the American continent and the states' righters who objected to this infringement of the states' traditional liberties.

The resulting conflict boiled over into civil war, despite every effort by the imperial government in London to mediate between the two sides. However, as so often in such conflicts, imperial influence was ultimately exercised in such a way as to tilt the balance in favour of the particularists. Following Lee's decisive victory at Gettysburg, the northern states were effectively forced by Palmerston and Gladstone to accept a compromise settlement, whereby the black slaves were given formal emancipation but no political rights (much as happened to the Russian serfs at around the same time); and the powers of the Viceroy, Abraham Lincoln, were substantially curbed. This settlement was formally agreed in April 1865, despite withering criticism from centralist or 'imperialist' supporters of the North like John Bright and Benjamin Disraeli. In fact, Disraeli's prediction that the tacit continuance of unfree labour would prove economically unsustainable was to prove false. However, where he was right was in his prediction that the two sides would never wholly forget the polarisation of the Civil War. Just as he predicted, post-bellum America increasingly divided into North and South.

Much the same happened when Gladstone and his successors sought to deal with the not dissimilar North–South division in Ireland. Here, the problem was not only an economic one (as in America, the North was industrial, the South agrarian, though reliant on poor peasant farmers rather than slaves). It was also a religious one, thanks to the seventeenth-century colonisation of the north of the island by Calvinists from Scotland. In the rest of Ireland there was a further division between the Dublin-based established church (as reformed by Laud) and the Catholicism of the peasantry. As in America, conflict arose from the resistance of one region to increasing centralisation. As the power of the Irish Parliament increased (which it did steadily under the influence of Grattan in the 1790s), so the Ulster Protestants came to fear for their traditional religious liberties. In an effort to avoid another civil war, Gladstone proposed Home Rule for Ulster – a separate parliament in Belfast for the six predominantly Protestant counties. But this was overwhelmingly rejected by the Irish Prime Minister John Redmond, who saw no reason to relinquish

Dublin's authority over the prosperous North of the island, and fervently opposed in London by imperialists like Joseph Chamberlain. As Alvin Jackson has shown, it was not until 1912 that the Asquith government was able to enact qualified Home Rule for the six counties of Ulster; and even this limited measure precipitated violence between Catholic Irish Volunteers and Protestant Ulster Volunteers, necessitating military intervention from England.

The second policy favoured by the nineteenth-century monarchies – emigration – led to rather different complications. From the 1840s onwards, millions of Irishmen, Scots, Germans, Italians, Poles and Russians were encouraged to depart their native lands. Russians mostly headed east to Siberia. But for most Europeans the most attractive destinations were undoubtedly in North America. However, both the Anglo-Americans and French-Canadians were profoundly hostile to any significant immigrations of people they regarded as foreigners. This did not present a problem for the Irish and Scots (curiously, the French did not prove to be such keen emigrants). But the Germans, Italians and Poles found themselves effectively without colonies to go to. It was partly the resulting sense of exclusion from the great global empires – and the growing fears of Central European governments about the social consequences of rural overpopulation – which inspired the great political changes which transformed the Central European map in mid-century.

The most important of these was the agreement of Austria and Prussia to settle their historic differences and to reform the Holy Roman Empire, making it into something more closely resembling a Western state – that is to say, a relatively decentralised federation under a single imperial head. After prolonged debate, agreement was finally reached in 1862–3 when the Austrian Emperor Franz Joseph secured the support of the Prussian King Wilhelm I for his scheme. Against the advice of his Austrophobe minister president Bismarck, Wilhelm accepted Franz Joseph's supremacy as emperor of a reformed empire on condition that its Foreign Ministry should be given permanently to Prussia – a concession which quickly changed Bismarck's attitude. As a consequence, the Habsburgs effectively extended their empire from Lombardy to Lübeck, from Mainz to Memel – though their power within the larger states was, like British power in America, in some ways more notional than real.

This 'reform era' was made easier by the wars waged by Britain and France to prevent a Russian takeover of the Ottoman Empire in the Balkans in 1854–5 (the Crimean War) and 1878–9 (the Bulgarian War). So long as the Tsar was kept from controlling the Black Sea Straits, the German Emperor was content to see the ancient kingdoms of Piedmont and Serbia extend their power in Italy and the Balkans. 'Patriotism' – the sense of loyalty to one's own historic kingdom – came to be one of the vital sources of Habsburg strength. Those few intellectuals who argued for alternative 'national' allegiances based on language and culture went largely unheeded, though some modern scholars of 'nationalism' believe their importance has been underestimated.

The ultimate loser in this process was France. In the wake of the defeat of Russia in Bulgaria, there were those at Versailles who dreamt of cementing a permanent alliance with Britain. True, the British Foreign Office was deeply suspicious of the new German Empire, particularly when it embarked on programmes of naval construction and colonial acquisition which some saw as a direct challenge to British maritime supremacy. This probably explains why the idea of an Anglo-German alliance came to nothing. But traditional hostility to France – the loss of Canada had never been wholly forgotten – and a growing belief on the part of English imperialists like Chamberlain in the natural cultural and economic affinity between an American Britain and a German Europe dashed the hopes of French Anglophiles like the Cambon brothers. Instead, the Bourbons turned to the Romanovs (a natural diplomatic convergence, perhaps, of the two most centralised monarchies). Unfortunately for Versailles, as far as most British politicians could see, the resulting Franco-Russian alliance simply made Habsburg–Hohenzollern fears of 'encirclement' more legitimate. The obvious ease with which the Royal Navy was able to maintain its superiority over the German fleet – and the lack of any real colonial friction between the two empires – soon dispelled City fears of an Anglo-German antagonism. By contrast, British interests seemed much more directly threatened by Russia's continuing expansion in Asia.

Russian and French military preparations undoubtedly did pose a direct threat to the security of the Habsburg–Hohenzollern Reich, which, because of its highly decentralised structure, lacked the financial resources to match its neighbours in terms of manpower. It was this threat to German security which made some sort of war more or less certain on the continent in the second decade of the twentieth century. Of course, there continued to be influential voices in British diplomatic and military circles who argued that Britain should align itself with France and Russia to avert what they claimed, rather implausibly, was a growing German threat to British security. Germanophobes like Eyre Crowe consistently pressed for some kind of continental commitment to France; and this view also had its adherents among the leaders of the Imperialist party. But the Francophiles remained in a distinct minority within the Home Rule party which came to power in 1905. Thus, when war broke out between the continental powers in August 1914 – ostensibly over Bosnia–Herzegovina, where there had been an unsuccessful attempt on the Archduke Franz Ferdinand's life – the majority of the Cabinet overwhelmingly supported the course of non-intervention urged by the Welsh Non-Conformist and ardent Home Ruler Lloyd George. This reflected not only the party's pacific traditions, but the realisation – confirmed by subsequent historical research in the Russian archives – that the war was to a large extent forced upon Germany by the Russian government's decision to mobilise its army rather than wait for a diplomatic settlement. Despite the resignations of the Home Rulers' Foreign Secretary Grey and the First Lord of the Admiralty, Churchill – which brought down the Asquith government – there was thus little the Imperialists under Bonar Law could do to influence the outcome of a continental war once the King had finally consented to their forming a government with Churchill and Grey. As Churchill ruefully remarked, to have sent the British Expeditionary Force would have been 'too little, too late' by the time the Germans had won the second battle of the Marne; and the naval sanctions imposed by Britain were no more than a warning to Vienna not to establish any naval bases on the French coast.

The German victory of 1915 and the subsequent treaties of Versailles and Brest-Litovsk came as no surprise to those who had followed the course of German policy before the outbreak of war. In addition to imposing substantial reparations on the French and Russian governments, the imperial Foreign Minister Bethmann Hollweg created a Central European Customs Union – *Mitteleuropa* – embracing France, the Netherlands, Piedmont and Sweden as well as the German Empire itself. Although formally nothing more than a free-trade area with a uniform system of external tariffs, it was not long before Anglo-American observers were referring to the new entity as the 'European Union'. Of particular importance from the British point of view were the limited military implications of the German victory. In return for territorial gains in Central Africa and the lifting of the Anglo-American blockade, Bethmann Hollweg agreed to end the military occupation of Northern France and the Netherlands. From the German point of view, this was an easy concession to make: it had never been their intention to threaten British security by establishing a naval foothold on the Channel coast.

Of course, it is impossible to say what form German war aims might have taken if Britain *had* acted as Grey and Churchill wanted, and intervened more effectively in early August 1914. As recent research has revealed, British plans certainly existed for the despatch of an 'expeditionary force' to France in the event of a German invasion. But they were merely contingency plans – strategic options – and, as the government repeatedly made clear before the war, they did not commit Britain in any way to the defence of France. It is sometimes suggested that, if Grey had only been heeded, the war on the continent might have been averted, in that a clear British commitment to France would have persuaded the Germans to halt their mobilisation. But this is wholly far-fetched. Once it was clear that the Russians were determined to mobilise, the Germans had no real alternative but to do the same. The most that Grey could have done, if he had been able to convince his Cabinet colleagues, would have been to send the expeditionary force. Given its size, the most this could have achieved would have been to halt the German advance (at worst, it would merely have shared in the ignominy of defeat at the Marne). But this would not have sufficed to defeat Germany. British intervention would simply have prolonged the war, perhaps for as long as two years.

The counterfactual of British intervention in 1914 is not as difficult to visualise as might be thought. In fact, contemporaries like Ivan Bloch and Norman Angell had done their best before the war to imagine what the consequences would be of a major European conflagration. The consensus was that the economic consequences of such a war would be so dire that it would be almost impossible to sustain it for long. During the July Crisis, Grey himself had warned of economic, social and hence political crises comparable with those of 1848. Numerous German commentators went further, predicting that a war would topple 'many a throne'. We can only guess which regime would have collapsed first, in the event of a war of long duration. At the time, it was argued by Bloch that Russia would outlast her enemies, as her population was used to greater hardship. The alternative view is that the Anglo-American Empire's superior economic resources would ultimately have been decisive, leading instead to a German collapse. At the very least, the established dynasties would have had to face unprecedented popular disaffection. Even the short war that was fought obliged the combatants to make significant political concessions. In both Russia and France, reigning monarchs were obliged to abdicate following the military failures of 1914–15. Under strong pressure from his own aristocracy and generals, Nicholas II stepped aside to make way for his haemophiliac son Aleksei. Even in victorious Germany, the ZPD (Zentralisierungspartei Deutschlands – German Centralisation party) was for the first time treated as a governing party in the postwar years, to the dismay of Prussian particularists; while in Britain the Imperialist coalition which had taken Britain into the war to so little effect was swept from power by a rejuvenated Home Rule party in the election of 1916.

Happily, the economic catastrophe of a long war did not become a reality. Instead, the years after 1916 brought unparalleled prosperity to the industrialised economies, though the continued decline of commodity prices put agricultural economies under increasing pressure. Moreover, the successful reform of the American monetary system in 1913 had brought the burgeoning financial markets of New York under closer supervision by the Bank of England, which continued to manage the global monetary system known as the bimetallic standard. The appointment of the young Cambridge economist John Maynard Keynes as governor of the Bank in 1920 – a reward by the Home Rulers for his seminal attack on Grey and Churchill, *The Economic Consequences of the War* – ushered in an era of highly successful monetary policy. Indeed, as Milton Friedman and others have argued, if it had not been for Keynes's decision to pursue countercyclical policies in the late 1920s, the minor downturn in world stock markets which occurred in September 1929 might have turned into a severe depression.

In economic terms, Keynes was certainly right to argue that British neutrality in 1914 would have been preferable to ineffectual intervention. As he pointed out, a Britain which had formally agreed to Bethmann Hollweg's neutrality offer on the eve of the war might have stood to gain a share of French and Russian postwar reparations to Germany. Yet there remained dissident voices – notably the maverick Imperialist Churchill – who regretted that the expeditionary force had not been sent in time to halt Moltke, and solemnly predicted a future conflict between Britain and an expansionist Germany.

This time Churchill was right. Germany had changed since 1914. As a result of the victory, as Bethmann Hollweg had feared, power had increasingly shifted away from the monarch and his bureaucracy towards the political parties: the ZPD and the two confessional parties, the German Protestant party (PPD) and the Catholic Centre party. Because of the system of proportional representation which had been introduced in 1918, this tended to give disproportionate power to small extremist parties like the radical Nordic Centralising German Aryan party (NZDAP) led by the Austrian demagogue Adolf Hitler, who preached a mixture of anti-Semitism and neo-paganism, and called on Protestant and Catholic Germans to bury their historic differences. When Hitler was installed as chancellor in 1933 – after much political manoeuvring in Vienna in which the new Emperor Charles failed to thwart the NZDAP's 'seizure of power' – there was an immediate shift in German domestic and foreign policy.

The possibility of German aggression had not wholly been ignored by the Anglo-American governments. In their meeting at Long Island in 1931, the three ministers who were to dominate the 1930s – the North's Herbert Hoover, the South's Huey Long and the Scottish Home Ruler Ramsay MacDonald – resolved to maintain security at levels 'sufficient' to deter any future agressor. Yet none of them had his heart in maintaining imperial security. MacDonald in particular saw his primary role as to improve church attendance in the British Isles; indeed, imperial considerations were an embarrassment to someone who, in 1914, had seen the war as an affront to God. For their part, Hoover and Long were simply uninterested in foreign affairs. As Hoover's unsuccessful opponent in 1932 complained, Americans were too busy enjoying Keynesian reflation and the relaxation of the American licensing laws to worry about Germany and Japan. 'We have nothing too dear', Franklin Roosevelt told listeners in a radio broadcast, 'but beer itself.'

When the German challenge came therefore, it found Anglo-America unready. Historians will doubtless never cease to ask if an earlier increase in the pace of rearmament could have averted 'the deluge'. But such speculation simply ignores the strength of the forces arrayed against any more assertive policy. The reality was that the German centralisers led by Hitler were able to tranform the federal Europe created in 1916 into an increasingly centralised 'leader-state' without paying the slightest heed to Anglo-American views. First the German states themselves were merged into a single state in 1938. Austrian troops marched into Berlin to a rapturous welcome, and the provinces of Moravia and Bohemia were formally deprived of their traditional rights – this in the wake of a summit meeting between Hitler and the new British Prime Minister Clement Attlee (who had succeeded MacDonald on the latter's death in 1937). Then, in 1939, the Germans turned to the rest of the European Union. Poland was partitioned in September 1939, its western provinces being absorbed into the Reich. The next year it was the turn of France and Italy.

What no one was prepared for, however, was the invasion of Britain which followed almost immediately after the German occupation of Paris. In fact, Hitler had been secretly preparing this for some time, so that immense amounts of shipping had been concentrated in the Maas and the Scheldt estuaries by late May. When this naval force was unleashed, the antiquated destroyers of the Royal Navy, some of which had been commissioned when Churchill was still at the Admiralty, were overwhelmed. Confronted by the combined might of the Luftwaffe and an invasion force equipped with superior weaponry (including tanks, an innovation of the previous war with which the British were unfamiliar), the defending forces stood no chance. The thirteen German divisions which landed on the morning of 30 May swept through the 1st London Division defending the vital line between Sheppey and Rye, and by 7 June had reached the outskirts of London.

Could this calamity have been avoided by an earlier acceptance of Hitler's peace offer, made repeatedly in the 1930s and repeated on the eve of the invasion? Some historians have suggested as much, and there were certainly influential voices urging such a deal. Yet the evidence indicates clearly that Hitler was insincere in his offers. From 1936 onwards, he was bent on the destruction of British power; and only the timing of his strike was left to be decided. An equally plausible counterfactual would have been a British pre-emptive strike in 1939 – over Poland, perhaps. This, of course, was what Churchill advocated. But such a course of action at the time seemed fraught with peril, not least because of British military unpreparedness and the conclusion, shortly before the partition of Poland, of Hitler's pact with the Russian government.

What of the alternative hypothesis – that any sort of resistance to German power was futile? Certainly, the costs of continued fighting against the occupation were higher than in areas (such as the Channel Islands) where the populations simply acquiesced. On the other hand, the 'Free English Government' set up by Churchill and Eden on the other side of the Atlantic enjoyed considerable popular support. Thousands of young men answered their appeal to fight on, no matter what the costs. Few had military experience, much less proper equipment; but they were able to maintain a persistent guerrilla war against the occupiers. The numbers of hostages shot in reprisals ran into thousands. Nevertheless, the exiled Churchill remained convinced that only such sustained resistance could secure him the support of the American Viceroy and his officials. There, in the neo-classical surroundings of the Northern capital, New York, Churchill urged America to mobilise for total war.

Yet what was in it for Roosevelt, who had finally become the North's prime minister at the third attempt? There was – or seemed to be – a legitimate government in England. A minor princeling from the House of Saxe-Coburg had been installed in the Stuarts' place as 'Edward VII'. Lloyd George had accepted the post of prime minister and had recruited a number of other senior politicians into his Cabinet including Samuel Hoare and R. A. Butler. True, this government was very clearly subordinate to the occupying authorities – the military under General von Brauchitsch and, more importantly, the senior SS officer in Britain, whose first act on arriving in Britain had been to take into 'protective custody' over 2,000 political suspect people listed in his notorious 'Black Book'. Yet (as Andrew Roberts shows) the propaganda broadcast by the BBC – now under a new Director-

General, William Joyce – was extremely persuasive. The Anglo-German Friendship Treaty signed in 1941 between Ribbentrop and Lloyd George was presented as the historic fulfilment of Britain's destiny as a European island. British membership of the new 'German-European Union' could be made to seem more geographically rational than the previous Anglo-American trans-atlantic empire. In any case, Roosevelt had no stomach for a fight with the German navy in the Atlantic.

However, when the Japanese launched their offensive into British Asia, sweeping into Singapore, Malaysia, Burma and India, he had to think again. 'What if the Japanese had attacked Pearl Harbor?' asked Churchill in his celebrated address to the American House of Commons (a reference to the principal Anglo-American naval base in the Pacific). Prophetically, Churchill warned of a 'Bamboo Curtain' across the Pacific if America did not bestir itself. He also pointed out that German military preparations, about which the Free English had some intelligence, implied a future naval and airborne attack on America.

The key to a victory over Germany in Europe, however, lay in Eastern Europe. On one key point, the radical right and the German conservatives agreed: in the belief that expansion into Eastern Europe and Russia was the essential precondition for a victory over Anglo-America. In fact, this proved surprisingly easy to achieve. The Russian aristocrats and generals who had forced the abdication of Nicholas II had found it extremely difficult to establish the kind of English-style monarchy they had originally envisaged. On the one hand, urban workers and many peasants continued to hanker after the kind of fundamentalist theocracy called for by the more radical religious sects. It was a major blow to the religious zealots when Ulyanov – one of the most prominent of their 'prophets' – was exposed as a German agent and executed in the summer of 1917. On the one hand, there was considerable centralist reluctance to adopt a devolved political system along Stuart or Habsburg lines. Not without reason, the Russians had reason to doubt their hold over such subject peoples as the Treaty of Brest-Litovsk had left them. Indeed, the real problem for the government was the same problem which was threatening Anglo-American power in Asia: the growing hostility of the non-Russian peoples to the power of the imperial government.

The Germans had, of course, begun the process of breaking up the Tsarist empire in 1916 by giving nominal independence to Poland, the Baltic states and the Ukraine. During the 1930s, other territories – notably Belorussia, Georgia and Armenia – began to press for greater autonomy. Ironically, the strongest opponent of the government's indecisive policy of half-measures and concessions to the minorities was himself a priest of Georgian origin. But Joseph Djugashvili's apocalyptic warnings that a rump Muscovy would be consumed by demonic foreign saboteurs – thought by many to refer to a second German attack – went unheeded. In June 1941, the Germans launched Operation Barbarossa. Just as Djugashvili had feared – and the new Minister for the Occupied Territories, Alfred Rosenberg, had hoped – the non-Russian nationalities flocked to the German standard, seizing the opportunity for a final decisive victory over their traditional oppressors. A Belorussian protectorate was set up, along with a Caucasian federation and a new Crimean Muftiate. Cossack, Kalmyk and Tatar formations were integrated into the Wehrmacht. The Germans allowed considerable political latitude to peoples like the Chechens and the Karachai in the Northern Caucasus.

Admittedly, as Michael Burleigh argues, Rosenberg's policies were not entirely to Hitler's taste, and still less to those of the Reichsführer-SS, Heinrich Himmler. But it was clear that their dreams of the ethnic transformation of Eastern Europe, involving massive population transfers, would have wasted precious economic resources which the Germans needed for their planned war against America. Only with respect to the European Jews, whom Hitler obsessively loathed, was a policy of forced resettlement and mass murder adopted. Of course, for many years it was denied by the German authorities that there had been a policy of genocide. Those who talked of 'death camps' during and after the war were simply not believed in the absence of tangible proof. Only the final defeat of Germany in 1952 allowed archaeologists to uncover the evidence of the existence of such camps at Auschwitz, Sobibor and Treblinka. It is striking that the Germans were able to carry out this appalling slaughter without any perceptible opposition from local non-Jewish populations, and with little disruption to their war effort. Indeed, in some camps (notably Auschwitz), prisoners were used as slave labour by major industrial concerns like IG-Farben. Jewish prisoners (including eminent scientists) were also used in the work on the German atomic bomb, which Hitler had become convinced would make him the master of the world.

It is difficult to say what might have happened if Hitler had lived long enough to see the work on the bomb completed. Very possibly there would have been an atomic strike against America. But thankfully it was not to be. The collapse of the Third Reich had for some time been predicted by exiled critics of Hitler's 'Behemoth', who believed that it would ultimately collapse because of its own internal contradictions. Yet although there was certainly a chaotic quality to the Reich as it expanded eastwards, the radicalisation of policy on the Eastern Front was in no way a harbinger of self-destruction. On the contrary, the rise of Himmler and his effective takeover of occupation policy gave the conquered empire a unique and terrible energy. In fact, what really doomed the Third Reich was simply the death of Hitler on 20 July 1944 – killed by a bomb planted inside his Eastern Front headquarters by an aristocratic army officer named von Stauffenberg. The subsequent *coup d'état* was resisted ferociously by Himmler's SS and sections of the army which believed Goebbels's claim that Hitler was still alive. But there was sufficient popular war-weariness for an apathetic acceptance of the new regime in most parts of the German Empire. Indeed, those who had remained faithful to their traditional religious faiths positively welcomed Helmuth von Moltke's new 'Kreisau' constitution, named after the place where the ideas were first drafted, the most important clauses of which restored the old federal system of the pre-Hitler Reich. Moltke's decision to seek a negotiated peace with Anglo-America was popular, despite the opposition of some of his older co-conspirators, notably von Hassell.

Von Hassell's fear was of a Russian recovery – the traditional 'threat from the East'. However, in 1944 such fears seemed exaggerated. The wave of religious fundamentalism which had overthrown the last Tsar the previous year looked more like the last phase of complete Russian collapse than the beginning of a military recovery. As recent research has shown, however, this was to be the beginning of a dramatic reversal in European politics. Once again, Churchill made the right decision in arguing for American recognition and financial support of the new theocratic regime. Once Djugashvili had been installed as patriarch and had consolidated his grip on Muscovy and Siberia, he and his advisers agreed on a policy of cooperation with the Anglo-Americans which promised exactly the division of the world into 'spheres of influence' – at Germany's expense – which Churchill had always desired. And although it was not until 1950 that the Russians were willing to launch their offensive against the German Empire, it is hard to imagine troops of the old Tsarist regime fighting with the near-suicidal fervour with which the 'Holy Army' fought from then on.

Realising too late that von Hassell's warnings had been justified, the German government turned to Hitler's unused – but now completed – secret weapon. As the Holy Army advanced into Belorussia and Poland, the Germans issued a threat: if Djugashvili did not pull his men back, the city of Volgograd would be destroyed. But the Germans exaggerated the deterrent power of their new weapon. As far as Djugashvili was concerned, Jonathan Haslam has shown, the bomb was merely 'designed to terrify those with weak nerves'. There had already been enough devastation in Eastern Europe to make the bomb seem like a bluff which could be called. The Patriarch ordered his troops to advance.

The explosion of the world's first atomic bomb and the destruction of Volgograd was without doubt a historic turning-point; for it not only revealed a new and unprecedented weapon of destruction, but also exposed its limitations in the face of numerous and highly motivated conventional forces. As Djugashvili saw, the Germans could drop at most two bombs on Russia; but they would not dare drop bombs on their own territory. When the first Russian troops crossed the Oder into Germany, the war was as good as over. Terrified civilians fled westwards in advance of what Goebbels had called, shortly before his suicide, the 'Asiatic horde'.

Meanwhile, Churchill and Roosevelt had at last opened the agreed 'second front'. The Anglo-American landings in Ireland and Scotland in 1945, and the subsequent campaign which drove the Germans south through England, had proved easier than pessimists (including the Commander-in-Chief Eisenhower) had feared. But the defending forces were known to be much stronger on the French coast. It was only the thought of Djugashvili claiming the credit for victory over Germany which finally prompted the Anglo-American invasion of Normandy in the summer of 1951.

The disastrous failure of the D-Day landings set the seal on the Russian victory. Arriving in Vienna while the Anglo-Americans were still picking up the pieces of the débâcle, the Holy Army found itself in effective control of Central Europe. The only question was whether the remaining German forces in the West, exhausted by their repulsion of the Anglo-American landings, would be willing to fight on. Once it was clear that the capital had fallen, they chose not to. Djugashvili lost no time in informing Churchill that he regarded their earlier agreement about 'spheres of influence' as having been overtaken by events. From now on all of Europe, with the exception of Paris (which he magnanimously divided into Eastern and Western zones) would be the Russian sphere of influence. This done, Djugashvili returned to Moscow and crowned himself Tsar Joseph I.

Yet the surrender to Russian dominance in Europe did not imply similar American pusillanimity in Asia. From an early stage, it had been clear to Churchill that the American states cared more about the Pacific theatre of war than about the European. The emergence after Roosevelt's death of a new generation of politicians, more committed than he had been to purely American rather than Anglo-American interests, paved the way for an era of recurrent conflict with the Japanese-dominated Asian Co-Prosperity Zone.

Despite their success in sweeping aside the old European colonial regimes, the Japanese had never wholly extinguished local resistance to their rule in China and Indo-China. Peasant wars, often led by messianic figures like Mao Zedong and Ho Chi Minh, tied down substantial numbers of Japanese troops. The costs of these wars also limited the extent to which the Japanese could build up their own naval defences. For any American government seeking to weaken the Japanese position still further, the temptation to intervene was obviously very great. Roosevelt began the process shortly before his death by publicly referring to China as a future great power. In 1948, his successor Dewey sent aid to Mao, who proceeded to drive the Japanese back to Shanghai. A similar strategy was adopted in Korea. This time, however, American troops were sent to assist the rebel North against the Japanese South.

No American Prime Minister did more to deepen American–Japanese confrontation than John F. Kennedy, the son of Roosevelt's Anglophobe consul in London, Joseph Kennedy. By a huge margin – mainly owing to the Catholic vote in the North's crowded cities – Kennedy won the 1960 election. The following year, he scored a minor triumph when a successful invasion reclaimed Cuba from the last remaining Nazi forces in Latin America. Emboldened, he began to examine the possibility of another military intervention, this time in support of Ho Chi Minh's Vietnamese revolt against the Japanese-backed regime of Ngo Dinh Diem.

In many ways, JFK was a lucky prime minister. He was spared the difficulties of the black suffrage movement which plagued the political career of his Southern counterpart Lyndon Johnson. He survived an assassination attempt while visiting Johnson in Dallas in November 1963. His Centralist party smashed the states' righters led by Barry Goldwater in the elections of 1964. But Kennedy's good luck deserted him in Vietnam. True, the war was popular; but Kennedy could not win it. When he was forced to resign in 1967, following revelations that his brother, the Attorney-General Robert Kennedy, had authorised phone-tapping of political opponents, no fewer than half a million American troops were fighting alongside the North Vietnamese forces. But the Japanese-backed regime was better equipped than had been expected, not least because of the rapid development of Japanese electrical engineering. When Richard Nixon swept to victory in the 1968 election, it was with a mandate to end the war. In a television debate with Nixon before his impeachment, a haggard Kennedy made his bitterness clear. 'If I had been shot dead back in 1963,' he exclaimed, 'I would be a saint today.' Although, as Diane Kunz argues, Kennedy had a point, his remark was universally derided at the time.

Looking back on the events of the two decades after Kennedy's fall from grace, it is tempting to see the subsequent break-up of the Anglo-American Empire as inevitable (there had already been considerable strains over the Vietnam War, which the British Prime Minister Harold Wilson opposed). However, as Mark Almond shows, the Russian economy was far from being in good health itself by the 1980s. Non-conformists had good cause to be critical of the policies of 'stagnation' which continued under Tsar Yuri, who succeeded his father Leonid in 1982. On the other hand, the policies of economic and political reform called for by reformers like Mikhail Gorbachev could very well have worsened the economic situation. If Gorbachev had succeeded in increasing the prices which Russia's satellite states in Europe paid for Russian oil, there could have been serious instability. And, if his arguments for free elections in France, Germany and elsewhere had been accepted, there is no knowing what might have followed. Even without new policies, it was still necessary to send the tanks into Leipzig in 1989, just as had happened in Berlin in 1953, in Budapest in 1956 and in Prague and East Paris in 1968.

What if the Anglo-American states had reacted more firmly to the crushing of the Leipzig rising? If nothing else, they might have dissuaded the Russians from taking further aggressive action elsewhere. But the governments in Britain and America in the 1980s were incapable of such assertiveness. George Bush was a trimmer, compared with his predecessor. More importantly, the Foot government in Britain – elected in 1983 and again in 1987 following the Thatcher administration's humiliating defeat by Argentina in the Falklands War – was widely accused of being sympathetic to Moscow. When the Sultan of Baghdad, Saddam Hussein, staged his long-anticipated attack against the Ottoman province of Kuwait, the West was caught unprepared. Already in the grip of a severe recession, the British and American economies were plunged into an acute and unprecedented slump as oil prices soared.

Today there are many competing theories designed to explain the 'collapse of the West' in 1989–90. Was it the excessive growth of public spending and debt and the monetary laxity of the decades after Vietnam? Or was it the consequence of a fundamentally political division between Britain and the Americas – the legacy, perhaps, of the German occupation of England fifty years before? Yet, as the debates continue, it is easy to forget that, at the time, no one expected anything so dramatic to happen. Most supposed 'experts' on the Anglo-American system were simply astonished at the speed with which the transatlantic confederation disintegrated in the 1990s. First, the American states declared their independence from Stuart rule. Then what seemed to be a chain reaction severed the historic links between England, Ireland, Scotland and even Wales.

Those who had been looking forward to celebrating four centuries of Stuart rule (in 2003) could only reflect bitterly on the unpredictable – even chaotic – quality of great historical events.

In Moscow, by contrast, the collapse of the West merely seemed to confirm the validity of the deterministic theory of history so dear to Tsar Joseph and his heirs.

Notes

VIRTUAL HISTORY

1. For an analysis of the appeal of these imagined alternative worlds, see Thomas Pavel, *Fictional Worlds* (Cambridge, Mass., 1986).

2. Robert Musil, *The Man without Qualities*, vol. I, trans. Eithne Wilkins and Ernst Kaiser (London, 1983), p. 12.

3. E. H. Carr, *What Is History?* (2nd edn, London, 1987).

4. Carr, *What Is History?*, pp. 44f., 90, 96, 105.

5. E. P. Thompson, 'The Poverty of Theory', in *idem, The Poverty of Theory and Other Essays* (London, 1978), p. 300.

6. Benedetto Croce, '"Necessity" in History', in *Philosophy, Poetry, History: An Anthology of Essays*, trans. Cecil Sprigge (London/New York/Toronto, 1966), pp. 557ff. Croce glosses over the possibility that it might in fact be easier for an historian to ask a counterfactual question about the past than about his own life.

7. Michael Oakeshott, *Experience and its Modes* (Cambridge, 1933), pp. 128–45.

8. Robert Harris, *Fatherland* (London, 1992). The idea of a German victory has inspired many less successful works, e.g. Philip K. Dick, *The Man in the High Castle* (New York, 1962); Gregory Benford and Martine Greenberg (eds), *Hitler Victorious: Eleven Stories of the German Victory in World War Two* (London, 1988); Peter Tsouras, *Disaster at D-Day: The Germans Defeat the Allies, June 1944* (London, 1994).

9. Kingsley Amis, *The Alteration* (London, 1976). A similar Catholic

utopia is imagined in Keith Roberts, *Pavane* (London, 1968). Not surprisingly, there have been comparable fictions based on a Southern victory in the American Civil War: Ward Moore, *Bring the Jubilee* (New York, 1953); Harry Turtledove, *The Guns of the South* (New York, 1992). Less well known to English readers are two fantasies based on a Republican victory in the Spanish Civil War: Fernando Diaz-Plaja, *El desfile de la victoria* (Barcelona, 1976); Jesus Torbado, *En el dia de hoy* (Barcelona, 1976). I am grateful to Dr Brendan Simms for these references.

10. To cite a few egregious examples of the genre: H. G. Wells, *The Shape of Things to Come: The Ultimate Revolutions* (London, 1933); R. C. Churchill, *A Short History of the Future* (London, 1955); Sir John Hackett, *The Third World War: The Untold Story* (London, 1982); William Clark, *Cataclysm: The North–South Conflict* (London, 1984); Peter Jay and Michael Stewart, *Apocalypse 2000: Economic Breakdown and the Suicide of Democracy, 1989–2000* (London, 1987); James Dale Davidson and William Rees-Mogg, *The Great Reckoning: How the World Will Change in the Depression of the 1990s* (London, 1992).

11. Edward Gibbon, *The Decline and Fall of the Roman Empire* (London, 1994 edn), vol. V (ch. lii), p. 445.

12. Charles Renouvier, *Uchronie (l'utopie dans l'histoire): Esquisse historique apocryphe du développement de la civilisation européenne tel qu'il n'a pas été, tel qu'il aurait pu être* (1st edn, Paris, 1876; 2nd edn, Paris, 1901), p. iii.

13. Renouvier dedicated the book 'to new partisans of human liberty, as it really was, in the past that it made'. 'Our primary salvation', he declared, 'is to decide for ourselves'; *ibid.*, p. 31.

14. G. M. Trevelyan, 'If Napoleon had won the Battle of Waterloo', in *Clio, a Muse and Other Essays* (London, 1930), pp. 124–35. For a more recent French riposte, see Robert Aron, *Victoire à Waterloo* (Paris, 1968).

15. J. C. Squire (ed.), *If It Happened Otherwise: Lapses into Imaginary History* (London/New York/Toronto, 1932).

16. For a pro-Lincoln counterfactual see Lloyd Lewis, 'If Lincoln Had Lived', in M. Llewellyn Raney, Lloyd Lewis, Carl Sandburg and William E. Dodd, *If Lincoln Had Lived: Addresses* (Chicago, 1935), pp. 16–35.

17. A list of reported legislation conveys the flavour of the piece:

'Compulsory Employment Act', 'Bill for the Censorship of Comic Newspapers' and 'Bill for the Dissolution of the City Companies'. While these conjure up a faintly droll vision of a Sovietised Britain, modern readers may find less unfamiliar such notions – which doubtless struck Knox as equally surreal – as a 'Bill Setting a Maximum Wage for Company Directors', a surplus milk lake and a 'rationalisation of the universities' to replace Greats at Oxford with Engineering.

18. D. Snowman (ed.), *If I Had Been ... Ten Historical Fantasies* (London, 1979).

19. Gibbon, *Decline and Fall*, vol. VI (ch. lxiv), p. 341.

20. Winston Churchill, *The World Crisis: The Aftermath* (London, 1929), p. 386.

21. William Dray, *Laws and Explanation in History* (Oxford, 1957), p. 103.

22. Bertrand Russell, 'Dialectical Materialism', in Patrick Gardiner (ed.), *Theories of History* (Glencoe, Illinois/London, 1959), pp. 294f.

23. J. M. Merriman (ed.), *For Want of a Horse: Chance and Humour in History* (Lexington, Mass., 1984). In fact, only about half of the essays are genuinely counterfactual.

24. Conrad Russell, 'The Catholic Wind', in *ibid.*, pp. 103–7.

25. Hugh Trevor-Roper, 'History and Imagination', in Valerie Pearl, Blair Worden and Hugh Lloyd-Jones (eds), *History and Imagination: Essays in Honour of H. R. Trevor-Roper* (London, 1981), pp. 356–69. The same lecture contains a more modern counterfactual setting out the 'four hypothetical accidents' which could have made a German victory in Western Europe 'final' after 1940: if there had been no Churchill; if there had been no Ultra intelligence; if Franco had joined the Axis; and if Mussolini had not launched his invasion of Greece.

26. John Vincent, *An Intelligent Person's Guide to History* (London, 1995), pp. 39f. See also his discussion of counterfactuals on pp. 45ff.

27. See in general R. W. Fogel, 'The New Economic History: Its Findings and Methods', *Economic History Review*, 2nd series, 19 (1966), pp. 642–51; E. H. Hunt, 'The New Economic History', *History*, 53, 177 (1968), pp. 3–13.

28. R. W. Fogel, *Railways and American Economic Growth: Essays in Interpretative Econometric History* (Baltimore, 1964). For an applica-

tion of the same methods to the British case, see G. R. Hawke, *Railways and Economic Growth in England and Wales 1840–1870* (Oxford, 1970).

29. See in general R. Floud and D. N. McCloskey, *The Economic History of Britain since 1700* (2nd edn, Cambridge, 1994), vol. II.

30. G. R. Elton and R. W. Fogel, *Which Road to the Past? Two Views of History* (New Haven, 1983).

31. R. W. Fogel and Stanley L. Engerman, *Time on the Cross: The Economics of American Negro Slavery* (Boston, 1974); R. W. Fogel, *Without Consent or Contract: The Rise and Fall of American Slavery* (New York, 1989). See for an opposing view H. G. Gutman, *Slavery and the Numbers Game: A Critique of 'Time on the Cross'* (London, 1975).

32. For a summary of the 'Borchardt debate', see J. Baron von Kruedener (ed.), *Economic Policy and Political Collapse: The Weimar Republic, 1924–1933* (New York/Oxford/Munich, 1990).

33. Geoffrey Hawthorn's seminal *Plausible Worlds: Possibility and Understanding in History and the Social Sciences* (Cambridge, 1991).

34. *Ibid.*, pp. 81–122.

35. *Ibid.*, pp. 123–56.

36. *Ibid.*, pp. 1ff., 10f.

37. R. F. Foster, *Modern Ireland, 1600–1972* (Oxford, 1988).

38. John Charmley, *Churchill: The End of Glory* (Dunton Green, 1993).

39. Herbert Butterfield, *The Origins of History*, ed. Adam Watson (London, 1981), pp. 200f.

40. Lucretius, *On the Nature of the Universe*, trans. R. E. Latham (revised edn, Harmondsworth, 1994), pp. 64f.

41. *Ibid.*, p. 66.

42. Polybius, *The Rise of the Roman Empire*, trans. Ian Scott-Kilvert (Harmondsworth, 1979), pp. 41, 44. My emphasis.

43. Tacitus, *The Histories*, trans. Kenneth Wellesley (Harmondsworth, 1975), p. 17.

44. Butterfield, *Origins*, p. 125.

45. Ecclesiastes I: 5–9. Cf. Stephen Jay Gould, *Time's Arrow, Time's Cycle: Myth and Metaphor in the Discovery of Geological Time* (London, 1987).

46. Butterfield, *Origins*, p. 207.

47. *Ibid.*, pp. 176–80.

48. Quoted in Ernest Nagel, 'Determinism in History', in William Dray (ed.), *Philosophical Analysis and History* (New York/London, 1966), p. 380. My emphasis.

49. Giambattista Vico, 'The New Science', in Gardiner (ed.), *Theories of History*, pp. 18f.

50. Pieter Geyl and Arnold Toynbee, 'Can We Know the Pattern of the Past? – A Debate', in Gardiner (ed.), *Theories of History*, pp. 308ff. On Toynbee's *A Study of History* see Arthur Marwick, *The Nature of History* (3rd edn, London, 1989), pp. 287f.

51. Pierre Simon de Laplace, *A Philosophical Essay on Probabilities*, trans. F. W. Truscott and F. L. Emory (New York, 1902), p. 4.

52. Ian Hacking, *The Taming of Chance* (Cambridge, 1990), p. 14.

53. Butterfield, *Origins*, p. 135.

54. Immanuel Kant, 'Idea of a Universal History from a Cosmopolitan Point of View' (1784), in Gardiner (ed.), *Theories of History*, pp. 22f., 29.

55. Michael Stanford, *A Companion to the Study of History* (Oxford, 1994), p. 62.

56. G. W. F. Hegel, 'Second Draft: The Philosophical History of the World' (1830), in *idem*, *Lectures on the Philosophy of World History* (Cambridge, 1975), pp. 26–30.

57. *Ibid.*, pp. 33–141.

58. Auguste Comte, 'The Positive Philosophy and the Study of Society', in Gardiner (ed.), *Theories of History*, p. 75.

59. Quoted in Isaiah Berlin, 'The Concept of Scientific History', in Dray (ed.), *Philosophical Analysis*, p. 28.

60. John Stuart Mill, 'Elucidations of the Science of History', in Gardiner (ed.), *Theories of History*, pp. 96–9, 104f.

61. Quoted in Fritz Stern (ed.), *The Varieties of History from Voltaire to the Present* (London, 1970), pp. 121ff., 127–32.

62. Henry Thomas Buckle, 'History and the Operation of Universal Laws', in Gardiner (ed.), *Theories of History*, pp. 114f.

63. Tolstoy, *War and Peace*, vol. II (London, 1978), pp. 1400–44.

64. See in general M. Rader, *Marx's Interpretation of History* (Oxford, 1979).

65. Karl Marx, *Capital*, vol. I, ch. 32.

66. Carr, *What Is History?*, p. 101.

67. P. Abrams, 'History, Sociology, Historical Sociology', *Past and Present*, 87 (1980), p. 15. See also Rader, *Marx's Interpretation*, pp. 4, 8f.; E. P. Thompson, 'The Poverty of Theory', in *idem* (ed.), *The Poverty of Theory and Other Essays* (London, 1978), p. 307.

68. Georgi Plekhanov, 'The Role of the Individual in History', in Gardiner (ed.), *Theories of History*, pp. 144–63.

69. Stanford, *Companion*, p. 284. For a similar allusion to Darwin by Trotsky, see Carr, *What Is History?*, p. 102: 'In the language of biology, one might say that the historical law is realised through the natural selection of accidents.'

70. Herbert Butterfield, *The Whig Interpretation of History* (London, 1931).

71. Lord Acton, 'Inaugural Lecture on the Study of History', in W. H. McNeill (ed.), *Essays in the Liberal Interpretation of History* (Chicago, 1967), pp. 300–59. My emphasis.

72. J. H. Plumb, *The Death of the Past* (London, 1969), esp. pp. 17, 77f., 97–100, 129f.

73. See esp. Michael Howard, 'The Lessons of History', in *idem*, *The Lessons of History* (Oxford, 1991), pp. 6–20.

74. Thomas Carlyle, 'On History' (1830), in Stern (ed.), *Varieties*, p. 95.

75. Fyodor Dostoevsky, *Notes from Underground*, trans. Andrew R. MacAndrew (London, 1980 edn), pp. 105–20.

76. Quoted in Stern (ed.), *Varieties*, p. 101.

77. *Ibid.*, p. 91. My emphasis.

78. Typical of this light-hearted mood was Maurice Evan Hare's limerick of 1905:

> There once was a man who said 'Damn!
> It is borne in upon me I am
> An engine that moves
> In predestinate grooves,
> I'm not even a bus, I'm a tram.'

79. H. A. L. Fisher, *A History of Europe* (London, 1936), p. v.

80. See J. B. Bury, *Selected Essays*, ed. H. W. V. Temperley (Cambridge, 1930), pp. 60–9.

81. G. M. Trevelyan, 'Clio, a Muse', in *idem, Clio, a Muse,* pp. 140–76, esp. pp. 157f.

82. A. J. P. Taylor, *The Origins of the Second World War* (2nd edn, London, 1963).

83. Quoted in Stern (ed.), *Varieties*, p. 142.

84. Dilthey stressed not only 'the relativity of every sort of human conception about the connectedness of things' but also the inevitably subjective construction of all historical evidence. See M. Ermarth, *Wilhelm Dilthey: The Critique of Historical Reason* (Chicago, 1978).

85. Friedrich Meinecke, 'Causalities and Values in History', in Stern (ed.), *Varieties*, esp. pp. 269, 273.

86. Friedrich Meinecke, *Die deutsche Katastrophe* (Wiesbaden, 1949).

87. R. G. Collingwood, 'The Nature and Aims of a Philosophy of History (1924–5)', in *Essays in the Philosophy of History: R. G. Collingwood*, ed. W. Debbins (Austin, Texas, 1965), p. 44.

88. R. G. Collingwood, 'Lectures on the Philosophy of History, 1926', in *The Idea of History: With Lectures 1926–1928*, ed. J. van der Dussen (Oxford, 1993), pp. 400ff.

89. Collingwood, 'Nature and Aims', pp. 36f., 39f.

90. Collingwood, 'Lectures', pp. 390f.

91. *Ibid.*, pp. 363f., 412f., 420. Cf. Marwick, *Nature*, pp. 293ff.

92. Quoted in David Hackett Fischer, *Historians' Fallacies: Toward a Logic of Historical Thought* (London, 1970), pp. 164f.

93. Croce, ' "Necessity" in History', p. 558.

94. Oakeshott, *Experience and its Modes*, pp. 128ff.

95. Michael Oakeshott, *On History and Other Essays* (Oxford, 1983), p. 71.

96. *Ibid.*, p. 79. My emphasis.

97. See Michael Bentley (ed.), *Public and Private Doctrine: Essays in British History Presented to Maurice Cowling* (Cambridge, 1993), esp. Bentley's 'Prologue', pp. 1–13.

98. G. R. Elton, *The Practice of History* (London, 1969), esp. pp. 42, 57, 63–6.

99. See the summary in T. J. Lears, 'The Concept of Cultural Hegemony: Problems and Possibilities', *American Historical Review*, 90 (1985), pp. 567–93.

100. *Ibid.*, pp. 88, 95–106, 126, 132, 164.

101. Thompson, 'Poverty', p. 227. See also D. Smith, *The Rise of Historical Sociology* (Cambridge, 1991), pp. 87f.

102. Carr, *What Is History?*, pp. 169f.

103. Eric Hobsbawm, *The Age of Extremes* (London, 1994).

104. Alexis de Tocqueville, *L'Ancien Régime et la Révolution* (Paris, 1856).

105. G. Roth and W. Schluchter, *Max Weber's Vision of History* (Berkeley, 1979).

106. Max Weber, *The Protestant Ethic and the Spirit of Capitalism* (London, 1985 edn).

107. *Ibid.*, pp. 91, 183.

108. Marc Bloch, *The Historian's Craft* (Manchester, 1992).

109. Fernand Braudel, *On History* (London, 1980), p. 76.

110. 'Perfectly and absolutely true [history] cannot be; for, to be perfectly and absolutely true, it ought to record *all* the slightest particulars of the slightest transactions ... [But] if history were written thus, the Bodleian library would not contain the occurrence of a week.' Quoted in Stern (ed.), *Varieties*, p. 76.

111. Braudel, *On History*, p. 51; Smith, *Historical Sociology*, pp. 104f. On the German roots of this geographical or ecological determinism, see Roth and Schluchter, *Weber's Vision*, pp. 169f. Montesquieu had of course thought in similar terms.

112. Smith, *Historical Sociology*, p. 114.

113. Fernand Braudel, *The Mediterranean and the Mediterranean World in the Age of Philip II*, trans. S. Reynolds (London, 1972, 1973). The three-tiered model evidently owed something to Meinecke; in the case of Lucien Febvre's three variables in historical causation – contingency, necessity and idea – the debt was more obvious.

114. *Ibid.*, vol. II, p. 901.

115. Braudel, *On History*, pp. 27f.

116. Quoted in Roth and Schluchter, *Weber's Vision*, p. 176.

117. Quoted in Smith, *Historical Sociology*, p. 111.

118. *Ibid.*, p. 120.

119. Braudel, *On History*, p. 12.

120. *Ibid.*, p. 72.

121. Bloch, *Historian's Craft*, p. xxi.

122. *Ibid.*, p. 162.

123. The historical sociologist Alexander Gerschenkron applied this model not only to Germany but to other European countries.

124. David Blackbourn and Geoff Eley, *The Peculiarities of German History* (Oxford, 1984).

125. A German historian would not dare ask what would have happened to German history if Hitler had not come to power, a question addressed in Henry A. Turner, *Geissel des Jahrhunderts: Hitler und seine Hinterlassenschaft* (Berlin, 1989).

126. Lawrence Stone, *The Causes of the English Revolution* (London, 1986), p. 58.

127. Paul Kennedy, *The Rise and Fall of the Great Powers: Economic Change and Military Conflict from 1500 to 2000* (London, 1989), esp. pp. xvi, xxiv–xxv.

128. I. Wallerstein, *The Modern World System*, 3 vols (New York/London, 1974–89); Michael Mann, *The Sources of Social Power*, 2 vols (Cambridge, 1986); Raymond Grew and David D. Bien (eds), *Crises of Political Development and the United States* (Princeton, 1978); Roberto Unger, *Plasticity into Power: Comparative-Historical Studies on the Institutional Conditions of Economic and Military Success* (Cambridge, 1987).

129. Alexander Woodcock and Monte Davis, *Catastrophe Theory: A Revolutionary Way of Understanding How Things Change* (London, 1991), esp. pp. 120–46. The highlight of this book is a three-dimensional graph purporting to depict the decline and fall of the Roman empire (p. 138). A more valuable attempt is made to relate modern views of natural selection to cultural development by W. G. Runciman, *A Treatise on Social Theory. II: Substantive Social Theory* (Cambridge, 1989), esp. p. 449.

130. For a good example of a loosely Freudian approach see Klaus Theweleit, *Male Fantasies*, 2 vols (Cambridge, 1987, 1989).

131. Though it is conceivable that a game-theorist Marxist could do the same with classes.

132. N. Z. Davis, 'The Possibilities of the Past', in T. K. Rabb and R. I. Rotberg (eds), *The New History: The 1980s and Beyond* (Princeton, 1982), pp. 267–77.

133. C. Geertz, *Local Knowledge: Further Essays in Interpretive Anthropology* (London, 1993).

134. W. J. Bouwsma, 'From the History of Ideas to the History of Meaning', in Rabb and Rotberg (eds), *New History*, pp. 279–93.

135. See G. Levi, 'Microhistory', in P. Burke (ed.), *New Perspectives on Historical Writing* (Cambridge, 1991), pp. 93–113.

136. See most recently and ambitiously Simon Schama, *Landscape and Memory* (London, 1995).

137. K. Thomas, *Religion and the Decline of Magic: Studies in Popular Belief in Sixteenth and Seventeenth Century England* (London, 1971).

138. P. Abrams, 'History, Sociology, Historical Sociology', *Past and Present*, 87 (1980), pp. 3–16. See also P. Burke, 'The History of Events and the Revival of Narrative', in *idem* (ed.), *New Perspectives*, pp. 233–48.

139. Louis O. Mink, 'The Autonomy of Historical Understanding', in Dray (ed.), *Philosophical Analysis*, pp. 182, 189.

140. Hayden White, 'The Historical Text as Literary Artefact', in R. H. Canary and H. Kozicki (eds), *The Writing of History: Literary Form and Historical Understanding*. See also Frederic Jameson, *The Political Consciousness: Narrative as a Socially Symbolic Act* (London, 1981); Paul Ricoeur, *Time and Narrative*, trans. Kathleen McLaughlin and David Pellauer (London, 1984–8).

141. J. Barzun, *Clio and the Doctors: Psycho-History, Quanto-History and History* (Chicago, 1974). Another traditionalist, Gertrude Himmelfarb, has recently rather confused the conservative argument by lumping together quantitative methods of the new economic history and the subjective methods of psycho-history: see G. Himmelfarb, *The New History and the Old: Critical Essays and Reappraissals* (Cambridge, Mass., 1987).

142. Barzun, *Clio.*, pp. 101, 123, 152f.

143. N. Z. Davis, 'On the Lame', *American Historical Review*, 93 (1988), pp. 572–603.

144. See for example G. M. Spiegel, 'History, Historicism and the Social Logic of the Text in the Middle Ages', *Speculum*, 65 (1990), pp. 59–86.

145. See J. W. Scott, 'History in Crisis? The Others' Side of the Story', *American Historical Review*, 94 (1989), pp. 680–92; P. Joyce, 'History and Postmodernism', *Past and Present*, 133 (1991), pp. 204–9. For a Marxist critique, see D. Harvey, *The Condition of Postmodernity: An Enquiry into the Origins of Cultural Change* (Oxford, 1989).

146. W. B. Gallie, 'Explanations in History and the Genetic Sciences', in Gardiner (ed.), *Theories of History*, pp. 389f.

147. Michael Scriven, 'Truisms as Grounds for Historical Explanations', in Gardiner (ed.), *Theories of History*, pp. 470f.

148. Martin Amis, *Time's Arrow or The Nature of the Offence* (London, 1992).

149. R. F. Foster, *The Story of Ireland: An Inaugural Lecture Delivered before the University of Oxford on 1 December 1994* (Oxford, 1995), p. 31.

150. Musil, *Man without Qualities*, vol. II, pp. 65–8.

151. *Ibid.*, pp. 69–71.

152. Jorge Luis Borges, 'The Garden of Forking Paths', in *idem*, *Labyrinths: Selected Stories and Other Writings*, ed. Donald A. Yates and James E. Irby (Harmondsworth, 1970), pp. 50ff.

153. Borges, 'Tlön, Uqbar, Orbis Tertius', in *ibid.*, p. 37.

154. Borges, 'The Lottery in Babylon', in *ibid.*, pp. 59ff.

155. Stéphane Mallarmé, *Igitur. Divagations. Un coup de dés*, ed. Yves Bonnefoy (Paris, 1976).

156. L. Untermeyer (ed.), *The Road Not Taken: A Selection of Robert Frost's Poems* (New York, 1951), pp. 270f.

157. Scriven, 'Truisms as Grounds for Historical Explanations', pp. 470f.

158. Hacking, *Taming of Chance*.

159. Stephen Hawking, *A Brief History of Time* (London, 1988), pp. 53ff.

160. Ian Stewart, *Does God Play Dice? The New Mathematics of Chaos* (London, 1990), p. 293.

161. Hawking, *Time*, pp. 123f.

162. *Ibid.*, p. 137.

163. Michio Kaku, *Hyperspace: A Scientific Odyssey through the 10th Dimension* (Oxford, 1995), pp. 234ff. Of course, it is conceivable that a successful time traveller would find his consciousness of being a time traveller wiped out in transit.

164. Richard Dawkins, *The Selfish Gene* (2nd edn, Oxford, 1989), pp. 267, 271.

165. *Ibid.*, pp. 4, 8, 15ff., 24f., 38f., 45. Hence also our instinct to defend the lives of other survival machines in proportion to the number of genes they share with us and their age and future fertility relative to ours. In Dawkins's model, even birth control is a matter of maximising the number of surviving offspring and hence giving the parental genes the best chance of survival.

166. Stephen Jay Gould, *Wonderful Life: The Burgess Shale and the Nature of History* (London, 1989), esp. pp. 47f.

167. The same point was in fact made by Bury: 'The appearance of the various botanical and animal species which exist and have existed seems to have depended on accidents. There was nothing in the logic of life that made the existence of an oak or a hippopotamus inevitable. Nor can it be proved that there was anything that made the existence of *anthropos* inevitable. At the remote threshold of history we seem to find a primordial contingency – the origin of man'; Bury, 'Cleopatra's Nose', p. 68.

168. *Ibid.*, pp. 238f., 309–21. For some unconvincing attempts to restore determinism in reaction to Gould's work, see Roger Lewin, *Complexity: Life at the Edge of Chaos* (London, 1995), pp. 23–72, 130ff. Some of Gould's critics make themselves ridiculous by their attempt to restore the notion of divine agency and a holistic universe in the guise of an earth goddess Gaia. This is New Age Hegel.

169. Stewart, *Does God Play Dice?*, pp. 2f., 6.

170. *Ibid.*, 57ff., 95ff. To give a concrete example, the logistic mapping $x \rightarrow kx(1-x)$ (i.e. the iteration of the non-linear equation

$x_{t+1} = kx_t(1-x_t))$ seems to become random once k has a value greater than 3. If k is increased very gradually, however, a pattern emerges: when x is plotted against k, the result is a diagram of infinite bifurcation: the so-called 'fig tree' (named after its discoverer Mitchell Feigenbaum): *ibid.*, pp. 145ff.

171. *Ibid.*, pp. 289–301.

172. See John Kay, 'Cracks in the Crystal Ball', *Financial Times*, 29 September 1995.

173. Stewart, *Does God Play Dice?*, p. 21.

174. Roger Penrose, *Shadows of the Mind: A Search for the Missing Science of Consciousness* (London, 1994), p. 23.

175. Carl Hempel, 'The Function of General Laws in History', in Gardiner (ed.), *Theories of History*, pp. 344–55; *idem*, 'Reasons and Covering Laws in Historical Explanation', in Dray (ed.), *Philosophical Analysis*, pp. 143–63. In the later piece, Hempel distinguishes between universal laws and probabilistic explanations, based on statistical relationships, suggesting that many historical explanations are based in the latter rather than the former. See also Nagel, 'Determinism in History', *passim*. In his defence of a qualified determinism, Nagel revives the Plekhanov–Bury metaphor of colliding chains to explain apparently 'chance' events; *ibid.*, p. 373.

176. The key texts are Karl Popper, *The Open Society and its Enemies* (London, 1945) and *The Poverty of Historicism* (London, 1957).

177. R. G. Collingwood, *An Essay on Metaphysics* (Oxford, 1940).

178. Popper, *Poverty of Historicism*, pp. 122, 128ff.

179. Charles Frankel, 'Explanation and Interpretation in History', in Gardiner (ed.), *Theories of History*, pp. 411–15.

180. Gallie, 'Explanations in History and the Genetic Sciences', p. 387. See also Michael Scriven, 'Causes and Connections and Conditions in History', in Dray (ed.), *Philosophical Analysis*, pp. 238–64.

181. H. L. A. Hart and Tony Honoré, *Causation in the Law* (2nd edn, Oxford, 1985), pp. 10ff.

182. *Ibid.*, pp. 22–63.

183. *Ibid.*, pp. 15f., 21n.

184. *Ibid.*, pp. 101, 109–14.

185. Patrick Gardiner, *The Nature of Historical Explanation* (London, 1952), pp. 107ff.

186. David Lewis, *Counterfactuals* (Oxford, 1973); Hans Reichenbach, *Laws, Modalities and Counterfactuals* (Berkeley, 1976); Igal Kvart, *A Theory of Counterfactuals* (Indianapolis, 1986).

187. Isaiah Berlin, *Historical Inevitability* (London, 1954). See esp. pp. 78f.: 'Those who hold [determinist views] use history as a method of escape from a world which has, for some reason, grown odious to them into a fantasy where impersonal entities avenge their grievances and set everything right.' See also P. Geyl, 'Historical Inevitability: Isaiah Berlin', in *idem, Debates with Historians* (The Hague, 1955), pp. 237–41.

188. Isaiah Berlin, 'Determinism, Relativism and Historical Judgements', in Gardiner (ed.), *Theories of History*, pp. 320f. My emphasis.

189. Berlin, 'Concept of Scientific History', p. 49.

190. *Ibid.*, p. 103.

191. Trevor-Roper, 'History and Imagination', pp. 363ff. Elton made a similar point in *The Practice of History*; as did Huizinga.

192. See Lewis Wolpert, *The Unnatural Nature of Science* (London, 1992), pp. 20f.

193. Indeed, Fischer adds several more types of causation: those based on 'abnormal antecedents', 'structural antecedents', 'contingent-series antecedents' and 'precipitant antecedents'. However, the utility of this typology seems questionable, as the distinctions are far from clear.

194. Dray, *Laws and Explanation in History*. See also *idem*, 'The Historical Explanation of Actions Reconsidered', in Sidney Hook (ed.), *Philosophy and History* (New York, 1963), pp. 105ff. For other critics of Hempel, see Alan Donagan, 'The Popper–Hempel Theory Reconsidered', in Dray (ed.), *Philosophical Analysis*, pp. 127–59.

195. Thomas Kuhn, *The Structure of Scientific Revolutions* (2nd edn, Chicago, 1970).

ONE:
ENGLAND WITHOUT CROMWELL

1. I am grateful to Dr Niall Ferguson, Professor Allan Macinnes, Dr John Morrill, Professor the Earl Russell and Dr David Scott for reading and commenting upon earlier drafts of this essay.

2. For the dating and analysis of this extensive series of plans and drawings by Webb, see the brilliant discussion by Margaret Whinney, 'John Webb's Drawings for Whitehall Palace', in *Proceedings of the Walpole Society*, 31 (1942–3), pp. 45–107. Although one of these drawings is marked as 'taken' by the King (plate XVIII), assessments of the chances of realising this project have usually been highly sceptical; see Timothy Mowl and Brian Earnshaw, *Architecture without Kings: The Rise of Puritan Classicism under Cromwell* (Manchester, 1995), pp. 85–7.

3. S. R. Gardiner, *History of the Great Civil War, 1642–49*, 4 vols (1893), vol. IV, p. 242. Gardiner was writing of the proposals put forward by Cromwell and Ireton in November 1648.

4. Caroline Hibbard, *Charles I and the Popish Plot* (Chapel Hill, 1983); Peter Donald, *An Uncounselled King: Charles I and the Scottish Troubles* (Cambridge, 1990); Conrad Russell, *The Causes of the English Civil War* (Oxford, 1990), and *The Fall of the British Monarchies, 1637–42* (Oxford, 1991); Allan I. Macinnes, *Charles I and the Making of the Covenanting Movement, 1625–41* (Edinburgh, 1991); Kevin Sharpe, *The Personal Rule of Charles I* (New Haven, 1992); Mark Charles Fissel, *The Bishops' Wars: Charles I's Campaigns against Scotland, 1638–40* (Cambridge, 1994); John Morrill's important contributions to the debate are conveniently collected in his *The Nature of the English Revolution: Essays* (London, 1993).

5. See, e.g., Esther S. Cope, *Politics without Parliaments, 1629–40* (London, 1987); L. J. Reeve, *Charles I and the Road to Personal Rule* (Cambridge, 1989). While Dr Reeve denies that 'England was on a high road to civil war from the beginning of the century', he argues that Charles I's personality was such that he stood 'to inherit the wind' (*ibid.*, pp. 293, 296): catastrophe, at some point, was virtually certain.

6. For the best modern account, see Macinnes, *Charles I and the Making of the Covenanter Movement*, chs 5–7.

7. Russell, *Fall of the British Monarchies*, ch. 9.

8. Nevertheless, a handful of studies have given serious consideration to some of these possibilities; see Geoffrey Parker, 'If the Armada Had Landed', *History*, 61 (1976), pp. 358–68; Roy Strong, *Henry, Prince of Wales and England's Lost Renaissance* (London, 1986); Conrad Russell, 'The Catholic Wind', in *idem, Unrevolutionary England, 1603–4* (London, 1990), pp. 305–8; Charles M. Gray, 'Parliament, Liberty and the Law', in J. H. Hexter (ed.), *Parliament and Liberty from the Reign of Elizabeth to the English Civil War* (Stanford, 1992), pp. 195–6.

9. Hugh Trevor-Roper, 'History and Imagination', in Valerie Pearl, Blair Worden and Hugh Lloyd-Jones (eds), *History and Imagination: Essays in Honour of H. R. Trevor-Roper* (London, 1981), p. 364.

10. British Library (hereafter BL), Add. MS 11045, fo. 45r–v, [Edward Rossingham to Viscount Scudamore], 13 August 1639.

11. Bodleian Library, Oxford (hereafter Bodl. Lib.), MS Tanner 65, fo. 100v, Sir Thomas Jermyn to Sir Robert Crane, 20 August 1640. (I owe this reference to Dr David Scott.)

12. Public Record Office (hereafter PRO), SP 16/464/71, fo. 159, Sir Francis Windebanke to Viscount Conway, 22 August 1640.

13. For a recent restatement of the traditional case, see Cope, *Politics without Parliaments*, pp. 153–4, 163–77.

14. Conrad Russell, 'The Nature of a Parliament in Early Stuart England', in Howard Tomlinson (ed.), *Before the English Civil War: Essays in Early Stuart Politics and Government* (London, 1983), p. 129.

15. Fissel, *Bishops' Wars*, p. 8.

16. Historical Manuscripts Commission, *Buccleuch and Queensberry (Montagu House) MSS*, 3 vols (1899–1926), vol. I, p. 276, Edward Montagu to the 1st Lord Montagu of Boughton, 9 February 1639. (I owe my knowledge of this reference to Professor Fissel.)

17. For the best recent account of the 1639 campaign, see Fissel, *Bishops' Wars*, pp. 3–39.

18. Macinnes, *Charles I and the Making of the Covenanter Movement*, p. 193; Fissel, *Bishops' Wars*, p. 5; and for the most thorough assessment of Hamilton's role see J. J. Scally, 'The Political Career of

James, 3rd Marquis and 1st Duke of Hamilton (1606–49) to 1643' (University of Cambridge, Ph.D. dissertation, 1993).

19. Bodl. Lib., MS Clarendon 16, fo. 20, Sir Francis Windebanke to Sir Arthur Hopton, 15 March 1639.

20. PRO, WO 49/68, fos 22v–23.

21. J. D. Alsop, 'Government, Finance, and the Community of the Exchequer', in Christopher Haigh (ed.), *The Reign of Elizabeth I* (London, 1984), pp. 101–23; Fissel, *Bishops' Wars*, pp. 137–43. Professor Fissel concludes (p. 151): 'The Exchequer was expected to perform a task which exceeded its capabilities at that time. The fact that the money [required by the King for the war-effort] *ultimately* was paid, however, demonstrates the resiliency of the institution and the tenacity of the staff.'

22. PRO, E 403/2568, fo. 72.

23. PRO, SP 16/414/93, fo. 219, deputy lieutenants of Yorks. to Sir Jacob Astley, c. 14 March 1639.

24. Hamilton, for one, realised the strategic significance of the north-east and diverted three of his warships to Aberdeen early in 1639, an action which did strengthen the royalist resistance to the Covenanting movement in the region. But it was too little to prevent Huntly's armed royalists from being overwhelmed by Covenanting forces (under Montrose) in April; though something of the potential damage which a properly supported royalist campaign in the north-east might have inflicted is suggested by the renewed campaign by Aboyne (Huntly's second son) during the spring of 1639. Although he was unaided by English military support, his insurrection was not quashed by the Covenanters until 20 June 1639, two days after the conclusion of the Pacification of Berwick. Macinnes, *Charles I and the Making of the Covenanter Movement*, p. 193; P. Gordon, *A Short Abridgement of Britane's Distempter, 1639 to 1649* (Spalding Club, Aberdeen, 1844), pp. 12–28. (I am grateful to Professor Allan Macinnes for a discussion of this point.)

25. Sheffield Central Library, Wentworth Woodhouse Muniments, Strafford Papers 10(250–1)a, Viscount Wentworth to the deputy lieutenants of Yorks., 15 February 1639. (I owe this and subsequent references in this paragraph to an important forthcoming paper by Dr David Scott,

of the History of Parliament Trust, London, on the reaction of Yorkshire to the two Bishops' Wars. I am grateful to Dr Scott for generously allowing me to cite from his paper prior to publication.)

26. John Rushworth, *Historical Collections*, Part II (1680), vol. II, p. 908; cf. Sheffield Central Library, Wentworth Woodhouse Muniments, Strafford Papers, 19(29), Sir William Savile to Viscount Wentworth, 26 April 1639.

27. Scottish Record Office, Hamilton MS GD 406/1/11144, 19 April 1639.

28. For the New Model's size, see Ian Gentles, *The New Model Army in England, Ireland, and Scotland, 1645–53* (Oxford, 1992), pp. 10, 392.

29. Yorks. Archaeological Society Library, Leeds, DD53/III/544 (Annals of York), unfol.

30. Bodl. Lib., MS Ashmole 800 (Misc. political papers), fo. 51v (first series of foliation), Colonel Fleetwood to his father, Sir Giles Fleetwood, York, 5 April 1639.

31. BL, Add. MS 11045, fo. 27, [Edward Rossingham to Viscount Scudamore], 11 June 1639.

32. There is the possibility that, in reporting the Covenanters' numbers to the King, Holland deliberately exaggerated their strength in order to discourage him from joining battle; see Russell, *Fall of the British Monarchies*, p. 63. The Covenanter leadership (probably accurately) believed Holland to be sympathetic to their cause, and had used him, a few weeks earlier, as their 'mediator' in making an approach to leading members of the English nobility. At Duns Law, it seems highly unlikely that he gave the King impartial advice. National Library of Scotland, Crawford MS 14/3/35 (formerly in the John Rylands Library, Manchester), 25 May 1639 (for the approach from the Covenanters). (I owe this point to Professor Russell.)

33. John Aston, 'Iter Boreale, Anno Salutis 1639', in J. C. Hodgson (ed.), *Six North Country Diaries* (Surtees Soc. 118, Durham, 1910), p. 24 (printing BL, Add. MS 28566). Henry Guthrie, Bishop of Dunkeld, *Memoirs [of] ... the Conspiracies and Rebellion against King Charles I* (1702), pp. 49–50 (printing Clark Memorial Library, Los Angeles, MS

O14M3/c. 1640/Bound, 'Observations upon the arise and progresse of the late Rebellion').

34. Scottish Record Office, Hamilton MS GD 406/1/1179, Sir Henry Vane Sr to Hamilton, 4 June 1639. This letter recounts the King's doubts: 'His Majesty doth now clearly see and is fully satisfied in his own judgement that what passed in the Gallery [at Whitehall] betwixt his Majesty, your lordship [Hamilton], and myself hath been but too much verified on this occasion.' Nalson, who prints the letter, is probably accurate in glossing this reference to the conversation in the Gallery as concerning the English nobility's and gentry's unwillingness 'to invade Scotland'. John Nalson, *An Impartial Collection of the Great Affairs of State*, 2 vols (1682–3), vol. I, p. 230.

35. Nalson, *An Impartial Collection*, vol. I, pp. 231–3. There seems to be no evidence for the suggestion that it was the king who opened negotiations: see S. R. Gardiner, *History of England*, 10 vols (London, 1891), vol. IX, p. 36; Sharpe, *Personal Rule of Charles I*, p. 808.

36. In practice, however, this condition was only partially met; the Fifth Table (or Covenanter executive) remained in being as a holding committee until February of the following year, in contravention of the treaty. (I am grateful to Professor Macinnes for a discussion of this point.)

37. Sharpe, *Personal Rule of Charles I*, p. 809.

38. E. M. Furgol, 'The Religious Aspects of the Scottish Covenanting Armies, 1639–51' (University of Oxford, D.Phil. dissertation, 1982), pp. 3, 7. Dr Furgol's estimates are accepted by Professor Fissel, who provides the most exhaustive modern account of the campaigns: *Bishops' Wars*, p. 31n.

39. J. Bruce (ed.), *Letters and Papers of the Verney Family* (Camden Soc. 56, 1853), p. 251.

40. BL, Add. MS 11045, fo. 32r, [Rossingham to Viscount Scudamore], 25 June 1639.

41. Fissel, *Bishops' Wars*, p. 31n; David Stevenson, 'The Financing of the Cause of the Covenants, 1638–51', *Scottish Historical Review*, 51 (1972), pp. 89–94.

42. Fissel, *The Bishops' Wars*, p. 38.

43. BL, Add. MS 11045, fo. 45, [Rossingham to Viscount Scudamore], 13 August 1639.

44. It has been recently argued that Charles's government was inherently 'never really stable' during the 1630s because 'it did not rest, like those of Elizabeth I and of his father [James I], upon a foundation of consent' (Reeve, *Charles I and the Road to Personal Rule*, p. 296). But this is to beg the question: whose consent? Charles did not depend upon a popular mandate to govern, and, although the gentry's reluctance to confer 'consent' could make the government of the localities problematic, in the absence of a successful rebellion the means by which Charles's subjects could vent their disapproval were distinctly limited.

45. Geoffrey Parker, *The Military Revolution: Military Innovation and the Rise of the West, 1500–1800* (Cambridge, 1988), ch. 1.

46. Conrad Russell, *The Scottish Party in English Parliaments, 1630–42, or, The Myth of the English Revolution* (Inaugural Lecture, King's College, London, 1991), p. 8. Although the kingdom had been 'demilitarized in the sense that all bu a handful of nobles had lost the power to raise and arm troops from among their retainers, the belief that military service was the proper concomitant of upper-gentry or noble status remained strong, well into the 1640s; and there are numerous examples of gentlemen or noblemen being aware of the latest developments in European warfare (either from their reading or from personal experience). Barbara Donagan, 'Codes and Conduct in the English Civil War', *Past and Present*, 118 (1982), pp. 65–95; J. S. A. Adamson, 'Chivalry and Political Culture in Caroline England', in Kevin Sharpe and Peter Lake (eds), *Culture and Politics in Early Stuart England* (London, 1994), pp. 161–97.

47. In a forthcoming study, Dr Barbara Donagan, of the Huntington Library, will offer evidence that a number of English households held substantial private stocks of arms during the 1630s. Even so, in the absence (during the intermission of Parliaments) of any generally acknowledged authority to sanction or coordinate their use, rebellion in England remained a distant prospect during Charles's Personal Rule; nor was there any general recognition within the political elite that armed resistance was a realistic or even a necessary option. (I am grateful to Dr John Morrill for a discussion of this point.)

48. Hugh Kearney, *Strafford in Ireland, 1633–41: A Study in Absolutism* (2nd edn, Cambridge, 1989). Rebellion in Ireland came only *after* Strafford had been removed as Lord Lieutenant, in 1641; and it was not directed against a tyrannical viceroy, but against an English parliament which appeared to have come under the control of a junta composed exclusively of the crown's militant Protestant opponents. See Conrad Russell, 'The British Background to the Irish Rebellion of 1641', *Historical Research*, 61 (1988), pp. 166–82.

49. For evidence of this collusion, see Peter Donald, 'New Light on the Anglo-Scottish Contacts of 1640', *Historical Research*, 62 (1989), pp. 221–9.

50. For contemporary evidence for this perception of Charles's regime, see John Morrill, 'Charles I, Tyranny, and the English Civil War', in *idem, The Nature of the English Revolution*, pp. 285–306.

51. Even the most 'revisionist' of historians accepts that the 'fear of Popery' was profoundly destabilising for Charles's regime during the late 1630s and early 1640s: see Sharpe, *Personal Rule of Charles I*, pp. 304, 842–4, 910–14, 938–9.

52. John Rylands Library, University of Manchester, Eng. MS 737 (Papers relating to Catholic contributions, 1639), fos 3a, 5–6; and see Caroline Hibbard, 'The Contribution of 1639: Court and Country Catholicism', *Recusant History*, 16 (1982–3), pp. 42–60.

53. During 1641 and 1642, reports of sinister 'Popish plotting' provided the King's critics within the Long Parliament with a cast-iron justification for arrogating to themselves 'emergency powers' and mustering a party (first in the two Houses and later in the country at large) to defend the Protestant religion and 'rescue' the King from the clutches of his evil counsellors. For these rumours see Caroline Hibbard, *Charles I and the Popish Plot* (Chapel Hill, 1983), pp. 168–238; Anthony Fletcher, *The Outbreak of the English Civil War* (London, 1981), chs 4–5.

54. Anthony Milton, *Catholic and Reformed: The Roman and Protestant Churches in English and Protestant Thought, 1600–40* (Cambridge, 1995), pp. 93–127.

55. Derek Hirst, 'The Failure of Godly Rule in the English Republic', *Past and Present*, 132 (1991), p. 66.

56. Conrad Russell, 'Parliament and the King's Finances', in *idem* (ed.), *The Origins of the English Civil War* (London, 1973), p. 107.

57. Of the six, the 4th Earl of Bedford died in 1641; the 3rd Earl of Exeter and the 2nd Lord Brooke (killed on military service at the siege of Lichfield) in 1643; the 3rd Earl of Essex, the 1st Earl of Bolingbroke and the 1st Earl of Mulgrave died in 1646.

58. D. Brunton and D. H. Pennington, *Members of the Long Parliament* (London, 1954), p. 16.

59. J. B. Crummett, 'The Lay Peers in Parliament, 1640–44' (University of Manchester, Ph.D. dissertation, 1970), appendix.

60. Kevin Sharpe, 'Archbishop Laud and the University of Oxford', in Pearl, Worden and Lloyd-Jones (eds), *History and Imagination*, p. 164.

61. John Twigg, *A History of Queens' College, Cambridge* (Woodbridge, 1987), p. 48.

62. BL, Harleian MS 7019, fos 52–93, 'Innovations in Religion and Abuses in Government in the University of Cambridge'; *Commons Journals*, vol. II, p. 126; David Hoyle, 'A Commons Investigation of Arminianism and Popery in Cambridge on the Eve of the Civil War', *Historical Journal*, 29 (1986), pp. 419–25, at p. 425.

63. Stephen Marshall, *A Sermon* (1641), p. 32; quoted in Russell, *Fall of the British Monarchies*, p. 26.

64. BL, Harleian MS 7019, fo. 82, 'Some of the scholars [of Emmanuel] have received harm by their frequent going to Peterhouse Chapel . . .'. Cf. Hoyle, 'A Commons Investigation', p. 424.

65. John Twigg, *The University of Cambridge and the English Revolution, 1625–88* (The History of the University of Cambridge: Texts and Studies, Woodbridge, 1990), vol. I, p. 41.

66. For further caution about the significance of Brunton's and Pennington's findings, see G. E. Aylmer, *Rebellion or Revolution? England, 1640–60* (Oxford, 1986), p. 42. (I am grateful to Professor Thomas Cogswell for a discussion of this point.)

67. Viscount Falkland and Sir Edward Hyde, for example, were royalists after 1642; but they had disapproved of many aspects of the government's conduct during the 1630s. Much of Charles's success in creating a royalist party in 1642 has been put down to the effectiveness

with which he reinvented his public persona during the first two years of the Long Parliament, presenting himself as the defender of the known laws and the established church, and depicting the two Houses as the body which threatened 'innovations' in church and state. See, in particular, the brilliant discussion of this theme by Russell, *The Fall of the British Monarchies*, pp. 230, 413, 420.

68. The most reliable estimates for England and Wales are as follows:

Year	Total population	Age				
		0–4	5–14	15–24	25–29	Total <30
		(% of total population)				
1631	4,892,580	12.45	19.87	18.19	7.89	58.40
1641	5,091,725	11.83	20.48	17.34	8.01	57.66

Private communication from Professor Sir Tony Wrigley. I am greatly indebted to Professor Wrigley for providing these detailed extrapolations from the statistics assembled for his massive survey, with R. S. Schofield, *The Population History of England 1541–1871* (Cambridge, 1981).

69. Esther Cope, 'Public Images of Parliament during its Absence', *Legislative Studies Quarterly*, 7 (1982), pp. 221–34. The medieval *Modus Tenendi Parliamentum* was probably the most widely circulated of all political texts in early Stuart England; see N. Pronay and J. Taylor (eds), *Parliamentary Texts of the Later Middle Ages* (Oxford, 1980), Appendix I. A copy of the *Modus* is the first item listed as having been found in Viscount Saye's study when it was searched for seditious papers at the conclusion of the Short Parliament: Bodl. Lib., MS Tanner 88*, fo. 115.

70. As Dr Gill has established, *Hampden's case* determined that, although the levying of ship-money writs was in accordance with the law, it was not permissible for sheriffs to distrain (that is, to confiscate property, in cases of non-payment, up to the value of the amount owed) on the authority of a writ from the Exchequer alone. Of course, this conclusion still left open to the crown the alternative of imprisoning those who refused to pay – an expedient which it had already shown itself willing to use. See A. A. M. Gill, 'Ship Money during the Personal Rule of Charles I: Politics, Ideology, and the Law, 1634–40' (University

of Sheffield, Ph.D. dissertation, 1990). If, hypothetically, another parliament had not been called during the 1640s, and ship money had become an annual imposition, it must remain an open question whether the crown would have been forced to imprison on a scale similar to the 1630s, or whether opposition to ship money would have progressively dwindled. (I am grateful to Dr John Morrill for a discussion of this point.)

71. For a lucid introduction to arguments deployed in this debate, J. P. Sommerville, *Politics and Ideology in England, 1603–40* (London, 1986), esp. pp. 160–2.

72. For some suggestive remarks about the impact of Coke's ideas on the generation entering the Inns of Court in the 1630s, see Alan Cromartie, *Sir Matthew Hale, 1609–1676: Law, Religion, and Natural Philosophy* (Cambridge, 1995), pp. 11–29.

73. 'The Lord Chancellor Egertons observacons upon ye Lord Cookes reportes' (1615), printed in Louis A. Knafla, *Law and Politics in Jacobean England: The Tracts of Lord Chancellor Ellesmere* (Cambridge, 1977), pp. 297–318. For the diversity of views on the status and purpose of the common law, see Clive Holmes, 'Parliament, Liberty, Taxation, and Property', in J. H. Hexter (ed.), *Parliament and Liberty from the reign of Elizabeth to the English Civil War* (Stanford, 1992), pp. 122–54.

74. Against this contention, it could be argued that Parliament, during the 1620s, was never given the opportunity by the crown to provide adequately for the defence of the realm; see Richard Cust, *The Forced Loan and English Politics 1626–8* (Oxford, 1987), pp. 150–85. But it remains highly questionable whether any Caroline Parliament would have passed subsidies to the value of the sums raised for, and exclusively expended upon, the king's ship-money fleet during the 1630s.

75. For the scale of the under-assessment, see Felicity Heal and Clive Holmes, *The Gentry in England and Wales, 1500–1700* (London, 1994), pp. 185–6; Conrad Russell, *Parliaments and English Politics, 1621–9* (Oxford, 1979), pp. 49–51.

76. K. R. Andrews, *Ships, Money, and Politics: Seafaring and Naval Enterprise in the Reign of Charles I* (Cambridge, 1991), pp. 128–39.

77. For the origins of this line of argument, see *The King's Prerogative in Saltpetre* (1607), printed in *English Reports*, vol. LXXVII,

pp. 1294–7; cited in Holmes, 'Parliament, Liberty, Taxation, and Property', p. 136.

78. Thomas Hobbes, *A Dialogue between a Philosopher and a Student of the Common Laws of England*, ed. Joseph Cropsey (Chicago, 1971), p. 63; and see the subsequent section: 'Also the king (as is on all hands confessed) hath the charge [i.e. duty] lying upon him to protect his people against foreign enemies, and to keep the peace betwixt them within the kingdom; if he do not his utmost endeavour to discharge himself thereof, he committeth a sin . . .' (*ibid.*).

79. For Hutton's views, see Wilfrid R. Prest (ed.), *The Diary of Sir Richard Hutton, 1614–39* (Selden Soc. supplementary series, IX, 1991), pp. xxvi–xxxv; *Dictionary of National Biography*, 'Sir Richard Hutton'.

80. Conrad Russell, 'The Ship Money Judgements of Bramston and Davenport', in *idem*, *Unrevolutionary England* (London, 1990), pp. 137–44.

81. Sir John Bramston (1577–1654), who found against the crown on a technicality (that, from the record, it did not appear to whom the money levied was due), nevertheless concurred with the majority on the question that the service was due to the King. Bramston had defended Sir John Eliot in 1629, and it is possible that he might have remained on the bench as a critic of the regime into the 1640s – albeit outnumbered on the bench, and probably ineffectual. See Russell, 'Ship Money Judgements', p. 143. Of course, age was not the only determinant of outlook among the legal profession; the young Matthew Hale, who was to be one of the most influential members of the post-Restoration bench, was thoroughly imbued with the traditions of Sir Edward Coke and John Selden; see Cromartie, *Sir Matthew Hale*, chs 1–2.

82. J. S. Cockburn, *A History of English Assizes, 1558–1714* (Cambridge, 1972), pp. 231–7. Professor Cockburn discusses the decline of 'popular confidence in the impartiality of [the judges'] proceedings' (p. 231) during Charles's reign. Whether or not this would have created an insuperable crisis in the English legal system – in the absence of a Parliament – must remain an open question.

83. The judges who found for the crown in *Hampden's case* stopped well short of any such endorsement, as the overall question of royal

fiscal policy was not at issue. What Finch and his colleagues determined was that the King had an obligation to defend the kingdom, and to take the measures necessary to achieve this end. (I am grateful to Professor Russell for his advice on this point.)

84. Francis Hargrave, *A Complete Collection of State-Trials*, 11 vols (1776–81), vol. I, col. 625.

85. BL, Add. MS 27402 (Misc. historical papers), fo. 79, Charles I to the Earl of Essex, 6 August 1644.

86. John Harris and Gordon Higgott, *Inigo Jones: Complete Architectural Drawings* (New York, 1989), pp. 238–40. The inscription on the entablature read: 'CAROLUS ... TEMPLUM SANCTI PAULI VETUSTATE CONSUMPTUM RESTITUIT ET PORTICUM FECIT' (Charles ... restored the Cathedral of St Paul, [which had been] consumed by age, and erected [this] portico).

87. John Rylands Library, University of Manchester, Eng. MS 737, fo. 3a, the Queen to Sir John Wintour, 17 April 1639. See also the circular letter from the Revd Ant[hony] Champney, dean of the English Catholic secular clergy, 30 November 1638, urging Catholics to be particularly earnest in their protestations of loyalty to the King at the time of the Scottish crisis (Eng. MS 737, no. 32).

88. Donald, *An Uncounselled King*, pp. 320–7; Fissel, *Bishops' Wars*, p. 4.

89. Jonathan Israel, *The Dutch Republic: Its Rise, Greatness, and Fall, 1477–1806* (Oxford, 1995), pp. 637–45.

90. House of Lords Record Office, Main Papers 29/7/1648, fos 59–60, lists of priests imprisoned or executed, 1643–7. In contrast, only three priests had been executed during the fifteen years of Charles's reign from his accession to 1640. See Robin Clifton, 'Fear of Popery', in Russell (ed.), *Origins of the English Civil War*, p. 164.

91. Scottish Record Office, GD 406/1/10543, Charles I to Hamilton, 18 April 1639, printed in Gilbert Burnet, *The Memoires of the Lives and Actions of James and William, Dukes of Hamilton* (1677), p. 155.

92. Northumberland to Strafford, 29 January 1639, printed in William Knowler (ed.), *The Earl of Strafforde's Letters and Dispatches*, 2 vols (1739), vol. II, p. 276; Northumberland to Leicester, 31 December 1640, printed in Arthur Collins (ed.), *Letters and Memorials of State ...*

from the Originals in Penshurst Place, 2 vols (1746), vol. II, p. 666. Northumberland, who disliked Hamilton, was exaggerating; but, if not the 'sole power' over the King, Hamilton was certainly one of the most powerful figures at court during 1639–41.

93. In the summer of 1638, for example, Lord Newburgh (the Chancellor of the Duchy of Lancaster) complained to Secretary Coke that it was Patrick Maule, one of the Bedchamber Scots, and the Marquess of Hamilton who were the King's principal confidants concerning the Scottish crisis. Kevin Sharpe, 'The Image of Virtue: The Court and Household of Charles I, 1625–42', in David Starkey (ed.), *The English Court: From the Wars of the Roses to the Civil War* (London, 1987), p. 251.

94. In what may have been a token of things to come, the Council of War (the Privy Council committee, presided over by Arundel and charged with the planning of the 1639 campaign) had succeeded in persuading the King to revoke a series of unpopular patents and monopolies over the winter of 1638–9. Bodl. Lib., MS Clarendon 15, fo. 36, Sir Francis Windebanke's and Lord Cottington's notes, 11 Nov. 1638; see also the discussion in Fissel, *Bishops' Wars*, p. 69n.

95. Scottish Record Office, Hamilton MSS GD 406/1/1505, 1506, 1509, 1510 (for Saye); GD 406/1/1427 (for Mandeville); GD 406/1/1316, 1319 (for Danvers). Such was Hamilton's reputation as a figure open to ideas about the reform of government that in 1642 Danvers sent him a presentation copy of a treatise he had commissioned on the reformation of the two kingdoms from Henry Parker, the nephew of Viscount Saye and Sele. Scottish Record Office, Hamilton MS GD 406/1/1700, Danvers to Hamilton, 1 July 1642; H[enry] P[arker], *The Generall Junto, or the Councell of Union* (1642), BL, 669, fo. 18/1; and see Michael Mendle, *Henry Parker and the English Civil War: The Political Thought of the Public's 'Privado'* (Cambridge, 1985), pp. 18–19, 54–5, 97. I am grateful to Dr John Scally for a discussion of this point.

96. Clark Memorial Library, Los Angeles, MS O14M3/c. 1640/ Bound ([Bishop Guthrie], 'Observations upon the arise and progresse of the late Rebellion'), p. 82. Hamilton was clearly out of favour with the Queen, whose Chamberlain had accused him of treasonable collusion with the Scots; see also Barbara Donagan, 'A Courtier's Progress: Greed

and Consistency in the Life of the Earl of Holland', *Historical Journal*, 19 (1976), p. 344.

97. For Arundel and the 'old nobility', see Kevin Sharpe, *Sir Robert Cotton, 1586–1631* (Oxford, 1979), pp. 140, 213–14; and his 'The Earl of Arundel, his Circle and the Opposition to the Duke of Buckingham, 1618–28', in Kevin Sharpe (ed.), *Faction and Parliament: Essays on Early Stuart History* (Oxford, 1978), pp. 209–44.

98. Arundel had originally wished to have Essex in the senior office of general of the horse: see Northumberland to Strafford, 29 January 1639, printed in Knowler (ed.), *The Earl of Strafforde's Letters*, vol. II, p. 276.

99. BL, Loan MS 23/1 (Hulton of Hulton corr.), fos 170–84, 190, letters from the Earl of Holland to Essex [undated].

100. The phrase is Burnet's, *Lives of the Hamiltons*, p. 518.

101. For the efforts of Hamilton and Vane on Gustavus' behalf see Scally, 'The Political Career of James, 3rd Marquis and 1st Duke of Hamilton', pp. 50–67.

102. Hibbard, *Charles I and the Popish Plot*, pp. 104–24.

103. BL, Add. MS 11045, fo. 27, [Rossingham to Viscount Scudamore], 11 June 1639. In June 1639, Hamilton was reported to have predicted that 'the business in Scotland will soon come to an end, the Covenanters do differ so much among themselves' (*ibid.*). This was an exaggeration, as Hamilton underestimated the solid support enjoyed by Argyll among the gentry and burghs; nevertheless, a split within the Covenanter leadership remained a real possibility, and would have been made a virtual certainty amid the recriminations which would have followed a Covenanter defeat in the summer of 1639. (I am grateful to Professor Allan Macinnes for a discussion of this point.)

104. Any long-term solution to Scottish rebelliousness depended on the King granting at least some of the demands of the National Covenant, and the construction of a pro-royalist party in Scotland to govern the country in the King's name. Even such prospective recruits to a new pro-royalist government as the Earl of Montrose would have been unlikely to have agreed to the wholesale abandonment of the aims of the Covenant. Of course, magnanimity in victory was not a quality for which Charles I was renowned; but, ironically, an English military

success in 1639 would have greatly strengthened the hands of precisely those English councillors who were most likely to have promoted a lenient post-war settlement with the Covenanter lords – particularly Holland (the Covenanters' chosen 'mediator') and Hamilton.

105. PRO 31/3/71, fos 85, 141v. (I owe my knowledge of this reference to Professor Kevin Sharpe.)

106. Israel, *Dutch Republic*, pp. 537–8; for a strongly argued alternative view of Charles's prospects, see Derek Hirst, *Authority and Conflict: England 1603–58* (London, 1986), pp. 174–7.

107. Collins (ed.), *Letters and Memorials of State ... from the Originals at Penshurst Place*, vol. II, p. 636, Northumberland to Leicester, 13 February 1640.

108. Valerie Pearl, *London and the Outbreak of the Puritan Revolution* (Oxford, 1961), p. 96.

109. Robert Brenner, *Merchants and Revolution: Commercial Change, Political Conflict, and London's Overseas Traders, 1550–1653* (Cambridge, 1993), pp. 281–306; for a more pessimistic view of the crown's relations with the City, Robert Ashton, *The Crown and the Money Market, 1603–40* (Oxford, 1960), pp. 152–3, 174–84; *idem, The City and the Court, 1603–43* (Cambridge, 1979), pp. 202–4.

110. For the decline in royal revenues from land in the early seventeenth century see R. W. Hoyle, 'Introduction: Aspects of the Crown's Estate, c. 1558–1640', in *idem* (ed.), *The Estates of the Crown* (Cambridge, 1994). Dr Hoyle points out that in c. 1600, about 39 per cent of the crown's overall income was derived from its landed estate; by 1641 that figure had declined to 14 per cent (*ibid.*, pp. 26–8).

111. Conrad Russell, 'Parliamentary History in Perspective', *History*, 61 (1976), pp. 1–27; Michael Braddick, *Parliamentary Taxation in Early Seventeenth-Century England* (Royal Historical Society, Studies in History, 70, London, 1994). I am grateful to Dr Braddick for a discussion of this point.

112. Edward Hyde, Earl of Clarendon, *The History of the Rebellion and Civil Wars in England*, ed. W. D. Macray, 6 vols (Oxford, 1888), vol. I, p. 85. Even without ship money, Charles could probably have balanced his books, so long as he avoided involvement in foreign wars (a point I owe to Dr Morrill).

113. Russell, 'Parliamentary History in Perspective', p. 9.

114. For the impact of taxation during the 1640s and 1650s, see Ann Hughes, *Politics, Society, and Civil War in Warwickshire, 1620–60* (Cambridge, 1987), pp. 262–6, 280–2; John Morrill, *Cheshire, 1630–60: County Government and Society during the English Revolution* (Oxford, 1974), p. 107.

115. Aylmer, *Rebellion or Revolution?*, p. 172; and see his 'Attempts at Administrative Reform, 1625–40', *English Historical Review*, 72 (1957), pp. 232–3. Of course, it may be objected that this was in the aftermath of a civil war; but, as recent studies have stressed, these were taxes collected by local men, not extracted by the army at the point of the sword: see Hughes, *Warwickshire*, ch. 5.

116. Richard Tuck, '"The Ancient Law of Freedom": John Selden and the English Civil War', in John Morrill (ed.), *Reactions to the English Civil War, 1642–49* (London, 1982), pp. 137–61.

117. Russell, *Fall of the British Monarchies*, p. 227.

118. I am grateful to Professor Olivier Chaline, of L'Ecole Normale Supérieure, for a discussion of this point.

119. For the limitations on French government in the later seventeenth century: Roger Mettam, 'Power, Status, and Precedence: Rivalries among the Provincial Elites in Louis XIV's France', in *Transactions of the Royal Historical Society*, 38 (1988), pp. 43–82; and *idem, Power and Faction in Louis XIV's France* (Oxford, 1988); see also Jeroen Duindam, *Myths of Power: Norbert Elias and the Early Modern European Court* (Amsterdam, 1995), pp. 43–56.

120. Clark Memorial Library, Los Angeles, MS W765M1/E56/ c. 1645/Bound, John Windover, 'Encomion Heroicon ... The States Champions in honor of ... Sr Thomas Fairfax' [c. 1646]; *The Great Champions of England* (1646), BL, 669, fo. 10/69.

TWO:
BRITISH AMERICA

1. In John C. Fitzpatrick (ed.), *The Writings of George Washington*, 39 vols (Washington, 1931–44), vol. III, pp. 244–7.

2. A handful have posed the question, but not seriously. See Roger Thompson, 'If I Had Been the Earl of Shelburne in 1762–5', in Daniel Snowman (ed.), *If I Had Been* ... (London, 1979), pp. 11–29, and Esmond Wright, 'If I Had Been Benjamin Franklin in the early 1770s', in *ibid.*, pp. 33–54.

3. Geoffrey Parker, 'If the Armada Had Landed', *History*, 61 (1976), pp. 358–68.

4. Conrad Russell, 'The Catholic Wind', reprinted in *idem, Unrevolutionary England, 1603–1642* (London, 1990), pp. 305–8.

5. 'But from the moment of using the conditional tense, we have begun to consider counter-factuals. There are obvious objections to doing so. History entails an infinite number of contingent variables, and for this reason our selection of counter-suppositions is necessarily undisciplined. But counter-history is not the study of what would have happened, so much as of what might have happened; and the case for considering outcomes which did not occur, but which those engaged in the happenings knew might occur – or we with the benefit of hindsight see might have occurred – is that it enables us to understand better the problematics in which the actors were entangled. Any event in history is both what did occur and the non-occurrence of what might have happened; nobody knows this better than we who spend our lives within the thinking distance of unthinkable possibilities, some of which happen from time to time': J. G. A. Pocock, 'The Fourth English Civil War: Dissolution, Desertion and Alternative Histories in the Glorious Revolution', *Government and Opposition*, 23 (1988), pp. 151–66, esp. p. 157.

6. Robert C. Ritchie, *The Duke's Province: A Study of New York Politics and Society, 1664–1691* (Chapel Hill, 1977).

7. Viola Florence Barnes, *The Dominion of New England: A Study in British Colonial Policy* (New Haven, 1923), pp. 35–6, 44.

8. David Lovejoy, *The Glorious Revolution in America* (2nd edn, Middletown, Conn., 1987).

9. The option of an America in which military governors and bureaucrats rather than representative assemblies were central is reconstructed in the works of Stephen Saunders Webb, *The Governors-General: The English Army and the Definition of the Empire, 1569–1681*

(Chapel Hill, 1979); *idem, 1676: The End of American Independence* (New York, 1984); *idem, Charles Churchill* (New York, 1996). This thesis runs counter to prevailing assumptions and has not received its due.

10. Geoffrey Holmes and Daniel Szechi, *The Age of Oligarchy: Pre-industrial Britain 1722–1783* (London, 1993), p. 97.

11. E.g. 'His Majestie's Most Gracious Declaration to all his Loving Subjects', 17 April 1693, in Daniel Szechi, *The Jacobites: Britain and Europe 1688–1788* (Manchester, 1994), pp. 143–5.

12. Belatedly, Charles Edward Stuart's note of points to be included in his next declaration, of 1753, included: '7th. An union between the three kingdoms to be proposed to a free Parliament': Szechi, *Jacobites*, pp. 150–1. But this was an unrealistic counterfactual, and French plans for the invasion attempt of 1759 still envisaged a dissolution of the Union of 1707: Claude Nordmann, 'Choiseul and the Last Jacobite Attempt of 1759', in Eveline Cruickshanks (ed.), *Ideology and Conspiracy: Aspects of Jacobitism, 1689–1759* (Edinburgh, 1982), pp. 201–17.

13. Richard Price, *Observations on the Nature of Civil Liberty, the Principles of Government, and the Justice and Policy of the War with America* (London, 1776), p. 28: 'An *Empire* is a collection of states or communities united by some common bond or tye. If these states have each of them free constitutions of government, and, with respect to taxation and internal legislation, are independent of the other states, but united by compacts, or alliances, or subjection to a Great *Council*, representing the whole, or to one monarch entrusted with the supreme executive power: In these circumstances, the Empire will be an Empire of Freemen.'

14. John Adams, 6 February 1775, in John Adams and Jonathan Sewall [sc. Daniel Leonard], *Novanglus and Massachusettensis; or Political Essays, published in the Years 1774 and 1775, on the Principal Points of Controversy, between Great Britain and her Colonies* (Boston, 1819), p. 30.

15. Gaillard Hunt (ed.), *The Writings of James Madison*, 9 vols (New York, 1900–10), vol. VI, p. 373.

16. James Otis, *The Rights of the British Colonies Asserted and Proved* (Boston, 1764), p. 23.

17. Richard Bland, *An Enquiry into the Rights of the British Colonies; intended as an Answer to 'The Regulations lately made concerning the Colonies, and the Taxes imposed upon them considered.' In a Letter addressed to the Author of that Pamphlet* (Williamsburg, 1766; reprinted London, 1769), p. 12.

18. Even Thomas Jefferson's *A Summary View of the Rights of British America* (Williamsburg, 1774), which echoed Bland's and Otis's doctrine on people's right to establish new societies (p. 6), was expressed in the old idiom of petitioning the crown for a redress of grievances as well as the new idiom of natural rights.

19. Barnes, *Dominion of New England*, p. 178; Charles M. Andrews, *The Colonial Period of American History*, 4 vols (New York, 1934–8), vol. I, p. 86n.

20. [Franklin], 'On the Tenure of the Manor of East Greenwich', *Gazetteer*, 11 January 1766, in Leonard W. Labaree *et al.* (eds), *The Papers of Benjamin Franklin* (New Haven, 1959–), vol. XIII, pp. 18–22.

21. *Novanglus and Massachusettensis*, p. 94.

22. [William Cobbett and T. C. Hansard], *The Parliamentary History of England from the Earliest Period to the Year 1803*, 36 vols (London, 1806–20), vol. XVIII, cols 957–8.

23. For recent versions of the claim that the causes of the Revolution were essentially internal to the colonies, see Gordon Wood, *The Radicalism of the American Revolution* (New York, 1992); J. C. D. Clark, *The Language of Liberty 1660–1832: Political Discourse and Social Dynamics in the Anglo-American World* (Cambridge, 1993).

24. Drew R. McCoy, *The Elusive Republic: Political Economy in Jeffersonian America* (Chapel Hill, 1980); Doron S. Ben-Atar, *The Origins of Jeffersonian Commercial Policy and Diplomacy* (London, 1993).

25. Carl Bridenbaugh, *Mitre and Sceptre: Transatlantic Faiths, Ideas, Personalities, and Politics, 1689–1775* (New York, 1962); William H. Nelson, *The American Tory* (Oxford, 1961).

26. T. H. Breen, 'An Empire of Goods: The Anglicization of Colonial America, 1690–1776', *Journal of British Studies*, 25 (1986), pp. 467–99; '"Baubles of Britain": The American and Consumer Revolutions of the Eighteenth Century', *Past and Present*, 119 (1988), pp. 73–104.

27. Durand Echeverria, *Mirage in the West: A History of the French Image of American Society to 1815* (Princeton, 1957); François Furet, 'De l'homme sauvage à l'homme historique: l'expérience américaine dans la culture française', in *La Révolution américaine et l'Europe* (Colloques Internationaux du Centre National de la Recherche Scientifique, Paris, 1979), pp. 91–105.

28. J. Hector St John de Crèvecoeur, *Letters from an American Farmer* (London, 1782); trans., Paris, 1787; Leipzig, 1788–9.

29. In Franklin, *Papers*, vol. XIII, pp. 124–59, at p. 135.

30. [Thomas Pownall], *The Administration of the Colonies* (London, 1764), p. 25.

31. Thomas Pownall, *The Administration of the Colonies* (2nd edn., London, 1765), Dedication, sigs A2v–A3r.

32. MS history of Virginia, Virginia Historical Society, quoted in Kate Mason Rowland, *The Life of George Mason 1725–1792*, 2 vols (New York, 1892), vol. I, pp. 123–4.

33. [Joseph Galloway], *Letters to a Nobleman, on the Conduct of the War in the Middle Colonies* (London, 1779), pp. 8–10.

34. Douglass Adair and John A. Schutz (eds), *Peter Oliver's Origin & Progress of the American Rebellion: A Tory View* (San Marino, 1961), pp. 3, 145.

35. Edward H. Tatum Jr (ed.), *The American Journal of Ambrose Serle, Secretary to Lord Howe 1776–1778* (San Marino, 1940), pp. 46–7.

36. [Daniel Leonard], *The Origin of the American Contest with Great-Britain, or The present political State of the Massachusetts-Bay, in general, and The Town of Boston in particular* (New York, 1775), p. 12; for these sources see Gordon S. Wood, *The Creation of the American Republic 1776–1787* (Chapel Hill, 1969), esp. pp. 3–4 for the 'strangely unaccountable' causality of the Revolution.

37. Within this older agenda, doubts began to be cast on the inevitability of a breakdown in such works as Ian R. Christie and Benjamin W. Labaree, *Empire or Independence 1760–1776* (Oxford, 1976). Still within this agenda, a powerful counterfactual analysis was provided by Robert W. Tucker and David C. Hendrickson, *The Fall of the First British Empire: Origins of the War of American Independence*

(Baltimore, 1982), a work which nevertheless often came to the conclusion that British policy could hardly have been other than it was.

38. The myth was most recently restated as an historical explanation by Jack P. Greene, 'Why Did the Colonists Rebel?', *Times Literary Supplement*, 10 June 1994.

39. An early attempt was made to diversify the secular litany of 'ostensible causes' of the Revolution by framing arguments about the effect of the Great Awakening in political mobilisation; but this was denied by a counterfactual claim that without the Awakening, 'colonial resistance would have taken very much the same forms it did and within the same chronology': John M. Murrin, 'No Awakening, No Revolution? More Counterfactual Speculations', *Reviews in American History*, 11 (1983), pp. 161–71, at p. 164.

40. Especially Bernard Bailyn, *The Ideological Origins of the American Revolution* (Cambridge, Mass., 1967) and *The Origins of American Politics* (New York, 1968).

41. Especially Jack P. Greene, *Peripheries and Center: Constitutional Development in the Extended Polities of the British Empire and the United States, 1607–1788* (New York, 1986), but anticipated in many of Greene's writings since the 1960s.

42. Tucker and Hendrickson, *Fall of the First British Empire*, p. 71.

43. Christie and Labaree, *Empire or Independence*, pp. 277–8.

44. John Shy, 'Thomas Pownall, Henry Ellis, and the Spectrum of Possibilities, 1763–1775', in Alison Gilbert Olson and Richard Maxwell Brown (eds), *Anglo-American Political Relations, 1675–1775* (New Brunswick, 1970), pp. 155–86.

45. This interpretation was stressed by Jack P. Greene, 'The Seven Years' War and the American Revolution: The Causal Relationship Reconsidered', *Journal of Imperial and Commonwealth History*, 8 (1980), pp. 85–105.

46. For a bibliography of the pamphlets, see Clarence W. Alvord, *The Mississippi Valley in British Politics*, 2 vols (Cleveland, 1917), vol. II, pp. 253–64; for the debate, William L. Grant, 'Canada versus Guadeloupe, an Episode of the Seven Years' War', *American Historical Review*, 17 (1911–12), pp. 735–53.

47. [Cobbett (ed.)], *Parliamentary History*, vol. XV, col. 1265.

48. William Burke, *Remarks on the Letter Address'd to Two Great Men. In a Letter to the Author of that Piece* (London, 1760), pp. 50–1.

49. [Benjamin Franklin], *The Interest of Great Britain considered, With Regard to her Colonies, And the Acquisitions of Canada and Guadaloupe* (London, 1760), in Franklin, *Papers*, vol. IX, pp. 47–100, at pp. 73, 77, 90.

50. Gerald S. Graham, *The Politics of Naval Supremacy: Studies in British Maritime Ascendancy* (Cambridge, 1965), p. 27.

51. Tucker and Hendrickson, *Fall of the First British Empire*, pp. 50–3.

52. Price, *Observations on the Nature of Civil Liberty*, pp. 43–4.

53. Richard Price to Benjamin Franklin, 3 Apr. 1769, in W. Bernard Peach and D. O. Thomas (eds), *The Correspondence of Richard Price*, 3 vols (Cardiff, 1983–94), vol. I, pp. 58–79, at pp. 76–7. When read to the Royal Society, the words 'unjust and fatal policy' were omitted.

54. Richard Price to Ezra Stiles, 2 November 1773, in Price, *Correspondence*, vol. I, p. 165; in response to Stiles to Price, 20 November 1772, *ibid.*, p. 149.

55. Quoted in Lawrence Henry Gipson, 'The American Revolution as an Aftermath of the Great War for the Empire, 1754–1763', *Political Science Quarterly*, 65 (1950), pp. 86–104, at p. 104.

56. John M. Murrin, 'The French and Indian War, the American Revolution, and the Counterfactual Hypothesis: Reflections on Lawrence Henry Gipson and John Shy', *Reviews in American History*, 1 (1973), pp. 307–18, at p. 309.

57. Alison Gilbert Olson, 'The British Government and Colonial Union, 1754', *William and Mary Quarterly*, 17 (1960), pp. 22–34.

58. Quoted in Sir Lewis Namier and John Brooke, *Charles Townshend* (London, 1964), pp. 39–40.

59. [Thomas Paine], *Common Sense; Addressed to the Inhabitants of America* (Philadelphia, 1776), p. 31.

60. Jack P. Greene, 'An Uneasy Connection: An Analysis of the Preconditions of the American Revolution', in Stephen G. Kurtz and James H. Hutson (eds), *Essays on the American Revolution* (Chapel

Hill, 1973), pp. 32–80, at p. 64. Greene argued (pp. 65, 72) that the 'salient condition' of the Revolution was 'the decision by colonial authorities in Britain [specifically Lord Halifax, President of the Board of Trade from 1748 to 1761] to abandon Walpole's policy of accommodation' in favour of 'a dependence upon coercion', a thesis now difficult to sustain against the evidence presented in Tucker and Hendrickson, *Fall of the First British Empire*.

61. Wood, *Making of the American Republic*, pp. 12–13.

62. [John Dickinson], *Letters from a Farmer in Pennsylvania, to the Inhabitants of the British Colonies* (Philadelphia, 1768), pp. 7–13, 16.

63. Franklin to Joseph Galloway, 9 January 1769, in Franklin, *Papers*, vol. XVI, p. 17.

64. Worthington Chauncey Ford (ed.), *Journals of the Continental Congress 1774–1789*, 34 vols (Washington, 1904–37), vol. I, pp. 84, 89.

65. Tucker and Hendrickson, *Fall of the First British Empire*, pp. 114–17.

66. *Ibid.*, pp. 117–27.

67. Jack P. Greene and Richard M. Jellison, 'The Currency Act of 1764 in Imperial–Colonial Relations, 1764–1776', *William and Mary Quarterly*, 18 (1961), pp. 485–518; Joseph Albert Ernst, *Money and Politics in America 1755–1775: A Study in the Currency Act of 1764 and the Political Economy of Revolution* (Chapel Hill, 1973).

68. J. Wright (ed.), *Sir Henry Cavendish's Debates of the House of Commons during the Thirteenth Parliament of Great Britain*, 2 vols (London, 1841–3), vol. I, pp. 494–5, cited in Tucker and Hendrickson, *Fall of the First British Empire*, p. 217.

69. Tucker and Hendrickson, *Fall of the First British Empire*, p. 226n.

70. *Ibid.*, p. 238.

71. Franklin, *Papers*, vol. XIV, pp. 110–16, at pp. 114–15.

72. Peter D. G. Thomas, *Revolution in America: Britain and the Colonies, 1763–1776* (Cardiff, 1992), pp. 29, 37.

73. [Thomas Whately], *The Regulations Lately Made concerning the Colonies, and the Taxes Imposed upon Them, considered* (London, 1765), p. 109.

74. For an important study which deals with divine-right monarchy

and representative democracy as equally 'fictions', see Edmund S. Morgan, *Inventing the People: The Rise of Popular Sovereignty in England and America* (New York, 1988).

75. [Cobbett (ed.)], *Parliamentary History*, vol. XVI, col. 100.

76. Sir Lewis Namier and John Brooke (eds), *The History of Parliament: The House of Commons 1754–1790*, 3 vols (London, 1964), vol. I, pp. 366, 419.

77. [Paine], *Common Sense*, p. 30.

78. Tucker and Hendrickson, *Fall of the First British Empire*, pp. 335–41.

79. Julian P. Boyd, *Anglo-American Union: Joseph Galloway's Plans to Preserve the British Empire 1774–1788* (Philadelphia, 1941), pp. 34–8.

80. Galloway, in Edmund C. Burnett (ed.), *Letters of Members of the Continental Congress*, 8 vols (Washington, 1921–36), vol. I, p. 59.

81. For the Commons debate on North's proposal on 20 February 1775, see [Cobbett (ed.)], *Parliamentary History*, vol. XVIII, col. 320.

82. Tucker and Hendrickson, *Fall of the First British Empire*, pp. 367–78.

83. Josiah Tucker, *The true Interest of Great Britain set forth in regard to the Colonies* in *idem*, *Four Tracts, together with Two Sermons, On Political and Commercial Subjects* (Gloucester, 1774), p. 195.

84. W. Paul Adams, 'Republicanism in Political Rhetoric before 1776', *Political Science Quarterly*, 85 (1970), pp. 397–421. In *Rights of Man*, part II (1792), Paine was to record an astonishing vagueness about just what republicanism meant.

85. Tucker and Hendrickson, *Fall of the First British Empire*, pp. 160–1. Such measures may have formed part of Charles Townshend's programme in the late 1760s (*ibid.*, pp. 241–8); by then it was, perhaps, too little and too late.

86. *Ibid.*, p. 304; Bernard Bailyn, *The Ordeal of Thomas Hutchinson* (Cambridge, Mass., 1974), pp. 212–20.

87. Tony Hayter, *The Army and the Crowd in Mid-Georgian England* (London, 1978); Tucker and Hendrickson, *Fall of the First British Empire*, p. 322.

88. Tucker and Hendrickson, *Fall of the First British Empire*, pp. 261–3, 322.

89. *Ibid.*, pp. 265–6.

90. *Ibid.*, p. 289.

91. John Shy, *Toward Lexington: The Role of the British Army in the Coming of the American Revolution* (Princeton, 1965), pp. 52–68, 82–3.

92. Tucker and Hendrickson, *Fall of the First British Empire*, p. 88.

93. Shy, *Toward Lexington*, pp. 142–3.

94. Tucker and Hendrickson, *Fall of the First British Empire*, p. 359.

95. Jeremy Black, *War for America: The Fight for Independence 1775–1783* (London, 1991), pp. 24–7.

96. *Ibid.*, pp. 14–15 and *passim*.

97. *Ibid.*, p. 23.

98. Shy, *Toward Lexington*, p. viii.

99. [Galloway], *Letters to a Nobleman*, p. 36.

100. Black, *War for America*, p. 249.

101. William Gordon, *The History of the Rise, Progress, and Establishment of the Independence of the United States of America*, 4 vols (London, 1788), vol. II, pp. 568–9.

102. Lester H. Cohen, *The Revolutionary Histories: Contemporary Narratives of the American Revolution* (Ithaca, NY, 1980), pp. 58–60, 67, 71–85. 'The historians thus preserved the ideological and cultural values traditionally associated with providence even as they rejected providence as an explanatory concept,' p. 82.

103. *Ibid.*, p. 83.

104. *Ibid.*, p. 185.

105. *Ibid.*, p. 119.

106. For the Indian question, see Tucker and Hendrickson, *Fall of the First British Empire*, pp. 87–95.

107. Benjamin Quarles, 'Lord Dunmore as Liberator', *William and Mary Quarterly*, 15 (1958), pp. 494–507.

108. Sidney Kaplan, 'The "Domestic Insurrections" of the Declaration of Independence', *Journal of Negro History*, 61 (1976), pp. 243–55; Sidney Kaplan and Emma Nogrady Kaplan, *The Black Presence in the Era of the American Revolution* (revised edn, Amherst, Mass., 1989).

109. Anne-Robert Jacques Turgot, *Mémoire sur les colonies américaines* (Paris, 1791), quoted in Anthony Pagden, *Lords of All the World:*

Ideologies of Empire in Spain, Britain and France c. 1500–c. 1800 (New Haven, 1995), p. 192.

110. I take this to be a central theme of a courageously innovative work, Raphael Samuel, *Theatres of Memory* (London, 1994).

111. W. B. Gallie, *Philosophy and the Historical Understanding* (2nd edn, New York, 1964), pp. 40–1, 72, 87–91, 125.

112. The tension between the counterfactual and the contingent is present in much recent historical writing which seeks to dissolve the old teleologies, and it is a tension as yet unresolved either in historical method or in the substance of the historical story.

THREE:
BRITISH IRELAND

1. *Hansard*, 5th ser., vol. XXXVII, col. 1721 (16 April 1912).

2. See, for example, Alan J. Ward, *The Irish Constitutional Tradition: Responsible Government and Modern Ireland, 1782–1992* (Dublin, 1994), pp. 30–8. See also R. B. McDowell, *The Irish Administration, 1801–1914* (London, 1964). For a succinct examination of the constitutional differences between Britain and Ireland see Lord Crewe's comments, *Hansard*, House of Lords, 5th ser., vol. XIII, col. 423 (27 January 1913).

3. For the prehistory of the Act of Union see James Kelly, 'The Origins of the Act of Union: An Examination of Unionist Opinion in Britain and Ireland, 1650–1800', *Irish Historical Studies*, 25 (May 1987), pp. 236–63. For the passage of the measure see G. C. Bolton, *The Passing of the Irish Act of Union* (Oxford, 1966).

4. There is a substantial literature on Irish nationalism. See, in particular, Tom Garvin, *The Evolution of Irish Nationalist Politics* (Dublin, 1981); *idem, Nationalist Revolutionaries in Ireland, 1858–1928* (Dublin, 1987); D. George Boyce, *Nationalism in Ireland* (2nd edn, London, 1991).

5. For a brilliant reflection on this theme see R. F. Foster, *The Story of Ireland: An Inaugural Lecture Delivered before the University of Oxford on 1 December 1994* (Oxford, 1995).

6. Elie Kedourie, *Nationalism* (4th edn, Oxford, 1993).

7. For an introduction to recent scholarship on Daniel O'Connell see Oliver Macdonagh, *O'Connell: The Life of Daniel O'Connell, 1775–1847* (London, 1991).

8. The only monograph devoted to Butt's career and achievement is David Thornley, *Isaac Butt and Home Rule* (London, 1964). For a stimulating analysis of Irish nationalist politics in this period see R. V. Comerford, *The Fenians in Context* (Dublin, 1985).

9. The best short introduction to Parnell's career is Paul Bew, *C. S. Parnell* (Dublin, 1980).

10. Alvin Jackson, *The Ulster Party: Irish Unionists in the House of Commons, 1884–1911* (Oxford, 1989), p. 52. For Irish Unionism in this period see also Patrick Buckland, *Irish Unionism I: The Anglo-Irish and the New Ireland, 1885–1922* (Dublin, 1972); Patrick Buckland, *Irish Unionism II: Ulster Unionism and the Origins of Northern Ireland, 1886–1922* (Dublin, 1973); Alvin Jackson, *Colonel Edward Saunderson: Land and Loyalty in Victorian Ireland* (Oxford, 1995).

11. Bew, *Parnell*, pp. 127–32.

12. H. C. G. Matthew (ed.), *The Gladstone Diaries*, 14 vols (Oxford, 1968–94), vol. XII, pp. xxxvi–xli.

13. James Loughlin, *Gladstone, Home Rule and the Ulster Question, 1882–1893* (Dublin, 1986), pp. 172–96.

14. One of the theses proffered in A. B. Cooke and John Vincent, *The Governing Passion: Cabinet Government and Party Politics in Britain, 1885–6* (Brighton, 1974).

15. Ward, *Irish Constitutional Tradition*, p. 60.

16. See, for example, Lord Welby, 'Irish Finance', in J. H. Morgan (ed.), *The New Irish Constitution: An Exposition and Some Arguments* (London, 1912), p. 154.

17. R. F. Foster, *Lord Randolph Churchill: A Political Life* (Oxford, 1981), p. 225; Bew, *Parnell*, pp. 72–3.

18. Jackson, *Ulster Party*, pp. 25–39.

19. Loughlin, *Gladstone*, p. 273.

20. Matthew, *Gladstone Diaries*, vol. XII, pp. lxi–lxii, lxxxiii.

21. Welby, 'Irish Finance', p. 140.

22. *Ibid.*

23. Jackson, *Ulster Party*, pp. 315–16.

24. *Ibid.*, p. 318.

25. Robert Blake, *The Unknown Prime Minister: The Life and Times of Andrew Bonar Law, 1858–1923* (London, 1955), p. 130.

26. H. M. Hyde, *Carson: The Life of Sir Edward Carson, Lord Carson of Duncairn* (London, 1953), pp. 286–7.

27. Austen Chamberlain, *Politics from Inside: An Epistolary Chronicle, 1906–14* (London, 1936), p. 193.

28. Blake, *Unknown Prime Minister*, pp. 69–70.

29. *Ibid.*, pp. 115–16.

30. Thomas Jones, 'Andrew Bonar Law', in J. R. H. Weaver (ed.), *Dictionary of National Biography, 1922–30* (London, 1937), p. 491.

31. Jeremy Smith, 'Bluff, Bluster and Brinkmanship: Andrew Bonar Law and the Third Home Rule Bill', *Historical Journal*, 36, 1 (1993), pp. 161–78.

32. Blake, *Unknown Prime Minister*, p. 165.

33. *Ibid.*, p. 181.

34. Alvin Jackson, *Sir Edward Carson* (Dublin, 1993), p. 37.

35. A. T. Q. Stewart, *The Ulster Crisis* (London, 1967), pp. 116–20.

36. Jackson, *Carson*, p. 35.

37. The best account of Devlin's career may be found in Eamon Phoenix, *Northern Nationalism: Nationalist Politics, Partition and the Catholic Minority in Northern Ireland, 1890–1940* (Belfast, 1994).

38. Patricia Jalland, *The Liberals and Ireland: The Ulster Question in British Politics to 1914* (Brighton, 1980), p. 56. Bentley Brinkerhoff Gilbert, *David Lloyd George: A Political Life: The Organiser of Victory, 1912–16* (London, 1992), p. 94. Even a comparatively neutral contemporary observer commented on the government's 'lack of political imagination to which I attribute the present *impasse*': Sir Horace Plunkett, *A Better Way: An Appeal to Ulster Not to Desert Ireland* (London, 1914), pp. 7–8.

39. Jalland, *Liberals and Ireland*, p. 59; Gilbert, *Lloyd George*, pp. 3–4.

40. Jalland, *Liberals and Ireland*, p. 67.

41. *Ibid.*, pp. 63–5.

42. *Ibid.*

43. The Bill was widely reprinted in contemporary publications. See, for example, John Redmond, *The Home Rule Bill* (London, 1912), pp. 103–53; Pembroke Wicks, *The Truth about Home Rule* (Boston, 1913), pp. 221–93.

44. Redmond, *Home Rule Bill*, p. 12.

45. *Ibid.*, p. 3.

46. *Ibid.*, pp. 5–6.

47. Jalland, *Liberals and Ireland*, p. 161. For a sustained Unionist critique of the financial settlement see A. W. Samuels, *Home Rule Finance* (Dublin, 1912).

48. Redmond, *Home Rule Bill*, p. 23.

49. Roy Jenkins, *Asquith* (London, 1964), p. 279.

50. Jalland, *Liberals and Ireland*, p. 47.

51. For a detailed discussion of earlier Home Rule novels see Edward James, 'The Anglo-Irish Disagreement: Past Irish Futures', *Linenhall Review*, 3/4 (Winter, 1986), pp. 5–8. See also I. F. Clarke, *Voices Prophesying War, 1763–1984* (Oxford, 1966); D. Suvin, *Victorian Science Fiction in the U.K.: The Discourses of Knowledge and of Power* (Boston, 1983). There were some distinguished literary contributors to the genre, including Lady Gregory: James Pethica (ed.), *Lady Gregory's Diaries, 1892–1902* (Gerrards Cross, 1996), p. 13.

52. For Frankfort Moore see Patrick Maume, 'Ulstermen of Letters: The Unionism of Frank Frankfort Moore, Shan Bullock, and St. John Ervine', in Richard English and Graham Walker (eds), *Irish Unionism* (London, 1996).

53. See, for example, Eoin MacNeill, 'The North Began', reprinted in F. X. Martin (ed.), *The Irish Volunteers, 1913–15: Recollections and Documents* (Dublin, 1963), pp. 57–61. See also Padraig Pearse, 'The Coming Revolution', reprinted in the same collection, pp. 61–5 ('I am glad that the North has "begun". I am glad that the Orangemen have armed, for it is a goodly thing to see arms in Irish hands.').

54. The best account of the Unionist gunrunning remains Stewart, *Ulster Crisis*.

55. George Birmingham, *The Red Hand of Ulster* (London, 1912), pp. 214–15.

56. A. W. Samuels, *Home Rule: What Is It?* (Dublin, 1911), p. 32.

See also A. V. Dicey, *A Fool's Paradise, Being a Constitutionalist's Criticism of the Home Rule Bill of 1912* (London, 1913), p. 106. Jackson, *Ulster Party*, p. 122.

57. W. Douglas Newton, *The North Afire: A Picture of What May Be* (London, 1914), p. 142.

58. George Bernard Shaw, 'Preface for Politicians' to *John Bull's Other Island* (new edn, London, 1926), pp. xxiii–xxvi.

59. *Ibid.*, p. xxiv.

60. *Ibid.*, p. xxx.

61. For MacSwiney and the context to the play see Francis J. Costello, *Enduring the Most: The Life and Death of Terence MacSwiney* (Dingle, 1995), pp. 38–40.

62. Redmond, *Home Rule Bill*, p. 65. Francis Sheehy-Skeffington, *Michael Davitt: Revolutionary Agitator and Labour Leader* (London, 1908), p. 261. William Redmond echoed his brother's line: *Hansard*, 5th ser., vol. XXXVII, col. 149 (15 April 1912). See also Joseph Devlin's remarks: *Hansard*, 5th ser., vol. LIII, col. 1548 (10 June 1913).

63. Redmond, *Home Rule Bill*, p. 67; A. V. Dicey, *A Leap in the Dark: A Criticism of the Principles of Home Rule as Illustrated by the Bill of 1893* (London, 1911), p. 127.

64. Redmond, *Home Rule Bill*, p. 23.

65. Richard Bagwell, 'The Southern Minorities', in S. Rosenbaum (ed.), *Against Home Rule: The Case for the Union* (London, 1912), p. 184.

66. Wicks, *Truth about Home Rule*, p. 204. Cecil Harmsworth, 'The State of Public Business', in Morgan (ed.), *New Irish Constitution*, p. 387.

67. Redmond, *Home Rule Bill*, p. 66; Dicey, *Leap in the Dark*, pp. 166–7. The reference to 'Committee Room 15' is to the venue for the notorious and acrimonious debates in November 1890 concerning Parnell's leadership of the Irish party.

68. Redmond, *Home Rule Bill*, pp. 75–6.

69. Sir John MacDonell, 'Constitutional Limitations upon the Powers of the Irish Legislature', in Morgan (ed.), *New Irish Constitution*, p. 111.

70. Revd J. B. Armour, 'The Presbyterian Church in Ulster', in Morgan (ed.), *New Irish Constitution*, p. 468.

71. Welby, 'Irish Finance', p. 146.

72. Jonathan Pym, 'The Present Position of the Irish Land Question', in Morgan (ed.), *New Irish Constitution*, p. 169.

73. T. F. Molony, 'Judiciary, Police and the Maintenance of Law and Order', in Morgan (ed.), *The New Irish Constitution*, pp. 157–65.

74. Redmond, *Home Rule Bill*, pp. 13, 65.

75. J. H. M. Campbell, 'The Control of Judiciary and Police', in Rosenbaum (ed.), *Against Home Rule*, p. 156.

76. Peter Kerr-Smiley, *The Peril of Home Rule* (London, 1911), p. 56.

77. Wicks, *Truth about Home Rule*, p. 196.

78. Dicey, *Leap in the Dark*, p. 127.

79. Kerr-Smiley, *Peril of Home Rule*, p. 53.

80. Bagwell, 'Southern Minorities', p. 187 ('Nothing will conciliate the revolutionary faction in Ireland, and there is every reason to think that it would become the strongest').

81. Thomas Sinclair, 'The Position of Ulster', in Rosenbaum, *Against Home Rule*, p. 177. See also the businessman H. T. Barrie's comment on 2 May 1912: *Hansard*, 5th ser., vol. XXXVII, col. 2159.

82. Phineas O'Flannagan (pseudonym for F. Frankfort Moore), *The Diary of an Irish Cabinet Minister: Being the History of the First (and Only) Irish National Administration, 1894* (Belfast, 1893), pp. 28–31.

83. Kerr-Smiley, *Peril of Home Rule*, p. 65.

84. Wicks, *Truth about Home Rule*, p. 220.

85. Earl Percy, 'The Military Disadvantages of Home Rule', in Rosenbaum (ed.), *Against Home Rule*, pp. 196–7. For a more extensive examination of this theme see Major-General Sir Thomas Fraser, *The Military Danger of Home Rule in Ireland* (London, 1912). The South African analogy was commonly mentioned: see, for example, W. F. Monypenny, *The Two Irish Nations: An Essay on Home Rule* (London, 1913), pp. 80–7.

86. Percy, 'Military Disadvantages of Home Rule', p. 196.

87. *Ibid.*

88. Jalland, *Liberals and Ireland*, p. 67, indicates that Asquith had for long recognised the need for (and possible shape of) a deal.

89. Devlin was able to deliver (admittedly with difficulty and in the context of the war) northern Nationalist support for temporary six-county exclusion in June 1916: Phoenix, *Northern Nationalism*, pp. 29–33.

90. For divisions within British Unionist support for Ulster see W. S. Rodner, 'Leaguers, Covenanters, Moderates: British Support for Ulster, 1913–14', *Eire-Ireland*, 17, 3 (1982), pp. 68–85. See also Smith, 'Bluff, Bluster and Brinkmanship', pp. 161–78. For an example of Chamberlain's prevarication on the issue of loyalist militancy see *Hansard*, 5th ser., vol. XXXVIII, col. 265 (7 May 1912). For evidence of Lloyd George's assessment of the likely Conservative difficulty see Gilbert, *Lloyd George*, p. 95.

91. Hardliners appear to have kept a brake on the more consensual impulses of some Ulster Unionist leaders in 1913–14: see Jackson, *Carson*, pp. 36–40.

92. Redmond, *Home Rule Bill*, p. 132.

93. Kerr-Smiley, *Peril of Home Rule*, pp. 52–3.

94. Paul Bew, *Ideology and the Irish Question: Ulster Unionism and Irish Nationalism, 1912–16* (Oxford, 1994), p. 6.

95. See, for example, Joseph Devlin's remarks in *Hansard*, 5th ser., vol. LIX, col. 2284 (19 March 1914): 'There will be an earnest desire on the part of Nationalists to do everything that is humanly possible to satisfy their wants and their desires and even to meet their most violent prejudices.' For the possible influence of the Hibernians see Lord Dunraven's remarks: *Hansard*, House of Lords, 5th ser., vol. XIII, col. 481 (27 January 1913).

96. Bew, *Ideology and the Irish Question*, pp. 120–3.

97. For evidence of the growing rapprochement between southern Unionists and Redmond as a result of the war see Buckland, *Irish Unionism*, vol. I, pp. 29–50.

98. Carson publicly considered the possibility of an excluded Ulster accepting Home Rule: *Hansard*, 5th ser., vol. LX, col. 1752 (29 April 1914).

99. See L. S. Amery's comments, *Hansard*, 5th ser., vol. XXXVII,

col. 1781 (16 April 1912): 'The revision of finance is a direct incentive to the beginning of a new and more advanced Nationalist agitation in Ireland.'

100. Shaw, 'Preface for Politicians', p. xxiv, for some interesting reflections on this issue. See also *Hansard*, 5th ser., vol. XXXVII, col. 149 (15 April 1912): 'events might conceivably so shape themselves in Ireland as to give the party from Ulster perhaps a preponderating influence in the Irish parliament' (William Redmond).

101. Public Record Office of Northern Ireland (PRONI), Crawford Papers, D.1700/2/17–18, 'Record of the Home Rule Movement', fo. 187. See also PRONI, Spender Papers, D.1295/2/7, 'Contingencies for the Carrying of Home Rule'. Charles Townshend, *Political Violence in Ireland: Government and Resistance since 1848* (Oxford, 1983), p. 252.

102. Townshend, *Political Violence*, p. 252.

103. *Ibid.*, p. 269. See also Jackson, *Carson*, p. 39, for some evidence of government strategy. For the Unionist leaders' fears that the government might provoke loyalist riots see Spender Papers, D.1295/2/16, Memorandum written by Spender for Revd Brett Ingram (1959). For the Unionist intention to boycott the new Home Rule Parliament see, for example, J. B. Lonsdale's remarks on 2 May 1912: *Hansard*, 5th ser., vol. XXXVII, col. 2119. See also J. H. M. Campbell's comments, *Hansard*, 5th ser., vol. LV, col. 160 (7 July 1913) and the perceptive remarks of Kellaway, *Hansard*, 5th ser., vol. LVIII, col. 119 (10 February 1914).

104. Townshend, *Political Violence*, p. 252.

105. Ian Beckett (ed.), *The Army and the Curragh Incident* (London, 1986), p. 9; Townshend, *Political Violence*, p. 269.

106. Stewart, *Ulster Crisis*, pp. 244–9.

107. See, for example, Philip Cruickshank, *The Tyrone Regiment, U.V.F.: Record of Camp of Instruction* (1913).

108. Phoenix, *Northern Nationalism*, p. 14.

109. Townshend, *Political Violence*, pp. 261–76.

110. Spender Papers, D.1295/2/7, 'Railway Policy'. This document – one of a series of UVF contingency plans for the enactment of Home Rule – recommended that 'a kind of fortified frontier post should be established on the [rail] lines after they enter Ulster at which all trains

should be compelled to stop'. It is difficult to see how this could have been achieved given the probable opposition of South Down Nationalists.

111. Beckett (ed.), *Army and the Curragh Incident*, pp. 1–29. See also A. P. Ryan, *Mutiny at the Curragh* (London, 1956); Sir James Fergusson, *The Curragh Incident* (London, 1964).

112. Beckett (ed.), *Army and the Curragh Incident*, p. 26.

113. *Ibid.*, p. 24.

114. Richard Holmes, *The Little Field Marshal: Sir John French* (London, 1981), pp. 179, 183.

115. For a fuller version of this argument see Alvin Jackson, 'Unionist Myths, 1912–85', *Past and Present*, 136 (1992), esp. pp. 178–83.

116. Townshend, *Political Violence*, p. 255. One Ulster Unionist MP, R. J. McMordie, claimed in debate that there were 100,000 revolvers in loyalist hands, but this seems highly unlikely: *Hansard*, 5th. ser., vol. XXXVIII, col. 289 (7 May 1912).

117. Townshend, *Political Violence*, p. 250.

118. Newton, *North Afire*, p. 200. Arthur Balfour speculated concerning this situation: see *Hansard*, 5th ser., vol. LIII, col. 1306 (9 June 1913).

119. Dicey had urged passive resistance by Ulster Unionists in the interlude between the enactment of Home Rule and a general election: *Fool's Paradise*, p. 124. See also J. B. Lonsdale's remarks on 2 May 1912: *Hansard*, 5th ser., vol. XXXVII, col. 2123. Lord Crewe dismissed the Unionist threat to withhold taxes: *Hansard*, House of Lords, 5th ser., vol. XIV, cols 871–2 (14 July 1913).

120. Analogies with the Balkans were being made in 1914: see Bonar Law's remarks in *Hansard*, 5th ser., vol. LX, col. 1751 (6 Apr. 1914).

FOUR:
THE KAISER'S EUROPEAN UNION

1. Viscount Grey of Falloden, *Fly Fishing* (first pub. 1899; Stocksfield, 1990), pp. 12, 15. I am grateful to Mr Sandy Sempliner for this reference.

2. Erskine Childers, *The Riddle of the Sands* (London, 1984 edn), p. 248.

3. A. J. A. Morris, *The Scaremongers* (London, 1984), pp. 156ff. See also I. F. Clarke, *Voices Prophesying War* (London, 1966).

4. Saki, *When William Came: A Story of London under the Hohenzollerns*, repr. in *The Complete Works of Saki* (London/Sydney/Toronto, 1980), pp. 691–814.

5. *Ibid.*, esp. pp. 706–11. The idea that Jews were pro-German, somewhat surprising to modern eyes, was a nostrum of the pre-1914 Right in England. Needless to say, the Boy Scout movement defies the defeatist mood.

6. V. R. Berghahn, *Germany and the Approach of War in 1914* (London, 1973), p. 203.

7. See D. E. Kaiser, 'Germany and the Origins of the First World War', *Journal of Modern History*, 55 (1983), pp. 442–74.

8. J. Steinberg, 'The Copenhagen Complex', *Journal of Contemporary History*, 3, 1 (1966), p. 41.

9. E. von Moltke, *Generaloberst Helmuth von Moltke. Erinnerungen, Briefe, Dokumente 1877–1916* (Stuttgart, 1922), pp. 13f.

10. General Friedrich von Bernhardi, *Germany and the Next War* (London, 1914). On Moltke's religious leanings, see A. Bucholz, *Moltke, Schlieffen and Prussian War Planning* (New York/Oxford, 1991).

11. James Joll, *The Origins of the First World War* (London, 1984), p. 186.

12. W. J. Mommsen, 'The Topos of Inevitable War in Germany in the Decade before 1914', in V. R. Berghahn and M. Kitchen (eds), *Germany in the Age of Total War* (London, 1981), pp. 23–44.

13. David Lloyd George, *War Memoirs* (London, 1938), vol. I, pp. 32, 34f., 47f.

14. W. S. Churchill, *The World Crisis 1911–1918* (London, 1922), pp. 45, 55, 188.

15. Lord Grey of Falloden, *Twenty-Five Years* (London, 1925), vol. I, pp. 143, 277; vol. II, pp. 20, 30.

16. C. Hazlehurst, *Politicians at War, July 1914 to May 1915: A Prologue to the Triumph of Lloyd George* (London, 1971), p. 52.

17. G. M. Trevelyan, *Grey of Falloden* (London, 1937), p. 250.

18. See, for an example of Marxist determinism, Eric Hobsbawm, *The Age of Empire 1875–1914* (London, 1987), pp. 312–14, 323–7. The American liberal tradition of blaming the war on a systemic crisis of international relations continues to have its adherents; as does the notion popularised by A. J. P. Taylor of 'war by timetable', i.e. a war caused by the inexorable 'logic' of military planning.

19. Hobsbawm, *Age of Empire*, p. 326; C. Barnett, *The Collapse of British Power* (London, 1973), p. 55.

20. H. H. Asquith, *The Genesis of the War* (London, 1923), p. 216.

21. Lloyd George, *War Memoirs*, vol. I, pp. 43f.

22. A. J. P. Taylor, *The Struggle for Mastery in Europe 1848–1918* (Oxford, 1954), p. 527. See also J. Joll, *Europe since 1870: An International History* (London, 1973), pp. 184ff.

23. M. Brock, 'Britain Enters the War', in R. J. W. Evans and H. Pogge von Strandmann (eds), *The Coming of the First World War* (Oxford, 1988), pp. 145–78.

24. Churchill, *World Crisis*, pp. 202f.

25. *Ibid.*, pp. 228f.

26. Grey, *Twenty-Five Years*, vol. II, p. 46. See also pp. 9f.

27. *Ibid.*, vol. I, pp. 77, 312.

28. *Ibid.*, vol. II, p. 28.

29. *Ibid.*, vol. I, pp. 335ff. Cf. Gordon Martel, *The Origins of the First World War* (London, 1987), pp. 89f.

30. K. M. Wilson, *The Policy of the Entente: Essays on the Determinants of British Foreign Policy, 1904–1914* (Cambridge, 1985), esp. pp. 96f., 115. See also T. Wilson, 'Britain's "Moral Commitment" to France in July 1914', *History*, 64 (1979), esp. pp. 382–90.

31. D. French, *British Economic and Strategic Planning, 1905–1915* (London, 1982), p. 87.

32. See for example M. Howard, 'Europe on the Eve of World War I', in *idem*, *The Lessons of History* (Oxford, 1993), p. 119; Martel, *Origins*, p. 69.

33. P. Kennedy, *The Rise of the Anglo-German Antagonism 1860–1914* (London, 1980), esp. p. 458: 'The ultimate decision was ...

predictable in advance, even without the Belgian issue being utilised as political camouflage.'

34. Crowe, Hardinge and Grey all accepted that 'the Germans have studied and are studying the question of invasion'; Morris, *Scaremongers*, p. 158. See also D. French, 'Spy Fever in Britain 1900–1915', *Historical Journal*, 21 (1978).

35. I. Geiss, *July 1914: The Outbreak of the First World War: Selected Documents* (London, 1967), pp. 29ff.

36. Wilson, *Entente*, p. 100; Z. Steiner, *Britain and the Origins of the First World War* (London, 1977), p. 42.

37. Wilson, *Entente*, pp. 66f.

38. P. J. Cain and A. G. Hopkins, *British Imperialism: Innovation and Expansion 1688–1914* (Harlow, 1993), pp. 450, 456ff.

39. Churchill, *World Crisis*, p. 120; Lloyd George, *War Memoirs*, vol. I, p. 6.

40. J. Gooch, *The Plans of War: The General Staff and British Military Strategy c. 1900–1916* (London, 1974), p. 25.

41. See the classic texts F. Fischer, *Germany's Aims in the First World War* (London, 1967); *idem, War of Illusions: German Policies from 1911 to 1914* (London/New York, 1975).

42. I. Geiss, *Der lange Weg in die Katastrophe. Die Vorgeschichte des Ersten Weltkrieges 1815–1914* (Munich/Zurich, 1990), esp. pp. 23f., 54, 123.

43. K. Burk, 'The Mobilization of Anglo-American Finance during World War One', in N. F. Dreisziger (ed.), *Mobilization for Total War* (Ontario, 1981), pp. 25–42.

44. Only the most tendentious reading of the historical record, as we shall see, could actually equate Germany's aims in 1914 with those of 1939.

45. B. H. Liddell Hart, *The British Way in Warfare* (London, 1942), pp. 12f., 29f.

46. J. M. Hobson, 'The Military-Extraction Gap and the Wary Titan: The Fiscal Sociology of British Defence Policy 1870–1913', *Journal of European Economic History*, 22 (1993), pp. 461–506.

47. L. Albertini, *The Origins of the War* (Oxford, 1953), vol. III,

pp. 331, 368, 644; Lloyd George, *War Memoirs*, vol. I, pp. 57f.; Hazlehurst, *Politicians at War*, p. 41. For similar views, see M. R. Gordon, 'Domestic Conflicts and the Origins of the First World War: The British and German Cases', *Journal of Modern History*, 46 (1970), pp. 195f.

48. Trevelyan, *Grey*, p. 257; Asquith, *Genesis*, p. 202. See C. Nicolson, 'Edwardian England and the Coming of the First World War', in A. O'Day (ed.), *The Edwardian Age: Conflict and Stability 1902–1914* (London, 1979), pp. 145–8.

49. Hobson, 'Wary Titan', pp. 495f., 499f. For similar suggestions, see A. L. Friedberg, *The Weary Titan: Britain and the Experience of Relative Decline 1895–1905* (Princeton, 1988), pp. 301f.; P. K. O'Brien, 'Reply', *Past and Present*, 125 (1989), p. 195. But see the perceptive critique in T. J. McKeown, 'The Foreign Policy of a Declining Power', *International Organisation*, 42, 2 (1991), pp. 259–78.

50. A rare exception is Paul Johnson, *The Offshore Islanders* (London, 1972), pp. 365f.

51. Asquith, *Genesis*, pp. 57f., 60, 63f., 83.

52. Grey, *Twenty-Five Years*, vol. I, pp. 75, 81, 85, 313, 334f. Cf. Trevelyan, *Grey*, pp. 254, 260.

53. Grey, *Twenty-Five Years*, vol. II, pp. 35ff.

54. On 'national efficiency' see G. R. Searle, 'Critics of Edwardian Society: The Case of the Radical Right', in O'Day (ed.), *Edwardian Age*, pp. 79–96; on Edwardian 'militarism', see A. Summers, 'Militarism in Britain before the Great War', *History Workshop*, 2 (1976), pp. 106–20.

55. C. Trebilcock, 'War and the Failure of Industrial Mobilisation: 1899 and 1914', in J. M. Winter (ed.), *War and Economic Development* (Cambridge, 1975), pp. 141ff.; Cain and Hopkins, *British Imperialism*, p. 452; Barnett, *Collapse*, pp. 75–83. See also G. W. Monger, *The End of Isolation: British Foreign Policy 1900–1907* (London, 1963), pp. 8f., 15, 110, 147.

56. Figures from Hobson, 'Wary Titan', pp. 478f. Cf. my own comparable estimates in N. Ferguson, 'Public Finance and National Security: The Domestic Origins of the First World War Revisited', *Past and Present*, 142 (1993), pp. 141–68.

57. Monger, *End of Isolation*, p. 13.

58. Lord Hankey, *The Supreme Command* (London, 1961), vol. I,

pp. 46, 49; Gooch, *Plans of War*, pp. 42–90; N. d'Ombrain, *War Machinery and High Policy: Defence Administration in Peacetime Britain* (Oxford, 1973), pp. 5f., 9f., 14, 76.

59. See C. Buchheim, 'Aspects of 19th Century Anglo-German Trade Policy Reconsidered', *Journal of European Economic History*, 10 (1981), pp. 275–89; Kennedy, *Anglo-German Antagonism*, pp. 46ff., 262ff.; Cain and Hopkins, *British Imperialism*, pp. 461f.; Z. Steiner, *Britain and the Origins of the First World War* (London, 1977), pp. 60–3.

60. J. L. Garvin, *The Life of Joseph Chamberlain*, vol. III: *1895–1900* (London, 1934), pp. 246, 250ff., 331–9, 502; J. L. Amery, *The Life of Joseph Chamberlain*, vol. IV, *1901–1903* (London, 1951), pp. 138ff., 159, 163; R. T. B. Langhorne, 'Anglo-German Negotiations Concerning the Future of the Portuguese Colonies 1911–1914', *Historical Journal* (1973), pp. 364ff.; Monger, *End of Isolation*, pp. 19f., 24–9, 39f., 119ff., 145, 186.

61. H. W. Koch, 'The Anglo-German Alliance Negotiations: Missed Opportunity or Myth', *History*, 54 (1968), p. 392; P. M. Kennedy, 'German World Policy and the Alliance Negotiations with England 1897–1900', *Journal of Modern History*, 45 (1973), p. 625. See also Grey, *Twenty-Five Years*, vol. I, p. 245.

62. See for details Garvin, *Chamberlain*, pp. 259–83, 332–41, 507–8; Amery, *Chamberlain*, pp. 144–55.

63. Kennedy, 'Alliance Negotiations', pp. 613. See Garvin, *Chamberlain*, pp. 268ff., 287–91, 503, 512; Amery, *Chamberlain*, pp. 148–51, 163.

64. Steinberg, 'Copenhagen Complex', pp. 27ff.; Kennedy, 'Alliance Negotiations', p. 610f., 619f.; Berghahn, *Germany and the Approach of War*, pp. 40f., 53.

65. See Garvin, *Chamberlain*, vol. III, pp. 498, 511–15; Amery, *Chamberlain*, vol. IV, pp. 153, 157, 167–80.

66. Monger, *End of Isolation*, p. 12.

67. Amery, *Chamberlain*, p. 197.

68. Kennedy, 'Alliance Negotiations', p. 618. See also *ibid.*, pp. 621, 625; Garvin, *Chamberlain*, p. 516.

69. A. J. Marder, *British Naval Policy 1880–1905: The Anatomy of British Sea Power* (London, 1964), p. 503.

70. Steinberg, 'Copenhagen Complex', pp. 31–8.

71. Wilson, *Entente*, p. 5.

493

72. Monger, *End of Isolation*, pp. 10, 17, 23–9.

73. B. Williams, 'The Strategic Background to the Anglo-Russian Entente of 1907', *Historical Journal*, 9 (1966), pp. 360–6; Monger, *End of Isolation*, pp. 2, 5, 7, 33f., 108, 115ff., 123f., 132, 140ff., 185, 216–20; Gooch, *Plans of War*, p. 175.

74. Monger, *End of Isolation*, pp. 200–2, 214–21.

75. *Ibid.*, pp. 39, 113, 129, 134, 144; C. Andrew, 'The Entente Cordiale from its Origins to 1914', in N. Waites (ed.), *Troubled Neighbours: Franco-British Relations in the Twentieth Century* (London, 1971), pp. 11, 19ff.

76. Garvin, *Chamberlain*, p. 275; Amery, *Chamberlain*, pp. 180, 202–6.

77. Wilson, *Entente*, pp. 71, 74; Andrew, 'Entente', p. 22; Monger, *End of Isolation*, pp. 129–33, 192.

78. *Ibid.*, pp. 187ff., 195f., 223.

79. A. Offer, *The First World War: An Agrarian Interpretation* (Oxford, 1989), pp. 223f., 230, 291; Monger, *End of Isolation*, pp. 188f., 206ff.; d'Ombrain, *War Machinery*, pp. 76–80; French, *British Planning*, pp. 22f.

80. PRO, CAB 16/5 XC/A/035374, Proceedings of a Sub-Committee of Imperial Defence Appointed by the Prime Minister to consider the Military Needs of the Empire, December 1908–March 1909.

81. Monger, *End of Isolation*, pp. 209f., 229. My emphasis.

82. Wilson, 'Grey', p. 173; Lloyd George, *War Memoirs*, vol. I, p. 1. See also the prescient warnings of Brodrick, Lansdowne and Salisbury quoted in Monger, *End of Isolation*, pp. 135, 212, 226, and the doubts of the radical *Speaker*, quoted in H. Weinroth, 'The British Radicals and the Balance of Power 1902–1914', *Historical Journal*, 13 (1970), pp. 659f.

83. The idea of war as an escape from domestic problems is applied to the British case in G. Dangerfield, *The Strange Death of Liberal England* (London, 1935); A. J. Mayer, 'Domestic Causes of the First World War', in L. Krieger and F. Stern (eds), *The Responsibility of Power: Historical Essays in Honour of Hajo Holborn* (New York, 1967), pp. 288f., 291f. For critical views see D. Lammers, 'Arno Mayer and the British Decision for War in 1914', *Journal of British Studies*, 11 (1973) esp. pp. 144, 153; P. Loewenberg, 'Arno Mayer's "Internal Causes and

Purposes of War in Europe, 1870–1956": An Inadequate Model of Human Behaviour, National Conflict, and Historical Change', *Journal of Modern History*, 42 (1970); Gordon, 'Domestic Conflicts', pp. 197f., 200, 203–13, 224f. But see also the comments by Nicolson, 'Edwardian England', p. 161, and K. M. Wilson, 'The British Cabinet's Decision for War, 2 August 1914', *British Journal of International Studies*, I (1975), p. 148.

84. M. Bentley, *The Liberal Mind 1914–29* (Cambridge, 1977), pp. 11–15.

85. Norman Angell, *The Great Illusion: A Study of the Relation of Military Power to National Advantage* (London, 1913).

86. M. Howard, 'The Edwardian Arms Race', in *Lessons of History*, pp. 82f.

87. Wilson, *Entente*, pp. 18–22; Monger, *End of Isolation*, p. 259.

88. See his warning to the Austrian ambassador during the July Crisis that war 'must involve the expenditure of so vast a sum of money and such an interference with trade, that a war would be accompanied or followed by a complete collapse of European credit and industry' comparable with that which occurred in 1848: Wilson, *Entente*, p. 13. For a similar comparison with 1848 by Morley, see French, *British Planning*, p. 87.

89. Lloyd George, *War Memoirs*, vol. I, pp. 28f., 60; Churchill, *World Crisis*, p. 203.

90. Monger, *End of Isolation*, pp. 257, 287; Wilson, *Entente*, pp. 34ff.

91. Cf. Bentley Brinkerhoff Gilbert, *David Lloyd George: A Political Life: The Organiser of Victory, 1912–16* (London, 1992), pp. 81ff.

92. Wilson, *Entente*, pp. 17, 30ff.

93. Searle, 'Critics', pp. 79–96.

94. Gooch, *Plans of War*, pp. 97ff., 265, 289; d'Ombrain, *War Machinery*, pp. 15–22, 88, 93–105, 135, 264, 271ff.; Hankey, *Supreme Command*, pp. 84, 118ff., 122; French, *British Planning*, pp. 74–84; Trebilcock, 'War', pp. 152f., 161.

95. As note 1. Cf. Trevelyan, *Grey*, esp. pp. 7–20; K. Robbins, *Sir Edward Grey: A Biography of Grey of Falloden* (London, 1971).

96. Grey, *Twenty-Five Years*, vol. I, pp. 153–9. Cf. Asquith, *Genesis*, p. 53.

97. Williams, 'Strategic Background', pp. 367–73; Wilson, *Entente*, pp. 6f., 76ff.; Monger, *End of Isolation*, p. 285.

98. H. Butterfield, 'Sir Edward Grey in July 1914', *Historical Studies*, 5 (1965), pp. 4f., 20f.; D. W. Sweet and R. T. B. Langhorne, 'Great Britain and Russia, 1907–1914', in F. Hinsley (ed.), *British Foreign Policy under Sir Edward Grey* (Cambridge, 1977), pp. 236, 245–54. Cf. Grey, *Twenty-Five Years*, vol. I, pp. 284, 297ff.

99. Wilson, *Entente*, pp. 35, 72; Weinroth, 'Radicals', pp. 657–61.

100. Monger, *End of Isolation*, p. 278.

101. Details in d'Ombrain, *War Machinery*, pp. 75–96, 103–9; Monger, *End of Isolation*, pp. 238–52; Wilson, *Entente*, pp. 63–7; M. Howard, *The Continental Commitment* (London, 1972), pp. 32–46. The talks had their origins in the CID conference at Whitehall Gardens in December 1905–January 1906. It was at this time – that is, during the first Moroccan Crisis – that the Director of Military Intelligence, Grierson, met the French military attaché in London to discuss the possibility of British intervention in a Franco-German war. The original impetus came from Esher and Clarke on the CID. However, the debate did not develop in quite the way they had intended, partly because Fisher was reluctant to make a naval commitment, but mainly because the French were far more interested in the idea of an expeditionary force. The talks therefore played into the hands of the advocates in the General Staff of a continental expeditionary force. The subsequent debates revolved around (a) where exactly such an expeditionary force should be sent, (b) what size it should be, (c) whether or not regular troops should be left to defend Britain itself, and (d) how long it would take to get troops to the continent.

102. K. A. Hamilton, 'Great Britain and France, 1911–1914', in Hinsley (ed.), *British Foreign Policy*, p. 331. Cf. Wilson, *Entente*, pp. 88f.; Monger, *End of Isolation*, p. 271.

103. PRO, CAB 2/2, Committee of Imperial Defence – Minutes of the 114th meeting, 23 August 1911. Cf. Hankey, *Supreme Command*, pp. 81f.; Nicolson, 'Edwardian England', p. 149; d'Ombrain, *War Machinery*, p. 102; French, *British Planning*, pp. 32f.; Wilson, *Entente*, p. 64.

104. B. Collier, *Brasshat: A Biography of Field Marshal Sir Henry Wilson* (London, 1961), pp. 117–21; Andrew, 'Entente', p. 27.

105. Churchill, *World Crisis*, p. 94.

106. Langhorne, 'Colonies', pp. 363–87.

107. Wilson, *Entente*, p. 10; Langhorne, 'Colonies', p. 369. See J. D. Vincent-Smith, 'Anglo-German Negotiations over the Portuguese Colonies in Africa 1911–1914', *Historical Journal*, 17 (1974), pp. 621f.

108. Max M. Warburg, *Aus meinen Aufzeichnungen* (privately printed), pp. 27f.

109. Grey, *Twenty-Five Years*, vol. I, pp. 117f. Cf. Monger, *End of Isolation*, pp. 266, 275ff.

110. W. A. Renzl, 'Great Britain, Russia and the Straits, 1914–1915', *Journal of Modern History*, 42 (1970), pp. 3f. Cf. Grey, *Twenty-Five Years*, vol. I, pp. 162ff., 176–89, 272.

111. Fischer, *Germany's Aims*, pp. 45f.; Grey, *Twenty-Five Years*, vol. I, pp. 272–5; Butterfield, 'Grey', p. 4.

112. *Frankfurter Zeitung*, 20 October 1913.

113. Brock, 'Britain Enters the War', p. 164. See also J. Gooch, 'Soldiers' Strategy and War Aims in Britain 1914–1918', in B. Hunt and A. Preston (eds), *War Aims and Strategic Policy in the Great War* (London, 1977), p. 23.

114. Ferguson, 'Public Finance and National Security', *passim*.

115. Grey, *Twenty-Five Years*, vol. I, p. 149; Berghahn, *Germany and the Approach of War*, pp. 67f., 119ff.; G. P. Gooch and H. Temperley (eds), *British Documents on the Origins of the War, 1898–1914*, vol. VI (London, 1930), No. 446; Churchill, *World Crisis*, pp. 96ff.; R. T. B. Langhorne, 'Great Britain and Germany, 1911–1914', in Hinsley (ed), *British Foreign Policy*, pp. 290ff. For the German side of the story, J. S. Steinberg, 'Diplomatie als Wille und Vorstellung: Die Berliner Mission Lord Haldanes im Februar 1912', in H. Schottelius and W. Deist (eds), *Marine und Marinepolitik im kaiserlichen Deutschland* (Düsseldorf, 1972).

116. Berghahn, *Germany and the Approach of War*, pp. 59f., 121f.

117. Langhorne, 'Great Britain and Germany', pp. 293f. My emphasis. Cf. Asquith's version in *Genesis*, pp. 55, 100.

118. Langhorne, 'Great Britain and Germany', pp. 299, 303f.

119. Asquith, *Genesis*, pp. 77f.; Churchill, *World Crisis*, pp. 103, 114f., 157; Grey, *Twenty-Five Years*, vol. I, pp. 249f.; Langhorne, 'Great Britain and Germany', pp. 296f.

120. Howard, 'Edwardian Arms Race', pp. 91f. Pessimists believed the Germans were aiming to accelerate their building 'tempo' so much that within a few years they would have more dreadnoughts than the Royal Navy. In fact, the German total in 1912 was nine to Britain's fifteen.

121. French, *British Planning*, p. 28; Offer, *Agrarian Interpretation*, pp. 232–41, 252, 260, 277–80, 296ff.; Hankey, *Supreme Command*, pp. 77, 88, 91, 97–100; Wilson, *Entente*, p. 106; Churchill, *World Crisis*, pp. 114f., 157.

122. Gooch and Temperley (eds), *British Documents*, vol. VI, No. 456, p. 611. Cf. Cain and Hopkins, *British Imperialism*, p. 458. Cf. D. W. Sweet, 'Great Britain and Germany, 1905–1911', in Hinsley (ed.), *British Foreign Policy*, p. 230.

123. Churchill, *World Crisis*, pp. 168–77; R. S. Churchill, *Winston S. Churchill*, vol. II. *Companion*, Part III: *1911–1914* (London, 1969), pp. 1820, 1825–37, 1856f.; K. O. Morgan (ed.), *Lloyd George Family Letters, 1885–1936* (Oxford, 1973), pp. 165f.; Lloyd George, *War Memoirs*, vol. I, p. 5; Wilson, *Entente*, p. 8.

124. Churchill, *World Crisis*, pp. 178f.; Asquith, *Genesis*, pp. 143f.

125. Monger, *End of Isolation*, pp. 260, 267ff.

126. Gooch and Temperley (eds), *British Documents*, vol. VI, No. 344, p. 461. Cf. Grey, *Twenty-Five Years*, vol. I, pp. 254f.

127. Sweet, 'Great Britain and Germany', pp. 229f.

128. Wilson, *Entente*, p. 93. Cf. Langhorne, 'Great Britain and Germany', pp. 290f.; Grey, *Twenty-Five Years*, vol. I, p. 251.

129. Sweet and Langhorne, 'Great Britain and Russia', pp. 243f.; Trevelyan, *Grey*, p. 114f.

130. Wilson, *Entente*, p. 101.

131. Nicolson's phrase, quoted in Wilson, *Entente*, p. 38. Grey may initially have been influenced by the fear that Russia and Germany might conclude an alliance, which the Kaiser and Tsar sought unsuccess-

fully to do in 1905. Cf. Butterfield, 'Grey', p. 2; Wilson, 'Grey', p. 193; Monger, *End of Isolation*, p. 293.

132. Wilson, *Entente*, pp. 35, 38f., 94, 111, 114f.; Monger, *End of Isolation*, p. 270; Howard, *Continental Commitment*, p. 57; Andrew, 'Entente', p. 25; Steiner, *Britain and the Origins*, p. 57; Grey, *Twenty-Five Years*, p. 252. See also Butterfield, 'Grey', p. 2.

133. Trevelyan, *Grey*, pp. 114f.

134. French, 'Spy Fever', pp. 355–8, 360–5; Andrew, 'Secret Intelligence', pp. 12ff.; Gooch, *Plans of War*, p. 33.

135. Bodl. Lib., Oxford, Harcourt MSS, 577. I am grateful to Mr Edward Lipman of Peterhouse for this reference.

136. Glen O'Hara, 'Britain's War of Illusions. Sir Edward Grey and the Crisis of Liberal Diplomacy' (Oxford University, BA thesis, 1996).

137. Gooch and Temperley (eds), *British Documents*, vol. VI, Nos 430, 437.

138. PRO, FO 371/10281, Goschen to Grey, 3 March 1913.

139. O'Hara, 'War of Illusions'.

140. G. Schmidt, 'Contradictory Postures and Conflicting Objectives: The July Crisis', in G. Schöllgen (ed.), *Escape into War? The Foreign Policy of Imperial Germany* (Oxford/New York/Munich, 1990), p. 144; Trevelyan, *Grey*, p. 244. As the *Nation* put it in March 1914, 'The Prussian military would be less than human if it did not dream of anticipating the crushing accumulation of force': Weinroth, 'Radicals', p. 680.

141. Fischer, *Germany's Aims, passim; idem, War of Illusions*, p. 470.

142. Butterfield, 'Grey', pp. 1f.

143. Fischer, *Germany's Aims*, pp. 103–6.

144. Point one raised the possibility of the cession from France of 'Belfort and western slopes of the Vosges, razing of fortresses and cession of coastal strip from Dunkirk to Boulogne'. The ore field of Briey was to be 'ceded in any case'. Point two stipulated that Liège and Verviers were to be ceded by Belgium to Prussia, and a 'frontier strip' by Belgium to Luxemburg. It left open the 'question whether Antwerp, with a corridor to Liège, should also be annexed'. 'Militarily important ports' were to be occupied by Germany; indeed, the whole Belgian coast

was to be 'at our disposal in military respects'. French Flanders with Dunkirk, Calais and Boulogne would then be taken from France and given to Belgium. Point three stated that Luxemburg would become a German federal state and might acquire Longwy from Belgium. Point seven raised the possibility that Antwerp might be ceded to Holland 'in return for the right to keep a German garrison in the fortress of Antwerp and at the mouth of the Scheldt': Fischer, *Germany's Aims*, p. 105.

145. Fischer, *Germany's Aims*, pp. 10, 28, 32ff., 101f.; Geiss, *July 1914*, pp. 21f.; Berghahn, *Germany and the Approach of War*, pp. 138ff. It is of course true that the Kaiser occasionally likened himself to Napoleon, but such flights of royal fancy should not be equated with German government policy. He was just as prone to remind British diplomats: 'We fought side by side a hundred years ago. I want our two nations to stand together again in front of the Belgian monument at Waterloo.... Do I want Australia? With its labour politicians? No thank you': Gooch and Temperley (eds), *British Documents*, vol. VI, No. 442.

146. The original German objectives are clearly set out in Jagow's letter to Lichnowsky of 18 July (Geiss, *July 1914*, doc. 30).

147. For a summary of the vast literature on German policy in 1914, see N. Ferguson, 'Germany and the Origins of the First World War: New Perspectives', *Historical Journal*, 35, 3 (1992), pp. 725–52. Zimmermann was one of the few German diplomats to admit openly to expecting that 'we should find our English cousins on the side of our enemies, inasmuch as England fears that France, in the event of a new defeat, would sink to the level of a power of the second class'; see Geiss, *July 1914*, doc. 33.

148. See Grey, *Twenty-Five Years*, vol. I, p. 325; Albertini, *Origins*, vol. II, p. 506. It should, however, be noted that Belgian integrity was only guaranteed 'assuming that Belgium does not take sides against us'; and that no assurance was to be given with respect to French colonies. It is possible to deduce from this that Bethmann already contemplated some changes to the extent and status of Belgium, as by this stage the chances of Belgian acquiescence were small. On the other hand, Moltke's draft decree 87 justifying the invasion of Belgium offered not only to guarantee Belgium's sovereign rights and independence in return for its

neutrality, but also to evacuate the country immediately after the war was over and to pay compensation for any war damage: Geiss, *July 1914*, doc. 91. The future of Belgium was to be a bone of contention in Berlin throughout the war, and it proved impossible to make the kind of unequivocal commitment to the restoration of Belgian integrity which might have satisfied British opinion; though it should be noted that the issue might have disappeared if, as nearly happened, the Germans had been able to persuade King Albert to drop his country's commitment to neutrality: Fischer, *Germany's Aims*, pp. 215–25; 420–8.

149. *Ibid.*, pp. 104f.

150. *Ibid.*, pp. 115ff.

151. D. E. Kaiser, 'Germany and the Origins of the First World War', *Journal of Modern History*, 55 (1983), pp. 442–74. Cf. P. Winzen, 'Der Krieg in Bülow's Kalkül. Katastrophe der Diplomatie oder Chance zur Machtexpansion', in J. Dülffer and K. Holl (eds), *Bereit zum Krieg. Kriegsmentalität im wilhelminischen Deutschland 1890–1914. Beiträge zur historischen Friedensforschung* (Göttingen, 1986).

152. For further details of the German conception of *Mitteleuropa* as it developed during the war, see Fischer, *Germany's Aims*, pp. 201–8, 247–56, 523–33.

153. Monger, *End of Isolation*, pp. 248–55, 273.

154. Wilson, *Entente*, pp. 39, 42f., 51, 123. See also Grey, *Twenty-Five Years*, vol. I, pp. 73–81, 95, 281.

155. PRO, CAB 16/5 XC/A/035374, Proceedings …, [23 March 1909]. My emphasis. Cf. d'Ombrain, *War Machinery*, pp. 95–8.

156. K. A. Hamilton, 'Great Britain and France', in Hinsley (ed.), *British Foreign Policy*, p. 324; Wilson, *Entente*, p. 37.

157. Grey to Asquith, 16 April 1911, quoted in Grey, *Twenty-Five Years*, vol. I, p. 94. He repeated this view to the CID the following month: Wilson, *Entente*, p. 85.

158. Wilson, *Entente*, pp. 57, 69. For Esher's similar views, see d'Ombrain, *War Machinery*, pp. 106ff., and Offer, *Agrarian Interpretation*, pp. 307f. Radicals and navalists alike suspected, rightly, that the expeditionary force was the thin end of a wedge which would widen into conscription.

159. Wilson, 'Decision for War', pp. 149, 156n.

160. Wilson, *Entente*, pp. 28f., 124; Offer, *Agrarian Interpretation*, p. 295; d'Ombrain, *War Machinery*, pp. 106f.

161. Wilson, *Entente*, pp. 29, 39, 48, 52f.

162. Hamilton, 'Great Britain and France', p. 332; Churchill, *World Crisis*, pp. 112f. My emphasis.

163. Grey, *Twenty-Five Years*, vol. I, pp. 97f. Cf. Wilson, *Entente*, p. 26; Offer, *Agrarian Interpretation*, p. 304; d'Ombrain, *War Machine*, pp. 109f.

164. Renzl, 'Great Britain, Russia', p. 3. For Nicolson's concern at this time about public lack of 'knowledge' as to 'the very great importance that Russia's friendship is [*sic*] to us', see Wilson, *Entente*, p. 404.

165. Grey, *Twenty-Five Years*, vol. I, pp. 289ff.

166. Monger, *End of Isolation*, pp. 281f. For Crowe's version of the same deterrent theory, see *ibid.*, p. 271. For Nicolson's, see Wilson, *Entente*, p. 40.

167. Langhorne, 'Great Britain and France', pp. 298, 306; Wilson, *Entente*, pp. 92, 98; Schmidt, 'Contradictory Postures', p. 139; Fischer, *Germany's Aims*, p. 32.

168. Brock, 'Britain Enters the War', p. 146. British non-intervention could also have been inferred from Lloyd George's emollient Mansion House speech of 1914: Hazlehurst, *Politicians at War*, p. 28. For the early German assumptions about British non-intervention, see Geiss, *July 1914*, p. 95, docs. 18, 28. It is possible that Bethmann was gambling on the timing of British intervention, rather than on British intervention itself, believing that it would come too late to determine the outcome of the crisis.

169. This possibility was discussed but dismissed by Bertie: Wilson, *Entente*, pp. 46ff.; Monger, *End of Isolation*, p. 279.

170. Albertini, *Origins*, vol. II, pp. 203–8; Cf. Butterfield, 'Grey', pp. 9f; Geiss, *July 1914*, pp. 95, 138. The Russian ambassador in Vienna made it clear as early as 8 July that 'Russia would be compelled to take up arms in defence of Serbia' if Austria 'rushed into war'. Grey's belief that a distinction could be drawn between cessions of territory from Serbia and some less serious form of reprisal was never really shared in St Petersburg. Revealingly, Grey warned the German ambassador

Lichnowsky that 'in view of the present unpopularity of England in Russia' he would 'have to be careful of Russian feelings'.

171. Albertini, *Origins*, vol. II, pp. 209–14, 329–38; Geiss, *July 1914*, docs 44, 46, 57, 80, 93.

172. Hence his characteristically convoluted statement to Lichnowsky on 24 July that 'there was no alliance ... committing us to ... France and Russia.... On the other hand ... the British government belonged to one group of powers, but did not do so in order to make difficulties greater between the two European groups; on the contrary, we wished to prevent any questions that arose from throwing the groups ... into opposition.... We should never pursue an aggressive policy, and if there was a European war, and we took part in it, it would not be on the aggressive side, for public opinion was against that.' Lichnowsky interpreted this, as Grey doubtless intended, as a warning that 'in case France should be drawn in, England would [not] dare to remain disinterested', a point he repeated with growing anxiety as the crisis intensified. But Bethmann and Jagow evidently concluded that a show of German support for four-power mediation would suffice to satisfy Grey: Geiss, *July 1914*, docs 68, 73, 81, 82, 83, 85, 94, 97, 98, 99; Grey, *Twenty-Five Years*, vol. II, pp. 304f., 317. See also Albertini, *Origins*, vol. II, pp. 336–9, 514; Asquith, *Genesis*, pp. 201f. The King took a similar ambiguous line with the German Crown Prince when they met on 26 July: 'I don't know what we shall do, we have no quarrel with anyone and I hope we shall remain neutral. But if Germany declared war on Russia and France joins Russia, then I am afraid we shall be dragged into it. But you can be sure that I and my government will do all we can to prevent a European war': *ibid.*, pp. 429, 497, 687. Prince Heinrich concluded that England would remain neutral 'at the beginning', though he doubted 'whether she will be able to do so in the long run ... on account of her relations with France'. However, neutrality in the short run was all the German government needed, provided victory over France could be achieved quickly enough.

173. Albertini, *Origins*, vol. II, p. 429.

174. Geiss, *July 1914*, p. 221, docs. 95, 96; Grey, *Twenty-Five Years*, vol. I, pp. 319f.

175. Albertini, *Origins*, vol. II, pp. 329–34, 340; Geiss, *July 1914*, docs 50, 79; Churchill, *World Crisis*, pp. 193f.

176. Geiss, *July 1914*, docs 103, 110, 112, 114. The Germans had begun to spread rumours of Russian mobilisation as early as 26 July: Albertini, *Origins*, vol. II, p. 343.

177. As Nicolson commented, 'One does not really know where one is with Mr Sazonov': Geiss, *July 1914*, docs 108, 119, 120; Albertini, *Origins*, vol. II, p. 509; Grey, *Twenty-Five Years*, vol. I, p. 319; Asquith, *Genesis*, pp. 190ff. Nor did one know where one was with Bethmann: he now argued that a four-power conference would amount to a court of arbitration, putting Austria and Serbia on an equal footing, while at the same time deliberately not mentioning Sazonov's proposal for bilateral talks to Lichnowsky, who, he complained, was 'informing Sir Edward [Grey] of everything': Geiss, *July 1914*, docs 90, 100.

178. Geiss, *July 1914*, docs 121, 122, 123, 128; Albertini, *Origins*, vol. II, pp. 510ff.

179. Geiss, *July 1914*, doc. 101. Sazonov declared himself willing to halt mobilisation only 'if Austria ... declares itself ready to eliminate from its ultimatum those points which infringe on Serbia's sovereign rights'. An increasingly desperate Bethmann seized on this as a basis for negotiation and the Austrian government actually accepted Sazonov's offer of talks on 30 July, but by this stage military considerations had taken over: *ibid.*, docs 140, 141a, 153.

180. The Russians in fact mobilised in the southern districts of Odessa, Kiev, Moscow and Kazan on 29 July – a decision which the Tsar later said had been taken four days before – assuring the German ambassador that this was 'far from meaning war'. But on being told by Pourtalès that Germany would nonetheless 'find herself compelled to mobilise, in which case she would immediately proceed to the offensive', the Russians concluded that a partial mobilisation would be inadequate, and might even jeopardise full mobilisation. There followed a series of hysterical meetings and telephone conversations as Sazonov and his colleagues tried to persuade the vacillating Tsar to agree to full mobilisation. He finally did so at 2 p.m. on 30 July and mobilisation began the next day. As in Berlin, the much vaunted power of the monarch proved

to be illusory at the moment of decision: Geiss, *July 1914*, pp. 271, 291, docs 118, 123, 124a, 137, 138, 147.

181. *Ibid.*, docs 91, 111, 114, 115, 125.

182. *Ibid.*, docs 133, 134, 143, 145, 154; Albertini, *Origins*, vol. II, pp. 523–6.

183. Albertini, *Origins*, vol. II, pp. 635–8, 645; vol. III, pp. 378f., 390f.

184. Geiss, *July 1914*, p. 270, doc. 158; Albertini, *Origins*, vol. II, pp. 634f.; vol. III, pp. 373, 378, 386.

185. Geiss, *July 1914*, docs 107, 148, 149.

186. *Ibid.*, doc. 152.

187. *Ibid.*, doc. 164. Cf. Hazlehurst, *Politicians at War*, p. 52; Andrew, 'Entente', p. 33; Wilson, *Entente*, p. 95; Albertini, *Origins*, vol. III, p. 374.

188. Kennedy, *Anglo-German Antagonism*, pp. 458f.

189. Between 24 and 30 July, consol prices dropped by around 5 points; European securities fell by similar amounts. The Bank of England's gold reserve fell by some 16 per cent, obliging it to increase its base interest rate (bank rate) to 8 per cent on 31 July. For the impression this made on Asquith see Albertini, *Origins*, vol. III, pp. 376ff.

190. Hazlehurst, *Politicians at War*, pp. 36–9; Churchill, *Companion*, Part III, pp. 1990f.

191. Hazlehurst, *Politicians at War*, pp. 78f. See also Grey's repetition of the same formula to Ponsonby: *ibid.*, p. 37. Cf. Wilson, 'Decision for War', pp. 149f.

192. Geiss, *July 1914*, docs 130, 133.

193. Albertini, *Origins*, vol. II, pp. 501, 514, 523–5.

194. The German offer to guarantee French territorial integrity (but not French colonial possessions) had in fact been trailed by the German ship-owner Albert Ballin in a conversation with Churchill at dinner on 24 July: Churchill, *World Crisis*, p. 196; Cecil, *Ballin*, p. 207. For Bethmann's offer see Geiss, *July 1914*, docs 139, 167; Albertini, *Origins*, vol. II, p. 506; Grey, *Twenty-Five Years*, vol. I, pp. 325f.

195. Geiss, *July 1914*, doc. 151; Albertini, *Origins*, vol. II, pp. 507,

519, 633; Grey, *Twenty-Five Years*, vol. I, pp. 327f.; Churchill, *Companion*, Part III, pp. 1989, 1993; Wilson, 'Decision for War', p. 153; Churchill, *World Crisis*, pp. 213ff.; Offer, *Agrarian Interpretation*, p. 308; Hazlehurst, *Politicians at War*, p. 23.

196. Albertini, *Origins*, vol. II, pp. 511ff., 521ff.; Asquith, *Genesis*, p. 198

197. Geiss, *July 1914*, docs 170, 173, 177. Cf. Albertini, *Origins*, vol. III, pp. 380–5.

198. Albertini, *Origins*, vol. II, p. 639.

199. Geiss, *July 1914*, docs 162, 177.

200. Albertini, *Origins*, vol. II, pp. 638f., 646–9; vol. III, pp. 373, 380, 384f., 392ff.

201. Beaverbrook, *Politicians and the War*, pp. 19ff. Cf. Hazlehurst, *Politicians at War*, pp. 49, 84–91; Wilson, 'Decision for War', pp. 150ff.; Wilson, *Entente*, p. 139. It is an error to regard Lloyd George as in some way committed to intervention on the basis of his Mansion House speech of 1911.

202. Albertini, *Origins*, vol. III, pp. 369f.

203. Wilson, 'Decision for War', p. 150.

204. Beaverbrook, *Politicians and the War*, pp. 28f.; Churchill, *World Crisis*, pp. 216f.; Churchill, *Companion*, Part III, p. 1997.

205. Wilson, *Entente*, pp. 138ff.; Hazlehurst, *Politicians at War*, p. 94; Geiss, *July 1914*, doc. 183; Albertini, *Origins*, vol. III, pp. 406f. Cf. Offer, *Agrarian Interpretation*, p. 317.

206. Wilson, 'Decision for War', pp. 154f.; Albertini, *Origins*, vol. III, pp. 403f. Asquith estimated that around three-quarters of his parliamentary party were for 'absolute non-interference at any price': Hazlehurst, *Politicians at War*, p. 33; Bentley, *Liberal Mind*, p. 17.

207. Albertini, *Origins*, vol. III, p. 405. Morley felt with hindsight that if Lloyd George had given a lead to the waverers, 'the Cabinet would undoubtedly have perished that evening'. Harcourt vainly appealed to Lloyd George to 'speak for us': Gilbert, *Lloyd George*, p. 109.

208. Albertini, *Origins*, vol. III, pp. 381f., 386, 399. Grey subsequently denied in the House of Commons that he had made the offer, claiming that Lichnowsky had misunderstood him. This is contradicted

by his letter to Bertie of 1 August: see Geiss, *July 1914*, doc. 177 – unless Grey had been deliberately misleading Cambon in describing his proposal to Lichnowsky.

209. Albertini, *Origins*, vol. III, p. 483; Hazlehurst, *Politicians at War*, pp. 116f.; Wilson, 'Decision for War', pp. 157f.; Asquith, *Genesis*, pp. 220f.

210. PRO, CAB 16/5 XC/A/035374, Proceedings ..., Foreign Office memorandum (CID paper E-2), 11 November 1908. Cf. Wilson, 'Education', p. 409.

211. Lloyd George, *Memoirs*, pp. 30f., 40; Churchill, *World Crisis*, pp. 65, 199, 219.

212. Albertini, *Origins*, vol. III, p. 513; Asquith, *Genesis*, p. 211.

213. Hazlehurst, *Politicians at War*, pp. 177, 303.

214. R. Graves, *Goodbye to All That* (Harmondsworth, 1977), pp. 60f.; S. Sassoon, *Memoirs of a Fox-Hunting* Man (London, 1978), p. 244. For other examples of the Belgian argument see Brock, 'Britain Enters the War', pp. 167f.; Hazlehurst, *Politicians at War*, pp. 47f.; Wilson, 'Decision for War', p. 159; A. Marwick, *The Deluge: British Society and the First World War* (London, 1991), pp. 85f.; Albertini, *Origins*, vol. III, p. 518; Bentley, *Liberal Mind*, pp. 19f.

215. Offer, *Agrarian Interpretation*, p. 305.

216. Hazlehurst, *Politicians at War*, p. 73; Wilson, *Entente*, p. 136; Wilson, 'Decision for War', p. 149.

217. Churchill, *Companion*, Part III, pp. 1991, 1996; Geiss, *July 1914*, docs 166, 174; Albertini, *Origins*, vol. III, pp. 388f., 399f.; Grey, *Twenty-Five Years*, vol. I, pp. 329f.; vol. II, p. 10; Asquith, *Genesis*, p. 209.

218. Beaverbrook, *Politicians and the War*, pp. 22f.; Brock, 'Britain Enters the War', pp. 149f.

219. Wilson, 'Decision for War', p. 153; Brock, 'Britain Enters the War', p. 151; Gilbert, *Lloyd George*, p. 110; Hazlehurst, *Politicians at War*, pp. 70f.

220. Albertini, *Origins*, pp. 409f., my emphasis. For vivid proof of Lloyd George's agonising on the subject, see Morgan (ed.), *Lloyd George Family Letters*, p. 167. See also Lloyd George's remarks to C. P. Scott in Gilbert, *Lloyd George*, p. 112.

221. Albertini, *Origins*, vol. III, p. 494; Brock, 'Britain Enters the War', p. 160.

222. Geiss, *July 1914*, docs 179, 184, 188; Albertini, *Origins*, vol. III, pp. 479, 489, 497.

223. Brock, 'Britain Enters the War', p. 145.

224. Albertini, *Origins*, vol. III, pp. 486f.; Grey, *Twenty-Five Years*, vol. II, pp. 14f.; Wilson, *Entente*, p. 144.

225. Asquith, *Genesis*, pp. 212f.; Wilson, *Entente*, p. 120; Hazlehurst, *Politicians at* War, p. 114; Brock, 'Britain Enters the War', p. 161. For a good example of the popular reception of the strategic argument, see G. Hodgson, *People's Century* (London, 1995), pp. 27f.

226. Wilson, *Entente*, p. 146. This was also the view of Frances Stevenson, Lloyd George's mistress, and Ramsay MacDonald, who dined with Lloyd George on the evening of 2 August: see Gilbert, *Lloyd George*, pp. 108, 111.

227. Wilson, 'Decision for War', *passim*.

228. Beaverbrook, *Politicians and the War*, pp. 13–19; Hazlehurst, *Politicians at War*, p. 41.

229. Beaverbrook, *Politicians and the War*, p. 31; Albertini, *Origins*, vol. III, p. 399. Churchill relayed a similar message from F. E. Smith to the Cabinet: Wilson, *Entente*, p. 141.

230. Lammers, 'Mayer', p. 159; Wilson, 'Decision for War', p. 155. Cf. Sir L. Woodward, *Great Britain and the War of 1914–1918* (London, 1967), p. 46, for the reciprocation of this sentiment from the Tory side.

231. Wilson, 'Decision for War', pp. 154f.

232. See for example his less than hawkish comments to the German Crown Prince on 26 July: Albertini, *Origins*, vol. II, pp. 429, 497, 687.

233. Before the war, the General Staff had envisaged mobilising simultaneously with France and getting the BEF to France within fifteen (at most twenty) days: PRO, CAB 16/5 XC/A/635374, Proceedings ... , Ewart testimony, 3 December 1908; PRO, CAB 2/2, Committee of Imperial Defence ... 23 August 1911; Monger, *End of Isolation*, p. 251.

234. Albertini, *Origins*, vol. III, p. 503; Hankey, *Supreme Command*, p. 165. Cf. Offer, *Agrarian Interpretation*, p. 5.

235. French, *British Planning*, p. 88; Offer, *Agrarian Interpretation*, p. 312. The maximum number of divisions contemplated before the war

was six. For this and other adverse comments on the size of the proposed expeditionary force see Wilson, *Entente*, pp. 47, 63, 65; d'Ombrain, *War Machinery*, pp. 103f.; Howard, *Continental Commitment*, p. 46. See also PRO, CAB 2/2, Committee of Imperial Defence ... 23 August 1911; Collier, *Brasshat*, p. 117.

236. PRO, CAB 16/5 XL/A/035374, Proceedings ..., General French testimony, 23 March 1909. Cf. Collier, *Brasshat*, p. 119; d'Ombrain, *War Machinery*, p. 109.

237. Kitchener in fact allowed Wilson to revert to Maubeuge six days later, and on 3 September the Cabinet agreed to send the 6th Division too: Wilson, *Entente*, p. 125; Albertini, *Origins*, vol. III, pp. 510f.; Hankey, *Supreme Command*, pp. 169ff., 187, 192; Gooch, *Plans of War*, p. 301; Beaverbrook, *Politicians and the War*, p. 36; Collier, *Brasshat*, p. 162ff.; Morgan (ed.), *Lloyd George Family Letters*, p. 169; d'Ombrain, *War Machinery*, pp. 113f.

238. The question was posed directly by McKenna and answered in the affirmative by Wilson at the CID meeting of 23 August 1911. Cf. Ollivant's memorandum on the subject of 1 August 1914, quoted in Hazlehurst, *Politicians at War*, pp. 63f.: 'There is reason to suppose that the presence or absence of the British army will ... very probably decide the fate of France.' Cf. Woodward, *Great Britain*, pp. 32–5.

239. See esp. G. Ritter, *Der Schlieffen Plan. Kritik eines Mythos* (Munich, 1956).

240. Hankey, *Supreme Command*, pp. 187–97; Collier, *Brasshat*, pp. 172–90; P. Guinn, *British Strategy and Politics, 1914–18* (Oxford, 1965), p. 37.

241. 570,000 men volunteered between August and December 1914. By 'First Ypres', two new divisions and two Indian divisions had been deployed.

242. See the evidence in (though not the argument of) Offer, *Agrarian Interpretation*.

243. Renzl, 'Great Britain, Russia'.

244. Guinn, *British Strategy*, pp. 122, 171, 238; Gooch, *Plans of War*, pp. 30, 35, 278. It is important to note that a German victory over France would *not* – as is often assumed – have shifted German politics to the right. The pan-Germans and the Kaiser may have thought so; but, as we

have seen, Bülow and Bethmann knew well that the price of a war, whether victorious or not, would be a further move in the direction of parliamentary democracy.

245. Woodward, *Great Britain*, pp. 227f. Robertson was no less suspicious of Italian and French ambitions.

246. Wilson, *Entente*, p. 79.

247. I. Geiss, 'The German Version of Imperialism: *Weltpolitik*', in Schöllgen (ed.), *Escape into War?*, pp. 114f.

FIVE:
HITLER'S ENGLAND

I would like to thank Professor Michael Burleigh and Dr Niall Ferguson for their comments on an earlier draft.

1. Among fictional presentations are Douglas Brown and Christopher Serpell, *Loss of Eden* (London, 1940); H. V. Morton, *I, James Blunt* (London, 1940); Noël Coward's play *Peace in Our Time* (1947); C. S. Forester, *If Hitler Had Invaded England* (London, 1971) and Len Deighton, *SS-GB* (London, 1978). Films on the subject include *Went the Day Well?* (1943) and *It Happened Here* (1960).

2. See Andrew Roberts, '*The Holy Fox': A Biography of Lord Halifax* (London, 1991), p. 103.

3. Paul Schmidt, *Hitler's Interpreter* (London, 1951), p. 320.

4. Robert Rhodes James, *Churchill: A Study in Failure, 1900–1939* (London, 1970). See also Robert Blake and Wm. Roger Louis (eds), *Churchill* (Oxford, 1993).

5. Martin Gilbert, *Prophet of Truth: Winston S. Churchill 1922–1939* (London, 1990 edn), p. 573.

6. *Ibid.*, p. 456n.

7. Roberts, *Holy Fox*, pp. 54–75.

8. *Sunday Times*, 5, 12 and 19 July 1992.

9. Roberts, *Holy Fox*, p. 108.

10. J. Noakes and G. Pridham (eds), *Nazism 1919–1945*, vol. III: *Foreign Policy, War and Racial Extermination* (Exeter, 1988), p. 741.

11. *Sunday Times, loc. cit.* See also Michael Bloch, *Ribbentrop* (London, 1992), esp. pp. 233–62.

12. Geoffrey Stokes, *Hitler and the Quest for World Dominion: Nazi Ideology and Foreign Policy in the 1920s* (Leamington Spa/ Hamburg/New York, 1986), pp. 93ff.

13. Noakes and Pridham (eds), *Nazism*, vol. III, p. 667.

14. *Ibid.*, p. 746.

15. Richard Griffith, *Fellow Travellers of the Right: British Enthusiasts for Nazi Germany, 1933–1938* (London, 1983).

16. Bloch, *Ribbentrop*, pp. 91–134.

17. See Andrew Roberts 'The House of Windsor and the Politics of Appeasement', in *Eminent Churchillians* (London, 1994), pp. 5–54.

18. Noakes and Pridham (eds), *Nazism*, vol. III, pp. 758f.

19. Willi A. Boelcke, *The Secret Conferences of Dr Goebbels, 1939–43* (London, n.d.), pp. 1–62.

20. Noakes and Pridham (eds), *Nazism*, vol. III, p. 777.

21. *Ibid.*, p. 783.

22. John Charmley, *Churchill: The End of Glory: A Political Biography* (London, 1993).

23. *Ibid.*, pp. 403f. See also Roberts, *Holy Fox*, pp. 210–28.

24. *The Times*, 2 January 1993.

25. Noakes and Pridham (eds), *Nazism*, vol. III, pp. 674f.

26. *Ibid.*, p. 683.

27. *Ibid.*, pp. 692–6.

28. *Ibid.*, p. 738.

29. John Keegan, *The Second World War* (London, 1989), p. 214.

30. Noakes and Pridham (eds), *Nazism*, vol. III, p. 760.

31. *Ibid.*, p. 790. Emphasis in original.

32. Gilbert, *Prophet of Truth*, p. 1000.

33. General Heinz Guderian, *Panzer Leader* (London, 1952), p. 117.

34. See Alistair Horne, *To Lose a Battle* (London, 1969), pp. 611–16.

35. Norman Rich, *Hitler's War Aims: Ideology, the Nazi State and the Course of Expansion* (New York/London, 1973), pp. 159ff.

36. Peter Fleming, *Invasion 1940* (London, 1957), p. 37. Cf. Noakes and Pridham (eds), *Nazism*, vol. III, pp. 783–6; Ronald Wheatley,

Operation Sea Lion: German Plans for the Invasion of England, 1939–1942 (Oxford, 1958).

37. Rich, *War Aims*, pp. 161ff. Further preparations were halted in August 1941 and the plan was effectively postponed *sine die* the following March.

38. Michael Glover, *Invasion Scare 1940* (London, 1990), p. 50.

39. In addition to the works already cited, a short bibliography must include Basil Collier, *The Defence of the United Kingdom* (London, 1957); David Lampe, *The Last Ditch* (London, 1968); Norman Longmate, *If Britain Had Fallen* (London, 1972); Adrian Gilbert, *Britain Invaded* (London, 1990); Peter Schenk, *Invasion of England 1940* (London, 1990); Kenneth Macksey, *Invasion: The German Invasion of England 1940* (London, 1980); *idem* (ed.), *The Hitler Options* (London, 1995).

40. See *Loopholes* (the journal of the Pillbox Study Group), vols I–VI.

41. Fleming, *Invasion 1940*, p. 35.

42. *Ibid.*, p. 293.

43. Glover, *Invasion Scare 1940*, p. 180; William Shirer, *The Rise and Fall of the Third Reich* (London, 1964), pp. 912–13.

44. Schenk, *Invasion of England*, pp. 263–70; Shirer, *Rise and Fall*, p. 912.

45. Collier, *Defence of the United Kingdom*, p. 494.

46. Madeleine Bunting, *The Model Occupation: The Channel Islands under German Rule 1940–45* (London, 1995), p. 6. For an opposing view see Charles Cruikshank, *The German Occupation of the Channel Islands* (Oxford, 1975).

47. *Sunday Times*, 29 January 1995.

48. *Spectator*, 8 April 1995.

49. Gilbert, *Britain Invaded*, p. 100.

50. Lampe, *Last Ditch*, p. 152.

51. Fleming, *Invasion 1940*, p. 266.

52. Bunting, *Model Occupation*, p. 6.

53. S. P. Mackenzie, *The Home Guard* (London, 1995), pp. 34ff.

54. Noël Coward, *The Lyrics of Noël Coward* (London, 1965), p. 275.

55. Lampe, *Last Ditch*, p. 60.

56. Philip Ziegler, *London at War* (London, 1995), p. 163.

57. *Ibid.*, p. 178.

58. *Sunday Telegraph*, 16 April 1995.

59. William Shirer, *The Collapse of the Third Republic* (London, 1969), p. 267.

60. Eugen Weber, *The Hollow Years: France in the 1930s* (London, 1995).

61. Nigel Nicolson (ed.), *Diaries and Letters of Harold Nicolson, 1939–45* (London, 1967).

62. Weber, *Hollow Years*, p. 19.

63. Shirer, *Collapse of the Third Republic*, pp. 188f.

64. Michael De-la-Noy, *The Queen Behind the Throne* (London, 1994), p. 119.

65. Longmate, *If Britain Had Fallen*, p. 115.

66. Fleming, *Invasion 1940*, p. 95.

67. Peter Wilkinson and Joan Astley, *Gubbins and SOE* (London, 1993), pp. 69–74.

68. Fleming, *Invasion 1940*, p. 293.

69. Wilkinson and Astley, *Gubbins*, p. 71.

70. Shirer, *Rise and Fall*, pp. 937f.

71. Bunting, *Model Occupation*, p. 113.

72. A. W. B. Simpson, *In the Highest Degree Odious* (London, 1992).

73. In fact, he was released in 1952, after serving just four years, joining the management of Porsche and the incipient West German secret service. I am grateful to Michael Burleigh for this reference.

74. Imperial War Museum, *The Black Book* (London, 1989).

75. Griffith, *Fellow Travellers of the Right*, pp. 222ff.

76. Interview with Sir Isaiah Berlin, 8 December 1988.

77. For the conspiracy theory see Gwynne Thomas, *King Pawn or Black Knight? The Sensational Story of the Treacherous Collusion between Edward, Duke of Windsor and Adolf Hitler* (London, 1995); *Guardian*, 13 November 1995, and *Observer*, 12 November 1995. For the historians' response see Michael Bloch in the *Spectator*, 18 November 1995; John Grigg in *The Times*, 14 November 1995; Philip Ziegler in the

Daily Telegraph, 17 November 1995; Andrew Roberts in the *Sunday Telegraph*, 19 November 1995.

78. William Joyce, *Twilight over England* (London, 1992), p. 50.

79. Allan Massie, *A Question of Loyalties* (London, 1989).

80. Hugh Trevor-Roper (ed.), *Hitler's Table Talk* (London, 1953), p. 260.

81. Nicolson (ed.), *Diaries and Letters of Harold Nicolson*, p. 35.

82. Templewood Papers, Cambridge University Library, XIII/17.

83. Colin Cross, *Life with Lloyd George: The Diary of A. J. Sylvester* (London, 1975), p. 281.

84. Oswald Mosley, *My Life* (London, 1968), p. 401.

85. *Ibid.*, p. 402.

86. Trevor-Roper (ed.), *Table Talk*, p. 255.

87. Quoted in Tomas Munch Petersen, 'Common Sense and Not Bravado: The Butler–Prytz Interview of 17 June 1940', *Scandia* (1986).

88. Private information.

89. Lucjan Dobroszycki, *Reptile Journalism: The Official Polish-Language Press under the Nazis 1939–45* (New Haven, 1995).

90. *International Currency Review*, Occasional Paper No. 4 (London, September 1993). See also Robert Edwin Herzstein, *When Nazi Dreams Come True* (London, 1982).

91. Interview with Christopher Beaumont, 5 February 1995.

92. Longmate, *If Britain Had Fallen*, p. 145.

93. *Ibid.*, p. 146.

94. Public Record Office, CAB 65/13 WM 142.

95. Guderian, *Panzer Leader*, p. 117.

96. Margery Allingham, *The Oaken Heart* (London, 1941), p. 163.

97. Douglas Dodds-Parker, *Setting Europe Ablaze* (London, 1983), p. 45.

SIX:
NAZI EUROPE

1. Horst Boog, 'Die Luftwaffe', in *idem et al.*, *Der Angriff auf die Sowjetunion* (Frankfurt am Main, 1991), p. 737. English-language work

includes John Erickson, *The Road to Stalingrad* (London, 1993) and John Erickson and David Dilks (eds), *Barbarossa: The Axis and the Allies* (Edinburgh, 1994). The best recent German works on the subject are Gerd Uberschär and Wolfram Wette (eds), *Der deutsche Überfall auf die Sowjetunion* (Frankfurt am Main, 1991); the outstanding collection edited by Wegner (see below n. 3) and the exhibition catalogue edited by Reinhard Rürup, *Der Krieg gegen die Sowjetunion 1941–1945* (Berlin, 1991).

2. Jeremy Noakes and Geoffrey Pridham (eds) *Nazism 1919–1945* (Exeter, 1988), vol. III, pp. 818–19.

3. B. Kroener, 'Der "erfrorene Blitzkrieg". Strategische Planungen der deutschen Führung gegen die Sowjetunion und die Ursachen ihres Scheiterns', in Bernd Wegner (ed.), *Zwei Wege nach Moscow* (Munich, 1991), p. 144.

4. Alan Clark, *Barbarossa: The Russian–German Conflict 1941–1945* (London, 1995), pp. 56ff., 80f., 88.

5. Bernd Wegner, 'The Road to Defeat: The German Campaigns in Russia 1941–43', *Journal of Strategic Studies*, 13 (1990), pp. 112f.

6. John Barber and Mark Harrison, *The Soviet Home Front 1941–1945* (London, 1991), p. 139.

7. A. M. Belikov, 'Transfer de l'industrie Sovietique vers l'Est (juin 1941–1942)', *Revue d'Histoire de la Deuxième Guerre Mondiale*, 11 (1961), p. 48. On the Soviet war-effort see also Richard Overy's outstanding *Why the Allies Won* (London, 1995), esp. pp. 63–100.

8. Noakes and Pridham (eds), *Nazism*, vol. III, p. 820.

9. *Ibid.*, p. 829.

10. *Hitler's Table Talk 1941–1944*, introduced by Hugh Trevor-Roper (Oxford, 1988), p. 319.

11. Wegner, 'Road to Defeat', pp. 115f.

12. For the most recent German work on the battle see Wolfram Wette and Gerd Uberschär (eds), *Stalingrad. Mythos und Wirklichkeit einer Schlacht* (Frankfurt am Main, 1993).

13. Wegner, 'Road to Defeat', p. 109.

14. Noakes and Pridham (eds), *Nazism*, vol. III, p. 1087.

15. For revisionist and post-revisionist views on the German army in Russia see O. Bartov, *Hitler's Army: Soldiers, Nazis, and War in the*

Third Reich (Oxford, 1991), and Theo Schulte, *The German Army and Nazi Policies in Occupied Russia* (Oxford, 1989). The most recent work in this field is comprehensively represented in Hannes Heer and Klaus Naumann (eds), *Vernichtungskrieg. Verbrechen der Wehrmacht 1941–1944* (Hamburg, 1995).

16. Matthew Cooper, *The Phantom War: The German Struggle against Soviet Partisans 1941–1945* (London, 1979), pp. 56f. This remains the most useful account of the partisan war.

17. Ruth Bettina Birn, 'Zweierlei Wirklichkeit? Fallbeispiel zur Partisanbekämpfung im Osten', in Wegner (ed.), *Zwei Wege*, p. 283.

18. Cooper, *Phantom War*, pp. 83–8.

19. Len Deighton, *SS-GB* (London, 1978); Robert Harris, *Fatherland* (London, 1992); Newt Gingrich and William R. Forstchen, *1945* (New York, 1995).

20. Ralph Giordano, *Wenn Hitler den Krieg gewonnen hatte* (Munich, 1989).

21. Kenneth Macksey (ed.), *The Hitler Options: Alternate Decisions of World War II* (London, 1995).

22. Jochen Thies, 'Hitler's European Building Programme', *Journal of Contemporary History*, 13 (1978); *idem*, 'Nazi Architecture – A Blueprint for World Domination', in David Welch (ed.), *Nazi Propaganda* (London, 1983); Robert Edwin Herzstein, *When Nazi Dreams Came True* (London, 1982). Aspects of fascist and Nazi conceptions of European unity are also explored in M. L. Smith and P. M. R. Stirk (eds), *Making the New Europe* (London, 1990).

23. James Lucas, 'Operation Wotan: The Panzer Thrust to Capture Moscow, October–November 1941', in Macksey (ed.), *The Hitler Options*, pp. 54ff.

24. Sergei Kudryashov, 'The Hidden Dimension: Wartime Collaboration in the Soviet Union', in Erickson and Dilks (eds), *Barbarossa*, p. 246. See also Jurgen Thorwald, *The Illusion: Soviet Soldiers in Hitler's Armies* (New York, 1975); Sergei Frohlich, *General Wlassow. Russen und Deutsche zwischen Hitler und Stalin* (Cologne, 1987); Joachim Hoffmann, *Die Ostlegionen 1941–1943* (3rd edn, Freiburg im Breisgau, 1986); *idem*, *Deutsche und Kalmyken 1942 bis 1945* (4th edn, Freiburg im Breisgau, 1986); *idem*, *Die Geschichte der Wlassow Armee* (Freiburg

im Breisgau, 1986); Catherine Andreyev, *Vlasov and the Russian Liberation Movement: Soviet Reality and Emigré Theories* (Cambridge, 1987); Samuel J. Newland, *Cossacks in the German Army 1941 to 1945* (London, 1991).

25. Alexander Dallin, *German Rule in Russia, 1941–1945: A Study in Occupation Policies* (2nd edn, London, 1981), p. 509.

26. *Ibid.*, p. 241.

27. Barber and Harrison, *Soviet Home Front*, pp. 114f.

28. *Table Talk*, 17 October 1941, p. 68.

29. *Ibid.*, 9–10 January 1942, p. 198.

30. *Ibid.*, esp. pp. 15, 23, 24, 33.

31. *Ibid.*, 17 September 1941, p. 34.

32. *Ibid.*, 19–20 February 1942, p. 319.

33. *Ibid.*, 17 October 1941, p. 69.

34. *Ibid.*, 8–9 and 9–10 August 1941, p. 24.

35. *Ibid.*, 6 August 1942, p. 617.

36. *Ibid.*, 17 September 1941, p. 34.

37. *Ibid.*, pp. 46ff. Dallin's rather dated study is essentially concerned with Rosenberg's effectively powerless agency, and hence is much weaker on both the military and the SS-police empire.

38. Karl-Heinz Janssen, 'Beherrschen, verwalten, ausbeuten!', *Die Zeit*, 27–28 June 1991, p. 45.

39. Ruth Bettina Birn, *Die höheren SS- und Polizeiführer. Himmlers Vertreter im Reich und in den besetzten Gebieten* (Düsseldorf, 1986).

40. Dallin, *German Rule*, p. 322. See also John Erickson, 'Nazi Posters in Wartime Russia', *History Today*, 44 (1994), pp. 14–19.

41. The best account of Himmler's ideological outlook remains Josef Ackermann, *Heinrich Himmler als Ideologe* (Göttingen, 1970), esp. pp. 195ff. for his views on the East.

42. Robert Koehl, *RKFDV: German Resettlement and Population Policy 1939–1945: A History of the Reich Commission for the Strengthening of Germandom* (Cambridge, Mass., 1957) is still the standard account.

43. Rolf-Dieter Müller, *Hitlers Ostkrieg und die deutsche Siedlungspolitik* (Frankfurt am Main, 1991), pp. 119–21 for the text of Himmler's address.

44. Helmut Krausnick, 'Denkschrift Himmlers über die Behandlung

der Fremdvölkischen im Osten', *Vierteljahreshefte für Zeitgeschichte*, 5 (1957), pp. 194–8.

45. Bundesarchiv Koblenz, NS 19 (alt), 184, 'Niederschrift Himmlers über Probleme der deutschen Ostsiedlung vom 24 Juni 1940'.

46. 'Planungsgrundlagen für den Aufbau der Ostgebiete', in R.-D. Müller, *Hitlers Ostkrieg* (Frankfurt am Main, 1991), pp. 130–8.

47. Michael Burleigh, *Germany Turns Eastwards: A Study of 'Ostforschung' in the Third Reich* (Cambridge, 1988), esp. pp. 155ff. See also *idem*, 'Die Stunde der Experten', in M. Rössler and S. Schleiermacher (eds), *Der 'Generalplan Ost'. Hauptlinien der nationalsozialistischen Planungs- und Vernichtungspolitik* (Berlin, 1993), pp. 346–55.

48. Gert Gröning and Joachim Wolschke-Bulmahn (eds), *Der Liebe zur Landschaft. Teil III: Der Drang nach Osten. Arbeiten zur sozialwissenschaftlich orientierten Freiraumplanung*, Bd. IX (Munich, 1987), p. 31, citing Konrad Meyer's autobiography.

49. 'Himmler über Siedlungsfragen', in Karl Heinz Roth, 'Erster "Generalplan Ost" (April/May 1940) von Konrad Meyer', *Dokumentationsstelle zur NS-Sozialpolitik, Mitteilungen*, 1 (1985), documentary appendix.

50. Dietrich Eichholtz, 'Der "Generalplan Ost". Über eine Ausgeburt imperialistischer Denkart und Politik', *Jahrbuch für Geschichte*, 26 (1982), documentary appendix, pp. 257f., for Heydrich's speech.

51. Helmut Heiber, 'Der Generalplan Ost', *Vierteljahreshefte für Zeitgeschichte*, 6 (1958), pp. 281ff.

52. Müller, *Hitlers Ostkrieg*, pp. 185–8, for Meyer's text.

53. Bruno Wasser, 'Die "Germanisierung" im Distrikt Lublin als Generalprobe und erste Realisierungsphase des "Generalplans Ost"', in Rössler and Schleiermacher (eds), *Der 'Generalplan Ost'*, pp. 272f.

54. For the details of the Zamosc resettlements see Czesław Madajczyk, *Die Okkupationspolitik Nazideutschlands in Polen 1939–1945* (Cologne, 1988), pp. 422ff.

55. Götz Aly and Susanne Heim, *Vordenker der Vernichtung. Auschwitz und die deutschen Pläne für eine neue europäische Ordnung* (Hamburg, 1991), pp. 436f.

56. H. R. Trevor-Roper, 'Hitlers Kriegsziele', *Vierteljahreshefte für Zeitgeschichte*, 8 (1960), pp. 121–33; Eberhard Jäckel, *Hitler's World*

View: A Blueprint for Power (Middletown, Conn., 1972); Gunter Moltmann, 'Weltherrschaftsideen Hitlers', in O. Brunner and D. Gerhard (eds), *Europa und Übersee. Festschrift für Egmont Zechlin* (Hamburg, 1961), pp. 197–240; Milan Hauner, 'Did Hitler Want World Domination?', *Journal of Contemporary History*, 13 (1978), pp. 15–32; Meier Michaelis, 'World Power Status or World Dominion?', *Historical Journal*, 15 (1972), pp. 331–60.

57. Michael Burleigh, '... And Tomorrow the Whole World', *History Today*, 40 (1990), pp. 32–8; Dimitry Oleinikov and Sergei Kudryashov, 'What If Hitler Had Defeated Russia?', *History Today*, 45 (1995), pp. 67–70.

58. *Table Talk*, 8–9 August 1941, p. 24.

59. *Ibid.*, 21–22 October 1941, p. 81.

60. *Ibid.*, 8 June 1942, p. 523. See also Hans J. Reichardt and Wolfgang Schäche (eds), *Von Berlin nach Germania. Über die Zerstörung der Reichshauptstadt durch Albert Speers Neugestaltungen* (Berlin, 1985).

61. Wolfgang Schäche, 'From Berlin to Germania: Architecture and Urban Planning', in David Britt (ed.), *Art and Power: Europe under the Dictators, 1930–1945* (Hayward Gallery, London, 1995), pp. 326ff.

62. For these plans see Karl-Heinz Roth (ed.), 'Versorgungswerk des Deutschen Volkes: Die Neuordnungspläne der Deutschen Arbeitsfront zur Sozialversicherung 1935–1943', *Dokumentationsstelle zur NS-Sozialpolitik*, vol. II (Hamburg, 1986).

63. Michael Burleigh and Wolfgang Wippermann, *The Racial State: Germany 1933–1945* (Cambridge, 1994) for the most comprehensive discussion of these policies.

SEVEN:
STALIN'S WAR OR PEACE

1. Interviewed by Michael Charlton, *The Eagle and the Small Birds – Crisis in the Soviet Empire: From Yalta to Solidarity* (Chicago/London, 1984), p. 50.

2. M. Lewin, *The Peasant and Soviet Power* (London, 1969).

3. B. Croce, *History as the Story of Liberty* (London, 1941), pp. 27–8.

4. The first work of this kind, recently reissued, was G. Alperovitz, *Atomic Diplomacy: Hiroshima and Potsdam* (London, 1994).

5. *Ibid.*, p. 313.

6. *Ibid.*, p. 63.

7. *Ibid.*

8. These are the Venona telegrams: partially decrypted intercepts of communications between the Soviet mission in New York and the government in Moscow, now released by the US National Security Agency.

9. This was the result of agreement with the International Advisory Group established in January 1992 at the initiative of the Nobel Foundation in Oslo. The Group – chaired originally by Arne Westad, and currently by the author – has, through raising money for the process of declassification, seen to the release of considerable documentation on Soviet foreign policy since 1917, including a significant proportion dating from 1945, though certainly not to the extent we would have liked or originally anticipated.

10. M. Sherwin, *A World Destroyed: The Atomic Bomb and the Grand Alliance* (New York, 1975).

11. Testimony of Marshal Zhukov, who was present: *Vospominaniya i razmyshleniya*, vol. III (Mosow, 1983), p. 316.

12. Indeed, the leading proponent closes the most recent edition of his book (appendix IV) with a Report from the Federal Council of Churches, 1946, and (appendix V) with excerpts from the US National Conference of Catholic Bishops' Pastoral Letter on War and Peace, 1983: Alperovitz, *Atomic Diplomacy*, pp. 321–39. At the very least this suggests that the author's dislike of atomic weapons may have influenced his writing.

13. *Washington Post*, 22 January 1952. The reader will find this argument and the evidence first published in J. Haslam, 'Le valutazioni di Stalin sulla probabilita della guerra (1945–1953)', in A. Natoli and S. Pons (eds), *L'eta dello stalinismo* (Rome, 1991), pp. 279–97.

14. *Bol'shevik*, No. 17–18, September 1946, reprinted in R. McNeal (ed.), *I. V. Stalin: Sochineniya*, vol. III: *1946–1953* (Stanford, 1967), p. 56.

15. Molotov dictated his memoirs to the poet Felix Chuyev over a

period of years. The tapes have been made available to at least one documentary film-maker. For the text: *Sto sorok besed s Molotovym: Iz dnevnika F. Chueva* (Moscow, 1991), p. 81.

16. *Sto sorok*, pp. 96–7. Molotov gets the year wrong, however, remembering it as 1944.

17. *Pravda*, 23 January 1947.

18. P. Nenni, *Tempo di Guerra Fredda: Diari 1943–1956*, ed. by G. Nenni and D. Zucaro (Milan, 1981), p. 537.

19. Quoted in the Forrestal diaries: Alperovitz, *Atomic Diplomacy*, p. 364.

20. Nenni, *Tempo*, p. 400.

21. Entry, 19 April 1948: V. Auriol, *Journal du Septennat 1947–1954*, vol. II: *1948* (Paris, 1974), p. 189. Auriol, President of France, was quoting the official in his diary.

22. *Washington Post*, 21 January 1952.

23. PRO, FO 371/56731, Roberts, Moscow, to Bevin, London, 6 September 1946.

24. Y. Modin, *My Five Cambridge Friends* (London, 1994), p. 47.

25. C. Andrew and O. Gordievsky, *KGB: The Inside Story of its Foreign Operations from Lenin to Gorbachev* (London, 1990).

26. Modin, *My Five Cambridge Friends*, p. 139.

27. *Ibid.*, p. 142. For the effects on the development of the Soviet bomb project from 1942: D. Holloway, *Stalin and the Bomb: The Soviet Union and Atomic Energy, 1939–1956* (New Haven/London, 1994).

28. NKGB documents quoted in G. Borovik, *The Philby Files: The Secret Life of the Master Spy – KGB Archives Revealed*, ed. with an introduction by P. Knightly (London, 1994), p. 236.

29. Quoted in *ibid.*, p. 240.

30. *Sto sorok*, p. 88.

31. P. Sudoplatov, *Special Tasks* (London, 1994), pp. 230–1. Sudoplatov, a former spy, may not always be a reliable source, but in this case his testimony is backed up by evidence from Foreign Ministry files: M. Narinsky, 'The Soviet Union and the Marshall Plan', in S. Parish and M. Narinsky, *New Evidence on the Soviet Rejection of the Marshall Plan, 1947: Two Reports* (Woodrow Wilson Center for Scholars, Washington DC, 1994), p. 45. This publication was issued by the Cold War

International History Project which is based at the Woodrow Wilson Center and is numbered working paper 9.

32. Modin, *My Five Cambridge Friends*, p. 168.

33. *Ibid.*, p. 193.

34. *Ibid.*, p. 142.

35. *Ibid.*, pp. 145–6.

36. This, of course, raises a further counterfactual question which cannot be dealt with here: What if the United States had *not* stood firm?

37. For more on this, see the author's *The Soviet Union and the Struggle for Collective Security in Europe 1933–39* (London/New York, 1984), and *The Soviet Union and the Threat from the East 1933–41* (London/Pittsburgh, 1992).

38. 'Kommissiya Livinova po podgotovke mirnykh dogovorov i poslevoennogo ustroistva. Protokoly i Zasedanii Kommissii', 31 March–21 September 1944, *Arkhiv vneshnei politiki Rossii* (hereafter AVPR), Fond Molotova, Op. 6, Papka 14, dela 141.

39. '1944. Komissiya t. LITVINOVA po podgotovke mirnykh dogovorov i poslevoennogo ustroistva', AVPR, Fond Molotova, Op. 6, Por. 143, Papka 14.

40. For the first detailed discussion of the Voroshilov committee: A. Filitov, 'Die UdSSR und das Potsdamer Abkommen. Ein langer und leidvoller Weg', presented to a conference at Otzenhausen, Germany, 22–26 May 1995, entitled 'Vor 50 Jahren: Die Potsdamer Konferenz. Vorgeschichte, Verlauf und Folge fur Deutschland, Europa und die Welt'.

EIGHT:
CAMELOT CONTINUED

1. McGeorge Bundy, 1993 Stimson Lecture at Yale University; Robert S. McNamara, *In Retrospect: The Tragedy and Lessons of Vietnam* (New York, 1995).

2. Stone's preposterous thesis received support from historian John Newman, who in *JFK and Vietnam* (New York, 1991) argued that Johnson, on taking office, immediately escalated the war beyond Ken-

nedy's intentions. See also George Bernau's novel *Promises to Keep* (New York, 1988). An antidote of sorts is provided by the British satirist Mark Lawson's recent *Idlewild* (London, 1995).

3. Doris Kearns Goodwin, *The Fitzgeralds and the Kennedys: An American Saga* (New York, 1987), pp. 246–53.

4. Gore Vidal, 'The Holy Family', in *idem, United States – Essays 1952–1992* (New York, 1992), pp. 809–26.

5. Stephen E. Ambrose, *Eisenhower: The President* (New York, 1984, 1985), vol. II, p. 190.

6. Richard Reeves, *President Kennedy: Profile of Power* (New York, 1993), p. 356.

7. Stephen E. Ambrose, *Nixon: The Education of a Politician 1913–1962* (New York, 1987), pp. 596f.; Taylor Branch, *Parting the Waters: America in the King Years 1954–1963* (New York, 1988), pp. 344–78.

8. *Inaugural Addresses of the Presidents of the United States – Bicentennial Edition* (Washington, 1989), p. 308.

9. Reeves, *Kennedy*, pp. 122–6.

10. *Ibid.*, p. 498.

11. *Ibid.*, p. 126.

12. *Ibid.*, pp. 498–502.

13. Harvard Sitkoff, *The Struggle for Black Equality 1954–1992* (New York, 1993), pp. 145–7.

14. Preamble to the Economic Opportunity Act 1964.

15. George M. Kahin, *Intervention: How America Became Involved in Vietnam* (New York, 1986), pp. 17–20.

16. George C. Herring, *America's Longest War: The United States and Vietnam 1950–1973* (2nd edn, New York, 1986), p. 57.

17. Herring, *Longest War*, pp. 51f., 57; Kahin, *Intervention*, pp. 75–7.

18. Reeves, *Kennedy*, pp. 254, 559.

19. Arthur M. Schlesinger Jr, *A Thousand Days: John F. Kennedy in the White House* (New York, 1965, 1971), p. 156.

20. Reeves, *Kennedy*, p. 112.

21. *Foreign Relations of the United States 1961–1963*, vol. I: *Vietnam 1961* (Washington, 1988), No. 42, Memorandum from the Deputy Secretary of Defense to the President, 3 May 1961, p. 93.

22. *Ibid.*, p. 97.

23. *FRUS*, vol. I, Attachment to No. 42, 'A Program of Action to Prevent Communist Domination of South Vietnam', 1 May 1961, pp. 93–115.

24. *Ibid.*, No. 52, National Security Action Memorandum, 11 May 1961, pp. 132–4.

25. Lloyd C. Gardner, *Pay Any Price: Lyndon Johnson and the Wars of Vietnam* (Chicago, 1995), pp. 54f.; Robert D. Schulzinger, *A Time for War*, (Oxford, forthcoming) ch. V.

26. *FRUS*, vol. I, No. 60, Report by the Vice-President, undated.

27. *Ibid.*, No. 99, Bundy to Lemnitzer, 19 July 1961, pp. 233f.

28. *Ibid.*, Komer to Rostow, 20 July 1961, p. 234.

29. Schulzinger, *A Time for War*, ch. V.

30. *FRUS*, vol. I, No. 210, Letter from Maxwell Taylor enclosing report and attachments, 3 November 1961, pp. 477–532.

31. *Ibid.*, No. 233, Memorandum from Rostow to the President, 11 November 1961, pp. 573–5.

32. *Ibid.*, No. 214, Draft Memorandum from the Secretary of Defense to the President, 5 November 1961, pp. 538–40.

33. *Ibid.*, No. 254, 'Notes on NSC Meeting', 15 November 1961, pp. 607–10.

34. *Ibid.*, No. 272, NSAM No. 111, 22 November 1961, pp. 656f.; Schulzinger, *A Time for War*, ch. V.

35. Herring, *Longest War*, p. 65.

36. Reeves, *Kennedy*, p. 444.

37. *New York Times*, 7 January 1963; Reeves, *Kennedy*, p. 446.

38. Reeves, *Kennedy*, p. 446; Schulzinger, *A Time for War*, ch. V.

39. *Foreign Relations of the United States 1961–1963*, vol. III *Vietnam, January–August 1963* (Washington, 1991), No. 112, Telegram from the Hue Consulate, 9 May 1963, pp. 277f.

40. Schulzinger, *A Time for War*, ch. V.

41. *FRUS*, vol. III, Nos 163 and 164, Saigon to State Department 11 June 1963, pp. 374–6.

42. *Ibid.*, No. 249, Michael Forrestal Memorandum to the President 9 August 1963, pp. 559f.; Schulzinger, *A Time for War*, ch. V.

43. *FRUS*, vol. III, No. 230, Telegram from the State Department to the Embassy in Vietnam, 19 July 1963, p. 517.

44. Reeves, *Kennedy*, p. 528.

45. *FRUS*, vol. III, No. 254, Editorial Note, p. 567.

46. *Foreign Relations of the United States 1961–1963*, vol. IV: *Vietnam: August–December 1963* (Washington, 1991), No. 167, Memorandum from the Chairman of the Joint Chiefs of Staff and the Secretary of Defense to the President, 2 October 1963, pp. 336–46.

47. Reeves, *Kennedy*, p. 620.

48. *Ibid.*, p. 638.

49. *FRUS*, vol. IV, pp. 427–537; Reeves, *Kennedy*, pp. 643–50.

50. Schulzinger, *A Time for War*, ch. VI.

51. McNamara, *Retrospect*, pp. 86f.; Reeves, *Kennedy*, pp. 586f.

52. Schulzinger, *A Time for War*, ch. VI. On Johnson's Vietnam travails as President see Gardner, *Pay Any Price*, and Schulzinger, *A Time for War*.

NINE:
1989 WITHOUT GORBACHEV

1. Timothy Garton Ash, *We the People: The Revolution of '89 Witnessed in Warsaw, Budapest, Berlin & Prague* (Cambridge, 1990), p. 139.

2. *Time*, 23 June 1980.

3. David Lane, *State and Politics in the USSR* (Oxford, 1985), pp. 257, 311, 313. My emphasis.

4. J. Hough, *Russia and the West* (New York, 1990), pp. 205–7.

5. Quoted in Denis Healey, *The Time of my Life* (Harmondsworth, 1990), p. 531. My emphasis.

6. Modrow was quoted in *Focus*, 44, 31 October 1994, p. 29. For a long but by no means definitive list of Stasi officers and informers in the Modrow government and the so-called Party of Democratic Socialism (PDS), see *Der Spiegel*, 9 October 1995, pp. 84–92.

7. For the underlying reinforcement of Soviet economic weakness by *perestroika*, see Marshall I. Goldman, *What Went Wrong with Perestroika?* (London, 1991).

8. For the GDR's 'objective' economic problems and its unconventional ways round them, see Wolfgang Seiffert and Norbert Treutwein,

Die Schalk-Papiere: DDR–Mafia zwischen Ost und West (Munich, 1992). For the ease with which it could still raise money in the West, see the testimony in Peter Wyden, *Wall: The Inside Story of Divided Berlin* (New York, 1989), p. 606.

9. See Robert L. Hutchings, *Soviet–East European Relations: Consolidation and Conflict* (Madison, 1983), p. 193.

10. Quoted in BBC, *Summary of World Broadcasts*, EE/2135, 25 October 1994, A9. See also Georges Mink and Jean-Charles Szurek (eds), *Cet étrange post-communisme: rupture et transitions en Europe centrale et orientale* (Paris, 1992), esp. pp. 75–6.

11. See Judy Shelton, *The Coming Soviet Crash: Gorbachev's Desperate Pursuit of Credit in Western Financial Markets* (London, 1989), pp. 171–2.

12. See my *Europe's Backyard War: The War in the Balkans* (London, 1994), pp. 31–57, for Western antagonism to small states seceding from either the USSR or socialist Yugoslavia. Bush's Kiev speech was echoed by Clinton's Secretary of State, Warren Christopher, three years later when he endorsed President Yeltsin's onslaught on Chechnya: 'It's not in our interests, or certainly in theirs, to have a sort of disintegrating Russia, so I think he has done what he had to do to prevent this republic from breaking away.... But I think you have to understand what's happening there is within the Russian Federation and this particular republic is trying to leave the Federation and President Yeltsin is dealing with that.' As broadcast on *Today*, BBC Radio 4, 14 December 1994.

The US State Department spokesman Michael McCurry made it clear that Washington would not let thousands of civilian dead in the ruins of Grozny disturb cosy relations with the Kremlin: 'By no means does Chechnya define the broad parameters of the US–Russian partnership' (quoted in the *Financial Times*, 14 December 1994). Hans van den Broek, the EU's External Affairs Commissioner, insisted to *Le Monde*, 'Nous ne pouvons pas refuser à la Russie le droit légal d'essayer de garantir l'integrité de son territoire' since the Chechen invasion was an 'affaire internale'; *Le Monde*, 17 December 1994.

13. See Bob Woodward, *The Commanders* (New York, 1991), p. 226.

14. See Jacques Attali, *Verbatim: III*, as quoted in 'Wir können

Deutschland schließlich nicht den Krieg erklären' in the *Frankfurter Allgemeine Zeitung*, 12 October 1995.

15. Quoted in J. Laughland, *The Death of Politics: France under Mitterrand* (London, 1994), p. 255. See also Georges Bortoli, *Une si longue bienveillance: les Français et l'URSS, 1944–1991* (Paris, 1994), pp. 222f.

16. For Andreotti's endorsement of military repression, see my *Europe's Backyard War*, pp. 42–6.

17. From left to right, the German establishment was cosy with the existence of the GDR and only a few of its doyens who actually made visits there ever questioned its viability. Jürgen Habermas may stand representative of a generation of the German 'critical' intelligentsia who noticed something was not quite right only in 1988 and even then never expected an end of the other German state. He told Adam Michnik: 'Naturally I was as astonished as most Germans [by the fall of the Wall]. I went to the GDR, to Halle, for the first time in the summer of 1988. The spiritual state of the people ... was devastating. They were cynical and desperate. Nothing remained of any kind of optimistic prospects. *Retrospectively* I was conscious of how far this system had eroded by then. But *of course* I did not anticipate the end'; see *Die Zeit*, 17 December 1993. The degree to which the West German elite rejected dissidents and defectors is illustrated by the way in which *even after reunification* the ex-Communists Stefan Heym and Gregor Gysi were able to block the participation of an ex-dissident Freya Klier in the television programme *Talk im Turm* because she had drawn attention to Gysi's past collaboration with the Stasi. Heym dismissed 'human rights activists' as 'neurotics who cannot abide that since the change [in 1989] they have lost significance'. See *Focus*, 28 November 1994, p. 25. The defector Oleg Gordievsky once told me that he had not been allowed on the platform at a conference in Aschaffenburg sponsored by the supposedly conservative Bavarian Christian Social Union, while unrepentant former KGB and Stasi generals, Leonid Scherbashin and Misha Wolf, were treated as honoured guests. In October 1989, Vaclav Havel recalled how stand-offish the West German elite had been towards dissidents like him whose critical activities they feared might damage the atmosphere of detente. The Germans were not alone. It was the Gaullist

'baron' Michel Debré who called the Soviet invasion of Czechoslovakia 'a traffic accident on the road to detente'. German conservatives too saw it as *removing* an obstacle to detente! See Timothy Garton Ash, *In Europe's Name: Germany and the Divided Continent* (London, 1994), pp. 280, 470 .

18. Any contemplation of the staggering degree of Stasi penetration of West Germany and the complete failure of West German intelligence (led by the future Foreign Minister Klaus Kinkel) to achieve any comparable successes leads one to question the value of bourgeois intelligence services and to ponder how the Chekists could not have noticed the impending fall of their own home base. For Kanter, see *Der Spiegel*, 7 November 1994, p. 17.

19. See 'Honeckers Wohlgefallen an Rot-Grün' in the *Frankfurter Allgemeine Zeitung*, 12 October 1995, p. 14.

20. According to Jacques Attali, *Verbatim: II*, 1986–8, quoted in *The Economist*, 15 July 1995, p. 91. For Mitterrand's preference for Jaruzelski over Walesa, see Laughland, *Death of Politics*, p. 245.

21. See Garton Ash, *In Europe's Name*, p. 109.

22. See the *Frankfurter Allgemeine Zeitung*, 20 January 1995, and the *International Herald Tribune*, 20 January 1995. Emphasis added.

23. See Elizabeth Drew, *On the Edge: The Clinton Presidency* (New York, 1994), p. 316.

24. Quoted in John Dunlop, *The Rise of Russia and the Fall of the Soviet Empire* (Princeton, 1993), pp. 121–2.

25. See Marcel Ophuls, *Walls Come Tumbling Down*, documentary for BBC television, 10 November 1990, which broadcast the contrasting reactions to the fall of the Berlin Wall. Even the Stalinist *fainéant* Herr Krenz thought Mrs Thatcher closer to the spirit of the moment than the EU's current Transport Commissioner.

26. General Powell apparently argued in August 1990, 'I don't see the senior leadership taking us into armed conflict for the events of the last 24 hours. The American people do not want their young dying for $1.50-gallon oil.' See 'Inside Story: Why the Gulf War Ended When It Did' in the *International Herald Tribune*, 24 October 1994.

27. The Senate voted 52–47 to endorse Desert Storm; see Woodward, *Commanders*, p. 362.

28. For the pipeline issue, see Garton Ash, *In Europe's Name*, pp. 70, 257; and p. 90 for the plan to supply 30 per cent of West Germany's natural gas from the Soviet Union by 1989 – which would have meant, if not a stranglehold, certainly a pressure on the Federal Republic's notoriously exposed fuel-importing jugular.

29. With the disruption of the Soviet economy caused by *perestroika*, Gorbachev was not in fact in a position to exploit the oil crisis resulting from the Iraqi invasion of Kuwait. Soviet oil production actually fell and, for instance, the USSR sold 30 per cent less oil to its former East European satellites in 1990–1. See Gale Stokes, *The Walls Come Tumbling Down: The Collapse of Communism in Eastern Europe* (Oxford, 1993), p. 188.

Index